ISRAEL-PALESTINE

Israel-Palestine
Lands and Peoples

Edited by
Omer Bartov

berghahn
NEW YORK · OXFORD
www.berghahnbooks.com

First published in 2021 by
Berghahn Books
www.berghahnbooks.com

© 2021, 2024 Omer Bartov
First paperback edition published in 2024

All rights reserved. Except for the quotation of short passages
for the purposes of criticism and review, no part of this book
may be reproduced in any form or by any means, electronic or
mechanical, including photocopying, recording, or any information
storage and retrieval system now known or to be invented,
without written permission of the publisher.

Library of Congress Cataloging-in-Publication Data

Names: Bartov, Omer, editor.
Title: Israel-Palestine: Lands and Peoples / edited by Omer Bartov.
Description: New York: Berghahn, 2021. | Includes bibliographical references and index.
Identifiers: LCCN 2021032943 (print) | LCCN 2021032944 (ebook) |
    ISBN 9781800731295 (hardback) | ISBN 9781800731301 (ebook)
Subjects: LCSH: Arab-Israeli conflict. | Land settlement—Palestine—History. | Zionism. |
    Nationalism—Israel—History. | Palestinian Arabs—Israel. | Settler colonialism—
    Palestine—History. | Decolonization—Palestine.
Classification: LCC DS119.7 .I82618 2021 (print) | LCC DS119.7 (ebook) |
    DDC 956.04—dc23
LC record available at https://lccn.loc.gov/2021032943
LC ebook record available at https://lccn.loc.gov/2021032944

British Library Cataloguing in Publication Data

A catalogue record for this book is available from the British Library

ISBN 978-1-80073-129-5 hardback
ISBN 978-1-80539-329-0 paperback
ISBN 978-1-80539-440-2 epub
ISBN 978-1-80073-130-1 web pdf

https://doi.org/10.3167/9781800731295

Contents

List of Illustrations	viii
Preface to the Paperback Edition	xi
Note on Transliterations	xviii
Introduction Lands and Peoples: Attachment, Conflict, and Reconciliation *Omer Bartov*	1

Part I. Trauma and Displacement

Chapter 1. The Political Theology of Eretz Israel: The Nakba and the Hasidic Immigration to Palestine *Hannan Hever*	23
Chapter 2. Western European "Philosemitism" and the Nakba in the 1950s *G. Daniel Cohen*	43
Chapter 3. "You Just Can't Compare": Holocaust Comparisons and Discourses of Israel-Palestine *Lital Levy*	58
Chapter 4. International Human Rights Aspects of Repatriating Israeli Settlers from the West Bank *Yaël Ronen*	78

Part II. Redrawing Space

Chapter 5. Oil and the Origins of Middle Eastern Sovereignty *Rachel Havrelock*	101
Chapter 6. Territory, Demography, and Effective Control: An Analysis of Israel's Biospatial Politics *Yinon Cohen and Neve Gordon*	118
Chapter 7. Come to Netanya: A New Reading of Israel's Planning History	137

Noah Hysler Rubin

Chapter 8. Architecture and the Struggle over Geography: Revisiting the Arab Village in Israel-Palestine   157
Haim Yacobi and Hadas Shadar

Part III. Education and Ideology

Chapter 9. Contested Pedagogy: Modern Hebrew Education and the Segregation of National Communities in Pre-state Palestine   183
Miriam Szamet

Chapter 10. The Biblical Borders between Theology and History: Israeli Schoolbook Maps, 1903–1967   198
Orna Vaadia

Chapter 11. Zionist Civic Rituals as Nation-Building Instruments   221
Avner Ben-Amos

Chapter 12. Rival Histories in a Deeply Divided Society: The Israeli Case   239
Majid Ibrahim Al-Haj

Part IV. Nationalism, Settler Colonialism, and Decolonization

Chapter 13. Three Paradigms for Understanding the Israel-Palestine Conflict   263
Sam Fleischacker

Chapter 14. Thinking about State Demise: The Case of Israel   282
Ian S. Lustick

Chapter 15. Decolonizing Israel-Palestine: A Discourse or a Political Program?   302
Ilan Pappé

Chapter 16. What Would a Decolonized Archaeology of Israel-Palestine Look Like?   315
Raphael Greenberg

Part V. Future Scenarios

Chapter 17. Reinstating Apartheid or Stating the Obvious? 1948 Palestinians and Israel's New Nation-State Law   333
Nida Shoughry

Chapter 18. Palestinians in Israel: The Undesirable Others   352
  Said Zeedani

Chapter 19. The Demography of Return   363
  Salman Abu Sitta

Chapter 20. When Utopia Becomes Topia: Mapping the Future
in Israel-Palestine   384
  Debby Farber and Umar al-Ghubari

Afterword
Between Talbiyeh and Me   402
Alon Confino

Index   426

Illustrations

Figures

6.1. Bedouin towns and villages in the Negev. 129

6.2. Israeli authorities with pickup trucks and tractors plowing "illegal" Bedouin fields east of Lakiya, 5 February 2014. 130

7.1. *Come to Netanya* (1937) cover. 143

7.2. Netanya plan, from *Come to Netanya* (1937). 150

7.3. Celebration photos, from *Come to Netanya* (1937). 152

8.1. A terraced housing project in Nazareth Illit, 1955–57. Architects: Arieh Sharon and Benyamin Idelson. 163

8.2. Housing project along the streets of Afula Illit (1958), planned by architects Ora and Ya'acov Ya'ar: internal street. A photograph from the 1960s taken by Ya'acov Ya'ar. 164

8.3. Terrace Houses in Nazareth Illit, planned by Avraham Ventura and Yehuda Drexler. 164

8.4. A residential building in Umm al-Fahm, in the planning of R. Bostoni. 167

8.5. Public housing in the village of Fureidis, in the planning of Bitosh Comforti. 168

8.6. Apartment for Kafr Qasim, in the planning of D. Shimshoni. 169

8.7. Construction plan for the expansion of Khirbet Yama village, planned by Moshe Lufenfeld and Giora Gamerman. 170

8.8. A building in the Gilo neighborhood. Public housing for Jews as planned by Salo Hershman. 171

8.9. Housing for the younger generation in the castle, designed by Salo Hershman—model of one inner courtyard. 173

8.10. The al-Lajun return project. 175

8.11. Architect Senan Abdelqader's private home located in Beit Safafa. 176

20.1. The Mi'ar mosque—before and after the village's mosque had been reconstructed digitally.	396
21.1. Salameh Square and the majestic villa of Constantin Salameh, which has been the Belgium consulate since 1948.	403
21.2. The gate of Villa Salameh.	404
21.3. Salameh Square in the 1940s.	420
21.4. The house where I grew up on 4 Marcus Street just off Salameh Square, previously the Montserrat house.	420

Maps

5.1. Haifa-Tripoli-Kirkuk pipelines map.	109
8.1. The New City of Be'er Sheva: assembly of neighboring units detached and abounding in greenery.	160
8.2. The Ashkelon urban scheme.	161
8.3. The Ramla urban scheme.	162
10.1. The Promised Land map.	201
10.2. The Kingdom of Israel in the Solomon era.	204
10.3. The Tribes' Estates Border map.	207
10.4. The conquest of the Land of Israel by Joshua.	209
10.5. Tribes' Estates.	213
10.6. Borders map.	214
10.7. Contemporary map of the State of Israel.	215
10.8. The Tribes' Estates Border map and Promise Border map.	216
19.1a. The Nakba.	364
19.1b. The refugee exile.	364
19.2. Population distribution.	368
19.3. Canton 1 Central.	374
19.4. Canton 2 Haifa.	375

20.1. The Miska return map, superimposition of historical aerial photo with a contemporary bilingual mental map created by the workshop members, including the names of the current Jewish settlements.   392

Tables

12.1. Stated objectives of history teaching in Arab and Jewish schools in the first period.   245

12.2. Percentage of all history hours devoted to world history, Jewish history, and Arab history in Jewish and Arab high schools in the first period.   246

12.3. Percentage of required units in the history curriculum for Arab and Jewish schools in the second period.   247

12.4. Stated objectives of the teaching of history in Arab and Jewish schools in the third period.   249

12.5. Wording of the new history curriculum for Jewish and Arab schools in Israel.   252

19.1. Elements of future Palestine.   366

19.2. Land use in Israel.   370

19.3. Phases of return.   372

19.4. Areas and population of cantons and blocks.   376

Preface to the Paperback Edition

I am delighted that Berghahn Books has decided to bring out a paperback edition of this book, published in hardcover in 2021. Since that time, profound changes have occurred in Israel-Palestine. In this brief preface I attempt to address these events and ask to what extent they have transformed our understanding of the underlying conditions and historical trajectory outlined in the book. I also consider what implications these developments have for any future scenarios we may sketch for this long-suffering region.

In May 2021, just as the hardcover edition went to press, Israel experienced a shocking explosion of communal violence in many of its so-called mixed cities. To some observers it appeared like a throwback to events that occurred in the country in the first half of the twentieth century—the riots in Jaffa in 1921, the massacres of 1929, the Arab uprising of 1936, and the events of 1948. But since then, Israel within the 1967 borders had never experienced anything on this a scale before. Many Jews and Palestinians worried that the speed in which violence flared up, its ferocity, popular nature, and breadth, were a harbinger of things to come, an indication that the seeming integration of Palestinian citizens in the state was fragile and precarious.

In the couple of years leading to the 7 October 2023 Hamas attack and the Israeli assault on Gaza that followed, the conditions under which 1948 Palestinians were living in Israel progressively deteriorated. This process accelerated as a consequence of the current Israeli government's policies, which included blatant indifference to the tremendous escalation in criminal violence and gang warfare within the Palestinian sector, with the police making almost no effort to enforce the law. As the number of assassinations of Palestinians mounted, along with numerous victims of "collateral damage" or intentionally targeted family members of rival faction leaders, the sense of insecurity in Arab communities grew by leaps and bounds. Palestinians in Israel began to realize that neglect of law and order by the Israeli police, under the overall control of extremist Minister of National Security Itamar Ben Gvir, was both malicious and deliberate, intended to convince those Palestinian citizens of Israel who could afford it to contemplate leaving the country altogether.

Things were also deteriorating in the occupied West Bank, as settlers empowered by the new "right-right" government (as its supporters refer to it), formed by Prime Minister Benjamin Netanyahu in December 2022, perpetrated ever more violence against the local Palestinian population. The attempted judicial overhaul announced by the Minister of Justice, Yariv Levin, the following month, brought tensions within Jewish Israeli society to a new height, with massive weekly demonstrations demanding that Israeli democracy be preserved. The goal of what was in reality an attempted governmental judicial coup was to weaken the Israel supreme court in a way that would prevent it from overruling undemocratic, bigoted, and racist legislation by the Knesset emanating from the ultra-religious and the national religious parties. Hoping to reverse recent gains in civil right, gender equality, and protection of LGBTQ rights, the messianic section of the national religious faction also sought to expand repressive policies against Palestinians with the ultimate goal of ethnically cleansing much if not all of the West Bank.

In an important sense, the protest movement against the judicial overhaul was concerned only with the first component of its program, fearing a diminution of its rights as a largely secular progressive sector in Jewish Israeli society. This sector has been declining in the last few decades, as the influence of religion in all its varieties, but including that of the extremist national religious political sector well represented in the settler population, has rapidly grown. As evidence of this reversal of the balance between the secular and the religious in Israeli society, we note not only the increased political representation of the ultra- and national religious parties in the Knesset, as well as the growing prevalence of various versions of religiosity in Israeli society as a whole, but also the penetration of these elements into the military—both in the upper command echelons and among members of elite and regular combat units.

Such developments notwithstanding, there was in fact a curious consensus in pre-7 October Israeli society over the question of the occupation. Years of Netanyahu governments promising that the Palestinian issue could be managed at no great cost—economic, military, or political—and a deepening separation between the bulk of the Jewish population and the increasingly fragmented occupied Palestinian population, maintained through a complex system of walls, fences, bypass roads, checkpoints, and siege, imposed a kind of "social death" on Palestinians and enabled most Israeli Jews to entirely ignore the oppressive reality of occupation only a few miles away from their homes.

In other words, the impressive protest movement in the months leading up to the 7 October attack by Hamas was engaged largely in trying to preserve the privileges of secular Jewish Israelis; apart from a small, if vocal minority of left-wing Zionists and communists, the protestors strenuously refused to raise the issue of the occupation. It was that reality which several colleagues and myself tried to point out when we issued a petition called "the elephant in the room" on 4 August 2023, drawing attention to the centrality of the occupation both specifically to the judicial overhaul and more generally to the unresolved fundamental conundrum of Israeli democracy. For here is a country whose 7 million Jewish citizens still enjoy democracy, while the 7 million Palestinians living in the same space and under one type or another of Israeli state control, either have no democratic rights whatsoever or can at best be described as second-class citizens. The petition, which underlined the emergence of a regime of apartheid in the West Bank—where two ethno-national groups live under two entirely different legal systems, and only Jewish settlers have the kinds of rights we associate with liberal democracy—warned of growing attempts to ethnically cleanse that territory. Within a few days, the petition was signed by close to 2,500 scholars from around the world, including many mainstream specialists in Jewish and Holocaust history, indicating how appalled they all were by the deterioration of democracy and the rule of law in Israel, and the growing violence in the West Bank. But the petition had little effect in Israel itself.

The devastating, heinous 7 October attack by Hamas seemed to change everything—both people's understanding of the past and their expectations of the future; it was also perceived as a moment when the elaborate rules of the game in Israel-Palestine were irreversibly broken. In Jewish society, the immediate response by the more liberal sector, with some important exceptions, was what people referred to as a process of "sobering up." What people had actually sobered up from was, however, less clear. Supposedly, the term implied that those who had previously still believed in some sort of reconciliation and peace process with the Palestinians, now "realized" that this was no longer possible, because, it was said, the massacre by Hamas clearly showed that "they just want to kill us all." Considering that there had been little inclination for compromise with Palestinians prior to 7 October, and that the liberal part of Israeli society had generally accommodated itself to the idea that the occupation could comfortably be shoved under the rug, this sobering up actually meant nothing more than a final confirmation of what most Jewish Israelis had believed long before—only now with no pangs of conscience—namely, that the only language Palestinians understand is that of the gun, combined with even higher walls and fences to separate "us" from "them."

On the Israeli right, the response was predictably one of schadenfreude vis-à-vis all those who had expressed in the past any criticism of settler violence and expansionism. Ultimately, it was argued, Hamas had shown that the entire land, from the Jordan to the sea, had to formally come under the sovereign rule of Israel; that those parts of it still populated by Palestinians had to be settled, and that the Palestinian population had to be removed. In other words, the Hamas attack had proven the necessity of ethnic cleansing and Jewish supremacy.

On the Palestinian side the Hamas attack seems to have initially triggered a fair amount of schadenfreude as well, not to speak of pride, at the sight of several thousand lightly armed Hamas militias surging out of the besieged Gaza Strip, killing hundreds of IDF troops, taking over Israeli towns and villages and massacring their populations for many hours, before the Israeli military finally showed up and managed to regain control. Considering the deep sense of powerlessness and utter vulnerability to IDF and settler violence among Palestinians under Israeli occupation, especially in the West Bank, this early response was not surprising. There appears to have been a similar, if not greater sense of victory and accomplishment by the population in Gaza, which for years had to watch the prosperous Jewish communities across the fence as the Israeli siege condemned them to ever greater poverty and despair.

Among 1948 Palestinians, however, there was a much greater measure of fear about the potential consequences the Hamas attack might have for their own safety. From their vantage point, they could easily observe the rage and will for revenge, as well as fear and sense of insecurity, among the Jews. In such sites of intense Jewish–Palestinian interactions as Israeli universities, any expressions by Arab students of pride in Hamas or empathy for the civilian population in Gaza as it came under massive Israeli aerial bombing, could bring quick retaliation, including expulsion, imposed by the heads of these institutions, which until then had prided themselves on being bastions of free speech and integration.

As I write, the tragedy unfolding in Gaza is almost incomprehensible. Nothing on that scale has happened to Palestinians since the Nakba. Indeed, depending on how things develop in the coming weeks and months, the Gaza Nakba may end up being worse than the expulsion of 1948. Close to two million Gazans have been displaced, the vast majority of the overall population there, and the destruction of their homes and of the infrastructure of Gaza surpasses anything we have seen in the past. With 30,000 people killed (by 24 February 2024), the majority of them civilians, thousands more buried under the rubble, and 70,000 wounded, a profound humanitarian crisis in the shrinking areas where the refugees—mostly descendants of 1948 refugees—are sheltering, and uncertain prospects as to whether they will be able to return to their homes or to newly built houses, one must concede that we are witnessing not only a human catastrophe but also a titanic paradigm shift whose outcome is unpredictable.

How does this situation impact the way we should read this book? And how can this book help readers imagine the future, beyond the images of devastation and despair, violence and vengeance that are spilling out of our screens every day? I suggest that the logic of events and ideologies, policies and perceptions traced in this book can definitely help explain the underlying and deep causes of the current crisis. Thus, we can say that the timing of the attack by Hamas may have been dictated by the fear that an approaching agreement between Israel, Saudi Arabia, and the United States would also seal the deal of perpetual Palestinian marginalization—clearly one of Netanyahu's topmost goals. But we must also recognize that the rise of Hamas as a radical Islamic organization needs to be understood as a manifestation of despair by the population of Gaza in the wake of the two intifadas and the collapse of the Oslo process. Similarly, it is true that the current attempt by extreme right wing political leaders in Israel to push for the removal of the Palestinian population from Gaza and its resettlement by Jews is presented—and thus appeals to not a few Israelis—as the appropriate response to the massacre of 7 October. But it is crucial to note that the deep roots of the settlement movement must be traced back to Israeli government policies, both on the left and on the right, since the 1967 War and the occupation of Gaza and the West Bank.

Indeed, we would not understand the current perceptions of reality by both Jews and Palestinians without going much further back to the beginning of Zionism and Jewish settlement of Palestine, on the one hand, and the growth of a Palestinian national movement in response, on the other. Especially crucial to current perceptions are the events of 1948, which are perceived to this day in polar ways by most Palestinians and Israeli Jews—either as a moment of national resurrection and the establishment of a sovereign Jewish state in the wake of the Holocaust, or as a national catastrophe and the destruction of any hope for an independent Palestinian state in the wake of a lost war and the victory of an aggressive, well organized and well supported national and settler colonial Zionist movement.

When we turn to future scenarios, the current discourse on both sides appears to be even more pessimistic than it was a mere three years ago. On the one side, we see the utter inability of Israeli moderates to show even a modicum of empathy for the tens of thousands of Palestinians killed by the IDF, along with the publicly expressed will by the Israeli right to use this moment to realize its dream of a purely Jewish state between the Jordan and the sea. On the other side, we have witnessed the refusal by many Palestinians to recognize the horrors of the 7 October massacre, and the growing popularity of Hamas even among those who had previously shunned it and its goal of creating a Jew-free Islamic state in all of "historical" Palestine.

Nonetheless, at this moment of darkness and anguish, there is another way to think about the possible long-term consequence of the calamity we are currently observing. The first thing to be said is that precisely because of the dimensions of the destruction, and despite the desire of some protagonists to go back to "normal," it is unlikely that things will ever be as they were before. Most important, it is now clear to all that the Palestinian issue can no longer be managed, but must be confronted and resolved. That land, which extremists on both sides want to have all for themselves, contains equal numbers of Jews and Palestinians, and both have shown time and time again that they have no intension of leaving, indeed, they have demonstrated an ability to mobilize ample reserves of resilience and perseverance, not to say brutality, to ensure that they will not be removed.

If the political paradigm has indeed irreversibly shifted, and if the insistence of both groups to hold on to the land has only intensified, what kind of future scenarios can we envision? To my mind, it is certainly possible that things will continue to go from bad to worse; that an increasingly authoritarian and violent Israeli regime will bank on further militarizing the Jewish population and seek to use this opportunity to "solve" the Palestinian issue with fire and sword. This will spell the end of liberalism and democracy in Israel, and bring untold suffering on the Palestinians. Such a course may last for years, even generations, as Israel will become increasingly isolated, impoverished, intolerant and violent against both Palestinians and its own citizens. Such regimes exist elsewhere and have shown an ability to survive, even if the case of South Africa demonstrates that in the long run, they may become increasingly fragile. An Israel of this kind will lose the support of much of the Jewish community elsewhere in the world, as well as the backing of its greatest allies, the United States in particular. Eventually, I believe, it will not be able to withstand its inner contradictions and go the way of other oppressive regimes. The long-term costs of this failure, however, to both Jews and Palestinians, will be tremendous.

There is, however, another future scenario that may possibly emerge from this paradigm shift, not least as a result of a mutual recognition that barring an ever-metastasizing cycle of violence in a struggle that neither side can win, another path out of the crisis must be found. Despair and hopelessness can coarsen and brutalize individuals and groups, especially when utilized by cynical or ideologically-driven leaders. But they can also serve as the basis for seeking compromise and reconciliation, and an opportunity for a new breed of leaders. The impetus for seeking a political resolution to a conflict that can never be resolved by military means will not come only from within. Precisely because events in the Middle East are showing ever more signs of spinning out of control, there will be more international pressure on local actors to seek an alternative path.

In this context, several factors need to be considered. First, it must be understood that both the Israeli settlement project in the West Bank and the extraordinary buildup of Hamas in Gaza were largely financed by external sources. By the same token, any change in the Israeli takeover of occupied territories, let alone its reversal, would call for significant international financial assistance. This would be even more the case in Gaza, whose rebuilding would entail enormous investment from Arab, European, and American sources. In other words, politics and economics would have to go hand in hand. In the long run, however, the potential for profits, not least from development in Gaza, would be similarly substantial.

This means, in turn, that a change in the political paradigm between Israel and the Palestinians can only come about as a result of a shift in the regional and international political and strategic balance. To some extent, such a shift had already begun before 7 October, as the United States reluctantly realized that in order to focus on its East Asia policy it first had to ensure that the Middle East would not blow up again. For a moment it seemed that creating a Saudi-Israeli-US axis would both isolate a resurgent and disruptive Iran and open up vast new economic prospects stretching from India to the Mediterranean. But by now it has become clear that rather than serving as a tool to marginalize the Palestinian question, such a grand rearrangement of Middle East politics cannot be accomplished without resolving the conflict over Israel-Palestine, just as that particular conflict cannot be resolved without a larger regional realignment. There are, it seems, many major Arab and European countries eager to participate in such a transformation of relations in the Middle East. But for other stakeholders such as Iran, Hamas, and the current holders of governmental office in Israel, precisely this link between resolving local and regional conflicts appears to be a major threat.

This brings us to a third, and no less crucial issue. Much of what has propelled the increasing violence between Jews and Palestinians, as well as such other players as Hizballah, the Houthis, and, of course, Iran, have been both fanatical religious faith and powerful religious establishments holding substantial political and military power. On the local level, one can argue that the transformation of Hamas from a social welfare religious movement to a radical, violently militant Islamic organization, shares similarities with the transformation of the moderate national religious party in Israel, which for decades served in coalition governments with the Labor Party, into the radical orthodox national religious party of today, with all its messianic, anti-democratic, and Jewish-supremacist elements. Both groups have a similar goal, namely, the creation of an Islamic, or halachic state between the Jordan and the sea, to the total or at least extensive exclusion of the other group. If a general malaise in many neoliberal societies has created a widespread desire for greater spirituality, the impoverishment and hopelessness among Palestinians—especially in Gaza—and the sense of power and impunity, along with messianic zealotry, among settlers, in both cases exploited by a fanatically ruthless leadership, has fueled the conflict as never before.

Historically, this kind of fanatic religious faith thrives at times of crisis, even as by its very nature it also both prophesizes and produces bedlam and catastrophe. In times of greater physical security, material comfort, and responsible, uncorrupt leadership, the fanatics find it much harder to recruit new zealots. One must hope that more moderate forms of faith and religiosity will emerge under a new theological and political leadership. Both Islam and Judaism have a long history of moderation, not only extremism, to draw on, which can be called upon in reforming education and advancing interfaith reconciliation. But these changes are likely to begin only in response to a change in the politics and economics of the region driven by other factors, and, simultaneously, through an effort to marginalize the extremists rather than allowing them to operate with impunity in the name of utopian schemes requiring rivers of blood.

All this must be predicated on the hope that just as people had swiftly claimed to have "sobered up," or had celebrated a temporary sense of triumph at the sight of violence by the underdog, so, too, when they inevitably come to terms with the vast carnage and destruction wreaked on their societies, will "sober up" once again, but this time from their dedication to aggression. This, too, has happened more than once in history, when nations seized by a fanatical will for dominance and vengeance had to face up to the mountains of debris they and their enemies had piled up; when they were compelled to accept the limits of their power and learned to recognize the blessings of peace; when they reluctantly had to acknowledge that the taste of peace was sweeter than that of victory; that strength was better manifested in renunciation and reconciliation than in subjugation and oppression, and that hope for the future of their children was more deeply felt and lasting than martyrdom in the name of one God or another. It is possible, if we try, to imagine such a turn of events, as well. This is a goal worth pursuing.

Omer Bartov, March 2024

Note on Transliterations

Transliterating Hebrew and Arabic into English is notoriously difficult and inconsistent. In this book, I have tried to maintain a degree of consistency, but that has not always been possible, especially where the common spelling of names of persons and places is concerned, or where cited authors transliterate their names in different ways. The main difficulty is in differentiating between *het* (ח) and *khaf* (כ) in Hebrew, and *ha* (ح) and *kha* (خ) in Arabic. Throughout this book, the *het* and *ha* have been rendered as "h," as in Hasidism and Ahmad, and the *khaf* and *kha* as "kh," as in *mamlakhti* and Khalidi. I have not used the letter "ḥ" because it is less commonly used and may be confusing to some readers. However, as noted, there are many exceptions to this rule. Hence the reader will find the organizations Zochrot and Palmach, rather than Zokhrot and Palmah, because that is how they are officially known; the site Kibbutz Yad Mordechai and not Mordekhai, because that is how it is normally spelled; the name Elhanan also spelled Elchanan, because this is how some people spell their name; the name Bar Kochba and not Bar Kokhba or Bar Kokhva, because this is how it is commonly spelled, and so forth.

Additionally, in transliterating Hebrew, the definite article "ha," the sound "ve" or "u" representing "and," and the sound "be," "ba," or "bi," representing "in," are either separated from the word following them by a hyphen or connected to it directly, depending on the ease of correct reading, whereas the apostrophe is used to facilitate correct pronunciation, as in the words *hano'ar* (and not *ha-noar*) and *ha-atzma'ut* (and not *haatzmaut*). In Arabic transliteration, the definite article "al" is separated from the word with a hypen, whereas the apostrophe is used either to separate between syllables, or to indicate a guttural, as *Ras al-'Ayn*.

INTRODUCTION
LANDS AND PEOPLES
ATTACHMENT, CONFLICT, AND RECONCILIATION

OMER BARTOV

Preliminary Comments

The century-long conflict over the Land of Israel-Palestine has raised a plethora of questions over historical narratives and rights of possession, the morality of return and the injustice of displacement, the correction of past wrongs and the imponderables of reconciliation, the promise of coexistence and the right to self-determination. At heart, this is a dispute over attachment and belonging, over what both Jews and Palestinians consider to be their historical and emotional home, the core of their existence and the fountain of their identity. For that very reason, it is exceedingly difficult for each side to recognize the other's link to the land.

This book is the culmination of a multiyear research project titled "Israel-Palestine: Lands and Peoples," which I led at Brown University's Watson Institute for International and Public Affairs in 2015–18. The main goal of the project was to gain a more nuanced and empathetic view of the myriad ways in which the inhabitants of this region and those who made it part of their mental, mythical, and religious landscape before and after coming to it have felt linked to the Land of Israel-Palestine. I should say at the outset that to my mind, the strength of that sense of connection to a place need not be questioned or disputed. The feeling of being at home, or the longing for it, is ultimately subjective, although it can clearly also be politicized and exploited. We have as little right to deny an individual's or group's sense of belonging or to assert that ours is more powerful or authentic as we have to deny an individual's or group's experience of suffering or to claim that ours is greater or more authentic. This is not to say that we cannot or should not charge individuals or groups with committing crimes or injustices against others in the name of establishing, regaining, or protecting their homes. But that is quite different from negating and denying their connection to the place they call home, that is, depriving them of what they perceive as the root of their individual and collective identity and culture.

Hence, this volume is based on the premise that beyond all the heated arguments and bloodshed, political manipulation and abuse, and before one begins imagining or planning future scenarios, there has to come an understanding, indeed there has to be a consensus, that all those involved have a right to a home, in the deepest sense of the word, somewhere in the land they claim to be their own, as long as they do not deny that right to others or attempt to violently oppress or remove them. This is not an argument about symmetry, however. In the current reality of Israel-Palestine, there is no symmetry of power. The State of Israel has more or less absolute political, economic, and military hegemony, and it uses this overwhelming power to control, oppress, and subjugate the Palestinians it rules, though to different degrees and in different ways depending on whether they are its citizens or an occupied population. But neither Israeli oppression of the Palestinians nor the growing international and academic criticism of the Zionist undertaking as a settler colonial movement has succeeded in undermining the prevailing sentiment in both groups that they belong to that place and that the land belongs to them, a sentiment that continuously overrides any particular political configuration or the vicissitudes of contemporary history.

As in the original project, this is an interdisciplinary volume, engaging the perspectives of historians and geographers, political scientists and sociologists, philosophers and archaeologists, scholars of literature, education, and international law, experts in architecture, urban studies, and development planning, as well as political activists. This wide variety of approaches, alongside the diversity of the contributors, provides a multilayered and complex response to the question at the heart of this volume: What makes for the bond between individuals and groups, on the one hand, and a place, on the other, be it real or imagined, tangible as its stones or ephemeral as the hopes and longings it evokes, and what are the myriad ways in which this bond is expressed, fortified, undermined, reconfigured, or, ultimately, shared?

To be sure, despite its ambitious scope, this volume cannot encompass the entire array of excellent scholarship produced in recent years on Israel-Palestine. Indeed, some of the most interesting presentations at the workshops on the topic I hosted at Brown University did not find their way into this volume, for reasons that were beyond the control of either the editor or the presenters. These included, to cite just two examples, a fascinating paper by the Palestinian sociologist Areej Sabbagh-Khoury, "Taking Possession of Village Lands and Expulsion of the Land Tenants: Kibbutzim at the Edges of the Jezreel Valley," based on her Tel Aviv University PhD dissertation; and a highly original presentation by the self-described Palestinian-Bedouin-Israeli anthropologist Safa Aburabia, "Land, Identity, and History: New Discourse on the Nakba of Bedouin Arabs in the Naqab," similarly related to her Ben Gurion University PhD research. It should also be stressed that this volume cannot and did not attempt to address all of even the most urgent questions that come to mind when we think about this region. Most important, as discussed below, this is not a volume focused strictly on the Israeli-Palestinian conflict, although doubtlessly this intractable, century-long struggle forms the backdrop of many chapters. Instead, this is a collective attempt to reach across some of the persistent scholarly and political boundaries in this contentious field by bringing in new thinking and approaches, even as we all acknowledge the enormous challenges we face as we strive for greater mutual understanding and compassion.

The two major axes of this volumes are space and time. By space I have in mind the changing and complex natural and built environment of these lands both over the longue durée and in reference to more recent environmental and man-made changes and challenges. On a less concrete level, this volume also grapples with the mindscapes of the region, namely the manner in which it has been imagined in myth and fiction, but also in cartography and urban/village planning. As for the temporal dimension, the volume contends with the varied and often disputed historical narratives about the Land of Israel-Palestine; the present political, socioeconomic, and cultural realities in all their complexity and diversity, the different prisms through which they are seen and interpreted, and the togetherness and apartness of human and group existence they reflect; and finally, the volume considers the starkly different, but perhaps increasingly converging future scenarios for these lands, where utopian yearnings and apocalyptic warnings are as old as their first inhabitants.

The twenty chapters in this volume, along with the afterword, provide a wide array of new research, original interpretations, and illuminating insights not merely on the conflict—a term that has rightly been disputed for assuming a nonexistent symmetry—but also on larger themes and deeper questions related to the lives of Jews and Palestinians in the lands of Israel-Palestine from the nineteenth century to the present. The authors of these chapters all have their different points of view on the history, present-day reality, and possible futures of Israel and Palestine. But what they have in common is an ability to go beyond the superficial political rhetoric and popular prejudices that so often cloud our understanding and to reconstruct with critical empathy the manner in which these lands and their inhabitants have profoundly changed, through tragedy and creativity, despair and hope, over decades of struggle and innovation. As Jews and Palestinians increasingly drifted apart, they also came together; as deep rifts of hatred and fear marked the landscape they traversed and transformed, their hopes for another future only swelled; as they demanded with ever greater vehemence to be separated from each other and to own as much of the land as they could, some of them have come to gradually internalize the fact that none of them were leaving, that they all had a stake in the land, its history and its future, and that they had no choice but to recognize each other's right to exist in peace with mutual respect. This volume, I believe, reflects these trends and allows us to express a modicum of cautious optimism for the future in these dark times.

Trauma and Displacement

The volume opens with a section on trauma and displacement. These two connected events are part and parcel of the experience of the peoples of Israel-Palestine. The two obvious traumas both connecting and dividing Jews and Palestinians are the Holocaust and the Nakba. To be sure, the Holocaust did not spark the first waves of Zionist immigration to Palestine. But the growing incidence of anti-Jewish violence in Europe from the latter part of the nineteenth century, subsequently seen as heralding the Holocaust, did stimulate a very different kind of immigration from earlier Jewish settlement in the Holy Land. Eventually the events leading to the Holocaust strengthened Zionism and intensified Jewish immigration to Palestine, which further expanded in the aftermath of the Shoah, as hundreds of thousands of survivors came to Palestine and to the newly established State of Israel in the first postwar decade. Yet even as escaping Jewish persecution and the experience of the Holocaust were main motivators of immigration, the traumas of anti-Jewish violence, and especially of the "final solution," came to increasingly dominate Jewish-Israeli consciousness and identity. At the same time, many of the displaced, unwanted, and deeply traumatized Jews who landed on the shores of Palestine ended up as participants in or witnesses and beneficiaries of the traumatic displacement of another people, the indigenous population of Palestine. The trauma of the Nakba, the catastrophe of Palestinian expulsion, thus similarly became the organizing principle of post-1948 Palestinian identity, and its reversal emerged as the cardinal aspiration of an uprooted people transformed into a nation of refugees.[1]

Things did not begin that way. As Hannan Hever argues in the opening chapter, the Hasidic immigration to Palestine in the decades that preceded the arrival of the first Zionists made no claims on the soil of Eretz Israel and perceived the move to the Holy Land as a spiritual rather than a political journey. Conversely, he notes, Zionism was a reaction to violence against Jewish communities in Europe, and its goal was to create a space where Jews would constitute the majority of the population. But in Palestine, the Zionist immigrants found themselves in a position not unlike the one they had left behind in Europe, since once more they were a minority, this time vis-à-vis the Palestinians. Hence, the logic of the Nakba was built into their very political theology. This stood in stark contrast to the Hasidim, for whom the land had a spiritual significance rather than a material one. Additionally, while the Zionists were engaged in what they perceived to be a transformation of Jewish existence and the creation of a "new Jew" by way of "redeeming" the land and returning it to the ownership of the newly emerging Jewish nation, Hasidism was focused on a closer relationship to God and on personal redemption by dint of living on the sacred land of Israel—hence the radical difference between the longing for and contact with the Holy Land experienced by Hasidic Jews retaining their links to their communities in Europe and the modern Zionist colonialist and nationalist project of taking over the land and "negating" the Diaspora.

If early Zionism was a response to the pogroms and other anti-Jewish measures since the early 1880s, the trauma of the Holocaust and the mass population displacement associated with it were on an entirely different scale. The hundreds of thousands of survivors transformed the nature of Zionism, the demography of the new state of Israel, and the way the "Jewish question" was perceived by the rest of the world. As G. Daniel Cohen has demonstrated elsewhere, the eventual recognition by the Allies and the United Nations that Jewish refugees in the displaced persons camps of postwar Europe differed in substantial ways from other refugees made both for a different attitude toward these Holocaust survivors specifically and for the creation of the new concept of political refugees, namely, those who cannot return to their countries of origin for fear of persecution and physical harm. In the case of the Jewish refugees, of course, the very notion of a country of origin was questioned, considering that they often came from states and societies that had collaborated in their attempted extermination and did not want them back. This made the Zionist argument, that the home to which such refugees should return was Eretz Israel, all the more compelling. But it also meant that the Palestinian refugees who resulted from the establishment of the Jewish state were largely relegated to a secondary position of importance in view of what was perceived as the Jewish refugees' purported homecoming.[2]

Cohen's contribution to this volume offers a wider look at the manner in which European attitudes toward Jews in the aftermath of the Holocaust tainted their perception of Zionism and the Palestinian victims of Israel's establishment. Cohen documents many instances of what has been called "the whitewashing of the yellow badge,"[3] that is, the transformation of European intellectual and religious antisemitism into a new brand of philosemitism, a kind of "love for Jews" that contained many of the antisemitic stereotypes that had been part and parcel of European culture for centuries. But as Cohen shows, when applied to Zionism and the establishment of the Jewish state, philosemites could transform their earlier desire to be rid of the Jews of Europe into a celebration of the Jewish success in building their old/new homeland. This adulation of the new Zionist pioneers—who had stripped themselves of their former detestable Jewish traits—was combined with the perception of Jewish rebirth as the polar opposite of old Europe's inability to recover from the legacy of fascism and wartime destruction. Conversely, in the period before 1967, Palestinians were often seen by Europeans both through the old Orientalist prism as a backward people that could profit from Zionist help in order to climb up the civilizational ladder and as largely irrelevant in view of the triumph of Jewish nationalism, a success story that had the additional benefit of seemingly alleviating European complicity in the Holocaust and diminishing the need for any lingering feelings of guilt and contrition.

From the Jewish Israeli perspective, over time the Holocaust came to be perceived by the state and many of its citizens as a constitutive trauma and the main justification for the existence of Israel. As Lital Levy's insightful chapter demonstrates, however, the trauma of the Holocaust played a much more ambivalent role in Jewish

Israeli perceptions of Palestinians. On the surface, the general argument has always been that since the Holocaust was an event of such magnitude and horror, it was essentially incomparable. At the same time, both critics and defenders of Zionism could not help but use it as a measuring rod, whether by asserting that Jewish Israelis were behaving like Nazis or by warning that the Palestinian/Arab urge to destroy the Jewish state would bring about another Holocaust. But as Levy points out, even those Jewish Israelis who are critical of their own conduct toward the Palestinians often rely on an implicit comparison that puts them, as the inheritors of Jewish fate and tragedy, on a higher moral plane and asserts their greater victimhood as compared to the suffering of Palestinians, even as they are in the process of observing or directly causing it. This can be seen as early as in S. Yizhar's 1949 novella *Khirbet Khizeh* and as late as in Ari Folman's 2008 film *Waltz with Bashir*. In both cases, the suffering of the Palestinians (expelled in Yizhar's story and murdered by Christian militias in the refugee camps of Sabra and Shatila in Folman's film) evokes vicarious memories of the Holocaust, thereby allowing for empathy with the Palestinian victim, yet also serving as evidence of the Israeli soldier's humanity, and simultaneously setting up a comparison whereby the Holocaust necessarily wins out as the greater trauma. Hence the Jews displaced from Europe to Palestine are always victims of a greater trauma than the one they are perpetrating on the Palestinians by displacing them, even as they are humanized by recognizing the suffering they caused.

Yaël Ronen's chapter takes us to a very different aspect of the discussion over trauma and displacement, namely the legal discourse over repatriating Israeli settlers from the West Bank. Following the 1967 War, Israeli settlements were established in the West Bank, a process that greatly accelerated in recent years, bringing hundreds of thousands of Israeli Jews to what are still officially recognized by both Israel and the international community as occupied territories. This massive settlement undertaking and the infrastructure it entails, along with intentional Israeli policies of segregation, have by now fragmented Palestinian territory to such an extent that it is difficult to envision the establishment of a viable Palestinian state alongside Israel, as proposed in the Oslo Accords of the early 1990s. Jewish Israeli settlement in the Occupied Palestinian Territories (OPT) also raises a host of legal questions. On the one hand, as Ronen notes, the legality of such settlements is greatly disputed, since by international law a state is not allowed to move large numbers of its citizens to territories it is temporarily occupying. Moreover, Israeli settlers in the OPT live under a different legal system from that of the Palestinian population there. Massive settlement is also creating increasing hardship for the Palestinians and increasing the pressure on them to leave. Since about a third of the Palestinian population in the West Bank is made up of refugees from the 1948 Nakba, one displacement is now being followed by the threat of another.[4]

Conversely, this question arises: what would be the fate of these Israeli settlers under various optional resolutions of the conflict, considering that their status as illegal settlers does not necessarily deprive them of just treatment in the future, particularly if they were motivated more by economic than by ideological reasons? Annexation of the OPT would presumably regulate the status of the settlers by bringing them directly under Israeli law; but it would also open up the possibility either of giving the entire population of the OPT Israeli citizenship, thereby threatening the Jewish majority in the state, or of depriving the Palestinian population of full citizenship and democratic rights, thereby officially creating an apartheid-like system. The alternative would be the creation of a Palestinian state, whose viability would depend on the removal of the majority of Israeli settlers from its territories. It is this process of repatriation that Ronen examines in detail, convincingly showing that it is both legally feasible and morally just. To be sure, the removal of Israeli settlers from the Gaza Strip in 2005 was presented by them as cruel and unjust displacement, and the far larger numbers of settlers in the West Bank would present immeasurably greater problems. But as Ronen indicates, considering the proximity of the settlers to their original homeland, the positive political outcome of such repatriation for the country as a whole, and the fact that this would bring about the elimination of a long-term illegal presence on occupied territory, there is every reason to include such an option of addressing the displacement of one population by the repatriation of another.

Redrawing Space

In Israel-Palestine, space is of paramount importance both because there is relatively little of it and because multiple religious, ethnic, and national groups fiercely lay claims to all or parts of it. At the same time, space in the region is malleable, its delineation and definition constantly shifting and never fully determined. It is concrete and imagined, ancient and envisioned, seen as both empty and yet also always already inhabited. Different individuals and groups attribute to it different meanings both at different times and in simultaneous opposition to each other. Its ownership is defiantly guarded and hotly disputed. Especially in the twentieth century, it has been repeatedly planned, restructured, and redrawn. Yet it is also always there, its main features unchanged, patiently waiting for what may still be in store for it.

As Rachel Havrelock shows in her highly original chapter, the main outlines of the Middle East as a whole, with major implications for what eventually became "historical" or, more precisely, Mandatory Palestine, were drawn by the colonial powers in the first half of the twentieth century, in large part under the impact of oil interests. Oil extracted in Iraq came to play an increasingly important role in the Western powers' economies and armed forces. The issue was not merely who owned the sites of extraction, but also who controlled the transportation of that oil to the most convenient ports, from which it could be shipped to Europe. The two main means of land transport were the railroads and underground pipelines. While the former served as a visible display and means of projecting power and modernity, they were also more vulnerable to attack and exposed the manner in which Western powers were draining the resources of their colonial territories or dependencies to their own benefit. Pipelines had the vast advantage of being invisible, requiring less protection and efficiently bringing the precious lifeblood of industry and armies across vast tracts of often sparsely inhabited terrain. These subterranean pipelines retained extraterritorial ownership by the companies that lay them down and, by extension, by the Western powers that provided for their protection. Additionally, as Havrelock argues, they largely determined the shape and location of the national borders that emerged at that time in the Middle East. Ironically, despite the artificiality of these state borders as mere indications of oil-carrying arteries laid down by competing imperial powers, they eventually came to be adopted and fiercely defended by local leaders and populations as the frontiers of the new postcolonial states of the region.

Focusing more closely on Israel-Palestine, Yinon Cohen and Neve Gordon's chapter brilliantly demonstrates how the struggle over space is translated into population policies geared to settle the land with one ethno-national group and to empty it of its indigenous inhabitants. As the authors argue, Israel's biospatial strategies, namely its policies of space and race, have always been motivated by the goal to acquire or take over as much land in the available territories of Israel-Palestine as possible and simultaneously to "Judaize" the land by both settling Jewish citizens there and removing or greatly restricting the Palestinian population already inhabiting these lands. This perspective on the sacred Zionist objective of "redeeming" Eretz Israel as an exercise in Jewish spatial and demographic expansion and settlement and, simultaneously, in spatial and demographic expropriation and removal of Palestinians allows the authors to show a clear continuity of Israeli state policies from 1948 to the present. The chapter therefore undermines the conventional argument for a sharp dividing line between Israeli policies before and after 1967, according to which the illegal settlements in the OPT can be criticized and should be removed, while the 1948 expulsion of the majority of Palestinians from what became the Jewish state, the expropriation of their lands and the destruction or takeover of their property, can be relegated to the annals of long-forgotten and irreversible history. It is in this context, according to Cohen and Gordon, that Israel's recent Nation-State Law should be understood, since it clearly relegates even national minorities within the legal borders of the state to the status of second-class citizens. Hence, whether the OPT are annexed or not, the law in fact sets the scene for the formal creation of an apartheid state, a potential that the authors argue was always inherent to the biospatial logic of the Zionist colonizing project.

This sweeping gaze of Zionist policies over many decades of settlement is complemented by Noah Hysler Rubin's test-case study of Netanya, a coastal town newly established in the 1920s about twenty miles north of Tel Aviv. As Rubin shows in vivid detail, the founders of Netanya viewed themselves very much as the originators of a modern resort town that would provide all the most up-to-date amenities to its inhabitants and visitors, who would come to enjoy its natural beauty, climate, beaches, and facilities. Yet they also saw themselves as coming into their own space, a land that had just been waiting for them since the exile. As their local foundation myth narrated, although they bought the site from its Palestinian inhabitants, the Arabs were glad to hand it back to them, so to speak, for a meager sum, since they had always allegedly seen themselves merely as its guardians on behalf of the true owners. In this sense, as Rubin notes, on one level the city founders could present themselves (just like the European settlers of New England) as the "firsting," those who would begin the cultivation of a wild and abandoned site, and present the local Arabs (akin to the Indigenous population of New England) as the "lasting," the last members of a dying, backward breed.[5] Yet on another level, in their own minds the founders of Netanya were also merely returning to their home and, in the process, returning the homeland to its original state of cultivation and development under Jewish ownership centuries earlier.

Another crucial dimension of spatial imagination and fabrication in Israel-Palestine is analyzed in Haim Yacobi and Hadas Shadar's chapter. Here the authors shed light on the often ignored, perhaps even hidden connection of Israeli architecture and built environment to the traditional Palestinian village. Initially, in the wake of the 1948 War, Israel systematically destroyed hundreds of the so-called abandoned Palestinian villages, whose inhabitants had fled or were expelled; this undertaking was intended to erase the traces and memory of prior Palestinian life in the land, to prevent Palestinian refugees from trying to return to their homes, and to make way for the complete spatial and demographic restructuring of the territory now controlled by the new state. In the master plan for building Israel, remaining neighborhoods and houses in former Palestinian towns were either demolished—often on the argument that they lacked modern facilities—or were used to accommodate newly arrived Jewish immigrants. Conversely, in the late 1950s and 1960s, not least under the influence of a new global trend, Israeli architects found new interest in the Arab village as an example of vernacular construction and tried to incorporate some of its features into their own plans for Jewish neighborhoods, such as its geographical spread, narrow alleys, inner courtyards, building materials, and so forth. Finally, under the impact of the 1967 War, with the turn to greater religiosity in the Jewish public and attempts to justify the occupation of the West Bank, Israeli architects incongruously used themes from the Palestinian village to construct housing projects on a grand scale that supposedly hinted at authentic ancient Hebrew edifices.

Education and Ideology

The irony of first erasing hundreds of villages, then building Jewish neighborhoods in a vernacular style, and finally, erecting imposing pseudo-ancient Hebrew structures by magnifying indigenous architectural features in order to legitimize a second takeover of Palestinian territory exemplifies the ambivalent relationship of Zionism to the land: an urge to modernize and allegedly "civilize" it, on the one hand, and a reliance on its own ancient Hebraic roots, for which Palestinian village life is the only surviving model, on the other. A similar irony can be found in the revival of the Hebrew language as an ancient Semitic tongue that links modern Jews to Eretz Israel, yet which functionally facilitated segregation between the growing numbers of Jewish immigrants from Europe and the local Arab-speaking Palestinian population.

The re-creation of ancient Hebrew as a modern language, with the subsequent construction of an entire culture and society, including literature and journalism, a legal system and popular entertainment, a military and a statewide educational network, all speaking and writing Hebrew, is arguably the single greatest achievement of Zionism. As Miriam Szamet's chapter lucidly shows, however, the very urge to shape a new generation of Jews in Palestine whose mother tongue would be Hebrew dictated that the very notion of a bilingual education, whereby children would become fluent in the two languages of the land, did not even occur to most of those engaged in this pedagogical revolution. Another irony exposed by Szamet is that while the new immigrants brought with them universalist pedagogical approaches both to Modern Hebrew language teaching and to classroom teaching more generally, under the circumstances of the Yishuv in the last decades of Ottoman Palestine and the first years of the British Mandate, and in deference to Zionist ideology, they eventually succumbed to ethnic and national segregation; thus the new Hebrew/Zionist teachers ended up adopting a nationalist pedagogy that their own original methods were intended to reform and replace. And yet, as Szamet argues, this was not an inevitable development, not least because the innovative methods introduced by these pedagogues for foreign language acquisition could have in fact contributed to overcoming the very segregation that nationalist Hebrew-centrism eventually perpetuated. It remains for us to contemplate how different relations between Jews and Palestinians in the land might have been had they all been fluent in each other's language, rather than the current situation in Israel, where only Palestinian citizens of the state are bilingual.

Reviving Hebrew was one way of asserting the link between modern Jewry and ancient Israel. Another was by inculcating a certain imaginary of the Promised Land, as depicted in ancient texts, in generations of elementary and high school students. In her fascinating contribution, Orna Vaadia analyzes how the incorporation of maps of various biblical borders into pre-state and Israeli school textbooks widely used in the national-secular education system molded a particular spatial imagination among the students. Despite the secular context in which they were employed as teaching aids, these maps were given profound theological and historical meanings, by dint of originating in biblical depictions and divine promises extracted from a text that was taught both as a true history of the Jewish people and as an expression of the nation's metaphysical and timeless link to the land. As Vaadia argues, the prevalence of such maps in secular school textbooks reflects a much more complex and less dichotomous relationship between Zionism and religion than the conventional view of the former constituting a nationalist rebellion against the latter. Moreover, Vaadia shows that the deeply embedded Zionist mental image of the nation-state's borders is malleable and fluid, stretching far beyond what political and demographic circumstances may dictate at any given moment, and thus allowing for ongoing fantasies of expansion.

Education takes place, of course, not only in schools but in the public sphere more generally, as nationalist movements going back to the nineteenth century have always appreciated. In his chapter, Avner Ben-Amos examines the manner in which the Zionist movement mobilized civic rituals as pedagogical tools to inculcate in children and adults the national values of the "new Jew." This healthy, muscular, uncomplicated, and patriotic type that Zionism hoped to fabricate was at the core of its effort to "normalize" Jewish existence by "negating" the Diaspora, or as the saying went, not only to take the Jews out of the Diaspora, but also to take the Diaspora out of the Jews. Surveying a series of newly invented or repurposed rituals over the last century, Ben-Amos identifies a similar "complex interplay of religious and national elements" in the self-presentation of secular Zionism to that detected by Vaadia. In the case of civic rituals, Ben-Amos takes note of how various elements of religious, traditional, and contemporary collective memory were cobbled together in order to create a sense of national solidarity. Because his analysis covers many decades, Ben-Amos is able to trace both significant changes in the combinations of religious and national ritual elements over time and to show how one set of rituals was replaced by another. Perhaps the most significant common characteristic of the civic rituals that came to dominate the national calendar is the manner in which they altered the traditional Jewish ritual by replacing its theological core with a focus on land, nature, or selected events from the historical or mythical past—a transformation of meanings akin to that explored from another perspective in Hannan Hever's chapter. And yet, Zionism's secularized religious ceremonies have retained what Ben-Amos describes as "an aura of sanctity," becoming, in that sense, sacralized civic rituals, attributing a transcendental, redemptive meaning to space and time—the soil of Eretz Israel and the ancestral link to the ancient Hebrews and the Maccabees. It is this seemingly timeless cycle of catastrophe and redemption, as represented by the quick transition from mourning the nation's genocide on Holocaust and Heroism Day to celebrating its rebirth on Independence Day, that has largely come to dominate Israel's self-perception.

For Palestinians in Israel this calendar of sacralized civic rituals serves as a constant reminder of their status as being outside the cardinal reference points of national-Zionist ideology and of the Jewish nation-state, of which they are formally citizens. As Majid Ibrahim Al-Haj carefully delineates in his chapter, the deep divide in Israeli society between Jewish and Palestinian perceptions of the past, their link to the land, and their relationship to the state can clearly be identified by analyzing the evolution of the history curriculum in Jewish and Arab schools in Israel. Al-Haj traces the main historical narratives taught to Jewish and Arab students since the establishment of the State of Israel, demonstrating the extent to which the school curriculum, dictated by the highly centralized Israeli education system, reflects the dominance of Jewish-Zionist political power and culture in Israel as a whole. Among Al-Haj's most instructive findings is that whereas the history curriculum in Jewish schools puts a heavy stress on Jewish history, the Jewish contribution to world culture, Jewish links to Eretz Israel, and Zionism's triumphant establishment of a Jewish state, it pays very little attention to Arab and Palestinian history and skirts over the Nakba altogether. Conversely, the Arab sector's history curriculum contains a great deal of the same kind of Jewish history taught in Jewish school but devotes almost as little attention to the history of Arabs and Palestinians (with the latter term appearing only belatedly and lacking any independent narrative). Another important finding is that while the curriculum for Arab high schools emphasizes the need for Jewish-Arab coexistence, as well as understanding and appreciation of the Jewish people's contribution to human culture and advancement, even the most recent version of the curriculum for Jewish schools makes no mention of Jewish-Arab coexistence or of understanding and appreciation of Palestinian culture. Similarly, while Palestinian students are urged to cooperate with Jews in building a state of all its citizens, the curriculum for Jewish students avoids this topic altogether. Consequently, Al-Haj concludes that the school curriculum in Israel mirrors the ethno-national character of the state, whereby formal education is employed as a tool in shaping an exclusive patriotism and national ethos among the dominant group, and practically works against any purported desire to promote peace and coexistence.

Nationalism, Settler Colonialism, and Decolonization

The perception of Israel as an ethno-national state—that is, a state that perceives itself as the political expression of a particular ethnos, or an ethnically defined nation—is related to a larger discussion over the nature of Zionism and its relationship to the Land of Israel-Palestine. As a national movement, Zionism had sought to instill in Jews throughout the Diaspora the idea that they all belonged to the same Jewish nation and to motivate them to immigrate to Eretz Israel and establish there a state of their own. At the same time, there can be little doubt that Jewish settlement in Palestine was the main cause of the conflict with the Palestinians. In his chapter, Sam Fleischacker proposes three distinct frameworks for understanding this conflict. The first perceives Zionism as being motivated by and practicing typical policies of European settler colonialism, albeit with some unique features. The second asserts that Zionism was largely a response to European antisemitism and that any opposition to it was and still is motivated by the same antisemitism that gave birth to it, thereby, in a sense, legitimizing Zionism's raison d'être. Finally, the third framework of understanding the conflict portrays it as a typical national struggle between Zionists (Jewish nationalists) and Palestinians, whereby, as in many similar national conflicts, the two groups are vying for the same territory. Fleischacker does not entirely dismiss any of these frameworks but ends up preferring the third paradigm of a clash of nationalisms, which he finds as having greater explanatory power, as well as being morally superior, in that it recognizes both groups as having equal rights rather than relegating either to an inferior position. It is, he believes, only through this prism that one can hope to bring Palestinians and Israelis to "a peaceful and mutually respectful resolution of their conflict."

To be sure, one could argue that there is no reason to choose between these three paradigms: Zionism was largely a response to the rise of territorial ethno-nationalism and the consequent modern antisemitism that swept Europe; Zionism established an ethno-national territorial national movement of its own, only its territory was not located where most Jews dwelled but in Eretz Israel; and, in realizing its project of settling that land, Zionism functionally acted as a settler colonial movement, borrowing much of the rhetoric and practices of other European settler colonists and being perceived as such by the indigenous Palestinian population. It can also be said that while now there certainly is a national struggle between Israeli Jews and Palestinian nationalism, the vast asymmetry of power between a strong state and a people made up of a national minority, an occupied population, and millions of refugees hardly merits the term "conflict." At the same time, it is just as true that no reconciliation between the two groups can begin without mutual recognition as nations with equal and inalienable rights over the land, their particular historical narratives, and their individual and collective dignity.

This is an optimistic scenario, not least because recognition of the other's rights is usually facilitated by a sense of confidence in one's own position and future. But as Ian S. Lustick argues in his chapter, that is far from the case in Israel. Lustick asks, why do Israelis regularly assert that the resolution of almost every major public issue will determine the survival of the state? The prevalent sense among Jewish Israelis that their state may not continue to exist, at least not in a form they find desirable or acceptable, he argues, is in itself a sign of the state's precariousness. Now, anyone who has spent any amount of time in Israel will be familiar with frequent predictions of catastrophe, though what might trigger it usually depends on people's political leanings. This may seem strange considering that Israel is recognized as a regional military and economic power and the majority of its Jewish inhabitants are highly patriotic. Additionally, as recently as March 2019, Israeli citizens were ranked among the happiest populations in the world, ahead of Britain, Germany, and the United States.[6] Yet, as Lustick points out, Israelis are simultaneously haunted by three main perceived threats: internal demoralization, the fate of the occupied territories, and the demographic balance between Jews and Palestinians. What these three have in common is that they threaten to undermine the existence of Israel as a Jewish and democratic state, namely, a state in which a Jewish majority can maintain a democratic system without endangering its privileges. However, because of its fear of internal implosion, Israel failed to agree to a two-state solution when that was still possible; by now, thanks to the massive settlement of the OPT, that option is no longer available—hence the current dilemma of having to choose between a state that will retain Jewish privilege but do away with democracy and a democratic state that will no longer maintain that privilege. In other words, according to Lustick, what Israelis mean by state demise is the end of the precarious balance—never truly accomplished in the first place, since Israel was never a real liberal democracy even for its Jewish population, and its Arab inhabitants were always treated as second-class citizens—between being a Jewish state and a democracy at the same time.

As Lustick sees it, "Israel was founded as a settler colonial state dedicated to the paramountcy of a particular ethno-national segment of the population, isolated in its region, and confronting a large aboriginal population." For that reason, "the two-state solution offered a historically unprecedented opportunity for Israel to avoid the fate of similarly situated and constituted states such as apartheid South Africa, Rhodesia, and French Algeria." But he is pessimistic about the future, because "opportunities for a negotiated two-state solution no longer exist," and no other viable solution is on the table. Ilan Pappé, for his part, while he has long described Israel as a settler colonial state complicit in the ethnic cleansing of the Palestinians in 1948, is somewhat more optimistic about the future, albeit not in the short run. According to Pappé, if we agree that the conflict in Israel-Palestine is indeed one between a settler colonial movement and an indigenous population, then the only way to resolve it is through decolonization, especially now that the two-state solution appears no longer viable. Pappé does not have in mind what occurred in French Algeria, where a violent struggle eventually ejected the European settlers altogether. Rather, he proposes the creation of a single democratic state in the entire territory of Mandatory Palestine as another form of decolonization. To be sure, this would be the possible outcome of a much darker near-term scenario. For, as indicated by the recent passage of the Nationality Law and growing pressures for further annexations in the West Bank, Israel may well be on the way to becoming a single state between the Mediterranean and the Jordan River overtly engaged in what has been termed "incremental apartheid."[7] It is under these changing circumstances, Pappé notes, that unlike the failed Israeli-led "peace process," and more in line with events in South Africa in the early 1990s, the process of decolonization in the emerging single state will be led by a Palestinian grassroots struggle against segregation and apartheid with the goal of creating a truly democratic and just society in the entire land.

Decolonization, then, can mean different things to different people, ranging from the removal of the colonizers (as in Algeria) to the creation of a new democratic society—albeit still replete with historically determined socioeconomic inequalities—with the colonizers and the colonized living side by side (as in South Africa), to a federation of states that recognizes both nations' historical and emotional links to the territory as a whole (as outlined in more detail below). But as Raphael Greenberg forcefully argues in his chapter, it can also entail a reformulation of the relationship to the past and to the land in a manner that no longer serves ethno-national interests. Archaeology, as Greenberg sees it, has long been a tool of colonialism and nationalism; this has greatly skewed its ability to provide a path to a shared understanding of the past, certainly in Israel-Palestine, with its particularly intimate relationship between identity, place, and collective memory. Instead, Greenberg proposes what he calls a "decolonized archaeology," which would tell the history of the land and its peoples not through a Western-, Jewish-, or Palestinian-centered perspective, but by focusing on "shared matters of concern" of all its inhabitants. Rather than seeking to justify a national narrative, which eliminates from view those who do not belong to it, a decolonized archaeology could thus enable sharing and empathizing with different ways of understanding the past in Israel-Palestine. To be sure, this is an immense disciplinary and national challenge, and Greenberg does not expect it to become public policy. But somewhat akin to Pappé, he believes that decolonized archaeology could emerge "from the bottom up, by personal example and through professional solidarity," in part because, in an era of growing authoritarianism, archaeology can survive as a discipline only be reaching out to the public and offering a new perception of the past as a web of intercommunal coexistence rather than constant ethnic conflict. This kind of decolonized archaeology will thus both enrich our knowledge of the land's ancient heritage and offer a more optimistic image of a possible future.

Future Scenarios

The final section of the book considers possible scenarios for the future of Israel-Palestine. As we saw above, different analyses of the nature of the conflict, as well as different disciplinary approaches to it, can play a significant role in how one imagines the future and what solutions may be proposed for resolving the conflict. Nida Shoughry focuses on the Palestinian citizens of Israel, whom she refers to as "1948 Palestinians," namely the Palestinians who remained in what became the State of Israel after the Nakba. As she points out, the recent enactment of the Nationality Law was a major turning point in Israel's relationship with its Palestinian citizens, in that it explicitly cast them as second-class citizens, raising significant concerns within this population about their rights, status, and sense of belonging, as well as about Jewish-Arab relations within the state. Yet Shoughry sees this law also as an opportunity for political mobilization among the often-splintered Palestinian population in Israel, as long as the issues concerned are framed in a manner that resonates with wide sectors of the population. And, indeed, it would appear that in the last several elections in Israel since the passage of this law, Palestinian politics has undergone a (hopefully lasting) sea change, demonstrating that when parties with very different ideologies and agendas unite as a national bloc, they can bring into play the unified voice of a fifth of the electorate, which is all the more significant because of the ongoing stalemate between the block of the Right and the Left among the Jewish parties. As many observers have noted, the only way for the more moderate part of Israeli politics to win a majority is by working together with the Arab minority. That this is so difficult to accomplish is clearly a sign of the state's ethno-national character and insidious racism. But an effective mobilization of the Palestinian vote may yet swing matters in the opposite direction, however reluctant even many members of the Jewish "Left" may be to accept this. Once such a coalition is formed, it could have its own positive dynamic and demonstrate to all the benefits of transforming Israel into a state of all its citizens.

Said Zeedani's chapter sets out from a similar recognition of the traumatic impact made by the Nationality Law. As he sees it, this law made explicit and legalized the basic condition of Israel's Palestinian citizens as undesirable others of inferior status in a state that defines itself as Jewish and democratic. From Zeedani's perspective, as long as in Israel Jewishness takes precedence over democracy, Palestinians would never be able to gain full equality. Moreover, he argues that no genuine peace between all Palestinians and Israeli Jews can be reached without a fair resolution to the Palestine question. But Zeedani believes that there is a way out of both conundrums—the second-class status of Israel's Palestinian citizens and the impasse over peace in Israel-Palestine. His detailed proposal, which informed what has come to be known as the "two states, one homeland" plan,[8] is grounded in a thoroughly revised two-state solution. The main components of this proposal include the establishment of a democratic Palestinian state along the lines of the 1967 borders, side by side with the State of Israel, which in turn would be able to maintain its status as a democratic state with a Jewish majority; an agreement by the two states to share, most importantly, the united city of Jerusalem; a mechanism to address both the question of Jewish settlers in the West Bank and of returning Palestinian refugees, which would be based on the distinction between the status of citizen and resident; and ensuring mutual respect for Israeli Jewish and Palestinian attachment to the country as a whole, presumably allowing a degree of freedom of movement and residence throughout the land (as more explicitly stated in the two states, one homeland plan).

Zeedani argues that this vision is "both fair and practicable." Although plans along these lines are now being discussed in various quarters in Israel-Palestine, they are still known to only a few people on both sides and supported by even fewer. Nevertheless, such proposals seem to be breaking the conventional mode, if only by dint of being discussed by both Palestinian nationalist activists and settlers in the West Bank. The very fact that at the core of proposals such as that of Zeedani lies a mutual recognition of each side's right to the land as a whole and an exploration of a mechanism that would enable both sides to live with dignity side by side as independent yet linked nations and states has a great potential to appeal to conventionally rival constituencies. As noted in several chapters, it is likely that, according to the Leninist maxim, things will get worse before they get better, in the sense that the creeping annexation of the land by Israel and the consequent burial of the original two-state plan will make the two states, one homeland idea the only alternative to either apartheid or the loss of a Jewish majority state (barring another bout of violent ethnic cleansing). As Zeedani beautifully puts it, in his own case, "as in the case of so many other Palestinians, feeling at home in the homeland" was never quite possible, since it "requires, among other things, overcoming discrimination (the case of the Palestinians in Israel), ending the occupation of 1967, and addressing the problem of the Palestinian refugees since 1948 (inside as well as outside the country) in a fair and compassionate manner." This could only be realized once Palestinian Arabs and Israeli Jews find a way to live together in a country they "know how to share or to both divide and share."

There is little doubt, as Lustick points out, that most Jewish Israelis view the return of the Palestinian refugees as an existential threat, just as most Palestinians would never consider a resolution of the conflict that does not address that very same issue. Salman Abu Sitta has thought long and hard about Palestinian return. He begins his chapter by contending (as Ronen argues regarding the repatriation of Jewish settlers in the West Bank) that there are no economic, political, or legal reasons for barring Palestinian refugees and internally displaced persons in Israel proper from returning to their properties. As in the case of many other cases of ethnic cleansing, expulsion, and forcible transfer, he adds, the Nakba constituted a serious violation of international law, including war crimes and crimes against humanity. The Palestinian refugees and displaced persons therefore have an incontrovertible right to return to their places of origin. But rather than delving into the complex and polarized politics and legal aspects of such an undertaking, the bulk of Abu Sitta's chapter is dedicated to a meticulous demographic study of the feasibility of the refugees' return. As he demonstrates, most Palestinian refugees, the majority of whom are villagers, could return to their lands with only minor dislocation to the current Jewish population; indeed, he finds that save for a few urban concentrations, the country as a whole would remain sparsely settled. While most of these refugees' villages were depopulated and destroyed, Abu Sitta believes that they could be reconstructed and repopulated by the returning Palestinians, not least on the basis of plans drawn up in recent years by Palestinian architects and engineers in Israel. Repatriation would spare the region from future wars and destruction, and its cost would constitute but a fraction of the foreign aid Israel regularly receives, while the billions of dollars spent annually on weapons could be used instead to promote peace and prosperity in the region.

Abu Sitta's is a blueprint for reverse engineering of the demographic upheaval of 1948. It involves the potential transfer of millions of people from their current place of residence into other sites yet to be built. It would also, of course, radically transform the demography of the State of Israel in ways that are unlikely to be acceptable to its majority Jewish population, tilting the precarious balance, as noted, for instance, by Lustick, Shoughry, and Zeedani, of being both a Jewish and a democratic state. However, considered within the larger context of an overall resolution of the conflict over the entire land of Israel-Palestine, such a blueprint, even if it is greatly modified and adjusted to political realities, demonstrates that the question of Palestinian refugees can be transformed from an unsurpassable roadblock on the path to peace to a bridge on the way to perceiving the viability and even profitability of envisioning and practicing coexistence. The Jewish Israeli insistence that what happened in 1948 is entirely irreversible and that any discussion of a resolution ought to begin only in the zero hour following the Nakba, and the Palestinian insistence that the right of return is a sine qua non in any future scenario are thus extracted from the realm of ideology, fear, and resentment and brought down to the practicalities of demographic, urban, and village planning.

This issue, namely, the healing and reconciliatory potential of return and reconstruction, is at the heart of the final chapter, by Debby Farber and Umar al-Ghubari. As the authors reiterate, for Jewish Israelis, the very idea of the return of the Palestinian refugees is anathema; indeed, it is conceived, in their words, as a "monstrous dystopia, a colossal collapse of the normative order." Thus the notion of return is literally a utopia, in the sense that the Palestinian demand for justice is perceived as simply unrealizable. As former and current activists in the Israeli NGO Zochrot, which since its establishment in 2002 has promoted Jewish Israeli knowledge of and accountability for the Nakba, Farber and al-Ghubari set out here to explore the organization's and perhaps their own radical shift from engagement with the erasure of the past to an effort to generate thinking about return in a practical or, as they call it, topian sense. Most intriguingly, in discussing return as the undoing of historical injustice, the chapter presents a number of recent highly imaginative and original projects by young Palestinians and Jewish Israelis that sketch plans for the reconstruction of specific sites of destroyed villages and their repopulation by their displaced inhabitants and their descendants, creating models, as well as three-dimensional simulations, of how these villages would eventually look. The models and virtual digital re-creations of the villages as habitable, modern sites with numerous references to their original structures and spread on the land, make the impossible and unimaginable appear a mere matter of creative planning and construction. What had been pushed out of memory and mind reappears as if it had never been destroyed and emptied and seems naturally and effortlessly connected to the land and geography of the site and to the people who will inhabit it. This is of course an exercise of the imagination, even as it is also easily conceivable and feasible. Here we are speaking of the return not as a threatening reversal of history, but in terms of a village rebuilt from its ruins and reconnected to the land to which it had always belonged. The utopia of return becomes topia; the no-place is a place once more. As Theodor Herzl said at the beginning of the historical cycle that brought us all to this place, each in their own way, "If you will, it is no fairy tale" (אם תרצו, אין זו אגדה).[9]

Acknowledgments

I would like to thank the Watson Institute for International and Public Affairs at Brown University, and especially its director, Edward Steinfeld, as well as Brown's dean of faculty, Kevin McLaughlin, for funding the research project on which this book is based. The Watson Institute generously hosted the project's workshops, and I owe enormous gratitude to its events manager, Christie Kilgus, without whose extraordinary organizational skills these workshops would never have happened. Additionally, the Watson Institute kindly funded my research assistant and former PhD student, Amy Kerner, who provided essential help, well beyond my expectations, in putting together this volume. Most important, I would like to thank the dozens of scholars who participated in the project's workshops and the many bright Brown undergraduates who took the seminars on the same topics I taught alongside these workshops. These three years of intense intellectual engagement have had a major and lasting impact on my own thinking and understanding and have hopefully been of some benefit to other participants. Finally, special thanks to the contributors to this volume for their patience with my endless comments and nagging. I hope they will be as pleased with the final outcome as I am.

Omer Bartov is the John P. Birkelund Distinguished Professor of European History at Brown University. He is the author of eight monographs, including *Hitler's Army* (1991), *Erased: Vanishing Traces of Jewish Galicia in Present-Day Ukraine* (2007), and *Anatomy of a Genocide: The Life and Death of a Town Called Buczacz* (2018), which received the 2018 National Jewish Book Award and the 2019 Yad Vashem International Book Prize for Holocaust Research, inter al. He has also edited or coedited six volumes, including *Shatterzone of Empires: Coexistence and Violence in the German, Habsburg, Russian, and Ottoman Borderlands* (with Eric D. Weitz, 2013), and *Voices on War and Genocide: Three Accounts of the World Wars in a Galician Town* (2020). Bartov's new monograph, *Tales from the Borderlands: Making and Unmaking the Galician Past*, is forthcoming with Yale University Press. He is currently researching a new project, tentatively titled "Remaking the Past: Israel, a Personal Political History."

Notes

1. Omer Bartov, "The Return of the Displace: Ironies of the Jewish-Palestinian Nexus, 1939–49," *Jewish Social Studies* 24, no. 3 (2019): 26–50.
2. Gerard Daniel Cohen, "The Politics of Recognition: Jewish Refugees in Relief Policies and Human Rights Debates, 1945–1950," *Immigrants & Minorities* 24, no. 2 (2006): 125–43.
3. Frank Stern, *The Whitewashing of the Yellow Badge: Antisemitism and Philosemitism in Postwar Germany* (New York and Oxford: Pergamon Press, 1992).
4. The total population of the West Bank is approximately 3.2 million. Over 750,000 Palestinians are refugees or descendants of refugees, making up about 30 percent of the population. About 390,000 Jewish Israelis live in the West Bank, with an additional 375,000 in East Jerusalem. See World Population Review: West Bank Population 2021, https://worldpopulationreview.com/territories/west-bank-population/.
5. Rubin cites Jean O'Brien, *Firsting and Lasting: Writing Indians Out of Existence in New England* (Minneapolis and London: University of Minnesota Press, 2010).
6. "Israelis Still Very Happy, but Slip Two Spots to 13th in World Ranking," Times of Israel, 20 March 2019, https://www.timesofisrael.com/israelis-still-very-happy-but-slip-two-posts-in-world-ranking/.
7. Oren Yiftachel, "The Dark Side of Modernism: Planning as Control of an Ethnic Minority," in *Postmodern Cities and Spaces*, ed. Sophie Watson and Katherine Gibson (Oxford: Blackwell, 1994), 216–34.

8. Two States, One Homeland, https://www.alandforall.org/english/?d=ltr. See also Elhanan Miller, "Two States, One Homeland: The Promised Land of Isra-stine?," *Tablet*, 25 July 2016, https://www.tabletmag.com/sections/israel-middle-east/articles/promised-land-of-isra-stine; Yossef Rapoport, "Two States in One Homeland: Solving the Riddle of Resolution 2334," *Open Democracy*, 8 January 2017, https://www.opendemocracy.net/en/author/yossef-rapoport/; Judy Maltz, "Explained: Two States, One and Other Solutions to the Israeli-Palestinian Conflict," *Haaretz*, English edition, 10 June 2019, https://www.haaretz.com/israel-news/israeli-palestinian-conflict-solutions/.premium-explained-two-states-one-and-other-solutions-to-the-israeli-palestinian-conflict-1.7044468.
9. In the original German: "Wenn ihr wollt, ist es kein Märchen." This is the motto of Theodor Herzl's *Altneuland* (Leipzig: Hermann Seemann Nachfolger, 1902).

Select Bibliography

Bartov, Omer. "The Return of the Displace: Ironies of the Jewish-Palestinian Nexus, 1939–49." *Jewish Social Studies* 24, no. 3 (2019): 26–50.

Golani, Motti, and Adel Manna. *Two Sides of the Coin: Independence and Nakba, 1948; Two Narratives of the 1948 War and Its Outcome*. Institute for Historical Justice and Reconciliation series. Dordrecht: Republic of Letters, 2011.

"Israel-Palestine, Lands and Peoples." Watson Institute for International and Public Affairs. https://watson.brown.edu/research/2019/israel-palestine-lands-and-peoples-initiative-led-omer-bartov.

Jamal, Amal. "Conflict Theory, Temporality, and Transformative Temporariness: Lessons from Israel and Palestine." *Constellations* 23, no. 3 (2016): 365–77.

Kadman, Noga. *Erased from Space and Consciousness: Israel and the Depopulated Palestinian Villages of 1948*. Bloomington: Indiana University Press, 2015.

Lustick, Ian S. *Paradigm Lost: From Two-State Solution to One-State Reality*. Philadelphia: University of Pennsylvania Press, 2019.

Rouhana, Nadim N., and Areej Sabbagh-Khoury. "Memory and the Return of History in a Settler-Colonial Context: The Case of the Palestinians in Israel." *Interventions* 21, no. 4 (2019): 527–50.

Two States, One Homeland (website). https://www.alandforall.org/english/?d=ltr.

Yiftachel, Oren. *Ethnocracy: Land and Identity Politics in Israel-Palestine*. Philadelphia: University of Pennsylvania Press, 2006.

———. "'Terra nullius' and Planning: Land, Law and Identity in Israel-Palestine." In *The Routledge Companion to Planning in the Global South*, edited by Gautam Bhan et al., 243–54. Milton: Routledge, 2018.

Zeedani, Said. "Recognition of the Other and His Past." *Israel Studies* 18, no. 2 (2013): 148–55.

Zochrot (website). https://zochrot.org/en.

Part I
Trauma and Displacement

CHAPTER 1

THE POLITICAL THEOLOGY OF ERETZ ISRAEL
THE NAKBA AND THE HASIDIC IMMIGRATION TO PALESTINE

Hannan Hever

Introduction

From the first half of the eighteenth century onward, groups of Hasidim began immigrating to Palestine, or Eretz Israel, as it was called in the Hebrew translation of the Balfour Declaration. From the early days of the British Mandate it was also called Palestine.[1] These immigrants were members of the Jewish pietistic movement known as Hasidism, which arose in Eastern Europe in the early eighteenth century and is believed to have been founded by Rabbi (R.) Israel ben Eliezer, better known as the Ba'al Shem Tov, or the Besht (1690/1700–1760). The motives for their immigration were religious—primarily the desire to be connected to the holiness of Eretz Israel, to pray and to be buried there.

The fact that Hasidic settlement in Ottoman Palestine did not entail any demand for Jewish sovereignty—focusing, rather, on internal Hasidic sovereignty under the guidance of the tzaddik (the Hasidic rabbi)—allowed Jews and Arabs to coexist in Palestine in relative peace, isolated incidents of violence notwithstanding. The Hasidim who went to Palestine did not do so for reasons of political messianism and therefore did not act as colonists with a claim to the "Holy Land." The Hasidic reason for the immigration had nothing to do either with an appropriation of territory or with a violent political theology of a sovereignty.

All of this changed, however, with very modest steps, in the course of the nineteenth century and following the beginning of Zionist settlement in Palestine in 1878. The Zionist reason for immigration to Eretz Israel was their desire to solve the "Jewish question" by importing it from Europe to Palestine. Contrary to the theological motives of the Hasidic immigrant, the Zionists left Europe because it became dangerous for Jews. Thus, the Zionists immigrated to Palestine for a negative reason, as well as for a positive theological reason, while the Hasidim immigrated to Eretz Israel largely for a positive reason.

Because they imported the Jewish question from Europe to the Middle East, the Zionists insisted on resolving it by creating a space without non-Jews. But the Zionist aspiration to a space without non-Jews also reflected a desire to avenge the violence of the pogroms, a dynamic that according to René Girard produces an urge to emulate the pogromists' violence against the Jews. Since "mimesis coupled with desire leads automatically to conflict," the relationship between the Zionists and the Arabs took on the character of an aggressive interaction informed by a desire for violence.[2] Following Girard, we can say that the mimetic desire brings with it a cycle of violence, whose perpetration is perceived as revenge.[3]

This kind of Jewish connection with the Holy Land could be found in Europe at the end of the eighteenth century. While besieging Acre in 1799 as part of his campaign in the Ottoman territories of Egypt and Syria, Napoleon Bonaparte allegedly issued a proclamation promising to establish a Jewish state in Palestine. Regardless of the questionable authenticity of this proclamation, there was clearly no realistic option of implementing such a plan at the time.[4] Another case of a foreign presence in Palestine was that of Christian tourists, who flocked there for theological reasons, thrilled by the opportunity to visit the land in which the revelation took place. Christian tourists used travel guides, which were very popular during the nineteenth century. Needless to say, these guides clearly indicated that the pilgrims had no claim to the territory itself and were only staying temporarily in the Holy Land. Conversely, the indigenous Arab population had a very strong claim to the land of Palestine.[5]

Up to the 1860s, the protection of the Jews, including the Hasidim, in Eretz Israel was extended by non-Jewish sovereigns, not least by foreign councils that offered the Jews an alternative protection to that of the Ottoman authorities.[6] It was only after the late 1870s that the purpose of Jewish settlement became the establishment of Jewish sovereignty, rooted in the Zionist political theology that chose Zion, a sacred site to the Jews, as the space in which to realize Jewish settler colonialism. This colonialism gave rise to waves of violence and a perpetual conflict that persists to this day between the indigenous Palestinian population and Jews who came to the country mostly from Eastern Europe. As opposed to the nonviolent Hasidic immigrants, the Zionist violence produced an ongoing conflict that culminated in the 1948 War. The victory of Israeli military forces in that war resulted in the Nakba, in which most of the physical infrastructure of the Palestinian people was destroyed, and approximately 750,000 Palestinians fled or were driven out of the land and became refugees. The primary role of the Nakba was the creation, by violent means, of a Jewish majority within the State of Israel, in order to realize the Zionist dream of a Jewish, democratic state.

Exile in the Homeland

In speaking about the Hasidic immigrants, it is important to recall the verses in Leviticus that establish the relationship between religious observance and the question of ownership over the Land of Israel. The Israelites are told that if they obey God's commandments, "your threshing will overtake the vintage, and the vintage will overtake the sowing, and you will eat your bread to the full, and you will dwell securely in your land" (Lev. 26:5).[7] Leviticus also details what will happen if the Israelites fail to obey the commandments—including those pertaining specifically to the Land of Israel. As religiously observant Jews, the Hasidim who immigrated to Eretz Israel would have accepted the terms set out in Leviticus 26:21–34, whereby failure to fulfill all of God's commandments would lead to the destruction of the land and their ultimate expulsion from it.

Observance of God's commandments is thus a condition for the realization of the Jewish people's sovereign political rights over the territory of Eretz Israel. As noted, in the case of the Hasidim, this sovereignty was entirely passive and, in light of the above passage from Leviticus, contingent, temporary, and historical—a sovereignty that depended on the Jewish people's observance of God's laws. It is the political theology of God as ultimate sovereign that dictates the terms under which the Jewish people enjoy sovereignty over Eretz Israel.

Israel Halpern has formulated the Hasidic path to redemption by employing kabbalistic terminology:

> The path to redemption is thus the "repair of the world" [*tikkun ha-'olam*] through the elimination of the "shells" [*kelipot*], by means of ascents [of the soul; *'aliyot*], and "unifications" [of God's name; *yihudim*]. The act of [*tikkun*] can be performed anywhere and by anyone who knows how to perform [such] ascents and unifications. *Residing in Eretz Israel is not a precondition for redemption*, for R. Israel Ba'al Shem Tov in the Diaspora did more to repair [the world] and unify [God's name] than R. Abraham Gershon [the Besht's brother-in-law, who immigrated to Eretz Israel] in the Holy City [Jerusalem].[8]

The finding that residing in the holy territory is not a precondition for redemption can clarify the assertion that the concept of Jewish exile has nothing to do with a territorial demarcation line that distinguishes between the "exile" (galut) and the Holy Eretz Israel. This is why the Hasidim, as opposed to the Zionists, have refrained from any claim for territory and, by so doing, have refrained from establishing sovereignty. The Hasidim understand the Jewish exile not as an issue of territory, but as an issue of time. They believe that the Jewish people as a whole, regardless of its location on the globe, lives in an exile of time, awaiting redemption. This long waiting blurred the sharp Zionist distinction between Diaspora and homeland and gave rise to a Jewish political format that Israel Bartal termed "exile in the homeland."[9]

Symbol and Allegory

Moshe Idel's critique of reading the language of each and every kabbalistic text as symbolic is directed at Gershom Scholem, the most important scholar of Jewish mysticism. Idel claims that this all-inclusive reading ignores a large number of such texts—such as those of R. Abraham Abulafia—that were written as allegories. Whereas Scholem reads these writings as symbolic texts based on theosophy, Idel points out that allegoric kabbalistic texts were based on ecstasy; this implies that while symbolism in Scholem's reading is characterized as dynamic, Idel highlights the stasis of allegories. If the symbol maintains a permanent link between the signifier and the signified, the mechanical, nonorganic allegory highlights the basic mismatch between the allegorical signifier and its signified. Correspondingly, the unmediated match between the symbolizing and the symbolized of the symbol envelops it with a fog of meanings as a direct result of the fact that such a perfect match cannot practicably exist in a symbolic sacred text; hence the symbol cannot be reduced to one, single meaning. According to Idel, Abulafia therefore distances himself from the fogginess characterizing the symbol, which he regarded as no more than a replacement for a precise definition. It can thus be deduced that the two opposing axes of the kabbalistic text are the symbolism that relates to incomplete mystic experiences, on the one hand, and the experiences of mystic unification, articulated in a nonsymbolic language, on the other hand. In other words, the mystic experience expressed through a symbol does not allow unification with God, which is only possible through allegorical language. In accordance with Goethe's famous definition of the symbol, it abides by the rule that unifies the mystical experience with reality outside of this experience. Idel defines Hasidism as a combination of the symbolic and the allegorical:

> The Hasid shares a unifying religious ritual with the social group, which is nevertheless fraught with an element of transcendence that enables the achievement of a singularly individual experience of union. The initial stages of the mystical path in Hasidism at times also involved some symbolic significance. According to some Hasidic masters, however, the Lurianic *kavvanot*[10] that is, the symbolical referents of the *Sefirot* or of the divine configurations must be respectfully rejected, at least in the usage among the masses of Hasidism. As for the final stage of Hasidic mysticism, this is expressed by such metaphors as the drop and the ocean, swallowing, and so on, with no significant use of symbolism.[11]

The ecstatic experience at the core of Hasidic texts resides at the very base of the Hasidic community. Yet this ecstatic experience of Hasidic texts, such as R. Nahman of Braslav's tales, can also attest to their allegorical facet, which always maintains an ongoing gap between the allegorical signifiers and their signified. This crucial gap highlights the stasis of the Hasidic allegory, which prevents a symbolic, dynamic, and matter-of-fact connection between the symbolizing and the symbolized. Therefore, when the Holy Land appears as the symbolized, the mechanic, static allegory maintains a principled, unbridgeable gap between the sacred land and its Jewish inhabitants. In contrast, however, the dynamic symbol can serve the national discourse. Indeed, Scholem's definition of the symbol as interpreted by Idel refers directly to nationality:

> I would like to address the possible form of the transformation of traditional concepts like exile and redemption into kabbalistic symbols. In Scholem's explanation, it seems that there are two crucial elements that conspire in the formation of the symbol. On the one hand the historical experience of the nation, or at least of a significant part of it, probably condensed into concepts like exile and redemption, to take Scholem's recurring examples, and on the other hand through his inner experience the mystic combined and recirculated these concepts in the form of symbols that express, at the same time, the experience of the nation and of the individual.[12]

This is so because the very act of linking the appearance of the symbol's signifier and the dynamism of its signified, which appears as a given, is founded, more or less, on a stable connection between the signifier and the signified, that is—it includes a potential for change—creating a dynamism that will make it possible to match the national symbol to the changing historical circumstances within which the nation operates.

And indeed, nationality, which, as is well known, repeatedly employs the symbols representing it, maintains its loyalty—regardless of said historical changing circumstances—to the national territory as the foundation of its identity. The symbol can explain an outside reality and grant meaning to parts of the community that exist outside the private mystical experience of the ecstatic texts separating between the body's materiality and the soul. Thus, as opposed to the role of the symbol, which merges body and soul, the allegory of the Hasidic text, such as that of national redemption, cannot express an unconditional, material and stable connection to the soil of the Holy Land. For in contrast to allegory, the symbol, as defined by Walter Benjamin, is founded on a narrative of salvation: "Whereas in the symbol destruction is idealized and the transfigured face of nature is fleetingly revealed in the light of redemption, in allegory the observer is confronted with the *facies hippocratica* [the face as it appears near death] of history as a petrified, primordial landscape."[13] It is about this contingency, which defines the connection of the Hasidim to Eretz Israel, that Idel writes, "According to Hasidic literature, the Hasid has to raise the sparks in his vicinity and thus to purify and make it into a kind of Eretz Israel. In fact, it is not impossible that the Hasid will experience such an exalted mystical experience without actually immigrating to Eretz Israel."[14]

A Turning Point

The seventeenth century marked a turning point for the "Old" Yishuv (the Jewish community of Palestine before the establishment of Zionism). The non-territorial Jewish sovereignty of the Ottoman Empire, which controlled the affairs of the Jews of Palestine in their interactions with the imperial authorities, now assumed a new form. All such interactions were now assigned by the Ottoman authorities to the community elders known as *sheikh al-yahud* (sheikh of the Jews), while spiritual matters were entrusted to the *hakham ha-kahal* (the wise man of the community), who served the function of chief rabbi. Rabbinical courts operating in the Jewish Ottoman communities were part of the Sanjaks of Jerusalem, Nablus, and Acre. Although a majority of Jews in Palestine were Sephardim, distinctions between Sephardim and Ashkenazim became blurred starting in the seventeenth century, with the exception of the Ashkenazic community of Jerusalem, which was stable and had its own leadership.

From the seventeenth century onward, most of the Jews of Palestine owed their livelihood to the *halukah*, that is, the distribution of funds collected in the Jewish communities of Eastern Europe for that purpose. Nevertheless, the economic pressure exerted by local rulers on the Jews, combined with the irregular nature of the *halukah* itself,[15] created a political situation in which local Jewish communal sovereignty lost its power and hence its ability to control the funds that did arrive from Eastern Europe, including those sent by the Hasidic courts to support the Hasidim in Palestine.

Hasidic Immigrants

In 1764, a group of Hasidim arrived in Palestine from Constantinople, including two of the Ba'al Shem Tov's closest followers, R. Menahem Mendel of Przemyślany and R. Nahman of Horodenka, and settled in Tiberias. Another wave of immigrants reached Palestine in 1777, which included an organized group of disciples of the Maggid of Mezherich. This wave numbered hundreds of immigrants, most of whom were not Hasidim, and was headed by three prominent Hasidic leaders from Belarus: R. Menahem Mendel of Vitebsk, R. Abraham of Kalisk, and R. Israel of Polotsk. These leaders instructed the new arrivals to settle in Safed. Although there was already a small Ashkenazic community there, the newcomers established their own institutions and immediately found themselves at odds with the Ashkenazim, probably as a result of interference by the Lithuanian *mitnagdim* (the Hasidic Orthodox opponents). Another conflict erupted between the Hasidim and the Sephardic community, stemming from disagreements over the division of *halukah* funds. There were also differences in religious practices, and Hasidim were suspected of Sabbateanism, the movement created after the massacres of the 1648 Khmelnytsky Uprising and led by the false messiah Sabbatai Zevi, who eventually converted to Islam. Despite the fact that a large group, headed by R. Menahem Mendel of Vitebsk, broke away from the Hasidim in Safed and moved to Tiberias, the disputes between the Hasidim and the Ashkenazic and Sephardic communities persisted.[16]

There are two basic approaches to the messianic element in Hasidism. The first was developed by the preeminent scholar of Hasidism Simon Dubnow, who described the Hasidic view of redemption as a transition from national to personal redemption and considered that to be the primary goal of establishing a Hasidic center in the Land of Israel in line with the tradition of earlier kabbalist immigration to the Holy Land.[17] Conversely, the Zionist historian Ben Zion Dinur highlighted the messianism of Hasidism, particularly in the Land of Israel, as a means to hastening redemption.[18] Hasidism initially emerged in the wake of the massacres of the seventeenth century in Ukraine as a movement offering both a renewal of Judaism and a new hope for redemption (with Sabbateanism and Frankism as its radical offshoots). Gershom Scholem, for his part, rejected the notion of a messianic element in Hasidism altogether, citing a decline in messianic tension in early Hasidism.[19]

A Spiritual Connection

A Hasidic homily by the well-known Hasidic rabbi Levi Isaac of Berdichev offers a different perspective on what we saw above in Leviticus 26:16. Although R. Levi Isaac accepts the logic of the verse about the connection between nonobservance and the punishment of losing possession of the Land of Israel, he also seeks to reverse its meaning:

> "*Pakadeti aleikhem behalah* [I will (direct) panic upon you]." The word *pakadeti* implies absence, as in "And David's place was vacant [*va-yipaked*]," that is to say, I will remove panic and other misfortunes from you, for they will not exist among you. "And you shall sow in vain," because the Land of Israel will put forth cakes and clothing of fine wool, and sowing will be in vain for there will be no reason to sow, and only your enemies will sow.[20]

The phrase "And David's place was vacant [*va-yipaked*]" appears in 1 Samuel (20:25 and again in verse 27): "And the king sat in his place as he was wont to do, in the seat by the wall, and Jonathan preceded him, and Abner sat by Saul's side, and David's place was vacant." It refers to the fact that David was hiding from Saul and therefore failed to appear at the king's table. In R. Levi Isaac's homily, the removal of panic by God is like the absence of the fleeing David, who would one day become king of Israel and perhaps even the Messiah King. This dialectic of panic revealed to be kingship results in the fact that the removal of other misfortunes will render the sowing of seeds in the Land of Israel unnecessary, as R. Levi Isaac explains, because Jewish life on the holy soil of Eretz Israel will be sustained by the grace of God, as the land will produce cakes without any need for the Jews to sow. What is more, the fact that the Jews would no longer have any need to sow brings R. Levi Isaac to explain that sowing will be left to their enemies. R. Levi Isaac thus creates a fascinating distinction between the Hasidic Jewish community in the Land of Israel, which will strive to live in purity and holiness, without physically cultivating the land, and the enemies of Israel, to whom that task will fall. According to this approach, the Jews have no connection to the physical settlement of Eretz Israel, which could lead to violence. What is clear here is that instead, R. Levi Isaac highlights the spiritual and theological connection that binds the non-Jews to them as agricultural laborers.

A Non-National Community

In general, the conflicts that arose between the Hasidim and the Palestinian Arabs stemmed from the dependence of the former on the latter, from their vulnerability to attack, theft, and derision, and subsequently from their reliance on the protection of European representatives in the region. This was by no means a national conflict. As European involvement in the area increased, the influence of the local Muslim majority declined, but the Jews—acutely aware of the asymmetry between their respective positions—persisted in their traditional contacts with the locals.[21] A letter sent to the Diaspora by R. Abraham of Kalisk and twenty other Hasidim in 1789 reflects the fact that the conflict with the Arabs was not perceived as a national or ethnic struggle, but rather concerned issues such as banditry—treated in the letter as but one of the many financial hardships the Hasidim of the Land of Israel were forced to endure.[22]

The reason for this is that the Arabs of Palestine did not see the Hasidic immigrants as a threat to their status as inhabitants of the region that the Hasidim called Eretz Israel. Neither the Ashkenazim nor the Sephardim in Palestine constituted what Benedict Anderson coined a transcendent imagined national community.[23] The members of this non-national community dwelled in places that were not perceived as greater than the sum of their parts, that is, what Aran and Gurevitch called "the Big Place."[24] So too, the notion of the Jewish people as "chosen" remained a purely theological concept, limited to Scripture and devoid of any desire for a national and actual political materialization.

As noted above, neither the various and disparate Jewish communities, nor the similarly fragmented "Holy Land," nor the Jews of the Old Yishuv in Jerusalem, Tiberias, Safed, and Hebron posed a threat to the Arab inhabitants of the land. In fact, the opposite was true, as can be seen from the Hasidic correspondence with the Diaspora. For although most of the letters were filled with complaints about the economic situation and with requests for help, they also included descriptions of daily life, especially of religious life.

A letter sent by R. Abraham Gershon of Kuty to his brother-in-law, the Ba'al Shem Tov, in the Hebrew year 5508 (1747–48) mentions the friendly relations between Jews and Muslims—who took part in Jewish religious ceremonies and celebrations, such as circumcisions, at which there was singing in both Hebrew and Arabic.²⁵

Most of the political clashes involving Jews in Palestine in the late eighteenth to mid-nineteenth centuries were not with Arabs but with other Jews, whether between Ashkenazim and Sephardim or within the Ashkenazic community. For example, in a joint letter written in Safed and Tiberias in 1781, R. Menahem Mendel of Vitebsk and R. Abraham of Kalisk appealed to Hasidic rabbis in the Diaspora: "Until now, I did not wish to distress my dear friend, but today it is my duty to say [these things]. When we arrived in the 'Holy Land,' we found it ruined and desolate, with not a soul to worship God. And the Ashkenazim who were here before are foolish people, who disrupt and disturb the worship of God."²⁶

A letter sent by R. Menahem Mendel of Vitebsk and R. Abraham of Kalisk from Tiberias in (1784–85) clearly indicates that the Hasidic development of an alternative local sovereignty was a result of an internal Jewish conflict, in the course of which the Hasidim presented a strong political stance against the Maskilim (members of the Jewish Enlightenment) struggling for Jewish emancipation in Russia.²⁷

According to Ya'acov Barnai's interpretation, the letter's authors feared the Jewish struggle for equal rights in Russia, believing that Jewish interference in the politics of the empire would lead to discord between Jews.²⁸ Indeed, from the Hasidic perspective, emancipation would have drawn the Jews into gentile politics by subsuming the theo-political Jewish sovereignty of the Hasidic court under the political emancipation granted by the non-Jewish state.

Facing the National Project

The political conduct of the Hasidim was transformed, however, with the beginning of Zionist settlement in Palestine, conceived as a national project, in the early 1880s. The Hasidim of Eretz Israel became the target of Zionism's sharp criticism of traditional Jewish society, focused as it was on study and unwilling to address the need to defend itself against gentile violence. Yet this contrast between Zionism and the Hasidic movement was not binary, and in the late nineteenth and early twentieth centuries, writers such as Martin Buber, Michah Joseph Berdichevsky, and others developed a form of neoromantic Hasidic Zionist literature, which reworked traditional Hasidic texts to create modernist Hebrew literature.

Partha Chatterjee (quoting John Plamenatz) describes this process of the constitution of nationality as an attempt that

> is deeply contradictory: "It is both imitative and hostile to the models it imitates...." It is imitative in that it accepts the value of the standard set by alien culture. But it also involves a rejection: "in fact, two rejections, both of them ambivalent: rejection of the alien intruder and dominator who is nevertheless to be imitated and surpassed by his own standards,

and rejection of ancestral ways which are seen as obstacles to progress and yet also cherished as marks of identity."[29]

Nevertheless, prior to the arrival of the Zionists, the conflict between Jews and Muslims in Jerusalem, Tiberias, Safed, and Hebron was light-years away from the manner in which the conflict between Jews and Arabs developed in the wake of the Zionist immigration of the late 1870s and early 1880s. For in the conflict between the Hasidim and the indigenous Arabs, the identity of the "enemy" was not national, but rather religious, ethnic, or economic, in the sense of relations between creditor and debtor.

Auto-Emancipation

The idea of Jewish colonialist expropriation of Eretz Israel won legitimacy in the wake of Leo Pinsker's foundational Zionist text *Auto-Emancipation*, published in 1882. Pinsker pointed to the frightening liminality of Jewish existence in Europe as the primary cause of the pogroms—the violent response of non-Jews to the specter of Jewish liminality, as a walking living dead that disseminates Judophobia. The solution that Pinsker proposed to the Jewish question in Europe was to relocate the Jews to a territory where their existence would not be threatened by non-Jews: "We need nothing but a large piece of land for our poor brothers; a piece of land which shall remain our property, from which no foreign master can expel us."[30] Pinsker's text did not include any clear indication of the specific territory to which the Jews might be relocated. Following pressure from the Hovevei Zion (Lovers of Zion) movement, however, Pinsker acceded to their demand to indicate Eretz Israel as the territory where his proposal could be implemented. The choice of the Land of Israel as the place in which the Jewish question would be resolved was a political decision based on Jewish theology, which viewed the Land of Zion as the locus of the Jewish people's future redemption.

It was at this moment that a contradiction arose between the rational, modern, and universal basis of Jewish political culture and the particularities of theological Jewish nationalism. At the heart of this contradiction lay the fundamental difference between the non-imagined face-to-face community of the Hasidim of Eretz Israel and the Zionist imagined national community.

Unlike the Hasidic community, which made no claim to eternal control over national soil, Zionism demanded and continues to demand eternal control over the soil of Eretz Israel, as a theological construct. The contradiction between Hasidism and Zionism is particularly evident in the Hasidic indifference to the identity of the sovereign, beyond the realm of the tzaddik, who is sovereign of the Hasidic court that exists as a "state within a state,"[31] in stark contradiction to the democratic civic sovereignty to which Zionism aspires. The fundamental reason for this contradiction is that "if nationalism expresses itself in a frenzy of irrational passion, it does so *because* it seeks to represent itself in the image of the Enlightenment and *fails* to do so. For enlightenment itself, to assert its sovereignty as the universal ideal, needs its Other."[32] Thus, after the implementation of the Partition Plan failed, what remained as the only feasible solution was the exercise of violence against the Palestinian other. It was the only viable option for establishing the apparently universalistic, enlightened Israeli citizenship, which was realized within a Jewish-majority democratic nation-state. In other words, in this very historical moment, the definition of the State of Israel as a Jewish and democratic nation-state created the necessity to expel the Palestinians from its territory, since they prevented the creation of a Jewish majority that purports to realize the political theology of Jewish sovereignty. The Nakba therefore enabled and continues to enable the existence of the State of Israel as a democratic state with a Jewish majority, founded on the destruction of the Palestinian people.

From the perspective of the Zionist political theology inspired by Pinsker, which ultimately lay at the heart of the Zionist solution to the Jewish question, the indigenous inhabitants of the land were an enemy, liable to respond with violence to the colonial Zionist project. As was noted above regarding René Girard's thesis, it looks like there is an explanation for the fact that the Jews turned their imitative revenge for the violence of the non-Jewish Eastern European pogromists against the indigenous Arabs and against potential Arab violence as an anticipated response to Jewish colonialism. It may thus be said that the project of transferring revenge from the violent Diaspora to the Land of Israel attests to the fact that *the Zionist project is ultimately one of revenge*.

Revenge

Revenge is a violent act that occurs outside the law. As noted, both the avenging God and the object of God's revenge, and the avenging people and the object of its revenge, are part of a cycle of revenge that exists outside the covenant—first by the people violating its law and second by God, who takes revenge by violating the law of the covenant. But, in principle, the difference between human beings and God is based on the idea that human beings are included in God and not vice versa. The fact that God takes revenge does not contradict the fact that God can avoid it if God wishes. This is a good reason for the dramatic shift in Leviticus 26, where God declares that despite all of the people's transgressions, God will not violate the covenant. At the current stage of Jewish history, however, which unfolds as Zionist national history, the unexpected shift in Leviticus 26 can also be explained differently. Contrary to the Hasidic tzaddik—a Jewish sovereign who makes no claim to control over the Land of Israel—the Zionist sovereign is a violent ruler who orders a Jewish colonial project that aspires to control all of the Land of Israel as an imagined space. As a result, the revenge that had previously been outside sovereign law becomes revenge that operates within sovereign law, as expanded by Zionism. This expansion affords legitimacy to revenge, effectively transforming illegal revenge into legal revenge. This transformation of illegal revenge into a legal revenge is justified in public by the Zionist political theology's claim over the soil of the Holy Land. Conversely, because Hasidic political theology has no political claim over the soil of the Land of Israel, Hasidim can avoid any need for such a transformation. Since there is no colonialism, there is no need to justify violent revenge.

The relocation of avenging Jewish violence from the Diaspora to the Land of Israel thus changes the illegitimate revenge of the Diaspora into a legitimate violent response, that is, violence subject to sovereign law. The revenge of a persecuted people, which should have been exacted in the Diaspora, is relocated to Eretz Israel, as a justification for the Zionist violence that creates a space without non-Jews, erasing the fact of its indigenous inhabitants' existence by means of the metaphoric "building of the land." The moment that Zionist colonialism imported the Jewish question from Europe to the Middle East, it constituted a sovereign charged with the task of resolving the Jewish question in Eretz Israel, thereby rendering revenge legitimate.

Dialectically, a Zionist sovereign in control of violence directed against the indigenous Arab inhabitants of the country negates the definition of the Jewish violence as revenge. Jewish revenge against the anti-Jewish pogromists in the Diaspora is thus afforded legitimacy in the form of violence directed against the indigenous Arabs in the Land of Israel. It is violence directed against those who seek to thwart the realization of Pinsker's solution to the Jewish question, based on the creation of a space without non-Jews. It is the Jewish colonial violence that has won legitimacy and creates a space without non-Jews by expelling the Palestinians from it, that is, by means of the Nakba. It is thus clear that the desire to realize the idea of the establishment of a Jewish state as a democratic state—that is, as a democratic state that relies upon a Jewish majority—made the Nakba a necessity.

Importing the Jewish Question

Zionism is based on rehabilitating the autonomy of the Enlightenment subject, which is antithetical to Hasidic subjects, who distinguish themselves from the former, constituting themselves instead in accordance with the tzaddik's instructions. Consequently, unlike Enlightenment subjects, whose universality allows them to fight for the legitimacy of their revenge under any sovereignty, Jewish or non-Jewish, the violence of Hasidism is barred from acting outside the Jewish context, as it is the only context in which it can obtain legitimacy.

God justifies revenge by God's people's violation of the covenant. It was the people who violated the "covenant of the pieces" (Genesis 15) forged with Abraham, as well as the Sinaitic covenant. The political theology of God as sovereign dictates the conditions that, in their fulfilment, allow the Jews to rule over the Land of Israel. The cyclical narrative of revenge, in which threats and warnings of the misfortunes that will befall the people for violating God's precepts give way to God's proclamation of the eternity of the covenant, is explicated by Rashi (the greatest Jewish commentator of the Hebrew Bible and Talmud) in his commentary on Leviticus (26:9), which marks an earlier stage in the cycle of avenging violence ("and I shall fulfill my covenant with you"): "A new covenant, not like the first covenant that you violated, but a new covenant that will not be violated, as it is written (Jer. 31:30–31), 'I will make a new covenant with the house of Israel and with the house of Judah, not like the covenant, etc.'"

Forging a new covenant between the people and God establishes a new sovereign law, the role of which is to justify the people's newly acquired control over the Land of Israel. As a result, however, divine revenge outside the law will now also be justified by the new law. Revenge in response to the violation of the covenant becomes legitimate, by virtue of the new covenant being enshrined in the divine sovereign's law. The new covenant is the modern Jewish covenant that places the relationship between the Jewish people and God on a new plane of obedience, although the contingency of obedience—even in the new, modern covenant—may, at any moment, arouse divine violence in response to violence on the part of the people, and so on and so forth.

As analyzed by Yotam Hotam,[33] the gnosticism of Zionism that allowed the Jews to import the Jewish question from Europe to Eretz Israel is what turns revenge against the non-Jews into violence that exists within the framework of sovereign law, that is, justified violence directed against the non-Jewish inhabitants of Palestine. Contrary to the transcendent evil God who resides in the Diaspora, for whom violation of the covenant justifies revenge against the Jews by means of violent pogroms outside the law, the immanent, organic good God eliminates the identification of Jewish violence as revenge and affords theological justification to the Zionist Jewish colonial violence. Unlike Rashi, who lived in the Diaspora and interpreted the biblical "revenge of the covenant" as the constitution of a new covenant that would enable continued Jewish existence in the Diaspora, the Zionists want to respond with violence to the actions of the non-Jews within a process that relocates revenge against the non-Jews from the Diaspora to the Land of Israel.

Following Yotam Hotam, the political theology at the heart of the Zionist aspiration to sovereignty may be understood as gnostic theology, that is, dualistic rather than monotheistic. The distinction between the good God and the evil God is a distinction between a good and immanent God, who is theologically connected to the Land of Israel, and an evil, transcendent God, who exists in the Diaspora. Fulfilling the demands of the good God to settle in the Land of Israel would thus suffice to eliminate the justification for God's revenge. In contrast to the Hasidic position, whereby *"residing in Eretz Israel is not a precondition for redemption,"*[34] the organic connection between the good God and the land is a gnostic national connection that rejects traditional Judaism and offers a nationalist and violent political theology without alternative ethical inhibitions. The quintessential representative of this theology in modern Judaism is Michah Joseph Berdichevsky, who, as mentioned above, was a leading exponent of Nietzscheanism in Zionism, created neoromantic and Zionist versions of Hasidic tales, and advocated the creation of a "new Jew" or "Hebrew" as the goal of Zionism. Berdichevsky, who criticized Jewish monotheism, embraced organic and irrational nationalism, and above all, stressed the importance of the soil of the national homeland as the immanent foundation of the Hebrew nation.

Nationalist Jews

From the late 1870s to the early 1880s, nationalist Jews—referred to collectively in Zionist historiography as the First Aliyah—began arriving in Palestine. At this initial stage of Zionist immigration to Palestine, the idea of sovereignty rooted in political theology—that is, national, theological, and imagined sovereignty over all of Eretz Israel—was not yet fully developed.[35] It was only at the time of the Second Aliyah (1904–14) that the sovereign and theological concept of *halutzim* (pioneers) came into being: an avant-garde representing the entire Jewish people. The underlying religious foundation of that people was, at that time, undergoing an accelerated process of modernization, secularization, and identity formation as a modern nation. Zionism thus saw in the constitution of "auto-emancipation" in the form of Jewish sovereignty a modern solution to the Jewish question—an alternative to Jewish efforts to obtain full civil rights within the countries of Europe.

Indeed, even before the founding of the Zionist movement at the First Zionist Congress in Basel in 1897, Jews immigrated to Eretz Israel in order to settle there for eternity. This was the violent appropriation of the Land of Israel by the Jews, ignoring the fact that according to the Bible, such violent, colonial appropriation can only be sanctioned on a temporary and conditional basis, not as an eternal possession. Zionism thus disrupted the theological continuity on which the Jewish people had relied for generations—a continuity that the Zionist critic Ahad Ha'am sought to preserve and in which Berdichevsky, who had a "torn heart," continuously sought to create ever-greater rifts. A fascinating example of this disregard can be found in the words of one of the Bilu (a First Aliyah pioneers group) immigrants, Ze'ev Dubnow, brother of the well-known historian Simon Dubnow, written on 1 January 1882:

> Our ultimate goal is to conquer the Land of Israel and restore the political independence stolen from the Jews two thousand years ago. To achieve this end, agricultural and industrial colonies must be established, numerous factories built and constantly expanded. In short, every effort must be made to ensure that land, commerce, and manufacture are controlled by Jews. Furthermore, the young people must be trained in the use of arms. And then that wonderful day will come, prophesized by Isaiah in his passionate words of consolation. Then the Jews themselves will declare, loudly and publicly, bearing arms (if necessary), that they are the masters of their ancient homeland.[36]

It seems eminently clear that Ze'ev Dubnow justified the violence of Jewish settlement as a means to the establishment of Jewish sovereignty. Following Carl Schmitt, the aspiration to sovereignty shared by Dubnow and his fellow Bilu immigrants may be characterized as the result of their having declared a state of emergency for the Jews of Eastern Europe, which demanded a revolutionary, Zionist solution to the Jewish question, entailing its relocation from Europe to Eretz Israel. Violent sovereignty is justified by the sovereign who constitutes himself by declaring a state of emergency based on the political theology that Dubnow expresses in terms of the connection between Jewish violence and the vision of the prophet Isaiah.[37]

Therein lies the fundamental difference between the nationalism of the Bilu immigrants, who brought a revolutionary tradition with them from Russia, which they translated into a Zionist political theology with a violent potential, as described by Dubnow, and the nonviolent Hasidim. The Hasidic nonviolent approach and their refrain from any national appropriation of Arab lands allowed them to comply with the divine condition for their presence in Eretz Israel, satisfied merely by observing the commandment to settle the land. From a Hasidic-Haredi (ultra-Orthodox) perspective, nothing seemed to have changed, and living in the Land of Israel without observing the commandments, including the prohibition of the "three oaths," offered sufficient reason for God's revenge.

Contrary to the Ashkenazic rabbis in Jerusalem, who vehemently opposed the establishment of the colonies,[38] there were a number of figures in Palestine, such as Yoel Moshe Salomon, Arieh Leib Frumkin, and Joseph Joel Rivlin, who in 1878 sought to bring about change in the economic and social life of the Old Yishuv, without departing from religious tradition.[39] The bitter conflict that ensued between the nationalist approach of the Hovevei Zion movement and the leaders of the Ashkenazic community in Jerusalem largely paralleled the clash between those who viewed agriculture as a romantic nationalist project and those, like Salomon, who saw it as an economic solution for the poor.[40] In contrast to the Bilu pioneers, however, the rabbis and the Old Yishuv reformers would seem to have shared a negative view of the use of violence in and of itself, rather than for the sole purpose of defending the young colonies.

This was the attitude of the settlers of the First Aliyah to violence directed against them—as, for example, in Petah Tikva, the first colony, established in 1878. The violence directed by local Arabs against the colony's farmers and the farmers' violent response were not yet the result of a national conflict. This violence was unrelated to the violent political theology of Zionism and thus did not bring about the creation of a national Hebrew defense force. It was only during the period of the Second Aliyah that the Bar Giyora (1907) and Hashomer (1909) associations were formed, as Hebrew—namely, modern—nationalistic military forces that responded with violence against the local Arabs who attacked the Jewish project described by Gershon Shafir as settler colonialism.[41] The Orthodoxy of the colonists of the First Aliyah thus differed from the Zionist theology that sought to constitute Jewish sovereignty in

Eretz Israel through their colonies, while the colonists themselves constituted the sovereignty of the New Yishuv through the violence they directed against Arab hostility, which in turn evolved into Arab resistance.

There can be no doubt that the message formulated by Pinsker in *Auto-Emancipation*—essentially that the Jewish question will be resolved by relocating the endangered Jews of Europe to a space without non-Jews—a message that guided the Jews to settle in Eretz Israel, was a constitutive moment in the history of the Jewish people. From a force that drove Jewish immigration to Eretz Israel for theological reasons, entirely devoid of any claim to control over the land or its inhabitants, such as that which motivated Hasidic immigration, immigration to the Land of Israel became an act of political theology intended to constitute Zionist sovereignty there. Indeed, the active and violent political theology of Zionism, which entailed a rejection of the religious observance of the Old Yishuv, stood in sharp contrast to the passive Hasidic theology, which made no claims to territorial control of any kind.

It was a slow process, and at its inception—the founding of Petah Tikva in 1878—the colonists still observed all of the religious precepts. As time passed, however, the tendency to reject religious observance grew, and Zionist political theology became a tool for the constitution of Jewish sovereignty, in the context of which the fulfillment of theological commandments was subjugated to extraneous violent political goals. Jewish political power transformed a Hasidic theology devoid of territorial claims in Palestine into an aggressive Zionist force that rained terror on the Arab inhabitants of the land.

It is Zionist political theology that provides the justification for ethnocentrism and affords legitimacy to the use of violence in order to rule over the Land of Israel and its inhabitants. Abandoning the monotheism of the Hasidim makes Zionism's principles of civic universalism and Enlightenment values into no more than a disguise for a violent tribal society. Commitment to a dualistic Zionist gnosis compels the Zionists to create a space controlled by the evil God, which is inhabited by non-Jews and stands in contrast to the space controlled by the good God. This good God's space does not include non-Jews and is based on the logic of Zionist political theology that culminated in the ethnic cleansing of the Palestinians by the Israel Defense Forces during the 1948 War. In keeping with Pinsker's proposal in *Auto-Emancipation*, the solution of the Jewish question must be realized by relocating the Jews from Europe to a space without non-Jews, later identified as Zion. One need not have an active political imagination to understand the direct connection between Pinsker's proposed solution to the Jewish question and the Nakba, which sought to resolve the Jewish question by creating a space free of non-Jews or at least a space with a Jewish majority that would enable the creation of a "Jewish democracy"—a regime founded on an oxymoron, between civic universalism and theological particularism. We may now clearly see how, in sharp contrast to the violent colonial logic of Zionist theology, Hasidic theology made no territorial claims in Eretz Israel, nor did it view the separation between Jews and non-Jews in the Diaspora in a theological and violent political light.

The Jewish theological aspect of Zionism, however, made the apostasy of rejecting religious observance into a new kind of apostasy: apostasy against apostasy. This is the moment in which the gnostic and dualistic nature of Zionism is revealed. The first apostasy, which was directed against observance of the religious precepts, appears to have created a clear dichotomy between nonreligious Zionism and secular Zionism. It is a dualistic scenario, in which the evil God represents flawed Jewish life in the Diaspora, while the good God represents healthy Jewish life in the Land of Israel. The Zionist political theological dimension of Jewish sovereignty, which renders it ethnocentric, denying full civil rights to the inhabitants of the land over whom it rules, results in the second apostasy, against the first heresy.

The Hasidic version of political theology is essentially that of Martin Buber, whose opposition to exclusive Jewish sovereignty brought him to support the idea of bi-nationalism, in the spirit of Hasidism that sets itself apart from political sovereignty. Buber's disregard of Zionist gnosis also received expression in his disregard of the kabbalistic element in Hasidism. Gershom Scholem, who was highly critical of Buber's views on this matter, adopted a gnostic Zionist position that aspired to exclusive Jewish sovereignty. Although a member of Brit Shalom (a group of intellectuals and scholars who advocated a binational state) in the 1920s, by the end of the 1930s and especially after the Holocaust, Scholem abandoned the idea of binational sovereignty, embracing the principle of exclusive Jewish sovereignty that provided the rationale of the 1948 War and justified the establishment of the "democratic" State of Israel.

It was Buber who, at the height of the 1948 War, wrote a trenchant article calling for an end to ambiguity regarding the existence of Jewish colonialism. In this article, "Let Us Make an End to Falsities,"[42] Buber examined the prevailing Jewish position, which ignored the existence of Jewish colonialism and claimed that it was the Palestinians who had started the war, immediately after the United Nations decided in favor of partitioning Palestine, on 29 November 1947. During the war itself, as the battles raged, Buber showed remarkable civic courage, arguing that the specific date on which the Palestinians had launched the 1948 War was irrelevant. It thus goes without saying that Buber utterly rejected the claim that since it was the Palestinians who had attacked first, due to their opposition to the UN partition plan, it was they who brought the Nakba upon themselves.

Conclusion

The Hasidim who immigrated to Eretz Israel left the Jewish question behind in Europe. More precisely, they left its solution—whether by emancipation or auto-emancipation—to the Maskilim and, later, to the Jewish nationalists. Hasidism preserved its independence within the Russian Empire, refusing to accept the acculturation that the authorities tried to force upon it. The Hasidim adopted a *politics of survival* vis-à-vis the Russian Empire, distancing themselves from non-Jewish politics, thereby allowing Hasidic immigrants to Eretz Israel to refrain from the kind of aggression and political violence that characterized colonial Jewish immigration.

For this reason, the Hasidim were not involved in importing the Jewish question from Europe to the Middle East and were therefore not compelled to resolve it by creating a space free of non-Jews. What is more, they did not share the Zionist demand for a violent response to the pogroms and thus had no part in the narrative that relocated revenge against the non-Jews to the Land of Israel. As noted above, this relocation of Jewish violence from the Diaspora to Eretz Israel ultimately changed the illegitimate violence of revenge in the Diaspora into a legitimate response. The revenge of the persecuted people, which should have been exacted in the Diaspora, was transferred to the Land of Israel as justification for Zionist violence aimed at creating a space free of non-Jews, erasing the fact of its indigenous inhabitants' existence by means of the metaphoric "building of the land." Thus, the legitimacy of revenge as a Zionist solution to the Jewish question affords legitimacy to the Nakba, that is, the expulsion of the Palestinians from the land. In light of the above, it is also clear that the idea of creating a Jewish majority that would allow for the establishment of a Jewish state as a democracy made the local Palestinian population an obstacle—one that could only be overcome by means of the Jewish violence that brought about the Palestinian Nakba.

Hannan Hever is the Jacob and Hilda Blaustein Professor of Hebrew Language and Literature and Comparative Literature in the Comparative Literature Department, and affiliated with the Program of Judaic Studies, at Yale University. He taught at the Hebrew University in Jerusalem, Tel Aviv University, Northwestern University, Michigan University–Ann Arbor, Jewish Theological Seminary, and Columbia University. His most recent books are *Nativism, Zionism and Beyond: Three Essays on Nativist Hebrew Poetry* (2014); *With the Power of God: Political Theology in Modern Hebrew Literature* (2014); *To Inherit the Land, To Conquer the Space: The Birth of Hebrew Poetry in Eretz Yisrael* (2015); *Suddenly the Sight of War: Nationalism and Violence in the Hebrew Poetry of the 1940s* (2016); *We Are Broken Rhymes: The Politics of Trauma in Israeli Literature* (2017); and *Hebrew Literature and the 1948 War: Essays on Philology and Responsibility* (2019).

Notes

1. Yehoshua Ben-Arieh, *Keytzad notzrah Eretz Israel ba-'et ha-hadasha 1799–1949* [The making of Eretz Israel in the modern era 1799–1949] (Jerusalem: Yad Yitzhak Ben-Zvi and Magnes, 2018).
2. René Girard, *Things Hidden since the Foundation of the World*, ed. and trans. Stephen Bann and Michael Metter (Stanford: Stanford University Press, 1987), 146, 169.
3. Paisley Livingston, *Models of Desire: René Girard and the Psychology of Mimesis* (Baltimore: Johns Hopkins University Press), 141.
4. Ben-Arieh, *Keytzad notzrah Eretz Israel*, 44.
5. Ben-Arieh, *Keytzad notzrah Eretz Israel*, 74–76, 84–85, 88.

6. Ben-Arieh, *Keytzad notzrah Eretz Israel*. 44.
7. Robert Alter, *The Hebrew Bible: A Translation with Commentary* (New York: W. W. Norton, 2018).
8. Israel Halpern, *Ha-'aliyot ha-rishonot shel ha-Hasidim le-Eretz Israel* [The Hasidic immigration to Palestine during the eighteenth century] (Jerusalem and Tel Aviv: Schocken, 1946), 2, 14–15 (emphasis added).
9. Israel Bartal, *Galut ba-aretz: Yishuv Eretz Israel be-terem tziyonut* [Exile in the homeland: Settling Eretz Israel before Zionism] (Jerusalem: Hasifriyah Hatziyonit, 1994). I want to thank Elhanan Reiner for his valuable help in writing this paragraph.
10. The kabbalistic practice of prayer intentions.
11. Moshe Idel, *Kabbalah: New Perspectives* (New Haven: Yale University Press, 1988), 219.
12. Moshe Idel, "Function of Symbols in Gershom Scholem," in *Old Words, New Mirrors, on Jewish Mysticism* (Philadelphia: University of Pennsylvania Press, 2010), 83–108.
13. Walter Benjamin, *The Origin of German Tragic Drama*, trans. John Osborne (London: Verso, 1985), 166.
14. Moshe Idel, "Al Eretz Yisrael bamahshava ha-mystit shel yemay ha-beynaim" [On the Land of Israel in the mystical thought of the Middle Ages], in *Eretz-Israel bahagut ha-yehudit biyemey ha-beynaim* [The Land of Israel in the Jewish thought of the Middle Ages], ed. Moshe Halamish and Aviezer Ravitzki (Jerusalem: Yad Yitzhak Ben-Zvi, 1991), 209–210.
15. Ya'acov Barnai, ed., *Igerot Hasidim me-Eretz Israel: Min ha-mahatzit ha-sheniyah shel ha-me'ah ha-18 u-me-reshit ha-me'ah ha-19* [Hasidic letters from Eretz Israel: From the second part of the eighteenth century and the first part of the nineteenth century] (Jerusalem: Yad Yitzhak Ben-Zvi, 1980), 17–18.
16. Barnai, *Igerot Hasidim*, 25.
17. Simon Dubnow, "Ha-hasidim ha-rishonim be-Eretz Israel" [The first Hasidim in the Land of Israel], *Pardes* 2 (1894): 206.
18. Ben Zion Dinur, "Reshitah shel ha-Hasidut ve-yesodoteha ha-sotziyaliyim ve-ha-meshihiyim" [The origins of Hasidism and its social and messianic foundations], in Ketaviym Historiyim, vol. 1, *Bemifneh ha-dorot: Mehkarim ve-'iyunim be-reshitam shel ha-zemanim ha-hadashim be-toledot Israel*, ed. Ben Zion Dinur (Jerusalem: Bialik Institution, 1955), 81–227.
19. Gershom Scholem, "The Neutralization of the Messianic Element in Early Hasidism," in *The Messianic Idea in Judaism and Other Essays on Jewish Spirituality* (New York: Schocken, 1995), 176–202.
20. Levi Isaac of Berdichev, *Sefer kedushat Levi 'al ha-Torah u-mo'adim* [Torah commentary], (Jerusalem: Or Haim, 2008), 725. All translations are mine, unless otherwise indicated (H.H.).
21. Bartal, *Galut ba-aretz*, 16, 60.
22. Barnai, *Igerot Hasidim*, 204–205.
23. Benedict Anderson, *Imagined Communities: Reflections on the Origins and Spread on Nationalism* (London: Verso, 2006).
24. Zali Gurevitch and Gideon Aran, "Al ha-makom: Antropologiyah Israelit" [On the place: Israeli anthropology], *Alpayim* 4 (1991): 9–44.
25. Barnai, *Igerot Hasidim*, 39. Incidentally, my partner Orly Lubin, who is a seventh-generation descendant of Karlin Hasidim who immigrated to Palestine in the early nineteenth century and settled in Tiberias, recalls how her father used to sing the songs of the Passover Seder in Arabic as well as Hebrew.
26. Barnai, *Igerot Hasidim*, 84.
27. Barnai, *Igerot Hasidim*, 119.
28. Barnai, *Igerot Hasidim*, 8–9.
29. Partha Chatterjee, *Nationalist Thought and the Colonial World: A Derivative Discourse* (Minneapolis: University of Minnesota, 1993), 2.
30. Leo Pinsker, *Auto-Emancipation*, trans. D. S. Blondheim (New York: Maccabaean, 1906 [1882]), 11.
31. David Assaf, *The Regal Way: The Life and Times of Rabbi Israel of Ruzhin* (Stanford: Stanford University Press, 2002).
32. Chatterjee, *Nationalist Thought and the Colonial World*, 17.
33. Yotam Hotam, *Modern Gnosis and Zionism: The Crisis of Culture, Life Philosophy and Jewish National Thought*, trans. Avner Greenberg (London: Routledge, 2013).

34. Halpern, *Ha-'aliyot ha-rishonot*, 15; emphasis added.
35. Margalit Shilo, "Mi-tfisa 'Moshavtit' le-tefisa 'Yeshuvit Klalit'" [From the concept of a "settlement" to the concept of "wholesale settlement"], *Zion* 57, no. 1 (1992): 65–88.
36. Shulamit Laskov and Alter Druyanow, eds., *Ketavim le-toledot Hibbat Zion ve-yishuv Eretz Israel* [Documents on the history of Hibbat Zion and the settlement of Eretz Israel], 7 vols. (Tel Aviv: Tel Aviv University, 1982), vol. 1, 22–523.
37. Carl Schmitt, *Political Theology: Four Chapters on the Concept of Sovereignty*, trans. George Schwab (Chicago: University of Chicago Press, 2005).
38. Israel Bartal, *Letaken 'am: Ne'orut u-le'umiyut be-mizrah Eiropah* [To redeem a people: Jewish nationalism and Enlightenment in Eastern Europe] (Jerusalem: Carmel, 2013), 195.
39. Yehoshua Kaniel, *Be-ma'avar: Ha-Yehudim be-Eretz Israel ba-me'ah ha-19 bein yashan ve-hadash u-vein yishuv Eretz ha-Kodesh le-vein Tziyonut* [The Jews of Eretz Israel in the nineteenth century between old and new and between settlement of the Holy Land and Zionism] (Jerusalem: Yad Yitzhak Ben-Zvi, 2000), 36.
40. Bartal, *Galut ba-aretz*, 18.
41. Gershon Shafir, *Land, Labor and the Origins of the Israeli-Palestinian Conflict, 1882–1914*, updated edition (Berkeley: University of California Press, 1996).
42. Martin Buber, "Let Us Make an End to Falsities," in *A Land of Two Peoples: Martin Buber on Jews and Arabs*, ed. Paul Mendes-Flohr, new edition (Chicago: University of Chicago Press, 2005), 226–28.

Select Bibliography

Barnai, Ya'acov, ed. *Igerot Hasidim me-Eretz Israel: Min ha-mahatzit ha-sheniyah shel ha-me'ah ha-18 u-mereshit ha-me'ah ha-19* [Hasidic letters from Eretz Israel: From the second part of the eighteenth century and the first part of the nineteenth century]. Jerusalem: Yad Yitzhak Ben Zvi, 1980.

Bartal, Israel. *Galut ba-aretz: Yishuv Eretz Israel be-terem tziyonut* [Exile in the homeland: Settling Eretz Israel before Zionism]. Jerusalem: Hasifriyah Hatziyonit, 1994.

Ben-Arieh, Yehoshua. *Keytzad notzrah Eretz Israel ba-'et ha-hadasha 1799–1949* [The making of Eretz Israel in the modern era 1799–1949]. Jerusalem: Yad Yitzhak Ben-Zvi and Magnes, 2018.

Benjamin, Walter. *The Origin of German Tragic Drama*. Translated by John Osborne. London: Verso, 1985.

Dubnow, Simon. "Ha-hasidim ha-rishonim be-Eretz Israel" [The first Hasidim in the Land of Israel]. *Pardes* 2 (1894): 201–14.

Girard, René. *Things Hidden since the Foundation of the World*. Edited and translated by Stephen Bann and Michael Metter. Stanford: Stanford University Press, 1987.

Halpern, Israel. *Ha-'aliyot ha-rishonot shel ha-Hasidim le-Eretz Israel* [The Hasidic immigration to Palestine during the eighteenth century]. Jerusalem and Tel Aviv: Schocken, 1946.

Hotam, Yotam. *Modern Gnosis and Zionism: The Crisis of Culture, Life Philosophy and Jewish National Thought*. Translated by Avner Greenberg. London: Routledge, 2013.

Idel, Moshe. "The Function of Symbols in Gershom Scholem." In *Old Words, New Mirrors: On Jewish Mysticism and Twentieth-Century Thought*, 83–108. Philadelphia: University of Pennsylvania Press, 2010.

———. *Kabbala: New Perspectives*. New Haven: Yale University Press, 1988.

Pinsker, Leo. *Auto-Emancipation*. Translated by D. S. Blondheim. New York: Maccabaen Publishing House, 1906 [1882].

Scholem, Gershom. "The Neutralization of the Messianic Element in Early Hasidism." In *The Messianic Idea in Judaism and Other Essays on Jewish Spirituality*, 176–202. New York: Schocken, 1995.

Shafir, Gershon. *Land, Labor and the Origins of the Israeli-Palestinian Conflict, 1882–1914*. Updated edition. Berkeley: University of California Press, 1996.

CHAPTER 2

Western European "Philosemitism" and the Nakba in the 1950s

G. Daniel Cohen

Introduction

"If there is a Jewish question, neutrality is inconceivable. I am a philosemite, let it be known," confided the famous French novelist and art critic André Malraux to a fellow resistance fighter during the last weeks of World War II. Although the French underground organization included Jewish fighters, it rarely singled out the tragic plight of Jews in occupied France and Hitler's Europe. Malraux, however, had since 1943 stressed the difference between concentration and extermination camps and understood the special place occupied by the Final Solution in Nazi war aims.[1] A rare occurrence in 1945, his self-declared "philosemitism" challenged the notion of Jewish enmity in post-Holocaust Europe. This statement also hinted at a prominent theme in Malraux's future writings on Jews and the State of Israel, that of Jewish courage, revolt, and "metamorphosis." From public opposition to antisemitism to lyrical admiration for the new Jewish state, Malraux's philosemitism illustrates the emergence of a positive discourse on Jews, Judaism, and Jewishness in the aftermath of the Holocaust.

To be sure, Jewish returnees from concentration camps were generally met with indifference in French, Dutch, Belgian, and Italian societies, where the experience of Jewish suffering did not easily find expression. And across the continent, the end of the war failed to spell the demise of antisemitism. In Soviet-controlled areas, violence against returning Jews between 1944 and 1946 quickly shattered such hope. In Poland, the Kielce pogrom of July 1946 triggered a Jewish exodus to the American occupation zone in Germany. In Western Europe, the return of democracy did not translate into a zero hour of unequivocal acceptance. In Germany, where Allied surveys monitored public opinion, the colossal legacies of racial antisemitism hampered improvement. After Nazism dreamed of a world without Jews, defeated Germans coped uncomfortably with the presence of survivors in their midst.

It is true, of course, that the Federal Republic's founding fathers praised the Jewish contribution to German culture, pledged to protect "Jewish *fellow* citizens" from antisemitism, and in 1952 agreed to the payment of reparations to survivors and the State of Israel. Pro-Jewish attitudes, however, afforded the Bonn Republic moral legitimation while collective denial and "secondary antisemitism" prevailed within the West German public. In Austria, the depth of antisemitic prejudice in a country nearly empty of Jews shocked numerous contemporary observers. Two years after the end of the war, representatives of the American Jewish Committee (AJC) noted that Vienna remained "as before the center of the ugliest and most treacherous antisemitism." Without the protection of the four-powers Allied occupation, they added, "not one of the 4, 000 Jews would be able to appear in the streets."[2] In liberated France, the question of restitution triggered fierce resentment among non-Jewish owners of aryanized Jewish properties. Organized in various associations, defenders of "property rights" couched their grievances in a language unadulterated by the demise of the Vichy regime. "What an injustice to expel a Frenchman in favor of a foreign Jew who wants to reclaim his pre-war lodging," exclaimed one of them.[3] In the Netherlands, AJC envoys found widespread prejudice against Jews in the months following the German defeat. "For the first time in the history of the Netherlands," they reported, "open attacks against Jews appeared in the press, indicating that anti-Semitism has become prevalent among some sections of the population."[4] Italy offered a brighter outlook, although in 1946 the liberal intellectual Benedetto Croce casually advised Jews to abandon "the surviving traits of a barbaric and primitive religiosity."[5] Hitler, he claimed, had appropriated the Jewish idea of the chosen people and thus demonstrated its dangerous potential. In England too, as George Orwell wrote in 1945, "humane and enlightened people" were not immune to anti-Jewish prejudice. At the start of August 1947, the so-called Sergeants affair gave way to short-lived but unprecedented antisemitic violence in Britain. After the killing of two British soldiers at the hands of paramilitary Irgun activists in Palestine, angry mobs beat up Jews, damaged synagogues, and tore down Jewish-owned shops in the economically depressed cities of Liverpool, Manchester, and Glasgow. With various degrees of intensity, antagonism subsided in Western Europe after Nazism. The French Jewish novelist Albert Cohen did not nurture any illusions. "The old wish for 'death to the Jews,'" he wrote in September 1945, "still awaits me on the walls of all capitals."[6]

From Antisemitism to Anti-antisemitism

If "death to the Jews" was now clandestinely written on walls, it was also the result of suppressed antisemitism in the *public* arena. In liberated France, for instance, De Gaulle's government reinstated the anti-defamation Marchandeau Law abolished under Vichy. But if France became the first European country to criminalize hate speech, a moratorium on public antisemitism was also enforced across Western Europe, including occupied Germany. What has been labeled "antisemitism without antisemites" indeed captures the mutation of Jew aversion in the immediate postwar period.[7] Although former collaborationists in France, Belgium, and the Netherlands, former fascists in Italy, and former Nazis in Germany and Austria swiftly walked free if they were prosecuted at all, "antisemites" disappeared from plain view.

With antisemitism *publicly* off-limits, negative statements on Jews lodged themselves within an ambiguous "philosemitic" discourse. Examples from early postwar cinema illustrate this evolution. In Austria, Georg Pabst's *Der Prozess* (The trial, 1948) sympathized with Jews falsely accused of ritual murder in a late nineteenth-century Hungarian village. But Pabst's disturbing portrayal of Jews preoccupied with financial dealings stirred up outrage among Jewish critics. "You don't love a person whom you depict that way," protested one of them.[8] In Italy *L'ebreo errante* (The wandering Jew, 1948), starring Vittorio Gassmann in the role of a wealthy but "cursed" Jew, replicated this pattern. His execution at the hands of the Germans inspired compassion, yet the film openly portrayed the Holocaust as expiation for the Jews' refusal to accept Christ. With good reasons, therefore, the few historians who have explored the possibility of philosemitism after 1945 have dismissed the phenomenon as a "code" dangerously flirting with the taboo of antisemitism or worse, as "whitewashing the yellow badge."[9] Likewise, postwar Jewish intellectuals in Europe rarely embraced signs of demonstrative sympathy. In a short poem entitled "Philosemite" (1967), the Dutch survivor and historian Saul van Messel did not hide his contempt: "Worse than / hate which / can offend: friendship / against which / I cannot / defend."[10]

Yet for philosemitism to become an irritant, it first needed to exist. In Western Europe from 1945 to 1989 and within the official European Union afterward, philosemitism—conceived as positive discourse on Jews or Judaism—gradually became the dominant framework of relations between Jews and non-Jews. That "love for the Jews" potentially recycled antisemitic images, reinforced Jewish otherness, or deflected away Holocaust guilt should not mask its migration toward *mainstream* public discourse. Periodization varies according to national cases, yet at a minimum, the Jew became in 1945 the enemy that we now must love. As the German case continues to demonstrate, "nervous philosemitism" fulfilled a central function of Holocaust *compensation*. On the other end of the spectrum, however, emerged new languages of *solidarity*, an attempt at rehumanizing the Jew, illustrated most famously, perhaps, by Jean-Paul Sartre's epoch-making *Réflexions sur la question juive* published in 1946.

One way to sketch out the historical trajectory of "philosemitic Europe," therefore, is to follow the figural "good Jews" who after 1945 started to populate the philosemitic imagination. Since the rise of philosemitism as a counterpart to antisemitism in late Imperial Germany, the good Jew/bad Jew dichotomy has regularly permeated expressions of empathy toward Jews. Following the Dreyfus Affair, the French Jewish intellectual Bernard Lazare already sensed this ambivalence among supporters of the banished Jewish captain. "Philosemites," he wrote in 1901, "go at length to establish that the Jew is perfectly similar to the people surrounding him . . . only to point out his certain inferiority."[11] In 1920 the British secretary of state for war Winston Churchill applied this principle to his inventory of admirable "good" Jews (those loyal to their country of residence or, revealingly, Jewish pioneers in Palestine), as opposed to Jewish "international terrorists" and followers of Bolshevism. Likewise, Christian humanists in the 1930s came to the defense of victimized Jews, yet looked askance at secular Jewish revolutionaries.

In the immediate aftermath of the Holocaust, preferences for certain types of Jews continued to characterize pro-Jewish empathy in Western Europe. Influential Christian thinkers such as Jacques Maritain, for instance, saw in the religious Jew a symbol of Jewish authenticity. Contrary to the secular renegade, the faithful Jew ensured the survival of Judaism and therefore "the relation of spiritual consanguinity" uniting Christians and Jews. The image of "consanguinity" formidably challenged the Nazi idea of Jewish pollution, yet chiefly pertained to observant Jews. Maritain, to be sure, respectfully referred to all Jews "as friends and brothers." Yet the faithful Jew, contrary to "the rationalistic minded Jew of today," understood that the "God of Israel is also the God of mankind": no longer limited to bear witness to the truth of Christianity, "carnal" Judaism now played a positive role in the salvation of the world.[12]

The German philosopher Karl Jaspers, who in his famous 1946 lectures on the question of German guilt enjoined his countrymen to accept responsibility, similarly viewed Jewish authenticity through the lens of religion. "What a Jew is seems clearer to me than what a German is," he wrote in July 1947. "Biblical religion and the idea of God and the idea of Covenant. . . . Something priceless would be lost," he added, "if there were no more Jews, aware of themselves as Jews, in the world."[13] Atheistic intellectuals such as Jean-Paul Sartre preferred for their part *authentic* Jews, who consciously chose "to derive pride from humiliation," over *inauthentic* Jews, who "only play at not being Jews." Only through the power of authenticity, argued the existentialist thinker, can the Jew defeat the antisemite. The Sartrean "good Jew" is never fully sketched out, but clearly takes the form of the secular Jew whether Zionist or Diasporic. In *The Origins of Totalitarianism*, Hannah Arendt had very unpleasant words for Sartre's musings. "Sartre's 'existentialist' interpretation of the Jew as someone who is regarded and defined as a Jew by others," she wrote, was no more than a "myth that has become fashionable in intellectual circles."[14] But her own distinction between the politically conscious "pariah" and the inauthentic "parvenu," however, was in line with Sartre's vision of Jewish authenticity.

From Philosemitism to Philo-Zionism

By 1947, however, the first signs of Christian or philosophical "philosemitism" in post-Holocaust Europe overlapped with the rise of pro-Zionist sentiment. Outside of

Britain, the future of Mandatory Palestine had not been at the forefront of Western European preoccupations. Yet in July/August 1947, the famous *Exodus* saga drew immense international sympathy for "humanity at sea."[15] Clandestinely brought to France from displaced persons camps in Germany, forty-five hundred Jewish refugees set sail from the port of Sète on 11 July 1947. Their goal was to run the British blockade of Palestine and advertise the plight of stateless Jews in search of a homeland. In a show of force, Royal Navy sailors boarded *Exodus 1947* and diverted it to Haifa. On 20 July, the refugees were put on board three deportation vessels and sent back to Port-de-Bouc near Marseilles. Despite an offer of permanent asylum from the French government, the majority of Jews refused to disembark. For more than a month, a large press corps highlighted the deplorable situation of Holocaust survivors confined in unsanitary conditions. After the French authorities refused to intervene, the Royal Navy transferred the refugees back to Hamburg. Under a glare of negative publicity, they were returned to displaced persons camps in Germany. The affair ended in a British fiasco and a decisive victory for Zionist propaganda. It also sapped the already weak British resolve to remain in Palestine. On 20 September 1947, Clement Attlee's government announced the withdrawal of its troops. Three months later, the United Nations voted in favor of the creation of a Jewish state on the partitioned territory of Mandatory Palestine.

Yet another consequence of the *Exodus* affair was the rise of a philosemitic humanitarian sentiment directed toward Holocaust survivors in transit to Palestine. Expectedly, it was in France that illegal Jewish immigrants came to be portrayed as exemplary victims of injustice. French Socialists, in particular, denounced British abuses in a language combining human rights rhetoric and humanitarian compassion. On 2 August, Léon Blum's *Le Populaire* described a "moral and physical suffering surpassing all human limits," which, after so much suffering, Jews felt like "a red iron on a bleeding wound."[16] Humanitarian photography further dramatized the events. On 1 August, *Libération* featured the mother of a young infant taken off one of the ships. A caption emphasized her sacrifice: "She only abandoned her companions of misfortune to save her child."[17] Virulently anti-British and at that time still favorable to Zionism, French Communists contributed their own imagery. On 30 July, the Communist organ *L'Humanité* compared the ships in Port-de-Bouc to a "floating Auschwitz, the only way to depict the hell in which the passengers of *Exodus 47* live." *L'Humanité* once again invoked Auschwitz on 9 September in an exaggerated report on British troops in Hamburg manhandling "the martyrs of *Exodus* with clubs and the sound of music."

Solidarity with Jewish refugees was also expressed through demonstrations organized in large French cities. Prominent intellectuals and artists entered the fray. The painter Henri Matisse, the Communist poet Louis Aragon, and the resistance writer Vercors (Jean Marcel Bruller, author of *Le Silence de la mer*, clandestinely published in 1941) added their names to an anti-British poster distributed in Paris. The architect Le Corbusier, who had courted the Vichy regime in 1940, was nonetheless also included among the known anti-fascists on this list. Former political deportees, for their part, made use of their moral prestige. The Buchenwald survivor David Rousset, the author of *L'univers concentrationaire* (1946), saw in Jews stranded at sea "the pathetic witnesses of our own bankruptcy." For this early critic of the Soviet Gulag, the British internment camps in Cyprus confirmed the perpetuation of totalitarian tyranny after Nazism. Even after the Final Solution, the Jew remained "the first sacrificed victim of the concentration camp world [*le monde concentrationnaire*]."[18]

Resisters and intellectuals who until then had remained silent on the Holocaust now waxed lyrical about Jewish suffering and resilience. For the left-Catholic review *Esprit*, the exemplary struggle of Jewish survivors against British power epitomized resistance "against all forms of barbarity."[19] The admirable *ma'apilim* (illegal immigrants), upon whom fantasies of heroism could be liberally projected, indeed placed Zionism under a favorable light. In West Germany, where Allied opinion polls revealed public support for the *Exodus* refugees as long as they did not settle permanently in the country, the affair also opened the possibility of guilt-free "Holocaust-talk." "One cannot blame us for the concentration camps and at the same time block the road to freedom for these oppressed people," a young German student told American interviewers in August 1947.[20] In Italy too, professed admiration for Jewish immigrants helped transcend the fascist past. Although the *Exodus* story is mostly remembered today thanks to Leon Uris's immensely popular novel published in 1958 and Otto Preminger's film adaptation of 1960—both were grossly inaccurate and blatantly caricatured Arabs—the cinematographic representation of the event began in Italy. In 1948, Duilio Coletti's *The Earth Cries Out* (*Il grido della terra*, 1948) offered a sympathetic portrayal of Jewish illegal immigrants to Palestine. The film's pro-Zionist tone was unmistakable, yet stemmed from specific motivations. Coletti had worked as a film director under Mussolini, and his tribute to Jews was presumably intended as compensation. Such a stance also allowed a defeated Italian to safely express anti-British resentment. And by treating Jewish refugees and citizens of the peninsula as equal war victims, the film strengthened the myth of the "good Italian people" untainted by fascism.[21]

All in all, however, warm responses to Jewish statelessness on the eve of the creation of the State of Israel sharply contrasted with the general indifference surrounding Jewish camp survivors upon their return to West European countries in May and June 1945. Until then rather silent on Jews and the Holocaust, the French philosopher Albert Camus entered the public arena to condemn the world's disregard for the "persecuted." After years of "indescribable martyrdom," he wrote, Jews were a people who no longer accepted to be "spat in the face." In his idyllic vision, an Arab-free landscape of "orchards and lakes" in Palestine awaited survivors, who only longed for "the right to have a burial place." Camus briefly counterbalanced this lyricism with a sobering question: "Mind you, what if the persecuted learned the lesson and became, one day, the persecutors?"[22] But he did not dwell long on this intriguing thought. His point was unambiguous: Nazism destroyed human dignity, and its survivors symbolized the struggle for its recovery. For Camus, then, the Holocaust refugee validated his famous distinction between noble moral rebellion—which he defined as "a revolt limited to the refusal of humiliation" perfectly fitting his embrace of therapeutic Zionism—and violent revolution. The authentic Jew as a *moral rebel*—this idea soon gained greater traction when after 1948 philo-Zionism became intertwined with philosemitic rhetoric.

In Western Europe, the first Arab-Israeli war did not receive extensive coverage. Major European newspapers published dispatches on the war but concentrated mostly on military operations and developments on the battlefield. In England, reports from the fighting in Palestine were rarely favorable to the Jewish cause, but in West Germany and France a pro-Israel narrative rapidly took shape. German newspapers simply hired local Jewish journalists to cover the events, whereas in France famous war correspondents expressed sympathy for the heroism of Jews confronting, as Joseph Kessel wrote, "enemies barely awakened from the Middle Ages."[23] Throughout the war, the renowned journalist of Jewish Russian background offered exalted dispatches on "a [Jewish] people both reborn and one thousand years old" opposed to the "immense and dark Arab world." Kessel spent several weeks in wartime Palestine yet rarely commented on the fate of Palestinians. Interviews with Jewish fighters assured him "that after the war . . . our Arab friends will recover their assets." His portrayal of the last Palestinian inhabitant of Kawkab al-Hawa, a village in the upper Jordan Valley seized and forcibly depopulated by the Haganah in mid-May 1948, did not reveal any particular solicitude for the plight of Arab refugees. "Unable to follow the villagers when they left," a lone elderly Arab woman remained behind. In her Joseph Kessel only saw a "smile, a toothless smile, otherworldly" while she magnanimously offered "Koranic blessings to the young Jewish fighters who fed her."[24]

The appearance of a Jewish polity in the Middle East quickly attracted the attention of religious figures, politicians, trade unionists, intellectuals, and artists. It is often forgotten today that between 1948 and 1967, and particularly so during the 1950s, the new Israeli Jew became an object of European fascination. Social democrats, but not exclusively, marveled at Israel's collectivist experiments. In 1947 the Labour politician Richard Crossman set the tone for the European socialist love affair with Israel. Writing during the last days of Mandatory Palestine, Crossman contrasted the achievements of the kibbutz movement to the "filthy tin-can settlements where the Arab peasants evicted from the Plain of Aesdralon huddle." Modernism, humanistic socialism, and advanced welfare policies compared poorly with the backwardness of Arab peasants, presented as fortunate to benefit from Israeli development.[25] Countless studies and adulatory observations of Israeli socialism later reinforced this view.

Likewise, numerous Christians expressed their identification with Israel. In accordance with the Vatican's position, Catholic churches in France, Italy, Belgium, and the Netherlands were not enthused with the birth of the Jewish state. Pioneers in Jewish-Christian dialogue, however, welcomed the "the return of Israel."[26] Although not endorsed by the Holy See, the myriad organizations dedicated to Christian-Jewish amity after the Holocaust included numerous supporters of Zionism. German Protestants, for their part, connected the birth of Israel with salvation history. Initially reluctant to see divine meaning in the creation of the Jewish state in 1948, the theologian Karl Barth believed in 1950 that Israel was proof of God's continuing love for the chosen people.[27] Prominent Protestants also favorably compared the Jewish state to the Federal Republic. Both, argued the theologian Helmut Gollwitzer in 1958, enjoyed "the grace of the zero hour," that is, the possibility of a new beginning. "With us, we have gambled it away," he wrote, "but there [in Israel], it has benefited them."[28] German visitors also found in Israel an outlet for their growing sense of guilt. "The heaviest baggage you are carrying with you," advised a West Berlin pastor to a fellow traveler to the Holy Land, "is our guilt over the Jews."[29] Documentary filmmakers such as the French Chris Marker and film directors like Pier Paulo Pasolini were both mesmerized by Israeli society. Numerous European intellectuals, including anticolonial figures such as Sartre, saw in Israel a miraculous "metamorphosis," while the British writer Stephen Spender waxed lyrical about Israel's youthful vibrancy. Indeed, a large corpus of West European travelogues, written between the early 1950s and 1967, reveals how the image of the "good Jew" found in Israel a new habitat.

Portraying Israeli Jews

Photographic coverage of the first Israelis, borrowing from the genre of "humanist photography," contributed to this emotionality. Embraced after World War II by Henri Cartier-Bresson and Robert Doisneau, "humanist photography" highlighted the dramatic humanity of common people.[30] In Israel, close-up photographs of diverse faces, soon a genre in itself, highlighted the dignity of the new Israelis. Photography thus added an aesthetic dimension to philosemitic sentiment: after antisemitic iconography had disfigured the Jewish face, it was now an object of admiration as well as a crucible of Jewish authenticity. But the photographic idealization of Israeli Jews also revealed attitudes toward the remaining Arabs present in the country; it is thus an invaluable source for gauging the place of the Nakba in the post-Holocaust philosemitic imagination during the first decade of Israel's existence.

With *Daybreak for a Nation*, a photo collection published in 1952, the Dutch photographer Willem van de Poll was one of the first major contributors to this genre. Van de Poll arrived in Israel after several assignments in postwar Europe, including in the Sudetenland, where he followed Czech settlers into the province whose ethnic German inhabitants had just been expelled. In Israel, too, Van de Poll documented resettlement. Several of his photographs showed Jewish newcomers (often with prominent concentration camps tattoos on their arms) on the background of abandoned Arab houses designated for Jewish gentrification. "A young father and his son on his arm," says one caption, "gazes at the dilapidated remains of the strife-ridden house." As in the case of the ethnic German properties in the Sudentenland, Van de Poll commented, the ruins left by the "departed Arab population must be cleared . . . and made habitable as soon as possible."[31]

Prefaced by the French Catholic François Mauriac, a photo-reportage published in Switzerland and France in 1957 similarly captured various Israeli Jews in former Arab landscapes. Mauriac's introduction to the book, however, entirely revolved around the virtues of Judeo-Christianity, a theme the French writer would also develop in his famous preface to Elie Wiesel's *La Nuit* (*Night*), published in France in 1958. "Through the images of resuscitated Israel," marveled Mauriac, "we believe in Resurrection and in Life."[32] The book provided puzzling glimpses of Jewish life in the Arab streets of Jaffa nearly emptied of its original inhabitants, yet Mauriac only saw in them moving images of the "[Jewish] people to whom the Almighty spoke and which has given birth to Christ." Yet the volume did not entirely ignore Palestinians. In one photograph, one of the last Arab inhabitants of historic Jaffa sits at the door of her house, seemingly sewing a piece of clothing. She is presented as an immemorial part of the landscape, yet without any particular identity. "How many centuries has she been sewing, peacefully, in front of her home?" asks the accompanying caption.

The most revealing humanist reportage on Israel published in the 1950s was a collection of photographs taken in 1955 by Izraels Bidermanas (most commonly known as Izis), a Lithuanian Jewish refugee who settled in France in the 1930s. Simply entitled *Israël*, the book, later translated into English for an American audience (1958), documented various Israeli types since the creation of the state.[33] In his emblematic preface, the novelist, art critic, and Gaullist politician André Malraux enthusiastically endorsed Izis's portrayal of Israel through the lens of "humanity": shoemakers in the streets of Tel Aviv, shepherds in the Galilee, soldiers and watchmen on the border, dancing children, kibbutz and construction workers as well as new immigrants in *ma'abarot* (reception and transit centers) all skillfully dramatized in their routine activities. For Malraux, this visual outburst of "humanity" across the Mediterranean sharply contrasted with the grim fate of "man" in post-1945 Europe. As he had already written in 1946, "ravaged and bloody Europe is no more ravaged and bloody than the figure of man it hoped to create." Israel, "the symbol of a metamorphosis which transformed a community of intellectuals and traders into a nation of peasant-soldiers," offered to his mind a welcome alternative to the "death of man" in Europe, at a time when humanism itself was beginning to fall into intellectual and academic disrepute. Thus Malraux extolled "a nation unlike the old nations of Europe," a blend of rabbinical wisdom and military courage, of "stubborn rationalism" and messianic aspirations.

Yet the "most beautiful photograph of the book" singled out by Malraux in his introduction does not evoke flourishing deserts, military power, or the possibility of "socialism with a human face" realized, away from Europe, by pioneer Israel. It simply features a beggar, likely of Jewish Yemeni origin, sitting or asleep at the doorstep of a condemned Arab house in the city of Ramla (al-Ramla in Arabic) from which Palestinian townsmen (and those of nearby Lod, or al-Lid) were expelled on 13 July 1948. Malraux's rather abstract description of the scene, however, makes no mention of this specific location and focuses instead on three flyers glued to the door: "A Chaldean arch with three announcements: from a state, from a party and from a movie theater promising blood and dreams: an American documentary on *Mein Kampf* and a film, *The Thief of Bagdad*." The photograph's appeal, according to Malraux, consisted in the poetic juxtaposition of these three posters with the image of the despondent "beggar reminiscent of Job, immersed in a prophet's sleep." An erudite specialist in ancient art, Malraux only saw in the walled Palestinian house a decontextualized "Chaldean arch" under which modernity ("state," "party") coexisted with the Jewish prophetic tradition, a testimony to Israel's singularity among the nations.

A few lines later, Malraux finds resemblance between the Ramla beggar and another detached Jewish elderly figure sitting on top of a hill near Jerusalem while schoolchildren plant the Forest of the Martyrs (Ya'ar Hakdoshim), "whose six million trees will grow in memory of Hitler's victims." Some of Malraux's favorite photographs, therefore, are situated at the crossline between the Shoah and the Nakba, in this case in the "naked hills of Judea"—that is, in the lands of the former Palestinian village Beit Mah'sir, today Moshav Beit Meir, where the Forest of the Martyrs continues to grow to this day. Malraux never acknowledges this intersection and altogether ignores the few photographs of Arabs included in the book. Indeed, Izis's humanist lens also beautifully captured several Palestinians inside the Israeli human landscape. Yet they consistently appear as fleeting, isolated, and faceless ghosts, such as a lone Arab woman hastily walking in Ramla (after the 1948 expulsion, the town took in internal Arab refugees from outlying emptied villages), a hunched old woman shepherding a few goats amid the Arab ruins of Lod, the back of a woman in Safed and of one in Ein Karem near Jerusalem, and a group of female Palestinian villagers near Haifa. Intense closeup portrayals of Jews are sharply contrasted with the invisibility of Arab faces, such as a young Jewish girl intensely gazing at the camera while preparing to plant a tree in the Forest of the Martyrs.

Malraux, who throughout his life (1901–76) never visited Israel, took his cue from Izis's uneven strategy of facial representation. Only the Jewish face was inscribed in history: "Although its ruins have all been destroyed, the Jewish people still bears on its face the oldest history of the world [*le plus vieux passé du monde*]." Only one photograph features clearly identifiable Palestinian faces, alongside Jews. In the "colorful" old city of Acre, Izis captured in a single frame "immigrants from Europe" (which in the early 1950s was generally synonymous with Holocaust survivors) and remnants of the town's Arab population. Strikingly, neither Palestinians nor Jews look at each other and instead depressingly gaze at the ground.

Visions of the Nakba: Erasure and Holocaust Guilt

I have chosen to dwell at length on Malraux's emblematic musings in order to raise the question of erasure. A common argument, particularly among Arab intellectuals, is that European—let alone American—philosemitism erased the Nakba from historical, political, and moral view. In this narrative, Holocaust guilt or atonement for shameful episodes of collaboration with Nazism not only legitimized the creation of Israel but also contributed to the long-lasting support for its cause, at the expense of Zionism's victims. Since the publication of Edward Said's *Orientalism* (1978), another explanation has complemented the old one: the Arab, and today the Muslim, has replaced the Jew as the most dangerous threat to European civilization. Nakba denial in the West, therefore, is commonly seen as the product of a guilty conscience, the perpetuation of a European colonial mindset and Orientalist stigmatization, with disastrous consequences for the claims of justice and recognition put forward since 1948 by Palestinians. Malraux's lyrical overtones, typical of many similar utterances across Western Europe in the 1950s, certainly fit this pattern.

Yet the "Holocaust guilt" argument warrants qualification. To be sure, the Nakba was in multiple ways played down, ignored, or erased in mainstream Western European public discourse in the 1950s despite notable exceptions: the Orientalist scholar Louis Massignon and the left-Catholic review *Témoignage Chrétien* in France; Arnold Toynbee in England ("the calamity that overtook the Palestinian Arabs in A.D. 1948 was on the heads of the Zionist Jews who seized a *lebensraum* for themselves in Palestine by force of arms in that year"); the West German legal scholar Otto Kimenich, who linked the plight of the German expellees to that of Palestinians and stressed their common "right to a homeland" (*das Recht auf die Heimat*); and German Protestants who similarly compared Israel's treatment of Palestinians in 1948 to the predicament of dispossessed ethnic Germans. As a German missionary wrote from the Jordan-ruled West Bank in 1952 about the Palestinian refugees, "these Arabs had fled from the territories assigned to Israel out of fear of Jewish terror. We Germans experienced this misery with deep sympathy, fully aware of the hardships in our own country."[34]

In the 1950s, however, the balance overwhelmingly tilted toward philo-Zionism, evident in a large body of books and articles on Israel published in Western Europe during that decade. An examination of this literature clearly shows, however, that Holocaust atonement was rarely an explicit factor justifying the negation of Palestinians. This should not come as a surprise: although recent historians have successfully challenged the idea of absolute "silence" or "repression" of the Holocaust in postwar Europe before the 1970s, the Shoah remained peripheral to mainstream memories of the war until the last part of the twentieth century. In the early postwar period, Holocaust guilt alone could not erase the Nakba, since the social demand for moral atonement was minimal, particularly so in Adenauer's Germany.

A case in point is *Ein Deutscher sieht Israel* (A German sees Israel), a travelogue published in 1955 by the journalist Erich Lüth, the founder of a group called Peace with Israel active in German reparations politics in the early 1950s. Lüth was also known for his call in 1951 to boycott a movie by Veit Harlan, the maker of the notorious antisemitic film *Jud Süß* (1940), leading to a legal suit brought against him and to an important constitutional precedent upholding freedom of speech in West Germany. Like similar German travel stories from Israel, Lüth's book starts with a reminder that "in their demonic incarnation of evil . . . the leaders of the Third Reich sought to destroy and expel the Jewish people" in Germany and beyond. Yet by doing so, he continues, "they" (the Nazis) also proved the "necessity of reestablishing the Jewish state in the beloved land of our Father." There is nothing unconventional in these lines written by one of the main proponents of Jewish-Christian understanding in the early Federal Republic: the Holocaust as a "Nazi" (and not German) deed, and the right of Jews to a state following their near destruction. What is significant is Lüth's justification of the "necessity," as he put it, of philosemitism and support for Zionism: "For us Germans, the salvation of Israel in the present and the future is a crucial admonition for our own transformation [*Umkehr*]."[35]

Because the figure of the Jew and the State of Israel now served a grand moral purpose, recognition of the Nakba stood in opposition to the reconstruction of German and West European ethics. The few pages dedicated to "Arabs" in Lüth's travelogue, following long segments on the miraculous achievements of the State of Israel, reiterated commonplace stereotypes about 1948 popularized by this form of literature: the order given to Arab villagers to temporarily flee until invading armies "throw Jews to the sea"; the democratic Israeli treatment of "Arabs loyal to the state"; the "seething hate" rampant in Palestinian refugee camps; and the obvious path to peace sadly obstructed by Arab rejectionism, namely, the mass resettlement of Palestinian refugees in neighboring Arab countries.

This standard narrative was already typical of Christian Zionism in the United States but also in England, where the Anglican churchman and scholar James Parkes promoted the struggle against antisemitism and advocated Christian-Jewish reconciliation. In the summer of 1950, Parkes published a twenty-six-page document in defense of the historical legitimacy of Zionism. In this study, conducted for the World Council of Churches, Parkes also researched the reasons behind the mass flight of Palestinian Arabs in 1948. Although "Jewish military commanders were clearly responsible for some expulsions," he believed that it was "quite inaccurate to blame any one cause for all the fugitives." Parkes nonetheless identified a single overarching factor explaining these events. In traditional Arab warfare, he argued, "the weaker party never stayed to fight. It 'retired,' knowing that the raid would soon be over and then it would be possible to return and rebuild." Thus the "inexplicably foolish" mistake committed by Arab combatants in Palestine was their failure to realize that "those on whom they had declared war in November 1947 were not Bedouin who intended to go back with their loot to the desert."[36]

Lüth's characterization of the Nakba, while less imaginative, illustrates the same mindset. So did the observations on Israel published in 1952 and 1955 by the Protestant theologian from Heidelberg Herman Maas, a wartime member of the anti-Nazi Confessing Church and the first German to be officially invited to Israel. After a few obligatory lines on the flight of Palestinians during the 1948 events, Maas marvels at the drained marshes, blooming deserts, and the kibbutz as an ideal social and economic structure.[37]

Conclusion

In all these cases, however, the invisibility of Palestinian suffering is not the product of an elusive "Holocaust consciousness" or reflective of a culture of collective atonement. It can be alternatively seen, as the historian Frank Stern has argued, as a "whitewashing" bargain: love for the Jews and Israel against a clean slate for newly anointed liberal-democratic Germans. Yet if this "whitewashing" explanation retains its overall interpretative validity, a different equation arises: indifference to the specificity of the Holocaust went hand in hand with Nakba denial both in Adenauer's Germany and in Fourth Republic France (1946–58). The 1950s was a decade of near-systematic Nakba erasure in the Western European public mind; it was also a moment when for noble, humanistic, and universal reasons (as in Alain Resnais's *Night and Fog*, 1956) or out of anti-totalitarian concerns, the Holocaust was historically relegated to mere "Nazi evil."

The dual trajectory of Holocaust and Nakba historiography illustrates the possibility of a reversed pattern. Although far from inexistent before the 1970s, historical knowledge of the Holocaust exploded in the United States and Europe, particularly in the wake of the Cold War. Similarly, while already a painful subject of investigation and introspection in the Arab world after the Nakba, awareness of the Palestinian catastrophe has grown dramatically since the 1980s, in part due to the publication of iconoclastic studies by the "New Historians" in Israel and of works by Palestinian scholars in English translation. Did the historical Shoah open a space for the historical recognition of the Nakba? Did Holocaust consciousness, seen by its critics as an industry stifling the Palestinian voice, paradoxically function as a portal into Nakba consciousness? If so, this new relationship announces a welcome departure from the one-sided, negationist, and discursively violent philosemitism of an earlier era.

G. Daniel Cohen teaches European history and Jewish studies at Rice University. He specializes in the history of Jewish migration and humanitarianism in the twentieth century. His current research focuses on philosemitism and attitudes toward Jews, Judaism, and Zionism in post-Holocaust Europe.

Notes

1. Michaël de Saint-Chéron, *Malraux et les Juifs. Histoire d'une fidélité* (Paris: Desclée de Brouwer, 2008), 11.
2. *American Jewish Yearbook* 47 (1946–47): 316–21.
3. See S. L. Fogg, *Stealing Home: Looting, Restitution, and Reconstructing Jewish Lives in France, 1942–1947* (New York: Oxford University Press, 2017), 68; Anne Grynberg, "Des signes de résurgence de l'antisémitisme dans la France de l'après-guerre," *Les Cahiers de la Shoah* 5 (2001): 171–224.
4. *American Jewish Yearbook* 47 (1945–46): 382–84.
5. Croce is cited by David Ward, *Antifascisms: Cultural Politics in Italy 1943–1946* (Madison, NJ: Fairleigh Dickinson University Press, 1996), 82.
6. Albert Cohen, "Jour de mes dix ans: Fragments," *Esprit* 114 (1945): 77–87.
7. See Bernd Marin, *Antisemitismus ohne Antisemiten. Studien zu Vorurteildynamik* (Frankfurt am Main: Campus, 2000).
8. Lisa Silverman, "Absent Jews and Invisible Antisemitism in Postwar Vienna: Pabst's *Der Prozeß* (1948) and *The Third Man* (1949)," *Journal of Contemporary History* (2017): 211–28.
9. Frank Stern, *The Whitewashing of the Yellow Badge: Antisemitism and Philosemitism in Postwar Germany* (New York and Oxford: Pergamon Press, 1992).
10. Saul van Messel, "Filosemiet" [Philosemite], in *Zeer zeker en zeker zeer. Joodse gedichten* [Very certain and certainly very: Jewish poems], Haagse Cahiers 10 (Rijswick Z.H: De Oude Degel, 1967), 10–11.
11. Antoine Compagnon, "Antisémitisme ou antimodernisme? Anatole Leroy-Beaulieu, Bernard Lazare, Léon Bloy," in *L'antisémitisme éclairé. Inclusion and Exclusion: Perspectives on Jews from the Enlightenment to the Dreyfus Affair*, ed. Ilana Y. Zinguer and Sam W. Bloom (Leiden and Boston: Brill, 2003), 423–47.
12. Jacques Maritain, cited by Richard Francis Crane, *Passion of Israel: Jacques Maritain, Catholic Conscience and The Holocaust* (Scranton: University of Scranton Press, 2010), 81.
13. See Lotte Kohler and Hans Sahner, *Hannah Arendt-Karl Jaspers: Correspondence, 1926–1969* (New York: Harcourt Brace, 1992), 95.
14. Hannah Arendt, *The Origins of Totalitarianism* (New York: Harcourt Brace, 1973), xv.
15. Itamar Mann, *Humanity at Sea: Maritime Migration and the Foundations of International Law* (New York: Cambridge University Press, 2016).
16. Léon Blum is cited by Laurence Coulon, *L'opinion publique française, Israël et le conflit israélo-arabe* (Paris: Honoré Champion, 2009), 38.
17. See David Lazar, *L'opinion française et la naissance de l'état d'Israël 1945–1949* (Paris: Calmann-Lévy, 1972), 86–95.
18. David Rousset, "Préface," in François-Jean Armorin, *Des juifs quittent l'Europe* (Paris: Juillard, 1948), 11–13.
19. Jean-Marie Domenach, "L'antisémitisme reste logique," *Esprit* 198 (1953): 146–49.
20. On reactions to the *Exodus* affair in occupied Germany, see Stern, *The Whitewashing of the Yellow Badge*, 155–57.
21. Asher Salah, "The Earth Cries Out: Aliya Bet and the War of Independence from an Italian Perspective," in *In Response to an Italian Captain: Aliya Bet from Italy, 1945–1948*, exhibition catalogue, ed. Galia Solev (Tel Aviv: Musa, Eretz Israel Museum, 2016), 82–94.
22. See Vincent Grégoire, "L'Holocauste dans les écrits de Camus," *French Review* 80, no. 5 (April 2007): 1070–84.
23. Gilad Margalit, "Israel through the Eyes of the West German Press 1947–1967," *Jahrbuch für antisemitismusforschung* 11 (2002): 235–48; Joseph Kessel, *Terre d'amour et de feu. Israël 1926–1961* (Paris: Texto, 2018), 117.
24. Kessel, *Terre d'amour et de feu*, 141.
25. Paul Kelemen, *The British Left and Zionism: History of a Divorce* (Manchester: Manchester University Press, 2012), 114–15.
26. Jacques Madaule, *Le Retour d'Israël* (Paris: Desclée de Brouwer, 1951).

27. Eva Fleischner, *Judaism in German Christian Theology Since 1945* (Metuchen, NJ: Scarecrow Press, 1975), 28.
28. W. Travis McMaken, "'Shalom, Shalom, Shalom, Israel!' Jews and Judaism in Helmut Gollwitzer's Life and Theology," *Studies in Christian-Jewish Relations* 10, no. 1 (2015): 1–22.
29. McMaken, "Shalom, Shalom, Shalom, Israel!"
30. Peter Hamilton, "A Poetry of the Streets? Documenting Frenchness in an Era of Reconstruction: Humanist Photography 1935–1960," in *The Documentary Impulse in French Literature*, ed. Buford Norman (Leiden: Brill, 2001): 177–226.
31. Willem van den Poll, *Daybreak for a Nation: Israel, the Country and Its People* (Amsterdam: J. A. Bloom, 1952), 6.
32. See François Mauriac, preface to Arielli, *Israël: Photographies* (Neuchatel and Paris: Editions Ides et Calends, 1957), 1–4.
33. Izraels Bidermanas, *Israël* (Lausanne: Éditions Clairefontaine, 1955).
34. Gerhard Gronauer, "Attitudes in West German Protestantism towards the State of Israel, 1948–1967," in *The Social Dimension of Christian Missions in the Middle East*, ed. Norbert Friedrich et al. (Stuttgart: Steiner, 2010), 205–29.
35. Erich Lüth, *Ein Deutscher sieht Israel* (Hamburg: Hamburger Buchdruckerei, 1955), 14.
36. On Parkes and Christian Zionism, see Gerard Daniel Cohen, "Elusive Neutrality: Christian Humanitarianism and the Question of Palestine, 1948–1967," *Humanity: An International Journal of Human Rights, Humanitarianism, and Development* 5, no. 2 (Summer 2014): 183–210.
37. Gronauer, "Attitudes in West German Protestantism," 18.

Select Bibliography

Arielli, *Israël*. Paris: Ides et Calendes, 1957.
Bidermanas, Izraels. *Israël*. Lausanne: Éditions Clairefontaine, 1955.
Grégoire, Vincent. "L'Holocauste dans les écrits de Camus." *French Review* 80, no. 5 (2007): 117–36.
Kelemen, Paul. *The British Left and Zionism: History of a Divorce*. Manchester: Manchester University Press, 2012.
Kessel, Joseph. *Terre d'amour et de feu. Israël 1926–196*. Paris: Texto, 2018.
Lazar, David. *L'opinion française et la naissance de l'état d'Israël 1945–1949*. Paris: Calmann-Lévy, 1972.
Lüth, Erich. *Ein Deutscher sieht Israel*. Hamburg: Hamburger Buchdruckerei, 1955.
Margalit, Gilad. "Israel through the Eyes of the West German Press 1947–1967." *Jahrbuch für antisemitismusforschung* 11 (2002): 235–48.
Poll, Willem van den. *Daybreak for a Nation: Israel, the Country and Its People*. Amsterdam: J. A. Bloom, 1952.
Stern, Frank. *The Whitewashing of the Yellow Badge: Antisemitism and Philosemitism in Postwar Germany*. New York: Pergamon, 1992.

CHAPTER 3

"You Just Can't Compare"
HOLOCAUST COMPARISONS AND DISCOURSES OF ISRAEL-PALESTINE

LITAL LEVY

The Problem: Comparison and Moral Equivalence

On a 2002 trip to the West Bank city of Ramallah, the late Portuguese author and Nobel laureate José Saramago proclaimed that in the Israeli occupation, one could feel "the spirit of Auschwitz." "This place is being turned into a concentration camp," he said, referring to the siege by the Israel Defense Forces (IDF) on the city. Asked pointedly by an Israeli reporter where the gas chambers were, he replied, "So far, there are none," but added that as a writer, it was his prerogative to "make emotional comparisons in order to shock people into understanding."[1]

In the summer of 2014, as bombs exploded over Gaza and rockets were shot down over Israeli cities, Saramago's prerogative was assumed by countless columnists, pundits, bloggers, and social media users. This was hardly the first time the Holocaust was mobilized for political purposes in the rhetorical crossfire of the Israeli-Palestinian conflict.[2] Similar episodes from the 2008–9 Israel-Gaza war are discussed by Michael Rothberg in his 2011 article on transcultural uses of Holocaust memory, in which he addresses the persistence of comparisons between Gaza and the Warsaw Ghetto. There, Rothberg dwells at length on one case involving William Robinson, a sociology professor at University of California–Santa Barbara, who emailed his students a photo-essay of workshopped images in which photographs of Nazis abusing Jews are paired with photographs depicting Israeli oppression of Palestinians, with the caption "Gaza is Israel's Warsaw." In one of the images, the famous Warsaw Ghetto boy is juxtaposed with a Palestinian child raising his hands in the air in a similar gesture of surrender. Rothberg maps such uses of public memory along what he characterizes as two "axes": the axis of comparison (with a continuum stretching from equation to differentiation) and the axis of political affect (ranging from solidarity to competition). Situating Robinson's image and caption at the intersection of *equation* and *competition*, Rothberg suggests that the sociology professor finds some surprising company: "The same conjunction [of equation and competition] characterizes the Israel right-wing 'second Holocaust' discourse, which sees any move toward peace as setting the scene for another, more horrific genocide."[3] Indeed, Israel's 2005 unilateral evacuation of Gaza was presented in this apocalyptic manner by religious settlers, many of whom wore yellow Stars of David on their clothing as they were forcibly removed by Israeli soldiers.

Moving to the context of contemporary American political life, the question of Holocaust comparisons made headlines in the United States in June 2019 when a furor erupted over Congresswoman Alexandria Ocasio-Cortez's description of detention centers at the US-Mexico border as "concentration camps" following reports that children were being held under inhumane conditions.[4] One week later, the United States Holocaust Memorial Museum (USHMM) in Washington, DC, stated that it "unequivocally rejects efforts to create analogies between the Holocaust and other events, whether historical or contemporary."[5] (This was not the first time the USHMM had taken a position on the question of Holocaust analogies in US political life; in December 2018, it issued a press release authored by staff historian Edna Friedberg entitled "Why Holocaust Analogies Are Dangerous."[6]) Ocasio-Cortez defended her statements, noting that the detention centers "'fit squarely in an academic consensus and definition [of concentration camps],' and asserting that calling something a concentration camp is *not the same* as comparing it to the Holocaust."[7] Hundreds of scholars, many of whom teach Holocaust history, signed an open letter in the *New York Review of Books* urging the USHMM to retract its statement, arguing that "the Museum's decision to completely reject drawing any possible analogies to the Holocaust, or to the events leading up to it, is fundamentally ahistorical."[8] The USHMM stood by its statement.

I first began thinking about comparison, analogies, and the problem of equivalence in public discourse five years earlier, during the 2014 Israel-Hamas war. Throughout those catastrophic seven weeks of summer, one couldn't escape the ubiquity of Holocaust comparisons wielded for pure shock value in the manner of Saramago's provocation. In the media fray, these comparisons usually emphasized the incommensurability of victim and aggressor while presenting an analogy between two historically different experiences of victimhood. Yet I was particularly struck by the double edges of Holocaust comparisons that were deployed rather differently. These other comparisons were not intended as provocations, nor did they subscribe to the usual competition of victims in which one party to the conflict (or its supporters) appropriates the Holocaust to cement its own moral standing in a zero-sum game. Rather, this particular category of Holocaust comparisons was leveraged to establish a *moral equivalency* or common ground between perpetrator and victim, ostensibly at what Rothberg terms the intersection of *equation* and *solidarity*.[9]

Specifically, I noticed that well-known Israeli authors, journalists, and filmmakers attempted to circumvent the "competitive" suffering mode by comparing traumatic episodes and ongoing situations in Palestinian history (e.g., the Nakba, Sabra and Shatila, the first and second intifada, the ongoing occupation) to the multigenerational, lingering trauma of the Holocaust. While my first indications of this particular instrumentalization of Holocaust comparisons came from media discourse, within it I heard reverberations of literary and cinematic expressions from past years. As I pursued this thread in Israeli culture, I discerned that such assertions of commensurability in the form of a *shared victimhood* were usually informed by the author or filmmaker's desire to deflect his (indeed, they were all male) own moral culpability in chapters of the ongoing conflict—or in other words, by his strong drive to preserve a liberal and humanistic Israeli self-image. Further, these comparisons were made on terms that assume Jewish Israelis are the arbiters of Holocaust memory and thus hold the exclusive right to compare the Holocaust (to anything).

In this chapter, I will discuss these dynamics in relation to the broader uses of Holocaust comparisons in media and cultural discourse surrounding the conflict. My purpose is to clarify how, in the political context of Israel-Palestine, extreme comparisons are mobilized as rhetorical instruments of power in a highly asymmetric situation—not only in the more immediately legible manner wherein the author of the comparison seeks to establish moral superiority over a perceived aggressor, but also in the less obvious manner wherein the author of comparison seeks moral absolution for wrongdoing, without making an outright admission of guilt. (Here I should note that the term "conflict" has itself been critiqued by some for implying a false symmetry between Israeli state violence and the Palestinian struggle.) While my focus is on liberal Israeli discourse, over the course of the essay I will examine statements by Israeli, Palestinian, and international figures across a variety of media. Through my analysis, I hope to complicate our understanding of rhetorical comparisons as a political tool and to shed light on the psychology of comparison as a mode of self-understanding, with an emphasis on how comparison may be used for the self-affirmation of the "moral" subject. I will close with thoughts on how we may move beyond competitive and appropriative uses of comparison.

The Backdrop: Holocaust-Nakba Comparisons

The question of Holocaust comparisons in the conflict between Jews and Palestinian Arabs most likely precedes the Nakba and establishment of the State of Israel in 1948. The Holocaust has been used as a point of comparison throughout many chapters of the long and bloody conflict, including the 1982 Sabra and Shatila massacres and the 2008 and 2014 Gaza wars. However, this discussion necessarily begins with the question of Holocaust-Nakba comparisons, not least because some scholars argue that the Nakba itself should be understood as encompassing post-1948 Palestinian experience right up through the present day. The prominence and persistence of comparisons between the Holocaust and the Nakba have attracted the attention of scholars and critics for decades. In an influential 1977 article, Edward Said discussed how supporters of Palestinians and Israelis have exploited Holocaust imagery and rhetoric to minimize the claims of the other side. As he puts it, although the Holocaust and the Palestinian catastrophe are linked, this linkage

> cannot be made rhetorically, or as an argument to demolish or diminish the true content both of the Holocaust and of 1948. Neither is equal to the other; similarly neither one nor the other excuses present violence; and finally, neither one nor the other must be minimized.... We must accept the Jewish experience in all that it entails of horror and fear, but we must require that our experience be given no less attention or perhaps another plane of historical actuality.[10]

Reading Said's essay, Shira Stav observes that "Said draws attention to the fact that both nations are dominated by deep and strong mechanisms of comparison, each used for multiple purposes, including justification of occupation and terror and as a tool to minimize the suffering of the other, who is portrayed as the real and only aggressor."[11] Here, Stav echoes Rothberg's analysis of "competitive" forms of comparison. The contributions to the recent volume *The Holocaust and the Nakba: A New Grammar of Trauma and History*—a major, highly important contribution to the discussion of these two tragic histories—are suffused with notions and questions of analogy and comparison (although the question of comparison as a cognitive, psychological, and discursive mechanism itself is left unexplored).[12] In his foreword to the volume, the Lebanese novelist and critic Elias Khoury, like Said over forty years earlier, also warns against comparing the two tragedies:

> The Palestinians refrained from utilizing the term "Holocaust" to describe their own catastrophe; they used different terminology for this purpose. This is further indication ... of the essential difference between the two historical events, in both the circumstances surrounding them and in what they signify. Even though some Israeli practices may be reminiscent of those of the Nazis, it is a mistake to fall into the trap of making such comparisons, as it would only lead to obscuring issues that color the present. This is an error committed by many Israelis, Jews, Palestinians, and Arabs, and it is no less grave than the mistaken belief by some of the Palestinian leadership in the 1940s that the enemy of their enemy was their friend, which led them into the great folly of cooperation with the Nazis.[13]

Khoury further argues that "refusing to fall into the trap of such a comparison is crucial" given the inherent differences between the two events.[14] Khoury is correct in seeing it as a "trap." Morally and logically, making comparisons to the Holocaust to prove one's point immediately digs oneself into the proverbial hole. However, there are fundamental psychological reasons for our inclination to compare and even to resort to such extreme comparisons.

Comparison is unavoidable in human thought and discourse; it is a cognitive, social, and cultural "imperative" and a constitutive tool of identity formation.[15] We use comparison to organize our thoughts, to evaluate new situations, and to assess ourselves in relation to others. It is also an essential tool for the historian; what cannot be compared or is termed "unique" escapes history into the metaphysical. Comparison is inevitable in any intersubjective encounter, and all the more so when we are confronted with the suffering of the other. Confronting suffering always elicits discomfort; when faced also with the question of our responsibility, our discomfort is heightened, requiring a response. Using comparison to minimize the other's suffering or to deflect our own responsibility is, in this sense, an expected response—a defense mechanism. Comparison is also integral to the maintenance of collective identity in the contexts of community and nation. As Bashir Bashir and Amos Goldberg note in the introduction to *The Holocaust and the Nakba*, "The Holocaust has become a central component of Jewish identity, particularly since the late 1970s and the 1980s, in Israel and around the world. The Nakba and its persisting consequences have become a crucial part of Palestinian and Arab identities since 1948."[16] It should thus come as no surprise that many Jewish Israelis use comparisons to the Holocaust, which is universally seen as a limit case, to defensively delineate and consolidate both individual and collective identity in the context of the protracted violence in Israel-Palestine. For Palestinians and supporters of the Palestinian cause, Holocaust comparisons may seem to offer an opportunity to question Israel's legitimacy as a necessary, self-evident response to the Holocaust (as per the "redemption" narrative), to call out the Israeli state's perceived hypocrisies, and to dislodge it from its moral high ground. "For the most part," write Bashir and Goldberg, "each group sees its own catastrophe as a unique event and seeks to devalue or even deny the catastrophe of the other."[17]

There is no doubt that many agents on both sides have sought to downplay or deny the "catastrophe of the other." Yet I would argue that competitive or antagonistic uses of Holocaust comparisons per se do not necessarily imply denial. Instead, such aggressive comparison straddles a liminal space between the recognition of an event and the contestation of rights to its ethical legacy. To compare the plight of Gazans in 2008 or 2014 to the plight of Holocaust victims is both to recognize the Holocaust as the limit case of evil *and* to contest the idea that the Holocaust bestows upon Israel an enduring claim to the mantle of ultimate victimhood. In other words, such comparisons entail *both* a baseline of recognition and a form of appropriation. This is far messier than "denial" would imply. On the other hand, as I will show, noncompetitive forms of comparison are messy and problematic in their own ways.

Other scholars have extensively critiqued Israeli discursive appropriations of Palestinian experience. My purpose here is thus neither to question the incontrovertible and inevitable impulse to compare nor to expose the (already well-known) practice of appropriating the trauma of others. Rather, in weaving together voices and examples from media discourse, critical theories of comparison, and literary and cultural studies of Israel-Palestine, I aim to elucidate a particular facet of the politics and the psychology of comparison and to disclose the various conflicting and sometimes even self-contradictory ways the Holocaust is used by Israelis vis-à-vis Palestinians. My own reading utilizes Gayatri Chakravorty Spivak's notion of "comparison in extremis" as "a mode of comparative analysis that focuses on situations of extreme violence to reveal underlying structures of power," in order to explore "the double bind of politics and ethics."[18] Ultimately, we will see that where comparison operates on an ethical fault line of asymmetric power relations, using a comparison to one's own historical experience—ostensibly as a lens for seeing or representing the other—may end up reinforcing one's self-view while saying very little about the other.

Two Approaches: From "No Comparison" to the Mirror

Riffing on Derrida's formulations of translatability ("nothing is translatable, everything is translatable"), Rita Felski and Susan Stanford Friedman claim that "nothing is comparable, everything is comparable."[19] In the Israeli-Palestinian context, this aphorism materializes with excruciating acuity. In the 2014 war, as in earlier conflicts, the notion of comparison itself became a prominent target of verbal crossfire. On the one side, a chorus of voices indignantly asked: How can you compare a momentary (if traumatic) disruption in the lives of Israeli civilians to the everyday, relentless suffering of Palestinians trapped in a strangulating occupation? You just can't compare! How can you compare over two thousand people, nearly five hundred of them children, killed in Gaza, with sixty-four soldiers and seven civilians killed in Israel? Don't the numbers speak for themselves? These voices were met by equal indignation on the other side: How can you compare the intentions of Hamas, a militant organization explicitly dedicated to Israel's destruction, which operates in densely populated areas and hides its leaders while leaving citizens without bomb shelters, to those of Israel, a Western-style democracy defending itself from indiscriminate rocket fire and underground infiltration?

In both cases, the offended questioner construes the very notion of comparison between these two situations as a *moral affront*. Here, comparing is equalizing, comparing is erasing the difference between oppressor and oppressed, perpetrator and victim. Yet paradoxically, even while insisting that "there is no comparison," in fact everyone is constantly comparing in order to prove one side's incommensurability. We compare the numbers of the dead, and we compare the *intentions* of Hamas to the intentions of Israel; supporters of Israel's actions often invoke Hamas's charter with its notorious references to the "Nazism" of the Jews and the *Protocols of the Elders of Zion*,[20] while critics of Israel refer to its semiprivate military doctrines such as the Dahiya Doctrine and the Hannibal Protocol, both of which called for the use of heavy and "disproportionate" firepower to be employed against civilian infrastructures.[21]

We also compare public discourse on both sides, analyzing statements by Hamas calling for the slaughter of Israelis[22] or the words of Israeli politicians and public figures who have called for the rape of Palestinian women[23] and for ethnic cleansing.[24] And finally, after insisting that the two parties to the conflict can't be compared to each other, we inevitably compare either one or the other side to the victims of the Holocaust—the outer limit of all comparison.

The Holocaust was invoked dozens of times in opinion columns and editorials on the 2014 Gaza war in the international media. Gabor Maté, a physician, author, and self-described "infant survivor of the Nazi genocide," wrote in the *Toronto Star*, "The Palestinians use tunnels? So did my heroes, the poorly armed fighters of the Warsaw Ghetto." He adds, "My heart tells me that 'never again' is not a tribal slogan, that the murder of my grandparents in Auschwitz does not justify the ongoing dispossession of Palestinians . . . that Israel's 'right to defend itself,' unarguable in principle, does not validate mass killing."[25] I saw this article posted on a colleague's social media post. Beneath it, one reader commented, "What an awful comparison to the Holocaust. No one denies the tragedy in this war. Why are people so afraid to call out Hamas and demand better leadership for the Palestinians?" Another response from a prominent historian read, "As a historian I find the comparison with the Warsaw Ghetto to be somewhere between ludicrous and laughable. However one might feel about the situation in Gaza, these kind[s] of comparisons are just silly." Indeed, the comparison suggests a fundamental kinship between the Warsaw Ghetto and Gaza as open-air prisons and between the ghetto fighters and Hamas fighters. In both cases tunnels were dug by desperate people and were used for purposes of smuggling and warfare. Yet those similarities don't account for the widespread belief that Hamas's tunnels are intended for the kidnap and murder of Israeli civilians, a belief that elicits the vehement rejection of comparisons to the Warsaw Ghetto. In short, where some would see profound similarities in terms of resistance to oppression, others find a moral dissimilarity that invalidates any comparison of similar experiences.

On 8 August 2014, the Norwegian doctor and pro-Palestinian activist Mads Gilbert, who had volunteered at al-Shifa (Gaza's main hospital) through the worst of the war, gave a speech upon his return to Tromsø, Norway, in which he said, "Imagine being back in 1945. And I beg to be understood when I say that I am not comparing the German Nazi regime with Israel. I do not. But I compare occupation with occupation." In the speech, he asked his audience to imagine what would have happened had Norway not won the liberation struggle and had remained occupied and if Tromsø had been bombed in the manner of Gaza. He concludes, "In 1938, the Nazis called the Jews 'Untermenschen,' subhuman. Today, Palestinians in the West Bank, in Gaza, in the Diaspora are treated as Untermensch, as subhumans who can be bombed, killed, slaughtered by their thousands, without any of those in power reacting."[26] So, he says, Israel is *not* Nazi Germany, but occupation is occupation and Palestinians *are* treated as Untermenschen. In other words: I don't equate *in toto*, but I do equate selectively; Gaza is what Norway might have become had history happened a little differently. Gilbert's uses of comparison exemplify Gayatri Spivak's observation that comparison is never simply a matter of comparing and contrasting, but rather of *judging and choosing*.[27]

Maté and Gilbert are two specific cases of foreigners who, when writing and speaking on behalf of Palestinians in Gaza, use Holocaust comparisons to elevate the moral status of Hamas fighters and Palestinian civilians, respectively. Let us now consider the case of another foreign journalist who neither uses Holocaust comparisons nor justifies such comparisons, but rather who critiques the common Israeli practice of wielding the Holocaust as the outer, unbreachable limit of comparison. On 9 August 2014, in a pitch-perfect satire of the liberal Zionist response to the war published in the online forum *+972 Magazine*, Adam Shatz, a contributing editor to the *London Review of Books*, "interviewed" a fictitious Israeli writer named Amos Yehoshua-Shavit, an obvious composite of the names of the leading Israeli writers Amos Oz, Ari Shavit, and A. B. Yehoshua. Even the title of the piece, extracted from the pseudo-interview, calls out the narcissism of Israeli liberal discourse: "Living with Political Depression in Tel Aviv Is Harder Than Dying in Gaza." The imagined interviewee, a self-described "peacenik," laments:

> And so I have come to the uncomfortable conclusion that they have too much invested in hating us. It's become their identity: they can't give it up. And so they try to kill us, and when we end up killing more of them, because we are more powerful, they say we are committing genocide. Come on! Yes, 2,000 deaths is a lot. But it's not six million. Look, I promised myself that I would not bring up the Holocaust, but I am afraid I can't avoid it. The Shoah looms over us like a dark cloud. We are a traumatized people, and we react—we over-react—in the way that traumatized people do.[28]

Shatz's satirization of the "Holocaust card" is meant to reveal how the singularity of the Holocaust is always the appeal of last resort, a transhistorical defense that reconstructs the perpetrator as the eternal victim.

In short, in situations of extreme violence, when comparing is implicitly understood as equating aggressor and victim, the rhetorical battle tends to favor extreme forms of comparison, which each side uses to claim the mantle of victimhood. Thus, in the midst of a situation in which both sides are wedded to the principle of incommensurability—the idea that "you just can't compare"—the Holocaust can play the role of trump card for everyone. Defenders of the Palestinians compare Gaza to the Warsaw Ghetto and compare the slaughter of innocents in Gaza to the Nazi genocide. Defenders of Israel, including many liberal Israelis, insist on the singularity of the Holocaust, maintaining that it defies all such comparisons.

But this is not the only approach to comparison that characterizes liberal Israeli discourse. Even as some interlocutors defend the incomparability of the Holocaust, others use the Holocaust as a filter for the Palestinian experience—either empathetically, to relate to the suffering of the other, or (to return to our fictitious Israeli author) as a narcissistic mirror onto the trauma of the Israeli psyche. In fact, as I will show, what begins with an apparent act of recognition may end up as narcissism. In Israeli cultural expression, one can trace the admixture of empathic intersubjective relation and narcissistic mirroring back to the foundational war literature of the Israeli author S. Yizhar in his 1949 novella *Khirbet Khizeh* and his 1948 story "Ha-shavui" ("The Prisoner").[29] "The Prisoner," first published in November 1948, depicts the brutal interrogation of a Palestinian shepherd taken prisoner by Israeli soldiers; it ends with the Israeli guard's internal monologue as he debates whether to free his prisoner. *Khirbet Khizeh*, named for a fictitious, representative Palestinian village, follows the thoughts and actions of an Israeli soldier assigned to the expulsion of the village's last remaining inhabitants: women, children, the disabled, and the elderly. Although the soldier sees the helpless civilians his unit is violently removing as the mirror image of Holocaust victims and Jewish refugees, he ultimately follows his orders and rationalizes his actions as a necessary evil for the establishment of the Jewish state. An instant bestseller in Israel, the novella was highly influential among younger authors such as Amos Oz.[30] Arguably, with "The Prisoner" and *Khirbet Khizeh*, Yizhar launched a counter-canon of internally conflicted Israeli literature that accepted the Zionist meta-narrative while questioning the morality of Zionism's treatment of Palestinians. Both works have been variously lauded for the empathy shown toward Palestinian suffering during wartime and critiqued for the narrators' inaction and self-serving moralizing.[31]

How can we analyze this countertendency in Israeli discourse—that of "mirroring" with the other—through the psychology of comparison? I believe that this discussion requires us to reconsider the problem of asymmetric comparison from a different perspective: not as a problem of asymmetry that manifests itself in the *object* of comparison (i.e., the Holocaust and Gaza, or the Holocaust and the Nakba), with their concomitant comparisons of scale, intent, and so forth, but rather as a problem of asymmetry in the material conditions of the *authors* of comparison. First, there is the question of power. What does it mean for the vastly more powerful party to make this kind of comparison? Shatz mocks the common Israeli complaint about a double standard when his faux author protests that after all, it's not Israel's fault that it has more power; why should it be held to a higher moral standard? Hannan Hever voices a similar critique regarding *Khirbet Khizeh*, faulting Yizhar for creating a "false symmetry" when, in the very moment the Israeli soldier-protagonist is driving Palestinian villagers into exile, he identifies their cruel fate with that of Jews in the Diaspora—as though the mere recognition amounts to absolution: "Such erasure of the asymmetry of power relations in representations of the expulsion opens the perpetrator's path to self-exoneration—which is the function of Yizhar's analogy between the Holocaust and the Nakba."[32] Then there is the question of reciprocity. What does it mean to say, as many left-leaning intellectuals (Israelis and foreigners) tend to do, that Israelis and Palestinians both are victims of a terrible situation or that they are caught together in an endless cycle of violence? Is this an expression of empathy, or is it a failure to assign responsibility? Or can it be something of both?

Comparison in Extremis: Reciprocity and Recognition

Here, I return to Spivak's notion of the double bind. Spivak invokes the double bind as a kind of catch-22 between ethics and politics that characterizes what she calls "comparison in extremis," which she identifies in acts of suicide bombing and other forms of non-state violence. For Spivak, the thinking that subtends such acts can be understood as a "comparativism of last resort," a "plea to the other to recognize equivalence," situating it "between ethics (I must not kill) and politics (I can have a 'response' from my non-respondent[s] only in a shared death)."[33] Spivak's "comparison in extremis" pivots on the problem of recognition, seeking to answer the question, what happens when the more powerful party fails to recognize the subaltern's cry for help and fails to respond? Although Hany Abu Assad's 2005 film *Paradise Now* is not among the cinematic examples she adduces, this idea is well illustrated in a late scene from the film in which one of the two Palestinian recruits for a suicide bombing explains his decision to carry out his destructive mission in Tel Aviv, arguing that "they [the Israelis] must understand that if there's no security for us, there'll be none for them either." He adds, "I tried to deliver this message to them, but I couldn't find another way. Even worse, they've convinced the world, and themselves, that they are the victims. . . . If they take on the role of oppressor and victim, then I have no other choice but to be a victim and a murderer as well."[34] Similarly, Spivak is interested in how the subaltern finds equivalence with the hegemon in a shared (and thus equalizing) death, when other means of demanding equivalence have been met with silence. Here, "equivalence" seems to imply a fundamental recognition of the subaltern's right to the same freedoms and privileges enjoyed by the hegemonic power. For Spivak, then, the double bind of ethics and politics emerges from the desperation of the suicide bomber. It is expressly *not* about how the hegemonic power asserts its *own* idea of equivalence with the subaltern. And yet I think that this notion of the double bind is also useful for characterizing the nonresponse of the Israeli public and leadership to examples of Palestinian nonviolent resistance, such as the protracted nonviolent protests by the inhabitants of Budrus, Bil'in, and Ni'lin against the intended bifurcation of their villages by the Separation Wall.[35]

In short, liberal Israeli discourse oscillates between the ideal of the ethical and the constraints it says are "imposed" on Israel by the political. It sees *itself* as caught in this double bind and claims that true equivalence on the macro level can be achieved only through a mutual recognition of both sides' narratives and suffering (the "dual narrative" thesis). It is hard to argue with the premise that the starting point for reconciliation is mutual empathy, and indeed, mutual empathy is the foundation of the difficult work undertaken by Palestinian and Israeli individuals active in organizations such as the Bereaved Family Circle and Combatants for Peace, both of which work toward nonviolent conflict resolution. But much of the liberal Israeli discourse of the type critiqued by Shatz adopts a basic and uncritical premise of *reciprocity* between the two parties. In another essay on comparison, the postcolonial critic R. Radhakrishnan asks, "How does an epistemology of comparison exacerbate or resolve the tension between the categories of 'reciprocity' and 'recognition'?"[36] The summer 2014 interviews published with leading Israeli authors David Grossman in the *New York Times* and the late Amos Oz in *Deutsche Welle* both frame comparison in terms of reciprocity and recognition, with Oz presenting Palestinians and Israelis as "two sides caught in a cycle of violence together,"[37] or, in Grossman's words, "Israelis and Palestinians are imprisoned in what seems increasingly like a hermetically sealed bubble."[38] This is precisely the kind of double-edged comparison that, on the one hand, empathetically recognizes the other and avoids outright self-centrism but, on the other hand, erases recognition of the fundamental asymmetry of power between the two parties in conflict. Ultimately, this type of comparison deflects agency and responsibility from individual human subjects to an externalized, self-generating, and self-replicating "cycle." Furthermore, it implies that the speaker occupies a neutral space vis-à-vis this "bubble." Contrast this rhetoric to that of Maté, Gilbert, or the fictitious but representative character Khaled in *Paradise Now*, all of whom assume a clear position in their judgment of aggressor versus victim and make an explicit moral judgment.

Bruce Robbins addresses such questions of position and judgment in his critique of anthropologist Talal Asad's well-known 2007 book *On Suicide Bombing*. According to Robbins, Asad displaces the normative criteria of morality by which we assess two sides in a conflict with the criteria of capability or power. Paraphrasing Asad, Robbins writes, "It's not that terrorist violence is virtuous; it's merely that it has less capability to harm than the violence of the state. True enough. Yet the implication here seems to be that the *lack* of the capability to harm becomes, if not virtue itself, then a new functional *substitute* for virtue, the basis for a new ethics."[39] In Robbin's view, this is problematic because it "dispenses you from making moral judgments." He elaborates:

> When Asad offers an anthropological "understanding" of suicide bombing in place of, and as opposed to, any normative judgment, one might say that he presents himself as an extraterrestrial, looking on with complete detachment from the urgencies of judgment that mere humans feel obliged to respond to. By this account scholarship itself would be . . . a space of *perfect nonbelonging*. This danger is most acute for anyone who depends on a politics of comparison.[40]

Robbin's argument reminded me of the familiar comparison made between Hamas's tunnels and rockets and Israel's massive military capabilities, which is often invoked along the lines that the lack of might makes right; and again I was reminded of Shatz's fictitious author bemoaning the unfairness of the responsibilities that come with an unequal share of power. But then Robbins surprised me with the following:

> I want to conclude by returning to the practice of comparison as seen against a troubling background of unequal power. It is of course true that the scale of power matters. Talal Asad's point was made and remade during the [2009] Israeli invasion of Gaza. It is grotesque to assume that a few rockets aimed at Israeli civilians by Hamas, however wrongly, can be properly met with the wholesale slaughter inflicted on the Palestinian inhabitants. Any norm that justifies the latter by equating or "balancing" the two, as mainstream American discourse has repeatedly done, deserves to be treated as worthless. But many of us in the humanities generalize this position . . . preferring, like Asad, to place ourselves outside norms.[41]

In other words, in being comparatists in the most general sense of the word—that is, in placing ourselves *outside* the act of comparison—and further, in situating our human objects of comparison as passive subjects trapped in a "cycle," a "bubble," or some other sphere outside the human world we share with them, we absolve *ourselves* of the responsibility to make a moral judgment. This in a sense is the perfect analogue to Shatz's caricature of the enlightened Israeli intellectual who uses comparison to depict his Palestinian other and himself as equal partners in a cycle of violence more powerful than either of them.

In a similar manner, Holocaust comparisons have also been used in Israeli cultural discourse to filter Palestinian suffering. The belief that, even as a participant in the conflict, you can place yourself outside the norms of judgment becomes the driving force of the 2008 Israeli film *Waltz with Bashir*. This award-winning film innovatively combined documentary material, including interviews, with animation, creating a unique form of representation that visualizes the innermost recesses of memory, dream, and fantasy.[42] It portrays director Ari Folman's personal quest to recover his repressed memories of Israeli's 1982 Lebanon war, culminating in his presence at the site of the massacre of Palestinian civilians in the Sabra and Shatila camps. The narrative unfolds as a psychological detective story in which Folman revisits former comrades, experts, and his therapist both to piece together the forgotten events and to process his trauma. As numerous critics have noted, this is not a film about social and political responsibility, but about the guilt or trauma of the perpetrator, or to use Dominick LaCapra's term, "perpetrator trauma"—part of a larger trend in Israeli cinema, as elaborated by Raya Morag.[43] As leading Israeli historian and critic Tom Segev put it, "The film *Waltz with Bashir* belongs to the kvetch genre: 'Oy, how traumatic that massacre in Sabra and Chatila was for us'"[44]—the same sentiment, of course, that Shatz parodies when his fictitious author laments his own "political trauma" while sitting safe and sound in Tel Aviv.

Throughout *Waltz with Bashir*, the Holocaust is invoked "as a cognitive device that enables Folman and his comrades to process their experiences."[45] As others have already addressed this point extensively, I will refer only to the film's two most important Holocaust references. At the climax of Folman's psychoanalytical quest, his therapist suggests to him that both his absent memories and his guilt actually originate in his parents' experiences as Holocaust survivors. The unconscious absorption of his parents' traumatic memories imposed on him "the role of the Nazi" when he was a soldier; thus, in the words of the therapist, his "interest in those [Palestinian] camps is actually in the 'other' camps."[46] This, apparently, is the key that unlocks the mystery of his psyche while simultaneously exonerating his past. For as Raya Morag explains, it displaces his "ambiguous guilt" over his indirect complicity in the massacres with the unambiguous past of the Holocaust.[47] At the same time, however, the Holocaust is also subtly invoked throughout the film in relation to the war's Palestinian and Lebanese victims.

Shira Stav has brilliantly analyzed how analogies between the Holocaust and Nakba in this film and in Noam Chayut's 2009 novel *My Holocaust Thief* "juxtapose Palestinian refugees and Holocaust victims (and less explicitly, Israeli soldiers and Nazi officers) as a way of rehabilitating a moral self."[48] As she notes, Holocaust comparisons are also used by Israeli liberals sympathetically, to create a presence for the Palestinian narrative "within a hostile political atmosphere." Yet this type of comparison, she argues, "relegates the Palestinian catastrophe . . . to secondary importance" and ends up insisting on the victimized position of the Israeli Jew.[49] Further, these comparisons become a form of appropriation of the Palestinian story:

> The Nakba is thus diminished and turned into an internal event of Jewish history, as if "their" catastrophe is impossible to understand without "our" catastrophe, which is, of course, *the* catastrophe. A common Israeli response to this comparison is, "There is no comparison!" The very comparison between the Holocaust and the life and fate of the Palestinian refugees is considered "monstrous."[50]

The film's most explicit Holocaust comparison is made during Folman's interview with Israeli war correspondent Ron Ben-Yishai, when the journalist, describing the exodus of refugees out of the camp, relates the images of the Sabra and Shatila massacre to those of the Warsaw Ghetto uprising. In particular, Ben-Yishai identifies a Palestinian child raising his hands in the universal gesture of surrender with the famous image of the Warsaw Ghetto child, the very image discussed earlier in this chapter.[51] In her analysis, Stav goes so far as to read the figure of the Palestinian boy not only as a visitation of the Warsaw Ghetto child but as a reincarnation of Folman himself: "The Israeli soldier assumes the role of the victim, staggering under the enormous burden of traumatic memories."[52]

This brings us back to reciprocity, recognition, and the "double bind." To return to Spivak's formulation of comparison in extremis, I propose that if the suicide bomber imagines achieving an equilibrium of power with his or her oppressor in a shared death, Folman (like Grossman and Oz before him) fantasizes about achieving *moral* equivalence with his or her victims through a shared *victimhood*. Ultimately, through the persistent thread of Holocaust comparisons that culminates in the ambiguous image of the Palestinian child, Folman implies that he himself is caught in this terrible "double bind" of ethics and politics. In a process of logical triangulation, Ben Yishai's comparison of the Palestinian boy with the Warsaw Ghetto child meets Folman's self-presentation as a second-generation Holocaust victim. Comparison A meets comparison B, effecting a transhistorical equivalence that transforms the perpetrator into the victim through the equation of shared victimhood. In other words, equivalence does not undergird this comparison; to the contrary, equivalence is an *effect* of the comparison, which proceeds in blatant disregard of all obvious circumstances of asymmetry on the ground.

I have adduced this scene as a prime example of a comparison that begins with a gesture of recognition but then reads the suffering of the other through one's own narrative, returning the reference of the comparison back to the self. As Rothberg writes of Holocaust comparisons, "While the discourse activates a universalizing framework of recognition through which underrecognized subjects become visible as victims, this framework serves not so much to acknowledge difference as to *translate difference back into a reduced vision of sameness*."[53] To summarize, then, Israeli liberal discourse tends to compare the Holocaust with Palestinian suffering in one of two ways: by insisting on the singularity of the Holocaust, which ends with the displacement of Israeli responsibility onto "the conflict," "the cycle of violence," and so forth; or by insisting on Palestinian similarity to Jewish experience, where the Jewish experience is the privileged standard of comparison. What is absent from this discourse is an ethics of recognition based on the value of difference (the particular) that manifests *within* the comparative frame of similarity. We have seen that comparisons to the Holocaust, a form of extreme comparison, do not generally serve to enhance mutual appreciation of suffering in a way that would genuinely open one up to the recognition of a different experience or narrative. To the contrary, it may *obscure* the experience of the other. As such it is monologic rather than dialogic and becomes part of the "nonresponse" Spivak describes in her articulation of "comparison in extremis."

Conclusion: Recognizing Difference

By now, we have seen ample evidence of the multiple uses and abuses of Holocaust comparisons in the conflict. It seems self-evident that comparison is never neutral—that, to quote R. Radhakrishnan, "behind the seeming generosity of comparison, there always lurks the aggression of a thesis."[54] So then, between the politics of competitive victimhood and the misplaced desire for shared victimhood, are we left with the bleak impression that Israel and Palestine are subjective worlds that can only be understood separately and exclusively? Is all comparison across lines of conflict doomed to reinforce self-centrism? I think not. I would not want to conclude this chapter with a one-sided indictment of comparison as a social and psychological practice, for comparison is also the very mechanism that generates empathy and enables us to find common ground with others. In *Comparing the Incomparable*, Marcel Detienne argues for the virtue of transcultural comparison in history and the social sciences, saying that it is precisely there that "one learns how to distance oneself from one's basic instincts and to bring a critical eye to bear on one's own traditions."[55] Similarly, Rothberg writes in *Multidirectional Memory* that "too often comparison is understood as 'equation'—the Holocaust cannot be compared to any other history the story goes, because it is unlike them all. This project [*Multidirectional Memory*] takes dissimilarity for granted . . . and then focuses its intellectual energy on investigating what it means to invoke connections nonetheless."[56] To reiterate, then, the problems I have identified are not intrinsic to comparison as a cognitive or rhetorical tool; rather, they stem from the deployment of comparison as a rhetorical tool *within an asymmetric power relationship* and its attendant problems of identification with the other. Comparison need not always proceed in a way that fails to recognize the value of difference. Rothberg sees transformative potential in art that creates new frameworks of recognition and reconfigures elements or at least draws attention to the fixity of the two narratives, tropes, or images at play, rather than simply producing "commensurability out of difference."[57] In this wager, Rothberg may well be channeling Ettiene Balibar's observation that "equivalence blurs differences, whereas equality requires them."[58] Similarly, in her 2012 book on post-memory in art, which includes a reading of Ghassan Kanafani's iconic story "Returning to Haifa" (itself a narration of a Holocaust-Nakba comparison), Marianne Hirsch offers a concept of "connective histories" that seeks to connect global events with intimate details and fragments, focusing on the minuteness of experience and enabling the discovery of connection.[59] Rather than comparing in a manner that reduces difference to similarity, we can consider points of connection between unique experiences in a way that does not transcend a larger appreciation of difference.

In short, I conclude with the proposition that intersubjective forms of comparison can be mutually enriching when they are conducted through a fundamental recognition of *difference*. When one values difference, one resists the impulse to subordinate the suffering of the other to one's own personal or historical trauma through competition (mine is greater than yours) or appropriation (yours is the mirror of mine). As Emmanuel Levinas writes in *Entre Nous*, our understanding of the other, in terms of the other's being in the most general sense, "carries out an act of violence and of negation." This, says Levinas, results from understanding being implicitly conflated with possession. When you meet the other, "despite the extent of my domination over him and his submission, I do not possess him."[60] In their introduction to *The Holocaust and the Nakba*, Bashir and Goldberg discuss how Dominick LaCapra's notion of "empathic unsettlement" offers an alternative to the problem of identification with the other. To see a glimpse of oneself mirrored in another, and vice versa, is the beginning of recognition and therefore of empathy; but to remain trapped in the mirror is the very essence of narcissism. Thus, while empathy is often "mistakenly conflated" with identification, LaCapra contrasts them. Identification, as we have seen in the discussions of *Waltz with Bashir*, is "always connected to narcissistic impulses" and "follows the risky fantasy of universal likeness, which seeks homogeneity and eradicates difference," ending in appropriation or subjugation.[61] By contrast, empathic unsettlement calls for empathy while recognizing a disturbing otherness and while resisting the urge to overpower that otherness by neutralizing it through self-identification. To reframe these thoughts in terms of the question of comparison, replace "identification" with "equivalence." When we are able to relinquish the need for equivalence, we can engage the work of comparison productively. Connective approaches such as those discussed by Rothberg and Hirsch offer glimmers of an alternative that, in the spirit of Balibar's words, would move the fulcrum of comparison from *equivalence* toward *equality*.

Lital Levy is associate professor of comparative literature at Princeton University, where she teaches comparative literature and theory, Hebrew literature, Arabic literature, and Jewish studies. She is the author of the award-winning *Poetic Trespass: Writing between Hebrew and Arabic in Israel/Palestine* (Princeton University Press, 2014) and numerous articles on literature, history, and cultural studies. She is working on two book projects: an intellectual history of Arab Jews and modernity, and a study of temporality in Palestinian and Israeli cultural discourse.

Notes

1. Amira Hass, "Nobel Winner: Ramallah Being Turned into Concentration Camp," *Haaretz*, 26 March 2002, http://www.haaretz.com/news/nobel-winner-ramallah-being-turned-into-concentration-camp-1.49362.
2. In 1990, the lawyer and author Mike Godwin famously ventured that in long online debates, "the probability of a reference or comparison to Hitler or to Nazis approaches 1," a proposition now widely known as "Godwin's Law."
3. Michael Rothberg, "From Gaza to Warsaw: Mapping Multidirectional Memory," *Criticism* 53, no. 4 (Fall 2011): 523–48; quotation from 535. Here and in his earlier monograph *Multidirectional Memory: Remembering the Holocaust in the Age of Decolonization* (Stanford: Stanford University Press, 2009), Rothberg investigates what happens when histories of extreme violence confront each other in the public sphere and questions whether a competition of victims is inevitable; he argues for a shift from competitive to "multidirectional" uses of memory. For more on settlers' uses of Holocaust imagery in the 2005 evacuation, see Harry de Quetteville, "Settlers Evoke Images of the Holocaust as Israeli Forces Move in to Clear Them from Gaza," *The Telegraph*, 14 August 2005, http://www.telegraph.co.uk/news/worldnews/middleeast/israel/1496201/Settlers-evoke-images-of-the-Holocaust-as-Israeli-forces-move-in-to-clear-them-from-Gaza.html.
4. Sheryl Gay Stolberg, "Ocasio-Cortez Calls Migrant Detention Centers 'Concentration Camps,' Eliciting Backlash," *New York Times*, 18 June 2019, https://www.nytimes.com/2019/06/18/us/politics/ocasio-cortez-cheney-detention-centers.html.
5. For the full statement, see https://www.ushmm.org/information/press/press-releases/statement-regarding-the-museums-position-on-holocaust-analogies.

6. Edna Friedberg, "Why Holocaust Analogies Are Dangerous," press release of the USHMM, 12 December 2018, https://www.ushmm.org/information/press/press-releases/why-holocaust-analogies-are-dangerous.
7. Leila Ettachfini, "Holocaust Museum Slams Concentration Camp Comparisons," *Vice*, 25 June 2019, https://www.vice.com/en_us/article/kzm5nn/holocaust-museum-concentration-camp-statement.
8. See Omer Bartov, Doris Bergen, Andrea Orzoff, Timothy Snyder, Anika Walke, et al., "An Open Letter to the Director of the US Holocaust Memorial Museum," *New York Review of Books*, 1 July 2019, https://www.nybooks.com/daily/2019/07/01/an-open-letter-to-the-director-of-the-holocaust-memorial-museum/.
9. Rothberg, "From Gaza to Warsaw," 535.
10. See Edward Said, "Usus al-ta'ayush," *al-Hayat*, 5 November 1977, n.p.; cited in Joseph Massad, *The Persistence of the Palestinian Question: Essays on Zionism and the Palestinians* (London: Routledge, 2006), 139, 141.
11. Shira Stav, "Nakba and Holocaust: Mechanisms of Comparison and Denial in the Israeli Literary Imagination," *Jewish Social Studies: History, Culture, Society* 18, no. 3 (Spring/Summer 2012): 85–98; 90.
12. Bashir Bashir and Amos Goldberg, eds., *The Holocaust and the Nakba: A New Grammar of Trauma and History* (New York: Columbia University Press, 2019).
13. Elias Khoury, "Foreword," in Bashir and Goldberg, *The Holocaust and the Nakba*, ix–xviii, xii.
14. He construes the Holocaust as "a major episode in human history" that should stand as a warning to humanity against the "insidious encroachment of racism," and the Nakba as "an embodiment of the same colonial expansionist reality that gave birth to the apartheid regime in South Africa." Furthermore, the Holocaust is a "collective human memory" that must be preserved, whereas the Nakba only *began* in 1948 and is ongoing in the present; here, he emphatically distinguishes between the moral responses demanded by memory of a past event versus present-day iniquity. Yet "they are both relevant to the essential struggle of humanity against racism." Khoury, "Foreword," xii–xiii, xv.
15. Susan Stanford Friedman, "Why Not Compare?," in *Comparison: Theories, Approaches, Uses*, ed. Rita Felski and Susan Stanford Friedman (Baltimore: Johns Hopkins University Press, 2013), 34–45, 36–37.
16. Bashir Bashir and Amos Goldberg, "Introduction—The Holocaust and the Nakba: A New Syntax of History, Memory, and Political Thought," in Bashir and Goldberg, *The Holocaust and the Nakba*, 1–42. Their book seeks to offer a non-comparative framework for addressing both events while honoring the uniqueness of each one (5).
17. Bashir and Goldberg, "Introduction," 3.
18. Rita Felski and Susan Stanford Friedman, "Introduction," in Felski and Friedman, *Comparison*, 1–12, 4, 9.
19. Felski and Friedman, "Introduction," 4.
20. These references appeared in an earlier version of the Hamas charter that was originally issued in 1988 and was still current at the time of the 2008 and 2014 Israel-Hamas wars. In 2017 Hamas replaced its charter and removed these references. The older version included phrases such as "The Nazi Zionist practices against our people" and "the despicable Nazi-Tatar invasion," and claimed, "Their scheme has been laid out in the Protocols of the Elders of Zion, and their present [conduct] is the best proof of what is said there" (Hamas Charter translated and annotated by Raphael Israeli for the Harry Truman Research Institute at The Hebrew University, Jerusalem, Israel; see https://fas.org/irp/world/para/docs/880818.htm). On the charter's replacement in 2017, see Patrick Wintour, "Hamas Presents New Charter Accepting a Palestine Based on 1967 Borders," *The Guardian*, 1 May 2017, https://www.theguardian.com/world/2017/may/01/hamas-new-charter-palestine-israel-1967-borders.
21. Jerome Slater, "The Walzer Problem," *Mondoweiss*, 13 August 2014, http://mondoweiss.net/2014/08/the-walzer-problem.html.
22. Yoram Hazony, "How a Hamas Anthem Became a Hit in Israel," 8 August 2014, *Tablet Magazine*, http://www.tabletmag.com/jewish-arts-and-culture/music/181478/hamas-anthem-israel#undefined.

23. Dr. Mordechai Kedar of Bar-Ilan University's suggestion that raping Palestinian women would serve as an effective deterrence against terrorism was widely reported; see, for instance, Ori Kashti, "Israeli Professor Suggests Rape Would Serve as 'Terror Deterrent,'" *Haaretz*, 22 July 2014 (repeated in *The Forward*), https://forward.com/news/breaking-news/202558/israeli-professor-suggests-rape-would-serve-as-ter/.
24. Moshe Feiglin, "My Outline for a Solution in Gaza," *Arutz Sheva/Israel National News*, 15 July 2014, http://www.israelnationalnews.com/Articles/Article.aspx/15326#.U-wa64BdUpw. Even the use of the term "war crime" is highly contentious in Israel, where both official discourse and public opinion insist that its military actions are always defensive in nature; when the IDF kills hundreds of children and noncombatants in Gaza, Israeli discourse blames Hamas for operating in civilian enclaves and using "human shields."
25. Gabor Maté, "Beautiful Dream of Israel Has Become a Nightmare," *Toronto Star*, 22 July 2014, http://www.thestar.com/opinion/commentary/2014/07/22/beautiful_dream_of_israel_has_become_a_nightmare.html.
26. Ali Abunimah, "Video: Palestinian Resistance in Gaza Is 'Fighting for All of Us,' Says Dr. Mads Gilbert," *Electronic Intifada*, 8 August 2014, http://electronicintifada.net/blogs/ali-abunimah/video-palestinian-resistance-gaza-fighting-all-us-says-dr-mads-gilbert.
27. Gayatri Chakravorty Spivak, "Rethinking Comparativism," in Felski and Friedman, *Comparison*, 253–70; 254.
28. Adam Shatz, "Living with Political Depression in Tel Aviv Is Harder Than Dying in Gaza (Satire)," *+972 Magazine*, 9 August 2014, http://972mag.com/satire-gaza/95249/.
29. S. Yizhar, "The Prisoner," in *Modern Hebrew Literature*, ed. Robert Alter, trans. V. C. Rycus (New York: Behrman House, 1975), 294–310; S. Yizhar, *Khirbet Khizeh*, trans. Nicholas de Lange and Yaacob Dweck (Jerusalem: Ibis Editions, 2008).
30. Anita Shapira, "Hirbet Hizah: Between Remembrance and Forgetting," *Jewish Social Studies* 7, no. 1 (Autumn 2000): 1–62.
31. See, for example, Yizhar, *Khirbet Khizeh*; Elias Khoury, "The Mirror: Imagining Justice in Palestine," *Boston Review*, July–August 2008; Stav, "Nakba and Holocaust"; Yochi Fisher, "What Does Exile Look Like? Transformations in the Linkage between the Shoah and the Nakba," in Bashir and Goldberg, *The Holocaust and the Nakba*, 173–86; and Hannan Hever, "From Revenge to Empathy: Abba Kovner from Jewish Destruction to Palestinian Destruction," in Bashir and Goldberg, *The Holocaust and the Nakba*, 275–92.
32. Hever, "From Revenge to Empathy," 280.
33. Spivak, "Rethinking Comparativism," in Felski and Friedman, *Comparison*, 258–60.
34. *Paradise Now* (dir. Hany Abu Assad), 2005.
35. See, for example, the documentary films *Bil'in my Love* (dir. Shai Carmelli-Pollak, 2006), *Budrus* (dir. Julia Bacha, 2010), and *Five Broken Cameras* (dir. Emad Burnat, 2011).
36. R. Radhakrishnan, "Why Compare?," in Felski and Friedman, *Comparison*, 20.
37. Amos Oz, "Lose-Lose Situation for Israel," *Deutsche Welle*, 30 July 2014, http://www.dw.de/oz-lose-lose-situation-for-israel/a-17822511.
38. David Grossman, "An Israel without Illusions," *New York Times*, 27 July 2014, http://www.nytimes.com/2014/07/28/opinion/david-grossman-end-the-grindstone-of-israeli-palestinian-violence.html?_r=0.
39. Bruce Robbins, "Chomsky's Golden Rule: Comparison and Cosmopolitanism," in Felski and Friedman, *Comparison*, 191–209; 201, emphasis in original.
40. Robbins, "Chomsky's Golden Rule," 204.
41. Robbins, "Chomsky's Golden Rule," 204.
42. Kamran Rastegar, "'*Sawwaru waynkum*?' Human Rights and Social Trauma in *Waltz with Bashir*," *College Literature: A Journal of Critical Literary Studies* 40, no. 3 (Summer 2013): 60–80; 63.
43. Raya Morag, "Perpetrator Trauma and Current Israeli Documentary Cinema," *Camera Obscura 80*, 27, no. 2 (2012): 93–132. See also Gil Hochberg, "Soldiers as Filmmakers: On the Prospect of 'Shooting War' and the Question of Ethical Spectatorship,' *Screen* 54, no. 1 (Spring 2013): 44–61.

For "perpetrator trauma," see Dominick LaCapra, *History and Memory after Auschwitz* (Ithaca, NY: Cornell University Press, 1998), 41; see also Rothberg, *Multidirectional Memory*, 90, 326n26.

44. Tom Segev, "Waltz with History," *Ha'aretz*, 5 February 2009, cited in Ursula Lindsay, "Shooting Film and Crying," *Middle East Research and Information Project*, March 2009, https://merip.org/2009/03/shooting-film-and-crying/.
45. David Shasha, "'Shooting and Forgetting': The 1982 Lebanon War as a Psychological Mystery in *Waltz with Bashir*," *Sephardic Heritage Update* 494, 14 September 2011 (privately circulated newsletter).
46. Morag, "Perpetrator Trauma," 99; Rastegar, "'Sawwaru waynkum?'," 68.
47. Morag, "Perpetrator Trauma," 100.
48. Stav, "Nakba and Holocaust," 86–67.
49. Stav, "Nakba and Holocaust," 88. For an earlier discussion of this dynamic in Israeli cinema, see chapter 4, "The Jew as Anti-Hero," in Omer Bartov, *The "Jew" in Cinema: From* The Golem *to* Don't Touch My Holocaust (Bloomington: Indiana University Press, 2005), esp. 264–75.
50. Stav, "Nakba and Holocaust," 89. In fact, the word "monstrous" was used by the head of Israeli educational television in March 2002 to describe the comparison made by the Nobel Prize winner José Saramago between actions of the IDF in the occupied territories and everyday life in the concentration camps; Morag, "Perpetrator Trauma," 89.
51. Rastegar, "'Sawwaru waynkum?'," 68; Stav, "Nakba and Holocaust," 95.
52. Stav, "Nakba and Holocaust," 95.
53. Rothberg, "From Gaza to Warsaw," 539; my emphasis.
54. R. Radhakrishnan, "Why Compare?," in Felski and Friedman, *Comparison*, 16.
55. Marcel Detienne, *Comparing the Incomparable*, trans. Janet Lloyd (Stanford: Stanford University Press), 39.
56. Rothberg, *Multidirectional Memory*, 18.
57. Rothberg, "From Gaza to Warsaw," 536–38.
58. Quoted in Spivak, "Rethinking Comparativism," 256.
59. Marianne Hirsch, *The Generation of Postmemory: Writing and Visual Culture after the Holocaust* (New York: Columbia University Press, 2012), 21, 24.
60. Emmanuel Levinas, *Entre-Nous: Essays on Thinking-of-the-Other*, trans. Michael B. Smith and Barbara Harshav (New York: Columbia University Press 1998), 9.
61. Bashir and Goldberg, *The Holocaust and the Nakba*, 22.

Select Bibliography

Bashir, Bashir, and Amos Goldberg, eds. *The Holocaust and the Nakba: A New Grammar of Trauma and History*. New York: Columbia University Press, 2019.

Felski, Rita, and Susan Stanford Friedman. "Introduction." In *Comparison: Theories, Approaches, Uses*, edited by Rita Felski and Susan Stanford Friedman, 1–12. Baltimore: Johns Hopkins University Press, 2013.

Hirsch, Marianne. *The Generation of Postmemory: Writing and Visual Culture after the Holocaust*. New York: Columbia University Press, 2012.

Levinas, Emmanuel. *Entre-Nous: Essays on Thinking-of-the-Other*. Translated by Michael B. Smith and Barbara Harshav. New York: Columbia University Press 1998.

Radhakrishnan, R. "Why Compare?" In *Comparison: Theories, Approaches, Uses*, edited by Rita Felski and Susan Stanford Friedman, 15–33. Baltimore: Johns Hopkins University Press, 2013.

Robbins, Bruce. "Chomsky's Golden Rule: Comparison and Cosmopolitanism." In *Comparison: Theories, Approaches, Uses*, edited by Rita Felski and Susan Stanford Friedman, 191–209. Baltimore: Johns Hopkins University Press, 2013.

Rothberg, Michael. "From Gaza to Warsaw: Mapping Multidirectional Memory." *Criticism* 53, no. 4 (Fall 2011): 523–48.

———. *Multidirectional Memory: Remembering the Holocaust in the Age of Decolonization*. Stanford: Stanford University Press, 2009.

Spivak, Gayatri Chakravorty. "Rethinking Comparativism." In *Comparison: Theories, Approaches, Uses*, edited by Rita Felski and Susan Stanford Friedman, 253–27. Baltimore: Johns Hopkins University Press, 2013.

Stav, Shira. "Nakba and Holocaust: Mechanisms of Comparison and Denial in the Israeli Literary Imagination." *Jewish Social Studies: History, Culture, Society* 18, no. 3 (Spring/Summer 2012): 85–98.

CHAPTER 4

INTERNATIONAL HUMAN RIGHTS ASPECTS OF REPATRIATING ISRAELI SETTLERS FROM THE WEST BANK

Yaël Ronen

Introduction

One of the obstacles to bringing the Israeli-Palestinian conflict to a consensual end is the failure to reach an agreement on the future of Israeli settlements in the West Bank. The solution to the conflict is primarily a matter of political choice, and the main criterion for evaluating its legitimacy is the free and genuine consent of the parties. This does not mean that international law has no role in shaping a solution. First, international law may contain mandatory rules that limit the range of measures that parties may lawfully adopt. Compliance with such rules is necessary for the agreement to obtain international legitimacy and validity. Second, international law may contain rules or principles from which the parties may deviate by agreement, but which, in the absence of consent, provide a default arrangement.[1]

Different political options raise different legal questions. For example, a "two states, one homeland" vision does not involve removal of settlements but would require clarifying the status of settlers in a Palestinian state;[2] by contrast, a two-state solution might involve a partial[3] or a complete removal of settlements. This chapter considers the constraints under international human rights law on a potential agreement between Israel and the Palestinians on withdrawal of Israel from the West Bank and the establishment of a Palestinian state. Admittedly, in light of developments in recent years, in particular the tenacious hold of Israel over the West Bank through the settlement project and the incorporation of the settlement regime into Israeli domestic law, even the proponents of this route within Israel and outside it have begun to doubt its feasibility. Nonetheless, at the time of writing this is still the route that commands international support and is formally the framework for negotiations between Israel and the Palestinians.[4] The question addressed is whether an agreement may be premised on (or even stipulate) the demand that Israeli settlers leave the West Bank (and return to Israel, if they so wish), or whether provisions must be made that would allow the settlers to remain in the territory (presumably with some guarantees of security, discussed below). The principal legal constraint on an Israeli-Palestinian agreement would be the prohibition on infringing on rights of affected parties, since the power of a state to make concessions, even on behalf of its own nationals, is not unlimited. The analysis is concerned not with what is possible, probable, or advisable, but with what is permissible or prohibited.

It may appear odd to speak of legal protection of Israeli settlers from forced repatriation, considering that their residence in the West Bank has long been considered by the international community to be both unlawful and an impediment to peace.[5] Indeed, academic literature rarely considers repatriation of settlers following the end of armed conflict or in the course of decolonization as a problematic forced transfer of population. There are a number of possible explanations for the lack of critical scrutiny. First, such repatriation is viewed favorably because it takes place in the course of establishing a goal desired by the international community, namely international peace and order. In addition, there is an assumption that repatriation is not detrimental because the settlers return to their natural environment rather than face displacement from it. Another explanation is that settlers do not belong to a category of persons regarded as needing international protection, such as refugees or stateless persons,[6] but rather to one that has been illegitimately privileged; settler repatriation is therefore perceived as bringing not only peace and order but also justice. Finally, it is not clear that repatriation of settlers can even be perceived as forced rather than voluntary.[7]

However, some of these assumptions may be factually incorrect, and others legally irrelevant. The state of nationality is not always the "natural environment" that it is assumed to be; and repatriation, even if not physically resisted, is hardly voluntary when no alternative is offered. The significance of the illegality associated with the conduct of an occupying or colonizing state also should not be overstated. International law distinguishes the rights and obligations of states from those of individuals. State conduct does not create individual responsibility, and accordingly the wrongfulness of a state's conduct cannot be vindicated through the treatment of the states' nationals individually. Since the wrongfulness in the act of settling the state's nationals in occupied territory of settlers attaches to the state and not to the individual, it does not negate the need to address the detriment that repatriation may cause the individual. This legal differentiation between states and individuals is reflected in international human rights law, on which I focus here.

This chapter may be naïve in that it entertains the possibility of Israel and the Palestinians agreeing on a two-state solution. At the same time, it is not as naïve as to imagine that the political and social context of such an agreement would be very different from the prevailing one. Accordingly, my premise is that there will not be a sudden rush of brotherly affection between Israeli and Palestinian societies: Israel will not concede the illegality of the settlement project, Israeli settlers will not come to a sudden appreciation of the desirability of leaving the settlements, and animosity between Israelis and Palestinians will persist. The assumption underlying this analysis is that the settlers will object to their removal.[8]

International Law and the Settlements Project

International Law in the West Bank

The West Bank is occupied territory as defined under international law, namely territory that "is actually placed under the authority of the hostile army."[9] The holding of territory under occupation is not, as such, unlawful under international law, and there is no absolute requirement that an occupying power withdraw from occupied territory.

The status of the West Bank as occupied territory is not denied by Israel. Israel acknowledges, indeed relies on, the applicability in the territory of the law of occupation as embodied in the 1907 Hague Regulations.[10] There is nonetheless a long-standing dispute over the applicability in the West Bank of the Fourth Geneva Convention of 1949 (GC IV), part III of which concerns occupied territories.[11] Israel claims that GC IV does not apply in the West Bank, on the ground that the convention applies only in territory that was previously under sovereign rule. Israel has nonetheless declared that it would voluntarily abide by the humanitarian provisions of the convention. The Israeli view has received the support of fewer than a handful of international legal scholars. According to the great majority of views, GC IV does not purport to define occupation differently from the Hague Regulations.[12] It, too, applies unreservedly in the West Bank.[13]

The applicability of GC IV appears to be crucial with respect to the settlements project, since Article 49(6) of the convention provides that the occupying power "shall not deport or transfer parts of its own civilian population into the territory it occupies."[14] Later international legal documents even characterize the violation of this prohibition (by state organs carrying out the transfer) as a war crime.[15] Even if GC IV, and consequently Article 49(6), applies in the West Bank, Israel contends that it covers only forcible transfers, and not permissive transfers and facilitation of settlement. The Israeli position is that Article 49(6)

> was intended to protect the local population from displacement, including endangering its separate existence as a race, as occurred with respect to the forced population transfers in Czechoslovakia, Poland and Hungary before and during the war. . . . [t]he case of Jews voluntarily establishing homes and communities in their ancient homeland, and alongside

Palestinian communities, does not match the kind of forced population transfers contemplated by Article 49(6).[16]

The other, overwhelmingly prevalent, view is that nothing in the language of Article 49(6) limits the prohibition to forcible transfers, and that its purpose is to protect the indigenous population in the occupied territory from the detrimental effect of the presence of the settler population. Therefore, the lack of coercion is immaterial to a finding that the prohibition is being violated.[17]

The nuanced distinction between the applicability of the Hague Regulations and that of GC IV is important because Israel relies on the Hague Regulations to justify measures that it takes to protect the settlements. It holds that protection of the settlements is a military necessity, which under the Hague Regulations allows the requisition of private lands or destruction of crops on cultivated land[18] for purposes such as the construction of military and security areas, the separation barrier, and access roads limited to use by Israelis.

Another body of international law of relevance to the West Bank is international human rights law. The prevalent view in international law is that the obligations of states under international human rights law extend beyond their sovereign territory.[19] The exact scope of these obligations is far from settled, but it is increasingly accepted that they extend at least to areas where states exercise effective control, that is, occupied territory.[20] Israel contests this view. It holds that international human rights treaties do not apply outside a state's sovereign territory and that even if they did, in situations of armed conflict (including occupation) they are displaced by the laws of armed conflict. Contrary to the flat rejection of the applicability of international human rights law by the government, the Israeli Supreme Court has acknowledged in a number of rulings that international human rights law may be utilized to fill lacunae in the law of occupation.[21] The regime that Israel maintains to support the settlements involves violations of the rights of Palestinians to equality, to an adequate standard of living, and to health and education, as well as of a host of civil and political rights.[22]

A state that has violated international law is obligated to cease the violation and return the situation to the *status quo ante*.[23] Accordingly, Israel is required to remove the settlements unconditionally[24] (irrespective of its military forces' presence in the occupied territory more generally). Cessation of governmental involvement in settlements means discontinuance of direct and indirect financial incentives and of security services to the settlements as such, and restoration of private lands to their owners.

Although dismantlement of the settlements is a legal obligation, it is unlikely that if Israel dismantles the settlements, it would admit that it is doing so because of a legal obligation, rather than as a policy choice. The former would constitute an admission of a decades-long violation of international law and entail an obligation of substantial reparation. It is also unlikely that Israel would dismantle the settlements unilaterally, as it did in Gaza and in Northern Samaria in 2005. Accordingly, the ensuing discussion assumes that such dismantlement would be undertaken by Israel only as part of a comprehensive agreement with the Palestinians.

International Law and Colonialism

The term "colonialism" has never had a distinct definition under international law. It is a descriptive term, which refers to the goals and character of a regime rather than to its formal provenance. Colonialism as a phenomenon of international relations is a practice of domination (originally territorial), which involves the subjugation of one people to another and exploitation of the territory's natural and human resources, for the economic and strategic benefit of the colonial power.[25] It is also a political and ideological concept, grounded in the conviction of the biological, cultural, and political superiority of the dominating power and its people.[26] Critical literature holds that Israel has adopted, ostensibly on grounds of security, a quasi-colonial governmental apparatus. This apparatus comprises the governance of the territory as if Israel were the legitimate sovereign power, turning the inhabitants into noncitizens devoid of any rights and undermining their sources of livelihood in the territory, thereby driving them to integrate into the Israeli economy as cheap exploitable labor.[27]

The review above of the applicable law indicates that Israel's quasi-colonial approach is embodied in the very normative framework that Israel applies in the West Bank. Although Israel acknowledges its non-sovereign status in the West Bank, formally it accepts the applicability in the West Bank only of the 1907 Hague Regulations, which are concerned with the powers of the occupying power as substitute for the sovereign; and it rejects the applicability of the GC IV, which focuses on protection of the population from those quasi-sovereign powers.[28] In addition, Israel rejects the applicability to its actions in the West Bank of the body of law that proclaims the universality of the human character, namely international human rights law, and applies different legal regimes to Israelis and Palestinians as individuals. This distinction is effected primarily through military orders applicable exclusively to the settlements; through application of Israeli law to Israeli settlers in the West Bank on a personal basis,[29] and since 2016 also on a territorial basis;[30] and through Israeli case law, which extends Israeli constitutional law to the Israeli settlers in the West Bank but not necessarily to the Palestinians residing there.[31]

Characterization of the administration of the West Bank as "colonial" entails Israel's obligation to terminate the regime altogether[32] or to reshape it in a manner consistent with the law of occupation and free from colonial characteristics. The viability of such change is highly doubtful, particularly if one accepts that Israel's motivation for maintaining the occupation is not security but the benefits of dominance in a colonial situation.[33]

Legal Regulation of Repatriation of Settlers

There are numerous historical examples of the status of settlers constituting a central issue in resolving territorial disputes. In many cases, the issue was "resolved" through mass repatriation, whether imposed by force or seemingly voluntarily. The second half of the twentieth century has seen the infamous expulsion of ethnic Germans and groups of other nationalities from East-Central European states following World War II, as well as the mass repatriation of European colonists from newly independent states in the era of decolonization.[34] There are also examples of subsequent instances where settlers had not been removed from occupied territories, leading some to question the status of the prohibition under GC IV Article 49(6).[35]

Only in a minority of cases was repatriation regulated by international agreement. The affected population was not consulted: the point of departure was that settlers did not have a legal right to remain in the new state, and that the former occupant or colonial state was obligated to receive them as its nationals. Legal arrangements, whether under domestic law of the new state or by international agreements, were conceived only in those instances where there was an interest in allowing settlers to remain.[36] From the settlers' perspective, international agreements have the advantage of allowing their state of nationality to act on their behalf rather than leaving them at the mercy of domestic politics in the new state.

International law does not regulate the manner in which the dismantling of settlements or bringing colonialism to an end should be carried out. Accordingly, the next section proposes to consider repatriation in light of generally applicable principles of international law, primarily international human rights law.

Obstacles to Repatriation Based on International Human Rights Law

States have a right to expel foreign individuals from their territory. This is a logical and necessary consequence of state sovereignty. In other words, unless otherwise agreed upon, individuals do not have a general entitlement to choose their place of residence in the world. However, the right to expel is limited by states' international obligations,[37] first and foremost international human rights law.

International human rights law is concerned with the protection of fundamental needs and interests that have been recognized as inherent to human nature. Human rights are distinct from those of states and sometimes run counter to them. Accordingly, the conduct of a state may generate rights for individuals even if it is unlawful under other bodies of international law. Thus, long-term residence of Israeli settlers in the West Bank may generate legal consequences under international human rights law that affect the right to remove the settlers, despite the original illegality of the settlement project.

Various international human rights may be implicated in repatriation. The present discussion focuses on rights that are inherently affected by the very notion of removal of settlers implanted by an occupying power. It does not address rights that may be implicated in the process of removal, such as the rights to liberty and bodily integrity, which may be at risk when physical force is applied in the removal. Not every encroachment on rights is a violation. Rights may be limited, provided that the limitations are necessary and proportionate for the pursuit of a legitimate purpose.

The present analysis therefore also addresses the grounds for demanding the repatriation of Israeli settlers. Its point of departure is the 1966 International Covenant on Civil and Political Rights (ICCPR), which is the universal human rights instrument to which both Israel and Palestine are parties.[38]

Rights Implicated by the Repatriation of Settlers

Prohibition on Mass Expulsion

Expulsion of settlers en masse is collective expulsion, generally understood as "an act or behavior by which a State compels a group of aliens to leave its territory."[39] It has been suggested that there is a general principle of international law that prohibits collective expulsion,[40] since the treatment of a group as such does not permit the consideration of individual circumstances, and thus there is a risk that human rights would be violated. In other words, the flaw in collective expulsion is not in the plurality of expellees but in denying each person a review of their particular case.[41] Expulsion would not be viewed as collective—and therefore would not be prohibited as such—if it followed a reasonable, thorough, and sufficiently objective examination of the particular case of each individual in the group. The need for separate consideration of the various cases does not mean that the competent authorities must reach decisions that vary in substance or wording. What is required is that every order be preceded by specific consideration of the situation of each member of the group of persons concerned.[42]

The right to individual review is guaranteed under ICCPR Article 13 only to "an alien lawfully in the territory of a State Party,"[43] who may be expelled therefrom only in pursuance of a decision reached in accordance with law and, except where compelling reasons of national security otherwise require, following a review by a competent authority. Israelis residing in the West Bank cannot be said to be "lawfully in the territory of" Palestine. They are therefore not protected under Article 13. Consequently, the prohibition on expulsion or collective expulsion as a denial of the right to review does not arise in their regard.

However, repatriation also implicates rights other than protection from expulsion. The absence of an obligation to maintain an *ex ante* review mechanism of expulsion under Article 13 does not obviate a state's obligation to ensure that a person who makes a reasonable claim of violation of a right has accessible and effective opportunity to vindicate that right through consideration by a competent authority, with the possibility of receiving a remedy.[44] Accordingly, the question remains whether repatriation encroaches excessively on substantive human rights.

Protection of Individuals' Attachment to Their Country

ICCPR Article 12(4) stipulates: "No one shall be arbitrarily deprived of the right to enter his own country." From this follows a corollary prohibition on arbitrary expulsion from one's "own country."[45] For deprivation not to be arbitrary, it must be by law; in accordance with the provisions, aims, and objectives of the ICCPR; and reasonable in the particular circumstances.[46] The common interpretation of this provision is that it protects first and foremost nationals. The prohibition on "arbitrary" deprivation has been interpreted as providing almost absolute protection for nationals. Under this interpretation, it is clear that Israeli settlers are not protected from removal from the West Bank. They do not become nationals of Palestine by virtue of the transfer of authority over the territory or its accession to independence, nor is the Palestinian state obligated to grant them its nationality. A state has discretion in determining the eligibility for acquiring its nationality, with the only qualification that it may not discriminate against any particular national origin.[47]

However, it is increasingly accepted that Article 12(4) also applies to other categories of persons. One such category would be those who, because of their long-term special ties or claims in relation to a given country, cannot be considered mere aliens in it. These include long-term residents who are either stateless persons or persons who cannot benefit from the right attached to their foreign nationality.[48] This category also does not apply to Israeli settlers, because their status as Israeli nationals is neither disputed nor undermined in practice.

An even more expansive view of Article 12(4) is that it also protects the "strong personal and emotional links an individual may have with the territory where he lives and with the social circumstances obtaining in it." Therefore a state should be regarded as "one's own country" not only by virtue of one's formal ties, but also because of "the web of relationships that form his or her social environment."[49] Under this view Article 12(4) invites consideration of such matters as long-standing residence, close personal and family ties, and intentions to remain, as well as the absence of such ties elsewhere.[50]

The Human Rights Committee (HRC), which monitors states' implementation of the ICCPR, adopted in 1999 the narrow, status-related interpretation of Article 12(4). Nonetheless, it also attached some weight to the factual links of a person with the place of residence. It stated that "other factors may in certain circumstances result in the establishment of close and enduring connections between a person and a country."[51] This addendum, which widens the scope of protection from removal under Article 12(4), echoes the jurisprudence of the European Court of Human Rights (ECtHR) on the right to private life under Article 8 of the European Convention on Human Rights and Fundamental Freedoms (ECHR), which encompasses the totality of social ties between individuals and the communities in which they live.[52] The right to private life under the ECHR protects "the right to establish and develop relationships with other human beings and the outside world" and "can sometimes embrace aspects of an individual's social identity."[53] This right may protect a person from expulsion in light of the solidity of his or her social, cultural, and family ties within the territory, measured, in part, against the ties with the state of origin (and destination). The longer a person has been residing in a particular place, the stronger his or her ties with that country and the weaker the ties with the state of nationality. Another factor to be considered is the seriousness of the difficulties that the person and family members are likely to encounter in the country to which they would relocate.

These criteria were developed in case law concerning the expulsion from West European states of long-term and second-generation immigrants, for the most part from North Africa. These persons often had no immediate contact with their states of nationality; some had never been there and did not speak its language. In some instances, this led the ECtHR to declare that expulsion would violate the right to private life.[54] Applying these criteria to Israeli settlers in the West Bank in order to determine whether it is their "own country" leads to entirely different findings. Granted, after five decades of occupation, the West Bank is home, both geographically and emotionally, to many settlers who have lived there much if not all of their lives. However, while there is no doubt as to their emotional attachment to the territory, they can hardly claim to be in any way attached to the surrounding human environment, namely the local Palestinian society. The right to private life is primarily concerned not with attachment to a *geographical* location but to a *society*. Perhaps somewhat ironically, then, repatriation of the entire community of settlers rather than of selected individuals does not raise concern of infringing on the right to private life.[55] It should nonetheless be acknowledged that a more expansive view of the right to remain in one's "own country" would accommodate a connection of Israelis to the West Bank that is not only social or material, but also ideological, religious, and spiritual. This connection will undoubtedly be severed even if the entire community is resettled together. As for connections with the state of origin and destination, the settlers obviously maintain strong links with the "metropole," namely sovereign Israel.

In conclusion, repatriation of Israeli settlers would infringe upon their right to remain in the West Bank as their "own country" only if this right is accorded a very expansive interpretation. Even then, the right may be subject to limitations, so long as they are not arbitrary. Although the HRC has opined that there are few, if any, circumstances under which deprivation of the right to enter one's own country could be reasonable and not arbitrary,[56] this was said with respect to status-based protection, namely of nationals and those with comparable status. If the right is interpreted expansively, so as to include a wide scope of factual attachments, including ideological, religious, and spiritual ones, then the scope of legitimate grounds for its limitation that would be regarded as reasonable may also expand. Such grounds are discussed further below.

The Right to Noninterference in the Home

A number of additional rights protected by the ICCPR may appear to be implicated in repatriation of settlers. Article 17 protects the individual from arbitrary interference with the "home." The use of the term "home" rather than "dwelling," "abode," etc. may suggest that the intention was to account for the emotional link of a person to his or her place of residence. The accepted interpretation of this provision[57] is limited to "home" as a tangible structure rather than as a social institution.[58] At the same time, at issue is not the right to property as such. Repatriation would undoubtedly encroach on the right of Israeli settlers in the West Bank to their homes. But this right, too, is not absolute and may be subject to limitation provided that it is not arbitrary. Grounds for such limitation are considered below.

The Prohibition on Torture or Other Cruel, Inhuman or Degrading Treatment
Historical experience shows that mass repatriation of settlers has often been a traumatic experience.[59] This refers not only to the departure from their homes, but also to the process of absorption in the country of destination. The experience of Israel's repatriation of settlers from Gaza in 2005 has also been traumatic for many. Half a decade after the disengagement, most of the evacuees were still living in temporary caravan sites, the construction of most of the permanent housing and public structures in the evacuees' new settlements had not yet been completed, the rate of unemployment among the evacuees was double the rate of unemployment in the general population, and the economic condition of some of the evacuees was lamentable.[60]

The question is whether the difficulty of repatriation can constitute a violation of the prohibition on torture or other cruel, inhuman, or degrading treatment[61] because of the conditions that await the returnees. The HRC and the ECtHR have in a number of cases dealt with such a claim by candidates for expulsion who suffered from physiological or mental handicaps that would have been inadequately accommodated in the states of destination, to such an extent that their lives and physical well-being would have been at risk. In some cases, the claim has been accepted and the proposed expulsion declared inhuman treatment.

The treatment that international jurisprudence considers to be potentially cruel, degrading, or inhuman has almost exclusively involved infliction of physical or mental pain (not necessarily intentionally). Economic destitution is not, in itself, inhuman treatment.[62] In *Jasin v. Denmark* (2015) the HRC went a little further and held that without guarantees of work and social benefits, expulsion of an asylum seeker and her three children to Italy would violate Article 7 because they were at risk of facing hardship and destitution at a level that would have jeopardized their ability to benefit from their status as asylum seekers.[63] Even in this case, however, the risk was indirectly physical, because the loss of effective asylum could have resulted in the applicants' return to the state of origin, in which their lives were at risk.[64] One exceptional view of inhuman treatment as encompassing social exclusion was put forward in the ECtHR with respect to the expulsion from France to Algeria of a second-generation immigrant who was born in France and had never been in Algeria in all his forty-odd years. In *Beldjoudi v. France* Judge de Meyer opined that expulsion would have constituted inhuman treatment.[65] This view has not garnered support. In any case, these extreme circumstances are not applicable to Israeli settlers. In conclusion, it seems that repatriation of Israeli settlers would not qualify as inhuman treatment.

Rights Implicated by the Reptriation of Settlers
Acknowledging that repatriation entails a limitation on rights does not render it impermissible. The right to remain in one's "own country" and the right to a home may be limited so long as the limitation is not "arbitrary." Examination of these factors requires an assessment of the necessity and proportionality of the harm caused by the limitation in comparison with the goal that the limitation is intended to realize. While such an assessment differs from one individual to another, the following are certain general considerations that are likely to inform an assessment of the expected harm and the justification for imposing it.

Grounds for Limitations on Rights

This section examines certain goals that may justify encroachment on the rights of Israeli settlers by demanding their repatriation. These goals relate directly to the circumstances surrounding the presence of Israeli nationals in the West Bank: public order and security interests, redress of historical injustice, and property concerns.

Public Order and National Security
If an Israeli population remains in the West Bank following the establishment of a Palestinian state, violence will likely ensue. Insofar as the risk of violence emanates from the settlers themselves, it is of course legitimate to limit their rights to prevent such violence. If, however, the settlers are held to be the potential victims, the question arises whether protection of their safety justifies the demand that they leave the territory. Ordinarily, a state cannot discharge its obligation to protect potential victims from the violation of their rights by placing limitations on them. Rather, the state must directly act to curb the potential threat. Nonetheless, the obligation to protect is not absolute; states are required to act with due diligence, and the burden that they would need to bear is a relevant consideration. Applying these principles to the protection of Israelis in the territory of a Palestinian state demonstrates the difficulties, as follows.

First, the population of Israelis remaining in the West Bank is likely to be miniscule, but the social and financial burden of protection might not be. Physical separation, through separate residential areas or access roads, cannot legitimately be demanded of the Palestinian government, being anathema to a human rights regime (without which the demands of Israeli settlers would not be considered in the first place). It would also undermine Palestine's integrity and self-determination. While the cost of protection would depend on specific measures, some indication of what it would involve can be taken from the present investment by the Israeli government in protecting the settlers.[66] Placing such a heavy financial burden on an emerging state is problematic. A third aspect is Israeli involvement. There is a whole range of possible arrangements that may be agreed upon to safeguard the rights and interests of settlers wishing to remain in the territory. However, if such mechanisms exceed the ordinary entitlements of expatriates (such as consular representation), there could be a legitimate concern that they would become a vehicle for Israeli intervention in the administration of the Palestinian state and would create a national security concern for Palestine. Even an abstract right to intervene would create such a risk.[67] There are milder forms of involvement, such as the legal coordination that already exists under the 1995 Interim Agreement, but such measures alone are unlikely to be sufficient to counter physical risk.

Admittedly, it is difficult to imagine a situation in which a non-national minority insists on remaining within a territory in which it faces a life-threatening situation, despite having a state of nationality in which it would be safe and to which it is easily able to move. It is all the more unimaginable that Israelis would demand the protection of the Palestinian state rather than that of Israel. It is this, among other reasons, that makes it unlikely that Israel and Palestine would reach an agreement that regulates the continued presence of Israelis in the West Bank.

Redress for Historical Injustice
The presence of an Israeli settler community in the West Bank has facilitated large-scale deprivation of the Palestinian community, through political alienation and economic marginalization. The question is whether redress of such historical injustice is sufficient ground for demanding the departure of this population, if such a demand encroaches on rights.

In the ECtHR the question arose of the right of military personnel who had been involved in preserving the Soviet regime of occupation in Latvia, as well as their family members, to remain in the territory of the newly independent country. In *Slivenko v. Latvia*[68] the majority held that requiring the departure of military personnel was necessary for ensuring the independence and national security of the new state. A separate, dissenting opinion considered that "the restoration of the independence of the Baltic States on the basis of legal continuity and the withdrawal of the Soviet/Russian troops has to be regarded as redress for a historical injustice," and that departure of military personnel (and their families) was "an appropriate way of dealing with the various political, social and economic problems arising from that historical injustice."[69]

The majority view, which did not attach a separate value to redressing the historical injustice that the occupation of Latvia had caused, should be preferred. Denial of a right to remain, where it has no conceivable role of prevention or deterrence, is a punitive measure. It must therefore be justified on grounds of personal fault. But historical injustice is not a matter of personal fault. Only when individuals are themselves responsible for acts of injustice would their exclusion from the state be justifiable.[70] Some cases appear clear-cut, for example, when the injustice amounts to an international crime. But reliance on other types of injustice to justify exclusion of individuals from the territory is debatable. Such injustice might include certain types of involvement in the administration of the settlements, such as formal participation in the land requisitioning. In contrast, participation in an administration that impacts the Palestinians less directly, such as running the education system within the settlements, seems too far removed to constitute a ground for removal of a person (even though that system is an element in the mechanism that perpetuates the settlements project).

In practice, differentiating levels of participation is problematic. A large share of the settler population is employed in the administration of the settlements themselves.[71] There is little merit in engaging in such classification, given that there are much stronger grounds for removal of the settler community in its entirety, making the present exercise moot. One ground justifying removal of settlers that may also be viewed as a matter of redress for historical injustice, and which implicates practically all settlers, is the matter of immovable property. This is considered next.

Economic Recuperation
Removal of settlers is crucial to the economic well-being of the country, for example, when they dominate the economy and its resources at the expense of the indigenous population. A particularly acute problem is that of immovable property, which occupying powers often engage in transferring from the local population to their own settlers.[72] One of the harshest injuries caused to Palestinian society by the settlements project is the deprivation of individuals and the public of private and public property, which has resulted in personal losses as well as in the inability of the economy to develop.[73] Restoration of land would restore to individuals their sources of income and protect their right to an adequate standard of living. It is also necessary for the recovery of the national economy.

Formally, restoration of property currently possessed by settlers to its original Palestinian owners and the settlers' right to remain in the territory are two separate issues that can be regulated independently of each other. In practice, however, the two are intimately linked. If Israeli settlers remain in the territory, they cannot be denied use of property and resources. If restoration of property and resuscitation of the Palestinian economy is the goal, it can hardly be achieved under the continued presence of the settler population.

Necessity and Proportionality

A general principle of international human right laws is that limitations on rights should only be imposed when they are necessary, namely, when no less harmful means is available for obtaining the same or similar result. Can the interests considered above be achieved by measures less injurious to settlers than their removal? In an ideal world, violence and animosity between population groups would be addressed not by enforcing separation but through the promotion of formal and substantive integration. However, insofar as concerns Israelis and Palestinians in the West Bank, integration does not seem to be a viable option. Reconciliation in the long term seems to require separation in the short term.

In the absence of less harmful means of achieving the desired goal, the question is whether the hardship caused by the infringement on rights is proportionate to the benefit that it is intended to achieve. In the case of removal of Israeli settlers from the West Bank, the benefits at stake are of the highest priority: the realization of the right to self-determination and the resolution of a century-long violent dispute and prevention of future armed conflict. The importance of these goals, which are embodied in peremptory norms of international law, cannot be overstated. Indeed, it could be argued that the normative superiority of these norms requires that they be given precedence over all other consideration and that no limitation on rights would be disproportionate if it is aimed at achieving these goals. However, human rights are inalienable and cannot be dismissed altogether. Accordingly, the detriment caused by repatriation has to be considered against the benefit that it would generate.

The level of social distress as a result of repatriation is likely to differ among population groups. For example, ideological settlers might cope more easily with repatriation than would quality-of-life settlers, because they are a cohesive, unified group led by inspiring leaders, factors that would provide the personal and communal crisis with an ideological outlook and meaning. On the other hand, the more ideologically committed settlers would likely face a more difficult emotional crisis.[74]

The assessment of potential harm must take into consideration the prospects of absorption in the country of destination. Needless to say, Israeli settlers speak the language of their state of origin and have cultural and family ties with it; moreover, the lives of Israelis in the West Bank are intricately linked to life in Israel. In fact, the long-term policy of blurring the geographical distinction between Israel and the West Bank has resulted in a popular perception that the territory of the settlements is Israeli territory. This perception would now undermine the claim that Israel is foreign to the settlers. Nonetheless, starting over is never easy. Older settlers and those whose livelihood is generated in the West Bank, such as farmers, are likely to encounter greater difficulties doing so than others.[75]

Israel has already had some experience with repatriation of settlers from the occupied territories. In 1982 Israel removed some six thousand settlers from the Sinai Peninsula, pending its return to Egyptian control. Within little over a year, most of the evacuees successfully rehabilitated their lives. The exceptions were those evacuees who continued in agriculture.[76] More recent experience is not encouraging. In 2005 Israel evacuated some nine thousand settlers from Gaza and dismantled five settlements in the northern West Bank. Various measures were adopted at the time in an attempt to alleviate the hardship of uprooting, including resettlement of communities in their entirety so as to maintain the integrity of the immediate social environment. However, the community relocation mechanism was riddled with failures, which constituted one of the main factors in delaying the rehabilitation of the repatriated settlers. This does not mean that repatriation is necessarily doomed to fail, and a government-appointed Commission of Inquiry has drawn lessons for future possible evacuation and resettlement of a large group of citizens.[77] However, it cannot be denied that a significant measure of hardship could befall the settlers.

One factor that may be taken into account in weighing the hardship caused by an infringement of rights by removal against its benefit is the extent to which the individuals are responsible for the predicament in which they find themselves. Two aspects of this matter are worth consideration.

First, it might be tempting to argue that Israeli settlers could not but know that their residence in the West Bank was internationally regarded as legally unlawful and politically illegitimate. Accordingly, in choosing to reside in the West Bank they had voluntarily undertaken the risk that they would eventually be required to leave. However, this assumption of prior knowledge is of little relevance as a matter of law and inaccurate as a matter of fact. Legally, as noted above, the responsibility for the violation of international law lies with the state, not with the individuals. Since they were not legally responsible for that violation, the burden of reversing it cannot be placed on them. Factually, it is at least questionable whether settlers are actually aware of the illegality of the settlements project. Few among them are familiar with the nuances of international law. Those who are familiar with Israeli law may even know that in 1993 the Israeli High Court of Justice refused to consider the legality of the settlements project on grounds of non-justiciability, effectively giving the project legal imprimatur.[78] Although many settlers may be familiar with the political debate concerning the settlements, there are others who at least when they first settled in the West Bank were not even aware of this debate, having been sent there upon immigrating to Israel, before becoming familiar with the political and legal conundrum into which they had been placed. Finally, there may well be settlers who are not even aware that they are living in occupied territory. This is especially true since the separation barrier was constructed, as a perception has gradually developed that everything on the "Israeli" side is or has become Israeli territory.[79]

It should be acknowledged, however, that if there are settlers who insist on remaining in the West Bank even if Israel withdraws from it, they are more likely to be the ones who have settled (or lived) there for ideological reasons and who are therefore more likely to be familiar at least with the political debate. Ironically, those who might be keenest to remain might be those who have the weakest claim to do so.

Another factor in assessing the severity of the encroachment on rights concerns the hardship in absorption within Israel, namely the stance taken by settlers in preparation for repatriation. The disengagement in 2005 is instructive in this context. According to the 2010 Commission of Inquiry, much of the responsibility for the settlers' dire state lay with the settlers themselves, who refused to communicate with state authorities prior to their return to Israel in the hope that their intransigence would obstruct the disengagement. The obligation to respect rights and minimize hardship lies in the first place with the government; but when the government provides the individual with appropriate and effective options, it discharges its obligation. Individuals who refuse to avail of them for ideological or strategic reasons bear the consequences of that refusal. The state would continue to be responsible for ensuring a reasonable absorption,[80] but the refusal does bear on the assessment of the detriment to the individuals when measured against the benefit in repatriation.

In conclusion, it appears that while repatriation of Israelis to Israel encroaches on recognized international human rights, the injury it causes is not excessive in comparison with the benefit pursued.

Conclusion

History demonstrates that notwithstanding the term "repatriation," removal of settlers often entails hardship, loss, and a sense of wrongdoing. The analysis above indicates that in the case of a potential repatriation of Israeli settlers in the context of an agreement with the Palestinians on an Israeli withdrawal from the West Bank, such hardship and loss would not amount to a violation of human rights. The geographical contiguity of the West Bank to Israel has made the Israeli settlement project unique in that settlers have never needed to separate from Israel, physically or otherwise. Accordingly, the negative impact of repatriation should not be exaggerated. This is not to belittle the hardship and loss that settlers might feel; at the same time, such hardship and loss need not bar repatriation.

Professor Yaël Ronen teaches public international law at the Academic Center for Science and Law in Israel; research fellow at the Minerva Center for Human Rights at the Hebrew University in Jerusalem; and academic editor of the *Israel Law Review*, published by Cambridge University Press. She received her PhD from the University of Cambridge, following an LLB and LLM from the Hebrew University in Jerusalem. Professor Ronen's areas of interest include statehood, occupation, and territorial status, particularly as they intersect with questions of human rights, humanitarian law, and international criminal law. She is coauthor with Professor David Kretzmer of *The Occupation of Justice: The Supreme Court of Israel and the Occupied Territories*, 2nd ed. (Oxford University Press, 2021).

Notes

1. Omar M. Dajani, "Shadow or Shade? The Roles of International Law in Palestinian-Israeli Peace Talks," *Yale Journal of International Law* 32, no. 61 (2007): 91–109.
2. E.g., Elhanan Miller, "Two States, One Homeland: The Promised Land of Isra-stine?," *Tablet*, 25 July 2016, https://www.tabletmag.com/jewish-news-and-politics/204997/promised-land-of-isra-stine.
3. E.g., the Geneva Initiative, http://www.geneva-accord.org/mainmenu/summary.
4. UN General Assembly Resolution A/RES/73/19 (30 November 2018); "'Act Now to Prevent Two-State Solution from Slipping Away Forever,' United Nations Secretary-General Warns during Security

Council Debate," UN Doc SC/12219, 26 January 2016; "The Peace Index: December 2015," *Israel Democracy Institute*, 4 January 2016; "Palestinian Public Opinion Poll No. 59," *Palestinian Center for Policy and Survey Research*, 21 March 2016.

5. UN General Assembly Resolution A/RES/73/98 (7 December 2018), ¶ 1.
6. Jaro Mayda, "The Korean Repatriation Problem and International Law," *American Journal of International Law* 47 (1953): 414.
7. Pamela Ballinger, "Entangled or 'Extruded' Histories? Displacement, National Refugees, and Repatriation after the Second World War," *Journal of Refugee Studies* 25, no. 3 (2012): 366, 368–73.
8. For a projection of expected reactions to evacuation of the West Bank of January 2007, see "Peace Now," www.peacenow.org.il. But see also "The Feasibility of Voluntary Evacuation of Settlers Living East of the Security Barrier Prior to an Agreement, Findings of the 2013 Survey," *Blue White Future*, February 2014; and "Psychological Preparation for Future Evacuation of Settlements in Judea and Samaria," *Blue White Future* (in Hebrew), http://www.bluewhitefuture.org.il/wp-content/uploads/2017/01/%D7%97%D7%95%D7%91%D7%A8%D7%AA-%D7%A1%D7%A7%D7%A8-%D7%A4%D7%99%D7%A0%D7%95%D7%99-%D7%9E%D7%A8%D7%A6%D7%95%D7%9F-%D7%A1%D7%95%D7%A4%D7%99.pdf
9. Regulations Respecting the Laws and Customs of War on Land Annexed to Convention No. IV Respecting the Laws and Customs of War on Land, 18 October 1907, 36 Stat. 2277 art. 42.
10. "The Hague Regulations . . . are binding on the military administration in Judea and Samaria, being customary international law." HCJ 390/79, *Dweikat and Others v. Government of Israel and Others* [Elon Moreh case], 22 July 1979; HCJ 1661/05, *Gaza Coast Regional Council and Others v. Israeli Knesset*, 2005 PD 59(4) 481 (in Hebrew).
11. Geneva Convention Relative to the Protection of Civilian Persons in Time of War, 12 August 1949, 6 U.S.T. 3516, 75 UNTS. 287.
12. *Prosecutor v. Naletilic and Martinovic*, International Criminal Tribunal for Yugoslavia Trial Chamber, 31 March 2003, ¶ 215.
13. Legal Consequences of the Construction of the Wall in the Occupied Palestinian Territory, Advisory Opinion, 2004 I.C.J. Rep. 136, ¶ 101 (9 July) (hereinafter *ICJ Wall Advisory Opinion*); ICRC Declaration, 5 December 2001, ¶ 2 "The ICRC has always affirmed the de jure applicability of the Fourth Geneva Convention to the territories occupied since 1967 by the State of Israel, including East Jerusalem," reproduced in IRRC No. 847; UN General Assembly Resolution A/73/97 (7 December 2018) ¶ 1 S.C. Res. 271(1969) of 15 September 1969. Also: S.C. Res. 446 (1979) of 22 March 1979; S.C. Res. 681(1990) of 20 December 1990; S.C. Res. 799(1992) of 18 December 1992; and S.C. Res. 904(1994) of 18 March 1994.
14. Other provisions of the law of occupation also bear on the issue of settlements. See David Kretzmer, *The Occupation of Justice: The Supreme Court of Israel and the Occupied Territories*, 2nd ed. (New York: Oxford University Press, 2021), 186–190.
15. Articles 85(4)(a) and 85 of the Protocol Additional to the Geneva Conventions of 12 August 1949, and Relating to the Protection of Victims of International Armed Conflicts (Protocol I), art. 96, 8 June 1977, 1125 UNTS 3, and Article 8(2)(b)(viii) of the Rome Statute of the International Criminal Court, 2187 UNTS 3. Israel is not party to either instrument.
16. Israeli Ministry of Foreign Affairs, "Israeli Settlements and International Law," 30 November 2015, https://mfa.gov.il/mfa/foreignpolicy/peace/guide/pages/israeli%20settlements%20and%20international%20law.aspx.
17. David Kretzmer, "The Advisory Opinion: The Light Treatment of International Humanitarian Law," *American Journal of International Law* 99 (2005): 88, 91. See also Commission on Human Rights, Sub-Commission on Prevention of Discrimination and Protection of Minorities, Human Rights and Population Transfer: Final Report of the Special Rapporteur, Mr. Al-Khasawneh, U.N. Doc. E/CN.4/Sub.2/1997/23 14–15 ¶ 46; *Wall* Advisory Opinion, ¶ 120. U.N. General Assembly Res. A/RES/73/19 (30 November 2018).
18. Hague Regulations art. 23, 52.

19. Human Rights Committee (hereinafter "HRC"), *Lopez Burgos v. Uruguay*, Communication No. R.12/52, view of 6 June 1979, U.N. Doc. Supp. No. 40 (A/36/40) 176 (1981), ¶ 12.3.
20. *Loizidou v. Turkey (Merits)* 1996–VI ECHR (18 December 1996), ¶ 56; *Wall* Advisory Opinion, ¶¶ 107–13; Marko Milanovic, *Extraterritorial Application of Human Rights Treaties: Law, Principles and Policy* (Oxford: Oxford University Press, 2011), 59.
21. Yaël Ronen, "Applicability of Basic Law: Human Dignity and Freedom in the West Bank," *Israel Law Review* 46, no. 1 (2013):135, 141–42, and sources cited there.
22. E.g., "By Hook and By Crook: Israeli Settlement Policy in the West Bank," *B'tselem*, July 2010; Human Rights Council, Report of the Independent International Factfinding Mission to Investigate the Implications of the Israeli Settlements on the Civil, Political, Economic, Social and Cultural Rights of the Palestinian People throughout the Occupied Palestinian Territory, Including East Jerusalem, UN Doc A/HRC/22/63.
23. ILC Draft Articles on Responsibility of States for Internationally Wrongful Acts (2001), U.N. Doc. A/56/10, art 30(1); Al-Khasawneh, ¶¶ 60–63.
24. UN General Assembly, U.N. Doc. A/RES/73/98 (7 December 2018), ¶ 3.
25. Margaret Kohn and Kavita Reddy, "Colonialism," in The Stanford Encyclopedia of Philosophy (Fall 2017 edition), ed. Edward N. Zalta, https://plato.stanford.edu/archives/fall2017/entries/colonialism/.
26. Jörn Axel Kämmerer, "Colonialism," in *Oxford Public International Law, Max Planck Encyclopedia of Public International Law* (New York: Oxford University Press, 2008), ¶ 2, https://opil-ouplaw-com.ezp-prod1.hul.harvard.edu/view/10.1093/law:epil/9780199231690/law-9780199231690-e690?rskey=I8tAS3&result=1&prd=MPIL.
27. Ariella Azoulay and Adi Ophir, *The One-State Condition: Occupation and Democracy in Israel/Palestine* (Stanford: Stanford University Press, 2012); Orna Ben-Naftali, Aeyal M. Gross, and Keren Michaeli, "Illegal Occupation: Framing the Occupied Palestinian Territory," *Berkeley Journal of International Law* 23, no. 3 (2005): 551, 610–11.
28. Eyal Benvenisti, *The International Law of Occupation* (Princeton: Princeton University Press, 1993), 210–11.
29. Limor Yehuda et al., "One Rule, Two Legal Systems: Israel's Regime of Laws in the West Bank," *Association for Civil Rights in Israel*, October 2014, https://law.acri.org.il/en/wp-content/uploads/2015/02/Two-Systems-of-Law-English-FINAL.pdf.
30. Yaël Ronen and Yuval Shany, "Israel's Settlement Regulation Bill Violates International Law," *Just Security*, 20 December 2016, https://www.justsecurity.org/35743/israels-settlement-regulation-bill-violates-international-law/.
31. Yaël Ronen, "Applicability of Basic Law: Human Dignity and Freedom in the West Bank," *Israel Law Review* 46, no. 1 (2013): 135.
32. Legal Consequences for States of the Continued Presence of South Africa in Namibia (South West Africa) Notwithstanding Security Council Resolution 276 (1970), Advisory Opinion, 1971 I.C.J. Rep. 16, 22 (21 June 1971).
33. Neve Gordon, *Israel's Occupation* (Berkeley: University of California Press 2008).
34. Andrea L. Smith, "Europe's Invisible Migrants," in *Europe's Invisible Migrants*, ed. Andrea L. Smith (Amsterdam: Amsterdam University Press, 2003), 9.
35. Eugene Kontorovich, "Unsettled: A Global Study of Settlements in Occupied Territories," *Journal of Legal Analysis* 9, no. 2 (Winter 2017): 285.
36. E.g., the 1962 Evian Agreement regarding the rights of Pied Noirs remaining in Algiers, and the proposed Annan Plan of 2004 for reunifying Cyprus.
37. UN Doc. A/CN.4/581 ¶ 8, 12, 22.
38. International Covenant on Civil and Political Rights (ICCPR), 999 UNTS 171.
39. UN Doc A/CN.4/581 ¶ 135.
40. UN Doc A/CN.4/581 ¶ 115.
41. Jean-Marie Henckaerts, *Mass Expulsion in Modern International Law and Practice* (The Hague: Martinus Nijhoff, 1995), 14.

42. U.N. Doc. A/CN.4/581 ¶ 107, 109, 110.
43. International Covenant on Civil and Political Rights, 999 UNTS 171, art. 13.
44. ICCPR art 2(3)(b), HRC, General Comment 31: "The nature of the general legal obligation imposed on States Parties to the Covenant," UN Doc CCPR/C/21/Rev.1/Add. 13 (26 May 2004) ¶ 15.
45. HRC, *Stewart v. Canada*, Communication No. 538/1993, U.N. Doc. CCPR/C/58/D/538/1993 (1996), individual opinion of committee member Bhagwati (dissenting in respect of other issues).
46. HRC, General Comment No. 16: Article 17 (Right to Privacy) (1988) in Compilation of General Comments, UN Doc HRI/GEN/1/Rev.9 Volume I ¶ 4.
47. International Convention on the Elimination of All Forms of Racial Discrimination, 660 UNTS 195, art. 1(3).
48. HRC, General Comment 27: Freedom of movement (Article 12), in Compilation of General Comments, UN Doc HRI/GEN/1/Rev.9 Volume I, ¶ 20.
49. Both quotes from *Stewart v. Canada*, individual opinion of committee members Evatt, Medina Quiroga, Aguilar Urbina, ¶ 5. See also HRC, *Giosue Canepa v. Canada*, Communication No. 558/1993, U.N. Doc. CCPR/C/59/D/558/1993 (1997), individual opinions by committee members Evatt and Medina Quiroga (dissenting), and Chanet (dissenting).
50. *Stewart v. Canada*, individual opinion by committee members Evatt, Medina Quiroga, Aguilar Urbina, ¶¶ 5–6. See also Manfred Nowak, *U.N. Covenant on Civil and Political Rights: CCPR Commentary* (Kehl am Rhein: Engel, 2005), 287–88; Stig Jagerskiold, "The Freedom of Movement," in *The International Bill of Rights: The Covenant on Civil and Political Rights*, ed. Louis Henkin (New York: Columbia University Press, 1981), 180–81; Henckaerts, *Mass Expulsion in Modern International Law and Practice*, 83; Hurst Hannum, "The Right to Leave and the Right to Return: A Declaration Adopted by the Uppsala Colloquium," *The Right to Leave and Return, International Migration Review* 7 (1972): 59–60.
51. HRC, General Comment 27, ¶ 20.
52. ECtHR, *Üner v. Netherlands*, ¶ 59.
53. ECtHR, *Pretty v. United Kingdom*, Application No. 2346/02 ECHR 2002-III ¶ 61; cf. ACHR Article 11(2), Report No. 4/01 Case 11.625 María Eugenia Morales de Sierra, Guatemala (19 January 2001), ¶ 46.
54. Yaël Ronen, "The Ties That Bind: Family and Private Life as Bars to the Deportation of Immigrants," *International Journal of Law in Context* 8, no. 2 (2012): 283.
55. But in a case concerning the dismantlement of a settlement established unlawfully on private Palestinian property, the Israeli Supreme Court has regarded the interest of relocating to a nearby location as a legitimate consideration. HCJ 794/17, *Ziada v. Military Commander in the West Bank and Others* (31 October 2017) ¶ 91 (in Hebrew).
56. HRC, General Comment 27, ¶ 21.
57. HRC, General Comment 16; HRC, *Giosue Canepa v. Canada*, Communication No. 558/1993, U.N. Doc. CCPR/C/59/D/558/1993 (1997) ¶ 11.5.
58. ECtHR, *Demopoulos and Others v. Turkey*, Application Nos. 46113/99, 3843/02, 13751/02, 13466/03, 10200/04, 14163/04, 19993/04, 21819/04 (1 March 2010), ¶¶136.
59. R. M. Douglas, *Orderly and Humane: The Expulsion of the Germans after the Second World War* (New Haven: Yale University Press, 2012); Smith, *Europe's Invisible Migrants*; Ballinger, "Entangled or 'Extruded' Histories?"
60. State Commission of Inquiry into the Handling of the Evacuees from Gush Katif and Northern Samaria by the Authorized Authorities, Report, 6 June 2010, Main Conclusions and Summary, 8 (in Hebrew).
61. ICCPR Article 7; Convention against Torture and Other Cruel, Inhuman or Degrading Treatment or Punishment (entered into force 26 June 1987), 1465 UNTS 85 Article 2, Convention for the Protection of Human Rights and Fundamental Freedoms (ECHR) 213 UNTS 221 Article 3.
62. Individual opinion of committee members Yuval Shany and Konstantine Vardzelashvili (concurring) HRC, Communication No. 2360/2014, *Jasin v. Denmark*, UN Doc CCPR/C/114/D/2360/2014, 25 September 2015, ¶ 1.

63. HRC, Communication No. 2360/2014, *Jasin v. Denmark*, UN Doc CCPR/C/114/D/2360/2014 25 September 2015, ¶¶ 8.8–8.9.
64. HRC, *Jasin v. Denmark*, Communication No. 2360/2014, U.N. Doc. CCPR/C/114/D/2360/2014, 25 September 2015, individual opinion of committee members Yuval Shany and Konstantine Vardzelashvili (concurring) ¶ 2.
65. ECtHR, Application No. 12083/86 *Beldjoudi v. France*, 26 March 1992, separate opinion of Judge de Meyer. See also ECtHR, *Nasri v. France*, *Nasri v. France*, Judgment (Merits and Just Satisfaction), Application No. 19465/92 (13 July 1995), partly dissenting opinion of Judge de Meyer.
66. Shlomo Swirski and Noga Dagan, "The Occupation: Who Pays the Price? The Impact of the Occupation on Israeli Society and Economy," *Adva Center: Information on Equality and Social Justice in Israel*, June 2017, https://adva.org/wp-content/uploads/2017/07/Price-of-Occupation-EN-Full-1.pdf.
67. For such a right, see the 1960 Treaty of Guarantee adopted upon the accession to independence of Cyprus, which in 1974 served Turkey as a pretext for military intervention on the island.
68. ECtHR, *Slivenko v. Latvia* Application No. 48321/99 Judgment (9 October 2003) ECHR 2003–10, ¶ 117.
69. ECtHR, *Slivenko v. Latvia* Application No. 48321/99 Judgment (9 October 2003) ECHR 2003–10, separate dissenting opinion of Judge Maruste.
70. CSCE, High Commissioner on National Minorities Letter to the Minister of Foreign Affairs of Latvia, Ref. No. 1463/93/L, 10 December 1993, contained in CSCE Communication No. 8, 31 January 1994.
71. Human Rights Watch, *Occupation, Inc.: How Settlement Businesses Contribute to Israel's Violations of Palestinian Rights*, 19 January 2016, https://www.hrw.org/news/2016/01/19/occupation-inc-how-settlement-businesses-contribute-israels-violations-palestinian.
72. As has been done, for example, in northern Cyprus. Yaël Ronen, *Transition from Illegal Regimes under International Law* (Cambridge: Cambridge University Press, 2011), 294–306.
73. World Bank, *Fiscal Crisis, Economic Prospects: The Imperative for Economic Cohesion in the Palestinian Territories*, 23 September 2012, http://documents1.worldbank.org/curated/en/350371468141891355/pdf/760230WP0GZ0AH02Box374357B00PUBLIC0.pdf.
74. Yair Sheleg, *The Political and Social Ramifications of Evacuating Settlements in Judea, Samaria and the Gaza Strip*, position paper 69 (Jerusalem: Israel Democracy Institute, 2007, in Hebrew).
75. Yair Sheleg, *The Political and Social Ramifications of Evacuating Settlements in Judea, Samaria and the Gaza Strip*, position paper 70 (Jerusalem: Israel Democracy Institute, 2007, in Hebrew).
76. Sheleg, *The Political and Social Ramifications* 70, 28–30.
77. State Commission.
78. HCJ 4481/91, *Bargil and Others v. Government of Israel and Others* (25 August 1993), unofficial translation at https://versa.cardozo.yu.edu/opinions/bargil-v-government-israel.
79. Yaël Ronen, "Taking the Settlements to the ICC? Substantive Issues," *AJIL Unbound* (2017) 111: 57.
80. State Commission of Inquiry into the Handling of the Evacuees from Gush Katif and Northern Samaria by the Authorized Authorities, Report, 6 June 2010, 52–53 (in Hebrew), http://www.moag.gov.il/tnufa/mismahim_hashuvim/Documents/doch_veadat_hahakira.pdf.

Select Bibliography

Books and Articles

Azoulay, Ariella, and Adi Ophir. *The One-State Condition: Occupation and Democracy in Israel/Palestine*. Stanford: Stanford University Press, 2012.

Ben-Naftali, Orna, Aeyal M. Gross, and Keren Michaeli. "Illegal Occupation: Framing the Occupied Palestinian Territory." *Berkeley Journal of International Law* 23, no. 3 (2005): 551–614.

Benvenisti, Eyal. *The Law of Occupation*. Princeton: Princeton University Press, 1993.

Gordon, Neve. *Israel's Occupation*. Berkeley: University of California Press, 2008.
Hannum, Hurst. "The Right to Leave and the Right to Return: A Declaration Adopted by the Uppsala Colloquium." *International Migration Review* 7 (1973): 62–66.
Henckaerts, Jean-Marie. *Mass Expulsion in Modern International Law and Practice*. The Hague: Martinus Nijhoff, 1995.
Kretzmer, David. *The Occupation of Justice: The Supreme Court of Israel and the Occupied Territories*. 2nd ed. New York: Oxford University Press, 2021.
Nowak, Manfred. *U.N. Covenant on Civil and Political Rights: CCPR Commentary*. Kehl am Rhein: Engel, 2005.
Ronen, Yaël. "The Ties That Bind: Family and Private Life as Bars to the Deportation of Immigrants." *International Journal of Law in Context* 8, no. 2 (2012): 283–96.
Swirski, Shlomo, and Noga Dagan. "The Occupation: Who Pays the Price? The Impact of the Occupation on Israeli Society and Economy." *Adva Center: Information on Equality and Social Justice in Israel*, June 2017. https://adva.org/wp-content/uploads/2017/07/Price-of-Occupation-EN-Full-1.pdf.

Documents

Human Rights Committee, General Comment 27: Freedom of movement (Article 12). In Compilation of General Comments, UN Doc HRI/GEN/1/Rev. 9 Volume I. https://www.ohchr.org/documents/hrbodies/tb/hri-gen-1-rev-9-vol-i_en.doc.
"State Commission of Inquiry into the Handling of the Evacuees from Gush Katif and Northern Samaria by the Authorized Authorities." Report, 6 June 2010. In Hebrew. http://www.moag.gov.il/tnufa/mismahim_hashuvim/Documents/doch_veadat_hahakira.pdf.

Part II
Redrawing Space

CHAPTER 5

OIL AND THE ORIGINS OF MIDDLE EASTERN SOVEREIGNTY

RACHEL HAVRELOCK

Pipelines in the Sand

Among the outcomes of World War I was the creation of the modern Middle Eastern state. Unlike the Ottoman Empire with its sanjaks and zones of administration, the nation-state emerged with definitive borders fixed during a series of conferences for Western victors between 1919 and 1925.[1] We tend to think of the resulting borders as arbitrary demarcations or, as James Barr named them, "lines in the sand."[2] A compelling counterargument comes from scholars like Elias Muhanna, who prefers to see pre-national "poetic borders" that informed where state thresholds eventually fell.[3]

My own work on the Jordan River as a border began with the premise that twentieth-century biblical interpretation informed the designation of the Jordan as a frontier. But I ultimately concluded that in fact this border resulted from the exigencies of late nineteenth-century British colonial cartography.[4] In short, members of the Palestine Exploration Fund (PEF) mapping team faced raids and attacks when they ventured east of the Jordan and so delegated the other side of the Jordan to the American Palestine Exploration Society (APES), which produced beautiful photographs, but no maps.[5] General Edmund Allenby then went into battle with the PEF maps and conquered the designated terrain. Taken together, the maps and the victory fixed Palestine in the British colonial imagination as a land between the river and the sea. Most Palestinians and Zionists internalized the colonial borders, then deployed religious and cultural traditions to domesticate them as national signifiers.

It remains correct to think of the Jordan River as an arbitrary colonial boundary that ultimately obtained existential significance for Palestinians, Israelis, and Jordanians. However, my sense of what caused its arbitrary nature changed dramatically as I began to examine the oil pipeline that crossed the Jordan and spanned its banks from

1935 to 1948. The planning and ultimate construction of the Iraq Petroleum Company (IPC) pipeline from Kirkuk to Haifa influenced the borders between the states that became Iraq, Jordan, and Israel, as well as Syria and Lebanon. Furthermore, the transport of petroleum from Iraqi wells to Western markets affected the very nature of Middle Eastern sovereignty, which means that understanding territorial sovereignty requires renewed attention to the subterranean realm.

I argue that plans for distinct British (from Kirkuk to Haifa) and French (Kirkuk to Tripoli) oil pipelines motivated the placement of nation-state boundaries. Even T. E. Lawrence, Britain's foremost proponent of Arab autonomy, knew of pre-existing limitations set by oil concessions. His utopian map of independent Arab states limits their jurisdiction in red zones of direct British control over Iraqi oil fields and Haifa Bay. The Sykes-Picot Agreement correlates plans for two separate pipelines—the French one from Kirkuk, in modern-day Iraq, to Tripoli, in modern-day Lebanon, and the British one from Kirkuk to Haifa—with the territorial divide between French and British colonial holdings. With the accord, Sir Mark Sykes and Francois Georges-Picot split the Middle East to reflect the fact that Britain and France did not want to share a pipeline, fearing that their alliance might someday fray while leaving one power in control of petroleum flow. Historians usually quote Sykes's 1915 statement to the British war cabinet—"I should like to draw a line from the 'e' in Acre to the last 'k' in Kirkuk"—as proof that the borders he drew were arbitrary. In fact, he was describing the path the British government had in mind for its pipeline. Herbert Kitchener, the British secretary of state for war, corrected Sykes after he spoke: "I think that what Sir Mark Sykes means is that the line will commence at the seacoast in Haifa." This explains how the dividing lines of the Sykes-Picot Agreement into British Area B and French Area A hardened into the borders between Syria, Iraq, and Jordan. After the war, Sykes-Picot figured as a primal demarcation on a map that came to define the oil-producing state of Iraq, the oil-transit states of Jordan and Syria, and the oil-export states of Lebanon and Palestine.[6]

Although the holders of concessions changed as a result of the war, the basic structure maintained—potential mineral stores and everything else underground belonged to private corporations. This structure involved a preordained disenfranchisement of citizens, as well as a scenario in which colonial governments protected assets not quite their own. Such disenfranchisement from mineral wealth meant that from the start, state governments were alienated from the resources of value. As much as they might have objected to the scenario, these governments adapted to the situation by forming a fierce attachment to national territory defined as it was by arbitrary colonial borders. In truth, other options were not available if they sought international recognition or interaction with financial institutions. The virulent attachment to territory diagnosed as native to Middle Eastern nationalisms should thus be understood as a by-product of oil concessions. Yet sovereignty—even after independence—was often restricted by concessions to exclude aquifers, oil, and minerals.

Subjects of Oil

Despite their underground existence, pipelines had effects that reverberated above. Beginning in 1931, communities along the pipeline route were subjected to scrutiny by an anthropological team commissioned by the Iraq Petroleum Company and, after oil began to flow, to an elaborate system of aerial surveillance. New social classifications arose, such as "moderate" and "extremist" based on whether certain communities supported or opposed the pipeline.[7] In general, colonial officials and oil men alike turned to the reclassification of the populace according to their stance on extraction as a means of transforming the multiethnic, inter-religious Ottoman landscape.

As a result, religious or ethnic affiliation played a role in who had political power and economic access and, in more quotidian terms, what job a person could hold. Such materialization of ethnicity or sect proved advantageous in disrupting both nationalist and socialist challenges to the tax-free shipping of resources out of the region. It was, furthermore, a point of origin for the famed sectarianism of Middle Eastern countries. During the 1919 boundary discussions in the British Colonial Office, for example, some argued that Zionist aspirations could be satisfied by settling Jews in Haifa, where they might develop the city with their own capital and labor. This plan followed the logic that Jews beholden to the British for the gift of relative autonomy in Haifa were preferable to a majority Arab population at a key point of petroleum transfer from pipeline to tanker. Without their knowledge, Zionist Jews came to be considered an asset to the oil industry.[8] This idea took hold and British Mandate policy maintained the wisdom of encouraging Jews to settle around the pipeline, which crossed the Jordan River south of the Sea of Galilee and arched toward Haifa through the spring-fed Jezreel Valley (Marj ibn Amr). Coincidentally, the easier path of a pipeline through a valley dovetailed with Zionist aspirations to settle in agricultural communities alongside sources of water.

Militarization accompanied the emergent political geography and social categories. Just as the borders of the nascent states were drawn to accommodate engineered paths of oil, so was the internal space militarized to thwart local claims to oil, surrounding land, and taxation. The companies owned the oil, yet the task of securing the paths of pipelines fell to colonial governments. As both a preliminary and an ongoing measure, various governmental bodies had to pledge their ability to keep the pipeline secure.[9] The British Air Ministry, for example, sent officers into the field to determine the threat level presented by residents of Haifa, Bedouin tribes, and the Wahabi Akhwan, whom they characterized as "religiously opposed to all forms of modernization such as motor cars, telegraphs, roads, etc."[10] The Air Ministry then assured the Foreign and Colonial Offices that it could secure a pipeline owned by the oil companies that became BP, Shell, ExxonMobil, and Total. Instead of companies bidding for government contracts, governments paraded their services in order to win companies' favor, while their own militaries would foot the bill.[11] Without much interrogation, it was widely believed that serving oil companies was good for home economies.

Much as the ownership of the subterranean sphere might be enforced through rule of the skies, the ground proved difficult to control. The solution took the form of local subcontractors where necessary or the more preferred proxy soldiers. There was competition among local groups for guarding the conveyance of resources out of the region, since this was one of the few sources of livelihood. Biding its time by entertaining elaborate bids from British and French ministries, the IPC subjected the residents around the future course of the pipeline to particular scrutiny. "The Company will, therefore, have to assure themselves that their pipeline services will be secure not only from actual hostile attack, but from any kind of interference by the local Governments or disorganization resulting from local unrest."[12] Anything stopping the flow of oil aside from company procrastination required military intervention.

While I am indebted to Timothy Mitchell's *Carbon Democracy*, I diverge from his argument when it comes to militarism.[13] Where Mitchell views the militarization of the Middle East as a largely American solution to lost profits following the nationalization of oil by producing countries (insofar as lost oil profits were recuperated through weapons sales), the archive proves that militarization occurred much earlier as a strategy simultaneous to the development of oil concessions. Militarization followed the ethnic or sectarian premise—certain groups were armed by particular companies to protect their assets from other locals or rival companies. When the young states later nationalized oil and its infrastructure, they simply absorbed the existing militarized spaces along with the concession structure that stressed ethnic and sectarian division.

Making Concessions

Petroleum and banking companies became active in the eastern Ottoman Empire at the beginning of the twentieth century, pursuing concessions through mercenary relationships with one another, local parties, and Ottoman officials. More than mandates or occupations, the concession best accounts for colonial policies. Conferring the right to exploit along with the outright ownership of resources, concessions were held by both individuals and private companies. For example, the Iraq Petroleum Company (which had nothing Iraqi about it), eventually held title to the *entire* subterranean level of what became known as the Middle East. Tax-free profit accrued directly to individuals or companies despite the fact that imperial agencies conferred the legal basis, advantageous labor conditions, and security. When we disentangle the private beneficiaries of concessions from the colonial bearers of risk and the disenfranchised locals, imperial rule resembles the neoliberal order.

By establishing private ownership of underground stores in Iraq, Jordan, Palestine, Syria, and Lebanon, oil concessions stripped resources of value from state sovereignty and encouraged competition among constitutive ethnic and religious groups for what might percolate up. In the prewar oil agreement of 1914, the Ottoman Empire's ally Germany secured a 25 percent share for Deutsche Bank along with Royal-Dutch Shell and British investors. The war prevented any further steps to secure the concession, yet England and France built the assumption of German shares into the Sykes-Picot Agreement. Much bloodshed and many postwar conferences later, a new concession covered the subterranean sphere of the states created by the Sykes-Picot Agreement. As the concession holder's name shifted from the Turkish to the Iraq Petroleum Company, Turkey surrendered all "petroleum resources discovered, and to be discovered" in the provinces of Mosul and Baghdad. The only Iraqi aspect of the Iraq Petroleum Company (IPC) was the source of its oil. The newly minted Compagnie Française de Pétroles (CFP, later Total) absorbed a 23.75 percent holding from Deutsche Bank. Through the Anglo-Persian Oil Company (APOC) and Royal Dutch-Shell (a Dutch and Jewish English company steadily becoming more British), Britain could count on a double share of 47.5 percent. Great Britain had planned for a larger share but the US Department of State and American oil companies used political, economic, and legal pressure to assert American claims to Iraqi oil. The American syndicate, stacked with Standard Oil interests, was called the Near East Development Corporation (NEDC). Thus, although the French and the British established the oil infrastructure and colonial institutions, ownership of the oil fell to multinational companies.[14] Keeping in mind the multinational shareholders and the symbolic morphing of corporate branding, we can identify the Iraq Petroleum Company with the global agent that would become British Petroleum and later still its more recent avatar, BP.[15] These were the interests served by the twin pipelines that ran from Kirkuk to Tripoli and Haifa.

To the extent that the concession was a quintessential apparatus through which private companies benefited from colonial projects, the Great War does not signify a rupture. The holders of concessions shifted, and nation-states were born into alienation from the resources of value, but the nature of concessions themselves did not change. How then to read the changes brought about by the war? I suggest that we can observe the difference between economic maneuvering in prewar imperialism and in postwar nation-states through the infrastructure built to convey oil to Western markets. The premise here is that the means of conveying energy have as much impact on social geography as its extraction. The infrastructure relevant to our case includes the railway and the pipeline, and the difference comes into view between Germany operating in the Ottoman Empire and oil companies at work in nascent nation-states.

Conveying Power

When it comes to transporting energy, a railcar and a pipeline are similar—both contain and move oil across vast distances—yet the visibility of a train and its overland transport of people, along with products, comes with expectations. Where a train's movement of multiple products and bodies reflects a range of interests, a pipeline invisibly dispossesses while directing benefit to a narrow group of investors. Until oil made its impact visible through global climate change, pipelines gave oilmen exactly what they wanted: profit refined through externalization of damage. Any spills, impairment of sources of water and food, or violence associated with the surveillance or defense of infrastructure did not impact the bottom line of the companies. As oil flowed beneath their feet, the residents impacted by such things found it difficult to see where the wealth was going. Trains are more obvious. When it came to the Orient Express and the Hijaz Railway, German-engineered technology run at an Ottoman pace was widely visible. Communities in the Ottoman Empire saw and therefore expected some service from trains. This gave them recourse to stopping trains during strikes as a way to force companies and government alike to heed their demands.

The trouble trains pose for corporate interests becomes apparent in the case of the Berlin-Baghdad Express, which the German government and Deutsche Bank had agreed to build in order to secure the Baghdad Concession for petroleum fields from the Ottoman government. Sean McMeekin describes how Ottoman rulers desperately sought rail lines stretching to Mesopotamia in order to move troops and cement influence in Arab lands.[16] Germany agreed, initially seeing the railway as "a pipeline on wheels" that would convey oil from their concessionary lands to Berlin and later as a way to leverage the Ottoman Empire to join the war.[17] Importantly, the nature of a train's visible existence in a sovereign space meant that commercial interests had to negotiate with the state.

The Ottoman state flexed its power by insisting that the 1899 Baghdad Concession be contingent upon construction of "a railway 'within a *maximum* period of eight years' from Konya to Basra via Baghdad."[18] Since Deutsche Bank held the concession, as well as the Anatolian Railway Company, it could be pressed to capitulate. Sultan Abdul Hamid displayed even more foresight about the nature of concessions when he included a last-minute clause that the Ottoman government reserved the right to buy the line, meant to preserve sovereignty, and then "announced a ban on all foreign mining concessions in the Ottoman Empire in February 1900, only several months after giving the Germans the Baghdad concession."[19] But, in much the same way that a freight train can appear to serve local residents as it dispossesses them of items of value, Abdul Hamid voiced his conditions but "quietly agreed to give German prospectors working for the railway company generous exploration rights inside his domains, including copper- and coal-mining grants and broad excavation rights within twenty kilometers of the Baghdad line on either side."[20] The "cosmopolitan nature" of the rail project (whose concession was renewed in 1911), which engaged advisers and workers from across lands united behind the Central Powers, was "one of the last great flowerings of the first era of globalization."[21] The impending end of this era was already apparent to the negotiating parties in 1917 when the Germans made any additional support to the Ottomans contingent on "concession guarantees to Turkish coal, copper, iron and phosphate deposits—and not least Mesopotamian oil" for Deutsche Bank and its investors.[22]

Even as Ottoman negotiators conferred subterranean concessions on German banks, they steered progress on the train line. No matter the actual financial agreements, they recognized the need for an optics of power on the terrestrial plane. Stretching across territory, the infrastructure of a train supports state sovereignty at the same time that it provides local populations with certain agency. In the case at hand, this becomes apparent in the refuge that completed sections of the railroad offered some Armenians during the Turkish onslaught in 1915. The train also allowed passengers and journalists to witness the scale and widespread nature of Armenian suffering even as it transported the troops that perpetuated genocide. This points to the dual impact of overland transport—it manifests the power of its operator through a physical network but also allows travelers to view the incongruity between the projection of power and actual social space. Like the Hijaz Railway, the Ottomans saw in the Berlin-Baghdad Express an overland network to convey imperial power, but the formation of a new world order stopped it in its tracks.

Seemingly, both the Ottoman Empire and the German bank got what they needed through the exchange—an empire projecting its power via a transportation network and unlimited, tax-free access to natural resources—but, in essence, it assured war. The Ottomans desired the train as a way to secure power through surveillance and deployment of troops, certain to impact both ethnic communities and political insurgents. As a move in the Great Game, Deutsche Bank's acquisition of the Baghdad Concession meant that other finance firms would likewise motivate national armies to turn eastward. The war brought these forces to a head. The outbreak of war and the demise of the Ottoman Empire truncated the line, which ended near the Turkish town of Bulgurlu.

The transport of materials by train also allows for abrupt stoppage. As dramatized in the film *Lawrence of Arabia*, the Arab Revolt disabled the Ottoman military by blowing up the Hijaz Railway. Paralyzing imperial networks opened up a space for political independence no matter how quickly it was foreclosed. In *Carbon Democracy*, Timothy Mitchell observes a similar dynamic operative in the English coal trains that brought energy from mines to cities and gave workers the power to shut down industrial life by halting train cars filled with potential energy.[23] Such effective powers of persuasion enabled the labor movement to achieve provisions for workers' rights and well-being and to mobilize politically. Rail strikes "spread through the interconnected industries of coal mining, railways, docking and shipping," culminating in massive worker action.[24]

Positioned at the crossroads of domestic politics and imperial power, Winston Churchill figures as a central character in the shift from coal to oil and trains to pipelines. In 1910–11, as head of the Home Office, Churchill responded to a strike of coal miners in South Wales by dispatching cavalry and armed infantry to oppose workers before ordering a military takeover of the trains. As head of the Admiralty during World War I, Churchill converted the navy's ships from coal to petroleum power. At the war's end, he assumed a seat on the board of the Iraq Petroleum Company and, as if to illustrate the very process of a revolving door, played a lead role as prime minister in the Kirkuk to Haifa pipeline scheme. Needless to say, the prime minister did not endorse the idea of a train running parallel to the Kirkuk-Haifa oil pipeline.

The Ghost Railway

Baghdad fell to the British in March 1917, effectively annulling the German concession and its train line. Taking a lesson from the power that trains conferred on workers, the Iraq Petroleum Company asked the Bechtel corporation to build a pipeline with only a parallel road. Oil, not rail, defined the path from Kirkuk to Haifa. Understanding that "the politics of energy involves acquiring the power to interrupt the flow of energy as much as securing its supply," the companies were sure to bury their evidence deep beneath the ground.[25] Still, concealing the conveyance of oil did not quell colonial fear of the locals.

After Indian battalions of the British army crushed the popular Iraqi uprising of 1920, the Foreign Office installed Feisal ibn Hussein as king. More precisely, Feisal was king over the thin surface of ground covering the IPC concession, but still he strove for a stable, prosperous country. Angry with the French for driving him out of Syria, Feisal pressed for a pipeline through exclusively British territory. Feisal's quasi-independent status conferred the right to negotiate with Sir John Cadman, president of the IPC. During concession negotiations in 1931, Cadman complained, "The question of the pipeline is excessively difficult, but again the Iraq Government appear at last to state their real case. What they have in mind is the construction of the railway from Haifa to Bagdad, and they only regard the pipeline as a means of forcing people to construct a railway."[26] Desperately pursuing a railroad to bring Iraqi products and people to regional markets, Feisal had indeed established a ministry to leverage his consent to the pipeline. Despite drawing it on maps, the IPC never intended to build the Baghdad-Haifa train. Strung along for decades, Feisal was not privy to Cadman's candid thoughts: "There are no concrete Haifa Baghdad railway schemes and therefore all suggestions as to what is required to obtain the railway are fantastic." To British colonial officials, he simply called the train "a ghost."[27]

The ghost railway had tragic implications. Everyone along the proposed route wanted the Baghdad-Haifa line, which would have promoted material connections among a range of ethnic and religious communities and potentially brought vibrancy to rather stagnant economic conditions. After a stark asphalt road was laid in sparsely populated areas parallel to the pipeline, company officials returned local collections for the train to disappointed donors. Rather than cosmopolitan circulation, the energy companies created corridors for automobiles and directed profits

OIL AND THE ORIGINS OF MIDDLE EASTERN SOVEREIGNTY | 109

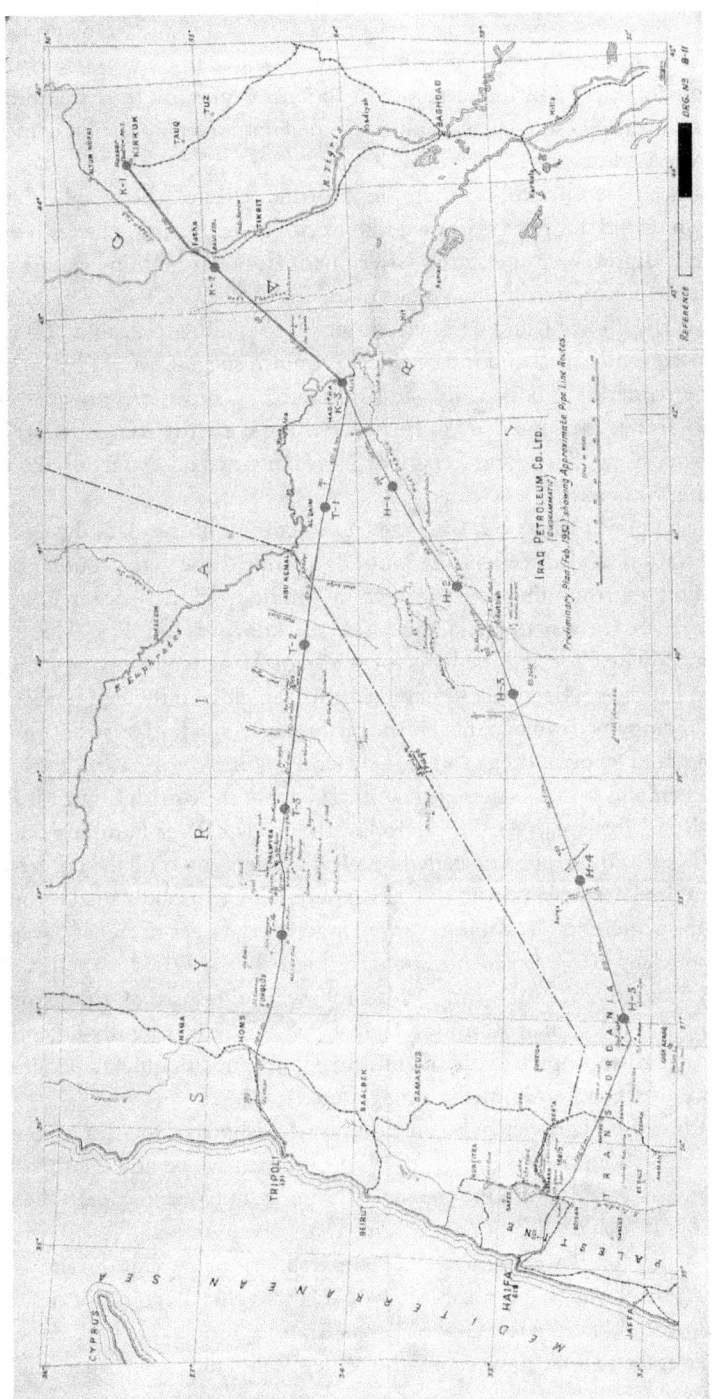

Map 5.1. Haifa-Tripoli-Kirkuk pipelines map. Drawn borders parallel the linearity of the pipelines, which contrast with the drainage systems of proximate rivers. K(1-3) stations pumped oil from Kirkuk. H(1-5) stations moved petroleum toward Haifa and T(1-4) stations pumped in the direction of Tripoli. Source: TNA CO732/70/2 (1), The National Archives, UK.

to themselves.²⁸ Instead of promoting local or regional economies, moving capital in this manner introduced competition for allegedly scarce resources. It was under these conditions that in 1932 Iraq attained its independence as a state that did not own what was beneath its surface, was subjected to aerial surveillance, and could not establish its own markets.

Where trains enabled networks of empire, pipelines enacted the Middle Eastern nation-state, which did not possess its own resources. Pipelines emptied wealth out of national space and prevented the acting government from determining export rates. The most shockingly counterintuitive point made in Mitchell's *Carbon Democracy* is that controlling the flow of Middle Eastern oil involved stalling its production in order to create need in the West and inflate price. A train, I suggest, would have altered the scenario by rendering it both visible and vulnerable. Concessions provided wide tax umbrellas—in our case one that covered everything currently recognized as Iraq, Jordan, Palestine, Israel, Syria, and Lebanon. No element of oil extraction, conveyance, or refining was taxed.²⁹

Along with no power to tax oil, the state lacked control of the skies. Five official bases, a relief station, and three landing grounds anchored the aerial route, policed the pipeline and its surrounding communities, and militarized the space in question. Because they marked the way to Haifa, the bases were known as the "H's." H1, 2, and 3 in the Anbar Province formed the basis for the Iraqi Air Force following nationalization. H4, in Ruwaysid, became a Jordanian army base close to the Iraq border, and H5 in the IPC company town of Safawi is the birthplace of the Jordanian air force. In 1931 IPC's Mafraq Depot landing ground—currently alongside of Za'atri, the largest Syrian refugee camp in Jordan—became an official base of the British Royal Air Force and later the Royal Jordanian Air Force. Today, the Jordan River Pumping Station, the unofficial H6, is a quiet outpost staffed by a few soldiers guarding the border with Israel, where retired Jordanian army officials raise fish in two pools made from oil tankers shot up by members of Kibbutz Neve Ur across the river in an act of reprisal in 1969. The nucleus of the Israeli Air Force complex Ramat David is the IPC base established by Roald Dahl in the early 1940s following the spate of attacks on the pipeline during the Palestinian Revolt of 1936–39.³⁰ While it is hardly exceptional for young nations to appropriate colonial infrastructure, the H's quickly became the staging ground for attacks on immediate neighbors.³¹

The view from the Haifa-Semakh (on the southern shore of the Sea of Galilee) branch of the Hijaz Railway was different. As an Ottoman-willed and German-built train, it predated the section of IPC pipeline that ultimately ran parallel. The train conveyed many a British soldier, but at the same time served Arab and Jewish workers headed to the Naharaim Power Station, the Haifa Refinery, or agricultural sites in the Marj ibn Amr/Jezreel Valley. Famously slow, it was said that Bedouin during their spring migration could keep pace. Glubb Pasha's Arab Legion guarded the cargo and allowed the contraband that moved on "the Valley Railroad." Even when the surrounding space was militarized in the 1930s, the Hijaz train stations remained lively sites of Arab-Jewish intermixing.

Marketing Scarcity

Along with the infrastructure that redirects resources, the notion of scarcity should undergo examination.[32] It proves insufficient to appraise a place as having scarce water, food, or money without attending to the extractive industries that appropriate those very resources. In the case of the Baghdad-Haifa Railway, the scarcity of funds resulted from the fact that the Iraqi government could only self-fund by choosing to either receive a loan against future profits or claim 20 percent of the profits from the IPC pipeline after its completion generated revenue. Other than this minority percentage, out of which Iraq was mandated to pay off Turkey's prewar claims, the Iraqi government had no means of deriving funds from the burgeoning oil industry.[33]

In place of a substantive development plan stood the blueprints of a ghost train. In 1936 independent Iraq "found the Treasury empty" and had no means of paying for its administration. Reluctant to step further into foreign debt, the Iraqi minister of finance filed a request with the Iraq Petroleum Company to postpone payment of Iraq's debts to the company. Between 1927 when the IPC struck oil and 1935 when the pipeline opened, the company loaned the government funds to be reimbursed after the pipeline began operation. Contrary to its hope, the opening of the pipeline actually brought Iraq into worse financial straits. In exchange for the stay, the IPC extended its concession into the Persian Gulf.

Transjordan, facing parallel financial shortfalls and a starving population, tried to leverage a pipeline transit tax. Yet, with tax- and tariff-free passage guaranteed by the 1925 concession, Transjordanians were given the option of working as pipeline guards. The pipeline had different effects in Mandate Palestine. Constructing the Haifa harbor, and later the refinery, did involve a significant labor force and the means of exporting a range of goods. The British desire for a beholden populace unlikely to disrupt the export of oil from the region entailed support for Zionist activities in Haifa among some British officials. This same impulse, evident in the 1920 law permitting Jewish land purchases, allowed the Jewish National Fund to purchase territory in the Jordan and Jezreel Valleys through which the pipeline moved. The kibbutzim in these valleys were largely focused on development of agriculture, so mainly interacted with the pipeline in its early stages when its construction upended their fields.

Initially, the mixed Arab-Jewish labor movement in Palestine unified around the restrictive conditions of IPC work. On 19 February 1935—about a month after the pipeline's opening ceremony—fifty workers at a subsidiary installation struck and received better wages. When the IPC announced layoffs and wage reductions a few weeks later, employees tested the possibilities of organizing. On 22 February 1935, a group of skilled workers laid out demands for improvements in conditions, inspiring a strike among "600 of the IPC's 800 workers" to cease labor.[34] Fearful of the precedent-setting power of the strike, IPC management agreed to several of the demands and restored the plant to its productive capacity. The IPC strike marked a high point for labor in Mandate Palestine. Zachary Lockman records how "leftist and prolabor accounts . . . routinely attached the adjective 'great' to it, and not a few contemporary observers, both Arab and Jewish, saw it as marking the beginning of a new stage in the emergence of a class-conscious Arab working class in Palestine."[35]

Worker solidarity in Palestine experienced only fleeting "greatness," for one year later the Palestinian Revolt erupted, exploding and militarizing Arab-Jewish tensions. The 1936–39 Palestinian Revolt in Palestine aimed at paralyzing infrastructure to protest British Mandate rule and increased Jewish immigration. Palestinian rebels blew up the pipeline at multiple junctures as far east as Irbid in Transjordan and as far west as Kibbutz Yagur near Haifa by sawing out pieces of pipe and igniting the flowing oil.[36] The seemingly local attacks on an exploitative industry that benefited the British were inspired by radio broadcasts by the mufti of Jerusalem, Hajj Amin al-Husseini, from Berlin. Hajj al-Husseini spent the years of the Palestinian Revolt (1936–39) in Berlin supported by Deutsche Bank, which we should note had lost its share in the Iraq oil concession after World War I. Never having fully accepted the loss, it seems, Deutsche Bank wagered on the mufti to rally Palestinians to the side of Germany or, at least, sabotage the pipeline and its profits.[37]

If Palestinians could act as proxies for Deutsche Bank, then Iraq Petroleum would have to turn to the Jews. As it had pledged to the IPC in preliminary reports, the Royal Air Force bombed suspected saboteurs from above but soon realized the need for ground patrol. To meet the need, British colonel Orde Wingate conceived of special night squads made up of Jews from local kibbutzim who could guard the pipeline and confront infiltrators. Local Jewish patrols, Wingate asserted, offered cost advantages, because they were out for guns instead of money. Members of the squads wanted access to weapons and the right to organize as Jewish militias, proto-national acts that the British had banned prior to the revolt. In need of the special night squads, the British changed the law and allowed for the arming of Jewish settlements on the condition that they use their weapons to protect the pipeline. The young Moshe Dayan, who lived in Nahalal, an agricultural collective alongside the pipeline, gained his first military training from Wingate and used his weapons to protect both the pipeline and his community.[38] Guarding the pipeline legitimized Zionist self-defense, and acts of self-defense soon evolved into retaliations and forays.[39] Where Arab and Jewish workers had united to demand better conditions from the IPC in 1935, their position vis-à-vis sabotaging or protecting the pipeline in 1936 marked a key moment of Arab-Jewish conflict, as well as the point at which the opposition became pointedly militarized. Similar to the force mobilized by Glubb Pasha in Transjordan to guard the pipeline, which grew into Jordan's national army, Wingate's special night squads formed the nucleus of the paramilitary Palmach, which folded and expanded into the elite of the Israel Defense Forces in the 1948 War.

When the Peel Commission arrived from Britain hoping to defuse the situation by drawing yet more lines across the terrain, the entire run of the pipeline in Palestine was placed in hypothetical Jewish territory.[40] The Peel Commission map, we might note, is the first proposal for the partition of Palestine, an idea that gained legitimacy through the 1947 UN vote, as well as the Israel-Palestine peace process of the 1990s. The 1947 map, not surprisingly, also designated the run of the pipeline in Jewish territory. Ultimately, Palestinian acts of sabotaging the pipeline most inspired right-wing Zionist paramilitary groups like Lehi and Etzel. Admiringly naming those acts "terrorism," the new Jewish saboteurs emulated them with zeal. Throughout the 1940s, members of Lehi and Etzel attacked the pipeline, its guard stations, and oil installations in Haifa. Some scholars have suggested that parallel to the Deutsche Bank support of Palestinian rebels in the 1930s, right-wing Zionist militias derived support from the French as part of their ongoing struggle with the British.[41] The net effect of the Palestinian Revolt and the struggles of the 1940s was thorough militarization of Zionist-Palestinian territorial competition that neither the labor movement nor any other large-scale Arab-Jewish association could survive.

End of the Line

At the oil refinery in Haifa, Arabs and Jews continued to work together in a fraught vestige of what had been a coordinated labor movement. Nationalistic pressures made the proximity increasingly tenuous.[42] After the Partition Plan for Palestine cleared the UN General Assembly, Arab and Jewish workers at the refinery engaged in a spontaneous strike and began attacking one another. The company sent in British soldiers and told the workers to return to work or the soldiers would begin firing on anyone in the vicinity.[43] Etzel saw the devolving coexistence as an ideal target and, one month later (30 December 1947), bombed the refinery entrance where Arab day laborers sought work, causing six deaths and forty-two injuries. Inside the refinery, Arab workers turned on their Jewish colleagues, resulting in thirty-nine casualties and fifty-one injuries.[44] Arab-Jewish opposition at the refinery was not total; in fact, several Arab workers saved the lives of Jews, and a Jewish nurse put herself in danger to treat the Arabs injured by Etzel's grenades. After about three hours of mayhem that Arab Legion guards and English management passively witnessed, the colonial army entered the refinery to put down the violence. The refinery incident began a chain of attacks and retaliations that forever transformed Haifa.

The year 1948 marked the end of the line from Kirkuk to Haifa. The IPC did not grant Iraqis the autonomy to advocate for commodity ownership, but did allow them to assert nationalism by shutting down the Haifa line in the name of boycotting the Jewish state.[45] At a cost of one million pounds to Iraq's treasury, finance minister

Ali Muntez spoke of it as "a sacrifice which Iraq cannot escape to attain her sublime aims."⁴⁶ The very last British troops remained in Palestine to guard oil infrastructure, but eventually even they evacuated. When the newly formed Israel Defense Forces marched on Haifa, Prime Minister David Ben-Gurion took his chances against global oil corporations by ordering its seizure. In a kind of Hanukkah story redux, Jews reopened part of the plant in order to refine the twenty thousand tons of crude remaining at the bottom of tanks and supplied their war machine with these dregs.⁴⁷ The IPC answered the severance of the Kirkuk-Haifa line by constructing another, larger pipeline that ended in the Syrian city of Banias.⁴⁸

The countries created by Britain to facilitate oil export could no longer accommodate the circuit that had so impacted their development. In other words, connections forged in the imperial context could not be sustained by Middle Eastern nationalisms. There are at least two ways to think about this outcome. On the one hand, European colonialism in the Middle East allowed for certain kinds of cosmopolitan circulations at the same time that it controlled access to the modes and commodities of circulation. On the other hand, the tandem corporate acquisition of subterranean resources and colonial creation of states resulted in nations with an undue attachment to their arbitrary frontiers and surface territory combined with a penchant for violating the space of both proximate states and internal others. The nationalisms that grew up around the pipeline were fierce enough to prevent future linkages.

But, finally, we should not take the process of oil's nationalization as a break so much as a continuation. Unfolding in stages and overlapping for Israel with war and for Iraq with coups, nationalization entailed an absorption of institutions configured to facilitate oil extraction and export. In contrast, we might note how in Jordan, where nationalization proved less disruptive, the concession was not dissolved. Worthy of further notice is the degree to which Israel, Jordan, and Iraq followed particular trajectories of nationalization reminiscent of their separate design as supply, transit, and export sites. Although they were created and distinguished through a system of oil circulation, the dissolution of this system broke the links among them as its end reinforced the states and their borders. And yet I don't want to fault the states for maintaining political structures set in place by the oil business while exonerating the corporations, with their new names and wider reach. After all, why should we expect states with origins tied to the oil industry to be able to transform the industry? In fact, a nation-state independent from the global oil industry has yet to arise.

Rachel Havrelock is a professor at the University of Illinois at Chicago and author of *River Jordan: The Mythology of a Dividing Line* (University of Chicago Press, 2011) and *The Joshua Generation: Israeli Occupation and the Bible* (Princeton University Press, 2020). Havrelock's current book project is *Pipeline: How Oil Created the Modern Middle East*. In 2014 the US Department of State honored her with a Professional Fellows Alumni Impact Award. Rachel serves on the International Advisory Committee of the trilateral (Israeli, Palestinian, and Jordanian) NGO EcoPeace, which promotes equitable water distribution and shared resource planning.

Notes

1. Salim Tamari identifies a stronger parallel between Ottoman Palestine and British Mandate Palestine, whereas I see the stronger hand of the Palestine Exploration Fund and colonial exigencies. Salim Tamari, *The Great War and the Remaking of Palestine* (Berkeley: University of California Press, 2017), 12–13.
2. James Barr, *A Line in the Sand: The Anglo-French Struggle for the Middle East, 1914–1948* (New York: W. W. Norton, 2012).
3. Elias Muhanna, "Iraq and Syria's Poetic Borders," *New Yorker*, 13 August 2014, https://www.newyorker.com/books/page-turner/iraq-syria-poetic-imagination.
4. Rachel Havrelock, *River Jordan: The Mythology of a Dividing Line* (Chicago: University of Chicago Press, 2011).
5. Rachel Hallote, Felicity Cobbing, and Jeffrey A. Spurr, *The Photographs of the American Palestine Exploration Society* (Atlanta: American Schools of Oriental Research, 2012).
6. Barr, *A Line in the Sand*, 144.
7. The High Commissioner of Iraq remarked, "Moderates can be strung along by our constitutional intentions, but extremists must be subject to military law." Sir Percy Cox, High Commissioner of Iraq, 21 June 1920, The National Archives (TNA), formerly the Public Records Office, FO 371/5227.
8. TNA FO 608/278. See also TNA FO 608/100; and Jacob Norris, *Land of Progress: Palestine in the Age of Colonial Development, 1905–1948* (Oxford: Oxford University Press, 2013), 66.
9. TNA AIR 8/90, Iraq Pipe Line 1927, 23/11.
10. From S/Idr. Paine, Baghdad to Bottomley, 1929 (associated notes from the Air Staff 28.11.1929, AIR 8/90).
11. TNA AIR 8/90.
12. *Decisions affecting the Route of the Pipeline*, TNA CAB 24/202/18.
13. Timothy Mitchell, *Carbon Democracy: Political Power in the Age of Oil* (London: Verso, 2011), 155–58.
14. The split among the CFP, NEDC, Shell, and APOC was 23.75 percent rather than 25 percent in order to accommodate the eternal 5 percent of Calouste Gulbenkian, the cosmopolitan Armenian gentleman whose survey maps had inspired the whole project.
15. HMG acquired a majority share in APOC in 1914—the Anglo-Persian Oil Company merged with the Iraq Petroleum Company, morphing into Anglo-Iranian in 1935 and British Petroleum in 1954. In 1998 BP merged with Amoco to become BP Amoco before settling on the current BP in 2000.
16. Sean McMeekin, *The Berlin-Baghdad Express: The Ottoman Empire and Germany's Bid for World Power* (Cambridge, MA: Harvard University Press, 2010).
17. Railways accounted for about two-thirds of German investment in Ottoman lands. Neil Faulkner, *Lawrence of Arabia's War: The Arabs, the British, and the Remaking of the Middle East in WWI* (New Haven: Yale University Press, 2016), 33.
18. McMeekin, *The Berlin-Baghdad Express*, 42.
19. McMeekin, *The Berlin-Baghdad Express*, 42–43.
20. McMeekin, *The Berlin-Baghdad Express*, 43.
21. McMeekin, *The Berlin-Baghdad Express*, 238–39.
22. McMeekin, *The Berlin-Baghdad Express*, 315.
23. Mitchell argues that coal as "a new energy system" enabled people to "forge successful political demands" on a mass scale. Mitchell, *Carbon Democracy*, 12.
24. Mitchell, *Carbon Democracy*, 23.
25. Mitchell, *Carbon Democracy*, 8.

26. 1931 Iraq Part I, Oil Concessions IPC's Agreement, TNA CO 730/160/8.
27. Paraphrase Telegram from the Secretary of State for the Colonies to the High Commissioner of Iraq, 29 January 1931, No. 4. CO 730/160/8.
28. For more on the railway survey and the building of the road, see Norris, *Land of Progress*, 115.
29. The 1925 concession in Jordan granted Royal Dutch-Shell a one-hundred-year claim on any minerals discovered underground. Never highly valued and therefore never abrogated, Shell initiated Hydraulic Fracturing in Eastern Jordan in 2013 under the enduring tax umbrella of the concession. In Israel, the concession expired in 2003, at which point the refineries were privatized.
30. In 1937 a landing strip was established alongside a pipeline pumping station. Following the revolt, Royal Air Force pilot Roald Dahl sanctioned the building of the base, which was completed in 1942. Interview with Ramat David museum docent, 29 May 2013.
31. In the 1967 War, Israeli planes from Ramat David blew up the Iraqi air force base at H2. H5 became the Prince Hassan air base in 1969 but did not see action until the following year when the Popular Front for the Liberation of Palestine hijacked Western passenger airplanes and grounded them in the nearby desert. Ten days after the hijacking, on 16 September 1970, Syrian tanks manned by Palestinian fighters engaged with the Jordanian army. When the Jordanian air force engaged in the battle from H5, the Iraqis threatened to shoot any aircraft taking off from the base. With a definitive knowledge of the trajectory, they fired at one squadron. In the first Gulf War, Saddam Hussein launched attacks on Haifa and its oil refinery from H3 along the IPC air route. US intelligence reports list H3 as a chemical weapon storage facility eventually captured by coalition forces during the second Gulf War in 2003.
32. Samer Alatout provides the methodology of interrogating this term, in "From Abundance to Scarcity (1936–59): a 'Fluid' History of Jewish Subjectivity in Historic Palestine and Israel," in *Reapproaching Borders: New Perspectives on the Study of Israel-Palestine*, ed. Mark LeVine and Sandy Sufian (New York: Rowan, 2007), 199–220.
33. Debts to Turkey—10 percent for 25 years—were to be paid out of this sum rather than out of company profits.
34. Zachary Lockman, *Comrades and Enemies: Arab and Jewish Workers in Palestine, 1906–1948* (Berkeley: University of California Press, 1996), 232.
35. Lockman, *Comrades and Enemies*, 233.
36. C. Townshend, "The Defence of Palestine: Insurrection and Public Security, 1936–1939," *English Historical Review* 103 (1988): 917–49.
37. McMeekin, *The Berlin-Baghdad Express*, 38–53.
38. Moshe Dayan, *Living with the Bible* (New York: William Morrow, 1978), 127.
39. Ted Swedenburg, *Memories of Revolt: The 1936–1939 Rebellion and the Palestinian National Past* (Fayetteville: University of Arkansas Press, 2003), 220.
40. The policy did not necessarily encourage welcoming more Jews into Palestine, as evidenced by the 1938 White Paper, which accompanied the Peel Commission map. A single strip of land seemed enough to achieve the goal of a buffer population.
41. Barr, *A Line in the Sand*, 257–59.
42. In a manner of return to Lawrence's map, the UN's 1947 internationalization plan called for Haifa to be a Transjordanian town in order to maintain the IPC concession.
43. Mordechai Naor, *The Oil Refinery: Sixty Years of Energy* (Haifa: Bazan, 2000, in Hebrew), 60.
44. Lockman calls the incident, "the largest and most brutal massacre of civilians which Palestine had witnessed since the UN vote a month earlier"; *Comrades and Enemies*, 353.
45. With the departure of the British from the country in 1948, the refineries were transferred to Israel's control. The Israeli government formally acquired them in 1958, holding them until a 2006 sale to private investors. Currently they are owned by the oligarchic Israel Corporation, which has about a 33 percent stake, while David Federman's firm, Israel Petrochemical Enterprises, has about 15 percent. The balance is publicly traded. Ownership fluctuates regularly through private equity bids and sales.
46. Interruption of production at the Haifa refinery reduced world production at an annual rate of four million tons. "In terms of refined products, the loss of 700,000 tons of motor spirit, 2,000,000 tons

of fuel oil, and nearly 1,000,000 tons of gas oil and kerosene a year. The markets in the Eastern Mediterranean and the UK were upset." See "The Haifa Refinery," *The Economist*, 29 May 1948.
47. TNA CAB/129/29.
48. Bechtel, a company significant in the water privatization sector, subcontracted from IPC to build the Kirkuk-Banias pipeline. Just as following the Kirkuk-Haifa line offers a lens into Arab-Israeli relations, so the Kirkuk-Banias line and its closure reveals much about Sunni-Shia relations. The Iraq Petroleum Company, the Israeli government, and Iraqi foreign minister Nuri al-Said all tried to reopen the pipeline in 1949 and the years immediately thereafter, but Iraqi public opinion had been stirred up against economic collaboration with Israel. Israel nationalized its oil infrastructure in 1956 after carefully studying Iraqi oil nationalization attempts.

Select Bibliography

Alatout, Samer. "From Abundance to Scarcity (1936–59): A 'Fluid' History of Jewish Subjectivity in Historic Palestine and Israel." In *Reapproaching Borders: New Perspectives on the Study of Israel-Palestine*, edited by Mark LeVine and Sandy Sufian, 199–220. New York: Rowan, 2007.
Barr, James. *A Line in the Sand: The Anglo-French Struggle for the Middle East, 1914–1948*. New York: W. W. Norton, 2012.
Havrelock, Rachel. *River Jordan: The Mythology of a Dividing Line*. Chicago: University of Chicago Press, 2011.
Lockman, Zachary. *Comrades and Enemies: Arab and Jewish Workers in Palestine, 1906–1948*. Berkeley: University of California Press, 1996.
McMeekin, Sean. *The Berlin-Baghdad Express: The Ottoman Empire and Germany's Bid for World Power*. Cambridge, MA: Harvard University Press, 2010.
Mitchell, Timothy. *Carbon Democracy: Political Power in the Age of Oil*. London: Verso, 2011.
Norris, Jacob. *Land of Progress: Palestine in the Age of Colonial Development, 1905–1948*. Oxford: Oxford University Press, 2013.
Swedenburg, Ted. *Memories of Revolt: The 1936–1939 Rebellion and the Palestinian National Past*. Fayetteville: University of Arkansas Press, 2003.
Tamari, Salim. *The Great War and the Remaking of Palestine*. Berkeley: University of California Press, 2017.

CHAPTER 6

TERRITORY, DEMOGRAPHY, AND EFFECTIVE CONTROL
AN ANALYSIS OF ISRAEL'S BIOSPATIAL POLITICS

Yinon Cohen and Neve Gordon

Introduction

Not long after the June 1967 War, at a meeting of the Labor Party, Golda Meir turned to Prime Minister Levi Eshkol and asked, "What are we going to do with a million Arabs?" Eshkol paused for a moment. "I get it," he said. "You want the dowry, but you don't like the bride!"[1]

This anecdote underscores that in the immediate aftermath of the 1967 War, Israel made a clear distinction between the land it had occupied—the dowry—and the Palestinians who inhabited it—the bride. While the distinction between the people and their land swiftly became the overarching logic informing the structure of Israel's colonial project in the Occupied Territories, it also informed Israel's land policies within the pre-1967 borders.[2] Indeed, the notion that there are "two Israels"—the virtuous liberal democracy west of the Green Line, or the 1949 armistice agreement border, and the iniquitous colonial regime within the territories Israel occupied in 1967—is a construct disseminated by liberal Zionists that conceals the intricate links between race and space produced by the Jewish state. This "good Israel" / "bad Israel" framing does not hold water once one acknowledges that the Judaization of land has been a prime objective of every government since Israel's establishment in 1948 and that the modes of Palestinian dispossession on both sides of the Green Line have been uncannily similar.

On its own, expropriating land does not guarantee spatial control or the Judaization of space. Critical social scientists have shown how from the 1920s in Mandatory

Palestine, through the establishment of Jewish towns in the Galilee and the Negev after 1948, to the construction of settlements and outposts in the West Bank following the 1967 War, Zionist leaders have always understood that without a civilian presence on the ground, effective control of Palestinian land could not be secured. Thus, alongside efforts to empty the land of its Palestinian inhabitants, Jewish civilians were relocated to the land seized from the indigenous population and deployed within the broader architecture of control as an integral part of the process of racializing space and rendering it "Jewish." This process has depended on a strict bifurcation between Jews and Palestinians, which may seem all too natural today but was, in fact, produced over time through the introduction of a variety of mechanisms, including decisions on demographic classifications. Underscoring how the Judaization of land is tied to the state's biopolitical techniques helps make sense of the interplay among territory, demography, and effective control.

Applying Israel's land-grabbing practices and demographic classifications as a conceptual lens, this chapter makes the following two claims: the first concerns *biospatial* strategies, including the construction of space as a racialized category; the second is historical and shows the continuity of the expropriation of Palestinian land from 1948 until today. We derive the term "biospatial" from Michel Foucault's notions of biopolitics and biopower. Biopolitics focuses on the administration of life and populations, while biopower is the way in which biopolitics is put to work in society.[3] Biopower uses statistical devices and scientific methods as well as mechanisms of surveillance to measure and intervene in a set of processes designed to administer, optimize, and multiply the population's productive capacities and at times to repress and subjugate the people. As opposed to discipline, however, these biotechniques operate on the level of the population as a whole rather than the individual. The term "biospatial" denotes the deployment of such biotechniques to demarcate, control, manage, shape, and ascribe signification to space. In other words, "biospatial" is a term that helps describe the diverse mechanisms and processes by which space is constituted as racialized or in racialized terms.

While the vast majority of the literature on Israel-Palestine has focused on national, religious, and ethnic differences, we maintain that Jewish nationality is also informed and even determined by race. Indeed, as we show below, only race renders some of the distinctions Israel draws, such as the one between "Arab Christians" and "non-Arab Christians," comprehensible. In a similar vein, it is not surprising that in Hebrew the term "racism," rather than "national, religious, or ethnic hatred," is widely used to describe Israel's treatment of its Palestinian population. In the Israeli context, race pervades nationalism and religion and helps explain the state's land-grabbing policies.

We show that the particular biospatial scaffolding underlying Israel's colonial project has deployed two major strategies—namely, legal-bureaucratic mechanisms of dispossession and the movement of Jewish civilians to settle Palestinian land—across the entire territory located between the Jordan Valley and the Mediterranean Sea, in order to grab and control as much land as possible.[4] We go on to draw a connection between these strategies and statistical classifications and techniques of enumeration that Israel has adopted in order to delineate its efforts to racialize the appropriated space. These classifications and forms of enumeration at times not only defy international standards of statistical reporting,[5] but are deployed to either cement or sever the connection between people and space. Historically, we identify a boomerang trajectory, beginning with the massive confiscation and Judaization of Palestinian land in the wake of the 1948 War, then extending and duplicating many of the practices originally developed inside Israel to the West Bank in 1967, and finally turning back inward to solidify the racialization of land within Israel.[6] When we consider that settler colonialism, as Patrick Wolfe has shown,[7] is a structure and not an event, this recoiling movement across space and time is neither surprising nor unexpected.

The Racial-Spatial Logic

Before the 1948 War, there were nearly three hundred Jewish and over six hundred Palestinian villages and towns in the territory that would later become Israel. During the war, Palestinian cities were depopulated, and about five hundred Palestinian villages were destroyed, while most of their inhabitants either fled or were expelled across international borders, becoming refugees in neighboring countries. In total, about 750,000 Palestinians were displaced in what today would be characterized as ethnic cleansing, while thousands more were internally displaced within the nascent Jewish state. By 1951 the Palestinians who had become refugees were "replaced" by a similar number of Jewish immigrants, both Holocaust survivors from Europe and Mizrahi Jews from Arab countries, thus transforming the state's ethnic composition without altering its overall population size.[8]

Soon after the war, Israel introduced a series of administrative and legal mechanisms to seize Palestinian land.[9] It classified property belonging to Palestinian refugees first as "abandoned" and then as "absentee property" and quickly appropriated it, while also confiscating much of the land owned by the Palestinians residing in the one hundred villages that survived the war (this includes the villages that were transferred from Jordan to Israel as a result of the 1949 armistice agreement). The establishment of a military government (1948–66) responsible for governing the Palestinian citizens within the fledgling state facilitated this massive confiscation of land.[10]

A twofold strategy was adopted: Israel confined the estimated 160,000 Palestinians who had remained in the Jewish state to their villages and simultaneously converted Palestinian land into closed military zones and nature reserves, confiscated what it defined as absentee property, and restricted the cultivation of Palestinian agricultural plots, all the while registering their estates as "state land."[11] As we will see, the post-1967 strategies implemented in the Occupied Territories and associated with the "bad Israel" by liberal Zionists (who in Israel are referred to as left Zionists) had their origins in these earlier practices. Indeed, as early as 1951, the state effectively owned 92 percent of the land within its territory, up from 13.5 percent in 1948.[12]

Yet, as mentioned, seizing land alone does not guarantee effective control or the racialization of space as Jewish. Using the rhetoric of "population dispersal," Israel consequently established new Jewish towns to attract large numbers of immigrants to areas still populated by Palestinians and created agricultural settlements to ensure control over large swaths of Palestinian land. Of the 370 new Jewish settlements established soon after 1948, 350 were built on or in proximity to Palestinian villages that had been destroyed.[13] While Jews of all stripes and classes settled on confiscated Palestinian land, the state sent mostly new Mizrahi immigrants—a weak socioeconomic group that came from Arab and Muslim countries—to Israel's periphery, especially to the frontiers along its borders.[14]

In later years, middle- and upper-middle-class Jews were offered incentives to relocate to the Galilee to live in hilltop communities overlooking Palestinian villages. As Alexander Kedar and Oren Yiftachel explain, the Palestinian settlement map was "frozen" in 1948 by prohibiting the establishment of new Palestinian villages and towns and arresting the development of those still intact after the war by confiscating most of their land reserves, preventing any construction outside the already developed area, and surrounding these villages with Jewish settlements. In this way, Israel created a "geography of enclaves" in which the vast majority of Israel's Palestinian citizens have remained to this day[15]—even as their population has increased tenfold. Not surprisingly, these policies maintained and reproduced extreme residential segregation between Jews and Palestinians.

Residential segregation—characterized by acute disparity in the state's investment in infrastructure and social services—is arguably the most salient feature informing the organization of Israeli space, with the vast majority of localities defined as either Jewish or non-Jewish by the Israeli Central Bureau of Statistics (CBS). To create and maintain such segregation, Israel adopted a variety of biopolitical techniques while harnessing statistical tools to produce and reproduce a series of classifications that create a clear demarcation between Jews and Palestinians; it did so by homogenizing the former and fragmenting the latter. From the outset, the CBS adopted religion as the population's primary classification, while framing the Jews as the norm and contrasting them with all "non-Jews" (or members of other religions) in its statistical reports. To this day the word "Palestinian" does not appear in Israel's statistical abstracts, while only in 1995 did the word "Arab" finally emerge after decades in which Palestinians were referred to as "non-Jews," reminiscent of how they were labeled in the Balfour Declaration and the 1922 British Mandate for Palestine.

Moreover, to determine their "origin," Jews are classified according to their (or their father's) country of birth. Possible "origins" do not include Mizrahi or Arab Jews (presumably because these terms are considered divisive), but only continents of birth. If, however, both respondents and their fathers were born in Israel, they are assigned an "Israeli origin." Kenneth Prewitt, a former director of the United States

Census Bureau, calls this "Israel's policy of ethnic erasure," explaining that it was "designed to solve any problem of [Jewish] ethnic cleavage."[16]

One of its outcomes was the rapid erasure of the Arab origin of Mizrahim, about half the Jewish population, thus contributing to the "cleansing," in Ella Shohat's words, of their Arabness, while ensuring that Arab Jews would swiftly become "Israeli."[17] By contrast, Palestinians have never been able to attain the status of "Israeli origin" irrespective of how many generations their ancestors had resided in Israel-Palestine.[18] In fact, they have no "origin," only religion. In other words, according to Israel's official statistics, all Jews ultimately become "Israeli" within the span of two generations, and no Palestinian can ever become "Israeli." This produces a bifurcated racial reality where Jewishness trumps all other categories of identification, in turn both reflecting and reproducing the state's mechanisms of control and spatial politics.

A case in point is nationality. The word "nationality" has never appeared in CBS statistical abstracts probably because adding nationality would undo the strict division between Jews and Palestinians. Nationality, however, is recorded in the state's population registry, which has a list of 137 acceptable nationalities, yet "Israeli" is not one of them. Common nationalities of Israeli citizens are Jewish, Arab (for Muslims and "Arab Christians"), and Druze. A 2008 petition filed by citizens of different registered nationalities, including Jewish, Arab, Buddhist, and Druze, asked the Jerusalem District Court to compel the state to register their nationality as "Israeli." The court rejected the petition, ruling that such a change has "far-reaching implications for the State of Israel's identity," while accepting in part the government's claim that an Israeli nationality would "undermine the foundation of the State of Israel."[19] In 2013 Israel's Supreme Court upheld this decision.

The statistical acrobatics carried out following the mass migration from the former Soviet Union in the 1990s underscores even further the steps the CBS has been willing to take in order to consolidate the strict Jewish-Palestinian divide: adding non-Jews to the Jewish group as long as they are not Palestinians.[20] Out of an estimated one million immigrants who arrived on Israel's shores, approximately 250,000 had Jewish relatives but were themselves either Christian or had no religious affiliation. The CBS decided to alter the way it classifies the entire population and labeled the new non-Jewish immigrants as "others," uniting them with Jews in a group called "Jews and others." This group is contrasted in the statistical abstracts with the newly created group designated "Arab population," which includes only Muslims, Druze, and Christians. Thus, since the mid-1990s, according to the CBS, there are two kinds of Christians in Israel: "Arab Christians" and "non-Arab Christians." The algorithm developed by the CBS to distinguish between these two groups is based in part on where they live, namely, in a "Jewish locality" or a "non-Jewish" one. This suggests that race and space are mutually constitutive; biotechniques are used to produce a population's racial (and other) identity and in this way to racialize the inhabited space, while space itself helps determine the population's identity.

Over the years, Israel has continuously monitored the changing proportions of Jews and Palestinians, not only at the national level but also in each region. Israel's demographic anxiety has manifested itself prominently in the state's spatial policies in the northern district, especially in the Galilee, where nearly two-thirds of the population after the 1948 War were Palestinians. This demographic imbalance led the state to devote massive resources to Judaize the land, and after decades of investment in the northern district, the proportion of the Palestinian population was reduced to 54 percent. As a consequence of the state's policy of halting all Palestinian development, Palestinians in northern Israel currently reside in 78 localities, all of which existed before 1948, while Jews reside in 307 localities, mostly established since 1948. Even though Israel did not succeed in creating a Jewish majority in this district, the size of the Jewish population relocated to the area has been sufficient to advance three major objectives. First, the establishment of Jewish towns and farming communities has helped restrict Palestinian development, transforming their villages into enclaves. Second, it has enabled Jews to exercise effective control over the land confiscated after the 1948 War and thus fulfill the plan to Judaize it. This was particularly important in the Galilee,[21] parts of which had been allotted to the Palestinian state in the 1947 United Nations (UN) Partition Plan. Israel's Labor-led government believed that if Palestinian development were left unchecked in the Galilee, it could potentially lead to demands for Palestinian autonomy or even Palestinian independence, a concern that has also informed the West Bank settlement project. Third, the Jewish civilians who were relocated to these areas served, wittingly or not, as a vital component in the state's apparatus of ethnic policing and surveillance.

The biospatial strategies adopted in the south, which is Israel's largest geographical region, known in Hebrew as the Negev (al-Naqab in Arabic), were even more pronounced. An estimated ninety thousand Palestinian Bedouin inhabited the region in 1947, but only eleven thousand remained in the years following the state's establishment, the rest having been pushed across the borders.[22] Moreover, not long after the 1948 War, Israel concentrated the majority of the remaining Palestinian Bedouin population into a restricted, 1,500-square-kilometer area known as al-Siyaj (meaning "fence" in Arabic) located in the northeastern Negev, the region's least arable land. After the military governorate ended, forced urbanization of the Bedouin community began.

For Israel, concentrating the Bedouin in urban areas meant that it could seize almost all of the Negev's land while concomitantly consolidating its control over the population. Indeed, after 1969, the state established seven Bedouin-only towns within the Siyaj area—the only Palestinian communities that have been established since 1948—touting them as paradigms of modernity.[23] The allocation of plots of land within these hastily fabricated towns was, however, contingent on the Bedouin surrendering at least some of their land claims, which drove almost half of the population to refuse to move into these designated towns.[24] Indeed, a significant portion of the Bedouin population remains in villages unrecognized by the state—villages whose borders are not demarcated and whose houses, unlike the Palestinian villages in the north, are dispersed over a relatively large area of confiscated land. The CBS does not include these Bedouin villages in the count of localities and asks the people inhabiting them to indicate the name of their tribe instead of an address, thus revealing, yet again, the CBS's power of interpellation—namely, the imposition of categories and classifications that constitute people as socially recognizable subjects. Simultaneously, this is how the CBS helps sever the Palestinian bio from space.

Attaining effective control of the Negev's land proved difficult also because of its size, which is five times larger than the entire northern district. Even though Israel took over Bedouin land for military training and gave local kibbutzim unusually large agricultural plots—less for their economic value and more in order to prevent Bedouin from settling on them—the Negev's size limited the state's ability to Judaize the whole terrain. As we will see, in recent years Israel has adopted new policies to mitigate this situation. Nonetheless, due to the overall success of its dispossessive practices, many strategies were exported to the West Bank following the 1967 War.

Territorial Expansion

On 27 June 1967, the day East Jerusalem was annexed by Israel, a group of Israeli archaeologists were appointed as supervisors of the archaeological and historical sites in the West Bank. In a press release issued by the military, these sites were defined as Israel's "national and cultural property." This act, which may appear relatively benign, nonetheless reveals that the ideology of a Greater Israel—namely, that the West Bank was part of the biblical Land of Israel and therefore Jewish, and should consequently be integrated into the state—informed Israel's policies from the moment it occupied these territories. Alongside this messianic ideology, a militaristic ideology that considered the West Bank to be a defensive corridor against invasion from the east also gained ground after the fighting had subsided. The spatial significance of the region was emphasized by the proponents of both of these ideologies, while the connection between the indigenous Palestinian inhabitants and their land was similarly and conveniently ignored.[25]

Israel, however, annexed more than what had been Jordanian Jerusalem, the main city in the West Bank, but also an area eleven times larger, including twenty-eight adjacent Palestinian villages with a total population of nearly 70,000. The "united" city's post-1967 borders were drawn according to a racial-spatial logic in order to maximize its urban territory while integrating the smallest possible number of Palestinians. Nonetheless, the city's population grew from 198,000 to about 266,000 residents overnight, while its ethnic makeup was transformed from 98 percent Jewish to 74 percent Jewish and 26 percent Palestinian. These Palestinians were not granted citizenship but rather classified as Israeli "residents," thus enhancing Palestinian fragmentation by distinguishing them from the Palestinian citizens of Israel and from the noncitizens in the West Bank and Gaza.

Following the annexation, Israel once again adopted a two-pronged approach of confiscating the newly captured land and sending civilian emissaries to settle it. Imposing its own legal system on the city's eastern part, Israel applied land-use codes, building restrictions, and regulations on infrastructure distribution in order to expropriate Palestinian land, prevent the development of Palestinian neighborhoods and disrupt their urban continuum, and transform them into enclaves by building new Jewish neighborhoods in ways similar to the state's actions in the Galilee. As Michal Braier explains, the government created a series of inner neighborhoods to ensure Jewish territorial continuity, while simultaneously establishing outer neighborhoods in order to deliberately facilitate suburban sprawl.[26] These colonial policies blurred the lines dividing West and East Jerusalem, creating an urban fabric that, on the one hand, is geographically interwoven yet, on the other hand, preserves a strict segregation between the city's Jewish and Palestinian areas.

Moreover, the densely built satellite "neighborhoods" nearly tripled the city's Jewish population, even though, thanks to higher Palestinian fertility and to a lesser extent out-migration of Jews, in the past fifty years the share of Jews in the city has actually declined from 74 to 64 percent. The rising proportion of Palestinians in Jerusalem, viewed as nothing less than a strategic threat, led Israel to implement a "quiet deportation"[27] policy, whereby legal-bureaucratic mechanisms have been used to strip thousands of Palestinians of their residency rights. More recently, the politics of space and race has moved up yet another notch, with the government contemplating ways to redraw the city's municipal boundaries either to include more Jews from neighboring settlements within its borders or to reduce its size in order to transpose 140,000 Palestinian residents of Jerusalem to the rest of the West Bank.

While Israel took over East Jerusalem in one fell swoop through de jure annexation and the application of Israeli laws, in the West Bank, by contrast, it carried out the confiscation piecemeal by utilizing a mixture of Ottoman and British Mandatory law, regulations from the Jordanian legal systems, and orders issued by military commanders. The West Bank is about seventy miles long and thirty miles wide, an area the size of Delaware; it is circumscribed on the east by a barren plateau and on the west by the Green Line. Before the 1967 War it contained about eight hundred thousand Palestinians living in 12 urban centers and 527 rural communities, including 19 refugee camps. During the war, Israel partially "cleansed" several West Bank areas of their Palestinian inhabitants.[28] The Jordan Valley (excluding Jericho) was partially cleansed of its population because Israel wanted to secure the border with Jordan. Similarly, the Latrun enclave was depopulated of Palestinians because their villages overlooked the highway leading from Tel Aviv to Jerusalem, and the Israeli military decided to destroy them as part of what Defense Minister Moshe Dayan called the "complex framework of the unpleasant and unpopular aspects of fulfilling Zionism."[29]

Additionally, demolitions were part of a broader policy aimed at clearing part of the area adjacent to the West Bank's western border—where, for example, more than 40 percent of the dwellings in the border town Qalqilyah were demolished—as well as the entire Magharbia Quarter located in Jerusalem's Old City in front of the Haram al Sharif and the Wailing Wall.[30] All in all, about two hundred thousand people, or 25 percent of the West Bank's inhabitants, fled to Jordan during the war and its direct aftermath.[31] Similar to the policies within the Green Line (the "good Israel"), Palestinians have not been allowed to build a single new village or town in the West Bank over the course of the fifty-year occupation, even as the population has grown fivefold.[32]

Israel has used several complementary methods to seize Palestinian land in the West Bank, many of which had their basis in the methods first developed within its pre-1967 borders. These include declaring land absentee property, transforming swaths of land into nature reserves, and claiming that land has been left uncultivated for many years or simply declaring that a particular area is needed for military or public use (where "public" denotes Jewish). Using these methods, by 1987 Israel managed to restrict Palestinians to living within a territory that composed less than 60 percent of the West Bank; consequently, and not unlike their co-patriots within the Green Line, many occupied Palestinians have lost all or parts of their land. This de jure land grab has translated into de facto annexation through the establishment of Jewish settlements, the construction of bypass roads, and eventually the erection of the separation barrier. Often the order of this process was actually reversed, whereby the de facto land seizure preceded de jure confiscation, as was the case with many "unauthorized" settlements.

While many observers view the Judaization of the West Bank as the outcome of a right-wing messianic ideology, the policy was, in fact, first enacted by Labor Zionists. Israel began Judaizing the land by establishing military bases in the region immediately following the war and then gradually converting some of them into settlements. One-fourth of the settlements that currently exist were built within the occupation's first decade, and if we include those that were already planned, almost one-third of the settlements existing today were initiated by the Labor Party before it lost the 1977 elections.[33] Young secular men and women, mostly aligned with the Labor Party, established the majority of the Jewish settlements during this first period, many of them located in the Jordan Valley, which was viewed as essential to Israel's security. Simultaneously, the Labor government allowed religious Jews, whose desires and interests were shaped by the messianic ideology of a Greater Israel, to establish a few settlements in densely populated parts of the West Bank.

Two points need to be emphasized here. First, even though the government presented the religious settlers as contrarians, in practically every case the two opposing camps ended up cooperating, with the government actually providing financial and other assistance to the settlers. Second, from the very beginning, settlements were established not only according to a military-strategic logic but also according to a national-religious one. Not unlike Jewish citizens in the Galilee, these West Bank settlers and settlements, which are usually located on hilltops overlooking Palestinian villages, serve as a means of social control. Not only do they restrict Palestinian development and movement, they also serve as mechanisms of civilian surveillance and ethnic policing.[34]

Once the right-wing Likud party assumed power, the cooperation between the government and the settler leadership—Jewish fundamentalists with clear goals and astute political skills—became even more intimate, and as a result, settlement construction was accelerated. Sixty-three new settlements were established during the seven-year period between 1978 and 1984. The Likud government's goal was to Judaize the entire "Land of Israel" and prevent the establishment of a Palestinian state, an option that seemed viable following the 1979 peace treaty with Egypt.[35] To accomplish these ends, other settlements were placed in close proximity to the Green Line, in an effort to attract nonideological Jews to settle in the West Bank. Indeed, while a minority of the settlers were religious fundamentalists, most were simply looking for a suburban home at an affordable price located not too far from the urban centers. To encourage their resettlement, the Israeli government, especially in the post-1977 period, proffered economic perks to anyone willing to relocate to the West Bank. Notwithstanding these policies, during the occupation's first two decades Israel failed to populate the West Bank with large numbers of Jews.

When Israelis and Palestinians first formally met to negotiate peace in 1991, twenty-four years into the occupation and fourteen years since the first Likud-led government, there were 132,000 settlers in East Jerusalem but only 90,000 settlers in the rest of the West Bank. Twenty-five years later, the number of settlers in East Jerusalem had increased by about 60 percent, while that of settlers in the West Bank has more than quadrupled, and this despite the freeze on new settlement construction to which Israeli was forced to agree during the Oslo process. An analysis of the increase in number of Jewish settlers in the West Bank during these years reveals that the level of Jewish migration to the West Bank does not fluctuate according to the changing composition of the Israeli government—led by Likud or Labor—but rather increases during periods of negotiations between Israelis and Palestinians, when there is less violence. This suggests that "the peace process" actually bolsters Israel's settlement project, while violence impedes it.[36]

Moreover, under the Oslo Accords, the West Bank was divided into Areas A, B, and C, which were drawn according to a biospatial logic and determined the distribution of powers by creating internal boundaries, each one with its own specific laws and regulations.[37] In Areas A and B, which were more densely populated with Palestinians, the Palestinian Authority was given more responsibilities, while in Area C, which contained almost 60 percent of the land and only about 4 percent of the Palestinian population, Israel retained full responsibility for security and public order, as well as for civil issues relating to territory (e.g., planning and zoning). Oslo reveals that the biospatial logic underlying Israeli settler colonialism not only racializes space but also divides and organizes it, thereby determining, in this case, its contiguity. Because Areas A and B were densely populated by Palestinians, they were divided into 131 clusters, scattered like an archipelago across the terrain and separated by strategic corridors that facilitated Israeli control, whereas Area C remained contiguous. It is also in the context of such biospatial strategies that one needs to understand the over one hundred Jewish outposts that were erected in the West Bank since the beginning of the new millennium. These outposts were built with government assistance, but labeled "unauthorized" because Israel had promised the US administration not to establish new settlements. They are populated by relatively few Jews—about ten thousand—many of them second- and third-generation settlers, but they manage to ensure effective control of large swaths of land.

The way Israel enumerates its population bolsters this logic. Since the 1967 War, the state includes in its population count all the people residing within the pre-1967 borders and annexed East Jerusalem, but in the West Bank it includes only those residing in Jewish settlements, leaving out the indigenous population. Statistical virtuosities of this kind—counting Jewish residents while ignoring the existence of millions of Palestinians within the same region—provide a distorted picture of reality. Such misrepresentations are exacerbated given that Israel includes the Palestinian population in East Jerusalem (which was also occupied in 1967 but had been annexed de jure shortly thereafter) in its count. These practices reflect and help reproduce the de facto annexation of this region by engendering a biospatial link between Jews and the land, while severing the Palestinians' connection to it.

Following Oslo, Israel has made immense strides in the demographic race in the West Bank. Of the 430,000 settlers living in the West Bank at the end of 2018 (excluding East Jerusalem), approximately 150,000 are ultra-Orthodox Jews. This settler group has grown thirtyfold—from 5 percent of the settler population in 1991 to 35 percent today—and is the major cause of the exponential growth of Jews in the region. The ultra-Orthodox community became Israel's demographic silver bullet, facilitating the rapid racialization of space. Not unlike its policies of moving the Mizrahi Jews to the periphery in pre-1967 Israel, the government exploited the poverty of the ultra-Orthodox and offered them inexpensive housing and an array of other subsidies as an incentive to relocate to the West Bank. In this case, however, the government also took advantage of this community's extremely high birthrate of approximately seven children per woman, thereby guaranteeing that the Jewish settlers' population growth rate is considerably higher than the Palestinian growth rate. Indeed, natural growth (births minus deaths) rather than immigration from pre-1967 Israel is now the main cause of settler proliferation. Consequently, even if the Israeli government were to stop moving its citizenry to the West Bank, the number of settlers would continue to increase substantially and the space would increasingly become more Jewish.

The Colonial Leviathan Recoils

Having succeeded in Judaizing large parts of the West Bank, Israel has now turned back inward and, in a boomerang-like trajectory, is now completing the project it left unfinished in the Negev. Approximately 695,000 people currently live in the Negev, which contains about 60 percent of the country's land but is home to only 8 percent of its population. Of this population in the Negev, 35 percent are Palestinians, the vast majority of them Bedouin, whose number has grown from about 11,000 in 1949 to about 230,000 in 2018, thanks to their extremely high fertility rate (similar to that of ultra-Orthodox Jews). Nonetheless, only 18 localities out of the 144 in the region are designated for the Bedouin community, while about 65,000 Bedouin citizens continue to reside in 35 villages classified as "unrecognized" by the Israeli government (see figure 6.1).[38] This means that these Bedouin are prohibited from connecting their houses to the electricity grid or the water and sewage systems. Construction regulations are strictly enforced, and in 2018 alone 2,326 Bedouin homes and animal pens—usually referred to by the government as "structures"—were demolished.[39]

No paved roads lead to the villages, and signposts on main roads indicating their location are prohibited.[40] Moreover, the villages do not appear on maps. As a matter of official policy these localities do not exist. Demographically their inhabitants (who are Israeli citizens) are linked to tribes rather than to a locality, thus officially erasing

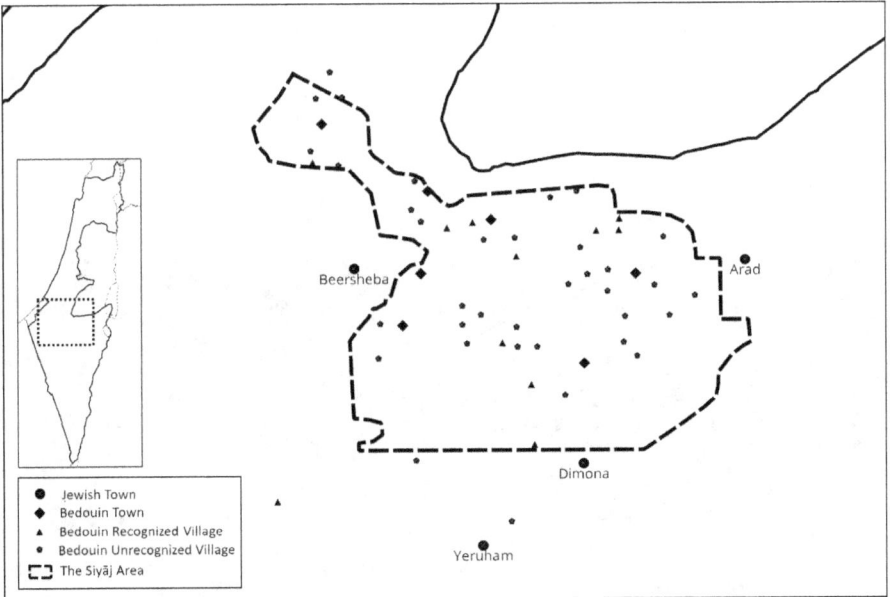

Figure 6.1. Bedouin towns and villages in the Negev. Source: Michal Rotem, Negev Coexistence Forum.

their connection to their land. Indeed, three of the eighteen Bedouin localities that were recently recognized by the state were considered "places" rather than "localities" in the state registry because according to the official records they were deemed empty. Informed by biotechniques that sever this group from their land, Israel's actions indicate that it plans to demolish most of the unrecognized villages and to relocate at least thirty thousand inhabitants into already established Bedouin towns.

While the confiscation of the Negev's land was accomplished in the state's early years, over the past decade the government has intensified its attempts to strengthen its effective control of this area and to Judaize it fully. The production of the biospatial link, which effectively racializes space, is achieved through the CBS's classification and the by now familiar twofold strategy of dispossessing and settling. On the one hand, the government is restricting Bedouin development within the confined borders of the towns it created and the eleven villages it recently recognized, while transferring many of its military bases to the Negev, deploying a draconian policy of home demolitions in the unrecognized villages, and until 2007, spraying "illegal" agricultural plots with poison. Since 2007, such plots have simply been plowed over (see figure 6.2). Simultaneously, the Israeli government has been reinforcing the Jewish presence on the ground, establishing new Jewish settlements and encouraging Jews to move to the region, while planting thousands of "Jewish trees" provided by the Jewish National Fund on large strips of Bedouin land.[41]

Initially the government decided to allocate plots of land to some sixty Jewish families, scattering farms across the Negev terrain in order to restrict and circum-

Figure 6.2. Israeli authorities with pickup trucks and tractors plowing "illegal" Bedouin fields east of Lakiya, 5 February 2014. Source: Michal Rotem, Negev Coexistence Forum.

scribe the space that its non-Jewish citizens could occupy. What is unique about these farms is that they connect existing strategies of Judaizing the land with neoliberal entrepreneurship projects. These new farms stifle Bedouin expansion as they prosper from boutique guesthouses and homemade wines and cheese catering to the bourgeois tastes of Tel Aviv tourists. Thus, space not only becomes increasingly Jewish, but it also acquires a specific entrepreneurial valence. More recently, the government has decided to build fifteen additional Jewish settlements in the region so as to consolidate the Judaization of the land. Indeed, Blueprint Negev, a Jewish National Fund flagship project, aims to attract 250,000 Jews to the Negev in the coming years.

An illustration of how the colonial leviathan is turning back inward is perhaps most obvious in Umm al-Hiran, a village of about 350 Bedouin citizens that was destroyed in 2018 and will be replaced by a Jewish settlement called Hiran. Just a few kilometers away from this Bedouin village, about thirty religious Jewish families have been living in a makeshift gated community, waiting patiently for the government to expel the Bedouin families from their homes. This gated Jewish community is made up of houses scattered around a playground and a new kindergarten. Needless to say, this bucolic setting is both unnerving and surreal, considering its violent undertow. Ironically, the people who are destined to dispossess the residents of Umm al-Hiran are West Bank settlers who made an ideological decision to return to Israel to "redeem Jewish land" from "Bedouin invaders." Because the land itself is constituted as Jewish, the Bedouin who have inhabited it for decades are rendered "invaders," thus revealing not only the classic colonial inversion between the colonist and the colonized,[42] but also how the spatial-racial nexus produces the "biocriminal"—the person who is deemed a felon due to the racial status ascribed to him or her.[43] In Israel, Foucault's notion of the biocriminal is further developed, since space itself is racialized and the racial mismatch between space and the subject who occupies it is sufficient to transform the latter into a criminal.

Conclusions

One obvious conclusion when examining the political ecology of the Jewish state is that the common tendency to single out Israel's policies in the occupied West Bank and East Jerusalem as representing an epiphenomenon or some kind of deviation is misguided. In the past seventy years, four related strategies have governed Israel's preoccupation with biospatial policies with remarkable regularity and little change. First, Israel has adopted biotechniques and has developed a series of classifications to help constitute Jews and Israelis while distinguishing them from Palestinians. The second strategy—even if only partially achieved—has aimed to create and maintain a solid Jewish majority not only in the entire territory between the Jordan Valley and the Mediterranean Sea, but also in each and every district (except Area A). The third has been the country's extreme residential segregation, where over 99 percent of the 1,214 localities listed by the CBS are either exclusively Jewish or Palestinian. This segregation is crucial to the state's biospatial project, since it not only encourages the Jewish localities to expand across space while stifling the development of the Palestinian localities, but it also helps ascribe and inscribe Jewishness to and in space. These three strategies inform the fourth, namely, the Judaization of land.

There are, of course, differences between the demographic and spatial strategies introduced on either side of the Green Line. Even though land has been seized using very similar mechanisms and the state's efforts to enhance effective control by dispossessing the colonized and settling the Jews are nearly identical in all areas under its control, Jews and Palestinians are segregated differently in each region. Due to these differences, the efforts to Judaize the land are beginning to produce contradictions within the pre-1967 borders that have yet to materialize in the West Bank. Consider Nazareth Illit (Upper Nazareth, recently renamed Nof Hagalil), a Jewish town that was built in 1957 on a hilltop overlooking Palestinian Nazareth. Notwithstanding the Jewish town's role in the Judaization of the Galilee, the acute housing shortage propelled by restrictions on the expansion of Palestinian municipal boundaries and on housing construction within Nazareth and nearby villages has led middle-class Palestinians to move to Nazareth Illit. Despite the fierce opposition of many of its Jewish residents and their elected officials, by the end of 2016 Palestinians made up 25 percent of the town's population of over forty thousand.

A similar process, albeit on a much smaller scale, has been identified in some of the Jewish "neighborhoods" in East Jerusalem.[44] The significant point is that the movement of Palestinian citizens to Jewish cities "contaminates" the Jewish city's purity and thus undermines, even if very gradually, the biospatial link and the construction of space as Jewish. The strict segregation in the West Bank does not allow for such "spatial miscegenation" processes. Indeed, the settlements in the West Bank consist only of Jews.

It is precisely in this context that one should understand the July 2018 legislation of Israel's "Nation-State Law."[45] Until 2018, Israel's mistreatment of Palestinians inside the pre-1967 borders, including the dispossession of their lands, stopped short of creating a legal structure that explicitly favored Jews. Rather, as we have seen above, for many years Israeli settlement policies have been implemented using seemingly racially neutral laws that nevertheless enabled the transfer of land from Palestinian to Jewish ownership and control.[46] The Nationality Law has changed this. Section 7a of the new law is not much more than a description of Israel's actions and policies since 1948: "The state views the development of *Jewish* [emphasis added] settlement as a national value and will act to encourage and promote its establishment and consolidation." Clearly, what Israel has done informally for seventy years is now the law of the land. Perhaps this is why liberal Zionists criticized this law first and foremost as "unnecessary" and "provocative"—for in the past this policy of favoring Jews over

Palestinians was achieved without the introduction of blatant racial language within the law. Hence, the law is deemed "unnecessary" and "provocative" not because it will lead to dramatic changes on the ground, but because it uncovers the true nature of the State of Israel.

Israel's obsession with demography and this obsession's intricate connection to space predate the establishment of the state. Indeed, the major distinguishing feature of the different camps within Zionism relates to the political significance each camp ascribes to demography and territory. Labor Zionists have always aspired to create a homogeneous Jewish society and, therefore, eventually preferred demography over geography, often resisting their desire for territorial expansion.[47] The Zionist right, by contrast, wanted the fledgling Jewish state to include parts of the East Bank (i.e., Jordan), thus emphasizing geography over demography. Over the years the language has changed somewhat, but the guiding principles continue to be the same. Liberal Zionists who currently support territorial compromise champion the creation of a Palestinian state primarily because they want to minimize the number of Palestinians within Israel's territory. Even for this camp, Palestinian basic rights and UN resolutions are of secondary importance, since the logic overriding everything else is biospatial: guaranteeing a solid Jewish majority within a given space.

By way of conclusion, it may be important to state the obvious. Historically, states have frequently connected the bio with the spatial since at least the eighteenth century, at times with horrific consequences. Contemporary manifestations also abound, ranging from the biospatial strategies Europe has recently adopted to deal with the massive refugee crisis, through US president Donald Trump's Muslim ban and asylum policies, and all the way to Myanmar, where Rohingya Muslims are being ethnically cleansed from Rakhine State. Nonetheless, excavating the specificities of each case remains vital. Before Israel's establishment, for instance, the 1937 Peel Commission and the 1947 UN Partition Plan clearly based their recommendations on a biospatial logic (i.e., the division of territory according to certain population classifications produced by the colonial power). The difference between these partition plans and the Oslo archipelago is instructive, however, since in the latter the biospatial logic was used not to harness and maximize the population's demographic and economic potential or to enable self-determination but rather to guarantee the ongoing subjugation of the colonized Palestinians.

Notwithstanding this difference, both the long history of biotechniques and the different geographical settings in which they are currently being mobilized suggest that Israel is not really an innovator. The novelty of Israeli colonialism is that for decades it has not merely managed to survive but has actually flourished. This is because it receives the unconditional support of almost all liberal democracies, a striking phenomenon in the postcolonial era that is due in part to these countries' perception of Israel as a democracy. The tragic irony is that Israel's biospatial politics have given birth to a reality of a single, Jewish-Palestinian, apartheid state.

Yinon Cohen is a professor of sociology and Yerushalmi Professor of Israel and Jewish Studies at Columbia University. His recent publications focus on income inequality and socioeconomic ethnic gaps in Israel and are available on his webpage, yinoncohen.com.

Neve Gordon is a professor of international law at Queen Mary University of London. He is the author of *Israel's Occupation* (2008) and coauthor of *The Human Right to Dominate* (2015) and *Human Shields: A History of People in the Line of Fire* (2020).

Notes

This is a revised and updated version of Yinon Cohen and Neve Gordon, "Israel's Bio-Spatial Politics: Territory, Demography and Effective Control," *Public Culture* 30, no. 2 (2018): 199–220. We acknowledge equal contribution and would like to thank Omer Bartov, Michal Braier, Isaac Cohen, Yosef Grodzinsky, Nicola Perugini, Moriel Ram, Michal Rotem, Catherine Rottenberg, and Niza Yanay for their comments and suggestions. Neve Gordon acknowledges the support of funding from the European Union's Horizon 2020 Research and Innovation Programme MSCA-IF-2015-701891.

1. Shlomo Gazit, *The Carrot and the Stick: Israel's Policy in Judaea and Samaria, 1967–68*, trans. Reuvik Danielli (Washington, DC: B'nai B'rith Books, 1995).
2. Edward Said, *The Question of Palestine* (New York: Vintage Books, 1980).
3. Michel Foucault, *"Society Must Be Defended": Lectures at the Collège de France, 1975–1976*, ed. Mauro Bertani and Alexandro Fontana, trans. David Macey (New York: Macmillan, 2003).
4. Ghazi-Walid Falah, "Dynamics and Patterns of the Shrinking of Arab Lands in Palestine," *Political Geography* 22, no. 2 (2003): 179–209.
5. Yinon Cohen, "Spatial Politics and Socioeconomic Gaps between Jews and Palestinians in Israel," *Israeli Sociology* 17, no. 1 (2015): 7–31 (in Hebrew).
6. Since Israel's withdrawal from the Gaza Strip in 2005, the methods through which it is controlled—without permanent presence on the ground—are radically different from the methods used in the West Bank. We therefore do not discuss the Gaza Strip in this chapter.
7. Patrick Wolfe, "Settler Colonialism and the Elimination of the Native," *Journal of Genocide Research* 8, no. 4 (2006): 387–409.
8. Yinon Cohen, "From Haven to Heaven: Changes Patterns of Immigration to Israel," in *Challenging Ethnic Citizenship: German and Israeli Perspectives on Immigration*, ed. Daniel Levy and Yfaat Weiss (New York: Berghahn Books, 2002), 36–56.
9. Elia Zureik, *The Palestinians in Israel: A Study in Internal Colonialism* (New York: Routledge, 1979).
10. Ahmad H. Sa'di, *Thorough Surveillance: The Genesis of Israeli Policies of Population Management, Surveillance, and Political Control towards the Palestinian Minority* (Manchester: Manchester University Press, 2013).
11. Rassem Khamaisi, "Mechanism of Land Control and Territorial Judaization of Israel," in *In the Name of Security*, ed. Majid Al-Haj and Uri Ben-Eliezer (Haifa: Haifa University Press, 2003, in Hebrew), 421–49.
12. Geremy Forman and Alexandre Kedar, "From Arab Land to 'Israel Lands': The Legal Dispossession of the Palestinians Displaced by Israel in the Wake of 1948," *Environment and Planning D: Society and Space* 22, no. 6 (2004): 809–30.
13. Alexandre Kedar and Oren Yiftachel, "Land Regime and Social Relations in Israel," in *Realizing Property Rights*, vol. 1 of *Swiss Human Rights Book*, ed. Hernando de Soto and Francis Cheneval (Zurich: Rüffer and Rub, 2006), 129–46.
14. According to Ela Shohat, the resemblance of these Jews to the Palestinians enhanced their anti-Palestinian sentiments and strengthened their non-Arab identity. For an elaborate explanation of this

claim, see Ella Shohat, "Sephardim in Israel: Zionism from the Standpoint of Its Jewish Victims," *Social Text*, no. 19–20 (1988): 1–35.
15. Kedar and Yiftachel, "Land Regime and Social Relations in Israel."
16. Kenneth Prewitt, *What Is Your Race? The Census and Our Flawed Efforts to Classify Americans* (Princeton: Princeton University Press, 2013), 217.
17. Shohat, "Sephardim in Israel."
18. Cohen, "From Haven to Heaven."
19. *Uzi Ornan et al. v. Ministry of Interior et al.* # 6092/07; clauses 58, 14.
20. Ian Lustick, "Israel as a Non-Arab State: The Political Implications for Mass Immigration of Non-Jews," *Middle East Journal* 53, no. 3 (1999): 417–33.
21. According to Ilan Pappé, *The Forgotten Palestinians: A History of the Palestinians in Israel* (New Haven: Yale University Press, 2013), 126, "*Yihud Hagalil* (Judaizing the Galilee) was a clandestine programme until 1976, when it became an open slogan of the Housing Ministry." The goal of Judaizing the Galilee and other regions has been to both transfer lands from Palestinians to Jews *and* to achieve solid Jewish majority in each region. See also Naama Blatman-Thomas, "Commuting for Rights: Circular Mobilities and Regional Identities of Palestinians in a Jewish-Israeli Town," *Geoforum* 78 (2017): 22–32. Though the term itself—Judaizing—no longer appears in government documents, some government ministers keep using this overtly racist slogan. As late as 2018, the minister of justice, Ayelet Shaked, claimed that "'Judaizing the Galilee' is not an obscenity." See *Calcalist*, 12 February 2018, https://www.calcalist.co.il/local/articles/0,7340,L-3731663,00.html.
22. Hanina Porat, *The Bedouin-Arab in the Negev between Migration and Urbanization, 1948–1973* (Beersheba: Negev Center for Regional Development, Ben-Gurion University, 2009, in Hebrew).
23. Michal Rotem and Neve Gordon, "Bedouin *Ṣumud* and the Struggle for Education," *Journal of Palestine Studies* 46, no. 4 (2017): 7–27.
24. Ahmad Amara, "The Negev Land Question: Between Denial and Recognition," *Journal of Palestine Studies* 42, no. 4 (2013): 27–47.
25. Neve Gordon, *Israel's Occupation* (Berkeley: University of California Press, 2008).
26. Michal Braier, "Zones of Transformation? Informal Construction and Independent Zoning Plans in East Jerusalem," *Environment and Planning A* 45, no. 11 (2013): 2700–2716.
27. B'Tselem, "The Quiet Deportation Continues: Revocation of Residency and Denial of Social Rights of East Jerusalem Palestinians," https://www.btselem.org/publications/summaries/199809_quiet_deportation_continues.
28. The removal of the population and land-grabbing policies in the Golan Heights, which we do not discuss in this paper, were more extreme. Of the 128,000 Syrians who lived on the Golan before the 1967 War, only 5 percent remained in the area in its aftermath, and of the 139 Syrian agricultural villages and 61 individual farms registered prior to the war, only 7 villages were not destroyed. See Neve Gordon and Moriel Ram, "Ethnic Cleansing and the Formation of Settler Colonial Geographies," *Political Geography* 53 (2016): 20–29. Currently the occupied Golan Heights is home to 22,000 Jews residing in 32 settlements and 25,000 Arabs (mostly Druze) residing in 5 villages.
29. Tom Segev, *1967: Israel, the War, and the Year That Transformed the Middle East*, trans. Jessica Cohen (New York: Metropolitan Books, 2007), 410.
30. Avi Raz, *The Bride and the Dowry: Israel, Jordan, and the Palestinians in the Aftermath of the June 1967 War* (New Haven: Yale University Press, 2012).
31. Gazit, *The Carrot and the Stick*.
32. The sole exception is the town of Rawabi, which is now under construction near Ramallah.
33. Gordon, *Israel's Occupation*.
34. Eyal Weizman, *Hollow Land: Israel's Architecture of Occupation* (London: Verso, 2012).
35. Seth Anziska, *Preventing Palestine: A Political History from Camp David to Oslo* (Princeton: Princeton University Press, 2018).
36. Neve Gordon and Yinon Cohen, "Western Interests, Israeli Unilateralism, and the Two-State Solution," *Journal of Palestine Studies* 41, no. 3 (2012): 6–18.
37. Edward Said, *The End of the Peace Process: Oslo and After* (New York: Vintage, 2007).

38. Rotem and Gordon, "Bedouin *Ṣumud* and the Struggle for Education."
39. Negev Coexistence Forum for Civil Equality, *Mechanism for Dispossession and Intimidation: Demolition Policy in Arab Bedouin Communities in the Negev/Naqab*, June 2019, https://www.dukium.org/wp-content/uploads/2019/07/Demolition-Report-Eng.2018-1.pdf.
40. Mansour Nasasra, *The Naqab Bedouins: A Century of Politics and Resistance* (New York: Columbia University Press, 2017).
41. Rotem and Gordon, "Bedouin *Ṣumud* and the Struggle for Education."
42. Nicola Perugini and Neve Gordon, *The Human Right to Dominate* (New York: Oxford University Press, 2015).
43. Foucault, "*Society Must Be Defended.*"
44. Wendy Pullan and Haim Yacobi, "Jerusalem's Colonial Space as Paradox: Palestinians Living in the Settlements," in *Normalizing Occupation: The Politics of Everyday Life in the West Bank Settlements*, ed. Marco Allegra, Ariel Handel, and Erez Maggor (Bloomington: Indiana University Press, 2017), 193–210.
45. See also in this context Raef Zreik, "The Day the 'Jewish State Bill' would take effect . . . ," *Tarabut Online*, 1 March 2018, http://www.tarabut.info/en/articles/article/israel-nationality-law-2018/.
46. For Israel's discriminatory laws, see "The Discriminatory Laws Data Base," *Adalah*, 25 September 2017, https://www.adalah.org/en/content/view/7771.
47. Gershon Shafir and Yoav Peled, *Being Israeli: The Dynamics of Multiple Citizenship* (Cambridge: Cambridge University Press, 2002).

Select Bibliography

Braier, Michal. "Zones of Transformation? Informal Construction and Independent Zoning Plans in East Jerusalem." *Environment and Planning A* 45, no. 11 (2013): 2700–2716.

Cohen, Yinon. "From Haven to Heaven: Changes Patterns of Immigration to Israel." In *Challenging Ethnic Citizenship: German and Israeli Perspectives on Immigration*, edited by Daniel Levy and Yfaat Weiss, 36–56. New York: Berghahn Books, 2002.

———. "Spatial Politics and Socioeconomic Gaps between Jews and Palestinians in Israel." *Israeli Sociology* 17, no. 1 (2015): 7–31. In Hebrew.

Falah, Ghazi-Walid. "Dynamics and Patterns of the Shrinking of Arab Lands in Palestine." *Political Geography* 22, no. 2 (2003): 179–209.

Gordon, Neve. *Israel's Occupation*. Berkeley: University of California Press, 2008.

Gordon, Neve, and Yinon Cohen. "Western Interests, Israeli Unilateralism, and the Two-State Solution." *Journal of Palestine Studies* 41, no. 3 (2012): 6–18.

Perugini, Nicola, and Neve Gordon. *The Human Right to Dominate*. New York: Oxford University Press, 2015.

Rotem, Michal, and Neve Gordon. "Bedouin *Ṣumud* and the Struggle for Education." *Journal of Palestine Studies* 46, no. 4 (2017): 7–27.

Sa'di, Ahmad H. *Thorough Surveillance: The Genesis of Israeli Policies of Population Management, Surveillance, and Political Control towards the Palestinian Minority*. Manchester: Manchester University Press, 2013.

Zreik, Raef. "The Day the 'Jewish State Bill' Would Take Effect. . . ." *Tarabut Online*, 1 March 2018. http://www.tarabut.info/en/articles/article/israel-nationality-law-2018/.

CHAPTER 7

COME TO NETANYA
A NEW READING OF ISRAEL'S PLANNING HISTORY

NOAH HYSLER RUBIN

Introduction

What is the secret of Netanya's magic?

>Its chosen location—whereby Netanya, like the tribe of Zebulun, "dwells by the haven of the sea," embracing great water and situated on blessed ground from which beautiful and fruitful trees grow.
>
>The vision of its creation—in that, since the days of its genesis, every soul within it shares the supreme recognition that greater Netanya is a precious link in the unbroken chain of the dream of generations, to restore the genius and the pride of our nation in its historic place of birth.
>
>The talent of its making—since [Netanya was] not meant to be a night shelter for passersby, but a fortress for the Yishuv and a secure stronghold for the return from the Diaspora. The people of Netanya are building a city upon its ruins [עיר על תילה], within which the people of this generation and all those that follow it will be blessed.
>
>And above all it is stirred by a profound belief that within the spacious kingdom of Judah, Netanya shall become a great city [עיר ואם] for God and for man.[1]

With these poetic words, one of Netanya's founders and eventually its first mayor, Oved Ben-Ami, described his vision of the city in a 1937 brochure advertising the town and its merits. Although it was an entirely new city, Netanya was depicted as the epitome of the Jewish return to Zion, as a reincarnation of the biblical promise of Jacob to his sons, and finally, as the coastal equivalent of ancient Jerusalem, the focus of Jewish yearning. It is almost self-evident to apply the notion of return to the Holy Land to the establishment of Netanya, a modern Jewish undertaking in the land of the ancient Hebrews. Told in biblical terms, the story of Netanya appears as a typical, albeit exaggerated, local manifestation of the nation's return to the land.

Netanya's short history is not well researched and so far has been recorded mainly in one urban monograph that relies heavily on personal memoirs, local biographies, centenary books, and annual publications.[2] This lacuna, unfortunately, reflects the historiography of Israeli cities as a whole, where other than in Jerusalem, Tel Aviv, and Haifa, much is still left to be discovered. Regarding Netanya, this lacuna might be explained by the fact that although it was established by prominent public figures, at the time their actions were ignored because of the predominant Zionist narrative's preoccupation with the agricultural endeavors of its leaders.

Moreover, at the time of Netanya's establishment, the "true" new Zionist city of Afula was also founded. The story of Netanya, as told today, resembles Israeli urban history in another way: recounting the story of a society settling into a land it regarded as empty and allegedly awaiting the miraculous return of its long-gone original, indigenous inhabitants, who would bring about, through them, its rebirth and reawakening—a story that overlooks the actual conditions within which this settlement took place. The story of Netanya thus fails to convey the harsh discrepancies between the settling Jews, the Arab inhabitants, and British rule. In terms of planning history, this implies ignoring the conflict in favor of urban images, sensitivities, and eventually design.

However, apart from Afula, Netanya was the only Jewish city established at the time as a new city, planned by Jews for themselves, and then planned again by a leading British official. Moreover, Netanya's founders were prolific writers and keenly aware of their initiative's symbolic importance and consequently of its documentation. Netanya's municipal historical archive provides one of the richest and best-preserved documentation of any city in Israel, where every event in the city's development was recorded, celebrated, and made public in daily papers, journals, and the memoirs of its inhabitants.

The goal of this chapter is to suggest a new reading of Netanya's early urban development by introducing concepts from settler colonialism and indigenous studies into the analysis of its urban planning and thus to propose a new framework for writing Israeli urban history overall. The textual analysis is carried out by comparing the terminology used by the settlers of Netanya to that employed by other established settler colonial societies, a terminology that was ironically derived from biblical notions and paradigms of a return to the land—originally conceived as the Holy Land. As will be shown, the same tactics used by settler colonialists in Australia and in New England—namely, of presenting themselves as the true indigenous society settling the land by divine right—were employed by the settlers of Netanya as self-evident justification for their actions. This analysis will facilitate a re-examination of Netanya's settlers' sense of identity, as well as the meanings ascribed to and the rhetoric depicting their settlement, and the means they used for its establishment.

Additionally, by analyzing the writing that preceded and accompanied the planning process, I will shift from the conventional path of only studying urban planning by way of city plans and official documentation, to viewing the plan as resulting from its planners' sense of identity and consequent spatial perception. In other words, I am interested in examining the discourse within which the city founders operated, as well as in exposing their larger aims, for which urban planning merely served as a practical tool.

After briefly contextualizing Israel's current planning history within the historiography of urban planning worldwide, I will propose a new framework for studying Israeli urban development and planning, on the basis of existing scholarship on the links between settler colonialism, indigenous studies, and Zionism. Finally, I will analyze a specific brochure, published in Netanya in 1937, in order to examine the resulting urban image of the city as it was portrayed by its inhabitants and as it eventually made its way into the city's planning.

Israeli Planning History: A New Paradigm

Amiram Gonen's 2003 study of the development of central Israel under the British Mandate demonstrates the importance of this critical period in the urban development of Palestine, soon to become the sovereign state of Israel.[3] The Mandate period brought an urban revolution to the land. In thirty years of British rule, the number and size of cities in Palestine grew, determining the local urban hierarchy and demography for years to come. Numerous plans made for the old and new towns were based on the modern discipline of town planning, which had been practiced throughout the British Empire since its conception in Britain in 1909 and its introduction into Palestine in 1921. The effect these processes had on the existing Palestinian villages, which were engulfed and surrounded in the process, their agricultural lands diminishing, is altogether missing from this analysis.[4]

Planning in Palestine, by both the British and the Jews, is generally described by the existing scholarship as drawing on joint theoretical and practical roots, aiming for similar development and betterment of the cities.[5] Moreover, written almost entirely from the Israeli point of view, the official planning history of Israel mirrors the needs and aspirations of the growing Jewish population and is described as a Zionist phenomenon. Accordingly, planners who worked in Palestine, including British ones, are described as serving the interests of the rising Zionist entity.[6]

Planner and historian Leonie Sandercock condemns planning historiography worldwide for its descriptive approach, whereby planning is viewed as part of the Western project of modernization.[7] Planning itself, she claims, is considered unproblematic, while its opponents are seen as reactionary,[8] a reading that leads unavoidably to historical omissions and exclusions. Additionally, as highlighted by others, such scholarship tends to repeatedly present undisputed and uncontested narratives.[9]

Israeli planning history can similarly be described as descriptive, monolithic, and unavoidably triumphant.

More recent scholarship, however, has begun to incorporate the Israeli city into new studies of Zionism, on the one hand, and of the origins of the Arab-Israeli conflict, on the other. Thus, describing the lives of abandoned children in the celebrated Tel Aviv of the Mandate era, Tami Razi explores what she terms the "backyard" of the otherwise successful city, focusing on the less appealing aspects of the Zionist discourse.[10] Several studies have examined the destructive effects of the national conflict on cities,[11] while others have explored the mutual production of space by both Arabs and Jews.[12] Still, very few of these studies examine the planning of such cities, and scholarship regarding Arab planners in Palestine is almost entirely nonexistent.[13]

Introducing Settler Colonialism into Israel-Palestine Urban Studies

Oren Yiftachel has recently proposed to update critical planning theories in order to explore new ways by which the Bedouins, as an indigenous society in Israel, respond to forced planning in the Negev (al-Naqab in Arabic).[14] While promoting the reading of contemporary Israeli city planning as colonial practice, Yiftachel also demands that we read the spatial conflict as one between a local or indigenous (ילידית) population and a foreign group, in this case Jewish or Israeli.

The study of Zionism as a form of colonialism is gaining purchase, both by Israeli Zionist scholars and by Palestinians.[15] A useful analysis for my case has been provided by Ilan Pappé's study of the link between Zionism and colonialism, which uses a political lens to examine the Zionist movement's national aims, economic tools, and demographic goals.[16] Pappé compares Zionism to settler colonial societies that regarded native populations as marginal: for the Zionists too, he claims, the locals were hardly visible or were presumed to eventually recede into oblivion once progress and modernity established themselves in the newfound land. This form of modernization, as shown in an earlier critical analysis by Gershon Shafir, was embedded in the colonial relationship.[17] Alternatively, claims Pappé, Zionist notions of exploitation were presented as a desire to promote the modernization of the local native population.[18]

Pappé also highlights the use of the Bible by settler colonial societies to justify colonization and "return," along with the introduction of the idea that no matter whether the land was barren or rich with natural resources, it could only be properly cultivated by true believers.[19] For Pappé, there is a clear similarity of motivation among all colonizers: "In the period of white man's penetration into Africa and Asia," he writes, "the Jews 'returned' to their 'homeland.'"[20]

While Pappé demonstrates how these ideas were realized through the conventional Zionist forms of settlement—the moshava, the moshav, and the kibbutz (private ownership, cooperative, and communal settlements, respectively)—recent research has turned to settler colonialism in urban contexts. In a recently edited volume of the journal *Colonial Settler Studies*, Libby Porter and Oren Yiftachel highlight the importance and impact of urban settlements on the colonial process, noting that urbanization was central to the making of European settler colonial societies since their inception.[21] They argue that the establishment of towns and cities was synonymous with "development" and "progress" in the colonial endeavor and that often the settler city was portrayed as a symbol of a "new world." Moreover, they claim, the "urban" is clearly not indigenous: creating an urban world advanced the colonial nation and assisted the settlers to sharply break from indigenous histories and geographies.[22]

Firsting and Lasting: A Basis for Comparative Discourse

Libby Porter, an Australian town planner and urban geographer, has provided a sound basis for studying the spatial impact of settler colonialism. In *Unlearning the Colonial Cultures of Planning*, she investigates spatial techniques used by settler communities in Australia, New Zealand, and Canada to explore, inhabit, and finally appropriate local lands. Porter goes on to show how these methods were finally amalgamated into the modern Western notion of planning, which she perceives as an inherently colonial practice.[23]

In a similar vein, American historian Jean O'Brien's study *Firsting and Lasting: Writing Indians Out of Existence in New England* examines the goals of white settlers in New England as regards the Native American population and their spatial and social implications.[24] The texts analyzed by O'Brien chronicle the history of land transactions from the white settlers' point of view, on which they based their claim to benevolent and just colonialism, notwithstanding the resulting unfortunate fate of the Indians and especially their disappearance.[25]

O'Brien and Porter thus both analyze the process whereby foreign settlers arrived in an unknown land with the purpose of giving it meaning and claiming it as their own. Using paradigms of progress and civilization and drawing on God and the Bible for support, the settlers justified their ownership of the land over the rights of the locals and legitimized their extinction. Making themselves into the "true" and "authentic" indigenous race, the settlers invested allegedly empty lands with their own meanings, while bringing about the extinction of the locals and their own spatial meanings. Devices of land acquisition, such as mapping, land parceling, and eventually planning, provided this process with objective justifications. Finally, chronicling these practices as local history supposedly sealed the settlers' claims to the land as rightful and authentic, making white people into *Firsts* on these lands, while designating the remaining Indians in America and Australian Aboriginals as *Lasts* of their races.

The national imperative of reclaiming the Land of Israel through "recovering" its Jewish roots had been thoroughly researched.[26] Much less attention has been given to the actual process of spatial appropriation, regulation, and settlement. In fact, as I have claimed above, the history of planning Israel's cities is almost entirely devoid of such studies. The rest of this chapter explores a 1937 brochure about Netanya, in order to demonstrate the similarities between the terminology and language employed by the settlers in that city and those associated with other settler colonial societies. This should present a new paradigm for further studies in Palestinian-Israeli planning history.

Netanya: A Case Study for a New Palestinian-Israeli Planning History

Netanya was established in 1929 by second-generation descendants of the settlers of the early moshavot (Zionist agricultural settlements). Their organization, Bnei Binyamin (The Sons of Benjamin), united young farmers who sought to establish new agricultural settlements. Politically they were identified with the right wing of Jewish society in Palestine and thus separate from the left-wing settlement department of the Zionist Organization. Oved Ben-Ami was the organization's secretary.[27] As Benjamin Hyman explains, what distinguished this project was its founders' entrepreneurial spirit: they coupled their Zionist and pioneering aims with the methods of capitalist free enterprise, as distinct from the socialist Zionist Organization.[28]

Anticipated by its founders to become a possible competitor with Tel Aviv, which soon after its establishment turned into an independent township, Netanya was hailed from its very beginning as a national success. Thus, although originally it was established as an agricultural citrus colony, a plan for Netanya's urban development was produced by the Jewish engineer Moshe Kesselman as early as 1929.[29] The British also recognized the appealing location and apparent potential, paving roads leading to the new town and using it for army resorts.[30] In 1932 Netanya was declared a village, by 1934 it was declared a site in need of a town plan, and in 1935 its mayor commissioned a modern town plan from the British architect and official planning adviser, Clifford Holliday, which was approved in 1936.[31] Expanding along the plan's lines, Netanya was finally declared a city in 1948.

The story of the founding of Netanya is well recorded by its founders and, later, by Israeli historians. The story of what preceded it is much less known. The area that was bought by Ben-Ami and his partners, on 8 September 1928, comprised fourteen hundred dunams from the lands of the village of Umm Khalid, following a negotiation with the village's sheikh Saleh Hamdan.[32] Very little research has been done on the village and its inhabitants. Israeli researchers refer to Umm Khalid (or Mukhalid) mainly in reference to the 1948 Nakba and the expulsion of the Arab villagers, briefly describing their fate and generally not detailing the specific numbers of village inhabitants nor the size of the villages.[33]

In his study *All That Remains: The Palestinian Villages Occupied and Depopulated by Israel in 1948*, Walid Khalidi describes Umm Khalid as one of seventeen small villages composing the Tulkarem district, and situated fifteen kilometers west of the city of Tulkarem and less than two kilometers east of the Mediterranean shore.[34] Various historical accounts by nineteenth-century travelers, quoted by Khalidi, claim that the ancient village, destroyed by Napoleon's troops in 1799, became a rest area between al-Tantura (in the Haifa district) and Ras al-'Ayn (a village in the Jaffa district), where Ottoman officials would stop and receive dignitaries. By that time, the village was described as small and poor, yet enjoying successful local agriculture.[35]

According to the 1922 census of Palestine, the village of Umm Khalid had a population of 307 people, all of whom were Muslim.[36] The number increased to 586 inhabitants in the 1931 census, of whom six were Christian, living altogether in 131 houses. At the village center a mosque, a boys' school, and four shops were located. However, as Khalidi notes, by this time most of the village lands had been taken over by Netanya's suburbs.[37] Later Jewish settlements founded in 1940 and 1941 took over other parts of the village's lands. According to the statistics of 1944–45, Umm Khalid had grown to 970 inhabitants and possessed 2,894 dunams of land (47 of which were used for growing citrus and bananas, while 1,830 dunams were sown with cereals). An additional 882 dunams originally belonging to the village were now under Jewish ownership, while 89 dunams were public property.[38]

Come to Netanya

Commissioned by the city council's department of health and recreation, *Come to Netanya* (*Bo le-Netanya*) was published in 1937 by a local printer, shortly after the completion of the long-awaited road connecting the city to the Palestinian town of Tulkarem in the east, and thereby to the main road from Jaffa to Haifa. This link

Figure 7.1. *Come to Netanya* (1937) cover. Source: Netanya Municipality Archives. Unlike the transliteration in the brochure, the current common spelling is *Netanya*.

changed Netanya's situation by putting an end to its isolation and facilitating its economic growth and expansion.[39] The brochure was obviously meant to celebrate Netanya's new accessibility and to encourage tourists to take advantage of it, since by then the city had become an established local resort. The unfortunate timing of the publication, amid the Palestinian Revolt, which broke out in 1936 and lasted until 1939, was not at all mentioned. The brochure also marked, albeit unofficially, ten years since the city's foundation. Among its contributors were several local and other prominent figures, including Netanya's mayor, Oved Ben-Ami; its cofounder, the journalist Itamar Ben-Avi, and his colleague Aharon Even-Chen; the city engineer, Zvi Korenfeld; the city doctor, Binyamin Beckman; and Walter Frenkel, an accomplished athlete and local gardening instructor, among others. The brochure's cover was designed by Zvi Raban, presumably the prominent teacher and leading artist in the Jerusalem art school Bezalel. The brochure also included a reprint of an article by Dorothy Kahn, which had been published the previous year in the newspaper *Palestine Review*, as well as three short contributions by "the children of Netanya," and many advertisements.

The main theme of the issue, as suggested by its cover, was Netanya's natural beauty and its benefits as a uniquely located resort town offering world-class services. The brochure discussed those benefits from aesthetic, scientific, and medical perspectives. Other themes included the miraculous land purchase of Netanya's site, its proper planning and development, and the warm relations with the British authorities. The advertisements in the brochure were reflective and supportive of those themes.

Scientific, poetic, and promotional, the brochure gives a good idea of the image of the city nurtured by its founders and inhabitants since its establishment a decade earlier. By analyzing some of these texts, I will demonstrate how the purchase of the site was presented as an act of auto-indigeneity, or Firsting, in Obrien's terms; how Netanya's celebrated climate and beauty were "sold" as scientific commodities that could only be used properly by Jews; and how the proper development and planning of the city, reinforced by a close allegiance with the British, echoed aspirations of modernity.

Netanya's Land Acquisition as an Act of Indigenous (Dis)Possession

In the process that O'Brien terms "Firsting," New Englanders (or non-Indians) appropriated the foreign land in which they arrived as they simultaneously appropriated the category "indigenous" from the Indians to themselves.[40] The indigeneity of Jews in Palestine was considered so self-evident that it did not even need to be asserted, and the right to "return to Eretz Israel" was taken for granted and therefore in no need of explanation. In his contribution to the brochure, titled "Natan-Ya!"—meaning "Given by God"—Itamar Ben-Avi analyzed the city's name (which also commemorated the name of a potential donor, the American Jewish businessman and philanthropist Nathan Straus). Echoing the sentiments expressed by Oved Ben-Ami cited in the opening of this chapter, Ben-Avi reminded his readers "that in this glorious place, the estate of the biblical tribe of Menashe, God gave them the honor and opportunity to reconstruct the ruins of the ancient Hebrew past by establishing a modern Zionist precinct in the midst of the deserts surrounding it."[41]

Nevertheless, the brochure did expose a perceived need to explain the presence of other claimants to the title of owners and to make a reasonable argument for their replacement. This too was done by employing the original terms that had legitimized the claim in the first place: God and the Bible. The story of the land acquisition of Netanya's site, told several times by Ben-Ami, was presented in the brochure in the lyrical words of journalist Dorothy Kahn, providing a good example of the displacement of the population and the dispossession of its land. This "simple narrative," as the author calls it, originally published in English in May 1937, appeared in a Hebrew translation in its entirety in the brochure (cited here in the original English):

> Six years ago, Netanya . . . was only a lyrical name and a complete wilderness, inhabited by a Sheikh and a few of his followers. The Mayor vividly tells the story of the day when he and a companion first sighted the spot.
>
> The Mayor also recalls the day, soon thereafter, when the first plot of land was bought from the Sheikh. The transaction took place in the Sheikh's vine-covered booth, over many small cups of coffee. The Sheikh asked for six pounds per dunam for his land. The site, which now fetches approximately four hundred pounds a dunam, was then a wilderness, and would require a large expenditure of money and labor. The Jewish settlers were poor, and aghast at the sum of six pounds.
>
> To their protest, the Sheikh replied: "Do you think that I want to sell you the land? The land in Palestine need not be bought by Jews; it was given to them by God.
>
> "When the Jews were driven out of Palestine, God decided to choose another people to watch over the land for them, for He knew that He would not always remain angry with His children. He chose the Arabs as watchmen.
>
> "Do you not think that we too could have developed the country and cultivated the soil as you are doing? We could have. But it was God's will that we should be no more than watchmen.
>
> "Now you have returned. The land is yours. I ask you six pounds a dunam for having guarded your land for fifteen hundred years. Is that too much?"[42]

The story recounts once again the high price paid for the lands of Netanya (now, clearly justified) and reminds the readers of its former inhabitants, highlighting, according to convention, their traditional, romantic setting among vines and their anticipated hospitality. It also unflinchingly hands them the role of recognizing the right of "God's true children" to the land, imposing on the Arabs an alleged acknowledgment of the Jewish right to Palestinian lands as the land of the Jews' ancient ancestors, thereby anointing them as the true indigenous race. In this manner, the Arabs are relegated, by their own "account," to the role of mere "watchmen."

This text also provides an explanation for the land's (alleged) barrenness. Here it is not the Jews who depict the land as empty, but rather the Arabs, who justify the lamentable condition of the land by conceding that it was not theirs to cultivate—that it was, in fact, God's will that it remain barren until the Jews return to it. And indeed, as Kahn concludes, in the end everyone is happy: "From that day on, even during the disturbances [i.e., the Palestinian Revolt] of 1936 . . . , peace has reigned between the Jews and the Arabs in the environs of Netanya."[43]

The Story of Netanya as a Modern Resort

In her analysis of settler communities in Australia, New Zealand, and Canada, Porter describes how a foreign, European "meaning of progress" led to the classification of "land devoid of obvious human activity," "'empty' or unsettled and thus 'unimproved,'" all because "human (European) activity had not (yet) shaped its form and function."[44] This interpretation allowed the settler to perceive of the land as "a 'blank slate,' a tabula rasa, a terra nullius, on which to dream and build [an] ideal human settlement."[45] O'Brien also shows how New Englanders perceived the "civilized" order of culture, science, and reason as replacing "uncivilized" peoples whose histories and cultures they represented as illogically rooted in nature, tradition, and superstition.[46]

Thus, claims Porter, for the settlers, land was not necessarily empty, but perhaps waiting for European labor to make it productive and yield its value.[47] On the one hand, those lands were obviously seen as lacking in cultivation and awaiting European improvement. Following John Locke, she explains, one came into possession of land by working it: claiming ownership through increasing its value. On the other hand, Porter illustrates how settler sensibilities to landscape were also powerfully shaped by romantic traditions, constructing a peculiar relationship between the colonists and the landscape as a sense of wonder emanating from the encounter with primeval nature.[48] In any case, she explains, even the most picturesque depictions of the land were not innocent of attempts to transform it into an exploitable, appropriable, and containable asset—fit for habitation by colonial powers. Thus, Porter claims, both accounts produced a view of nature as having a sole, utilitarian purpose: as "an object to be valued according to its ability to please and serve [white] human beings,"[49] and later, as a space rescued from waste thanks to the presence of appreciative European eyes.[50]

Such mechanisms of investing the (empty) land with (European) value, both for the sensual pleasures they provided and for their more calculable benefits, can be seen also in the appreciation of Netanya's natural position expressed in the brochure. In his article "Netanya—a Place of Health and a Marine-Climate Station," Dr. Beckman explained at length, using scientific terminology, why Netanya exceled as a unique combination of physical-medical elements that endowed it with the full potential of developing into a world-class health resort.[51] "Netanya began gaining fame for the merits of its climate and its wonderful shore even before meteorological-scientific data was methodically collected," he wrote, thanks to the appreciation of the people who spent a few hours or days on its beaches, sunbathing "under the invigorating influence of ultra-violet rays." Thus, while the merits of the sea and the sun were always there, they could now be truly appreciated. Additionally, it was now the mission of the municipality to make them available to the modern masses, "installing sanitary, hygienic and aesthetic improvements, as is customary in first-rate medical resorts." Dr. Beckman further advised "the university" to establish a meteorological station in Netanya, in order to study more carefully the "physical, chemical and biological state of its atmosphere."[52]

The contemporary journalist Aharon Even-Chen coupled the natural merits of Netanya with its apparent modernization, highlighting the successful marriage of the city's natural traits with its recent development. He thus attributed the abundance of resort sites in Netanya to it being a place "where the beach and the citrus groves meet, where the sea breeze and the scents of the citrus caress your face all through the day," and where "a unique natural beach" encounters "a wide and long plaza."[53] Even-Chen proudly quoted Mr. Sibley, "the head of the British Scouts," who had exclaimed during a recent visit to Netanya, "I have been to all the beaches of the Mediterranean and visited the French Riviera, yet I have never seen a beach so wonderful and rich with natural merits as the beach of Netanya."[54]

Finally, the athlete and gardener Walter Frenkel described the children's summer camps held by the beach, where the children played hide-and-seek and ballgames, learned to row boats, and of course, bathed in the sea. "Why Netanya?" he asked and immediately explained that nowhere else in the land had a local authority shown more appreciation of physical health and sports; that was why the city had already hosted three gatherings of the local sports associations and provided a large sports field "in an ideal location." Nor could athletes and horseback riders find a more ideal spot than Netanya to practice their sports, while the "wonderful streets paved with concrete and asphalt" allowed bicycle races for the locals and others.[55]

These ideas seem to be the major message of the tourist brochure, as highlighted by the three images on its cover. The first depicts the path to the beach, dotted with bathers, and located beyond, the citrus-tree-lined hills that shield it from the city; the second shows the bathers lying on the narrow strip of sand between the coastal cliffs and the water, with some children playing in the sand; and the third depicts a couple resting in their garden, surrounded by fruit trees, next to their white house and dog.

The advertisements in the brochure follow the same logic. Hanoteah (The Planter), the local "Colonizers and Orange-Grove Planters Association," was founded by the three committee members of Bnei Binyamin with the goal of raising funds to acquire lands and establish settlements in Palestine.[56] Its advertisement invited visitors to purchase orchards, mixed farms, and plots for construction "in the colonies" and pointedly asked, "Why are you going abroad, when you can find rest and health in Netanya, a city which resides by the beach and under the shade of forests?"[57] The Netanya Sea-Shore Development Company was established by Hanoteah in 1932 in order to implement the town plan in an area along the coast that was leased from the British government for development purposes, and it eventually became an important engine for developing the city, paving roads, and constructing rental homes, public buildings, gardens, and boulevards;[58] its advertisement invited visitors to the "Garden City on the Mediterranean," describing it as providing "a unique panorama, a mild climate throughout the seasons of the year, [and] a long beach endowed by nature with unparalleled charm and picturesqueness." It also called on guests to spend their vacations and weekends at Netanya to enjoy its grace and beauty.[59] Additional ads were published by local cafes, such as Zamir ("a place of rest, resort and pleasure in Netanya"), and hotels.[60] Finally, the "United Sharon," a Tel Aviv–based cooperative of drivers, offered tourists transportation services to the southern and northern parts of this coastal region, using its ancient Hebrew name.

Lasting by Urban Planning

"Lasting," as described by O'Brien, implied the extinction of the local population by dispossession and displacement, whether physically or through delegitimation. Porter highlights the role of towns as part of a military strategy in wars with indigenous peoples: they afforded protection to colonists and allowed easy policing and patrol of borders. This strategy was accompanied by a variety of land policies such as fees, taxes, grants, and sometimes even land reservations—a spatial mechanism for containment and regulation of the native "problem."[61]

Porter describes the stages of settler urbanization as follows: starting with the imaginary spot on which a colonist "stood and surveyed territory that was not yet known to Europe, not yet given European shape, sensibility and function";[62] through the employment of mapping and other techniques in order to make the territory navigable, legible, known, and ultimately conquerable;[63] and culminating with planning that made it possible to determine which bodies belonged where by defining certain types of people as too primitive to own land.[64] Planning, in other words, assisted in sustaining the idea of Lasting, while allowing the process, initialized with Firsting, to bring spatial subjugation to completion.

Come to Netanya celebrated the modernization of the site that became Netanya—its paved concrete streets, public spaces, and resorts—and finally, its modern planning. After the first plan was made for the city in 1929, it was planned again in 1934. This time, Clifford Holliday was privately commissioned. Holliday, who arrived in Palestine in 1922, was the third official British planner; he first worked as town planning adviser to the city of Jerusalem and in 1927–35 served as adviser to the Central Town Planning commission. As of 1927 Holliday also maintained a private practice as architect and town planner and over time did planning in Jerusalem, Jaffa, Tiberias, Ramla, Lydda, and Haifa.[65] Benjamin Hyman reflects on this private appointment of Holliday in Netanya:

> Why Holliday? One can only speculate. Ben-Ammi was determined not to make the same mistakes as Tel-Aviv. His town would be planned to the highest standards and its development tightly controlled. There was no doubt that Holliday, by now experienced and well-established, could give him the desired product. Holliday's name and official position could also be effective in marketing plots abroad.
> ... On the other hand, Government decisions were very important for Netanya: the lease of Government land, the early construction of an approach road to the site, and the determination of a Town Planning Area, among others.[66]

According to Hyman, Holliday was chosen because he could supply the best planning product available at the time, but also because he was a British official; it seems that both these components were picked up by the writers contributing to the brochure. Describing the plan in 1937, Korenfeld highlighted its main features, giving it due credit for Netanya's success as a resort town, alongside the site's obvious natural beauty: "Our principal point of departure was Netanya's beautiful nature and clean air. This was the foreground for our embroidery. Thinking ahead, for Netanya to make itself a place of rest on the shores of the Mediterranean, we planned its streets, its gardens and its boulevards."[67]

Next, the new plan for the city followed the most advanced novelties of modern planning:

> We did not spare spaces to provide the necessary distances between the houses. The size of Netanya's plots and the height of its buildings were fixed in a manner that would allow one to enjoy the fresh air and to view the glory of nature.
> For the future of Netanya we left large spaces for public gardens and playgrounds. . . . We separated commercial zones from residential zones and took care to ensure that zones intended for living and recreation would retain their quiet character. By providing an abundance of greenery and trees and all the other public improvements, we strove to offer the individual and the public the scenery and space needed for their health and pleasure.[68]

Finally, just like the white settlers of New England who contrasted Indians with their own European background, positing a stark break with "the irrational feudalism of Europe as a bedrock of their claims to be modern,"[69] the plan for Netanya portrays the Zionist desire to replace the settlers' shameful European background with a new world. In the process, the plan did away with anything local that stood in the way of this dichotomy, between the land they left and the one they were settling, thereby producing, as was the case in numerous other settler states, "chances which did not exist in the metropole":[70]

Figure 7.2. Netanya plan. Source: *Come to Netanya* (1937), Netanya Municipality Archives.
Translation: "First there was the plan" [abridged]

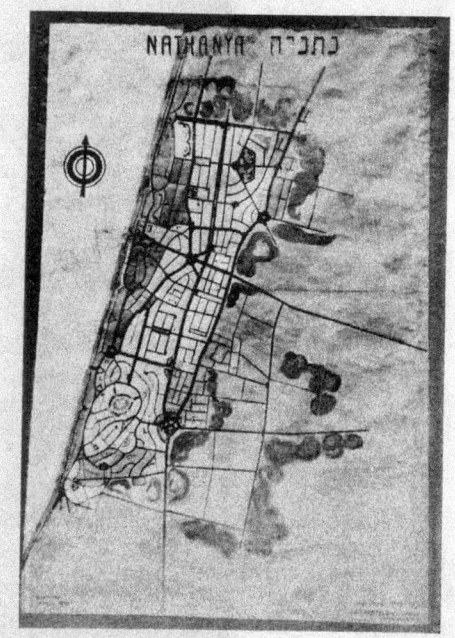

The foundation of Netanya as a center for recreation and relaxation emanates from its initial planning and building, the main point of departure for these being the beautiful nature and clean air of Netanya.

Thus, planning the city, its founders claim: "We did not sell short on space to give the necessary distances from the houses. The building plots of Netanya and the height of the buildings were fixed in a way which allows to breathe [fresh air] easily and to view the magnificence of nature. In future Netanya, we left large spaces for the needs of public gardens and playgrounds. Of these we have already prepared [several] and planted a large part [of them], and the crowd can already stroll in the garden lanes and view/watch over the beach from a height of 40 to 50 meters."

The plan also supplied spacious parking places and separated between commercial areas and places of residence, strictly guarding that the areas intended for residence and relaxation retain their quiet nature.

All the opportunities of a city and its preparation as a site of relaxation emanate from the guidelines given to its development in terms of building and planning. No one could make a dense city into a health resort without any gardens. This could only be done if the city fathers tended to it from its very establishment. This principle did not escape us when we set about drawing the plan for Netanya.[71]

The imperial sentiments of Netanya's settlers were similarly apparent. From the outset, the city greatly benefited from the unofficial patronage of the British Mandate; yet it seems that the sentiments were reciprocal. The city thus displayed a clear attachment to the British government at home and beyond, naming its landmarks after the king and his officials. Next to the celebration of the Jewish holiday of Pentecost (Shavuot), photos in the brochure depict the celebration of planting trees in the king's garden and a picture of "decorated Pitt square." Another picture shows the king's coronation day, vividly described by thirteen-year-old Aliza Halperin, as bringing together locals, tourists, and Britons on the background of the blue sky, the sea, the dunes, and the Zionist flag:

> A pretty day, a summer day. The sky is blue, the sun shines over the young city, a city of wonders. A straight line separates between the blue sky and the blue sea. The streets of the city are full of people, strangers and locals. . . .
> The buses stop next to "Pitt square." The tourists disembark and make their way westwards. The school children are dressed in uniforms that combine the colors of the sky and the sea. We are wearing light blue shirts and dark blue pants. We pass Herbert Samuel street and reach Wauchop plaza, where the coronation celebration will take place. . . . Night has fallen. The lights put up to decorate the streets and the gardens, the council house, the synagogues and the school are turned on. . . . The people of Netanya and all its visitors are walking in the brightly lit streets and wondering how the sands of the desert were turned into a blossoming settlement in such a short period of time.[72]

Conclusion

The story of building Netanya, as told by its Jewish settlers, made the land into their own. Moreover, it impeded the possibility of any alternative story, either of the place or of its former inhabitants. In this sense, Netanya's story resembles the story of the white settlers of New England and of Australia, whose official histories, which began only with their arrival, were presented as authentic and incontrovertible. Based on texts produced by the new arrivals, these accounts made implicit arguments about what counted as legitimate history and who counted as legitimate peoples.[73]

Figure 7.3. Celebration photos. Source: *Come to Netanya* (1937), Netanya Municipality Archives.

The story of Netanya's planning began much earlier than the actual official process, with the dismissal of the local Arabs as traditional and uncivilized and the portrayal of their lands as uncultivated. Even before the first plan for the city was drawn, tactics of dispossession were employed, culminating in the celebration of the perceived desert's transformation into a flourishing city. Biblical symbolism was naturally combined with the perception of Palestine as an empty land, to be transformed through the values of beauty, leisure, and health, by its *first* ever Jewish settlers. Supported by the (modern) British, the Jewish urban revolution, as it happened in Netanya, appeared to justify the dispossession of the land and its transformation according to the latest scientific planning criteria.

However, as detailed above, the bare facts tell a different story: Netanya was not established on barren land, as the land acquired for its settlement was a part of a close-knit web of existing settlements, modest in size yet evidently lively and steady in their growth. Thousands of dunams, cultivated by locals, continued to flourish alongside the growth of Netanya as the village and its people maintained their existence alongside the Jewish settlement process well into the 1940s; it was only the 1948 War which caused the final *lasting* of the indigenous population.

Yet the image of the city, as portrayed in the 1937 brochure, which in turn captured the spirit of the 1934 city plan, had no place for an alternative story. Proposing the construction of a clean, modern, and spacious town with all the necessary facilities and urban amenities, the plan for Netanya was hailed as a natural continuation of its natural beauty, allegedly untouched, undiscovered, and certainly unused. The new settlers, who bought the land only as a gesture of returning it to its original owners, could not accommodate a more complex vision. Depicting themselves as totally replacing the locals, they made the latter invisible; despite the continuing and growing proximity of the ancient village and the new town, they were not part of its present setting or its modern future. They were, in fact, gone.

The planning history of the cities of Palestine, whether old or new, is a partial history. It provides no account of alternative geographies, alternative people, or alternative visions; not only descriptive and monolithic, it is bluntly committed to the classical Zionist narrative. In order to tell the full story of Israeli urbanism, an alternative analytic paradigm, viewing Zionism as settler colonialism and relating to the local Arabs as an indigenous society, must be implemented. Using relevant analytical tools, devised in relation to similar settler colonial societies elsewhere, would make it possible to produce a more balanced and comprehensive story of the place and its people and assist in remedying the overall biased local historiography. Although the result will be complex and inevitably disputed, it will nonetheless be more informative and, most importantly, more respectful to the indigenous inhabitants of Palestine.

Noah Hysler Rubin is a town planner and a historical geographer. Her MA thesis and PhD research, both written at the Hebrew University of Jerusalem, examined colonial town planning in Palestine and throughout the British Empire, analyzing the works of Charles Robert Ashbee and Patrick Geddes. Hysler Rubin teaches at the Bezalel Academy of Arts and Design. She also writes the annual report for UNESCO regarding the state of conservation of the Old City of Jerusalem. Her current research interests include urban planning in Palestine during the time of the British Mandate, the conflicted planning of Jerusalem, and critical analysis of Israeli conservation theory and practice.

Notes

1. Oved Ben-Ami, introduction to *Come to Netanya* (Netanya: Ofek, 1937, in Hebrew).
2. Rachel Klineman, Yehushua Ben-Arieh, and Dan Giladi, "The Genesis of an Urban Settlement Alongside the *Moshava* Netanya (1933–1939)," in *The Book of Netanya*, ed. Avshalom Shmueli and Moshe Brawer (Tel Aviv: Am Oved, 1982, in Hebrew), 123–38. See also Klineman, Ben-Arieh, and Giladi, "The Genesis of Netanya as an Agricultural Settlement (1928–1933)," in Shmueli and Brawer, *The Book of Netanya*, 115–38. On the economic development of the city, see Nahum Karlinsky, *California Dreaming: Ideology, Society, and Technology in the Citrus Industry of Palestine, 1890–1939*, trans. Naftali Greenwood (Albany: State University of New York Press, 2005); on its role in tourism, see Kobi Cohen-Hattab, *Tour the Land: Tourism in Palestine during the British Mandate Period 1917–1948* (Jerusalem: Yad Yitzhak Ben-Zvi, 2006, in Hebrew).
3. Amiram Gonen, "How the Center of Israel Was Established," in *Society and Economics in the Time of the Mandate, 1918–1948*, ed. Avi Bareli and Nahum Karlinskly (Beer Sheva: Ben-Gurion Institute for the Study of Israel and Zionism, Ben-Gurion University, 2003, in Hebrew), 439–88.

4. Walid Khalidi, ed., *All That Remains: The Palestinian Villages Occupied and Depopulated by Israel in 1948* (Washington, DC: Institute for Palestine Studies, 1992) is a unique monument to many of those villages that eventually disappeared in 1948.
5. See, for example, on Jerusalem: Elisha Efrat, "British Town Planning Perspectives of Jerusalem in Transition," *Planning Perspectives* 8, no. 4 (1993): 377–93, and Saul E. Cohen, "Greenbelts in London and Jerusalem," *Geographical Review* 84, no. 1 (1994): 74–89; on Tel Aviv: Yaacov Shavit and Gideon Biger, *The History of Tel Aviv*, vol. 1, *The Birth of a Town, 1909–1936* (Tel Aviv: Ramot, Tel Aviv University, 2001, in Hebrew); on Haifa: Gilbert Herbert and Silvina Sosnovsky, *Bauhaus on the Carmel and the Crossroads of Empire: Architecture and Planning in Haifa during the British Mandate* (Jerusalem: Yad Yitzhak Ben-Zvi, 1993); on smaller cities: Oded Avisar, *The Book of Tiberias* (Jerusalem: Keter, 1973, in Hebrew), and Nathan Shor, *The History of Acre* (Tel Aviv: Dvir, 1990, in Hebrew).
6. Most widely known is Patrick Geddes, whose work in the three main cities is still hailed; see, for example, Hellen Meller, "Conservation and Evolution: The Pioneering Work of Sir Patrick Geddes in Jerusalem, 1919–1925," *Planning History Bulletin* 9 (1987): 42–9; Gideon Biger, "A Scotsman in the First Hebrew City: Patrick Geddes and the 1926 Town Plan for Tel Aviv," *Scottish Geographical Magazine* 108 (1992): 4–8.
7. Leonie Sandercock, "Introduction: Framing Insurgent Historiographies for Planning," in *Making the Invisible Visible: A Multicultural Planning History*, ed. Leonie Sandercock (Berkley: University of California Press, 1998), 2.
8. Leonie Sandercock, *Cosmopolis II: Mongrel Cities in the 21st Century* (London and New-York: Continuum, 2003), 39–40.
9. Donald A. Krueckeberg, "Planning History's Mistakes," *Planning Perspectives* 12, no. 3 (1997): 269–79; Mary Corbin Sies and Christopher Silver, eds., *Planning the 20th Century American City* (Baltimore: Johns Hopkins University Press, 1996), 8; Oren Yiftachel, "Planning and Social Control: Exploring the Dark Side," *Journal of Planning Literature* 12, no. 4 (1998): 403–4.
10. Tami Razi, *Forsaken Children: The Backyard of Mandatory Tel Aviv* (Tel Aviv: Am Oved, 2009, in Hebrew).
11. Haim Yacobi, "The Architecture of Ethnic Logic: Exploring the Meaning of the Built Environment in the 'Mixed' City of Lod, Israel," *Geografiska Annaler*, Series B, Human Geography 84, no. 3–4, Special Issue: "The Dialectics of Utopia and Dystopia" (2002): 171–87.
12. Menachem Klein, *Lives in Common: Arabs and Jews in Jerusalem, Jaffa and Hebron*, trans. Haim Waitzman (London: Hurst & Company, 2014); Itamar Radai, *Palestinians in Jerusalem and Jaffa, 1948: A Tale of Two Cities* (New York: Routledge, 2016); Mustafa Abbasi, *Safed during the Time of the Mandate, 1918–1948: Arabs and Jews in a Mixed City* (Jerusalem: Yad Yitzhak Ben-Zvi, 2015, in Hebrew).
13. New scholarship is making an impact through the Institute for Palestine Studies and its publications, *The Journal of Palestine Studies* and the *Jerusalem Quarterly*.
14. Oren Yiftachel, "Critical Theory and 'Gray Space': Mobilization of the Colonized," *City* 13, nos. 2–3 (2009): 246–63.
15. Rana Barakat, "Writing/Righting Palestine Studies: Settler Colonialism, Indigenous Sovereignty and Resisting the Ghost(s) of History," *Settler Colonial Studies* 8, no. 3 (2018): 349–63; Omar Jabary Salamanca et al., eds., "Past Is Present: Settler Colonialism in Palestine," *Settler Colonial Studies* 2, no. 1 (2012): 1–8.
16. Ilan Pappé, "Zionism as Colonialism: A Comparative View of Diluted Colonialism in Asia and Africa," *South Atlantic Quarterly* 107, no. 4 (2008): 616.
17. Gershon Shafir, "Israeli Decolonization and Critical Sociology," *Journal of Palestine Studies* 25, no. 3 (1996): 17.
18. Pappé, "Zionism as Colonialism," 617; see also Shafir, "Israeli Decolonization," 25.
19. Pappé, "Zionism as Colonialism," 623.
20. Pappé, "Zionism as Colonialism," 621.
21. Libby Porter and Oren Yiftachel, "Urbanizing Settler-Colonial Studies: Introduction to the Special Issue," *Settler Colonial Studies* 9, no. 2 (2017): 1–10.

22. Porter and Yiftachel, "Urbanizing Settler-Colonial Studies."
23. Libby Porter, *Unlearning the Colonial Cultures of Planning* (Burlington, VT: Ashgate, 2010), 11–12.
24. Jean M. O'Brien, *Firsting and Lasting: Writing Indians Out of Existence in New England* (Minneapolis: University of Minnesota Press, 2010).
25. O'Brien, *Firsting and Lasting*, xvii–xviii.
26. See mainly Yael Zerubavel, *Recovered Roots: Collective Memory and the Making of Israeli National Tradition* (Chicago: University of Chicago Press, 1995).
27. Klineman, Ben-Arieh, and Giladi, "Netanya as an Agricultural Settlement," 115.
28. Benjamin Hyman, "British Planners in Palestine, 1918–1936" (PhD diss., London School of Economics and Political Science, 1994), 493.
29. Yossi Ben-Arzi and Avraham Labas, "Document: The First Plan of Nathanya," *Horizons in Geography* 6 (1982): 65–68 (in Hebrew).
30. Kleinman, Ben-Arieh, and Giladi, "The Genesis of an Urban Settlement," 134.
31. Kleinman, Ben-Arieh, and Giladi, "The Genesis of an Urban Settlement," 129.
32. The authors rely mainly on personal interviews with Ben-Ami and other Jewish sources to describe the story. See Kleinman, Ben-Arieh, and Giladi, "The Genesis of an Urban Settlement," 116, notes 4–8.
33. Benny Morris, *The Birth of the Palestinian Problem Revisited* (Cambridge: Cambridge University Press, 2004), 129; Meron Benvenisti, *Sacred Landscape: The Buried History of the Holy Land Since 1948*, trans. Maxine Kaufman-Lacusta (Berkley: University of California Press, 2000), 296.
34. Khalidi, *All That Remains*, 562–63.
35. Khalidi, *All That Remains*, 562–63.
36. "Palestine: Report and General Abstracts of the Census of 1922," compiled by J. B. Barron, superintendent of the census, https://users.cecs.anu.edu.au/~bdm/yabber/census/PalestineCensus1922.pdf.
37. Khalidi, *All That Remains*, 562.
38. Khalidi, *All That Remains*, 563.
39. Klineman, Ben-Arieh, and Giladi, "The Genesis of an Urban Settlement," 134.
40. O'Brien, *Firsting and Lasting*, xxii.
41. Ben-Avi, "Natan-Ya!," in *Come to Netanya*.
42. Dorothy Kahn, "Tel Aviv's Young Rival," *Palestine Review* 2, no. 4 (14 May 1937): 71–72.
43. Kahn, "Tel Aviv's Young Rival." This story has many versions, many told by Ben-Ami himself.
44. Porter, *Unlearning the Colonial Cultures of Planning*, 63.
45. Porter, *Unlearning the Colonial Cultures of Planning*, 59.
46. O'Brien, *Firsting and Lasting*, xxi.
47. Porter, *Unlearning the Colonial Cultures of Planning*, 58.
48. Porter, *Unlearning the Colonial Cultures of Planning*, 61.
49. Anaya Roy, "Praxis in the Time of Empire," *Planning Theory* 5, no. 1 (2006): 57, 72.
50. Porter, *Unlearning the Colonial Cultures of Planning*, 63.
51. Binyamin Beckman, "Netanya—a Place of Health and a Marine-Climate Station," in *Come to Netanya*.
52. Beckman, "Netanya."
53. Aharon Even-Chen, "Sea Breezes and Citrus Perfumes," in *Come to Netanya*.
54. Even-Chen, "Sea Breezes and Citrus Perfumes."
55. Walter Frenkel, "Why Netanya?," in *Come to Netanya*.
56. Klineman, Ben-Arieh, and Giladi, "Netanya as an Agricultural Settlement," 117.
57. Advertisement, in *Come to Netanya*.
58. Klineman, Ben-Arieh, and Giladi, "The Genesis of an Urban Settlement," 124–29, 132.
59. Advertisement, in *Come to Netanya*.
60. By 1937 there were five hotels in Netanya (a sixth was being built) and a cinema. See Klineman, Ben-Arieh, and Giladi, "The Genesis of an Urban Settlement," 134.
61. Porter, *Unlearning the Colonial Cultures of Planning*, 72–75. See also Porter and Yiftachel, "Urbanizing Settler-Colonial Studies."
62. Porter, *Unlearning the Colonial Cultures of Planning*, 59.

63. Porter, *Unlearning the Colonial Cultures of Planning*, 70.
64. Porter, *Unlearning the Colonial Cultures of Planning*, 67.
65. Hyman, *British Planners in Palestine*, 431.
66. Hyman, *British Planners in Palestine*, 495.
67. Zvi Korenfeld, "First was the Plan," in *Come to Netanya*.
68. Korenfeld, "First Was the Plan."
69. O'Brien, *Firsting and Lasting*, 5.
70. O'Brien, *Firsting and Lasting*, 5.
71. Korenfeld, "First Was the Plan."
72. Aliza Halperin, "Coronation Day in Netanya," in *Come to Netanya*.
73. O'Brien, *Firsting and Lasting*, xviii.

Select Bibliography

Abbasi, Mustafa. *Safed during the Time of the Mandate, 1918–1948: Arabs and Jews in a Mixed City*. Jerusalem: Yad Yitzhak Ben-Zvi, 2015. In Hebrew.

Barakat, Rana. "Writing/Righting Palestine Studies: Settler Colonialism, Indigenous Sovereignty and Resisting the Ghost(s) of History." *Settler Colonial Studies* 8, no. 3 (2018): 349–63.

Klein, Menachem. *Lives in Common: Arabs and Jews in Jerusalem, Jaffa and Hebron*. Translated by Haim Waitzman. London: Hurst & Company, 2014.

O'Brien, Jean. *Firsting and Lasting: Writing Indians Out of Existence in New England*. Minneapolis: University of Minnesota Press, 2010.

Pappé, Ilan. "Zionism as Colonialism: A Comparative View of Diluted Colonialism in Asia and Africa." *South Atlantic Quarterly* 107, no. 4 (2008): 611–633.

Porter, Libby. *Unlearning the Colonial Cultures of Planning*. Burlington, VT: Ashgate, 2010.

Porter, Libby, and Oren Yiftachel. "Urbanizing Settler-Colonial Studies: Introduction to the Special Issue." *Settler Colonial Studies* 9, no. 2 (2017): 1–10.

Sandercock, Leonie, ed. *Making the Invisible Visible: A Multicultural Planning History*. Berkley: University of California Press, 1998.

Yiftachel, Oren. "Critical Theory and 'Gray Space': Mobilization of the Colonized." *City* 13 (2009): 246–63.

CHAPTER 8

Architecture and the Struggle over Geography
Revisiting the Arab Village in Israel-Palestine

Haim Yacobi and Hadas Shadar

Introduction

Fauda, which means "chaos" in Arabic, is a successful Israeli TV show about an Israeli special operations force in the Occupied Territories. The unit's tactics are based on the idea of integrating Israeli special forces who "look Palestinian" and speak Arabic with a "Palestinian accent" into Palestinian villages and towns, so as to be able to arrest or assassinate Palestinian activists. The gaze at the Palestinian landscape in this show is twofold: it is distanced (due to security, danger, etc.) and moderated through surveillance technology; but at the same time, it is also intimate, observing an exotic, colorful, chaotic, and sensual landscape. This contradictory yet complementary representation, we suggest, epitomizes the construction and imaginary of the Arab built environment in the national-Zionist culture.

This parallel gaze contributes to the "struggle over geography." As noted by Edward Said, this is a complex struggle, since "it is not only about soldiers and cannons, but also about ideas, about forms, about images and imaginings."[1] In this context, the contribution of spatial practices such as architecture and planning is significant. On the one hand, they codify within their professional discourse the ideologies they serve; on the other hand, they transform the built environment, urban form, and space. Their power, we argue, is in their allegedly unquestionable effect of framing daily experience and accumulating meaning, which can be decoded through analyzing the discourses in which they are produced.

Based on critical readings of historical moments, this chapter discusses the Palestinian built environment in Israel as a vernacular object, one repeatedly subject to creative destruction—and as an object of colonial desire. We begin this discussion with Israel's first three decades, which included two significant wars: the 1948 War, also known as the War of Independence or the Nakba, and the 1967 War, in which Israel conquered the Golan Heights, Judea and Samaria, and the Gaza Strip and occupied over a million Palestinians (in addition to its Palestinian citizens within the 1948 borders).[2] We focus on residential planning by Jewish institutional architects, because through them we can learn about the hegemonic ideology.[3]

1950s: The Arab Village as "A Unique Planning Problem"

As we will discuss in this section, following the establishment of the State of Israel in May 1948, the destruction strategy toward the existing Palestinian built environment gained momentum for a mundane reason: the state, employing its sovereign powers, initiated the spatial and demographic planning of the territory defined as the State of Israel.[4]

The map of the State of Israel differed from that of Mandatory Palestine. Within that newly created, smaller space, the state took ownership of 93 percent of all lands and built structures and defined them as abandoned property, since their Arab owners had fled or were expelled from the country. A survey of the Custodian of Absentees' Property from 1949 counted 45,000 residential apartments, about 7,000 businesses, 500 industrial plants and workshops, more than 1,000 warehouses, and around 3,250 million dunams of agricultural land. The Absentee Property Law of 1950 transferred this land to the state.[5] Importantly, 24 percent of the recently arrived Jewish immigrants (160,000 people) resided in Palestinian property immediately after the establishment of the state, and a remarkable 85.6 percent of the Arab villages disappeared or were occupied by Jewish residents.[6] At the same time, thirty-four different laws and regulations were enacted to help the government establish its policy of balancing the distribution of the Jewish population throughout the country with preventing Arab territorial contiguity.[7] In other words, until the late 1970s, the state's planning and housing policy was geared specifically to Jewish interests and excluded the planning needs of the remaining Palestinian population.[8]

The well-known "Sharon Plan" of 1951, the first master plan for the State of Israel, outlined the development of the state for the coming years in several respects: landscape, industry, roads, and settlements.[9] Developed by the architect Arieh Sharon, head of the Planning Division of the Prime Minister's Department, the plan reflected the centralized policies that characterized the Israeli regime during the 1950s and is best known as providing the blueprint for shaping the state's territory and "planning a new land."[10] The plan was heavily influenced by European ideas and defined three principles of development: land, people, and time,[11] thereby facilitating the formation of Israel's new geography and identity. Accordingly, Sharon's plan called for the construction of thirty new towns and about four hundred new agrarian settlements, designed to replace a similar number of Palestinian villages and towns. It was thereby intended to provide housing for the Jewish population, which tripled during the first decade of the state. In this sense it provided for the construction of a *new place* and a *new identity* in what was ideologically, socially, and culturally constructed as a homeland and was geared toward the transformation of the immigrants into "Israelis" through a process of modernization and Israelization.[12]

The plan did not refer to the Palestinian communities as such, even though they appeared on the Mandatory maps that formed its basis.[13] For instance, in the plan for Be'er Sheva (Beersheba), the pre-state Arab city was represented as a neighborhood of a new Jewish city that would be developed to its north. The planners highlighted the urban blocks of the Arab city since they were settled by Jews. However, the Arab city was sketched as a marginal neighborhood within the new urban scheme (see map 8.1). In the urban scheme for Ashkelon, the former Palestinian village of Majdal and its surrounding orchards were located in the center of the new Jewish city. However, from functional point of view, Majdal was planned as a marginal neighborhood and not as an urban center (see map 8.2). Similarly, in planning the city of Ramla, another former Palestinian town, only a few Palestinian buildings were designated to form part of a residential neighborhood, while others were to be demolished in favor of green areas. In other cases, Palestinian houses were to form part of the urban center. In other words, the Israeli planners did not regard the Arab city as a planning unit in its own right, and certainly not as a significant urban unit (see map 8.3).[14]

David Zaslavsky, head of the Planning and Development Department in the Ministry of Labor and Construction in 1949–53, clearly explained in 1954 the government's approach toward the built environment of Arab cities and villages:

> The abandoned [Palestinian] cities were—and still are—a unique planning problem. With the beginning of the large [Jewish] migration, following the establishment of the state, the city houses were taken over by immigrants. After the better-quality houses were populated, they were renovated by the Custodian of Absentees' Property. In the abandoned cities, with their narrow streets and alleys, there were no modern facilities, and sometimes even such basic services as water and sewage were lacking. It was impossible to accept such backwardness, and those responsible for planning felt that an important goal of their work was to redesign, as far as possible, the built-up areas, especially the demolished quarters, in order to improve the architectural and transportation aspects of these cities.[15]

In practice the plans were directly translated into residential construction, mostly for Jews. During the first decade of the state's existence, approximately 290,000 new dwellings were built in Israel.[16] The government financed, located, planned, built, and populated 75 percent of all housing units in the years 1951–61. The hastily

Map 8.1. The New City of Be'er Sheva: assembly of neighboring unites detached and abounding in greenery. Source: Arieh Sharon, *Physical Planning in Israel* (Jerusalem: Government Printing Office, 1951, in Hebrew), 58.

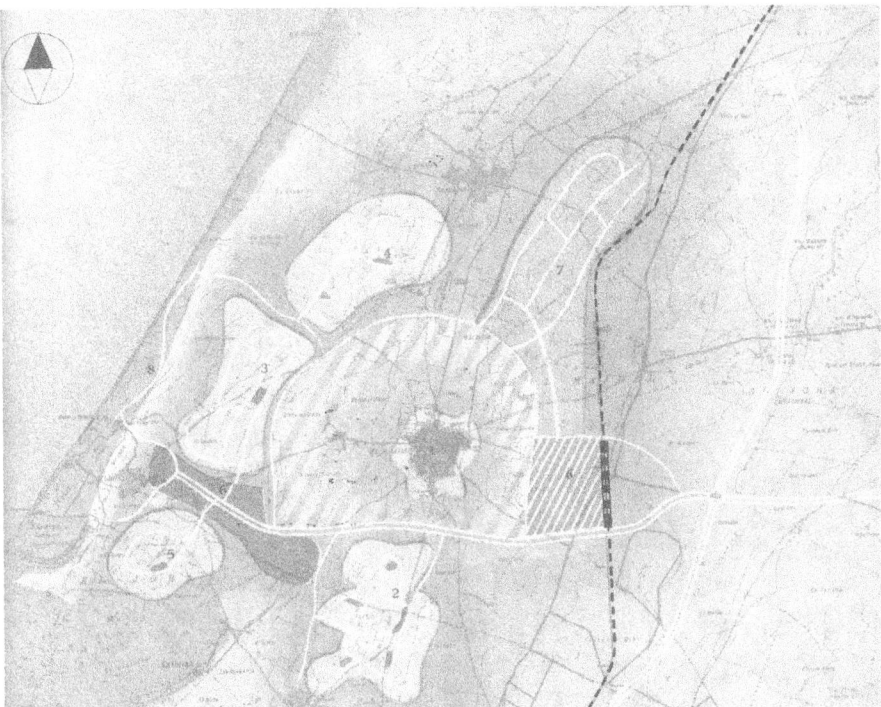

Map 8.2. The Ashkelon urban scheme. Source: Arieh Sharon, *Physical Planning in Israel* (Jerusalem: Government Printing Office, 1951, in Hebrew), 56.

built houses were one- or two-story structures with one or two rooms, planned by the Technical Department of the Housing Division. The construction technology stemmed from budgetary limits and a shortage of professional manpower.[17]

While construction of housing was a major enterprise in 1950s Israel, no housing projects for the remaining Palestinian population of Israel were undertaken, despite the fact that many had become internal refugees. For instance, the Arabs in El Maker—a Palestinian village near Acre to which internal refugees from Acre were expelled in order to diminish the Arab population of the city—were housed in white, one-story, four-square-meter cubes, built in 1950 and positioned directly on the ground.[18] These shelters were similar to those built by the UNRWA in Palestinian refugee camps on cheap agricultural land outside towns.[19]

Furthermore, from the modernist perspective of architecture and planning, the cities were evaluated according to their potential to provide for the inhabitants' quality of life, which included such requirements as running water, clean air, and easy access to transportation. These requirements were not and could not be met in the existing Palestinian towns and villages. The physical inventory was therefore considered uninhabitable.

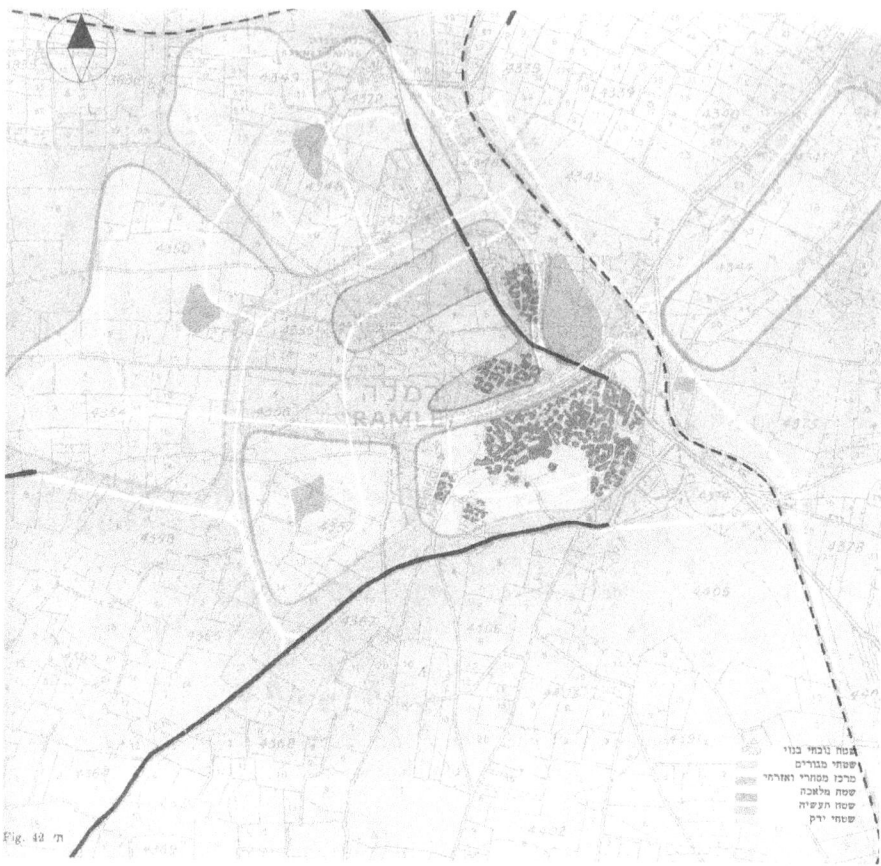

Map 8.3. The Ramla urban scheme. Source: Arieh Sharon, *Physical Planning in Israel* (Jerusalem: Government Printing Office, 1951, in Hebrew), 52.

1960s: Vernacular "but Not Quite"

During the 1960s, the Arab village became an object of interest in Israeli architectural discourse. The Arab village vernacular's morphology, its spread on the surface, the alleys between its houses, the inner courtyards, as well as the structure of the houses, which included separation between women and men, were incorporated into the unique public housing projects discussed in this section.[20] Importantly, this new appreciation of the vernacular in Israel—namely, the built environment characterized by the use of local materials, knowledge, and skills, often independently of professional architects—was also part of a global trend. This new direction came largely in the wake of the influential 1965 *Architecture without Architects* exhibition at the MoMA in New York, which was dedicated to communal architecture produced not by specialists but rather by spontaneous undertakings in traditional communities.

The Terrace Houses project can serve us to understand how Israeli architects interpreted the Palestinian vernacular. The project was built in 1957 at the request of the Planning Department of the Housing Division. Architects Arieh Sharon and Benyamin Idelson planned a housing complex in the new Jewish town of Nazareth Illit (Upper Nazareth), overlooking Palestinian Nazareth (see figure 8.1). It should be noted that the Jewish town of Nazareth Illit was established on confiscated Arab land as part of the national strategic plan for the Judaization of the Galilee.[21] The complex contained 48 one-story housing units, each covering an area of fifty-five square meters. All housing units were located on the same level, bordered by a terrace. The entrances to the units were through a terraced passageway. The terraces, built from local unchiseled stone, delimited the courtyards of the houses and the external longitudinal walls of the housing units.

The following year, 1958, the Planning Department of the Housing Division requested the architects Ora and Ya'acov Ya'ar to submit a plan for a housing project in the new town of Afula Illit (Upper Afula). Known as the Street Project, in 1960–61 the plan led to the construction of seventy-four housing units, each covering an area of fifty-four square meters in long rows of two-story buildings (see figure 8.2). The buildings enclosed two streets from which the apartments could be entered.[22] This complex was exceptional in the public housing urban landscape of the time, which was characterized by free and loose organization on the ground.

One other project, known as the Terraced Carpet, was built in Nazareth Illit in 1961. The project was planned by the architects Avraham Ventura and Yehuda Drexler and built by the Ministry of Housing. The housing units were designed as square block masses, angled at forty-five degrees in order to face the hill. Tilting the units toward the slope created complexes of units surrounding paved, well-structured, and spatially defined common courtyards. Entry into the apartments was through the courtyards, which were connected by a system of terraced alleys that ascended the hill (see figure 8.3).

Figure 8.1. A terraced housing project in Nazareth Illit, 1955–57. Architects: Arieh Sharon and Benyamin Idelson. Source: Ministry of Housing, Physical Planning Division, *Israel Builds 1967* (Jerusalem: Ministry of Housing, 1967).

Figure 8.2. Housing project along the streets of Afula Illit (1958), planned by architects Ora and Ya'acov Ya'ar: internal street. A photograph from the 1960s taken by Ya'acov Ya'ar. Courtesy of Ya'acov Ya'ar.

Figure 8.3. Terrace Houses in Nazareth Illit, planned by Avraham Ventura and Yehuda Drexler. Source: Yehonatan Golani and Gersom Schwarze Dieter, *Israel Builds* (Jerusalem: Ministry of Housing, 1970), 4.6.

As far as their arrangement on the ground was concerned, the designs of the projects elaborated above were indeed unusual for the time as compared to most housing projects surrounding them. The Terraced Carpet project, for its part, integrated an additional visual characteristic: a vernacular aesthetic created by the use of natural stone in the construction. What, then, were the origins of these projects, and how was it that their Jewish planners relied on the free arrangement of buildings in open areas in a manner not seen in other projects (particularly of public housing) in Israel?

The best explanation for the type of modernism shared by all three projects can be traced back to their origins. All the planners involved received a modernist professional education. Sharon, one of the Terrace Houses planners, studied at the Bauhaus in 1926–29.[23] Yehuda Drexler, Avraham Ventura, and Ora and Ya'acov Ya'ar were trained at the Technion, the Israel Institute of Technology, where they studied under architects of European origin with a Western-modernistic professional education. The modernist style of most of the apartments' plans and structures was, therefore, a natural and unconscious outcome of the architectural model these planners had internalized. But what about the outdoor spaces? It is here that the vernacular aspect of these projects can be identified; the planners were influenced by the nearest and most accessible vernacular construction: the Palestinian built environment and the local ancient cities such as Safed, Tiberias, and Jaffa.

In order to arrive at the construction site in Nazareth Illit, the planners of the Terrace Houses had to drive through Palestinian Nazareth in the valley below, which could also be seen from the hill on which the Terrace Houses were subsequently built.[24] Additionally, as noted in an interview with the architect Yehezkel Rozenberg, the concept of the Terrace Houses was borrowed directly from the local terraced agriculture, as were the materials (using the same local stone of which Palestinian houses in Nazareth were typically constructed). The entire pattern was taken from Palestinian design, including the definition of the courtyards and the narrow public passageways between individual plots.

The architects Ora and Ya'acov Ya'ar, who planned the Street Project, also were familiar with the Palestinian landscape. The Palestinian clay houses with thatched straw roofs built along alleys in Wadi Aara served as an inspiration for their planning.[25] Needless to say, the Terraced Carpet pattern, also located in Nazareth Illit, was similarly influenced by the local vernacular village. Pertinent environmental characteristics were ubiquitous in this project, which was primarily composed of terraced carpet construction. The square structural masses served as a reminder of the square housing units of local vernacular construction (a feature that originally stemmed from the size limitations of the openings imposed by the stone construction technology). Passage to the apartments was through narrow terraced alleys, similar to village alleys, and one entered the houses through shared, spatially defined courtyards. This characteristic was also taken from vernacular construction. The massive and obvious presence of this precedent was, indeed, the source of the nickname given to the project by its

Jewish residents: the "Kasbah," namely, low and dense construction that characterized the core of the Arab village.

While it is not surprising that the Palestinian vernacular was appropriated by Israeli architects, as part of the colonial gaze, an interesting question remains: why acknowledge the Arab vernacular when planning for Arab citizens of Israel in the 1960s? In an official publication issued by the Ministry of Housing titled "Housing for the Arab and Druze Sector," the following reference is made to the cultural values of the Arab population: "The special needs of the Arab and Druze citizens necessitated a different approach."[26] This alludes to the ministry's perceived need for adjustment between lifestyle and modern planning. As the report indicates:

> The common residential structure among the Jews, especially the internal division, is foreign to [the Arabs'] demands and needs. Various environmental conditions, traditions, generations, and social conventions necessitated finding ways for a different and unique structure for the Arab resident. . . . Prior to planning, a thorough preliminary study was undertaken, exploring the [construction] material in coordination with the potential *residents*. After that, a modern and functional home was planned—the use of the apartment area, easy access, hygienic conditions, ventilation, etc.[27]

Under the subheading "The House," the report details the planned architectural solutions, arguing that "the special character of the [Arab] family and the rate of its growth necessitated the possibility of expanding the house in the future. . . . Therefore, the possibility of expansion was planned in advance."[28] As concerns its recognition of the necessary separation between the male hospitality area and the female family section, the report states, "The house is divided into two 'wings,' which can be called 'the guest wing' and 'the family wing.' There is a direct entrance from the street, so that the women can thus go out without passing through the living room."[29] The report further acknowledges that "the roof of the house—as is customary in the village—is flat and can be used to dry various crops and for sleep on hot summer nights."[30]

Architectural understanding of the cultural and communal needs of the Arab population was inspired by the international architectural discourse of the time, highlighting the qualities of the vernacular built environment. Obviously, the power relations stemming from the colonial context between the Jewish architects and planners and the Palestinian subjects were ignored, paving the way for a seemingly apolitical, purely architectural discussion and leaving aside questions of land expropriation and the unequal distribution of resources. In the Arab town of Umm al-Fahm, R. Bostoni designed a single-story family house, separating the family wing from the guest wing (see figure. 8.4). In the area designated for the expansion of the village of Fureidis, ninety housing units were planned by Bitosh Comforti as a complete neighborhood of single-family homes with educational and health institutions (see figure 8.5).[31]

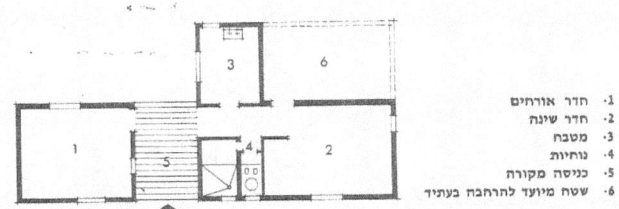

Figure 8.4. A residential building in Umm al-Fahm, in the planning of R. Bostoni. The house includes a separation between the hospitality wing and the living quarters through a covered passageway and an option for expansion. Source: Ministry of Housing, *A Collection of Publications* (Ministry of Housing, 1964), n.p.

In Kafr Qasim—the same village where a massacre by the Israel Defense Forces occurred in 1956—a new neighborhood of one hundred housing units, gardens, and public institutions was planned by D. Shimshoni. Here too, these were single-family homes, built on a family plot that allowed for comfortable expansion. In addition to a private entrance to the "guest wing" and an area designated for expansion, the design of the apartment had two additional characteristics: an inner courtyard, which paid homage to the Palestinian vernacular inner courtyard; and a unique aesthetic reminiscent of mud houses (see figure 8.6). In Khirbet Yama, described as a "small village in the Sharon region," whose residents were Bedouins, Moshe Lufenfeld and Giora Gamerman designed one-story family houses. In addition to the features mentioned above, these had another iconic characteristic: an inner courtyard that was expected by the architects to remain in the same form even after the expansion of the housing

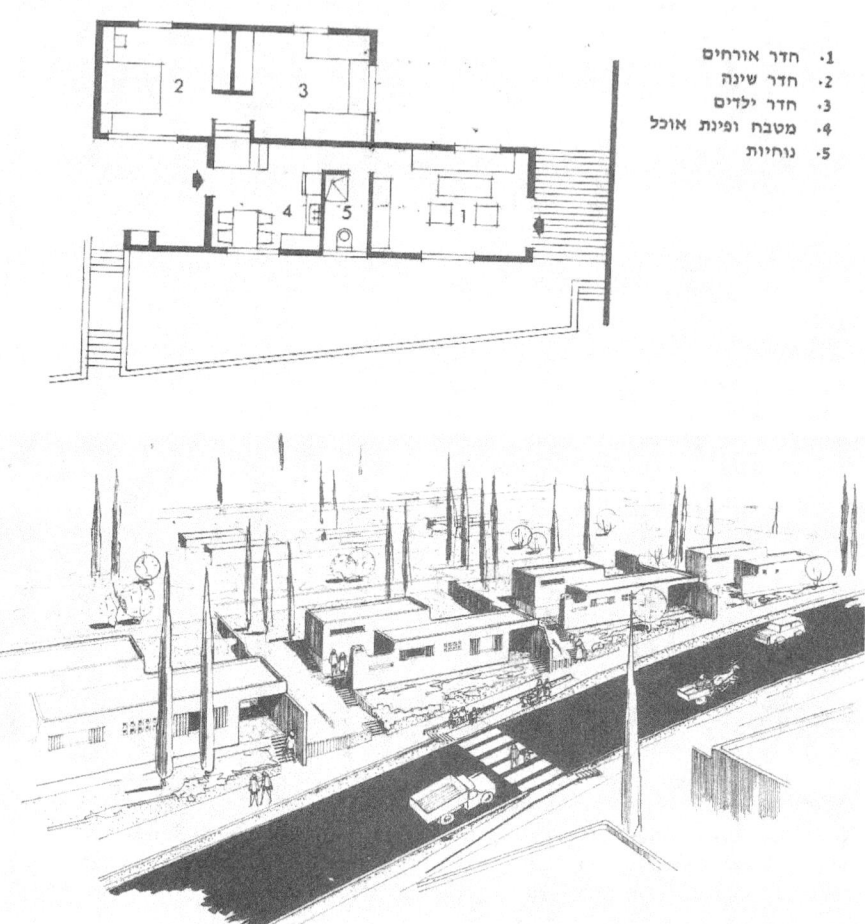

Figure 8.5. Public housing in the village of Fureidis, in the planning of Bitosh Comforti. *Top:* The apartments program has a separate entrance to the accommodation wing and enough space for self-expansion. *Bottom:* The land-based placement provides privacy and the possibility of comfortable family expansion without dependence on the neighbors. Source: Ministry of Housing, *A Collection of Publications* (Ministry of Housing, 1964), n.p.

unit. In fact, the open inner courtyard was to serve as the core of the house; it was planned for circulation and access to the guest wing, the residential wing (with two rooms after the expansion), the bathroom, and the kitchen (see figure 8.7).[32] The inner courtyard for the nuclear family was planned alongside an open courtyard for every family, which was not at all part of the traditional village nucleus. Did this indicate a lack of understanding by the planners of the residents' culture? This is possible,

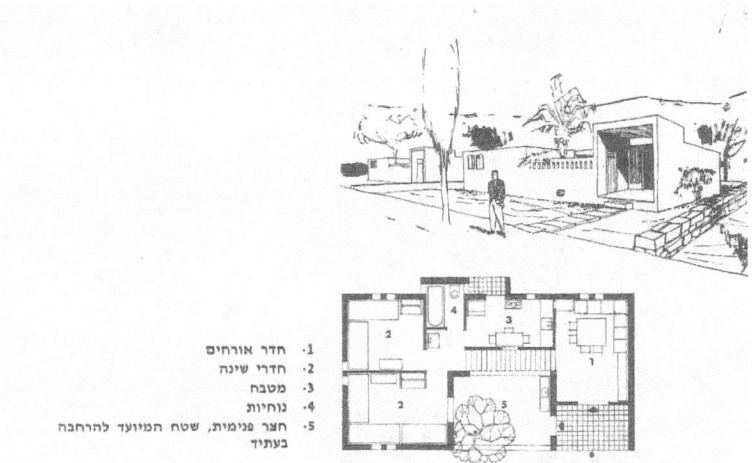

Figure 8.6. Apartment for Kafr Qasim, in the planning of D. Shimshoni. The apartment plan was added to an inner courtyard, which paid homage to the traditional inner courtyard, and a unique aesthetic, which mentions the construction of mud. Source: Ministry of Housing, *A Collection of Publications* (Ministry of Housing, 1964), n.p.

but clearly there was a desire to take into account the cultural use of space, as opposed to the previous period discussed in the first section of this chapter, which ignored or turned against the qualities of the Palestinian vernacular.

To sum up this section, it seems that during the second decade of the state, the Jewish-Zionist planners acknowledged and recognized the qualities of the Arab built environment. The Arab vernacular was recognized as an expression of the *local* identity, and therefore its outdoor definition of spaces was studied by Israeli architects, who were inspired by it and integrated it into the planning of Jewish residences. Conversely, the Arab home was seen as an expression of *ethnic* identity. Therefore, its principles were assimilated into the institutional planning for the Arabs, while denying the political dimensions within which such planning and architecture were taking place.

The Arab village during the 1960s did indeed become naturalized as a still-life, depoliticized, and ahistorical object. This rhetorical appropriation of the village implied none other than a process purification based on interpretation, revealing the duality of the Israeli colonial culture. This was characteristic not only of the Israeli context. In some other colonial contexts one can similarly identify this phenomenon, whereby the indigenous architectural object is appropriated and assimilated into the settlers' culture. This tendency, as we show below, is central to the discourse and practice of the professional elite that continued to work more extensively along these lines after the 1967 War, when the geopolitical conditions changed with the colonization of the Occupied Territories.[33]

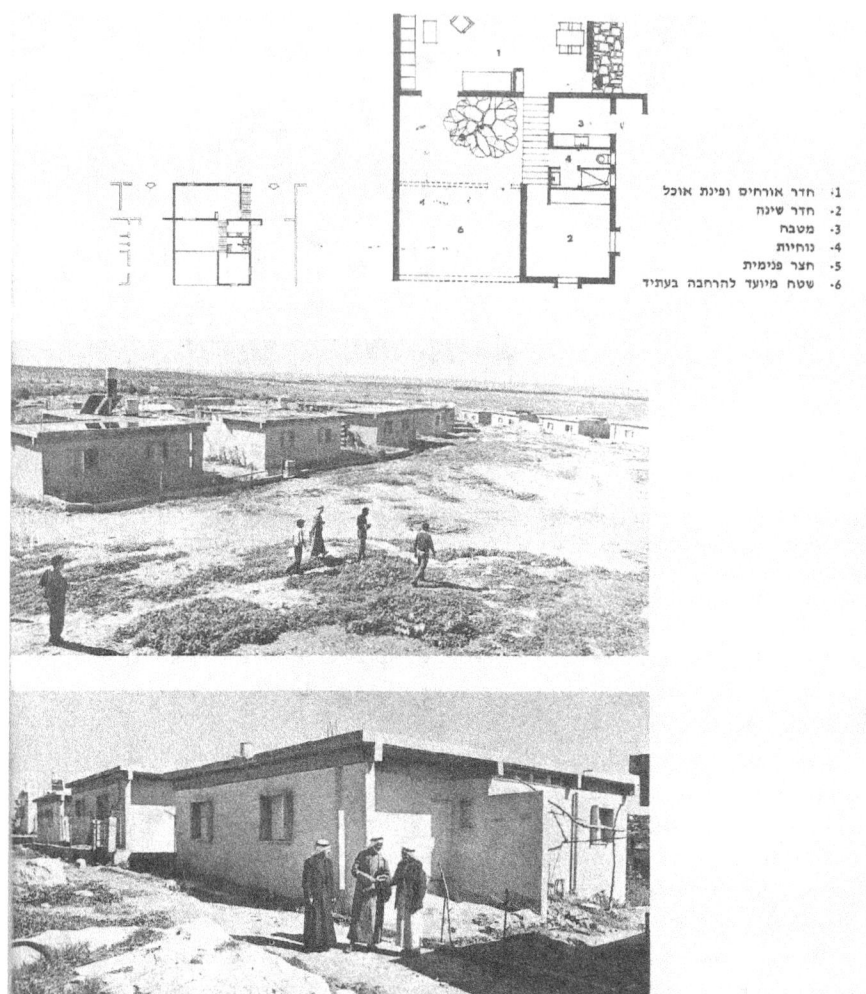

Figure 8.7. Construction plan for the expansion of Khirbet Yama village, planned by Moshe Lufenfeld and Giora Gamerman. The inner courtyard is supposed to be the center of the house, from which one can enter the accommodation wing, the residential wing with its two rooms after the expansion, the bathroom, and the kitchen. Source: Ministry of Housing, *A Collection of Publications* (Ministry of Housing, 1964), n.p.

1970s: Architecture as an Exhibition

The fascination with the picturesque qualities of the Palestinian vernacular intensified after the 1967 War, during which the State of Israel conquered the Golan Heights, Judea and Samaria, the Gaza Strip, and the Sinai Peninsula. As a result, the inventory of Arab construction within Israel's boundaries swelled immeasurably. We suggest that one should distinguish between the fascination of architects with the Arab landscape during the 1970s and in the 1960s, when the Arab village was first "discovered." In the 1970s, these sentiments included a religious content (such as the connection to the holy places in Judea and Samaria in general and Jerusalem in particular),[34] which in turn concerned claims of historical right to the land.[35] The decision of the Israeli government to build around Jerusalem[36] coincided with this new outlook, and thus the new Jewish construction in Jerusalem reflected the evolving image of Arab architecture, or rather, of the ancient native-Hebrew architecture. This was especially the case in the new colonial settlements/neighborhoods in East Jerusalem such as Gilo, whose complexes were designed by the best architects of the day, each providing a unique interpretation of the Palestinian vernacular.

Architect Salo Hershman's structural cluster of three interconnected courtyards was the best-known design in Gilo.[37] The courtyards are delimited: their side walls, four stories high, define them unequivocally. Only four dramatically designed entrance gates were provided for each courtyard. Stairways ascend toward each gate, and thus climbing them leads into the "unknown." The entrances are designed as great arches. The buildings surrounding the courtyards, with stone facings and arched windows, cling to one another, forming a monolithic unit. The interface between the buildings and the ground is diagonal, resembling that of stone buildings (see figure 8.8).

Figure 8.8. A building in the Gilo neighborhood. Public housing for Jews as planned by Salo Hershman. Source: Amiram Harlap, ed., *Israel Builds 1988* (Jerusalem: Ministry of Housing, Israeli Construction Center, 1988, in Hebrew), 114.

Supposedly, all the elements of Arab architecture are present in this cluster: the courtyards, the gates, the arches. Yet, something is different, and that difference pulls the rug from under the entire analogy: *the scale*. While the courtyard of the vernacular Arab construction is used by a single clan, each one of Hershman's courtyards serves approximately one hundred unrelated nuclear families. Whereas the owners spent years building a vernacular Arab construction, Hershman's cluster was built all at once by an external contractor—the Ministry of Construction and Housing. And, if the residential compound of the vernacular Arab construction borders a dense alleyway, Hershman's residential compounds borders parking lots and open spaces. Furthermore, all the design gestures—the stone facing, the sloped interfaces between the construction and the ground, the dramatic gates, the spacious stairways, and the arched windows—are merely external structural citations of the traditional vocabulary of stone construction and stone technology. The arches are neither made from the same substance (concrete rather than stone) nor inherent to the structure (which is in fact supported by reinforced concrete); much like the stone facings, they are merely a facade.

The focus of architectural attention at the time was Jerusalem. The "reunion" with Jerusalem, after nineteen years of separation, evoked previously unspoken emotions and facilitated the creation of a supertemporal metaphoric, apolitical space. The chief architect of the Ministry of Construction and Housing, Ram Karmi (1974–79), wrote about the architectural characteristics of East Jerusalem, employing not only an architectural jargon, but also a national and social message. As he saw it, the national architectural syntax of the Jewish people should have the characteristics of Mediterranean architecture. In his canonical article "Human Values in Urban Architecture," Karmi asserted, "We should therefore observe the traditional Mediterranean architecture that surrounds us, and examine the timeless basic values this architecture has developed, in order for us to learn some lessons about current architecture."[38] In another words, we should translate the traditional building (by which, in view of the photographs he included in the article, Karmi also meant Arabic houses) to the current buildings for the Jews, with their different scale and different apartment planning. Not coincidentally, the picture of Salo Hershman's residential compound in Gilo was attached to the paper with the caption "Combining values in Mediterranean construction and current architecture: structures, gates, internal courtyards, pedestrian walkways, covered alleys."[39] These characteristics stood by themselves as decorations, rather than as part of a more extended cultural statement, certainly not one related to the Arabic nation.

Interestingly, the architectural discourse and practice discussed above also infiltrated the design of the Arab environment. In an official publication by the Ministry of Housing in the 1970s, mostly dealing with public buildings for the Arab population, a housing project for the younger generation in the village of Tira stands out. This four-story housing cluster, designed by Salo Hershman, introduces vernacular elements, yet does so with the idea that since young people are more "modern," a more urban architectural typology would be appropriate. The rationalization of the project adheres to the usual terminology used to describe public housing for the Jewish population.[40] Phrases such as "social interaction among the residents"[41] and "neighborhood micro-square" reflect the essence of the project, which consists of nothing more than variations on the theme of the Arab inner courtyard, while the decorative arches on the facades of the buildings may indicate the project's cultural origin.

The 116 residential apartments are grouped into arched structures around three inner courtyards. Each has 32 housing units designated for nuclear families; each apartment has four bedrooms, a living room, and a patio. The three courtyards open onto a fourth inner courtyard, which is well defined by the extension of the residential buildings. The spacious living rooms, as well as the bathroom and the kitchen, open onto an interior space intended for eating around a table. The inner courtyard of the Arab village, which constitutes the center of the extended family to which all the entrances are directed, is ostensibly repeated twice. They are both communal areas designated for pedestrians only and residential spaces (see figure 8.9).

Figure 8.9. Housing for the younger generation in the castle, designed by Salo Hershman—model of one inner courtyard. Source: Amiram Harlap, ed., *Israel Builds 1977* (Jerusalem: Ministry of Housing, Department of Planning and Engineering, 1977, in Hebrew).

This structure, intended for the village of Tira, was almost perfectly duplicated in the early 1980s in Neve Yerek, a neighborhood built for the Arab inhabitants of Lod, a Palestinian city before 1948 that became a "mixed city" following the expulsion of most of its original Palestinian inhabitants. The overall plan remained, as did the aesthetics of the arches. The difference lay in the apartments' outline. This time there were four-room apartments (three bedrooms and a guest room) that opened up to a central dining room, which was combined with a kitchen. Theoretical options for variable expansion were sketched in the architectural plans. The traditional elements included an inner courtyard, a patio as part of the residential culture, the separation of women (in the house) from the men (in the hospitality space), and the internalization of the housing units. The architectural gestures of this project, according to Salo Hershman, amounted to a reproduction of the Arab village. However, this artificial "village" was derived from formal gestures (arches, courtyards, and patios) rather than from a deep understanding of Arab residential culture. While the evolving village was built by its residents, who were connected by close family ties and living on their own land, this "village" was built by a Jewish planner in the public housing service of the State of Israel.

Conclusion

This chapter has shown that in the course of three decades Zionist architects developed three different architectural approaches. First, in the early years of the State of Israel, the dominant architecture was modernist, whereas Arab villages and towns were wiped out both physically and conceptually by way of plans that reduced what remained of them to neighborhoods in new Jewish cities. Second, in the 1960s the approach was interpretive, as ideas about the Arab village gained access into public spaces built for Jews, as well as public housing planned for Palestinians, which were supposed to include elements from the traditional Arab house. Third, in the aftermath of the 1967 War, the Arab village continued to be viewed as providing a model for the architectural expression of the (Jewish) nation's antiquity, now increasingly seen also through the prism of intensifying religious sentiments. But this Arab presence was only external: in architectural terms, these were mere facades covering the arches and stone cladding of the new structures. Finally, in the 1980s—the fourth decade of the State of Israel—even these modes of appropriation disappeared. Thus the Arab village no longer retained any presence in the buildings of the Jewish state.[42]

However, the built environment was not singularly addressed through the prism of Zionist society. We claim that an alternative architectural production has emerged, whose counter-products have transformed the Arab village from being seen primarily as the enemy's (obliterated or appropriated) landscape into a national emblem for Palestinian society in Israel. This was, of course, the very same society that had created the Arab village in the first place and was consequently not expected to view it as a symbol, but rather as a self-evident, natural, indigenous environment. Our conclusion is derived from the finding that subjects are not indifferent to external initiatives aimed at shaping their lives. Rather, they associate their environment with the values and goals they view as significant, even if these are at odds with the hegemonic social and spatial order.[43] This observation regarding the Arab village is incompatible with its presentation in the Jewish-Israeli architectural discourse as a neutral object devoid of inhabitants or as a mere source of inspiration.

Let us illustrate this with two examples. At a conference held in September 2013, Zochrot, an Israeli NGO focusing on raising an awareness of the Nakba among the broader Jewish public, discussed the possibility of a return of Palestinians to Israel. One of the projects presented at this conference was by a group of Palestinian internal refugees from the village of al-Lajun, who planned a return to their lands. Using professional architectural displays, they presented their vision of re-establishing their village, which had been deserted and demolished in 1948. In their plan, the refugees designed a large square surrounded by public buildings. These buildings included a museum, art galleries, craft workshops, coffee shops, and a visitor center. The modern residential and industrial zones would be located outside the planned village core, and while they would appear to be "modern," the center of this utopian city would be inspired by traditional Palestinian architecture. The construction would employ stone facings and be designed in a traditional oriental style, including arches and domes (see figure 8.10).

The internal al-Lajun refugee community, headed by the architect Shadi Habib-Allah, deliberately used the architectural features of an "Arab village" in planning the village center; this was neither a coincidence nor an expression of personal taste. Habib-Allah justified this choice by invoking the need to re-create the pre-Nakba

Figure 8.10. The al-Lajun return project. Source: Architect Shadi Habib-Allah Archive.

architectural images seared into the memories of the village's original residents.[44] The village center thus reconstructs traditional houses as a reflection of the desired identity of the returning al-Lajun residents. These were traditional villagers and peasants living simple lives in an unchanging, intergenerational sequence since time immemorial. This architectural realization produces an image of their return, consisting of collective elements associated with the colonization and expulsion experienced by Palestinians even as they reconstructed their national identity. Nevertheless, comparing the imaginary al-Lajun architecture with Israeli architecture reveals that it makes the same symbolic use of the familiar images of "the village" as did the institutionalized Israeli architecture of the 1970s, the third decade of the State of Israel.

Another example of the counter-hegemonic image of the Arab vernacular can be seen in an architectural project that serves as the home and office of the architect Senan Abdelqader, located in Beit Safafa, a Palestinian enclave village in the midst of West Jerusalem. Abdelqader's home, which was praised by the Israeli architectural discourse of the 2000s, is encased in a perforated envelope inspired by the traditional *mashrabiya*—a semitransparent screen, often made of wood, which is typical in Arab architecture and shields windows from public view. The envelope is a skeleton construction made of bare, right-angled, reinforced concrete. The steel bars protruding from the top correspond with the continuous foundations characteristic of Arab village construction. The *mashrabiya* itself is no longer made of wood but rather built from bare cement blocks (see figure 8.11).

Figure 8.11. Architect Senan Abdelqader's private home located in Beit Safafa. Photograph by Haim Yacobi.

Like other creators who let their work reflect an ideological message even as their overt discourse refers to practice, Abdelqader told an interviewer, "When I thought about planning my house, I did not think of an 'Arab house.' I was pragmatically calculating construction percentages, mass, height. I thought of an envelope that could contain the various stages of construction."[45] Indeed, we can claim that Abdelqader's approach shares some similarities with the second decade of Israeli architecture that derived motifs from the Arab village.

As demonstrated throughout this chapter, the Arab village was transformed from a literal site into an image and an ingredient of both Zionist and Palestinian national identity. As we have shown, the transformations of the Arab landscape have taken it from a representation of the backward "other" and of the national-Zionist project's progress to a "rediscovered" and appropriated object. This was a Palestinian landscape reconceived as a native Jewish landscape, namely, the landscape of the Jewish nation's homeland, and more recently as a source of Palestinian national identity, an object of yearning for the times that preceded the Nakba and of inspiration for the future.

Haim Yacobi is a professor of development planning at University College London (UCL). His research focuses on (post)colonial architecture, planning and development in Israel-Palestine, the Middle East, and Africa. He has published work on Jerusalem, contested urban spaces in Israel-Palestine, and the politics of Jewish-Arab communities. He earned an MSc in development planning unit from UCL, and a PhD from the Department of Geography and Environmental Development at Ben-Gurion University of the Negev. He has recently been awarded the Wellcome Trust Grant to undertake a research project on health and violence in Gaza.

Dr. Hadas Shadar is an architect, researcher of public housing in Israel, senior lecturer at the NB Haifa School of Design and at the Technion, and conservation adviser. Her books include *The Construction of Public Housing: Six Decades of Urban Construction Initiated by the State of Israel* (Ministry of Construction and Housing, 2014, in Hebrew); *Beer-Sheva: Brutalist and Neo-Brutalist Architecture* (Bauhaus Center, 2014), and the edited volume *Sunstroke: Brutalist Construction in Be'er Sheva: Re-examination of National Architecture* (Yad Ben Zvi, 2016, in Hebrew).

Notes

1. Edward Said, *Culture and Imperialism* (New York: Knopf, 1994), 6.
2. It is important to note that this discussion was central to the Zionist architecture discourse already during the 1930s. However, the scope of this chapter does not allow a discussion of that period. For more details see Haim Yacobi and Hadas Shadar, "The Arab Village: A Genealogy of (Post)Colonial Imagination," *Journal of Architecture* 19, no. 6 (2014): 975–97.
3. Hadas Shadar, Zvika Orr, and Yael Maizel, "Contested Homes: Professionalism, Hegemony, and Architecture in Times of Change," *Space and Culture* 14, no. 3 (2011): 269–90.

4. Noga Kadman, *At the Sides of the Road and the Edges of Consciousness: The Repression of Palestinian Villages Emptied in 1948 from of the Israeli Discourse* (Jerusalem: November Books, 2008, in Hebrew).
5. Rasem Khamaisi, *Planning and Housing among the Arabs in Israel* (Tel Aviv: International Center for Peace in the Middle East, 1990, in Hebrew).
6. Khamaisi, *Planning and Housing*.
7. Khamaisi, *Planning and Housing*.
8. Al-Lajnah, al-Arabiyah, Hawla lil-Tansiq al-Haqq, and Mulaim bi-Sakan, *Housing for All? Implementation of the Right to Adequate Housing for the Arab Palestinian Minority in Israel: A Report for the UN Committee on Economic, Social and Cultural Rights, on the Implementation of Article 11.1 of the United Nations CESCR*, ed. Arab Association for Human Rights (Nazareth: Arab Coordinating Committee of Housing Rights, 1996).
9. Arieh Sharon, *Physical Planning in Israel* (Jerusalem: Government Printing Office, 1951, in Hebrew).
10. Sharon, *Physical Planning in Israel*.
11. Arieh Sharon, *Kibbutz + Bauhaus* (Stuttgart: Kramer, 1976), 12–84, 92–93.
12. Haim Yacobi, "Architecture, Orientalism and Identity: A Critical Analysis of the Israeli Built Environment," *Israel Studies* 13, no. 1 (2008): 94–118.
13. Khamaisi, *Planning and Housing*.
14. Sharon, *Physical Planning in Israel*.
15. David Zaslavsky, *Housing Immigrants in Israel: Housing Planning and Development* (Tel Aviv: Am Oved, 1954, in Hebrew), 80.
16. Haim Darin, "Economic and Social Trends of Housing in Israel during the Decade," in *Public Housing: Reviews and Assessments on Public Housing in Israel during the Decade 1948–1958*, ed. Haim Darin (Tel Aviv: Sifrei Gadish, 1959, in Hebrew), 13–80.
17. Asher Allweil, "The Development of Construction Methods in Housing Projects in Israel," in *Public Housing: Reviews and Assessments on Public Housing in Israel during the Decade 1948–1958*, ed. Haim Darin (Tel Aviv: Sifrei Gadish, 1959, in Hebrew), 87–92.
18. Fatina Abreek-Zbeidat, "And It Gave Them These Rooms: Architecture of Dispossession," *Sedek* 5 (2010): 20–25 (in Hebrew).
19. Henri Rueff and Alain Viaro, "Palestinian Refugee Camps: From Shelter to Habitat," *Refugee Survey Quarterly* 28, no. 2–3 (2009): 339.
20. Hadas Shadar, "Evolution and Critical Regionalism," *Journal of Urban Design* 15, no. 2 (2010): 227–42.
21. Dani Rabinowitz, *Overlooking Nazareth: The Ethnography of Exclusion in Galilee* (Cambridge: Cambridge University Press, 1997).
22. Jacob Yaar and Ora Yaar, "Afula Housing," in *World Architecture Today*, ed. Johan Donat (New York: Viking Press, 1964), 115.
23. Sharon, *Kibbutz + Bauhaus*.
24. Interview with the architect Yehezkel Rozenberg, an employee of the Sharon-Idelson firm since 1950, on 7 June 2001.
25. Interview with the architect Ya'acov Ya'ar, planner of the Afula Illit project, on 7 June 2001.
26. Ministry of Housing, *A Collection of Publications* (Ministry of Housing, 1964), n.p.
27. Ministry of Housing, *Collection of Publications*.
28. Ministry of Housing, *Collection of Publications*.
29. Ministry of Housing, *Collection of Publications*.
30. Ministry of Housing, *Collection of Publications*.
31. Ministry of Housing, *Collection of Publications*.
32. Ministry of Housing, *Collection of Publications*.
33. Alona Nitzan-Shiftan, "Capital City or Spiritual Center? The Politics of Architecture in Post-1967 Jerusalem," *Cities* 22, no. 3 (2005): 229–40.
34. Michael Feige, "The Beginning of the Gush Emunim Movement," in *The Third Decade*, ed. Zvi Zameret and Hanna Yablonka (Jerusalem: Yad Ben-Zvi, 2008, in Hebrew), 362–43.

35. Gershon Shafir and Yoav Peled, *Being Israeli: The Dynamics of Multiple Citizenship* (New York: Cambridge University Press, 2002).
36. Asher Olnik, "Introduction," in *Israel Builds 1973*, ed. Amiram Harlap (Jerusalem: Ministry of Housing, Department of Planning and Engineering, 1973, in Hebrew), 6.
37. Amiram Harlap, ed., *Israel Builds 1977* (Jerusalem: Ministry of Housing, Department of Planning and Engineering, 1977, in Hebrew); Amiram Harlap, ed., *Israel Builds 1988* (Jerusalem: Ministry of Housing, Israeli Construction Center, 1988, in Hebrew).
38. Ram Karmi, "Human Values in Urban Architecture," in Harlap, *Israel Builds 1977*, 315–28, citation on 326.
39. Karmi, "Human Values in Urban Architecture," 324.
40. Harlap, *Israel Builds 1977*, 150–52.
41. Harlap, *Israel Builds 1977*, 150–52.
42. Uri Ram, *The Globalization of Israel—McWorld in Tel Aviv, Jihad in Jerusalem* (Tel Aviv: Resling, 2005); Hadas Shadar, *The Construction of the Public Housing: Six Decades of Urban Construction Initiated by the State of Israel* (Tel Aviv: Ministry of Construction and Housing, 2014, in Hebrew).
43. Arun Appadurai, *Modernity at Large: Cultural Dimensions of Globalization* (Minneapolis: University of Minnesota Press, 1996).
44. Shadi Habib-Allah, quoted in Ester Zandberg, "A Utopian Arab City in Israel? Turn Left at Route 65," *Haaretz*, 6 October 2013.
45. Interview with the architect Senan Abdelqader, on 2 October 2013.

Select Bibliography

Oxman, Robert, Hadas Shadar, and Ehud Belferman. "Casbah: The Brief History of a Design Concept." *Architectural Research Quarterly* 6, no. 4 (2002): 321–36.

Shadar, Hadas. "Vernacular Values in Public Housing." *Architectural Research Quarterly* 8, no. 2 (2005): 171–81.

Yacobi, Haim, ed. *Constructing a Sense of Place: Architecture and the Zionist Discourse*. London: Ashgate, 2004.

Yacobi, Haim. *The Jewish-Arab City: Spatio-Politics in a Mixed Community*. London: Routledge, 2009.

Part III
Education and Ideology

CHAPTER 9
Contested Pedagogy
Modern Hebrew Education and the Segregation of National Communities in Pre-State Palestine

Miriam Szamet

Introduction

This chapter explores the modernization of Zionist Jewish education in Ottoman Palestine from the late nineteenth century, when a new system of education in Modern Hebrew (Ivrit) was devised. While discussing the Hebraization of the educational system, a particular emphasis is put on the tension between a universalist pedagogy, on the one hand, and segregation by ethnic and national affiliations, on the other. I argue that the full potential of the modern, even progressive, pedagogy used to revive the Hebrew language was not fulfilled, especially but not exclusively in the area of language acquisition. Rather than bridging between two ethnic groups in conflict—Jews and Arabs—the emergence of the modern education system in Palestine deepened their mutual alienation and created two opposed national groups, Zionists and Palestinians. In other words, whereas in Europe modern pedagogy had two strands—namely, child-centered education free from nationalism and government-run education—in the Yishuv these were merged, thereby transforming "modern pedagogy" from liberationist to segregationist. This same Hebrew education system based on modern pedagogy was subsequently adapted to the Israeli national education system, simultaneously bringing with it also the ethnic segregation that had prevailed in the Ottoman Empire.

The modernization of education in Palestine in general and of Jewish education in particular began in the mid-nineteenth century with the establishment of European schools by missionary and philanthropic organizations, both Christian and Jewish, and continued until the 1920s. Over time, the educational discourse underwent tremendous changes thanks to the growing movement of Jewish immigrants from Eastern Europe to Ottoman Palestine as of the 1880s and the Zionist ideals they brought with them. Among them were teachers and cultural entrepreneurs who were very influential in creating the new Hebrew culture, its educational contents, and its institutions. Inspired by pedagogical ideologies and methods emerging from the European Enlightenment of the eighteenth and nineteenth centuries, they made Ivrit (Modern Hebrew) the language of educational instruction, trying to promote its daily use throughout Jewish society.

However, because of the intrinsic conflict between universalist and partisan views among Zionist educators, tensions soon emerged between the new, Enlightenment-inspired pedagogical ideologies and the nationalist views some of these early educators endorsed. Largely ignored, both at the time and in later historiography of Hebrew education, this late nineteenth-century conflict in fact led to the social and linguistic segregation of students in the new modern schools along the lines of the opposing nationalist movements: Zionism and later Palestinian nationalism. This chapter will focus primarily on the Zionist pedagogical discourse.

Analysis of this tension can deepen our understanding of the complex history of Hebrew education and of the origins of the separation into ethnic and national groups in Palestine–Eretz Israel during the decades preceding the establishment of the state. Exploring the work of these early Hebrew teachers in Palestine raises many questions. For instance, how did the revival of Hebrew as a modern vernacular in school impact pedagogical principles? Was it perceived as a necessary component of excellence, or was Hebrew simply used as a means to the end of educating Jewish children in the Yishuv (the pre-state Jewish community in Palestine), just one element in a broader pedagogical and political apparatus? Did the revival of Hebrew by teachers and their pedagogical methods clash or coincide with their political views? How did Hebrew teachers (teachers teaching in Hebrew) view the local Palestinian population? What was lost when schools were enrolled into the project of reviving the Hebrew language in the service of a unilingual ideology?

The Revival of Hebrew and Modern Jewish Education in Palestine

The beginnings of modern education in Palestine did not include significant moves toward cooperation between new Arab and Jewish schools. During the waning years of Ottoman rule, separate schools were established for each of the ethnic and religious groups living in Palestine, despite the proximity in which they lived and traded with each other and the essentially Ottoman Jewish-Arab identity of the major cities in late nineteenth-century Palestine. Such intimate ties between the native Jewish and Arab communities notwithstanding, their religious and administrative autonomy expressed itself, among other things, in their traditional and separate community schools.[1]

Western European Jewish philanthropic organizations, as well as the immigrant Zionist teachers hailing mostly from the Pale of Settlement in czarist Russia, adopted the modern pedagogical methods. Both parties were viewed by the local communities as agents of modernization in education. This is an essential point in understanding the tension analyzed in this chapter between Hebrew teachers as agents of knowledge, on the one hand, and the nationalist ideologies they brought with them, on the other. Modernization and nationalism coalesced in the new schools to undo the intricate fabric of old local Ottoman identities through the segregation and ethnic socialization of the children attending them. Ultimately, as Menachem Klein has argued, the rival nationalist movements deliberately sought to "dominate local identity and define those living in Palestine as Zionist-Jewish or Palestinian-Arab."[2]

The decisive overriding goal in the revival of Hebrew was to raise a generation of children speaking the language as their mother tongue. Hebrew as a vernacular in the home was prevalent in the Yishuv since the beginning of the 1880s among adults, for whom it was a second or third language, and by the end of that decade, schools had been established in Jaffa, Rishon LeZion, Rosh Pina, and Jerusalem, where some or most of the lessons were conducted in Hebrew. When the first Hebrew kindergarten was opened in Rishon LeZion in 1898, it created the earliest cohort of native Hebrew speakers.[3] Several studies have addressed the important role played by children in the revival of Hebrew,[4] as well as the important role of school and kindergarten teachers, who, in addition to their work as educators, also served as cultural entrepreneurs dedicated to the creation and dissemination of a new, Hebrew culture.[5]

The revival of Hebrew was only part of a broader process of creating a new culture in the Yishuv within (and in conformity with) the political framework of Zionist ideology. During this process, Hebrew was converted from a sacred to a secular language; from a language studied by adults to one naturally acquired by children; from a written language to a spoken one, incorporating a new vocabulary in order to meet the needs of everyday life and constituting a "polysystem" for the construction of a new culture and society.[6] Regardless of the relative importance assigned by scholars to the various factors contributing to its success, there is a consensus that the revival of Hebrew constituted a unique linguistic event.[7]

Ivrit be-Ivrit: Instrument of Pedagogy or of Segregation?

Until the early modern period, foreign languages were taught by way of translation. Thus, Biblical Hebrew was learned in Hebrew school (*heder*) just as Latin and Greek were taught by private tutors or in monasteries. During the Enlightenment, with the development of modern pedagogy, psychology and the scientific study of the human mind, a new approach to teaching languages emerged, which took acquisition of the mother tongue as its model in what was termed "the natural method." This modern pedagogy placed the child at the center. Successful teaching, it was argued, used the senses, trial and error, and proximity to nature and was driven by the child's curiosity and interest. Later in the nineteenth century, the "natural" or "mother tongue" method of teaching modern languages emerged from this new approach. Under this rubric, many methodologies were employed, but all involved teaching exclusively in the language being studied right from the very first lesson, using visual aids, with grammar being incorporated only gradually.[8]

The "natural" method was Hebraized as *Ivrit be-Ivrit* (Hebrew in Hebrew), and the first forays into using it in teaching Hebrew were made in the Alliance Israélite Universelle schools in Istanbul (1874) and Jerusalem (1883).[9] From the late 1890s until World War I, the method was promoted by teachers in the Yishuv, who also composed the teaching materials. It eventually became the dominant method employed in modern Jewish education in Israel to this day. In what follows, I would like to highlight the distinction between the revival of the language and the use of the *Ivrit be-Ivrit* method: the revival of the language does not necessitate the use of the *Ivrit be-Ivrit* method, and the use of the *Ivrit be-Ivrit* method does not testify to the revival of the Hebrew language.

There were many reasons for Jewish educators in Palestine to adopt the natural method. School principal Nissim Behar (1848–1931) put forward a practical argument, according to which Hebrew was the only language his diverse pupils had in common, and therefore the translation method was not applicable to them.[10] Eliezer ben Yehuda (1858–1922), the first teacher to adopt the method in Jerusalem, supported the method with political arguments, asserting that modern education in Hebrew was the only way to ensure the modernization and homogeneity of the entire community.[11] While the natural method was originally intended to facilitate the acquisition of a second, foreign language, ben Yehuda sought to replace the children's disparate mother tongues with the new "mother tongue."[12] He was not the only one to undertake this endeavor. Haim Margaliot Kalvarisky also wanted to replace other European languages with Hebrew and to "imprison" students in the exclusive knowledge of that language.[13] By means of the natural method—which seemed to render European languages superfluous within the Hebrew school system—Kalvarisky sought to dictate the direction of his students' lives, ensuring that they would remain in the Yishuv.[14]

Yitzhak Epstein (1863–1943), one of the first teachers to compose teaching materials specifically for this method, put forward pedagogical arguments in its favor in an article titled "Ivrit be-Ivrit" published in 1898. Among other arguments, he pointed out that the method was easy, did not rely exclusively on memory, could be used even with very young children, brought the children close to nature, encouraged close observation by the children of their environment, and in its initial stages did not require the use of textbooks.[15] Epstein distinguished between the ideal of reviving the language (which he also supported) and the pedagogical merit of the method. He even went so far as to argue publicly that although the Zionists were extremely fond of this pedagogical tool and saw it as suiting their aspirations, this should not deter ultra-Orthodox Jews both in the Yishuv and elsewhere from adopting it. The merits of the method should be the determining factor, he argued, not any ideological bias that might be attributed to it.[16]

The above analysis shows the difference between the pedagogical merit of the method as such and the uses to which it was put for political purposes. Below I will address another aspect of the new Hebrew pedagogy's political significance in Palestine: the extent to which essentially isolationist nationalist ideologies intersected with the monolingual ideology. In the years preceding World War I, as nationalism spread in the Yishuv, support for the *Ivrit be-Ivrit* method resulted in de facto segregation between the Jewish and Arab populations.

Language and Segregation: Attitudes toward Arabs and Arabic

Scholars of Zionist history have identified the few instances in which Jews attended Arab schools and Arabs attended Jewish institutions.[17] As Menachem Klein points out, on the eve of World War I, local Ottoman Jewish-Arab identity was unraveling, and despite the fact that the two communities lived side by side, education remained mostly segregated, even if "it was not uncommon to find Jewish children having Arab teachers or studying in Arab schools and vice versa."[18] Jewish and Arab children also sometimes attended Christian missionary schools, such as the Collège des Frères de Jaffa.[19]

Nevertheless, two decades later there were those who nostalgically recalled mixed education for Arabs and Jews in the late nineteenth century. In 1931, for example, Haim Margaliot Kalvarisky recalled the prewar Torah u-Melacha (Torah and work) school: "It was astonishing: [the Muslims] were eager to get their children into Jewish schools. It was thanks to Nissim Behar, the principal of the Alliance Israélite Universelle schools in Jerusalem, that they opened their doors to Arab children. He understood that there was no better way to win over hearts and minds than shared education."[20] Yet the integrated education Kalvarisky describes never actually existed on any significant scale, and the few exceptions to ethnic segregation only served to prove the rule. David Yellin recalled, "In those days many effendi [Arabic term for a person of high academic or social status] children, whose parents held senior government posts, attended Behar's Jewish school. They mainly came to learn French because there were no modern Muslim schools in the country."[21] But these were middle-class Arab children whose parents wanted them to obtain a better education and viewed the Jewish school as a local agent of modernization.

Yeshayahu Press, principal of the Lämel school in Jerusalem, reported that the few Arab students attending his school, which was financed by a private Jewish fund, participated fully in the curriculum:

> Two Muslim brothers attended the school, the sons of Ottman Effendi Al Khaledi, a senior civil servant in the local government, along with one Armenian student. When these children reached the fourth grade, in

which students began studying the Mishnah, the principal excused [the non-Jewish students] from those classes. The next day Ottman Effendi came to the school, complained about this discrimination, and demanded that his sons participate in all classes taught in the school without exception. From the sixth grade these children also studied four hours of Talmud each week. They graduated successfully. Ottman's eldest son went on to study at the Technical High School in Darmstadt and would correspond from there with his teachers in excellent Hebrew.[22]

Another interesting instance of Arab children attending a Jewish institution took place in the Mikveh Israel agricultural school, established in 1870 by the Alliance Israélite Universelle with the permission and support of the Ottoman authorities.[23] The Alliance's aspirations to vocational education in modern agriculture and agronomics suited the authorities' goal of importing European know-how in order to promote various fields throughout the Ottoman Empire, ranging from agriculture to law. Ultimately, this was part of a broader program of reform that included compulsory primary education for boys and the establishment of a chain of educational institutions for the benefit of all the empire's subjects, Muslims and non-Muslims alike. The target population of the school was laid out explicitly in a firman, an imperial decree that authorized the establishment of Mikveh Israel just as other firmans had authorized other projects, including the Christian Mission School, noting that "although the school would be built for the children of the Jewish sect, it would nevertheless accept students from other sects and religions."[24] The protocol issued before Mikveh Israel opened its doors was even more explicit, noting that it would accept Jewish students but that it was permissible for "children of another faith to attend the school, as long as their number does not exceed the number of Jewish students at the school."[25] Thus in 1903 two Arab students completed their studies at the school for the first time.[26]

Amin Khalef and Dotan Halevy argue that "Arabs in Eretz Israel viewed the school as an Ottoman institution and as such wanted to study there. It seems that the governing board of the school regarded the acceptance of Arab students as a kind of tax they had to pay the Ottoman authorities in return for permission to operate the school on imperial territory."[27] Khalef and Halevy and also suggest that later on, under the British Mandate, and with increasing Zionist involvement in the school, there were other considerations on both sides. Zionist institutions exploited Mikveh Israel for closer contacts with the Palestinian elite who, for their part, sent their children there to ensure their upward social mobility in a rapidly shifting society.[28] Mikveh Israel was, however, an exception, and education in Palestine remained for the most part segregated.

The language of instruction at Mikveh Israel was not in dispute, since the predominant language spoken in philanthropic schools was that of the funding organization's country, in this case French. It is therefore more interesting to examine the teaching of Hebrew and Arabic specifically and to explore the effects of the teaching methods on segregation, starting with the teaching of Arabic in the Yishuv.

In the early days of modernization of Jewish education, Arabic was part of the curriculum in all schools.[29] I have not found firsthand reports of the pedagogical methods employed,[30] but at the very first meeting of the teachers' union held in Zichron Ya'akov in 1903, there were already arguments about the importance of Arabic. Moshe Smilansky, a prolific Zionist author and advocate of Arab-Jewish coexistence in Palestine, reported on the meeting in the newspaper *Hatzofeh*, where he wrote, "I agree with [Simhah] Wilkomitz that there is no reason to teach a foreign language in schools in the rural communities. But I do strongly demand that they study Arabic, which is very useful for people living in Eretz Israel." He noted that another teacher had commented "on his insistence on the study of Arabic in order to establish good relations with the Arabs," while yet another teacher requested permission to speak in Yiddish but was refused.[31]

David Yellin, Nissim Behar's beloved student in the Torah u-Melacha school, who acquired his excellent Arabic in private lessons Behar had arranged for him, was opposed to the teaching of Arabic in Jewish villages:

> I oppose introducing a foreign [European] language or Arabic in a rural school. Literary Arabic is not likely to promote the students' development or to be of real use. Moreover, it is very difficult to learn, so much so that even after several years of study, students of literary Arabic will not really be able to use it [for reading, writing, or intellectual purposes]. And in any case our children already speak fluent colloquial Arabic. We don't need to make our sons in the villages into scholars but rather into diligent farmers.[32]

Yellin differentiated between spoken (colloquial) Arabic, which he said "would be easier for the children to learn through commercial dealings with Arabs than in school, as experience proves,"[33] and literary Arabic. We may therefore conclude that the village children's fluency in spoken Arabic, at least until World War I, was not influenced by the introduction of literary Arabic into the syllabus. At any rate, the Zichron Ya'akov meeting concluded with a decision that "only one language would be taught in the village schools: Hebrew, with Arabic as an elective in the final two years of study, and that students studying literary Arabic should not be under thirteen years old."[34]

In his study of the changes in the status of Arabic instruction in Jewish schools during the Yishuv period and in the State of Israel, Yonatan Mendel has shown how the teaching of Arabic serves as a gauge for the intensification of the Arab-Jewish conflict. In the early years there was a desire to familiarize Jewish immigrants with the Orient through knowledge of Arabic, Hebrew's "sister" language. Later on, Arabic was taught as a means of knowing the enemy and in the service of reinforcing the segregation of the two populations.[35]

One may similarly ask about the status of Hebrew in Arab education in Eretz Israel–Palestine. Granted, Arabic was the language spoken by the people of Palestine, while Hebrew was a developing phenomenon. Haim Keller, a teacher from Rosh Pina, described Haim Margaliot Kalvarisky's initiative in the early 1900s to set up a school in the nearby Palestinian village of Jauni, where Keller was employed as a Hebrew teacher, on request of the village elders.[36] Keller's article, titled "A Hebrew-Arab school in the Upper Galilee," makes it evident that this was not an attempt to promote integration and cooperation between the children of Jauni and of Rosh Pina but intended to provide the children of Jauni with the benefits of a modern education. Thus Keller explained to the local teachers that it was pointless to beat the children and instead proposed that they adopt his modern pedagogical methods, eschewing force or violence. In Rosh Pina, Keller taught Hebrew as well as (literary) Arabic by the natural method and claimed that his students were more advanced in Arabic than the Jauni children. Yet the Arab and Jewish students did not all study Hebrew and Arabic by the natural method together, despite strong pedagogical considerations in favor of enabling child speakers of different languages to come together in the classroom to learn a new language. It simply did not occur to any of the teachers involved to integrate their classes, and Keller sums up his work in the "Hebrew-Arab" school thus: "Most of the pupils knew how to read . . . and write . . . and speak fluently and to read the map of our country. . . . But the theory I taught them and the progress I brought to them only increased their own national consciousness."[37] Interestingly Keller believed that modern education, including the teaching of Hebrew as a foreign language to Arab students, promoted a Palestinian national consciousness among them. It seems that the carriers of this modernization and modern pedagogy were imbued with nationalist ideas and consequently nationalized their students rather than encouraging coexistence between the two communities.

Ivrit be-Ivrit taught to Arab Muslim children in their villages by Jewish teachers is also mentioned in Alexander Dushkin's memoirs. Duskhin was the inspector of Jewish education under the British Mandate from 1920 to 1921:

> I also visited some Hebrew schools for Arab children. Despite government assistance, only a minority of Arab boys and very few Arab girls were receiving even the minimal elementary education. Some Jews, like [Haim] M. Kalvarisky of PICA [Yiddish acronym for the Palestine Jewish Colonization Association], were interested in establishing Hebrew schools for Arab children. I recall some of those Jewish schools for Arab children in Rosh Pina (Jauni) and in Nablus, housed in miserable, one-room, windowless and floorless huts, in which brave Jewish teachers were struggling in vain "to kindle the spark." But the government frowned on such efforts; nor was the official Jewish leadership at the time in favor.[38]

At a meeting of the temporary committee of the Jews of Eretz Israel,[39] convened to discuss future relations with the Arabs, Kalvarisky remarked that this was actually not a Jewish initiative: "I have one more pleasant thing to tell you. In several places in Palestine, schools have been opened for Arabs to learn *Hebrew* at the request of the Arabs."[40] As Dushkin points out, however, these were individual initiatives that did not support Kalvarisky's fantasy of a "common education," as exemplified by Nissim Behar's activity in the Torah u-Melacha school in Jerusalem at the end of the nineteenth century.

An endowment established by the Jewish philanthropist Sir Ellis Kadoorie was used in the early 1930s to set up two schools, one in Tavor (Tabor) and one in Tulkarem, where a drive to segregate, regardless of pedagogy, was clearly apparent.[41] When Kadoorie's endowment for education in Palestine was received, it was not at first clear for which ethnic group the money was intended. Humphrey Bowman, the director of the Education Department of the British government in Palestine suggested setting up an English-style public school where Jews and Arabs would study together in Hebrew and Arabic in the lower grades and in English in the higher grades. This idea encountered opposition from Zionist bodies. Frederick Kisch, head of the Political Department of the World Zionist Organization branch in Jerusalem, recorded a meeting with Humphrey Bowman and Yosef Luria, head of the Education Department of the Zionist Organization, in his diary:

> Bowman put all his cards on the table . . . setting out in detail the government proposal for a combined Arabic-Hebrew Secondary School on the lines of an English public school, with separate boarding houses for boys of the two communities. In accordance with the decision of the Executive as representing the almost unanimous consensus of opinion throughout the country, I opposed the scheme as firmly as possible on the main ground that at the present stage of development of our national home it was essential that our education should be national in character, emphasizing that the Mandatory Government was really pledged to support us in our desire to secure this. Bowman made no attempt to conceal his disappointment with our position as he had set his heart on creating this institution before leaving the country, believing that it would create a real Palestinian spirit and do much to bring the two races together [in English], while also being an enthusiastic believer in English public-school methods.[42]

The upshot of Zionist opposition to the public-school plan was segregation: a Hebrew school and a separate Arab one, each for the exclusive use of its target population, each to be taught in its own language.[43]

Given the above examples, it seems clear that segregation was the inevitable result of nationalist views and not of the pedagogical preference for *Ivrit be-Ivrit*. That is, neither the natural method nor pedagogy determined this segregation, since they could have been effective for all students in the acquisition of both Hebrew and Arabic. The compatibility between an effective method for teaching foreign languages and the needs of nation building, especially in the linguistically complex case of the modern Jewish community in Eretz Israel, did not lead to de facto segregation in the education system. On the contrary—implementing the method could have contributed to overcoming the segregation that resulted from the different languages and was a remnant of the ethnic segregation that had existed previously in Eretz Israel (even within the Jewish community); this segregation was subsequently further encouraged by the national views that by the 1920s became established on both sides.[44]

Conclusion: Exclusiveness versus Mobilizing Pedagogy for Reviving Hebrew

This chapter has explored the segregation of the Jewish and Arab communities in the early days of modern education in the Yishuv, from the perspective of the pedagogical approaches to Hebrew language education. As we saw, because of its isolationism, the Hebrew education system was complicit in the segregation of the local Arab and Jewish populations in Palestine. To be sure, particularly in educational institutions, segregation preceded the arrival of the new Zionist teachers. These teachers brought with them new educational approaches that centered on the child and might have therefore facilitated teaching and learning regardless of national affiliation and could have thus served as a bridge between the local populations.

But this natural child-centered method of teaching Hebrew existed within a particular political and ideological framework, notwithstanding the highly developed professional skills of the teachers who introduced it to Yishuv. The teaching of Hebrew in Jewish schools in Palestine, rooted as it was in innovation and modern methods, was seen by both contemporaries and subsequent historians of education as one of the greatest revolutions in Jewish education. But these revolutionary methods ultimately fell in line with the nationalist idea, leading to the segregation of Arab and Jewish children. The best that modern, progressive education could offer ultimately served the nationalists. As mentioned, this chapter focuses on the Zionist pedagogical discourse and does not offer an analysis of the Palestinian pedagogical discourse and a study on its development. Further research is necessary in order to clarify this aspect.[45]

In Central Europe, where this modern pedagogy had evolved, two apparently opposing trends emerged: first, the child and his or her freedom were made a priority, thereby distancing the method from nationalism, which by definition focused on the collective rather than the individual. The second trend was toward a compulsory, nationalist, government-run education system that sought to limit the freedom of teachers and students alike and to mold the character of the nation.[46] Conversely, in the Jewish Yishuv, teachers wanted to integrate both these trends into their efforts to construct a modern Jewish education system almost from scratch. The idea that pedagogical ideology could exist regardless of national identity was never even discussed, since the overall priority of nationhood was taken for granted. The result was that even at the margins of the educational sphere, there were no truly nonsegregated schools.

Dr. Miriam Szamet is currently a post-doctorate fellow at the DFG (German Research Foundation) on the project "Jewish National Youth Movements Education in Germany and Palestine in the Interwar Period" at the Technische Universität in Braunschweig and the Hebrew University of Jerusalem. Her first book, *"We Are the Novelty": Jewish Pedagogues and the Pedagogical Discourse in Palestine*, was awarded the Shlomo and Bella Bartal Prize for the promotion of historical research and is forthcoming with Magnes Press Jerusalem.

Notes

1. Menachem Klein, *Lives in Common: Arabs and Jews in Jerusalem, Jaffa, and Hebron* (Oxford: Oxford University Press, 2014). For more on local Ottoman identities shared by Jews—especially but not exclusively the Sephardic communities—and Arabs, see Mahmoud Yazbak, "In the Shadow of the Empire: Palestinian Responses to the Zionist Movement, 1882–1914," in *Zionism and the Empires*, ed. Yehouda Shenhav (Jerusalem: Van Leer Institute, 2015, in Hebrew), 183–211; Abigail Jacobson, "Practices of Subjecthood and Loyalty to Empire: The Ottomanization Movement as a Test Case," in Shenhav, *Zionism and the Empires*, 169–70.
2. Klein, *Lives in Common*, ix.
3. Ivy Sichel and Miri Bar-Ziv Levy, "Women's Contribution to the Creation of a Hebrew-speaking community during the First Aliyah," *Cathedra* 169 (2018): 75–108 (in Hebrew). This study points to the unilingual ideology prevalent at that time and its incorporation into the historiography of revival of the language. According to this ideology, the revival of spoken Hebrew depended on speaking Hebrew exclusively.
4. Zohar Shavit writes about how children spoke Hebrew as early as the First Aliyah period, concluding that "children were entrusted with the burden, not always to their advantage, of the revolution." Yaakov Shavit and Shoshanna Sitton show how the needs of children dictated the creation of an entire literary and cultural repertoire for kindergartens and schools. Basmat Even-Zohar claims that children initiated the new culture and presents evidence of the extent to which they were conscripted into the creation of a Hebrew culture, despite their minority status in the population at the time of the First Aliyah. Tzipora Schori-Rubin demonstrates that the Hebrew spoken by children in the Ezra kindergarten in Jerusalem impacted the languages of instruction at the Lämel school, where they went for their primary education. Hebrew displaced the German that had been the language of instruction there for many years. Rachel Elboim-Dror writes of the creation of a native Hebrew Zionist youth culture centered around spoken Hebrew, emerging as soon as the early 1880s. Zohar Shavit, "Children as Agents of the Hebrew Revolution," in *Children as Avant Garde: Childhood and Adolescence in Times of Crises and Social Change*, ed. Yael Darr, Tal Kogman, and Yehudith Steiman (Tel Aviv: Tel Aviv University and the Mofet Institute, 2010, in Hebrew), 23; Yaacov Shavit and Shoshanna Sitton, *Staging and Stagers in Modern Jewish Palestine: The Creation of Festive Lore in a New Culture, 1882–1948* (Detroit: Wayne State University Press, 2004), 29–40; Basmat Even-Zohar, "Children's Participation in the Hebrew Enterprise, 1880–1905," in Darr, Kogman, and Steiman, *Children as Avant Garde*, 63–64; Tzipora Shehory-Rubin, "Hebrew Kindergarten Teachers during the First and Second Aliyot," *Dor Le'Dor* 19–20 (2002): 156 (in Hebrew); Rachel Elboim-Dror, "'Look Who Is Coming and Going, the New Hebrew Is Coming from among Us.' On the Youth Culture of the First Aliyot," *Alpayim* 12 (1996): 104–35 (in Hebrew).

5. Educators involved in such initiatives include David Yellin, Ephraim Cohen-Reiss, Yosef Meyuchas, Eliezer ben Yehuda, Yehuda Grazovsky, Israel Belkind, David Yudilevitz, Yizhak Epstein, Simhah Wilkomitz, and Eliyahu Ze'ev Levin-Epstein. See Basmat Even Zohar, "Construction of Children's Literature within the Creation of Hebrew Culture in Eretz-Israel" (PhD diss., Tel Aviv University, 1999, in Hebrew).
6. Benjamin Harshav, *Language in Time of Revolution* (Berkeley: University of California Press, 1993), 89–92. For discussion of the concept of polysystem, see Itamar Even-Zohar, "Polysystem Theory," *Poetics Today* 1, no. 1–2 (1979): 287–310.
7. Uzi Ornan, *In the Beginning Was the Language* (Jerusalem: Academy of Hebrew Language, 2013, in Hebrew); Benjamin Harshav, *Language in the Time of Revolution*. There is disagreement with regard to the term "revival" much used by scholars. See, for example, Shlomo Morag, "Modern Hebrew: Some Sociolinguistic Aspects," *Cathedra* 56 (1990): 70 (in Hebrew).
8. Bella H. Banathy and Jesse O. Sawyer, "The Primacy of Speech: An Historical Sketch," *Modern Language Journal* 53, no. 8 (1969): 537–44; Emily C. Rose, "Maximilian D. Berlitz," Immigrant Entrepreneurship, German Historical Institute, 8 June 2011, http://www.immigrantentrepreneurship.org/entries/maximilian-d-berlitz/.
9. For more on the role of the Jewish philanthropic organizations in the Mediterranean region, see Eli Bar-Chen, "For My Brethren's Sake? The Alliance Israélite Universelle, the Anglo-Jewish Association and the Hilfsverein der Deutschen Juden: Jewish Solidarity in the Age of Information, Industrialization, Nationalism, and Colonialism" (PhD diss., Tel Aviv University, 2002, in Hebrew).
10. The children's mother tongues included Ladino, Yiddish, and Arabic, among other languages. In Jewish schools endowed by philanthropic organizations, several languages were taught besides Hebrew: the language of the organization's country, Turkish, and Arabic. Hebrew was taught in these schools as a signifier of the New Jew, since although organizations such as the Alliance Israélite Universelle, Hilfsverein der deutschen Juden, and the Anglo-Jewish Association were not at all Zionist, they still embraced Jewish national solidarity. There is evidence recorded by principals of the Alliance and Ezra schools at the turn of the twentieth century that their multilingual and multiethnic pupils constituted a major challenge to attempts to establish a unified curriculum in a single language. See Nissim Behar, "Letter to Menachem Ribolov," *Hado'ar* 10, no. 12 (30 January 1931): 193 (in Hebrew); Yishayahu Press, *One Hundred Years in Jerusalem* (Jerusalem: Mass Publishing House, 1964, in Hebrew), 108–9.
11. Eliezer ben Yehuda, "On the Matter of Education," *Havatzelet* 10, no. 13 (2 January 1880): 91 (in Hebrew).
12. Yosef Lang, "Eliezer ben Yehuda—A Hebrew Teacher in the Hatorah ve-Hamelachah School," *Cathedra* 56 (1990): 93–108 (in Hebrew); Shlomo Harmati, *The Pioneer Teachers in Eretz Israel* (Jerusalem: Modan, 2000, in Hebrew).
13. Hemda ben Yehuda, "Yishuv Matters: An Interview with Haim Margaliot Kalvarisky," *Hashkapha* 82 (7 July 1905): 1–2 (in Hebrew). The notion of "imprisonment" in a language was also raised in the context of gender. In the first meeting of teachers in Zichron Ya'akov in 1903, for example, David Yellin asked, "Is it absolutely essential to teach the girls—whom we want to stay in Palestine to be mothers and educators and industrious housewives—a European language as well? Hebrew is sufficient for their education." Cited by Margalit Shilo in *The Challenge of Gender* (Bnei Brak: Hakibbutz Hameuchad, 2007, in Hebrew), 28.
14. For more about Kalvarisky, see Yizhak Cytrin, "Chaim Margalit-Kalvarisky, Land Acquisition and the Arab Question: Anatomy of Jewish-Arab relations–Utopia and Reality," *Cathedra* 162 (2017): 35–66 (in Hebrew).
15. Yitzhak Epstein, "Hebrew in Hebrew: The Natural Method in the Early Days of Teaching the Hebrew Language," *Ha-Shiloah* 4, no. 23 (October 1898): 396 (in Hebrew).
16. Epstein, "Hebrew in Hebrew," 391. In his article, Epstein is deeply critical of the way Hebrew was taught among the ultra-Orthodox and in traditional education, arguing that the translation method prevalent in their Hebrew schools (*heder*) makes it impossible to separate the wheat from the chaff. Contemporary research supports his argument, with Mordechai Zalkin going so far as to argue that

many graduates of the traditional Hebrew schools could be called partially illiterate. See Mordechai Zalkin, *Modernizing Jewish Education in Nineteenth Century Eastern Europe: The School as the Shrine of the Jewish Enlightenment* (Leiden: Brill, 2016), 24. For a discussion of learning in the *heder*, see Chava Turniansky, "Heder Education in the Early Modern Period," in *The Heder: Studies, Documents, Literature and Memoirs*, ed. David Assaf, Immanuel Etkes, and Uriel Gellman (Ramat Aviv: Institute for the History of Polish Jewry and Israel-Poland Relations, 2010, in Hebrew), 33–36.

17. Klein, *Lives in Common*, 51. Amin Khalef and Dotan Halevy, "As Strangers in the Land: The Agricultural School Mikveh Israel and Its Arab Students, 1870–1939," *Zmanim* 135 (2016): 82–99 (in Hebrew). A joint education initiative that never came to fruition emerged after the period addressed in this chapter, envisioned by Mordechai Shenhavi, one of the founders of the educational institute of the Hashomer Hatzair youth movement in Mishmar ha-Emek in the early 1930s. Shenhavi (working from political rather than pedagogical premises) wanted the Hashomer Hatzair high school to cater to all children in the region, Jews and Arabs alike. In that instance pedagogy overcame politics, as Yaakov Hazan later pointed out, since the cultural differences were considered too great to bridge in a joint educational framework. For more on this episode, see Yitzhak Paltek, *The Mosad* (Ramat Efal: Sifriyat Poalim, 1989), 29–30 (in Hebrew).
18. Klein, *Lives in Common*, 51.
19. Klein, *Lives in Common*, 58–59.
20. Haim Margaliot Kalvarisky, "The Relations between Jews and Arabs before the War," *Brit Shalom Weekly* 2, no. 2 (Nisan 1931): 52 (in Hebrew).
21. David Yellin, "Nissim Behar," *Hado'ar* 7, no. 8 (23 December 1927): 119.
22. Press, *One Hundred Years in Jerusalem*, 112.
23. On Mikveh Israel, see Eliyahu Krauze, "The Birth-Pangs of Mikveh Israel," *Zion* 7, no. 2 (1942): 104–8 (in Hebrew).
24. Khalef and Halevy, "As Strangers in the Land," 86.
25. Joseph Shapira, *A Century of Mikveh-Israel, 1870–1970* (Tel Aviv: Tarbut ve-Hinuch, 1970, in Hebrew), 68.
26. Shapira, *A Century of Mikveh-Israel*, 186. According to Shapira there is no mention of Arab students in other reports.
27. Khalef and Halevy, "As Strangers in the Land," 84.
28. Khalef and Halevy, "As Strangers in the Land," 84.
29. Moshe Rinot notes, for example, that in the German Jewish seminar in Jerusalem, Arabic was taught almost as much as German. David Yellin was responsible for Arabic instruction and worked to expand hours and not only ensured that pupils were taught to speak, read, and write Arabic, but also trained teachers of Arabic. See Moshe Rinot, *"Hilfsverein der Deutschen Juden"—Creation and Struggle* (Jerusalem: School of Education of the Hebrew University and the Ministry of Education, 1972, in Hebrew), 122–23.
30. Uzi Ornan presents the only firsthand report on the subject, by Yoel Moshe Salomon, who reported that Arabic was taught by private tutors in the first half of the nineteenth century in Jerusalem. For another report about Yechiel Michal Pines's goal of setting up a school when he arrived in Eretz Israel in 1878, which would teach "God's Torah, and the rudiments of Hebrew and Arabic," see Ornan, *In the Beginning*, 22 and 42 respectively. Mention is made of a later instance, this time of teaching Arabic in the Reali school in Haifa, in 1913. During a meeting of the Education Department in 1938 dealing with the teaching of Arabic in Jewish schools of Knesset Israel, Dr. Yisrael ben Ze'ev, a senior member of the department, reported on Arabic teaching: "Before the war Arabic teachers were sheikhs, mostly students from Azahar, with no pedagogical training. There were a few Jewish teachers too, whose level was higher than that of the sheikhs. After the war the sheikhs stopped teaching in our schools and veteran teachers were joined by young teachers from Eretz Israel and abroad" (Minutes of Meeting, 10–11 April 1938, Central Zionist Archive, J17–319, in Hebrew). I am indebted to Yonatan Mendel for this source.
31. Moshe Smilansky, "Teachers' Meeting in Zichron Yaakov," *Hatzofeh* 217 (cont. from 215) (2 October 1903): 926 (in Hebrew).

32. Smilansky, "Teachers' Meeting," 926. This passage also tells us of teachers' attitudes to the village schools and the differences between them and urban schools.
33. Anonymous, "Inaugural Meeting in Zichron Yaakov, 1903," in *Jubilee Book of the Teachers Union 1903–1928*, ed. David Kimchi (Tel Aviv: Teachers Union Center, 1928, in Hebrew), 389.
34. Smilansky, "Teachers' Meeting," 927.
35. Yonatan Mendel, *The Creation of Israeli Arabic: Political and Security Considerations in the Making of Arabic Language Studies* (New York: Palgrave Macmillan, 2014), 25–29; Yonatan Mendel, "From German Philology to Local Usability: The Emergence of 'Practical Arabic' in the Hebrew Reali School in Haifa, 1913–1948," *Middle Eastern Studies* 52, no. 1 (2016): 1–26; Liora Halperin, "Orienting Languages: Reflection on the Study of Arabic in the Yishuv," *Jewish Quarterly Review* 96, no. 4 (2006): 481–89.
36. Haim Keller, "A Hebrew Arabic School in the Upper Galilee," in *Jubilee Book of the Teachers Union 1903–1953*, ed. Dov Kimchi and Y. L. Riklis (Tel Aviv: Teachers Union Center, 1956, in Hebrew), 549–51.
37. Keller, "A Hebrew Arabic School," 551.
38. Alexander M. Dushkin, *Living Bridges: Memoirs of an Educator* (Jerusalem: Keter, 1975), 44.
39. The temporary committee of the Jews of Eretz Israel was the organizational body that established the Jewish Assembly of Representatives in Palestine and operated in Jaffa at the end of World War I.
40. Kalvarisky's speech to the Va'ad Hazmani (emphasis Kalvarisky's) (Central Zionist Archive, L4/881), 7 (in Hebrew). See also an extensive discussion of the subject of language and Jewish-Arab relations at the end of World War I and Kalvarisky's plans in Tom Segev, *One Palestine Complete: Jews and Arabs under the British Mandate*, trans. Haim Watzman (New York: H. Holt, 2002), 283–84.
41. Segev mentions the episode in *One Palestine Complete*, 283–84. It is reported in greater detail in an article by Eliezer Domke, "Birth-Pangs of the Kadoorie Agricultural School," *Cathedra* 35 (1985): 91–108 (in Hebrew).
42. Frederick H. Kisch, personal diary. Entry for 2 February 1924. Central Zionist Archives S25/565/1, 114–15.
43. See also Bowman's recollection of the matter in Humphrey Bowman, *Middle East Window* (London: Longmans, Green, 1942), 264–65.
44. Moreover Ornan, for example, argues that the Zionist Organization was forced to accept Hebrew as the official language of the Zionist movement at the Eighth Zionist Congress of 1907, as a result of developments in the Yishuv, "from a desire to preserve the leadership mandate," given "the demonstratively strong place of the Hebrew language in the Hebrew Yishuv which long predates the war of languages. . . . But in fact, this statement was merely lip service paid under pressure." It appears that Hebrew was not a supreme value for European Zionists, who differed on this as in other matters from their Eretz Israel brothers. See Ornan, *In the Beginning*, 66.
45. See, for example, the following research about teaching history among Jews and Arabs in Mandatory Palestine: Yoni Furas, *Educating Palestine: Teaching and Learning History under the Mandate* (Oxford: Oxford University Press, 2020).
46. See, for example, two test cases in Germany contemporary with these trends: Christine Mayer, "Circulation and Internationalization of Pedagogical Concepts and Practices in the Discourse of Education: The Hamburg School Reform Experiment, 1919–1933," *Paedagogica Historica* 50, no. 5 (2014): 580–98; and Marjorie Lamberti, "Radical Schoolteachers and the Origins of the Progressive Education Movement in Germany, 1900–1914," *History of Education Quarterly* 40, no. 1 (Spring 2000): 22–48.

Select Bibliography

Bowman, Humphrey. *Middle East Window*. London: Longmans, Green, 1942.
Dushkin, Alexander M. *Living Bridges: Memoirs of an Educator*. Jerusalem: Keter, 1975.

Harshav, Benjamin. *Language in Time of Revolution*. Berkeley: University of California Press, 1993.
Klein, Menachem. *Lives in Common: Arabs and Jews in Jerusalem, Jaffa, and Hebron*. Oxford: Oxford University Press, 2014.
Mendel, Yonatan. *The Creation of Israeli Arabic: Political and Security Considerations in the Making of Arabic Language Studies*. New York: Palgrave Macmillan, 2014.
Segev, Tom. *One Palestine Complete: Jews and Arabs under the British Mandate*. Translated by Haim Watzman. New York: H. Holt, 2002.
Shavit, Yaacov, and Shoshanna Sitton. *Staging and Stagers in Modern Jewish Palestine: The Creation of Festive Lore in a New Culture, 1882–1948*. Detroit: Wayne State University Press, 2004.
Zalkin, Mordechai. *Modernizing Jewish Education in Nineteenth Century Eastern Europe: The School as the Shrine of the Jewish Enlightenment*. Leiden: Brill, 2016.

CHAPTER 10

THE BIBLICAL BORDERS BETWEEN THEOLOGY AND HISTORY
ISRAELI SCHOOLBOOK MAPS, 1903–1967

ORNA VAADIA

Introduction

This chapter examines how biblical borders were represented in Israeli textbook maps. The period under study begins in 1903, when the first Hebrew textbook containing a map of the Land of Israel was published.[1] In the beginning of that era, the Hebrew textbook maps of the Land of Israel did not present borders in general and biblical borders in particular. As will be shown below, the discussion over these borders emerged only twenty-five years later, and thus they also came to be represented in Hebrew textbook maps. The Six Day War marks the beginning of a new era of schoolbook mapping, thanks to the territorial changes resulting from the war and modifications in the Israeli education system. The discussion below will illuminate the designated role of biblical borders' representations in Israeli textbook maps within the context of the Zionist movement's nation-building process and the construction of a spatial imagination.

"Spatial imagination" is the cognitive mental action through which we produce a perception of space. This perception is based on both concrete experiences in space and spatial knowledge as mediated by culture and society. By emphasizing that spatial consciousness is the result of social systems, the term "spatial imagination" also highlights the ontological gap between physical space or "space itself," which is not accessible to us, and social space, which is accessible only through social and cultural systems such as language, science, religion, and so forth. These systems imbue space with meaning, and through them we perceive reality in general and space in particular. In other words, the inaccessibility of "space itself" requires the existence of an imaginary relationship to space that allows us to develop spatial awareness through cultural systems.[2]

A national education system is in essence an active cultural system; as such it can play a central role in strengthening the students' relationship to the land and in creating a deep commitment to the ideals and beliefs they are taught.[3] Examining how biblical borders were cartographically represented in textbook maps allows us to trace the ways in which space was imagined and to explore the meanings attributed to biblical texts by the national-secular education system in the pre-state Yishuv and the first two decades of the State of Israel.[4]

Despite the conventional view, according to which Zionism was a secular ideology opposed to religion, the school textbooks examined below demonstrate a more complex and less dichotomous relationship between Zionism and religion. By analyzing the representation of biblical borders in textbook maps throughout the abovementioned period, this chapter suggests that the maps and the accompanying texts embodied the spatial socialization processes promoted by the Zionist movement.

The rationale for focusing on school textbooks relies on the argument that the content of such texts is the result of negotiations between various groups in society and thus reflects the cultural and political processes that shaped it. As an agent of national socialization, the textbook therefore constitutes a rich research source, allowing us to trace modes of spatial imagination that the Zionist movement wished to promote through delineating the biblical borders.

It has not been possible to identify a clear correlation between the many historical upheavals that occurred during the period under discussion and the diverse ways in which the biblical borders were represented during this time. They were, however, certainly influenced by some of the more prominent textbook authors. Chief among them was Abraham Brawer, who, besides his geographic and cartographic academic training, was also a rabbinical authority. His 1928 textbook was the first to discuss the issue of biblical borders. As Yoram Bar-Gal points out, Brawer's authority as a geographer and his central position among other authors influenced the structure and content of such textbooks, which in turn influenced the emergence of biblical border representations in textbooks maps from that point on.[5]

My goal here is to examine textbook maps as evidence of their cartographers' spatial imagination, which they sought to disseminate to the students. My approach rejects the concept of the map as an objective scientific product and perceives it rather as an intersubjective interpretation of reality containing visible and invisible data and political meanings. Defining maps as culture-dependent representations undermines the traditional distinction between the "truth" value of scientific maps and political maps. As Michael Feige notes, the use of scientific rhetoric and appearance in maps in order to give them an apolitical and nonideological semblance is essentially political.[6] Additionally, Jeremy Crampton and John Krieger argue that maps not only are a representation of our spatial perception, but simultaneously also construct reality.[7] Finally, Denis Wood and John Brian Harley have asked how maps create social practices and make use of the spaces differentiated by them, suggesting that maps can be perceived both as spatial representations and as a practice of spatial construction.[8] Similarly, in this chapter, maps are perceived not only as representations of space but also as constructing it.

Accordingly, this chapter explores first, how were biblical borders represented in textbooks maps? Second, what meanings were ascribed to these borders by the authors? And third, what do such meanings tell us about the spatial imagination that textbook authors sought to instill in students?

Generally speaking, the meanings ascribed to biblical borders were at times theological and at other times historical. Such distinctions can be identified in several ways: first, by how the text in the book describes the maps in question; second, by whether the textbook's author perceives the Bible as a religious or a historical text (the prevailing opinion during this period among most secular textbook authors was that the "history of our people should be taught from the Bible itself");[9] and, finally, according to the actual cartography used in representing the border.

In discussing these maps, I will focus on two additional factors. First, their *narrative aspect*, that is, the extent to which they served the educational system's goal of creating and imparting a bequeathed tradition as the foundation of the contemporary Zionist narrative. Second, the maps' *territorial aspect*, that is, the space they actually demarcated and its relationship to the political options that existed or were being discussed at the time of the maps' production, as compared to the imagined space of the Land of Israel and the manner of constructing this scheme.

The Promised Land Map: A Borderless Border

The Promised Land map, which appears in several textbooks,[10] presents the paradoxical image of a borderless border map (see map 10.1). The only indication of a border, citing God's promise to Abraham, "from the river of Egypt to the great river Euphrates,"[11] appears in two geophysical elements: the Egypt river in the south and the Euphrates river in the north.

In examining the textbooks in which this map appeared, we find that the same geographical demarcation appears in the written texts under three different names: the "Patriarchs' Border," the "Promise Border," and the "Intended Border." While the Promised Land's borders under these different names do share some meanings, each name embodies unique meanings. These meanings appear in various discourses and represent different arguments, which in turn construct a different imaginary space.

These unique meanings show that, unlike approaches that refer to Zionism as a secular creation that situated itself in opposition to religion, the textbooks used in the secular school system rejected the notion of a dichotomy between the theological and national-historical readings of the Bible and presented them rather as complementary arguments in support of the Zionist undertaking, as will be discussed below.

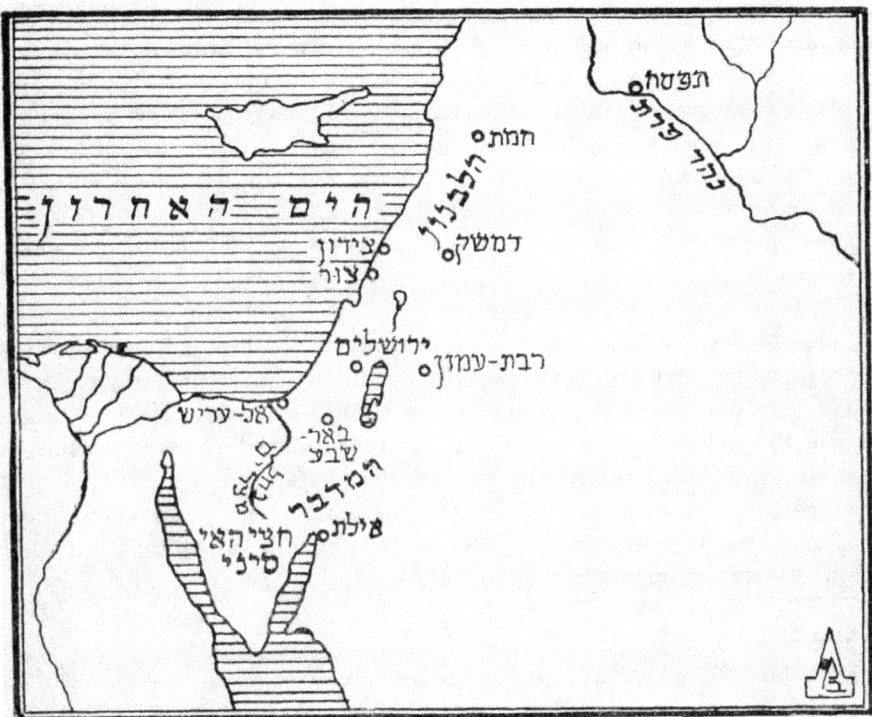

Map 10.1. The Promised Land map. Source: David Shifman and Zvi Ariely, *Netivot Hamikra: Yehoshua* [Paths in the Bible: The book of Joshua] (Tel Aviv: Yavne, 1953), 12.

Narrative Aspects of the Promised Land Map

The Patriarchs' Border

The Patriarchs' Border refers to the three forefathers of the Hebrew nation: Abraham, Isaac, and Jacob, who, as indicated in the Bible, were promised by God to inherit the Land of Israel.

The textbooks' discussion of the Patriarchs' Border as the object of the promise refers not only to the theological aspects of God's promise, but also to the historical aspects related to the story. In this context the Patriarchs constitute the beginning of history, from which an imaginary line stretches all the way to the present. This line serves as the grounds for legitimizing the territorial claims over the land demarcated geophysically by two rivers: the Egypt river and the Euphrates river. By speaking of the Patriarchs' Border, these textbooks establish three building blocks of national conceptual thinking. First, the Patriarchs' Border presents the origin of the people in antiquity, thus providing an ancient source for imagining the community as a nation. One of the textbooks laid the foundation for national thinking by opening the discussion as follows: "The borders of the land, as promised to the Patriarchs."[12]

Second, the textbooks using this map strive to demonstrate the affinity between the nation and the territory. As one of the books asserts, "The Land of Israel is ours. Thousands of years ago, our ancestors—the first Hebrew men—settled there."[13] This wording transposes the Patriarchs' Border from a theological context to a historical-national narrative, even as it fuses the two together: nation and territory; the Patriarchs and the Land of Israel. In addition, the Patriarchs' Hebrew identity blurs the years of Jewish exile, strengthens an indigenous identity of contemporary Zionist students in Palestine-Israel, and obscures the intervening history of the land and its residents.

Finally, several textbooks using this map highlight the claim to hereditary rights by stressing the promise repeatedly made to the Patriarchs that the land was a legacy to be passed from father to son: "It is told in the Bible that this land was promised to our Patriarchs: Abraham, Isaac and Jacob—to be their sons' forever."[14]

The Patriarchs' Border is thus inserted into the national discourse by evoking the three building blocks of modern nationalism, which together create a territorial claim on the basis of linear historical continuity.[15] For Zionism, the nation was not created but rather re-created, since it viewed the national community as a direct continuation of the biblical era community.

The Promise Border

The Promise Border was discussed in textbooks both from the theological and the national-secular perspective. The manner in which the Promise Border is represented from the theological perspective places the validity of the border in a metaphysical sphere derived from the relationship between God and man, as manifested in the biblical citations made in these textbooks and discussed below.[16]

David Shifman's book *Israel My Homeland* is a national-secular example of applying the Promise Border concept.[17] Shifman intertwines the biblical and the Zionist narratives into a seemingly unified historical continuum, as can be seen from such consecutive chapter headings as "The Patriarchs Promise," "The First Temple—Moses and Joshua Conquer the Land," "The Second Temple—The Koresh Declaration," "The National Home—The Balfour Declaration," "The United Nations Resolution on the Establishment of the State of Israel," and finally, "The Declaration of the State of Israel."

These landmarks in the history of the Jewish people, the historical declarations that accompany them, and God's promise to the Patriarchs present a collection of histories and political documents from different periods, all geared to solidify the argument for the Jewish people's settlement in the Land of Israel from time immemorial to the present. Assimilating God's promise into the Zionist historical narrative, while secularizing a theological text in the process, is at the core of this exercise in expropriating the Bible for the purposes of a national-secular ideology.

Along these lines, Amnon Raz-Krakotzkin has argued that this process of secularization does not actually make for a complete break from the religious tradition;

indeed, rather than seeing nationalism as a mere substitute for religion, he argues that it provides a different interpretation of the religious and the biblical perception.[18] As part of this interpretation, the religious concepts of choice and promise were formulated in terms borrowed from the romantic colonial language of designation and rights. Similarly, Ruth Firer has concluded that representations of the promise narrative in Israeli history textbooks transform it into a story that "turns the connection between the land and the people, as determined by God, into a progressive human and cosmic timeline." This "meta-historical approach," she argues, "has a distinct deterministic nature."[19]

The Intended Border

The third name used in the context of the Promised Land map, the Intended Border, places the border in a transcendent context as a border located beyond the bounds of historical time. Authors describe it as the redemption border, the border of the kingdom to come, or the nation's border in the end of days. Being an "ideal border" that is located beyond historical time, it acquires the qualities of a theological concept that represents an eternal and unchanging gauge of spatial dimension. This border stands in contrast to borders that result from human action and as such are provisional and changeable. Such definitions set the theological border apart from the ephemeral and temporal historical border. The textbooks' authors had to address the tension between the Intended Border and the borders of the kingdoms of David and Solomon (see map 10.2), which occupied the same territory.[20] This territorial overlap might have been viewed as the historical embodiment of a theological demarcation, thereby destabilizing the status of the Intended Border as a "border of the kingdom to come" by being interpreted as already representing the beginning of redemption.

The authors resolved this tension by distinguishing between occupying the area as conquerors and settling only part of the region. For "the kingdom's borders are one thing and the borders of settlement are another," as Brawer puts it.[21] Indeed, Brawer contrasts the theological or ideal borders with the political borders: "The common denominator of the ideal borders is their permanency, unlike the political borders that are constantly changing."[22] This proposition sets out from the ideal, theological, and permanent borders and then examines the historical realization of different borders in relationship to this ideal border.

In this sense, while the theological discourse presents the Intended Border as an ideal beyond the bounds of time, within the political discourse, the ahistorical permanence of the Intended Border is contrasted with the transience of the political border. These qualities highlight the deficiencies of the political borders vis-à-vis the Intended Border—temporary versus eternal, ephemeral versus permanent, human versus divine. This contrast can be interpreted in two ways: theologically, this can simply be a distinction between the sacred and the profane; politically, however, the contrast can be between existing borders and designs for the future.

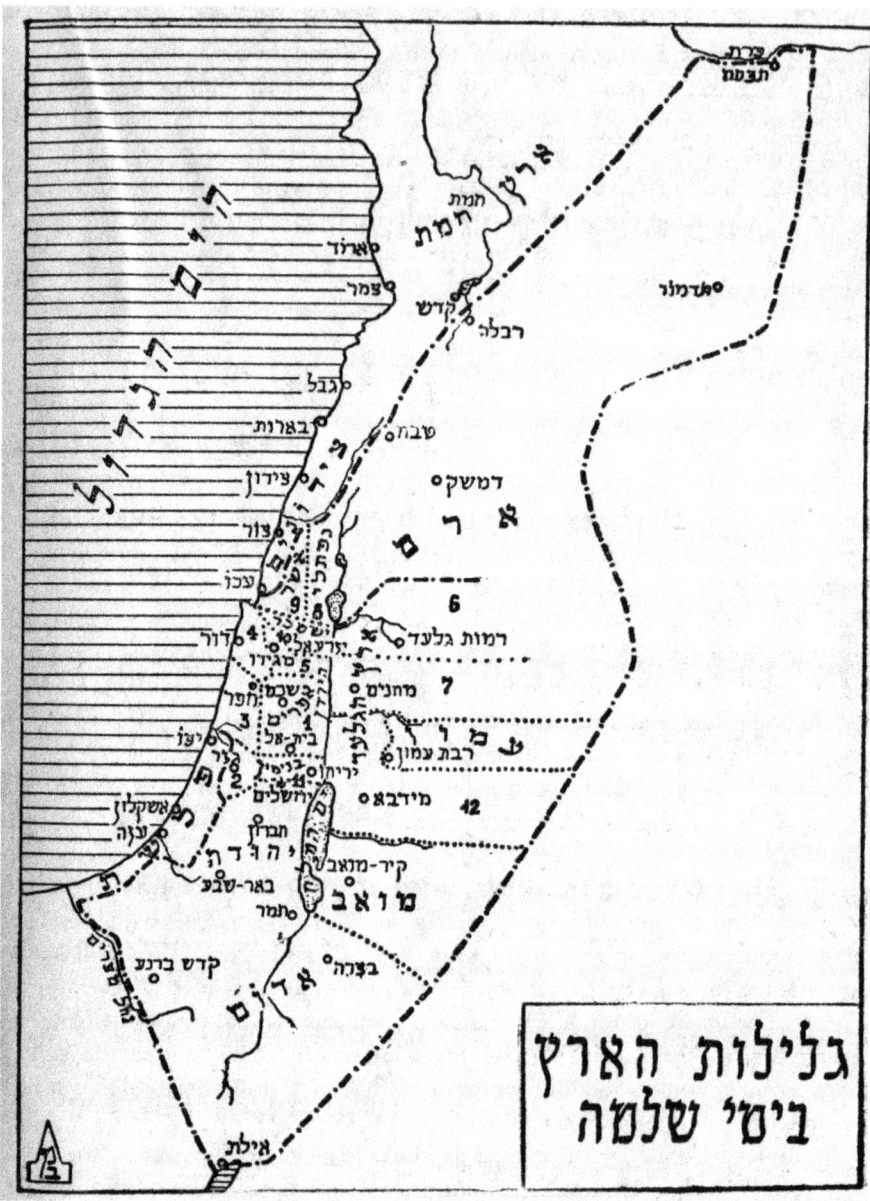

Map 10.2. The Kingdom of Israel in the Solomon era. Source: N. Gutman and D. Dovnikov, *Tanach Lebiet Hasefer: Melachim Alef* [Bible for school: 1 Kings] (Tel Aviv: Yavne, 1957), 16.

The Promised Land Map: Theology, History, Nation

The narrative components derived from the various meanings ascribed to the theological border, under its three names, appear in different compositions and arrangements, performing different functions and operating in several discourses. The theological discourse proposes a territorial claim of metaphysical origins and divine promise; granted to the nation's forefathers, it is an ahistorical, eternal, and permanent border, as well as an ideal "border to come" embodying a perpetual potential of realization. The historical discourse, for its part, proposes the Patriarchs' Border, providing the Zionist narrative with an ancient national origin, from which it can draw a line to the present and to a historical claim to the land, and creating an affinity between the land and the people. Finally, the national discourse embraces the origins of the nation asserted in the historical discourse and argues for the connection between the land and the people on the basis of hereditary birthright, thereby legitimizing the idea of the people's return to its old-new homeland. As for the future borders of that homeland, those were to be ultimately measured against the standard of the ahistorical and eternal Intended Border.

We can thus conclude that differently from those interpretation that present Zionism as a new, secular undertaking that set itself apart from religion, the "Borderless Border Map" and the school textbooks discussed here call for a more complex and nuanced reading of the Zionist nation-building educational undertaking.

Territorial Aspects: Between the Borderless Map and the Tribes' Estates Border Map

One of the questions that confronted the Zionist attempt to realize a theological border within a geophysical reality was: Where is the Land of Israel? This in turn raised another question: How could one draw a theological line in a geographical space? These questions arose in the late nineteenth century, when the Land of Israel did not exist as a territorial, political entity marked on world maps and its imagined space was a part of the Ottoman Empire. The Promise Border, which offered a transcendent, borderless geographical space, could not provide the necessary demarcation. One solution to this issue was found in Christian cartography. Early Zionist demarcations of the Land of Israel follow the borders of the twelve tribes' estates. This scheme, as pointed out by Rehav Rubin, was in fact borrowed from Christian maps of the Holy Land.[23]

Borders in Practice: The Exodus Border and the Tribes' Estates Border

The "Exodus Border" and the "Tribes' Estates Border" share the same spatial demarcation but differ in the meanings attributed to each one of them. The Exodus Border is a theological border, but unlike the Promise Border, which embodies ideal and transcendent characteristics, the Exodus Border is a border in practice—the border of the land that God commanded the Israelites who left Egypt to conquer and to bequeath to the future generations.[24] As such, it is located between the theological and the historical and invites interpretations ranging from divine will to human action: God's command to conquer and settle, and its historical human implementation. The distinction between the theological border—the Exodus Border—and the historical border—the Tribes' Estates Border—stems from the context of their presentation. When the demarcation of the border appears as metaphysical, originating in and validated by God, the border is defined as theological. It is defined as a historical border when the space is described as the land settled by the tribes of Israel as a result of human action at a specific moment in history, that is, the conquest of the land after the Exodus.

Narrative Aspects of Borders in Practice

The Exodus Border as a Theological Border

The Exodus Border represents God's repeated biblical promise, retaining a theological affinity with the narrative potential of the Promise Border, despite differences in their spatial demarcation. Its theological representation in the textbooks relies on a verse from the Bible, repeating God's promise to Abraham: "And I will set your border from the Red Sea to the Sea of the Philistines, and from the wilderness to the Euphrates."[25] It also relies on the sanctity of the physical space of the Land of Israel: "For this is the land God showed Moses before his death."[26] Unlike the Promise Border, this Exodus Border is practiced. As such, it is the border that requires action and demarcates the space "which the Israelites were commanded to conquer, and which the spies roamed"[27] and is the "border of the region conquered from the Canaanites by the Israelites who came from Egypt and settled there."[28] The acts of conquering and settling the land within this border and the territorial rights derived from them, as well as the territorial demarcation it offers and its theological validity as a promised border, form an important repository in the national discourse concerning the Israeli border.

The Exodus Border allowed the textbooks' authors to unite the theological and the historical, by preserving the spatial demarcation of the territory and using different compositions and interpretations to move along the spectrum between religion and secularism. By requiring action, the Exodus Border grants the Zionist movement an activist component. For instance, while Brawer defines the demarcation of the Exodus Border as a theological border and points to its eternal existence outside the bounds of human time, he simultaneously creates contexts that open a path for him to use this demarcation within the political arena. This narrative background is then harnessed to position the Exodus Border as a standard for examining the system of political borders: the current and the future demarcations of the Land of Israel, as discussed below.

The Tribes' Estates Border as a Historical Border

Most of the maps in textbooks published within the period of this study and relating to the time of Joshua present the lands of the tribes (see map 10.3).[29] But when we

Map 10.3. The Tribes' Estates Border map. Source: N. Gutman and D. Dovnikov, *Tanach Lebiet Hasefer: Yehoshua* [Bible for school: Joshua] (Tel Aviv: Yavne, 1959), 3.

examine the relationship between maps presenting the estates of the tribes and maps presenting Joshua's conquests on a timeline, we find that during the Yishuv period from 1903 to 1948, the vast majority of textbook maps of Joshua's time presented the tribes' estates. Conversely, following the founding of the State of Israel, from

1948 to 1967, over 40 percent of the maps presented Joshua's conquest rather than the tribes' estates.

Unlike the Promise Border map, which represents a transcendent geography, the Tribes' Estates Border map is historical, in that it represents territorial ownership within a defined and demarcated geographical space. During the Yishuv period, when the Zionists pursued land redemption, the Tribes' Estates Border map therefore offered a visual image that matched the settlers' vision. As the narrative components of the books containing these maps demonstrate, the main themes they were intended to highlight included the demarcation of the imagined space as the Land of Israel, the presentation of a spatial visual image of a free people in its own land, and a model for reimaging settlement in the old-new homeland, providing reassurance to young readers of the validity of the territorial claim as based on dynastic ownership and antiquity and supplying an image that enabled students to reimagine the biblical period in general and the period of the settlement of the tribes in particular, while obscuring the two thousand years of Jewish exile and the intervening geographical history of the space imagined as the Land of Israel.

Joshua's Conquests as Historical Maps

As we have seen, the ratio of maps of Joshua's conquests in textbooks published after the founding of the State of Israel rose from 10 percent to close to half of all maps of that historical period. This dynamic map (see map 10.4) represents the progression of Joshua's conquests in space with thick black arrows. As Mark Monmonier notes, the arrow is among the most persuasive and effective cartographic signifiers in maps.[30] But while cartographic depictions of military engagements often represent both sides, in the map of Joshua's conquests the opposing forces are absent. The black arrow thus reinforces the impression of action, initiative, aggression, and ownership of the land, all in contrast to the passivity of exile that the Israeli public was taught to reject. Furthermore, this dynamic map represents two temporal dimensions: while the arrows mark movement through space, the border demarcations are created by means of this movement. This reinforces the spatial imagination of the border as a temporary and fleeting demarcation. During the Yishuv period and following the founding of the state, this image preserved the potential for territorial expansion in view of the gap between the actual political borders and the space imagined as the Land of Israel.

In discussing the tendency of the Israeli public to link the 1948 War and the book of Joshua, Lea Mazor points out two elements that undergird the mechanism of transforming a biblical-religious text into a secular-national one in the service of nation building and territorial expansion.[31] The first is the reference to Joshua's story as a historical event and the time of the conquest and settlement of the land as a crucial moment in the national narrative. The second is the creation of a direct analogy between this biblical story and current events, while consciously skipping over two thousand years of Jewish history.

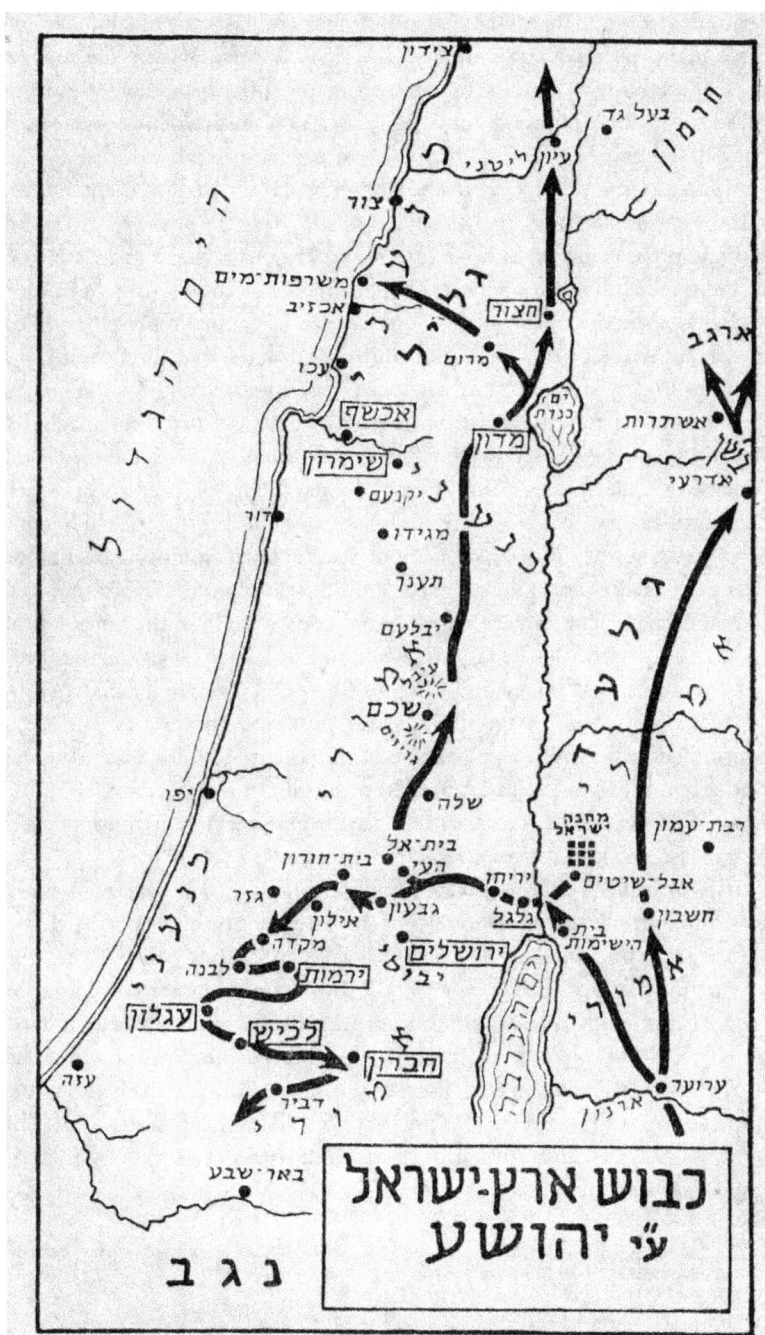

Map 10.4. The conquest of the Land of Israel by Joshua. Source: Y. Ben-Yehuda and M. Bitan, *Avoda Azmit Betanach: Yehoshua* [Self-study in the Bible: Joshua] (Tel Aviv: Yesod, 1962), 77.

We can further argue that reference to Joshua's conquests provided the young state with three main narrative components. The first concerned using the maps of the conquests to establish a claim on the land. If maps of the tribes' estates purportedly legitimized the claims of inherited ownership, those of Joshua's conquests established legitimacy based on action, the ability of man to change reality and shape destiny. This secular reasoning differed from the divine promise based on metaphysical will. In one of the textbooks, students were asked to use the maps of the conquest in order to follow the progression of Joshua's forces; similarly to a board game, this exercise enabled them to symbolically experience the triumph of conquering the land.[32]

The second component involved using the map as a visual representation of state ideology. In the wake of the Holocaust and the struggle for existence of the Israeli population in the early years of the state, maps of military operations in general and of Joshua's conquests in particular promoted a worldview that celebrated activism and militancy. By identifying with the generation of Joshua's warriors and understanding the conquest of Canaan as a Zionist utopia, Israel's citizens tried to draw strength from the mythical past to overcome the ordeals of the present.[33] As Firer has also observed, Jewish history textbooks in those years tended to emphasize the military actions of the Israelites and to incorporate militaristic expressions into their texts.[34]

The final narrative component concerns the construction of the image of the new Hebrew man and warrior—the sabra.[35] Reference to Joshua's warriors reinforced the image of the sabra as a fighter and a man of action, who could be favorably contrasted with the opposite image of Diaspora Judaism. The creation of the sabra's image within the education system was not an academic undertaking, but rather a concerted attempt to put in place a process of socialization geared toward molding a generation of fighters. To this end, the educational establishment enlisted the curriculum in general and Joshua's conquests in particular.

The maps of Joshua's conquests can therefore be classified as part of a larger group of maps printed in the school textbooks of the early 1950s, known as battle heritage maps. These maps presented historical as well as recent battles. Indeed, one other factor that explains the appearance of maps of Joshua's conquests at that time is the general preoccupation with battle heritage after the 1948 War. The focus on battlefield heritage reflected the role and justification of military operations as border-shaping acts. Furthermore, these maps were used to promote affinity with the Land of Israel among the youth, using battle stories and school walking trips to these battle sites as a part of a militaristic education meant to instill in students a love for the land and a will to make sacrifices for their country.

Territorial Aspects of Borders in Practice

As we saw, in the early years of the period under study there were no maps demarcating the political borders of the Land of Israel, but only approximations of the estates of the twelve tribes of Israel. It should be noted that even after the boundaries of Mandatory Palestine were determined, the construction of the imaginary space of the Land of Israel continued. Thus, for example, while Brawer's map of 1925, which was being used in Israelis schools, indicated the eastern political border of Mandatory Palestine along the Jordan River, it also included the eastern bank of the Jordan River according to the Exodus Border. This framing constituted a political statement, which sought both to represent the territory of the Land of Israel under the British Mandate and to include the rest of the territories excluded from the space imagined as the Land of Israel, thus also demonstrating the relative size of this imagined space as compared to the area demarcated by the Mandate.

This cartographic statement coincided with a lively debate in the Yishuv and Zionist institutions over the demarcation of the Land of Israel. Throughout the British Mandate, Brawer served as a geographical adviser to the Zionist Organization's institutions in the negotiations with the British authorities over the future of the national home. With this in mind, it is interesting to examine space demarcations in Brawer's map in relationship to his discussion of the Exodus Border in the textbook. Unlike Brawer's use of the Intended Border as an eternal and invariable unit of measurement, the Exodus Border is embodied in a geophysical reality, allowing Brawer to examine the demarcation of concrete political borders. In this manner, Brawer could argue for the Exodus Border as an actual basis for designing the imagined future space of the land during the Yishuv period.

An example of the use of the Exodus Border as a unit of measurement in demarcating the territory of the Land of Israel can be found in Brawer's books *Our Homeland*, published in 1929, and *The Land and Its Regions*, published in 1946.[36] These books illuminate the manner in which spatial geopolitical changes were reflected in his writings. In 1929 Brawer compared what he called the "natural territories" of the Land of Israel to the Exodus Border: "Within the natural territory of our country 60,000 [square kilometers] are included.[37] The Exodus border covers 40,000 [square kilometers]."[38] This passage indicated that the Land of Israel's "natural territory," as well as the Exodus Border, included the east bank of the Jordan. But in 1946, Brawer presented the Exodus Border as demarcating two units placed on either side of the Jordan.[39] This reflected his internalization of the spatial political changes that had taken place. The territory of the British Mandate had been divided into two entities, Mandatory Palestine west of the Jordan, and Transjordan east of the river, already in 1922. Yet while in 1929 Brawer ignored this political reality, by the 1940s he appears to have partly accepted it: on one hand, he presented the space as split by the Jordan River; but on the other hand, it remained united as the Exodus Border.

It should be emphasized that even after the State of Israel was established and its political borders were drawn, this spatial imagination remained. For instance, in discussing the fertility of the soil in a book published in 1954, Brawer comments that "the State of Israel includes the most fertile regions in the entire Exodus range."[40]

Brawer's reference to the Exodus range as a spatial standard after the establishment of the state attests to the prominent position of this imaginary territory both in the spatial demarcations he presents and in highlighting his view of the inferiority of the current political border in relation to it.

Territorial Continuity: From the Tribes' Estates Border to the Israeli State Border

Maps 10.5, 10.6, and 10.7 appear in a textbook on the book of Joshua published in 1957.[41] The maps are titled: "Tribes' Estates," "Borders map," and "Contemporary map of the state of Israel." In analyzing these maps, I will highlight the narrative and territorial expressions prevalent in the period under discussion and their firm connection to the imagined space of the Land of Israel. The maps' titles indicate a historical narrative that begins in the tribes' era and ends in the time of the maps' production, that is, after the founding of the State of Israel. In the original textbook, these maps are placed side by side. Thereby the author creates the appearance of an affinity of territory and sovereignty between the units represented. However, upon closer examination we can see that the space represented in these maps is not identical. In comparison to the Tribes' Estates map (map 10.5), the Borders map (map 10.6) represents a wider space that includes the Negev region and the Bay of Eilat—a region that is not included in either the Tribes' Estates Border map next to it or in other Exodus Border maps related to it.

How then, is this territorial addition to be interpreted? The source of this additional territory is the political spatial demarcation of the early twentieth century, namely, the delineation of the border between the Ottoman Empire and Egypt in 1906, which later became the southern border of Mandatory Palestine and eventually of the State of Israel. The Negev region, which was not included in the tribes' estates territory and was not a part of the imaginary space of the Land of Israel at the beginning of the twentieth century, appeared in maps of Israel from the beginning of the 1940s, thereby indicating its assimilation into the imaginary space of the Land of Israel.

With this in mind and given the political borders of the State of Israel, which included this region, the Borders map (map 10.6) acts as a hybrid spatial link that presents the territories of the tribes' estates (map 10.5) in addition to the contemporary borders of the State of Israel (map 10.7). This duality is also reflected in the sovereign identity of the territory represented. While the Tribes' Estates map presents a tribal organization of the twelve tribes and the Contemporary map of the State of Israel presents the national sovereignty of the State of Israel, the Borders map presents a hybrid entity aimed at bridging the gap between Joshua's tribal society and the nation-state of Israel in the second decade of its existence. Across the territory delineated within the Borders map, the words "the State of Israel in Joshua's Era" are inscribed, although even according to the Bible such an entity never existed. In order to strengthen the map's role as a mediator between the other maps' territorial and sovereign dimensions, the students were instructed to "color the territory of the State of Israel in the Joshua era." In doing so, the assignment reinforced and perpetuated the

THE BIBLICAL BORDERS BETWEEN THEOLOGY AND HISTORY | 213

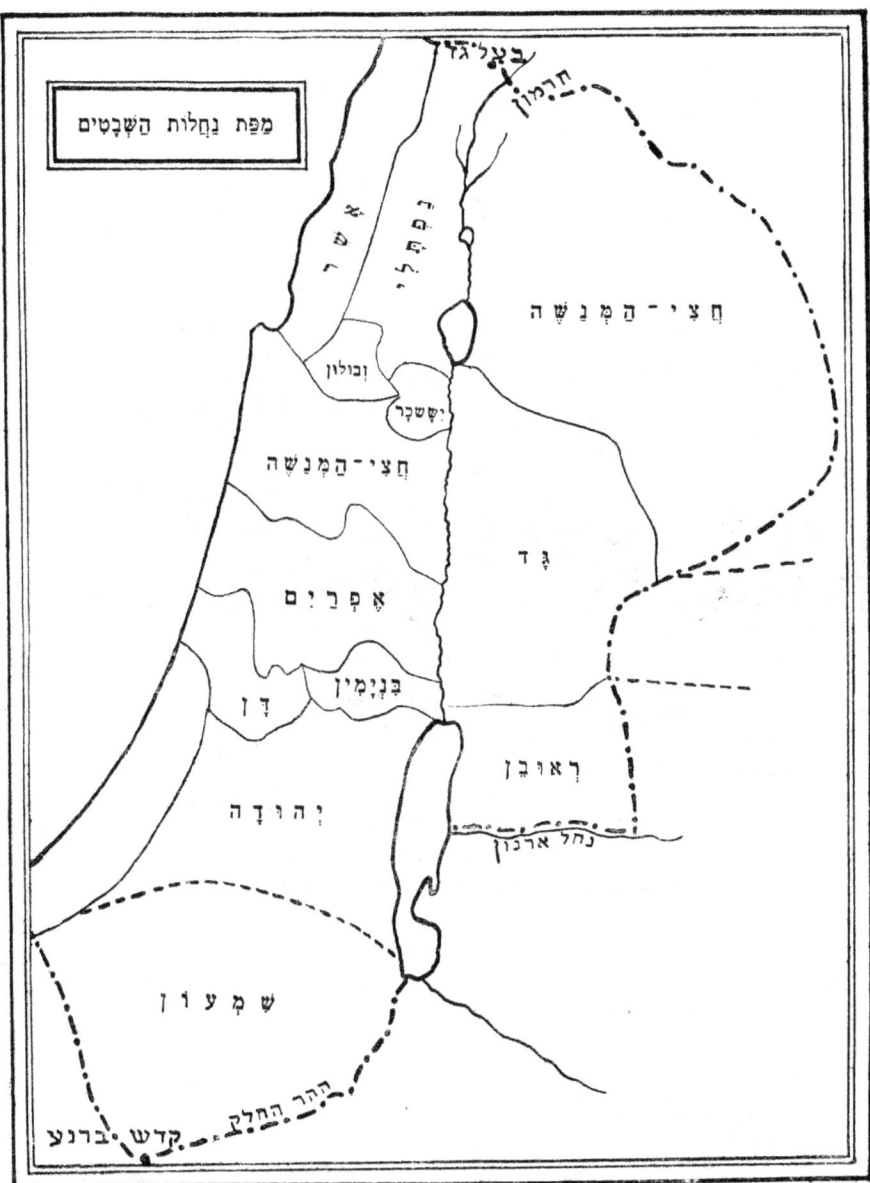

Map 10.5. Tribes' Estates. Source: Moshe ben Elazar Kenan, *Yehoshua: Hovert le-Avoda u-le-Sikkum le-Sefer Yehoshua* [Joshua: Workbook and summary for the book of Joshua] (Jerusalem: Kiryat-Sefer, 1957), 4.

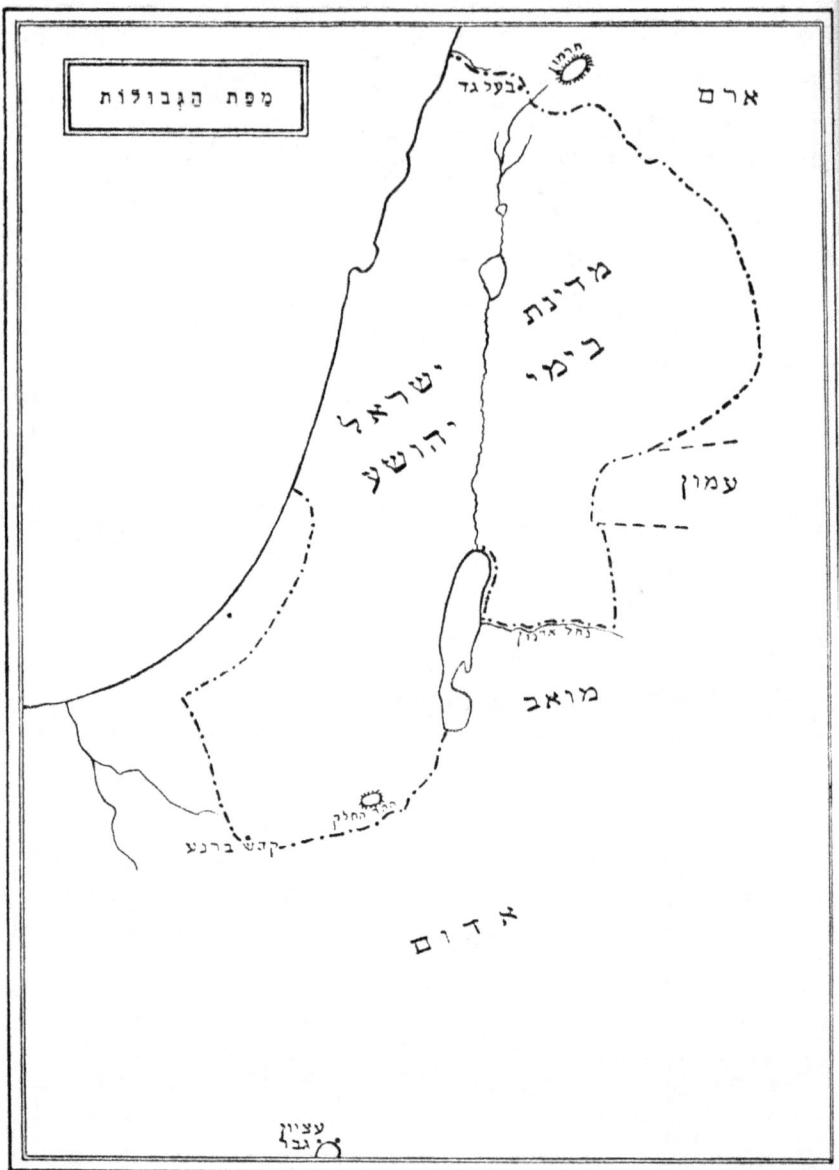

Map 10.6. Borders map. Source: Moshe ben Elazar Kenan, *Yehoshua: Hovert le-Avoda u-le-Sikkum le-Sefer Yehoshua* [Joshua: Workbook and summary for the book of Joshua] (Jerusalem: Kiryat-Sefer, 1957), 29.

THE BIBLICAL BORDERS BETWEEN THEOLOGY AND HISTORY | 215

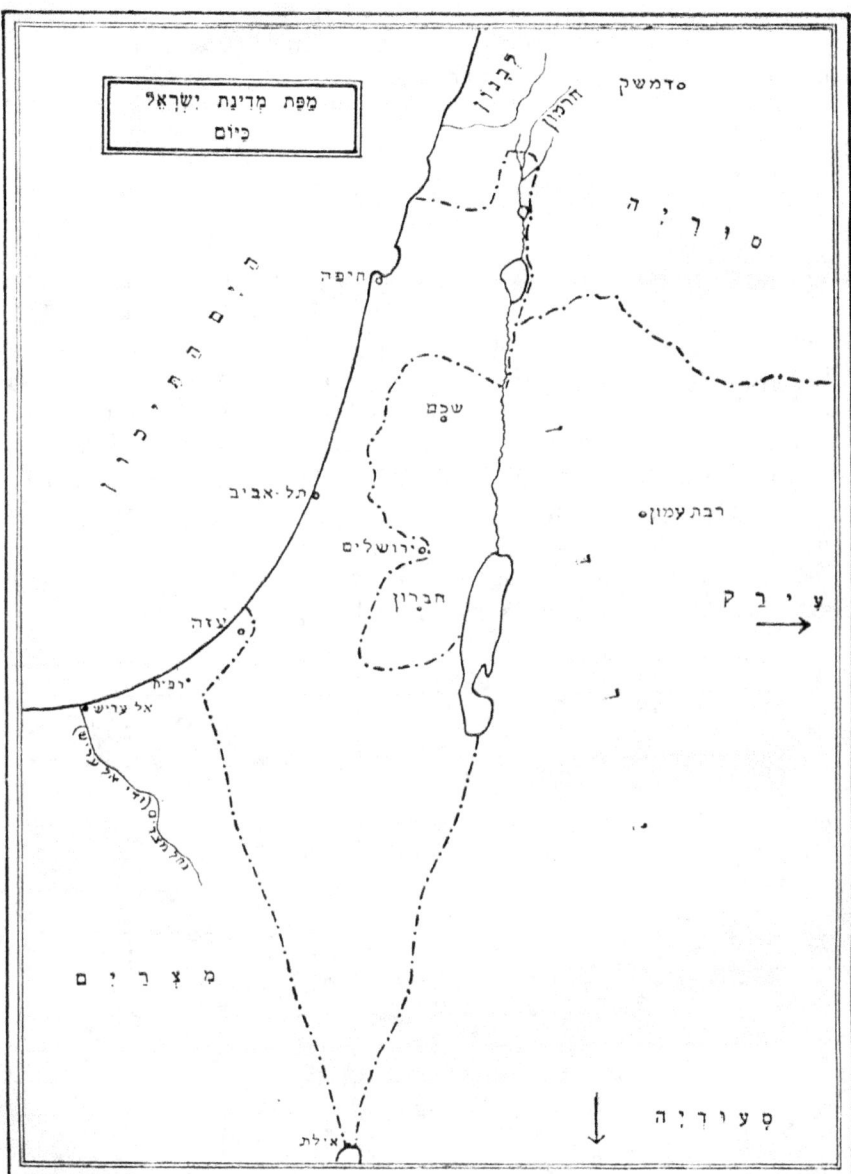

Map 10.7. Contemporary map of the State of Israel. Source: Moshe ben Elazar Kenan, *Yehoshua: Hovert le-Avoda u-le-Sikkum le-Sefer Yehoshua* [Joshua: Workbook and summary for the book of Joshua] (Jerusalem: Kiryat-Sefer, 1957), 39.

existence of this fictitious sovereign territorial entity in the student's consciousness and made the case that Israel's political borders at the time were merely a fraction of what they had been and should be again.

Conclusion

A school textbook by David Shifman and Zvi Arieli published in 1953 included two maps on opposite pages that illustrate the main argument of this chapter (see map 10.8).[42] The maps display a dichotomous representation: on the right, the borderless map of the Promise Border presents the theological border, transcending time and territory, and implying an eternal potential for realization; on the left, the Tribes' Estates Border map provides a concrete historical embodiment of the Promise Border. These dichotomous representations sharpen the distinction between theological and historical borders. The Promise Border map represents transcendent geography, whereas the Tribes' Estates Border map represents territorial ownership, defined and delimited in a geographical space.

The layout of the maps from right to left creates a chronological order that follows the direction of reading Hebrew: first, the theological realm—God's promise—

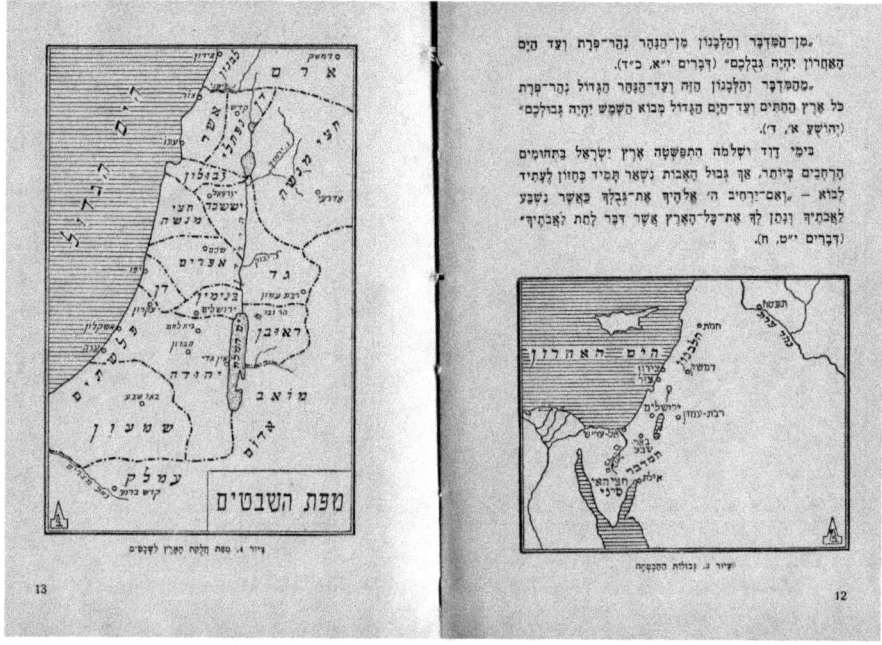

Map 10.8. The Tribes' Estates Border map (*left*) and Promise Border map (*right*). Source: David Shifman and Zvi Ariely, *Netivot Hamikra: Yehoshua* [Paths in the Bible: The book of Joshua] (Tel Aviv: Yavne, 1953), 12–13.

followed by its historical embodiment, the tribes' estates. This layout produces a historical narrative that endows theological time with a historical dimension and a metaphysical validity. The historical time, in which God's command to conquer and settle the land was issued, is thereby realized through human action. This narrative aspect undermines the dichotomous facade of theological versus historical time, since the narrative continuity requires placing both on the same basis.

This common basis was produced in the national discourse, which appropriated the theological and historical dimensions as needed. In this act of appropriation, carried out within the framework of a nation-building process, the distinction between these temporal categories collapses and a new temporal dimension is created: a hybrid entity of metaphysical historical time. But contrary to Firer, who refers to this time as an essentialist and determinist category, I define it as an instrumental time category characterized by its fluidity.[43] According to this definition, this category of time was interpreted and exploited by the Zionist movement as an instrument in the nation-building process for defining and demarcating the Land of Israel. Tracing the manner in which this undertaking was presented in Israeli textbook maps reveals that this category of instrumental time was not subjected to a monolithic interpretation and that different textbook authors and cartographers endowed it with meanings raging from the theological to the historical according to the needs and dictates of the national discourse over land, borders, and rights.

Orna Vaadia is a postdoctoral fellow at the Faculty of Architecture and Town Planning in the Technion—Israel Institute of Technology. Her research interests lie at the intersection of cartography, technology, and socio-spatial power relations. Her 2016 dissertation is titled "Maps in Schoolbooks and the Spatial Imaginary: The Education System in Israel: 1903–1967." As a postdoctoral fellow in the Department of Geography and Environmental Development of Ben-Gurion University, Vaadia researched the uses of the new spatial media for counter-mapping and memory activism among Bedouins and Palestinians in Israel-Palestine. She is currently working on mobile mapping and conflict spaces in the West Bank.

Notes

1. Yehuda Grazowski, *Eretz Israel: Sefer Limud ha-Geografya shel Eretz Israel (im mapah be-Ivrit)* [The Land of Israel: A geography textbook of the Land of Israel (with a map in Hebrew)] (Warsaw: Hotsa'at Tushiya, 1903). Grazowski (1862–1950) was later known as Gur or Goor and spent much of the rest of his life in Palestine-Israel.
2. Derek Gregory, *Geographical Imaginations* (Cambridge, MA: Blackwell, 1994). For further discussion, see Jen Jack Giesking and William Mangold, eds., "The People, Place, and Space Reader," section 11, "The Spatial Imagination," https://peopleplacespace.org/toc/section-11/.
3. For scholars of nationalism, see Benedict Anderson, *Imagined Communities* (London: Verso, 2006); Ernest Gellner, *Nations and Nationalism* (Ithaca: Cornell University Press, 1983); Eric J. Hobsbawm,

Nation and Nationalism since 1780 (Cambridge: Cambridge University Press, 1990). These scholars attribute importance to the centralized education system organized by the nation-state that provides a national education. This is despite their disagreement over the role of the education system in the national order, arising from the way in which each of them defines the nature of the nation.

4. The Yishuv period refers to the era between the beginning of Zionist immigration to the Land of Israel in the late nineteenth century and the establishment of the State of Israel in 1948. The Hebrew term *Yishuv* refers to both the settlement and the establishment of a civil community—specifically, the Zionist society in the Land of Israel during this period.
5. Yoram Bar-Gal, *Moledet ve-Geografya be-Mea Shnot Hinukh Tsiyoni* [Homeland and geography in a century of Zionist education] (Tel Aviv: Am-Oved, 1993), 131.
6. Michael M. Feige, "*Yesha ze Kan, Shetahim ze Sham: Praktikot Mada'iot ve-Kinun ha-Merhav be-Israel*" [Judaea-Samaria is here, the territories are there: Scientific practices and the establishment of space in Israel], *Teorya ve-Bikoret* 14 (1999): 111–31.
7. Jeremy W. Crampton and John Krygier, "An Introduction to Critical Cartography," *ACME—An International Journal for Critical Geographies* 4, no. 1 (2005): 11–33, https://www.acme-journal.org/index.php/acme/article/view/723/585.
8. Denis Wood, *The Power of Maps*, rev. ed. (London: Routledge, 1992); J. B. Harley, "Deconstructing the Map," *Cartographica* 26, no. 2 (1989): 1–20.
9. Haim Arie Zuta and Aharon Sternberg, *Kadmoniyot: Toldot Amei Kedem ve-Am Israel ad Galut Bavel* [Antiquity: The history of the ancient peoples and the people of Israel until the Babylonian Exile] (Tel Aviv: Masada, 1935).
10. Yaakov Gutman, *Tanakh le-Vatey ha-Sefer: Yehoshua* [The Bible for schools: The book of Joshua] (Tel Aviv: Yavne, 1956); David Shifman and Zvi Ariely, *Netivot ha-Mikra: Yehoshua* [Paths in the Bible: The book of Joshua] (Tel Aviv: Yavne, 1953).
11. Genesis 15:18.
12. Yehoyakim Paporisch, *Eretz Israel* [The Land of Israel] (Tel Aviv: Yehoshua Chechik, 1949), 44.
13. Baruch Avivi and Elchanan Indelman, *Ba-Moledet ha-Ivrit* [In the Hebrew homeland] (Warsaw, Tel Aviv: Hinukh Leumi, 1938), 6.
14. Naaman Razieli, *Artzi Israel* [Israel—my land] (Tel Aviv: Karni, 1956), 9.
15. The validity of these concepts is contested by national researchers employing two approaches. The primordialist approach views modern peoples and nations as belonging to a continuum of peoples and nations that existed in the remote past. Conversely, the constructivist approach rejects the idea of an ancient ethnic core that establishes ethno-national identity. It regards these components as invented or imagined, aimed at creating communal and social coherence among the nation's citizens. See Henry Wasserman, *Am, Uma, Moledet: Al Reishitam, Toldotei'hem ve-Aharitam shel Shelosha Musagim Meholeley-Le'umiuot* [People, nation, homeland: On the genesis, history, and aftermath of three nation-making concepts] (Tel Aviv: Open University, 2007), 13–14.
16. For example, see Ephraim Arni and Elisha Efrat, *Ha-Geografya shel Artzenu* [The geography of our land] (Tel Aviv: Ahiasaf, 1960), 7; David Benvenisti, *Artzenu* [Our land] (Jerusalem: Kiryat-Sefer, 1947), 7–8; David Benvenisti and Ben Zion Luriya, *Eretz Israel: Mapot le-Avoda Atzmit* [The Land of Israel: Maps for independent work] (Jerusalem: Kiryat-Sefer, 1957), 4; Abraham Jacob Brawer, *Ha-Aretz* [The land] (Tel Aviv: Bialik Institute and Dvir, 1950), 7; David Shifman, *Moladeti Israel* [Israel my homeland] (Tel Aviv: Yavne, 1954): 9.
17. Shifman, *Moladeti Israel*, 5–8.
18. Amnon Raz-Krakotzkin, "Ha-Shiva el ha-Historiya shel ha-Geulah, o: Mahi ha-'Historiya' she-eleiha Mitbaza'at ha-'Shiva' ba-Bituy 'ha-Shiva el ha-Historiya'" [The return to the history of salvation, or: What is the "history" into which the "return" is made with the expression "the return to history"], in *Zionism and the Return to History: A Reevaluation*, ed. S. N. Eisenstadt and Moshe Lissak (Jerusalem: Yad Yitzhak Ben-Zvi, 1999, in Hebrew), 269.
19. Ruth Firer, *Sokhnim shel Hinukh Zioni* [Agents of Zionist education] (Tel Aviv: Sifriyat Poalim, 1985), 110.

20. Johanan Aharoni, *Zot Artzi* [This is my land] (Tel Aviv: Ma'arakhot, 1967), 16; Brawer, *Ha-Aretz*, 2–3; Abraham Jacob Brawer, *Eretz Moladeteynu* [Our homeland] (Tel Aviv: Devir, 1929), 2–3; Abraham Jacob Brawer, *Ha-Aretz ve-Gliloteiha* [The land and its regions] (Tel Aviv: Ha-Va'ad ha-Artzi le-Ma'an ha-Hayal ha-Ivri, 1946), 2–3; Paporisch, *Eretz Israel*, 6–7; Yehoyakim Paporisch, *Yediat ha-Aretz: Geografya Fizit shel Eretz Israel* [Israeli geography: Physical geography of the Land of Israel] (Tel Aviv: Yehoshua Chechik, 1957), 13.
21. Brawer, *Ha-Aretz*, 5–6.
22. Abraham Jacob Brawer, *Eretz Israel* [The Land of Israel] (Tel Aviv: Bialik Institute and Devir, 1954), 5–6.
23. Rehav Rubin, *Portraying the Land: Hebrew Maps of the Land of Israel from Rashi to the Early 20th Century* (Berlin, Boston, Jerusalem: De Gruyter and Magnes, 2018); for comparison see reference on pp. 238–40 and 274–76 to the impact of Heinrich Kiepert's Palestine maps and the Eliyahu Sapir and Ephraim Krause maps of 1914 and 1918. See also *Neue Handkarte Palästina*, bearbeitet von H. Kiepert (Berlin: Dietrich Reimer, 1883), National Library of Israel, https://www.nli.org.il/en/maps/NNL_MAPS_JER002645042/NLI#$FL7073599.
24. Numbers 34:1–13; Deuteronomy 2:1–23 and 3:8; Joshua 12:1 and 13:1–3.
25. Exodus 23:31.
26. Deuteronomy 34:1.
27. Brawer, *Eretz Moladeteynu*, 3–4.
28. Paporisch, *Eretz Israel*, 21.
29. The biblical chronology refers to the period of Joshua as described in the book of Joshua—the period from the beginning of the history of the settlement of the tribes of Israel in the land of Canaan, until the death of Joshua.
30. Mark S. Monmonier, *How to Lie with Maps*, 2nd ed. (Chicago: Chicago University Press, 1996), 107–8.
31. Leah Mazor, "Aliyato ve-Sheki'ato shel Sefer Yehoshua ba-Hinukh ha-Mamlakhti le-Or Temurot Ide'ologiot ba-Hevra ha-Israelit" [The rise and decline of the book of Joshua in public education as a consequence of ideological changes in Israeli society] *Cathedra* 100 (2005): 1–41.
32. Oved Amiti, *Hora'at Nevi-im Rishonim be-Vatey ha-Sefer ha-Yesodiyim* [Teaching the first prophets in elementary schools] (Tel Aviv: Association of Hebrew Teachers in Israel, 1957), 73, 76.
33. Mazor, "Aliyato ve-Sheki'ato shel Sefer Yehoshua," 34.
34. Firer, *Sokhnim shel Hinukh Zioni*.
35. *Sabra* refers to the generation of children who grew up in Israel in the early 1930s and who were intended to become "new Jews" by performing as the new generation of native warriors during the Yishuv period and the 1948 War. The term *tzabar* (prickly pear) refers to the fruits of a cactus that are prickly on the outside and sweet on the inside. Today this nickname refers to a Jewish person who was born in Israel.
36. Brawer, *Eretz Moladeteynu*; Brawer, *Ha-Aretz ve-Gliloteiha*.
37. The term "nature" in the context of the border issue requires a separate discussion, as the textbooks attribute to it several meanings: a geophysical border, a border with the validity of natural law, a justified border, the border of biological living space, and more. Brawer's use of the phrase "natural territories" refers to the geophysical demarcation of the Land of Israel but also implicitly folds in the meanings of a territorial validity by natural law and territory defined by justice and for historical and theological reasons that Brawer establishes in his books throughout the biblical borders discussion.
38. Brawer, *Eretz Moladeteynu*, 5.
39. Brawer, *Ha-Aretz ve-Gliloteiha*, 17
40. Brawer, *Eretz Israel*, 5.
41. Moshe ben Elazar Kenan, *Yehoshua: Hovert le-Avoda u-le-Sikkum le-Sefer Yehoshua* [Joshua: Workbook and summary for the book of Joshua] (Jerusalem: Kiryat-Sefer, 1957).
42. Shifman and Ariely, *Netivot Hamikra*, 12–13.
43. Firer, *Sokhnim shel Hinukh Zioni*.

Select Bibliography

Bar-Gal, Yoram. *Moledet ve-geografya be-Mea Shnot Hinukh Tsiyoni*" [Homeland and geography in a century of Zionist education]. Tel Aviv: Am-Oved, 1993.

Brawer, Abraham Jacob. *Eretz Israel* [The Land of Israel]. Tel Aviv: Bialik Institute and Dvir, 1954.

———. *Eretz Moladeteynu* [Our homeland]. Tel Aviv: Dvir, 1929.

———. *Ha-Aretz* [The land]. Tel Aviv: Bialik Institute and Dvir, 1928, 1950.

Mazor, Leah. "Aliyato ve-Sheki'ato shel Sefer Yehoshua ba-Hinukh ha-Mamlakhti le-Or Temurot Ide'ologiot ba-Hevra ha-Israelit" [The rise and decline of the book of Joshua in public education as a consequence of ideological changes in Israeli society]. *Cathedra* 100 (2005): 1–41.

Paporisch, Yehoyakim. *Eretz Israel* [The Land of Israel]. Tel Aviv: Yehoshua Chechik, 1949.

———. *Yediat ha-Aretz: Geografya Fizit shel Eretz Israel* [Israeli geography: Physical geography of the Land of Israel]. Tel Aviv: Yehoshua Chechik, 1957.

Raz-Krakotzkin, Amnon. "Ha-Shiva el ha-Historiya shel ha-Geulah, o: Mahi ha-'Historiya' she-eleiha Mitbaza'at ha-'Shiva' ba-Bituy 'ha-Shiva el ha-Historiya'" [The return to the history of salvation, or: What is the "history" into which the "return" is made with the expression "the return to history"?]. In *Zionism and the Return to History: A Reevaluation*, edited by S. N. Eisenstadt and Moshe Lissak, 249–76. Jerusalem: Yad Yitzhak Ben-Zvi, 1999.

Rubin, Rehav. *Portraying the Land: Hebrew Maps of the Land of Israel from Rashi to the Early 20th Century*. Berlin, Boston, and Jerusalem: De Gruyter and Magnes, 2018.

CHAPTER 11
ZIONIST CIVIC RITUALS AS NATION-BUILDING INSTRUMENTS

AVNER BEN-AMOS

Introduction

A ritual, as Clifford Geertz remarks, has two functions: it offers its participants a powerful experience, but it is also an event that communicates a certain message.[1] During a ritual, participants form a group in order to celebrate an event or a person through music, dance, or speech. They wear special garments, their bodies and senses are entirely engaged in the action, and their emotions intensify. Yet a ritual also has a cognitive, communicative facet. Its meaning is transmitted through words, symbolic objects, and physical gestures, as well as the space and time in which it takes place. It has the ability to convey a narrative that concerns the participants, and it can evoke collective memories and represent a shared future. This renders rituals effective pedagogical tools; they can inculcate their participants with the values of the community in a manner that incorporates all dimensions of consciousness.

It is therefore no wonder that the Zionist movement has used rituals as pedagogical tools in Palestine since its inception in the late nineteenth century. Rituals have helped Zionism reach not only schoolchildren but adults as well and have molded a heterogeneous immigrant society into a cohesive community. For Zionists, the relocation of Jews from Europe to what they called Eretz Israel (Land of Israel) meant far more than a mere change of residence. It was a transition destined to bring about a massive change of consciousness to both the Jewish individual and to Jewish society as a whole. The bid to create a "new Jew" and a "new Jewish nation" provided Zionism with an educational agenda, and culture became one of the movement's major spheres of activity. At the very root of this activity was a particular cultural principle, the "denial of the Diaspora." This entailed rejecting all traits associated with Jewish life in Europe and adopting alternative modes of behavior meant to gradually transform the new Jewish nation and individual.

This fundamental urge to transform Jewish existence and consciousness generated a range of positions and practices that reflected various aspects of Zionism; yet they all shared some common traits. Zionism's model individual was envisioned as a native pioneer whose feet were planted firmly on the ground: a man dedicated to working and defending his land while shunning commerce and intellectual activities. This transformation entailed also the collective: Zionism perceived the Jewish community through a modern national lens and clearly aimed at obtaining national sovereignty. From a temporal perspective, Zionism tended to "cast aside" the two millennia of Jewish exile associated with inferiority and subservience and to concentrate on the more ancient historical epoch during which the Jewish people was sovereign in its land. It was this historical period that the movement sought to revive. In the territorial/spatial dimension, this aspiration to resurrect Jewish sovereignty merged with an emphasis on Eretz Israel as the sole location in which the national yearnings of the Jewish people could be realized.

Above all else, however, Zionism was marked by a transition from a religious, God-centric worldview to a secular one in which individuals, along with their community, were responsible for their own actions. This new approach did not eliminate references to Jewish religion—to the contrary, it often drew heavily upon religious tradition—but it did so by imbuing ancient Jewish texts and symbols with new meanings. The result was a profound change in self-definition as compared to that of Diasporic Jewish communities.[2]

An integral part of the new national culture in Eretz Israel were the Zionist ceremonies and festivals that expressed the movement's new values. As Itamar Even-Zohar has argued, despite relinquishing its previous culture, the immigrant society in Eretz Israel did not attempt to adopt the seemingly alien and "primitive" Arab culture of their new country.[3] Instead, the newcomers invented a new culture to serve their needs and reflect their identity. Inventing a culture that also offered a new perspective on the past (i.e., "inventing a tradition") was characteristic of many national movements in nineteenth- and twentieth-century Europe and served them to legitimize their endeavors.[4] In fact, this was how the social change brought on by modernization and the rise of national entities was naturalized and consecrated. One of the most effective cultural tools employed in this invention of tradition was the ritual: an event with fixed features that took place on a fixed date on the annual calendar and that quickly came to be seen as axiomatic and unquestionable.

This chapter aims to provide an overview of the Zionist civic rituals used as an educational means from the end of the nineteenth century to the beginning of the twenty-first century. Considering the length of the period under investigation, I do not delve fully into the complexity of this phenomenon and instead delineate the development of these rituals in very broad strokes. However, this focus on the *longue durée* allows me to trace changes in the various combinations of religious and national ritual elements, as well as to identify transitions over time from one set of rituals to another.

Reflecting the "negation of the Diaspora" mindset, Zionist rituals altered traditional Jewish rituals: while maintaining their external characteristics, they replaced their theological core with an emphasis on land, nature, the seasons of the year, or certain historical events. Still, these ceremonies preserved an aura of sanctity. Although they referred to a tangible space and time—the geography of Eretz Israel and linear historical periods dotted with sociopolitical events produced by human beings—they also evinced faith in a different reality, where both time and place took on a transcendental, redemptive significance. Thus, Eretz Israel also constituted the "great place," that is, a sacred place—the only place in which the Jewish people could resume its connection to the past and its symbolic essence.[5] Additionally, the specific time in which these ceremonies took place assumed a mythical and cyclical quality, with the Jewish people repeatedly oscillating between the opposite poles of catastrophe and redemption, that is, between the Holocaust (Holocaust Day) and Jewish sovereignty (Independence Day).[6]

The Zionist ceremony is not a static event. It has undergone various transformations since its inception at the end of the nineteenth century and into the early twenty-first century and will likely continue to evolve in line with future changes in Israeli society. Thus far, we can discern three main stages in the development of the Zionist ceremony: first, the time of initial trial and error—from the First Zionist Aliyah (wave of immigration) until World War I; second, the period of maturation—from the onset of the British Mandate until the establishment of Israeli independence; and third, the era of statehood—from independence to the dawn of the twenty-first century. During the second and the third periods, the Zionist ceremonial system became an efficient tool that mobilized the Jewish community and created a sense of national solidarity. However, civic rituals could also have a divisive role, as demonstrated by the Rabin Day's contentious ceremonies, which commemorated the assassinated prime minister who had made peace with the Palestinians. At the end of the twentieth century and the beginning of the twenty-first century, the power of rituals to create a national consensus clearly encountered certain limits.

Early Attempts: From the First Zionist Aliyah to the End of World War I

The early beginnings of Zionist festivals can be traced back to the first two waves of immigration (1882–1903; 1904–14), reflecting an attempt to develop a native culture unlike that of the Diaspora. However, these initial efforts failed at the time to constitute a consistent and inclusive system. In this period, we must distinguish between the people who came with the First Aliyah, who generally still adhered to their religious practices, and those who came with the Second Aliyah. The latter had abandoned their religious traditions and were now in search of symbols, imagery, and activities to express their new values. For all of the immigrants, however, these rituals acquired new meanings. Their very location in Eretz Israel distinguished them from the manner in which they were experienced in the Jewish Diaspora and imbued them with an eschatological dimension.[7]

The experience of being in the land affected the agrarian festivals in particular, because they were directly related to the land. While festivals relating to time—such as the Jewish New Year (Rosh Hashanah) and the Day of Atonement (Yom Kippur)—maintained their exclusive religious significance, the agrarian festivals offered an opportunity to re-create ceremonies from biblical times and use them to cultivate a love for the fatherland. On the festival of Shavuot (Pentecost, or the Feast of Weeks) in 1897, the farmers of Petah Tikva fulfilled a religious duty: "They acquitted themselves of all the religious duties that were related to the land: 'The forgotten sheaf and the poor man's tithe' . . . and they loaded it all on the backs of camels so as to convey it to Jerusalem in a beautiful ceremony."[8] In this way the biblical festival of Shavuot was given an additional, concrete meaning, specific to life in Eretz Israel. Quite apart from fulfilling an ancient religious injunction, the pilgrimage to Jerusalem also constituted an opportunity to further develop the bond with the land, its scenery, and the local Jewish communities.

"Historical" festivals, by contrast, gained a patriotic, militaristic dimension in this era of the First Aliyah, with the goal of emphasizing the link between existing Jewish communities in Eretz Israel and those of the ancient past. This was the case, for example, with Hanukkah, which came to be called the Festival of the Maccabees and offered the occasion for pilgrimage to the Maccabees' tombs, supposedly located in Modi'in, and for glorifying their heroism. Lag Ba'Omer (the thirty-third day of the Omer period, which begins with Passover) underwent a similar transformation: here the focus was shifted from the Kabbalah scholar Bar Yochai to the warrior Bar Kochba. These festivals were also celebrated with militarist displays, including gymnastics performances, wrestling matches, sharpshooting, and horseback marksmanship—all of which were added to the traditional festivities. Another notable source of influence were the ritual traditions of the local Arab population, considered by the newcomers to represent the authentic native culture; indeed, the Arabs were at times regarded as the guardians of archaic Hebrew customs. Elements of local Arab culture were, however, adopted selectively, through a Western-Jewish perspective, and only those features that suited the renewed Jewish experience were borrowed.[9]

The immigrants of the Second Aliyah went even further in their search for a new ritual language, although they, too, failed to develop a full alternative repertoire. On the whole, they were younger than the people of the First Aliyah, had no families, and worked as itinerant laborers. They tended to be either indifferent or hostile to Jewish religion; yet since they saw themselves as the next generation of the Jewish nation, they did not reject the traditional Jewish calendar but only eliminated its theological meanings. They were clearly looking for another type of sacredness that would center on the group of celebrators as a kind of extended family, a collective, egalitarian "self" that was destined to radically transform Jewish society.

The two most distinctive components of their celebrations were communal song and the circle dance. With these, the members of the Second Aliyah marked every celebration and often the end of the working day. These spontaneous, ecstatic events reflected—and created—a sense of comradeship among the members of the group. At times, parodic elements were also added to these transformed ceremonies. They were aimed not only against the Diasporic Jewish tradition but also took a stab at the more bourgeois Jews in Eretz Israel. Sometimes they even made fun of themselves.[10] It should be noted that inserting parodic elements in a celebratory event or even contriving a celebration that carries an inverted meaning does not usually evince a wish to totally do away with the sacred tradition; rather, it suggests an attempt to enter into some sort of dialogue with it. Often it signals a stage on the way toward a new ritual tradition.

Maturation: From the Onset of the British Mandate to Israeli Independence

Although the various rituals conducted by the First and Second Aliyah immigrants did already include most of the features that became typical of the new Zionist celebrations, they remained sporadic events that depended on local initiatives and lacked continuity. It was only under the British Mandate (1917–1948)—a crucial period in the endeavor to construct the vaunted "national home"—that a relatively homogeneous, semi-officially instituted calendar of rituals evolved and was followed by most communities and educational institutions. This homogeneity was spatial as well as temporal in character: it consisted of a more or less fixed formula for each holiday, conducted simultaneously in diverse sites and repeated annually with only minor adjustments.

This uniform calendar and manner of celebration were achieved with the help of various Zionist organizations established in Mandatory Palestine: the autonomous educational system, the youth movements, the kibbutz movement, the cultural section of the General Federation of Workers (Histadrut), and the Zionist Council of Teachers affiliated with the Jewish National Fund. These collective celebrations contributed to the creation of a shared identity for the Jewish-Zionist population of Eretz Israel. The new Zionist calendar was based on the Jewish one, but with additional days of celebration marking important moments in the history of the Yishuv (the pre-1948 Jewish community in Palestine).[11] Thus, the framework for the new calendar was religious, but the meaning ascribed to the holidays was national. Put differently, the rituals developed in the Mandate period fused two traditions that arose before World War I: the religious rituals of the First Aliyah, and the national rituals of the Second Aliyah. The result was a new kind of national ceremony that sacralized Eretz Israel and the Jewish nation by using components derived from the new Hebrew culture.

We can distinguish between three main types of Zionist rituals: *rituals of time*, or traditional rituals, based on the Jewish holidays, that marked major events in Jewish history; *rituals of place*, or traditional rituals that marked the link with the soil and the seasons; and the newly instituted *rituals of memory*, which marked contemporary events. These rituals, despite their differences, were all celebrated according to the Jewish calendar, thus underscoring the connection between Zionist, historical time and Jewish, theological time—attributing to both the same pace. No wonder, then, that one overriding purpose of all these celebrations was to bolster the connection to and identification with the Jewish people and the fatherland. Indeed, according to the Zionists in Palestine, the people and the fatherland were two sides of the same coin: if the Jewish people could only come fully into its own in the historical fatherland, so too it was the fatherland that endowed the nation with its unique qualities. And while the fact that an Arab population already resided on the same land was not denied, the Zionist movement believed that the indigenous inhabitants' right to the territory paled in comparison to that of the Jewish people.[12]

From a pedagogical point of view, there was a clear "division of labor" between rituals of time and memory, on the one hand, and rituals of place, on the other. The former, which dealt with historical events—whether from the remote or from the recent past—were intended to foster love for the nation. The latter enhanced patriotic feelings for the fatherland. This division was, of course, not absolute or watertight. Since the nation's momentous events took place in the fatherland, the connection with the place arose of its own accord. Conversely, rituals of place stressed the characteristic features of the nation that arose as a result of its connection with the Holy Land, its scenery and climate. Nonetheless, for the sake of analysis I will discuss rituals of time, place, and memory separately.

The most prominent festival of time on the Zionist annual calendar was Hanukkah, which had only been a minor holiday in the Diaspora. As noted above, it became a central event in the Hebrew schools even before World War I. While European Jewry celebrated Hanukkah as a religious festival that emphasized the desecration of the Jewish Temple, the miracle of the cruse of oil lasting eight days, and the holy martyrdom of Hanna and her seven sons, in Eretz Israel the festival became an event that marked national liberation. The new heroes were Matityahu and his five sons, the "Maccabees"; their struggle against the Greek Seleucids in the second century BCE was presented as a small nation's armed struggle for independence from a powerful occupying power. The religious dimension of the festival was consigned to the background in favor of its nationalist facet. Thus the Jews who had chosen to assimilate into the hegemonic Greek culture were no longer seen as having abandoned Jewish religion, but rather as traitors to the nation. The festival, moreover, gained a territorial dimension in Eretz Israel because it was now possible to make an annual pilgrimage to the Maccabees' tombs. The pilgrimage was especially popular among the younger generation, in schools and youth movements.[13]

The Zionist festivals of place were in fact Jewish celebrations of nature that the Zionist movement used to mark its new connection to the Land of Israel, its soil, landscape, and climate. Since these festivals were celebrated according to the seasons, they offered an opportunity to emphasize the agricultural nature of the Jewish Yishuv and its self-perception as the continuation of the ancient, biblical Jewish nation—despite the fact that most of the Jews in Palestine were actually living in cities. One such holiday was Tu Bi-Shvat (the sixteenth of the Jewish month of Shvat). In the Diaspora this day had been celebrated with special prayers and eating of dried fruits, marking the beginning of a new cycle of fruits ripening, while in Eretz Israel, from as early as the First Aliyah, it became a holiday dedicated to the planting of trees. For example, the Zionist Council of Teachers considered Tu Bi-Shvat to be one of the cornerstones of its educational endeavor and transformed the tree-planting ceremony into an elaborate ritual, uniting the concrete with the symbolic by alluding to the Jewish people striking new roots in Eretz Israel. It sponsored the writing and publication of appropriate texts and successfully disseminated the new model among the schools of the Yishuv.[14]

But the most significant holiday for the Zionist movement was Passover. The fact that this was both a ritual of time and a ritual of place made the traditional ceremony particularly amenable to new and different interpretations. The kibbutz movement invested a great deal of time and effort, especially during the 1920s–40s, in re-creating the traditional Seder celebration—the ceremonial meal at the start of the seven-day festival. The original family gathering around the dinner table was transformed into a community gathering in the communal dining hall—the symbolic center of the kibbutz—thus creating a kind of extended family. The ancient text of the Haggadah was no longer read, and in its place came a kibbutz Haggadah, tailor-made in each individual kibbutz. The new text was subject to changes over the years, but it had a stable core. That it was so relatively easy to adapt the old Haggadah to the new circumstances was surely connected to the fragmented and performative nature of the original text, since the Haggadah did not present a coherent, seamless narrative, and the ceremony traditionally involved "theatrical" elements that erased the difference between actors and audience.[15]

Among the rituals of memory, only the annual commemoration of the deaths of Joseph Trumpeldor and his seven comrades—who died in a gunfight with local Arabs at the Jewish settlement of Tel Hai, in the northern part of the Galilee, on 1 March 1920—became a notable event. Their deaths immediately acquired symbolic, mythic dimensions, thanks to the efforts of the commemorators.

One main contribution of this type was a eulogy published in the aftermath of the battle by Labor Zionist leader and intellectual Berl Katznelson, which became a template for subsequent commemorations. It was based on the Jewish prayer for the dead, known as the Yizkor, but as Anita Shapira has pointed out, the text included a call to the "people of Israel" to remember those who had fallen, substituting the religious invocation to "the God of Israel."[16] The new meaning given the event at Tel Hai should be understood in the context of the commemoration of similar events in the Diaspora; but now religious martyrdom was replaced by national martyrdom as the price for repossessing the land.[17] Thus a connection was made between the spilled blood, the settlement of the land, and the commemoration of the fallen men and women. Trumpeldor's purported last words—"It is good to die for our land"—which further underlined this connection, came to be frequently quoted during commemorative rituals for Zionist martyrs.[18]

What was new about the ritual that developed around the Tel Hai victims was that commemoration was not limited to texts, as was common in the Diaspora, but also gained a temporal dimension (an annual memorial on the eleventh of the Jewish month of Adar) and a spatial one (in the form of a memorial sculpture, known as *The Roaring Lion*, at Tel Hai). This form of commemoration, commonly found in many European nation states, testified to the fact that the local Jewish Yishuv was turning itself into a community with a notion of place and time of its own.

The structure of the Tel Hai ritual was unlike that of the other Zionist rituals of time and place. Because it focused on contemporary deaths and tried to give them an unambiguous Zionist significance, the result was a two-part ritual that included a commemorative ceremony and a playlet. The first part of the event was meant to mourn the death of the heroes and to mark the participants' identification with them by means of a series of symbolic acts: lighting memorial candles, blowing a trumpet, lowering the flag to half-mast, reciting Berl Katznelson's Yizkor and observing a minute of silence. The playlet, which formed the second part of the celebration, consisted of reciting a number of texts that dramatically recounted the battle of Tel Hai and held up Trumpeldor and his comrades as heroic models. The figures, who at times directly addressed the audience, performed thereby as the living-dead, endowing their sacrifice with meaning and symbolizing the collective victory over death. Such living-dead figures were typical of European national rituals surrounding fallen soldiers but were also part of popular Jewish culture.[19] Zionism, however, used them in its own particular way. Its ancient heroes (such as Bar Kochba or Judah Maccabee) appeared together with its modern ones (like Trumpeldor and his companions) in various playlets. Together they formed an entire gallery of characters that seamlessly skipped over the historical chasm of the Diaspora and directly conveyed a patriotic message to the audience.[20]

The Tel Hai ritual was a new model of commemoration that remained relevant even after the foundation of the state. An emotionally charged event, it linked the idea of self-sacrifice with the notion of national revival. The basic and simple mold of the memorial service could be similarly applied to other fallen heroes who had sacrificed themselves for the fatherland, and the playlet's complex textual patchwork could easily be adjusted to accommodate new victims. While this was only one of the many rituals created for and by the new Jewish community in *Eretz* Israel, the commemorative ritual, in its various shapes, came to constitute the central patriotic event of the new state.

Statehood: From the Foundation of the State to the Early Twenty-First Century

The establishment of the State of Israel changed its Jewish population's national cast of mind; as Shmuel Eisenstadt put it, "The vision has become a reality."[21] The patriotic fervor, which had been widespread in the Jewish community during the British Mandate, gradually diminished once the main objective of the Yishuv had been attained, namely, sovereignty over large parts of Mandatory Eretz Israel. There was no more pressing need for united action to achieve the Zionist ideal, and people could turn inward and focus on their families, trusting that the new state would look after the needs of the collective. The result was a "weakening and crumbling of the erstwhile institutional and ideological model of Israeli society,"[22] starting in the 1950s and accelerating in the first half of the following decade.[23]

The patriotic spirit, however, did not disappear; it only underwent several changes. Likewise, the system of national rituals remained, even though its main features were revised. While the public prominence of the traditional holidays of time and place gradually diminished, new national days of remembrance were instituted, overshadowing the Tel Hai commemoration. The relations between these different types of holidays can be compared to a set of connected vessels. The traditional holidays, which had been very important until 1948, continued to be celebrated but lost their national significance to a considerable extent. Their meaning was now invested in five new memorial days and celebrations. This was not precisely the same brand of patriotism, since now a love for the state was added to and came to embody the earlier love of the people and the fatherland. This was one outcome of the statist (*mamlakhti*) approach, which presented loyalty to the state as the primary value, above either political or class loyalty, because the state represented the entire nation as a whole. And so, the symbols of the state—the flag, the emblem, and the anthem—became patriotic symbols that occupied a central place in all ceremonies and created foci of identification. Although the state should have represented all of its citizens, including those who were not Jewish, these exclusively Jewish symbols testified to its unique nature.[24] In this sense, the new state continued to represent the old patriotism of the Zionist movement, focusing on the Jewish community under its rule as well as on its imagined historical past.[25]

As noted, with the establishment of the state, the old rituals of time and place now came to mean something else, turning into occasions for consolidating family ties, making trips into the countryside, and social activities. The only social space in which they survived as patriotic rituals was the kindergarten, where their mode of celebration became infantile.[26] Although certain segments of the population continued to regard them as opportunities to reinvigorate their sense of national-historical belonging, this ceased to be the rituals' principal role.[27] Conversely, while the five new national days of remembrance continued to feature some leisure-time activities, their major purpose was to facilitate public identification with the fatherland, the nation, and the state. Three of these hallowed days were created shortly after the 1948 War: Independence Day, Remembrance Day for Fallen Soldiers of the Israel Defense Forces (IDF), and Holocaust and Heroism Remembrance Day. The remaining two days were added at later stage: Jerusalem Day was instituted in 1968, and Yitzhak Rabin Memorial Day in 1996. All five days recalled events in the twentieth century, and while three of them were national days of mourning and remembrance, the remaining two marked national revival and triumph.

How can we explain these changes in the Zionist rituals? The struggle for "the redemption of the land," epitomized by holidays like Tu Bi-Shvat and Shavuot, had been won, at least in part, thereby making their patriotic component redundant. In the 1940s, two new types of warrior-heroes were added to the Zionist pantheon: the Warsaw Ghetto rebels and the soldiers of the Israeli army. These new heroes made their ancient forebears, such as the Maccabees and Bar Kochba, who had played a central role in the time holidays, superfluous. Even Trumpeldor, the twentieth-century martyr, became marginalized, as the influence of the pioneer-farmer ideal that he embodied gradually diminished.[28] The new days of remembrance and national rituals, for their part, were dedicated to modern Jewish and Zionist history and its heroes. These events, too, had their spatial concomitants, but those sites were no longer tracts of land that had to be cultivated, but rather battlefields on which the soldiers of the Israeli army fought—and fell.

Although there were similarities between the five new Israeli holidays, each had its own character and stressed a different aspect of the Zionist viewpoint. I will therefore first separately analyze each holiday and only then consider their overall meaning. I will present them not in their calendrical order, but in the order of their respective foundation, starting with Independence Day and concluding with Rabin Memorial Day.

Independence Day was the first of the new holidays to be legally instituted (in April 1949) by the state and to this day remains the most important of them. Its Hebrew date, 5 Iyar, coincides with the Declaration of Independence on 14 May 1948 and marks the longed-for achievement of sovereignty. The reference to the Jewish calendar came to underline the link between the new state and the Jewish religion, inserting the day among the traditional holidays of time and place. The Independence Day rituals, therefore, were transitional celebrations, marking the nation's passage from "slavery" to "freedom," from living under foreign rule in Eretz Israel to gaining Jewish sovereignty over a demarcated territory. In establishing such a day on its calendar, Israel was following in the footsteps of other countries, such as the United States, whose national celebration marks the day of liberation and independence from foreign colonial rule. Yet in the case of Israel, the struggle of the Yishuv was in fact against the Palestinians and the armies of its Arab neighbors and not against the British colonial rulers, who had already agreed to leave.

This emphasis on achieving statehood also suited the prevailing statist approach, which played up the holiday's significance regarding national unity, that is, the need to stand united above and beyond political disagreement. And so Independence Day celebrations stood under the sign of joy and pride in the nation's achievements, which were put on grand display for the Israeli public and the rest of the world to admire, through rituals such as the Mount Herzl torch-lighting ceremony.[29]

The date for Independence Day was chosen relatively rapidly, since 5 Iyar seemed a "natural" choice. In contrast, finding a date for Remembrance Day took longer, because here, alongside state authorities, the parents of the fallen soldiers were also involved. Its place on the calendar was finally determined in 1951 as the day before Independence Day—the outcome of a compromise involving constraints relating to the calendar, pressures from the bereaved parents' organizations, and the Ministry of Defense's own preferences. Eventually, however, the choice came to be seen as deeply significant because it appeared to forge a connection between the sacrifice of the fallen soldiers and the attainment of independence.[30] And thus, by way of selecting the date for Remembrance Day and shaping the ceremonies, a clear meaning was given to the soldiers' deaths: they died for the sake of their people and fatherland.

Since the Six Day War, the main event with which Remembrance Day opens (paralleling the torch-lighting ceremony on Independence Day the following day) is a national ceremony that takes place in the evening at the Wailing Wall in Jerusalem, first held in 1969, and broadcast live on television.[31] The following day two types of nationwide events take place: one focused on mourning, with large public gatherings at military cemeteries throughout the country, and the other dedicated to immortalization, with commemorative ceremonies held at schools and various communities, usually at a local monument. While the first type has been relatively simple and includes the lighting of memorial candles and the placing of wreaths, the latter have tended to be more elaborate and have incorporated the dual structure originating in the Tel Hai ceremonies. Here, a number of symbolic actions are followed by a playlet that serves to commemorate the fallen soldiers by means of poems, songs, and prose readings from letters and diaries, with the occasional addition of dance. But there are two fixed components that help forge a sense of national uniformity above and beyond the diversity represented by these playlets. The first is the activation of air raid sirens that are sounded throughout the country on Remembrance Day Eve to mark its onset and the following morning to indicate the beginning of the ceremonies at the military cemeteries. This creates two distinct moments in which ordinary life is "frozen" and the people are supposed to become united as an imagined national community while standing at attention wherever they may be and contemplating the memory of the soldiers.[32] The second is the Yizkor service—which comes in both a religious and a secular version—the latter based on the eulogy written by Katznelson for the fallen of Tel Hai. This text, which is usually recited at the beginning of the playlet, forms the core of the ceremony and defines its purpose: to perpetuate the memory of those who fell for the fatherland.[33]

Even though legally instituted only in 1963, Remembrance Day already occupied a central place in the public consciousness in the early 1950s and has kept this place up to the present day. Independence Day, by contrast, has gradually lost its initial aura. This can be explained by the fact that the latter related to the one-time event of the declaration of independence, while the former commemorates not only the fallen of the War of Independence but also those of all subsequent military actions. The overall number of the fallen soldiers since 1948, approximately 23,000, constitutes a relatively high proportion of the general population (about 1.8 percent), with two "peaks": the 1948 War (approximately 5,000) and the 1973 Yom Kippur War (approximately 3,000). Similarly to interwar Europe, the large number of casualties means that a considerable portion of the population has a more or less direct experience of loss.[34] There is, therefore, a perpetual need for a day of remembrance that gives expression to the families' mourning and enables the state to provide a patriotic meaning to the soldiers' deaths.

Unlike Remembrance Day, Holocaust Day remained a rather marginal event throughout the 1950s and only slowly came to occupy a more central role in Israeli society. Here too, the decision on the date was the result of negotiations and compromises among various parties. As early as the second half of the 1940s, both in Eretz Israel and in Europe, the Warsaw Ghetto uprising was commemorated on 19 April—the day in 1943 (on the first night of Passover) when the fighting began. In 1951, the Knesset (Israeli parliament) debated which date to designate as the official Holocaust Day and finally chose 27 Nisan, one week after the end of Passover. This was a compromise between the religious Zionists, who preferred 10 Tevet, which commemorates the beginning of the siege of Jerusalem that culminated in the destruction of the First Temple and was declared by the Chief Rabbinate of Israel as the general Kaddish day for the victims of the Holocaust; and the Workers Party (Mapam), which identified the Warsaw Ghetto uprising with their own Zionist youth movement, Hashomer Hatzair, and felt that for educational reasons Holocaust Day should be associated with the ghetto fighters. The date of 27 Nisan was chosen so as not to commemorate Holocaust Day during the week of Passover, but the following week.

Although the date chosen referred to the uprising, it was also incorporated into the Jewish calendar by being fixed on a Hebrew date. This allowed the religious segment of the population to connect the date with the Holocaust, since it fell within the annual Omer period of religious mourning for the mass death of Rabbi Akiva's students, allegedly in the rebellion against Roman rule in the second century CE. The official name of the day—"Day of Remembrance of the Holocaust and the Warsaw Revolt"—as well as its mode of celebration, showed that the memory of the Holocaust victims, which religious Jews had been trying to emphasize, was marginalized in favor of those who had fought against the Nazis. A mindset that contrasted a putatively "passive" Diaspora Jewry with an "active" Zionist approach seems to have been behind this outcome as well. Israeli society, which had triumphed in the 1948 War, could not identify with the "passive" victims of the Holocaust—only with those who had taken up arms.[35]

Unlike the case of Independence Day and Remembrance Day, in the 1950s there was no central ritual on Holocaust Day. Throughout the country, however, Holocaust Day rituals were held—by local authorities, kibbutzim, and political parties. The most prominent of these were the ceremonies at Yad Vashem—the World Holocaust Remembrance Center in Jerusalem (once it was opened in 1953) and at Kibbutz Yad Mordechai and Kibbutz Lochamey Hageta'ot—both communities established by survivors specifically in commemoration of the Holocaust. As far as the general public was concerned, however, Holocaust Day was an ordinary workday, and the ceremonies held to mark it remained inconspicuous. Israeli society's complex attitude toward the victims of the Holocaust stemmed from the arrogance it generally displayed vis-à-vis Diaspora Jews, the shame that they went "like sheep to the slaughter," and the guilt felt by members of the Yishuv for not having extended much help to the victims (often family members) during those dark days.

This, together with the survivors' tendency to remain silent about their past, contrived to relegate the Holocaust to the margins of the public sphere. A 1959 law instituting "Remembrance Day for the Holocaust and Heroism"—and a 1961 amendment—were intended to change this state of affairs by prohibiting entertainment activities on the eve of Holocaust Day, broadcasting special radio programs, and conducting ceremonies in military camps and schools. But the turning point occurred with the Adolf Eichmann trial, which opened in the spring of 1961 and for months dominated the public agenda. After this trial it became no longer possible to ignore the Holocaust as a major chapter in the history of the Jewish people. Since then, Holocaust Day and its rituals, including the official event at Yad Vashem, are no longer attended by a limited public; they now bring the entire country to a standstill.[36]

The fourth memorial celebrated in the spring, Jerusalem Day, came into being in the late 1960s. The date for it was fixed on 28 Iyar, marking the Israeli army's conquest of eastern Jerusalem in the 1967 Six Day War, but only in 1998 did it received legal ratification. The ceremonial activities of Jerusalem Day, therefore, evolved gradually throughout the late 1960s and into the 1970s, under the guidance of Jerusalem's municipality and several government ministries. In 1971 schools were ordered by the Ministry of Education to celebrate Jerusalem Day, and the ceremony was reminiscent of the way Holocaust Day had been marked in the 1950s: teachers were asked to speak with their students, either in class or in general assemblies, about the significance of a "liberated, united, and integrated city of Jerusalem, the capital of Israel."[37] As of the 1992–93 school year, when Jerusalem was selected by the Ministry of Education as that year's educational theme, some schools began to celebrate annual rituals on Jerusalem Day.

While this did not amount to a consistent commemorative tradition, sites within Jerusalem itself did become a major focus for rituals on that day. In the years following the legal ratification of the day, an annual ritual has been held on Jerusalem's Ammunition Hill that resembles the other memorial days in Jerusalem. Additionally, Jerusalem Day has featured special youth activities, such as, for instance, the "flag parade" held in the Old City, whose population is predominantly Arab, or large public dances. Still, despite considerable efforts, Jerusalem Day has never attained a major significance in the Zionist calendar. The day was apparently intended to exalt historical Jerusalem as the capital of the three monotheist religions while simultaneously also emphasizing its special status in the history of the Jewish people. But the date on which it is celebrated, marking a military-patriotic event, rendered it a one-sided day, of importance mainly for the Right and incapable of attaining a consensual status. Most of the rituals are actually dedicated to the Israeli soldiers who fell in the battle for eastern Jerusalem in 1967, and this leaves them indistinguishable from Remembrance Day ceremonies. Thus, Jerusalem Day has remained a pale copy of Remembrance Day, with the same ceremonial shape, but lacking the latter's wide appeal and emotional intensity.

Conclusion

The placement of these four main celebrations on the annual calendar, as explained above, was the result of several constraints: the state's preferences, pressures from interest groups, and the dates of adjacent events. The upshot has been a dense cycle of national holidays, starting with Passover and concluding on Jerusalem Day—a cycle that annually imbues the Jewish nation's history with meaning. The fact that the Jewish calendar was used has put these memorial days into a wider Jewish context and forged a link between traditional Jewish festivals and modern national memorial days. According to the narrative told by this cycle of holidays, there exists, at the very root of Jewish history, a mythic structure that represents movement between exile and Eretz Israel, between catastrophe (or threatened catastrophe) and redemption, and between slavery and liberation.[38] The ancient version of this structure is that of the Jewish people's exodus from Egypt, and the other memorial days enact it in the context of contemporary, twentieth-century history: Holocaust Day marks the modern attempt to destroy the people, offering "proof" of the failure of the Diaspora to end the suffering of the Jewish people (the Warsaw Ghetto revolt is the one flash of heroism in the Diaspora, which will reappear in Eretz Israel); Remembrance Day honors the memory of the sacrifices that must be made in order to gain the much vaunted sovereignty, celebrated on Independence Day; and finally, Jerusalem Day symbolizes a further stage toward full liberation and redemption. And thus, the foundation of Israel and the extension of its borders are presented as the *telos* of Jewish history and the one lesson to be learned from the attempt to annihilate the Jewish people in the Diaspora.

Rabin Day, the fifth national celebration, does not belong to the cycle of spring holidays. Its date, 12 Heshvan, the day in 1995 (4 November) on which Prime Minister Yitzhak Rabin was assassinated, falls in autumn. This, though, is not the only difference between Rabin Day and the aforementioned days. While the other two memorial days refer to the victimization of the Jewish/Israeli collective by an external (German or Arab) enemy, Rabin Day concerns a single hero who was killed by an "internal" assassin (Yig'al Amir). There is, moreover, an almost unanimous consensus in Israel over the meaning of the two other commemorated events: according to their narratives, they led from loss to redemption in the form of the State of Israel. Rabin's politics, by contrast, in the period leading up to his assassination, was and remains controversial in Israel. He held prominent positions in the IDF and in Israeli politics—chief of staff, minister of defense, and prime minister—but after signing the 1993 Oslo Accords with the Palestinian Liberation Organization, he became the target of a hate campaign orchestrated by the Right, while being supported by the Left. Hence the narrative of Rabin Day is ambiguous and open to various interpretations. This inability to create national unity around the life and death of Yitzhak Rabin hampers the efforts to turn Rabin Day into a truly national celebration. The day's commemorative rituals bear out the political split between the Left and Right by being held on two disparate dates—one Jewish, the other Gregorian (12 Heshvan and 4 November, respectively)—which rarely fall on the same day, and at two different geographical sites: Jerusalem and Tel Aviv.

The education system has nonetheless generated a patriotic message for Rabin Day by means of a selective approach to his legacy. According to the Rabin Memorial Day law (1997), on that day schools must engage in "activities that highlight Rabin's personality and his achievements," as well as "activities dedicated to the importance of democracy in Israel."[39] As a result, school ceremonies focus on the heroic aspects of Rabin's life, especially its military components, while passing in silence over the circumstances that led to his assassination. In this manner it has been possible to erase the political dimension of his death and to transform his life into an exemplar of patriotism—addressing the students in the same manner as for the other memorial days. Because it is different from the other national memorial days, Rabin Day demonstrates the limits of the post-1948 Zionist ritual system. Since the commemorated event was the result of an inner split in Israeli society, its commemoration failed to produce the much-desired national unity.[40] However, the failure of the Rabin Day commemoration highlights the strength of the other, springtime Zionist holidays, which have so far succeeded in creating a coherent, powerful national narrative.

Professor Avner Ben-Amos is a historian of education and a member of the School of Education, Tel Aviv University. His major research interests include the formation of collective memory and national identity through civic rituals and history teaching in late modern France and Israel. Among his publications is "The Palmach Museum in Tel-Aviv: The Past as a Space of Education, Entertainment and Discipline," *Museum History Journal* 8, no. 2 (July 2015): 147–67.

Notes

1. Clifford Geertz, *Local Knowledge: Further Essays in Interpretive Anthropology* (New York: Basic Books, 1983), 26–30. See also Catherine Bell, *Ritual: Perspectives and Dimensions* (New York: Oxford University Press, 1997).
2. Oz Almog, *The Sabra: The Creation of the New Jew*, trans. Haim Watzman (Berkeley: University of California Press, 2000); Yafa Berlovitch, *To Invent a Land, to Invent a Nation: Literature and Cultural Infrastructure in the Formation of the First Aliya* (Tel Aviv: Hakibbutz Hameuhad, 1996, in Hebrew); Rachel Elboim-Dror, *The Hebrew Education in the Land of Israel*, vol. 1, *1854–1914* (Jerusalem: Yad Yitzhak Ben-Zvi, 1986, in Hebrew); Benjamin Harshav, *Language in Time of Revolution* (Berkeley: University of California Press, 1993); Rina Peled, *The New Man of the Zionist Revolution: Hashomer Hatza'ir and Its European Roots* (Tel Aviv: Am Oved, 2002, in Hebrew).
3. Itamar Even-Zohar, "The Formation and Evolution of Local and Native Culture in Israel, 1882–1948," *Cathedra* 16 (1980): 165–89 (in Hebrew). See also Charles Liebman and Eliezer Don-Yehiya, *Civil Religion in Israel: Traditional Judaism and Political Culture in the Jewish State* (Berkeley: University of California Press, 1983).
4. Eric Hobsbawm and Terence Ranger, eds., *The Invention of Tradition* (Cambridge: Cambridge University Press, 1983).
5. Zali Gurevitz and Gideon Aran, "About the Place: Israeli Anthropology," *Alpayim* 4 (1991): 9–44 (in Hebrew).
6. Mircea Eliade, *The Sacred and the Profane: The Nature of Religion*, trans. Willard Trask (New York: Harper & Row, 1961); Gurevitz and Aran, "About the Place"; Don Handelman, *Models and Mirrors: Towards an Anthropology of Public Events* (Cambridge: Cambridge University Press, 1990), 223–33; Naomi Yoeli, "The *Masechet* as a Zionist Ritual" (PhD diss., Tel Aviv University, 2001, in Hebrew); Yael Zerubavel, *Recovered Roots: Collective Memory and the Making of Israeli National Tradition* (Chicago: University of Chicago Press, 1995), 3–12.
7. Elboim-Dror, *Hebrew Education in the Land of Israel*, 387–90; Yoeli, "The *Masechet* as a Zionist Ritual," 55–82.
8. Berlovitch, *To Invent a Land, to Invent a Nation*, 221.
9. Berlovitch, *To Invent a Land, to Invent a Nation*, 222–23; Even-Zohar, "Formation and Evolution of Local and Native Culture," 174–75; Yigal Tsalmona and Tamar Manor-Friedman, *Kadima: The East in the Israeli Art* (Jerusalem: Israel Museum, 1985, in Hebrew).
10. Yoeli, "The *Masechet* as a Zionist Ritual," 82–84.
11. The Jewish calendar, according to which the Jewish holidays are celebrated, is a lunar calendar with twelve months consisting of twenty-nine or thirty days and an additional thirteenth month added every third year to create a fit with the solar calendar. The Jewish calendar is the official calendar of the State of Israel, but the Gregorian calendar is also used by the government and the population for commercial and civic activities.
12. Yoram Bar-Gal, *Homeland and Geography as School Disciplines during One Hundred Years of Zionist Education* (Tel Aviv: Am Oved, 1993, in Hebrew); Ruth Firer, *The Zionist Education Agents* (Tel Aviv: Sifriyat Poalim, 1985, in Hebrew); Orit Ichilov, *Civic Education in an Emerging Society* (Tel Aviv: Sifriyat Poalim, 1993, in Hebrew).
13. Orit Bashkin, "The Zionist View of Hanukkah, according to 'Hamoadim Book,'" *Zmanim* 61 (1997–78): 38–50 (in Hebrew); Eliezer Don Yehiya, "Hanukka and the Myth of the Maccabees in Zionist Ideology and in Israeli Society," *Jewish Journal of Sociology* 34, no. 1 (1992): 5–23.
14. Shoshana Sitton, *Education in the Spirit of the Fatherland: The Education Program of the Jewish National Fund's Teachers' Council, 1925–1953* (Tel Aviv: Tel Aviv University, 1998, in Hebrew); Yoram

Bar-Gal, *The Jewish National Fund (KKL): An Israeli Propaganda Agency* (Haifa: Haifa University Press, 1999, in Hebrew).
15. Arie Ben-Gurion, "The Passover Seder in the Kibbutz," *Mibefnim* 1, no. 2 (1988): 121–24 (in Hebrew); Shimon Levy, "Salvation on the Scene: The Passover Night Tale as a Performative Text," in *Scents on Stages* (Tel Aviv: Or Am, 1992, in Hebrew), 76–92; Liebman and Don-Yehiya, *Civil Religion in Israel*, 49–50; Sitton, *Education in the Spirit of the Fatherland*, 162–63; Yoeli, "The *Masechet* as a Zionist Ritual," 150–55.
16. Anita Shapira, *Land and Power: The Zionist Resort to Force, 1881–1948*, trans. William Temple (Oxford: Oxford University Press, 1992), 102–3.
17. Moshe Glickson, quoted in Idith Zertal, *Israel's Holocaust and the Politics of Nationhood*, trans. Chaya Galai (Cambridge: Cambridge University Press, 2005), 23.
18. For a discussion of Trumpeldor's last words, see Zerubavel, *Recovered Roots*, 41, 252n7.
19. George Mosse, *Fallen Soldiers: Reshaping the Memory of the World Wars* (Oxford: Oxford University Press, 1990).
20. Yoeli, "The *Masechet* as a Zionist Ritual," 330–58.
21. Shmuel Eisenstadt, "The Contours of the Struggle around Collective Symbols in Israeli Society," in *Zionism: Contemporary Polemic*, ed. Avi Bareli and Pinhas Ginosar (Sede-Bocker and Tel Aviv: Ben Gurion Research Institute, 1996, in Hebrew), 21.
22. Eisenstadt, "The Contours of the Struggle around Collective Symbols."
23. Liebman and Don-Yehiya, *Civil Religion in Israel*; Dan Horowitz and Moshe Lissak, *Troubles in Utopia: The Overburdened Polity of Israel* (Albany: State University of New York Press, 1989).
24. All three symbols of the State of Israel are of a Jewish nature: the flag—a blue hexagram (Star of David) and two blue stripes on a white background; the emblem—the Menorah, that is, a seven-armed candelabra; and the anthem—the song "Ha-Tikva," whose subject is the hope of the Jewish people to return to its land. See Elik Mishori, *Look Ahead: Zionist Icons and Visual Symbols in Israeli Culture* (Tel Aviv: Am Oved, 2000, in Hebrew).
25. For the education of the Arab minority in Israel, see Majid Al Haj, *Education, Empowerment and Control: The Case of the Arabs in Israel* (Albany: State University of New York Press, 1995).
26. Don Handelman, "Holiday Celebrations in Israeli Kindergartens," in *Models and Mirrors: Towards an Anthropology of Public Events* (Cambridge: Cambridge University Press, 1990), 162–89.
27. Shlomo Deshen, "Secular Israelis in the Passover Fête: the Family and Religious Symbols," *Megamot* 4 (1997): 528–46 (in Hebrew); Elihu Katz and Michael Gurevitz, *Leisure Culture in Israel: Leisure Modes and Cultural Consumption* (Tel Aviv: Am Oved, 1973, in Hebrew); Elihu Katz et al., *Leisure Culture in Israel: Changes in Cultural Activity Patterns 1970–1990* (Tel Aviv: Open University, 2000, in Hebrew).
28. Zertal, *Israel's Holocaust and the Politics of Nationhood*, 91–127; Zerubavel, *Recovered Roots*, 147–177.
29. Maoz Azaryahu, *State Cults: The Day of Independence Celebration and the Commemoration of the Fallen Soldiers 1948–1956* (Sede-Boker: Merkaz le-Moreshet Ben Gurion, 1995, in Hebrew); Eliezer Don-Yehiya, "Festivals and Political Culture: Independence-Day Celebrations," *Jerusalem Quarterly* 45 (1988): 61–84; Don Handelman and Elihu Katz, "State Ceremonies of Israel: Remembrance Day and Independence Day," in *Models and Mirrors: Towards an Anthropology of Public Events*, ed. Don Handelman (Cambridge: Cambridge University Press, 1990), 191–233; Rebecca Kook, "Changing Representations of National Identity and Political Legitimacy: Independence Day Celebrations in Israel, 1952–1998," *National Identities* 7, no. 2 (2005): 151–73.
30. Azaryahu, *State Cults*, 140–44.
31. According to the Hebrew calendar, a calendar day begins in the evening, with the setting of the sun.
32. Benedict Anderson, *Imagined Communities: Reflections on the Origin and Spread of Nationalism*, rev. ed. (London: Verso, 2016).
33. Azaryahu, *State Cults*, 137–63; Avner Ben-Amos and Ilana Bet-El, "Holocaust Day and Memorial Day in Israeli Schools: Ceremonies, Education and History," *Israel Studies* 4, no. 1 (1999): 258–84; Dan Miron, *In Front of the Silent Brother: Essays on the Poetry of the War of Independence* (Jerusalem: Keter, 1992, in Hebrew).

34. Mosse, *Fallen Soldiers*, 70–106.
35. Tom Segev, *The Seventh Million: The Israelis and the Holocaust*, trans. Haim Watzman (New York: Hill and Wang, 1993), 421–45; Roni Stauber, *Lesson for This Generation: Holocaust and Heroism in Israeli Public Discourse in the 1950s* (Jerusalem: Yad Yitzhak Ben-Zvi, 2000, in Hebrew), 48–60.
36. Zertal, *Israel's Holocaust and the Politics of Nationhood*, 91–127; James E. Young, "When a Day Remembers: A Performative History of Yom ha-Shoah," *History and Memory* 2, no. 2 (1990): 54–75.
37. Ministry of Education, "Memorandum of the General Director of the Ministry of Education," distributed to schools and other educational institutions (1 May 1974, in Hebrew), 4.
38. Handelman and Katz, "State Ceremonies of Israel," 198–99; Michael Walzer, *Exodus and Revolution* (New York: Basic Books, 1985).
39. Ministry of Justice, *Reshumot*, official Ministry of Justice publication of laws and governmental rulings (26 May 1997, in Hebrew), 342.
40. Lev Greenberg, ed., *Memory in Dispute: Myth, Nationalism and Democracy: Controversies after Rabin's Assassination* (Beer-Sheva: Ben Gurion University, 2000, in Hebrew); Yoram Peri, ed., *The Assassination of Yitzhak Rabin* (Stanford: Stanford University Press, 2002); Vered Vinitzky-Seroussi, *Yitzhak Rabin's Assassination and the Dilemmas of Commemoration* (Albany: State University of New York Press, New York, 2010).

Select Bibliography

Al-Haj, Majid. *Education, Empowerment and Control: The Case of the Arabs in Israel*. New York: State University of New York Press, 1995.

Ben-Amos, Avner, and Ilana Bet-El. "Holocaust Day and Memorial Day in Israeli Schools: Ceremonies, Education and History." *Israel Studies* 4, no. 1 (1999): 258–84.

Eliezer Don-Yehiya, "Festivals and Political Culture: Independence-Day Celebrations." *Jerusalem Quarterly* 4 (1988): 61–84.

Handelman, Don. *Models and Mirrors: Towards an Anthropology of Public Events*. Cambridge: Cambridge University Press, 1990.

Kook, Rebecca. "Changing Representations of National Identity and Political Legitimacy: Independence Day Celebrations in Israel, 1952–1998." *National Identities* 7, no. 2 (2005): 151–73.

Liebman, Charles, and Eliezer Don-Yehiya. *Civil Religion in Israel: Traditional Judaism and Political Culture in the Jewish State*. Berkeley: University of California Press, 1983.

Vinitzky-Seroussi, Vered. *Yitzhak Rabin's Assassination and the Dilemmas of Commemoration*. New York: State University of New York Press, 2010.

Young, James E. "When a Day Remembers: A Performative History of 'Yom ha-Shoa.'" *History and Memory* 2, no. 2 (1990): 54–75.

Zertal, Idit. *Israel's Holocaust and the Politics of Nationhood*. Cambridge: Cambridge University Press, 2005.

Zerubavel, Yael. *Recovered Roots: Collective Memory and the Making of Israeli National Tradition*. Chicago: University of Chicago Press, 1995.

CHAPTER 12

RIVAL HISTORIES IN A DEEPLY DIVIDED SOCIETY
THE ISRAELI CASE

MAJID IBRAHIM AL-HAJ

Introduction

History constitutes a central subject in school curricula and is often used to shape collective identity and promote patriotism and national cohesion.[1] This becomes especially problematic in deeply divided societies marked by ongoing conflict. In such societies, majority and minority groups may have different and even contradictory historical narratives, thus presenting a significant challenge to multicultural education.

This chapter examines the history curriculum in Jewish and Arab schools since the establishment of the State of Israel. It traces the goals and content of this curriculum and the changes that have taken place over time. The analysis is situated within the context of Jewish-Arab relations in Israel and the impact of the Palestinian-Israeli conflict. Based on this analysis, I attempt to examine the role of school curricula in the development of a national ethos and the implications of this role for the possibility of promoting education for peace and multiculturalism in Israel.

Theoretical Framework

Various approaches in the sociology of education have attempted to explain the link between education and social change. Noteworthy among them are the positivist approach, the conflict-critical approach, and approaches that place education in a multicultural context. The positivist approach views the formal educational system as the central institution for socialization, vocational and professional training, skill development, and shaping the younger generation's attitudes, values, and behavior.[2] According to this approach, the educational system helps train elites and political leadership and confers the technical and administrative knowledge essential for the construction of modern institutions and economic expansion.³

The positivist approach does not deal with the dynamics of the relationship between the educational system and the power structure outside the school walls. Reliance on the positivist principle ignores the concepts of conflict, conflicting interests, and state control of minority and weaker groups by means of the educational system.⁴

Unlike the positivist approach, the conflict approach sees formal education as a mechanism for economic exploitation and sociocultural control by the dominant group.⁵ The advocates of the critical approach see the educational system as an obstacle to the development of weaker groups and as a tool for preserving the status quo.⁶ Unlike the positivist approach, the conflict approach sees the educational system not as a neutral institution, but rather as one that in practice reflects the power relations prevailing in the broader society.⁷ Like the positivist approach, the conflict model views the educational system as preserving cultural traditions. But whereas the former sees this preservation as serving society as a whole, the conflict approach sees it as working to benefit the dominant group, which uses the educational system to transmit its ideology and values. In this way the educational system becomes an instrument for legitimizing the dominant ideology, through which social, cultural, and political ideologies are reconstructed.⁸ Consequently, the critical approach sees the curriculum as a tool for imposing the cultural hegemony of the dominant group and rejecting the rival narratives of weaker groups.⁹

The consideration of education in the context of multiculturalism has come to occupy an increasingly central place in the sociology of education over time.¹⁰ The positivist approach allows minority groups to develop separate curricula in order to learn about their culture and history, except for contents that might contradict the majority's preferred narrative. At the same time, students from the majority group learn about other groups in a factual manner, devoid of any attempt to direct students toward personal development and social change.¹¹

The critical multiculturalism approach contends that in societies with rigid ethnic stratification in which minority groups have absolutely no control over their own educational systems, the existence of one set of objectives and curricula for the minority and one for the majority is intended to further marginalize minority groups rather than to empower them.¹² Hence, authentic multiculturalism requires an egalitarian distribution of resources and equal access by the minority to the power system and structure of opportunities.¹³

The study of history occupies a central place in all models of education for multiculturalism. The positivist approach emphasizes the need to expose students to the narratives of other groups. The study of history from a critical perspective requires not only presenting other narratives but also challenging the conventional historical narrative and preparing students to question "the historical facts and narratives" that form part of the state's curriculum.¹⁴ This is because the critical approach believes that in most countries, history curricula present the past as it is seen by the dominant group so as to study it in a manner that justifies the present.[15] Therefore, in a conflict situation the curriculum will generally reflect alienation and enmity between the various groups. It follows that in order to do away with narrow nationalism, students must be given alternative curricula that seek to expand their horizons and provide them with a more nuanced perspective.[16]

This finding is of special importance in societies transitioning from war to peace. Conservative curricula teach about war in an active fashion that encourages the sense of "we" among students. On the other hand, peace is described as a process that is done by "others." As a result, students develop overidentification with the "we" group—their nation—and hostility and hatred toward "them"—the enemy, or the rival group.[17]

Liberal multicultural democracies have been investing growing efforts in formulating an inclusive history curriculum that strengthens national cohesion and does not provoke conflicts between the groups composing the wider society. This is because the way the past is presented and constructed and/or reconstructed is of crucial importance to shaping future citizenship among majority and minority groups.[18] For a curriculum to be inclusive, it must recognize the "alternative narratives" of the majority and the minority alike.[19] Yet introducing alternative narratives in any school system is possible only within a broad multicultural ideology that is adopted by policy makers and forms part of the state's national policy. Such conditions are crucial, but they are not easy to bring about. The development of multicultural education shows that even in liberal democracies these issues are problematic, in particular under the shadow of continuing conflicts or upon a transition from war to conflict resolution.[20] Nevertheless, despite these controversies, multicultural education has established itself both as a scholarly field and as a basis for school curricula in Western as well as non-Western democracies.[21]

The Educational System in Israel

From the very beginning of the state, Jewish and Arab schools in Israel have been completely separate. In practice, this separation is an extension of residential and social segregation. About 90 percent of the Arabs in Israel live in Arab localities, while only 10 percent live in the mixed cities. Even there, they live in slum-like neighborhoods, so in the mixed cities as well, Jews and Arabs are kept apart in the educational system.

The model that came to guide policy toward Arab education was based on administrative and sectarian separation, with Jewish control of the administration, staffing, and resources of the educational system and, crucially, of the curricular content. Within the context of this centralized policy, the educational system among the Arab population became "education for Arabs" controlled by Jews through the state and a channel for conveying the ideology and narrative of the dominant Jewish majority.[22]

The background outlined thus far raises a number of key questions about the educational system in general and the history curriculum, which is the focus of this chapter, in particular: Have there been any attempts to introduce education for multiculturalism to Israeli students over the course of time? Has the Israeli education system been, and can it be, a resource for peace and reconciliation? What is the narrative that has been conveyed through the history curriculum in Jewish and Arab schools in Israel?

In what follows I attempt to answer these questions through a comparative analysis of the history curricula in Jewish and Arab high schools since the establishment of the State Israel.

History Curriculum

Several studies have focused on the teaching of history in Arab schools. Despite differences in their points of departure, they have by and large emphasized that some changes took place over time. Nevertheless, there has been a clear dominance of the Jewish-Zionist narrative and a lack of an independent Palestinian narrative.[23]

Based on an analysis of the history curriculum and textbooks in Arab schools in Israel, Hana Shemesh differentiates between four main periods/generations according to the textbooks produced by the Ministry of Education during each one. In the first period, 1948–70, which Shemesh refers to as the "Zionist generation," the textbooks in the Arab schools mirrored those used in the Jewish schools, with their dominant Jewish-Zionist content. The second period or generation, 1970–90, is called the "ambivalent generation." In this period, Arab (but not Palestinian) content was introduced into textbooks for Arab schools, along with universal-democratic content emphasizing the common elements between Islam and Judaism and with the aim of enhancing the integration of Arabs within Israeli society. Shemesh refers to the third generation of textbooks (1990–2003) as the "challenging generation," when for the first time a number of chapters on the Arab-Israel conflict and the Palestinians were added. Yet, a large gap still remained between the declared goal of the official curriculum "to deepen among Arab students the sense of belonging to the Palestinian people, the Arab nation and the State of Israel," on the one hand, and the presentation of these subjects in textbooks, on the other. Thus, very few textbooks corresponding to the curriculum were written.[24] In the fourth period (2003–8), known as the "generation of challenge," more Palestinian content was added and more Arab scholars were involved in preparing the history textbooks for Arab schools, yet no independent Palestinian narrative was introduced.[25]

Hourani, who analyzed the history syllabus through 1999, contends that the curriculum designed for Palestinian-Arab schools in Israel passed through three main periods. The first period, from the 1950s to the 1970s, was characterized by "assimilation into the Jewish nationhood and de-nationalism from the Palestinian identity." The period from the 1970s to the 1980s "witnessed a trend of citizenship education," although this type of citizenship was oriented toward strengthening the loyalty to the

State of Israel, rather than 'patriotic affiliation to the State of Israel.'" The third period was between 1982 and 1999, where national-Arab values were introduced into the syllabus for Palestinian-Arab schools, but it "remained detached from Palestinian-Arab national values."[26] Likewise, Abu-Saad concludes that the history curriculum and textbooks in Arab schools have been oriented to re-educate Arab students to "accept the loss of their history and identity" and to suppress their Palestinian-Arab narrative.[27]

As far as the curriculum in the Jewish schools is concerned, Bar-Tal concludes that despite changes that took place over time, all in all, the textbooks in the Jewish schools reflect the "intractable conflict," whereby the education system creates an ethos that supports the continuity of the conflict and produces psychological conditions that enable students to cope successfully with a state of conflict.[28]

It should be noted that some modifications were introduced into the education system in the 1980s, with the aim of enhancing democratic values and civil society in the Hebrew schools.[29] By and large, however, the main content of school curricula has remained particularistic and very much loaded with nationalist-religious content.[30] This conclusion is based on Julia Resnik's comprehensive analysis of curricula in public (nonreligious) Hebrew schools since the establishment of Israel. After a thorough analysis of school curricula in Bible, history, literature, and civics, Resnik concludes, "The picture that emerges from this description is a gloomy one from the standpoint of democracy and the rule of law. The idea of civil society in the construction of the national subject is mere flotsam in a sea of Jewish religious particularism."[31] Hence, the school curriculum in Israeli-Jewish schools has basically conveyed a negative image of Arabs, thereby internalizing the stereotypes of the "backward" and "hostile" Arabs among Jewish students.[32]

The aforementioned situation is especially evident in the history curriculum, which is heavily based on local-national content.[33] Arie Kizel reaches a similar conclusion. Based on his analysis of four versions of the history curriculum over nearly sixty years (1948–2006), he concludes that both the history curriculum and the textbooks have been systematically used to convey the official narrative of the Israeli establishment with its three main components: Zionist, Jewish, and Western.[34] In addition, since the establishment of Israel, the writers of history textbooks have tended to devote major attention to political and military history at the expense of social and cultural history.[35] As a matter of fact, this trend is part of the "militaristic" education that is heavily conveyed in the Jewish state schools in Israel.[36]

A Comparative Analysis of the History Curriculum in Arab and Jewish Schools

The observations of the aforementioned studies have made a major contribution to understanding the education system in Israel as a whole and the history curriculum in particular. Yet this curriculum must also be situated within a systematic comparative analysis that simultaneously delineates the main developments in the teaching of history in Arab and Jewish schools from a multicultural perspective.

To this end, I conducted a content analysis of the history curricula taught in Arab and Jewish high schools in Israel over nearly seven decades, from the establishment of the State of Israel to the present time. For the purpose of my analysis, I divided the main developments into three main periods: the 1950s to the 1970s, the 1970s to the 1990s, and the 1990s to the present. In what follows, I briefly outline the main characteristics of each period.

The First Period: 1950s–70s

Until the end of the 1950s there was no special history curriculum in the Arab schools. As in the case of other subjects, instruction depended on the teachers, each of whom prepared a course book that contained all the material to be taught. Obviously, this book was subjected to the supervision and monitoring of the inspector, who could control the material.[37] Only in 1961 did the Ministry of Education begin to prepare an Arabic version of history textbooks. In practice, books were translated from Hebrew into Arabic almost word-for-word. The only difference was the addition of a chapter on the history of the Arabs, which was nowhere to be found in the Hebrew textbooks.[38]

A comparison of the objectives of teaching history in Jewish and Arab schools during this period reveals consistency in everything associated with the goals mentioned in table 12.1. Whereas in the Jewish schools the emphasis was on the Jewish national theme, the curriculum for Arab students ignored the Arab national theme. Arab students were taught "that human culture is the fruit of the combined endeavors of all peoples of the world," whereas Jewish students learned that the Jewish people played a central role in shaping human culture. Curricular goals aimed to inculcate in Arab students a belief in Jewish superiority through repeated emphasis on the shared role played by Jews and Arabs in history and the shared destiny of the two peoples. Values of coexistence were not conveyed to Jewish students, for whom the Arabs as a people were included under the term "other nations." What is more, Arab students were expected to understand the importance of the State of Israel to the Jewish people and not to Jews and Arabs alike.

The asymmetry between Arab schools and Jewish schools was also reflected in the allocation of teaching hours for world history, Arab history, and Jewish history. As shown in table 12.2, World history occupied about 60 percent of the curriculum in both Arab and Jewish schools. Other historical topics were divided quite asymmetrically. Whereas Jewish schools devoted about 40 percent of their history classes to Jewish history, Arab schools dedicated only about half as much time to Arab history. What is more, whereas Arab students devoted about 20 percent of their history classes to Jewish and Zionist history, Jewish students spent less than 2 percent of their history studies on parallel Arab topics.[39]

Table 12.1. Stated objectives of history teaching in Arab and Jewish schools in the first period (curricula drafted in the 1950s through the early 1970s).

Jewish Schools	Arab Schools
1. To present human culture as the fruit of the combined efforts of the Jewish people and other nations	1. To present human culture as the fruit of the combined efforts of all nations
A. To evaluate our part in the creation of this culture	A. To evaluate the part of the Jewish people, the Arab nation, and other nations in the creation of this culture
B. To reinforce recognition of human cooperation	B. The same
C. To develop a desire for peace and goodwill	C. The same
2. To establish a Jewish national consciousness and strengthen the sense of a shared national destiny	2. No parallel section
A. To plant in students' hearts a love of the Jewish people throughout the world	
B. To strengthen their spiritual experience as part of the Jewish people as a whole	
3. To inculcate recognition of the importance of the State of Israel as a means to guarantee the biological and historical existence of the Jewish people	3. To inculcate recognition of the importance of the State of Israel to the Jewish people through the generations and to establish a feeling of shared destiny of the two peoples
A. To develop individual responsibility for the development of the state	A. The same
B. To create a willingness to serve the state in all ways	B. The same
4. To mold the students' character in light of the endeavors of great national and world figures	4. To mold the students' character in light of the endeavors of the great world figures and particularly great Jews and Arabs
5. To train and accustom students to examine social problems, draw conclusions from them, and attempt to solve them by means of independent critical thinking	5. The same

Source: The formal goals of the history curricula as formulated by the Ministry of Education. Based on Khalil Nakhleh, "The Goals of Education for Arabs in Israel," *New Outlook* (April–May 1977): 29–35.

Table 12.2. Percentage of all history hours devoted to world history, Jewish history, and Arab history in Jewish and Arab high schools in the first period (curriculum drafted in the 1950s).

Topic	Arab Schools	Jewish Schools
World history	60.7	59.8
Jewish history	20.2	38.8
Arab history	19.1	1.4
Total	100.0	100.0

Source: Based on Mahmoud Miari, *A Comparative Study of Curricula in the Arab Sector* (Jerusalem: Educational Planning Project, 1975, mimeographed, in Hebrew).

The Second Period: 1970s–90s

In 1971, the Ministry of Education set up a special committee under then deputy minister Aharon Yadlin to outline objectives for Arab education. The committee submitted a document with general recommendations, which were received as controversial and roundly criticized by Arab public figures and academics.[40] As a result, the Ministry of Education set up another committee, this time headed by Dr. Mati Peled, which for the first time included Arab representatives.[41]

The report of the Peled Committee proposed significant changes in two key areas. For the first time, distinct objectives were formulated for the education of Arabs, Jews, and Druze. The proposed objectives of Arab education included the following statement, considered far-reaching by both Jews and Arabs: "The objective of public education for the Arab sector in Israel is to ground education on the foundations of Arab culture; the achievements of science; the aspiration for peace between Israel and its neighbors; and love for the land that is shared by all its citizens, and loyalty to the State of Israel."[42]

But this achievement evaporated when, in an updated document published on 29 September 1976, the Ministry of Education (now under the directorship of Minister Aharon Yadlin) deleted the words "shared by all its citizens" and defined the objective as simply "love for the land."[43] By contrast, the ministry approved the objectives drafted for Jewish schools without modification.

Thus, even after revision of the objectives proposed by the Peled Committee, it remained state policy to educate Jewish students to love Israel as their homeland and the state of the Jewish people. Arab students, on the other hand, were educated to internalize the message that they were not full citizens but rather marginal members of Israeli society who must obey the rules set by the Jewish majority that are consistent with the basic state ideology.[44]

This lack of balance and symmetry in the official objectives proposed for Arabs and Jews came under criticism.[45] The core of this criticism was that the proposed objectives included no recognition, explicit or implicit, of the fact that the Arabs in Israel constituted a national minority and were an inseparable part of the Palestinian people. What is more, the goals emphasized the aspiration for peace only in Arab schools, while the goals drafted for Jewish schools made no mention of the aspiration for peace or of Jewish-Arab coexistence.[46]

The aforementioned goals were reflected in the second version of the history curriculum, which went into effect in the early 1980s for both Jewish and Arab schools. In its statement of objectives, this curriculum made a distinction between information and values. In addition to the study of "historical facts," information also included developing an analytical approach and the ability to analyze social phenomena in the present and the past.[47]

With regard to values, the following objectives were defined:

1. To develop skills to judge historical events on the basis of general human values.
2. To instill a spirit of tolerance and understanding for the feelings, traditions, and way of life of other peoples and other nations.
3. To develop a spirit of identification with the Arab nation and its culture and with the State of Israel and all its inhabitants.

The main change in the new history curriculum was its reference to identification with the Arab nation as a central objective. Yet this new version was also vague, cautiously stated, and far from parallel to the objectives set for teaching history in Jewish schools. Identification with the Arab nation was not necessarily associated with an intensification of national consciousness. What is more, the Arab nation was mentioned in general terms, without any reference to the Palestinian people.

The revised curriculum for Arab high schools emphasized Jewish-Arab coexistence, including an understanding and appreciation of the Jewish people's contribution to human culture and advancement. The curriculum for Jewish schools did not incorporate parallel objectives. Only the curriculum for Arabs mentioned the principle of cooperation and the joint efforts of Arabs and Jews in building a state of all its citizens.[48]

The marginal nature of Arab history in general and of Palestinian history in particular is even more conspicuous if one analyzes the allocation of teaching hours by units (see table 12.3). The curriculum included twenty-five units, of which only four were required and included on the matriculation exams; all the rest were optional.

Table 12.3. Percentage of required units in the history curriculum for Arab and Jewish schools in the second period (curriculum drafted in the 1970s).

Arab Schools		Jewish Schools	
Arab and Muslim history	22.2	Modern Jewish history	33.4
Modern Jewish history	22.2	History of Zionism, history of the rebirth of Israel	44.4
History of the 20th Century	22.2		
Modern Middle Eastern history	33.4	The Arab-Israeli conflict	22.2
Total	100.0		100.0

Source: Ministry of Education and Culture, *History Curriculum for Senior High Schools in Arab Schools* (Jerusalem: Curricula Center, 1982, in Arabic), 13; Naif Farrah, "History Curriculum and Textbooks," in *Education and the Arab Minority in Israel: Situation, Problems, and Needs*, ed. Muhammad Habiballah and Atallah Kopti (Haifa: al-Karameh, 1991, in Arabic), 109–13.

In practice, the new history curriculum (1982) for Arab schools contained no substantial modifications compared to the previous one. The required units devoted to Jewish history even increased slightly, from 20.2 percent to 22.0 percent. Modern Palestinian history and the annals of the Arab national movement were optional units. Students who did not take the detailed history curriculum had no chance of studying anything related to the Arab-Israeli conflict or the relations between Israel and the Palestinians. World history constituted the lion's share of the required units, because it was included both in the units on the history of the twentieth century and in those on the contemporary Middle East.

The Third Period: The New History Curriculum, Late 1990s

The new history curriculum for junior high schools (7th–9th grades) in the Jewish sector was published in 1998, while an experimental history curriculum for senior high schools (10th–12th grades) in the Arab sector was published in 1999.[49]

The section referring to the general objectives of teaching history in the Jewish schools includes the following statement: "The abundance of past events and the sources that deal with them make it impossible to become familiar with all of history. Historical study is selective by its very nature, in accordance with various criteria."[50] This is an important statement and reflects the familiar principle of "selective information" that almost every educational system follows. It is true that the authors left a number of key points unanswered: What is the basis for selection in the curriculum under discussion? What standards are used to determine which information should or should not be conveyed to pupils? And what precisely are the "various criteria" referred to, which in the final analysis set the goals and content of the study of history in Arab and Jewish schools?

The main section in the curriculum for Jewish schools (section 4) speaks of the objective of the study of history: "In the teaching of history we must provide the students with a knowledge and understanding of Jewish history and human history, with an emphasis on the distinctive course of the Jewish people."[51] This section in fact demonstrates continuity rather than change in the history curriculum. Similar to the situation in the 1950s, the enhancement of Jewish national awareness is the central axis of the history curriculum. There is also no mention of exposing Jewish pupils to the rival narrative of the Palestinian national movement or that of pan-Arab nationalism. This goal is subsumed under the general objective of familiarity with human history.

The other three sections in the curriculum for Jewish schools are general and relate to pedagogical principles relevant to the study of history, such as the need to emphasize social and cultural variety and to learn about earlier generations, the need for perspective on trends in human development, and the importance of seeing the present as the outcome of the past.[52]

In accordance with the guidelines, the general goals associated with information and values were defined as shown in table 12.4.

Table 12.4. Stated objectives of the teaching of history in Arab and Jewish schools in the third period (new curricula, since the late 1990s).

Jewish Schools	Arab Schools
Information	
1. Familiarity with important historical events	Same
2. Acquiring the skills necessary for the study of history	Same
3. Acquiring the historical concepts used in the description and explanation of historical events	Same
4. Viewing current events in their historical context	Same
5. Development of historical thinking (analytical, imaginative, and synthetic)	Same
Values	
1. Fostering judgment of historical events on the basis of human values	Same
2. Fostering understanding for and tolerance of the feelings, traditions, and ways of life of other peoples and nations	Same
3. Fostering a sense of identification with the people and state	Fostering a sense of affiliation with the Palestinian Arab people and the Arab people, on the one hand, and with the State of Israel and its citizens, on the other

Source: Ministry of Education and Culture, *History for Jewish Junior High Schools* [Grades 7–9] (Jerusalem: Ministry of Education, Culture, and Sport, 1998, in Hebrew), 10–12; Ministry of Education and Culture, *History for Arab Senior–High Schools* [Grades 10–12] (Jerusalem: Ministry of Education, Culture, and Sport, 1999, in Hebrew), 4–7.

The goals associated with information were conventional and, as noted, were also included in the previous version of the history curriculum published in the early 1980s. Under the heading of values, however, was something new, although not far-reaching. The first two sections referred to very important educational values, such as fostering judgment of historical events on the basis of humane and ethical values, and fostering understanding for and tolerance of the feelings, traditions, and ways of life of other peoples and nations. But having stated these liberal generalities, the curriculum in practice failed to engage with the cardinal point of placing the Palestinian narrative alongside the Zionist narrative throughout the teaching of history in Jewish and Arab schools.

In addition, because the history curriculum was drafted after the beginning of the peace process in the region, and specifically after the signing of the Oslo Accords with the Palestinians (1993), the peace treaty with Jordan (1994), and the first steps toward a comprehensive peace in the Middle East, one might have expected the Ministry of Education to confront the central question: What is the role of the history curriculum in the transition from conflict to peace? What new themes, both informational and values-driven, should have reflected the historical change taking place in the region?

These questions were overlooked in the enumeration of the general goals, which related to information, the acquisition of skills, types of historical concepts, analysis of social phenomena, development of historical thinking, fostering judgment of historical events, fostering understanding and tolerance, and fostering identification with the people and the state.

In fact, the only innovation with regard to values could be found in the goals set for Arab schools: "Fostering a sense of affiliation with the Palestinian Arab people and the Arab people, on the one hand, and with the State of Israel and its citizens, on the other."[53]

This statement about fostering a sense of affiliation with the Palestinian Arab people appeared for the first time as a central objective of the history curriculum in Arab schools (1999). In the previous curriculum (1982), the goals, as stated, related to developing "a feeling of identification with the Arab nation and its culture," with no specific reference to the Palestinian people.

It may be assumed that this innovation reflected the change that was taking place in the attitudes of the Israeli public in general and Israeli policy makers in particular with regard to the Palestinian people and Palestinian identity. The recognition of the PLO by the government of Israel and the establishment of the Palestinian Authority in the Occupied Territories increased the legitimacy of Palestinian identity in Jewish eyes and the extent to which the Arabs in Israel identified with it.

It should be mentioned that in the Arab curriculum (1999), the goal of "fostering a sense of affiliation with the Palestinian Arab people" was followed by the additional goal of fostering a sense of affiliation "with the State of Israel and its citizens," without any reference to the nature of the State of Israel. What is more, one of the key goals in the curriculum for Jewish schools was "recognition of the role of the state in the life of society and fostering a desire for active participation in shaping its destiny."[54] This section, which was missing from the curriculum for Arab schools, aimed at perpetuating the status quo in order to internalize the perception that Israel is a Jewish state rather than a civil state shared by Jews and Arabs. Unlike Jewish students, Arab students were not called upon to participate actively in shaping the destiny of the state and to feel as full members of the society.

From this perspective, then, whether consciously or unconsciously, the new curriculum of the 1990s urged Arab students to enhance their sense of belonging to the State of Israel as a *Jewish state* and not as a binational or a multicultural democratic state.

Noteworthy was the section on values. In both Arab and Jewish schools the general clauses were phrased in a balanced fashion, referring to the need "to foster humane ethical values to permit judgment of historical events, fostering critical thinking and avoiding dogmatism, fostering recognition of the reciprocal influences among peoples, and evaluation of individuals according to their actions and not their group affiliation." With regard to knowledge and understanding of different historical narratives, the curricula for Jews and Arabs alike emphasized the following goals: "To foster the ability to understand the position of the other from the other's point of view and to foster the recognition that there are other points of view (and not just one) that can be accepted with regard to national problems as well."[55]

In considering the translation of these general principles into the specific national context, however, an asymmetric picture emerges, with different standards for Jews and Arabs. In the Arab schools, the general principles were applied meticulously and with a broad multicultural perspective. The curriculum presented the two narratives, Jewish-Zionist and Arab-Palestinian-Muslim, in the same breath. Students were required to grasp the place of Palestine in the Palestinian-Arab and Islamic consciousness vis-à-vis the place of the Land of Israel in the history and consciousness of the Jewish people. The exact wording of the goals as articulated in the two curricula is outlined in table 12.5.

A comparison of the goals prescribed for Arab schools and for Jewish schools reveals that the principle of fostering an ability to understand the other's position and get to know other points of view of the same events and national problems was applied in Arab schools. In Jewish schools, however, a one-sided picture was given, weighted in favor of Jewish nationalism and providing a historical perspective based on learning about the distinctiveness of the Jewish people "with regard to its essence and destiny." There was simply no mention of the state's Arab-Palestinian citizenry or of their connection to the land.

What is more, in Jewish schools the specific goals of fostering a sense of identification with the Jewish people emphasized sentiment and were based on knowledge, understanding, and appreciation of the most important historical figures in Jewish history. Conversely, the general goals of enhancing Arab students' sense of affiliation with the Palestinian people and the Arab nation were presented in the specific goals in a dry and factual manner, emphasizing knowledge rather than the cultivation of sentiment and attitudes as part of the educational process.

Similarly, the difference between the textbooks for Arab and Jewish schools was profound. It was mainly reflected in the way the Palestinian and Zionist narratives were presented to students of both groups. Whereas Arab students were exposed to the Zionist narrative, Jewish students, as we have noted, were given no opportunity for direct exposure to the Palestinian narrative. What is more, Arab students learned about the Zionist movement as having come into being of its own initiative, with defined goals that integrated pragmatism and ideology. Jewish students, as we have seen, were exposed to the Arab national movement in general or its Palestinian section only in the shadow of the Zionist movement and not as a movement in its own right (see part two of the history textbooks of Arab schools).[56]

Table 12.5. Wording of the new history curriculum for Jewish and Arab schools in Israel.

Jewish Schools	Arab Schools
Fostering a sense of identification with the people and state will be achieved to the extent that students arrive at:	Enhancing the sense of belonging of Arab students with the Palestinian Arab people and the Arab nation and its culture, on the one hand, and with the State of Israel and its Israeli citizens, on the other hand, requires the following:
• Recognition of the distinctiveness of the Jewish people among the nations with regard to its essence and destiny	• Knowledge of the history of Palestine and the history of the Palestinian Arab people and the place of Palestine in the Arab consciousness
• Recognition and appreciation of the cultural traditions and ways of life that crystallized among our people over the generations in Israel and the Diaspora	• Familiarity with the history of the Arab nation and its culture
• Recognition, understanding, and appreciation of the main historical figures in the history of our people	• Familiarity with the history of Islam (religious tenets and stages in the expansion of Islam) and the place of Palestine in Islamic belief
• Recognition of the shared destiny and unity of the Jewish people in all its communities and Diasporas	• Familiarity with the history of the Jewish people (in Israel and the Diaspora) and familiarity with the place of Palestine/Eretz Israel in the history and consciousness of the Jewish people
• Recognition of the role of the state in the life of society and fostering a desire for active participation in shaping its destiny	[Missing]

Source: Ministry of Education and Culture, *History for Jewish Junior High Schools* [Grades 7–9] (Jerusalem: Ministry of Education, Culture, and Sport, 1998, in Hebrew), 12; Ministry of Education and Culture, *History for Arab Senior–High Schools* [Grades 10–12] (Jerusalem: Ministry of Education, Culture, and Sport, 1999, in Hebrew), 8–9.

The first version of the history textbook for Arab schools treated topics related to the Israel-Palestinian conflict, such as the massacres that took place during the 1948 War and the debate over the creation of the Palestinian refugee problem, with extreme caution or ignored them altogether, since they were considered "sensitive" or deeply controversial.[57] Additionally, unlike the textbooks intended for Hebrew schools, books used in Arab schools ignored a number of important points regarding the Palestinian national movement after 1948, Jewish-Arab relations in Israel, and the Middle East peace process. Thus, the Arabic textbook concluded with the establishment of Israel and made no mention of subsequent events, whereas the chapters that dealt with the Arab world generally continued through to the early 1990s. In this regard, there was a wide gap between the stated general principles in terms of history curricula for Arab schools and their reflection in the written textbooks. The stated general principle of "fostering a sense of affiliation with the Palestinian Arab people" was marginalized in the textbooks and class discussions. Consequently, Arab students had no chance whatsoever to be exposed to an independent Palestinian narrative.[58]

A revised version of the textbook for Arab schools was published in 2009. This version, like the old one, includes only one chapter on the Palestinian issue. A careful comparison of the two versions leads to the conclusion that there is almost no difference between them. Both versions conclude with the establishment of Israel. The only minor difference is that while the first version used a neutral term for the 1948 Arab-Israeli War,[59] the second version refers to the different names given to this war by Jews and Arabs. But this revision appears only through a single question directed to the students, without any discussion whatsoever, as follows: "The Jews call the 1948 War the War of Independence, while the Arabs call it Nakbat Falastine—the Catastrophe of Palestine. What do you think of these names?"[60]

In recent years we have witnessed an increasing trend in the Ministry of Education in Israel to intensify the teaching of the Zionist ideology and narrative in Jewish and Arab schools alike. At the same time, nothing has been done to expose students in these schools to the Palestinian narrative.[61] On 1 November 2012, the director general of the Ministry of Education published a circular to all Arab schools in Israel informing them that the history of the Zionist movement and the Holocaust should be taught as a compulsory unit. This means that Arab students will not be able to acquire a matriculation certificate without passing the exam on this specific unit. This decision ignited a dispute between the Follow-Up Committee on Arab Education and the Ministry of Education. While representatives of the Follow-Up Committee do not oppose inclusion of the Holocaust in the history curriculum for Arab schools, they used this step to request two main changes in the history curriculum: first, that a Palestinian narrative should be introduced to Arab students alongside the Zionist narrative, and second, that the history curriculum in Israeli schools should give equal treatment to the Palestinian and Zionist narratives. In other words, just as the Zionist narrative is taught to Arab students, the Palestinian narrative would also be introduced in Jewish schools.[62]

Needless to say, these demands have no chance whatsoever of being adopted by the Ministry of Education, in particular after the Israeli government approved the Nationality Law (July 2018). This law defines Israel as an exclusively Jewish-Zionist state, denies the principle of equality to other non-Jewish groups (even at the declarative level), and annuls the status of Arabic as an official language.[63]

The new Nationality Law found expression in the education system soon after its passage, as reflected, among other things, in a number of changes in the new version of the civics textbook for Arab high schools. In the textbook, which is an Arabic translation of the text taught in Jewish schools, several expressions are employed with the aim of emphasizing the Jewish character not only of the State of Israel, but also of the entire territory of Mandatory Palestine. Thus, instead of "Al-Quds" (the Arabic name of Jerusalem), the new book uses the name "Or-Shalim-Al-Quds" (which is the name used by official Israeli authorities), and instead of "Palestine" ("Filastin" in Arabic), the translators use the term "Palestina" (commonly employed in Zionist writings).[64] In addition, the new textbook exclusively teaches the Jewish-Zionist narrative and completely overlooks the Palestinian narrative. It is noteworthy that the committee of the Ministry of Education that issued the translation of this book did not include a single Arab member. These changes have already drawn wide protests from Arab public figures and politicians against the textbook, which is intended to be introduced to Arab schools.[65]

The aforementioned trend has most recently been reinforced with the appointment of Rafi Perez as the new minister of education (June 2019). Perez, chair of the right-wing Habayit Hayehudi party and one of the leaders of the extreme right in Israel, declared his intention to include teaching the Nationality Law as an integral part of the civics curricula in both Jewish and Arab high schools, starting from the following school year (2019–20).[66]

This step has aroused strong opposition among the Arab population. The Follow-Up Committee on Arab Education and other public figures expressed their intention to oppose these plans. Moreover, the parents' association in Nazareth urged Arab teachers to reject the Ministry of Education's decision in this regard.[67] In an interview on the Arabic website Bokra, Sharaf Hassan, chair of the Follow-Up Committee, had this to say:

> We reject the intention of the Ministry of Education with regard to teaching the Nationality Law [in Arab schools]. This step aims to internalize the content of the [Nationality] Law that considers us [the Arabs] foreigners in our homeland and wants us to accept our inferior status in the State [of Israel], which defines itself exclusively as the state of the Jewish people. We totally reject this racist trend. This dominant trend in the school curricula has been directed against our collective national identity and ignores our needs as a [national] group. Thus, it deepens the crisis in Arab education and exacerbates alienation and helplessness in educational institutions.[68]

Concluding Remarks

This chapter has attempted to trace the development of the history curricula in Arab and Jewish schools in Israel over time. The analysis was based on a comparison of the goals that served as guidelines for the two curricula and the specific content of each curriculum. The analysis leads to the conclusion that the history curriculum, which is one manifestation of the Israeli educational system, reflects the dominant ethnonational culture of the Jewish majority. The asymmetrical relationship between Jews and Arabs in Israel is thus also manifested in the educational and cultural system. Throughout the years of Israel's existence, the message internalized by Jewish students has been that Israel is a Jewish state that exists for Jews. No attempt has been made to foster a civic culture in which the Arab citizens are a separate but equal component. Conversely, Arab students are called on to identify with the state, although the nature of this identification remains vague. Moreover, unlike Jewish students, Arab students are not called on to play an active role in the state.

A comparison of the successive versions of the curricula of Jewish and Arab schools reveals a number of changes in both the general goals that have to do with the values of teaching of history and the specific goals concerning the particular subjects in the curricula. This is especially true in Arab schools, where there has been a shift from a curriculum quite devoid of Arab national content in the 1950s to one that refers to fostering identification with the Arab nation in the 1970s, and finally to identification with the Arab nation and the Palestinian people in the late 1990s. Simultaneously, these goals encourage fostering Arab students' affiliation with the State of Israel without noting how the professed nature of the state hampers such affiliation.

The Arab-Israeli and Israeli-Palestinian conflict that forms the core of the curriculum for Jewish schools is presented in a one-sided fashion that reaffirms the Jewish-Zionist narrative, with no reference to the Palestinian or pan-Arab narrative. By contrast, the history curriculum for Arab schools refers to the conflict in a balanced fashion with a dry presentation of the historical facts from the points of view of the Jewish people and of the Palestinian Arab people. In addition, in the curriculum for Jewish schools, the conflict is taught in an active manner that aims to shape the collective memory of the new generation. Conversely, peace negotiations are presented in a detached and passive manner, making no attempt to turn students into active partners in the public discourse regarding the transition from conflict to peace.

From a theoretical perspective, the curriculum for Jewish schools is still very far from providing a multicultural education, even from the positivist perspective. Such phrases as "critical thinking," "non-dogmatism," and the like are thus purely declarative and are nowhere to be found in the values-oriented part of the Jewish schools' curriculum. The curriculum in the Arab schools, by contrast, reflects a multicultural perspective. But this multiculturalism is incompatible with the positivist approach, let alone the critical model. The curriculum does not emphasize the cultural and national distinctiveness of the minority group, nor does it highlight its partnership in the state and society. Furthermore, it does not encourage questioning the status quo, instead presenting citizenship in a conservative and passive fashion.

This analysis of the content of education intended for the Arabs in Israel, and especially the history curriculum, leads to the notion that there is a third multicultural approach, namely "controlled multiculturalism." This concept applies to two separate educational systems in which the majority group has absolute superiority and controls the minority system, both administratively and in terms of content. This form of multiculturalism does not offer the majority any conception of a multiculturalism in which the minority is a legitimate partner. At the same time, the minority is required to internalize the values of coexistence, multiculturalism, and pluralism, even as it accepts the superiority of the majority group and its role in defining the nature of state and society.

We may conclude that the education system in Israel is not and in its current form cannot be a resource for peace and reconciliation between Jews and Arabs. To the contrary, the way history is conveyed to Jewish students perpetuates the conflict and reinforces the sense of "we—Jews," against "them—Palestinians-Arabs." On the other hand, the way history is taught to Arab students and the denial of their Palestinian-collective narrative reinforce alienation among them as far as school and the State of Israel are concerned.

The aforementioned situation has become even more complicated with the approval of the Nationality Law in 2018. By defining Israel as an exclusively Jewish state while overlooking the Palestinians and other non-Jewish minorities in Israel, this law will prevent any chance of creating a shared sense of Israeli identity. Needless to say, such a nondemocratic political culture will most likely penetrate the school system and hamper any possibility of introducing egalitarian-multicultural education in Israel.

Majid Ibrahim Al-Haj is professor emeritus of sociology and the founding director of the Center for Multiculturalism and Educational Research at the University of Haifa, where he also was a vice president for research. He was visiting professor at Carleton University (Canada), Duke University, and Rutgers University (USA) and a senior research fellow at the University of North Carolina at Chapel Hill. Professor Al-Haj has published extensively on the social and political structure of the Palestinians in Israel, Russian immigrants in Israel, and multicultural education. His books include *Education, Empowerment and Control: The Case of the Arabs in Israel* (State University of New York Press, 1995), and *The Russian Immigrants in Israel: A New Ethnic Group in a Tribal Society* (Routledge, 2019).

Notes

1. Richard J. Evans, "Introduction: Redesigning the Past—History in Political Transitions," *Journal of Contemporary History* 38, no. 1 (2003): 5–12; Baktygul Ismailova, "Curriculum Reform in Post-Soviet Kyrgyzstan: Indigenization of the History Curriculum," *Curriculum Journal* 15, no. 3 (Autumn 2004): 247–64; Maria Grever and Tina van der Vlies, "Why National Narratives Are Perpetuated: A Literature Review on New Insights from History Textbook Research," *London Review of Education* 15, no. 2 (2017): 286–301.
2. See Michael Armer and Robert Youtz, "Formal Education and Individual Modernity in an African Society," *American Journal of Sociology* 76 (1971): 604–26.
3. Michael W. Apple, *Education and Power* (London: Routledge and Kegan Paul, 1982).
4. Henry A. Giroux, *Theory and Resistance in Education: A Pedagogy for the Opposition* (London: Heinemann Educational Books, 1983); Apple, *Education and Power.*

5. Paulo Freire, *The Politics of Education: Culture, Power and Liberation*, trans. Donaldo Macedo (South Hadley, MA: Bergin & Garvey, 1985); Michael W. Apple, "Social Crisis and Curriculum Accords," *Educational Theory* 38, no. 2 (1988): 191–201; Henry A. Giroux, *Ideology, Culture and the Process of Schooling* (Philadelphia: Temple University Press, 1981).
6. Achim Leschinsky, "Educational Theories School Development in Germany in Historical Perspective," *Education* 37 (1988): 97–110.
7. Jonathan Jansen, "The State and Curriculum in the Transition to Socialism: The Zimbabwean Experience," *Comparative Education Review* 35, no. 1 (1991): 76–91.
8. Apple, "Social Crisis and Curriculum Accords"; Henry A. Giroux, *Pedagogy and the Politics of Hop: Theory, Culture and Schooling* (Boulder, CO: Westview Press, 1997).
9. Raymond Williams, "Base and Superstructure in Marxist Cultural Theory," in *Schooling and Capitalism: A Sociological Reader*, ed. Roger Dale, Geoff Esland, and Madelaine MacDonald (London: Routledge and Kegan Paul, 1976), 202–10.
10. See Kelly Estrada and Peter McLaren, "A Dialogue on Multiculturalism and Democratic Culture," *Educational Researcher* 22, no. 3 (1993): 27–33; James Banks, *Multiethnic Education, Theory and Practice* (Boston: Allyn and Bacon, 1981); James Banks, "Multicultural Education: For Freedom's Sake," *Educational Leadership* 49, no. 5 (December 1991/January 1992): 32–36; James Banks, "Failed Citizenship and Transformative Civic Education," *Educational Researcher* 46, no. 7 (2017): 366–77; Jim Cummins and Dennis Sayers, "Multicultural Education and Technology: Promises and Pitfalls," *Multicultural Education* 3, no. 3 (1996): 4–10; Majid Al-Haj, "Multiculturalism in Deeply Divided Societies: The Israeli Case," *International Journal of Intercultural Relations* 26, no. 2 (2002): 169–83; Audrey Osler, "The Stories We Tell: Exploring Narrative in Education for Justice and Equality in Multicultural Contexts," *Multicultural Education Review* 7, no. 1–2 (2016): 12–25.
11. Lynne Goodstein, "Achieving Multicultural Curriculum: Conceptual, Pedagogical and Structural Issues," *Journal of General Education* 43, no. 2 (1994): 102–16.
12. Sanza Clark, "The Schooling of Cultural and Ethnic Subordinate Groups," *Comparative Education Review* 37, no. 1 (1993): 62–68.
13. Banks, "Multicultural Education: For Freedom's Sake"; Banks, "Failed Citizenship and Transformative Civic Education"; Will Kymlicka, *Multicultural Odysseys: Navigating the New International Politics of Diversity* (Oxford: Oxford University Press, 2007); Magdalena Gross and Luke Terra, "What Makes Difficult History Difficult?," *Kappan* (May 2018): 51–56.
14. Marilynne Boyle-Baise, "Teaching Social Studies Methods from a Multicultural Perspective," in *Developing Multicultural Teacher Education Curriculum*, ed. Joseph Larkmand and Christine Sleeter (New York: State University of New York Press, 1995), 159–70.
15. Gundara Jagdish and Crispin Jones, "Ethnic Diversity and Public Policy: The Role of Education," in *Ethnic Diversity and Public Policy: A Comparative Inquiry*, ed. Crawford Young (New York: Palgrave, 1998), 108–32.
16. Jagdish and Jones, "Ethnic Diversity and Public Policy."
17. Elise Boulding, *Building a Global Civil Culture: Education for an Interdependent World* (New York: Teachers College Press, 1988), 41.
18. See Simon Laumann Jørgensen, "The History We Need: Strategies of Citizen Formation in the Danish History Curriculum," *Scandinavian Journal of Educational Research* 59, no. 4 (2015): 443–60, http://dx.doi.org/10.1080/00313831.2014.907200; Banks, "Failed Citizenship and Transformative Civic Education"; Gross and Terra, "What Makes Difficult History Difficult?"
19. Sirkka Ahonen, "Politics of Identity through History Curriculum: Narratives of the Past for Social Exclusion—or Inclusion?" *Journal of Curriculum Studies* 33, no. 2 (2001): 190.
20. See reviews on multicultural education by James A. Banks, ed., *The Routledge International Companion to Multicultural Education* (New York: Routledge, 2009); James A. Banks, ed., *Cultural Diversity and Education: Foundations, Curriculum and Teaching*, 6th ed. (New York: Routledge, 2016); Sonia Nieto, "Re-imagining Multicultural Education: New Visions, New Possibilities," *Multicultural Education Review* 9, no. 1 (2017): 1–10.
21. See review by Banks, *The Routledge International Companion to Multicultural Education*, and Banks,

Cultural Diversity and Education, on multicultural education in Western societies such as Great Britain, Canada, and Australia; on the United States, see Nieto, "Re-imagining Multicultural Education"; on Northern Ireland, see Claire McGlynn, "Negotiating Difference in Post-conflict Northern Ireland: An Analysis of Approaches to Integrated Education," *Multicultural Perspectives* 13, no. 1 (2011): 16–22; on Asian countries, in particular South Korea, see Jonghun Kim, "The Politics of Inclusion/Exclusion: Critical Discourse Analysis on Multicultural Education Policy Documents in South Korea," *Multicultural Education Review* 6, no. 2 (2014): 1–24.

22. See Sami Mari, *Arab Education in Israel* (Syracuse, NY: Syracuse University Press, 1978); Khalil Nakhleh, "The Goals of Education for Arabs in Israel," *New Outlook*, April–May 1977, 29–35; Majid Al-Haj, *Education among the Arabs in Israel: Control and Social Change* (Jerusalem: Magnes Press, 1996, in Hebrew); Muhammad Amareh and Abd al-Rahman Mari, *Issues in Linguistic Education Policy in Arab Schools in Israel* (Givat Haviva: Institute for Peace Studies, 1999, in Hebrew); Ismael Abu-Saad, "Present Absentees: The Arab School Curriculum in Israel as a Tool For De-Educating Indigenous Palestinians," *Holy Land Studies* 7, no. 1 (2008): 17–43.

23. See, for example, Said Bargout, "The New History Curriculum for Arab Schools," in *Education and the Arab Minority in Israel: Situation, Problems, and Needs*, ed. Muhammad Habiballah and Atallah Kobti, (Haifa: al-Karameh, 1991, in Arabic), 114–23; Majid Al-Haj, *Education, Empowerment and Control: The Case of the Arabs in Israel* (New York: State University of New York Press, 1995); Al-Haj, "Multiculturalism in Deeply Divided Societies"; Majid Al-Haj, "National Ethos, Multicultural Education, and the New History Textbooks in Israel," *Curriculum Inquiry* 35, no. 1 (2005): 47–71; Abu-Saad, "Present Absentees"; Hana Shemesh (Rash), "Shaping the Past in History Textbooks in Arab Schools in Israel (1948–2008)" (PhD diss., The Hebrew University of Jerusalem, 2009); Rida Blaik Hourani, *What Palestine Do We Teach? The History Curriculum for Palestinian Arabs, 1861–1999* (Saarbrücken: Lambert Academic Publishing, 2010).

24. Shemesh, "Shaping the Past in History Textbooks," 15.

25. Shemesh, "Shaping the Past in History Textbooks," 18.

26. Hourani, *What Palestine Do We Teach?*, 304–305.

27. Abu-Saad, "Present Absentees," 39.

28. Daniel Bar-Tal, "The Arab-Israel Conflict as an Intractable Conflict and Its Reflection in Israeli Text-Books," *Megamot* 39, no. 4 (1999): 445–91 (in Hebrew).

29. Julia Resnik, "Particularistic Versus Universalistic Content in The Israeli Education System," *Curriculum Inquiry* 29, no. 4 (1999): 485–511.

30. Resnik, "Particularistic Versus Universalistic Content."

31. Resnik, "Particularistic Versus Universalistic Content," 507.

32. See Ismael Abu-Saad, "Separate and Unequal: The Role of the State Educational System in Maintaining the Subordination of Israel's Palestinian Citizens," *Social Identities* 10, no. 1 (2004): 101–27; Abu-Saad, "Present Absentees."

33. See Miri Yemini, Hed Bar-Nissan, and Oria Yardeni, "Between 'Us' and 'Them': Teachers' Perception Between the National Versus International Composition of the Israeli History Curriculum," *Teaching and Teacher Education* 42 (2014): 11–22.

34. Arie Kizel, *Subservient History: A Critical Analysis of History Curricula and Textbooks in Israel, 1948–2006* (Tel Aviv: Mofet Institute Press, 2008, in Hebrew).

35. Kizel, *Subservient History*.

36. See Avner Ben-Amos and Ilana Bet-El, "Militaristic Education and Commemoration: Nationalistic Memorial Ceremonies in Israeli Schools," in *In the Name of Security: The Sociology of Peace and War in Israel in Changing Times*, ed. Majid Al-Haj and Uri Ben-Eliezer (Haifa: Haifa University Press and Pardes Publishers, 2003, in Hebrew), 369–400.

37. Bargout, "The New History Curriculum for Arab Schools," 115.

38. Bargout, "The New History Curriculum for Arab Schools," 116.

39. See Al-Haj, *Education among the Arabs in Israel*, 104–6.

40. Mari, *Arab Education in Israel*, 58.

41. Ministry of Education and Culture, *Report on Arab Education* (Jerusalem: Educational Planning Project for the 1980s, 1975, mimeographed, in Hebrew).
42. Ministry of Education and Culture, *Report on Arab Education*, 14.
43. Ministry of Education and Culture, *Director-General's Bulletin* (Jerusalem: Ministry of Education and Culture, 1977, in Hebrew).
44. Al-Haj, *Education among the Arabs in Israel*.
45. Nakhleh, "The Goals of Education for Arabs in Israel"; Mari, *Arab Education in Israel*; Sa'ad Sarsour, "Arab Education in a Jewish State: Major Dilemmas," in *One of Every Six Israelis*, ed. Alouph Hareven (Jerusalem: Van Leer Jerusalem Institute, 1981, in Hebrew), 113–31.
46. Sarsour, "Arab Education in a Jewish State."
47. Ministry of Education and Culture, *History Curriculum for Senior High Schools in Arab Schools* (Jerusalem: Curricula Center, 1982, in Arabic), 2–3.
48. Ministry of Education and Culture, *History Curriculum for Senior High Schools*, 5–6.
49. Even though the two stages are not parallel, it is possible to remain faithful to the comparative perspective, because the analysis will focus on the overarching declared goals that guide the curricula, in which there is no significant difference between junior and senior high school. This fact is conspicuous in the general guidelines, which explicitly state that the two curricula are complementary: the curriculum for junior high school is the stage of studying chronology, while the curriculum for senior high school is the stage of going deeper. Ministry of Education and Culture, *History for Jewish Junior High Schools* [Grades 7–9], (Jerusalem: Ministry of Education, Culture, and Sport, 1998, in Hebrew), 6.
50. Ministry of Education, *History for Jewish Junior High Schools*, 9.
51. Ministry of Education, *History for Jewish Junior High Schools*, 9.
52. Ministry of Education, *History for Jewish Junior High Schools*, 9–10.
53. Ministry of Education and Culture, *History for Arab Senior–High Schools* [Grades 10–12] (Jerusalem: Ministry of Education, Culture, and Sport, 1999, in Hebrew), 8–9.
54. Ministry of Education, *History for Jewish Junior High Schools*, 12.
55. Hebrew curriculum—Ministry of Education, *History for Jewish Junior High Schools*, 12; Arabic curriculum—Ministry of Education, *History for Arab Senior–High Schools*, 8.
56. Said Bargout et al., *The Modern History of the Middle East*, part 2 (Jerusalem: Ministry of Education and Culture, Pedagogic Secretariat, and the University of Haifa, 1998, in Arabic), 276–318.
57. Bargout, *The Modern History of the Middle East*.
58. See Shemesh, "Shaping the Past in History Textbooks."
59. See Bargout, *The Modern History of the Middle East*, 307.
60. George Salameh, *The Modern History of the Middle East—A Revised Version* (Haifa: n.p., 2009, in Arabic), 185.
61. See Moran Zilikovitz, "History: Teaching Holocaust will be compulsory for Arabs," *Ynet*, 16 May 2010, https://www.ynet.co.il/articles/0,7340,L-3889791,00.html (in Hebrew).
62. Elfger, 9 November 2012, http://www.elfger.net (in Arabic).
63. See "The Nationality Law: The Full Version," *Yisrael Hayom*, 24 July 2018, https://www.israelhayom.co.il/article/573919 (in Hebrew).
64. Adir Yanko, "Without 'Alquds' and 'Palestine': The Storm over the Civics Textbook to the Arab Sector," *Ynet*, 31 January 2019, https://www.ynet.co.il/articles/0,7340,L-5455308,00.html (in Hebrew).
65. "Knesset Member Jabareen: Minister Benet Distorts History in the New Civics Textbook," *Bokra* website, 31 January 2019, https://www.bokra.net/Article-1404911 (in Arabic).
66. "Starting from the New School Year: The Nationality Law Will Be Included in the School Curriculum," *Arutz 7* website, 15 August 2019, https://www.inn.co.il/news/410257 (in Hebrew).
67. "The Follow-Up Committee Calls Arab Schools to Reject Teaching the Nationality Law," *Maan News*, 25 August 2019, https://www.maannews.net/news/993043.html (in Arabic).
68. Yehya Amal Jabareen, "Sharaf Hassan Speaks to Bokra about the Preparations to Open the School Year," *Bokra* website, 27 August 2019, https://www.bokra.net/Article-1418570 (in Arabic).

Select Bibliography

Al-Haj, Majid. *Education among the Arabs in Israel: Control and Social Change*. Jerusalem: Magnes Press, 1996. In Hebrew.

———. "National Ethos, Multicultural Education, and the New History Textbooks." *Curriculum Inquiry* 35, no. 1 (2005): 47–71.

———. *The Russians in Israel: A New Ethnic Group in a Tribal Society*. London and New York: Routledge, 2019.

Banks, James. "Failed Citizenship and Transformative Civic Education." *Educational Researcher* 46, no. 7 (2017): 366–77.

Bargout, Said, et al. *The Modern History of the Middle East*. Part 2. Jerusalem: Ministry of Education and Culture, Pedagogic Secretariat, and the University of Haifa, 1998. In Arabic.

Freire, Paulo. *The Politics of Education: Culture, Power and Liberation*. Translated by Donaldo Macedo. South Hadley, MA: Bergin & Garvey, 1985.

Kizel, Arie. *Subservient History: A Critical Analysis of History Curricula and Textbooks in Israel, 1948–2006*. Tel Aviv: Mofet Institute Press, 2008. In Hebrew.

Kymlicka, Will. *Multicultural Odysseys: Navigating the New International Politics of Diversity*. Oxford: Oxford University Press, 2007.

Ministry of Education and Culture. *History for Jewish Junior High Schools* [Grades 7–9]. Jerusalem: Ministry of Education, Culture, and Sport, 1998. In Hebrew.

Ministry of Education and Culture. *History for Arab Senior High Schools* [Grades 10–12]. Jerusalem: Ministry of Education, Culture, and Sport, 1999. In Hebrew.

Part IV
Nationalism, Settler Colonialism, and Decolonization

CHAPTER 13

THREE PARADIGMS FOR UNDERSTANDING THE ISRAEL-PALESTINE CONFLICT

SAM FLEISCHACKER

Introduction

Much of my philosophical work has concerned the moral and political thought of Adam Smith. Smith was both a moral philosopher and a founder of modern social science, and one thing that attracted me to his writings was the way he brought out the degree to which moral premises shape modes of explanation in social science, even while social-scientific explanation shapes our moral and political decision-making. The factual and the normative are especially tightly interwoven in political matters, and much of the work that needs to be done to move people toward proposals for addressing a problem is already over once they take up a particular way of explaining that problem.

As regards Smith, I've argued that he helped transform how we think of poverty by trying to understand the situation of the poor through their own eyes. This marks a sea change from the condescending view of the poor that dominated literature on poverty before his time. I believe that Smith's empathetic approach to poverty has explanatory as well as moral advantages over its rivals, but as long as it does no *worse* as an explanation than its competitors, I would commend it for its moral advantages alone. It is always better to account for human actions in terms that the agents themselves can recognize and accept, in order to maintain our respect for them.

Exactly this is something we need to bear in mind as regards the Israel-Palestine conflict. The way we explain a conflict has consequences for the proposals we make for resolving it, and where two modes of explanation are so much as roughly equal from a descriptive standpoint, we have reason to prefer the one that is morally superior. And once again, the best explanations from a moral perspective will be those that most enable us to empathize with and respect all agents involved in the conflict. Such explanations are also likely to help the agents themselves to empathize with and respect one another.

Now explanations for the Israel-Palestine conflict generally work within one of three frameworks. There is a settler colonial paradigm, by which Zionism is just one of many European attempts to take lands from indigenous peoples. There is an antisemitism paradigm, by which opposition to Zionism is just one of many manifestations of the hatred of Jews. And there is a clash of nationalisms paradigm, by which the struggle between Zionists and Palestinians is one of many examples of the clashes that arise when two nationalist movements lay claim to the same territory.

Each of these frameworks provides both a way of explaining the conflict and a way of assessing and potentially resolving it. If Zionism is just an expression of settler colonialism, then Zionism amounts to a racist denial of self-determination to the people from whom it took land and should be brought to an end. It may be possible to exculpate some Zionist Jews from conscious racism and to allow most of the Jews currently in Palestine to remain there,[1] but that would be a pragmatic compromise, falling short of what justice truly demands.

If most or all opposition to Zionism is essentially antisemitism, on the other hand, then it is easy to defend both the foundation of Israel and most of its subsequent policies. It may be regrettable that so many Palestinians have been displaced or have had their rights curtailed by Israel, but according to the antisemitism model, the Jewish state has been fighting a war of self-defense against implacable enemies of the Jews since its inception, and rights violations and even mass deportation can be justified in self-defense. This model may also allow for some sort of territorial compromise and for some compensation for Palestinian refugees, but that would again be a pragmatic compromise and a derogation from the justice of the Zionist cause.

So the settler colonial and antisemitism frameworks put the blame for both the initiation and the continuation of the conflict squarely on one party to it. The moral motivation for the clash of nationalisms paradigm is a commitment to not doing that. The clash of nationalisms paradigm views the conflict as a classic tragedy, in which both groups have some right on their side. Both can indeed plausibly see their side as the primary rightful agent in the conflict, but their interests and actions have nevertheless led, more or less inexorably, to a bloody clash. The solutions to the conflict envisioned by those with this view of it explicitly emphasize compromise. Even where those solutions may resemble what advocates of the other paradigms can accept, therefore, the reasoning behind them is different. The clash of nationalisms paradigm sees no ideally just way to resolve the conflict. So compromise does not involve giving up on justice, but is itself the right way to resolve the conflict, morally as well as pragmatically.

After first laying out the explanatory pros and cons of each of these paradigms, I will argue that the third model is preferable on both normative and explanatory grounds.

The Settler Colonial Paradigm

It is worth noting that when people speak of settler colonialism, they usually have in mind a modern, Western project linked to a specifically Western, virulent kind of racism. One of the defining marks of "colonization," according to D. K. Fieldhouse, is "the creation of permanent and distinctively European communities in other parts of the world."[2] And Maxime Rodinson is typical in the way he applies this colonization model to Israel: "The creation of the State of Israel on Palestinian soil is the culmination of a process that fits perfectly into the great European-American movement of expansion in the nineteenth and twentieth centuries, whose aim was to settle new inhabitants among other peoples or to dominate them economically and politically."[3]

But attempts to "settle new inhabitants among other peoples or . . . dominate them economically and politically" are by no means limited either to modernity or to the West. The world was filled with empires in ancient and medieval times, and the modern kind of "expansion" described by Rodinson, where changes in demography were used for the purposes of domination, was by no means exclusive to the West. Consider, for instance, the takeover of Taiwan from its native Malay inhabitants by the Chinese, which began in the seventeenth century and followed a pattern very similar to the English, Dutch, Spanish, and Portuguese colonial projects that got underway at the same time.[4] Saddam Hussein's Arabization of Iraq, which displaced half a million Kurds, Assyrians, and other minorities over little more than a decade, is a similarly clear example of settler colonialism, as is the Moroccan government's attempt to settle its citizens in Western Sahara in order to wrest control over it from its native Sahrawi inhabitants. The term has also been applied to Myanmar's settlement of Buddhists in areas where the Muslim Rohingya live, China's policies in Tibet, and the Philippine government's settlement of Christian Filipinos in Mindanao—all policies that have led to violent ethnic cleansing, just as European colonialism has often done.

This is a point of some analytic significance. Some features of European colonialism, like the attempt to form "distinctively European" communities, are ill-fitted to Zionism, many of whose adherents were interested in reawakening or creating distinctively *non*-European aspects of Jewish culture (hence its revival of Hebrew, among other things). In addition, the effect of calling Zionism a settler colonial movement is to present Jews, culturally, as simply Europeans—typical inhabitants of the countries they came from—which distorts both their history and their self-understanding. Finally, elements of settler colonialism in places like Iraq and Myanmar suggest that it cannot be sharply separated from nationalism. It may indeed be an outgrowth of nationalism.

Let's turn now to the reasons for favoring the settler colonial paradigm. Advocates of this paradigm usually make four main points:

1. Early Zionists themselves used the words "colony" and "colonization" for what they were up to. The sociologist Gershon Shafir mentions, for instance, the

fact that Arthur Ruppin, the director of the World Zionist Organization's Jaffa office, titled his 1926 book *The Agricultural Colonization of the Zionist Organization in Palestine*.[5]

2. Zionism sought and received the support of two imperial powers throughout its history: the British Empire, in its founding period, and the United States in later years.
3. Zionists have often displayed the same racist condescension and contempt toward the indigenous inhabitants of Palestine that other colonialists showed toward the native peoples where they settled.
4. The socioeconomic structure of the Zionist settlement in Palestine, which exploited Arab labor even while denying political rights to Arabs, closely resembled the socioeconomic structure of other colonialist projects.

These points are of varying import. To the first point, one may note that the words "colony" and "colonization" have a variety of meanings, not all of which reflect the project usually meant by "colonialism." "Colony" just means a group of people from the same place or with similar interests who live in close proximity to one another or in a formal community of some sort. The word has agricultural connotations in particular—its root is *colonia*, Latin for "settled estate" or "farm," which in turn derives from *colonus*, a husbandman or tenant farmer—so a group that lives together in a farming community is especially likely to be given such a name. Ruppin titled his book with precisely this connotation in mind; his central concern was the need for Jews to adopt an agrarian way of life if they wanted to live in Palestine.[6] Nothing about these uses of the term suggests that the community in question is sponsored by a distant foreign power or expects to exert control over an indigenous population on behalf of that power. Perhaps the word's meaning has shifted enough that in modern times it can be applied only to communities established far from where its founders come from. In that case, the Zionist project, calling for Jews dispersed all over the world to gather in a new territory, necessarily involved "colonies." But again, this use of the term carries none of the racist and imperialist connotations that are essential to "settler colonialism" as that phrase is used in modern-day political analysis and polemic.

The second point has more merit but is also questionable. Zionism had no imperial sponsor for its first thirty-five years (from 1882 to 1917) and for all intents and purposes lost its British sponsorship in 1939. Even between 1917 and 1939, its relationship with Britain was rocky, as Britain tried to balance its commitment to the movement with its interest in cultivating a relationship with the Arab world. These points bring out the fact that Zionism was not a project run *by* the British Empire, but a separate entity—serving *Jews* around the world, not British people—and that Zionism's interests sometimes agreed, sometimes disagreed, with British interests.[7] This is entirely unlike the relationship between Britain or Spain or France and their colonists in the Americas, Africa, India, and Australia.

The third point is undeniable. As early as 1891, Ahad Ha'am complained that "our brethren in the Land of Israel . . . behave toward the Arabs with hostility and cruelty, infringe upon their boundaries, hit them without reason, and even brag about it."[8] Ahad Ha'am was unusual among early Zionist leaders in acknowledging this problem. Most of them, while disapproving of the sort of open thuggery that Ahad Ha'am described, shared the contemptuous attitudes underlying such behavior. They either held, contrary to the evidence on the ground, that most Palestinian Arabs actually welcomed the Zionists for the material benefits they had to offer[9] or that European Jews, as representatives of a higher civilization, had a right to rule over Arabs. Chaim Weizman declared that "there is a fundamental difference in quality between Jew and native" and regarded the Palestinian Arabs as "a demoralized race."[10] Ze'ev Jabotinsky quoted Max Nordau approvingly, to the effect that "we [Jews] come to the Land of Israel in order to push the moral frontiers of Europe up to the Euphrates."[11]

But pointing out that some or even many Zionists talked this way or acted in racist ways is not enough to tell us that racism defined the movement. In the first place, there were Zionists who pushed back against the Eurocentrism of figures like Weizman and Jabotinsky, some of them even calling on their fellow Jews to "consolidate our Semitic nationality and not obfuscate it with European culture."[12] In the second place, pronouncements by leaders do not of themselves tell us what defines a movement. Karl Marx and Friedrich Engels made racist remarks; Adolf Hitler condemned the inequities of capitalism. That does not turn socialism into racism or racism into socialism. And in the third place, what defines a political movement is the aim or set of aims that primarily motivates people to join it and work for it. They may have all sorts of other views and aims as well—they typically bring along with them the usual prejudices of their time and place, among other things—but they do not join their movement because of these other views. Thus many socialists in the nineteenth century, not just Marx and Engels, were racist. But that was not the reason they were socialists. Similarly, many European Zionists, not just Weizman and Jabotinsky, were racist. But that was not why they were Zionists.

We'll encounter the same point when we come to the antisemitism paradigm: the fact that some or even many Palestinians, including Palestinian leaders, have espoused antisemitic views does not tell us what their movement stands for or display its defining aims.

The fourth point is the strongest of the arguments for the settler colonial view. Gershon Shafir has shown how the early Yishuv and the World Zionist Organization looked to the French colonization of Algeria and Tunisia and to German colonization in Prussia as models in designing their own communities.[13] In particular, the Zionists learned from these examples ways of organizing labor and land that exploited or excluded the native population. Shafir also suggests that the legacy of these strategies persisted in the social structures of the State of Israel—both directly, in that the state maintained the Jewish National Fund and Jewish Agency as its means for acquiring land (collectively, and for Jews only), and indirectly, in that a tendency toward exploiting or excluding Palestinians has characterized Israeli society throughout its history.

Shafir makes these points in careful historical detail, and they are hard to gainsay. He and Baruch Kimmerling, another sociologist who employs the settler colonial paradigm, have also shed light on aspects of Israeli society that cannot be easily explained otherwise. That said, some of Shafir's points would equally well fit a nationalist explanation of Zionism. This comes out sharply when he describes early Zionists as seeking "to emulate in Palestine the 'internal colonization' model developed by the Prussian government in order to create a German majority in its eastern, Polish, marches"—to emulate, that is, a *nationalist* policy pursued by the late nineteenth-century German government within its own borders.[14] Shafir also acknowledges that there are several ways in which Zionism does not fit the settler colonial mold—the fact that many of the incoming Jews were refugees from European countries, rather than their representatives, being a primary one.[15]

That fact is indeed important. French settlers in Algeria, German settlers in Namibia, Portuguese settlers in Mozambique and Goa, and virtually all other settler colonialists saw themselves as French, German, Portuguese, and so on and their new communities as extending the power of their home countries. The Jews from Russia, Poland, Hungary, and Germany who came to Palestine from the 1880s through the 1940s did not identify culturally as Russian, Polish, Hungarian, or German. They saw being Jewish instead as their cultural identity, identifying more with Jews from other countries than with the non-Jews in their countries of origin. They had also been regarded in their countries of origin as an alien "race" or ethnicity. To be sure, many recognized that their Jewishness had been influenced by Russian, Polish, or German culture, and some sought to preserve distinctively Russian, Polish, or German ways of being Jewish in their new home. But they had no interest in extending the power of Russia, Poland, or Germany; they wanted to build a *Jewish* home in Palestine, not a Russian or Polish or German one. Their relationship to their countries of origin was not one of representation or even of belonging, but of alienation and persecution. This is characteristic of groups that seek a new national home for themselves, not of groups that want to extend the political entity to which they already belong.

An alternative way of making this point is to note, as opponents of the settler colonial model often do, that Zionism had no "metropole" to refer back to or to return to if their project failed. Even when the incoming Jews were not refugees, strictly speaking—when they were fleeing poverty and cultural alienation rather than outright persecution—they can hardly be regarded as peripheral representatives of a distant center. No European power regarded them as its representatives; no European power devoted its resources to their settlements; they did not swear allegiance to any European nation. They may have wanted Britain to help them, but they were willing to take such help from any great power. Britain was an ally for them, not a sovereign; nor did they regard any other European nation as their true ruler or home.

But without a metropole, it is hard to maintain the settler colonial paradigm. The absence of a metropole explains why the Jews could not just "go home" if their project failed and why they regarded their buying up of indigenous land not as expanding the power or resources of some faraway country, but as the necessary condition for a hitherto landless group to establish a national home for itself. These points are crucial to understanding Zionism, however one wants to judge it.

They also make for a sharp distinction between the establishment of the State of Israel and the settlement project that Israel embarked on after the 1967 War. Israel's settlement of Gaza and the West Bank after 1967 does fit the settler colonial paradigm. Israel in 1967 was an established state, and its citizens went out from there into the territories it conquered very much like frontier settlers moving from the metropole to a periphery. These settlers had a home to return to and saw themselves as representing Israel and expanding its power, and the state in return used its power to protect them and develop their communities, all the while oppressing and dispossessing the indigenous inhabitants of the area. There has moreover been a debate within the Israeli metropole for decades, much like debates in Britain when it ruled India and in France when it ruled Algeria, over whether the settlers should pull up stakes and come home—a debate that did not take place, *could* not take place, within the Jewish community that established itself in Palestine before 1948. Relatedly, there is a clear moral case for uprooting these settlements. "Sending back" the Jews of 1882–1948, which would have rendered many of them homeless or dead, would have been much harder to justify.

Applying the settler colonial paradigm to Israel's actions in the territories it captured in 1967 therefore makes both explanatory and moral sense. That is not true of the settler colonial model as applied to Zionism before 1948. There, the model renders unintelligible how the Jews saw themselves, how they were viewed in their countries of origin, and the political relationship in which they stood to their imperial sponsor. But a mode of explanation that runs against the grain of how people conceived of themselves over a long period of time must attribute deep dishonesty or self-deception to that people. It is generally both implausible and offensive to view an entire people as deceptive or self-deceptive, however. While the settler colonial paradigm makes sense of some elements of Zionism, therefore, it has both explanatory and moral failings as an account of the movement as a whole.

Anti-Zionism as Antisemitism

Let's turn now to the approach to the conflict that reduces anti-Zionism to anti-Semitism. This view begins by maintaining that the right of self-determination has been granted to every people except the Jews, so its denial to Jews must reflect the long-standing hatred of Jews among Christians and Muslims.[16] Advocates of the view add that antisemitism can be found throughout the rhetoric and practice of

Palestinian activists, from the Nazi ravings of Hajj Amin al-Husseini to the Charter of Hamas, which includes passages lifted from the conspiracy theories of the *Protocols of the Elders of Zion*.

Much about this view is obviously wrong. The right to political self-determination has not been granted to every people; the Acehnese, Basques, Catalans, Ibos, Kurds, and Tamils are among the many groups who have not realized such a right and whose agitations to do so have been unfavorably received by most of the world community. Realizing such rights by granting a people its own state generally comes at a serious cost to other peoples and states. So there is no need to appeal to antisemitism to explain why there has been resistance to the idea of a Jewish state. There is even less need to appeal to antisemitism to explain why *Palestinians* might reject arguments that justify turning the land where they live over to the Jews or reducing them to second-class citizens in order to make room for a Jewish state.

That said, it is true that major Palestinian leaders, including the grand mufti and the leaders of Hamas, have often employed openly hateful rhetoric about Jews generally, not just about Zionists, calling for their subordination or extermination. A strand of virulent antisemitism has indeed run through anti-Zionism throughout its history. Following are a few examples:

- Neguib Azoury, whose 1905 *Le Réveil de la Nation Arabe* is regarded as the founding document of Arab nationalism and a prescient critique of Zionism, presents Jews as the enemies of the rest of humankind, and his case against Zionism is infused by these views. He tells his reader in the preface of his book that it should be read together with a larger project that he expects to bring out soon: *Le Péril juif universel*. He also mentions the advantages to Europe of siding with Arab nationalism: it is the Arabs who can nip the contemporary success of the Jews in the bud and thereby destroy their project of world domination.[17]
- In 1913 the influential Jaffa daily *Filastin* published a poem by a local Palestinian leader that included the lines "Jews, sons of clinking gold, stop your deceit. We shall not be cheated into bartering away our country! . . . The Jews, the weakest of all peoples and the least of them, are haggling with us for our land." The following year, an anonymous anti-Zionist pamphlet asked the people of Palestine, "Do you want to be slaves and servants to people who are notorious in the world and in history?" The Jerusalem notable Aref Pasha Dajani told the King-Crane Commission, dispatched by the Paris Peace Conference in 1919 to ascertain how people in the former Ottoman Empire wished to be governed, that "in all the countries where [Jews] are at present they are not wanted . . . because they always arrive to suck the blood of everybody." A year later, Palestinian rallies chanted, "We will drink the blood of the Jews!" and "Palestine is our land and the Jews are our dogs," while holding up signs with messages like "Death to the Jews" and "Shall we give back the country to a people who crucified our Lord Jesus?"[18] In the Hebron riots of 1929, many of the Jews killed were indig-

enous inhabitants of the land, not Zionists; the grand mufti of Jerusalem, Hajj Amin al-Husseini, also used the *Protocols of the Elders of Zion* as evidence that the Jews were responsible for these riots when testifying to the British commission investigating them.[19]

- The grand mufti is of course Exhibit A in the case that gets made for anti-Zionism as pervasively antisemitic. Friendly with Hitler, he was a thoroughgoing hater of Jews from early on in his career. No doubt his importance is often exaggerated, as Gilbert Achcar has argued.[20] It is also true, and significant, that he achieved prominence partly thanks to the misguided hope of Herbert Samuel, the pro-Zionist high commissioner for Palestine under the British Mandate, that appointing him grand mufti would conciliate Arab opponents of Zionism.[21] But it is also important that he was regarded as the leading political figure in Palestine until at least the end of the 1940s, as well as the likely head of a Palestinian state had one been founded in 1948. Had the Palestinian national movement been truly free of antisemitism, let alone opposed to it, one would have expected most of its adherents to condemn the mufti and reject his claims to leadership. Moreover, the mufti was not alone among advocates for the Palestinian cause in the 1940s in his enthusiasm for Nazism. The most important leader of the Palestinian military forces in the 1947–49 war, Fawzi al-Qawuqji, also spent World War II in Berlin, calling for a German-Arab alliance based on their shared opposition to "the role of Jews and their intrigues."[22]

- A fondness for Hitler and Nazism was rife in the Arab world after World War II. In 1956 a Muslim Brotherhood newspaper in Damascus declared, "One cannot forget that Hitler enjoys high esteem in the Arab world, unlike in Europe. His name awakens sympathy and enthusiasm in the hearts of our supporters." On the eve of Adolf Eichmann's trial, the Jordanian *Jerusalem Times* published an open letter to him, calling his role in the Holocaust "a blessing to humanity" and looking forward to "the liquidation of the remaining six million." At a meeting with Kamal Jumblatt in 1974, Hafez el-Assad also noted that the Arabs thought of Hitler "in a positive way," upon which Jumblatt added, "National Socialism should be revived a bit."[23]

- One argument against the creation of a Jewish state in 1947, used in the UN by representatives of the Arab states bordering Palestine, was that the response to such a thing would be attacks on Jews throughout the Arab world. And this indeed occurred. Dozens of Jews were murdered and homes, stores, and synagogues were destroyed in Egypt, Syria, Iraq, Morocco, Yemen, and Bahrain after the Partition Plan was approved.[24] Persecution of indigenous Jews in these countries also continued for decades after Israel's creation, despite the fact that the result of such policies was to lead more Jews to go to Israel. And Palestinian terror attacks in the 1970s and 1980s targeted synagogues, kosher restaurants, and other Jewish communal centers all over the world, despite claims by the movements they represented that their enemy was Israel and Zionism, not Jews and Judaism.

So it is not hard to find language and strategic choices in the history of anti-Zionism that suggest it has been fueled and informed by a hatred for Jews and a desire to destroy them, just as it is not hard to find language and strategic choices in the history of Zionism that suggest it has been fueled and informed by a colonialist mentality. But what do these bits of language and practice show? Can they really tell us what most drove the people who flocked to movements that presented themselves as promoting Jewish or Palestinian self-determination? I submit that the answer is a clear "no" in both cases. Rashid Khalidi rightly describes the idea "that the Palestinians [have been] motivated by no more than anti-Semitism in their opposition to Zionism" as "ludicrous."[25] It is bizarre to suppose that Palestinians seeking their own individual and collective rights have been motivated merely by a hatred of Jews. But it is equally bizarre to suppose that Jews fleeing European persecution and trying to set up a polity of their own were motivated merely by a European desire to dominate non-European peoples. To read Zionism as a colonialist rather than a nationalist movement is to run roughshod over the true relationship between Jews and Europe and to dismiss uncomprehendingly the way Zionists have seen themselves and built support for what they were doing in Jewish communities.

A Clash of Nationalisms

The clash of nationalisms paradigm has the immediate advantage of fitting with the way most Zionists and most Palestinians both see themselves; no mass deception or self-deception need be attributed to either group. There is also no need to attribute racist and hateful attitudes to either group as the prime motivator for its political behavior. In the clash of nationalisms paradigm, we can see both Zionists and Palestinians as concerned above all with securing political rights for their own peoples, not with harming anyone else.

This paradigm, moreover, fits the history of both movements. The Zionist movement has seen itself as a nationalist movement from its beginning, modeling itself on the Greek and German and Italian nationalist movements that built states for their peoples in the nineteenth century and on contemporaneous efforts to form or transform a state along nationalist lines among Magyars, Poles, Russians, and other Slavs. The movement drew on figures like Johann Gottlieb von Herder, the main intellectual inspiration of nationalism in Europe, and was accompanied by and in part arose out of a revival of Hebrew that parallels the move to renew indigenous languages among nationalist activists elsewhere in Europe.[26] It did not for the most part aim—and many of its adherents did not aim at all—to extend European rule beyond

Europe. On the contrary, it aimed to provide a people that it regarded as having no home in Europe with a home elsewhere.

Palestinians opposed to Zionism have for the most part similarly identified themselves as members of a national movement, with institutions bearing names like "the Palestinian National Council."[27] They have also always stressed that being Palestinian entails being Arab—that it is a specifically ethnic identity, not a civic one open to people of any ethnic group. Both the 1964 and the 1968 versions of the Palestinian National Covenant proclaim the Palestinian national movement to be an integral part of Arab nationalism more generally, and the 2003 Constitution of Palestine follows them in this. To be sure, some Palestinians have been Marxists, whose ultimate goal could not possibly be a state that prioritizes an ethnicity. But the same can be said of some Zionists. Like Lenin, these figures have presumably seen nationalist states—including a Jewish or Palestinian state—as a way station in the dialectical movement of history toward its ultimate, non-nationalist goal.[28]

Now nationalism involves a very specific view of politics.[29] Unlike both liberalism and Marxism, it maintains that ethno-cultural groups need or deserve some kind of self-rule; it rejects the idea that the mission of states is merely to protect the individual rights treasured by liberals or to promote the socioeconomic equality emphasized by Marxists. Nationalism also takes nonpolitical forms in which it promotes a cultural revival alone; early nationalists in many places were more interested in promoting their people's language or literature than in building a state. The basic idea is that human beings are deeply shaped by culture and cannot be characterized in the baldly universalist ways favored by Enlightenment ideologies like liberalism and Marxism. There is something attractive about this idea, and many who do not identify with nationalist movements politically have welcomed its emphasis on culture and resistance to Enlightenment universalism. Moreover, the political demands of nationalism have varied widely. Depending on the geopolitical circumstances of the group that takes it up, a nationalist group may call for a degree of political autonomy within a larger state, for secession from that state, or for the transformation of a liberal or Marxist state into one that represents and promotes a particular culture.[30]

Both Zionism and Palestinian nationalism fit this profile perfectly. They have very much been cultural as well as political movements, giving rise to bodies of literature, film, and music as well as to organizations pursuing political strategies. Zionism has been as much a revival and reworking of what it means to be Jewish as a movement of settlement and state-building; it was indeed divided over its political aims for some time, issuing an official call for a Jewish state only in 1942.[31] Both movements have also had the complex relationship to religion that other nationalist movements have had.[32] On the one hand, the two movements have been largely built by secular activists and intellectuals, seeking a way of being Jewish or Arab that is not tied to religion. On the other hand, these secular leaders have turned to the religious roots of the communities they represent in order to build support for themselves—with the result that religious versions of the movements have, over time, threatened their own leadership. Both movements, in this regard, resemble Indian nationalism and the place of Hindu nationalism within it, as well as Arab nationalism in its relationship to the Muslim Brotherhood. Nationalism throughout the world has tended to start up among people seeking a mode of collective identity that is not religious, but then had to deal with a "return of the repressed," as the religious forces still smoldering within their communities lay claim to constituting the real identity of those communities.[33] These religious forces also tend to be far more illiberal than the original secular movements. All of these features have been true of both Zionism and Palestinian nationalism.

Both movements thus exemplify the problems with nationalism as well as what is attractive about it. Above all, they both display the illiberal, violent, and xenophobic characteristics to which nationalism is prone. This brings us to another advantage of the clash of nationalisms paradigm: it can make sense of the colonialist elements in Zionism and the antisemitic elements in anti-Zionism.

Nationalist movements have not infrequently engaged in colonialist projects. Italy and Germany followed up their struggles for national unity and independence with a takeover of parts of Africa and eventually sought to establish imperial rule over much of Europe as well. Greece, having won its independence from the Ottoman Empire in 1832, went on to pursue territorial claims in Thessaly, Macedonia, Cyprus, and Anatolia and to Hellenize the areas it conquered, transforming Macedonia from a largely Turkish and Muslim area (in Thessaloniki, a Turkish and Jewish area) into a Greek and Christian one.[34]

Even the new states of Asia and Africa, the model products of anti-colonial nationalism, have engaged in forms of colonialism. As noted earlier, Saddam Hussein tried to Arabize Iraq, Morocco has used its military power to subdue the Sahrawis, and the Philippines has tried to Christianize Mindanao. China has done something similar in Tibet. Many countries throughout the world have tried to squelch or assimilate ethnic minorities, whether by moving representatives of their majority populations into their minorities' areas or by refusing to teach minority languages in local public schools and ignoring claims by their minorities for collective rights.

The simple point to make here is that there is nothing about trying to achieve self-rule for one nation that bars that nation from seeking to bring other nations under its rule. Indeed, the dynamic is often the reverse: those who set out to establish a state for their own group often seek, for the sake of that group's glory or material well-being, to extend its rule widely. To some extent, the pressures here go deeper than a desire for glory or wealth. In order to ensure that a territory, hitherto inhabited by a variety of groups, functions from now on as the state of group X, it may be essential to squelch the political claims of other groups or to expel them or dilute their numbers. So the Hellenization of Macedonia, the Christianization of the Philippines, and the Arabization of Iraq may be necessary elements of statecraft if these areas are to constitute nation-states.

Seen in this light, the Judaization of the Galilee and of the West Bank is far from an abandonment of the nationalism that founded the State of Israel; it is rather an extension of it. More generally, to call Zionism a nationalist movement is not to exempt it from the charge of having colonialist features. But that charge is quite different from saying that Zionism was part of the colonialist expansion of nineteenth-century Europe. We should instead compare Zionism with Arab, Filipino, and other nationalisms in developing countries. All of these movements have similar sources and similar profiles, for good and for bad, and their tendency to colonialist expansion derives from their nationalist structure, not from European influence.

By the same token, viewing Palestinian nationalism as prone to antisemitism because nationalist movements in general are prone to xenophobia helps both to explain that aspect of the movement and to reduce its importance. The xenophobic hatred that has pockmarked the history of Palestinian nationalism is by no means unusual in the history of nationalism—among other things, it has parallels in the history of Zionism, as we have seen—and it should not obscure the fact that the main Palestinian goal is not to oppress other groups, but to achieve self-determination for the Palestinian people.

Finally, nationalisms clash in many places, over issues similar to the ones that divide Zionists and Palestinians. Serbs and Croats, Indians and Pakistanis, Greeks and Turks, and many other groups have battled fiercely, often for decades, over which group should dominate territories that both claim. Sometimes this takes the form of two states battling over border areas; sometimes it takes the form of groups within a state contending for power (Christians, Muslims, and Druze in Lebanon; Kurds and Arabs in Iraq); sometimes it takes the form of a secessionist movement (Sikhs in India, Tamils in Sri Lanka). The groups involved also may have more or less equal strength (India and Pakistan), or there may be a great asymmetry of power between them (Russia and Ukraine, China and Tibet, Turkey and the Kurds). The struggle between Jewish and Palestinian nationalists, at least since 1949, belongs in this latter category.

In practically every clash of nationalisms, we find the following features:

1. Ardent nationalists on each side tend to see no merit at all in the claims of the other side and to slap the label "traitor" on members of their group who do see reason in those claims. The emphasis of nationalists on group solidarity goes along with a rejection of the liberal some-truth-on-both-sides approach to political conflicts.
2. Both sides engage in historical mythmaking, rooting their rights to territory in events of ancient and medieval history and exaggerating the connection of their contemporary population to its distant ancestors—all the while calling out the lies and exaggerations made by the other side.
3. Both sides see violence as a legitimate tool, rejecting the belief of liberals that it is better to work through nonviolent procedures as much as possible; both sides also often employ violence against noncombatants as well as combatants.

4. Each group appeals where it can to great powers. Examples of this sort include the help that Greeks received from Britain in their struggle for independence, and the support of Russia for Serbia in its claims to Kosovo.
5. Fervent activists on each side, who often dominate nationalist politics, regard compromise as dishonor.

It hardly needs saying that we find all of these features in the struggle between Jewish and Palestinian nationalists. The blind confidence of each side that its claims are wholly justified and the other's are wholly wrong; the lies and exaggerations about history; the racism; the constant resort to violence, including violence against civilians; the appeal to powerful outside sponsors (the United States on one side, the Soviet Union on the other); the rejection of compromise—all of these are just what we should expect of a clash of nationalisms. Meanwhile, the debate that typically takes place within a colonialist power over whether its members should return to their homeland is nowhere to be seen in Israel within the Green Line and would make no sense there, since few of its inhabitants regard themselves as having a homeland other than Israel. Nor is it imaginable that if Palestinians were wholly free of antisemitism, they would then acquiesce in the deprivation of political and civil rights they face daily at the hands of their Zionist rulers.

Conclusion

On an explanatory level, then, the clash of nationalisms paradigm fits the Israel-Palestine conflict better than either the settler colonial or the antisemitism paradigm. It also has the normative advantage of allowing people on both sides to see their opponents as human beings with respectable ideals of their own, rather than as hateful and manipulative liars. That is not to say that regarding one's opponent as a nationalist is altogether a good thing; it is not an altogether good thing to regard *oneself* that way. As we have seen, nationalism has the merit of respecting the importance of culture to people, but it is also prone to mythmaking, xenophobia, and violence. And there will be normative advantages to regarding the Israel-Palestine conflict as a nationalist one only if Zionists and Palestinian nationalists recognize that both movements partake of the bad as well as the good sides of nationalism. If they do that, however, they will be in a position from which they can be alert to and work to amend the dangerous aspects of their own movement and ideology—in addition to seeing the good, and not just the evil, in the movements and ideology of the other side.[35]

The fact that the clash of nationalisms paradigm encourages each side to come to such a position means that it can also help them resolve the conflict between them. In the first place, no proposed solution—whether one-state, two-state, or some compromise between the two—can be reached and maintained peacefully unless the two parties are able to respect one another. But only the clash of nationalisms paradigm allows each side to respect the collective aspirations of the people on the other side. So the clash of nationalisms paradigm is essential to building the trust and mutual respect that would enable any solution to the conflict to work.

In the second place, the clash of nationalisms paradigm encourages the compromise solutions that are most likely to gain the acceptance of people on both sides. The clash of nationalisms paradigm keeps all parties to the conflict from expecting a solution to it that they will regard as wholly just. In this paradigm, no awakening from the false consciousness of colonialism or antisemitism will lead decent people on one side or the other simply to give up their claims. There is also no use in proposing cosmopolitan ideologies like liberal democracy or a Marxist state of the proletariat as the solution to the conflict. The success of Palestinian nationalism, if that came about, would almost certainly not be followed by a liberal democratic state; it would be followed instead by a state that identified itself as Arab and Muslim and favored those groups in much the way that Israel favors Jews.[36] At the same time, Israel is not and has never been the liberal democracy that it boasts of being and is unlikely to become one anytime soon. Recognizing these points makes for an approach to solving the conflict that emphasizes compromise and slow change. That compromise might take the form of a two-state solution along with robust minority rights in both states, a single binational state with separate cantons for Jews and Palestinians, or a confederation of some sort between two autonomous regions.[37] But in any of these forms, it will require both Jewish and Palestinian nationalists to give up a good deal of what they have struggled for.

And while one can expect such a pragmatic, compromising approach to be resisted by some people on both sides, it is in the end both more likely to succeed and more respectful of the people on both sides than one based on the ideologies that lie behind the settler colonial paradigm and the attempt to reduce anti-Zionism to antisemitism. The clash of nationalisms paradigm encourages solutions to the conflict that respect the individual rights as well as the collective aspirations of Jews and Palestinians alike. That alone is reason to uphold it.

Sam Fleischacker is LAS Distinguished Professor of Philosophy at the University of Illinois in Chicago (UIC), and co-director of UIC's Jewish-Muslim Initiative. He is the author of eight books, including *A Short History of Distributive Justice* (Harvard, 2004), and *Being Me Being You: Adam Smith and Empathy* (University of Chicago, 2019). He has been active in Americans for Peace Now and Partners for a Progressive Israel and has previously written on the Israel-Palestine conflict in "Owning Land vs. Governing a Land: Property, Sovereignty, and Nationalism," *Social Philosophy and Policy* 30, no. 1 (2014).

Notes

1. See, for instance, Mohammed Ali Khalidi, "Formulating the Right of National Self-Determination," in *Philosophical Perspectives on the Israeli-Palestinian Conflict*, ed. Tomis Kapitan (Armonk, NY: ME Sharpe, 1997), 92–93.
2. David Kenneth Fieldhouse, *Colonialism 1870–1945: An Introduction* (London: Weidenfeld and Nicolson, 1981), 5. The assumption that colonialism is essentially a European project is pervasive in the literature on this subject. See, for instance, George Fredrickson, *The Arrogance of Race: Historical Perspectives on Slavery, Racism, and Social Inequality* (Middletown, CT: Wesleyan University Press, 1988), 219–23; and Lorenzo Veracini, *Settler Colonialism: A Theoretical Overview* (London: Palgrave Macmillan, 2011), 2, 6 (although Veracini does acknowledge that non-Europeans have also been settlers). A welcome exception is Hyung Gu Lynn, "Malthusian Dreams, Colonial Imaginary: The Oriental Development Company and Japanese Emigration to Korea," in *Settler Colonialism in the Twentieth Century: Projects, Practices, Legacies*, ed. Caroline Elkins and Susan Pedersen (New York: Routledge, 2005).
3. Maxime Rodinson, quoted in Uri Ram, "The Colonization Perspective in Israeli Sociology," in *The Israel/Palestine Question: A Reader*, ed. Ilan Pappé (London: Routledge, 1999), 56.
4. To be sure, the Chinese colonization of Taiwan began under Dutch auspices. But in 1662, the island became a formal Chinese colony. See Tonio Andrade, *How Taiwan Became Chinese* (New York: Columbia University Press, 2008).
5. Gershon Shafir, *A Half Century of Occupation: Israel, Palestine, and the World's Most Intractable Conflict* (Oakland: University of California Press, 2017), 54.
6. Ruppin says in the preface to his book that the main problem he plans to address is how "to bring back townsmen, and Jewish townsmen, to agricultural life in Palestine," and in the first sentence of the main text he announces that "agriculture must be the economic basis for Jewish immigration into Palestine." Arthur Ruppin, *The Agricultural Colonisation of the Zionist Organization of Palestine*, trans. R. J. Feiwel (Westport: Hyperion, 1976, reprint of the 1926 Hopkinson edition), vi, 1.
7. Susan Pedersen, although a critic of Zionism, writes, "Unlike the cases in South West Africa or Tanganyika, . . . Zionist settlers in Palestine were not British nationals or settling at the mandatory power's behest. Although it took place under the protection of the League [of Nations] and the British Empire, and adapted methods common to other settler efforts, Zionism was in conception a nationalist and not an imperialist project: it was an effort to constitute a new nation within an already colonized space." Susan Pedersen, "Settler Colonialism at the Bar of the League of Nations," in Elkins and Pedersen, *Settler Colonialism in the Twentieth Century*, 128.
8. Ahad Ha'am, quoted in Shlomo Avineri, *The Making of Modern Zionism* (London: Weidenfeld and Nicolson, 1981), 123.
9. Mark Tessler, *A History of the Israeli-Palestinian Conflict*, 2nd ed. (Bloomington: Indiana University Press, 2009), 134.
10. Chaim Weizman, quoted in Tom Segev, *One Palestine, Complete* (New York: Henry Holt, 1999), 109.
11. Ze'ev Jabotinsky, quoted in Avineri, *Making of Modern Zionism*, 180.
12. Nissim Malul, quoted in Tessler, *History of the Israeli-Palestinian Conflict*, 135.
13. Gershon Shafir, "Zionism and Colonialism: A Comparative Approach," in Pappé, *The Israel/Palestine Question*, 87, 89. Shafir says that Baron de Rothschild actually enlisted French experts who had worked in North Africa to help him reorganize the Yishuv in the late nineteenth century. He does not mention any direct connection between Zionist organizations and German experts.
14. Shafir goes on, explicitly, to throw nationalism and colonialism together: "It was [the German] state-initiated, non-market based colonization, motivated by nationalist considerations, which found its way into Zionism" (Shafir, "Zionism and Colonialism," 89). Ram also concedes that "the colonization of Palestine" was "not . . . brought about by an imperial power, but rather by a nationalist movement" (Ram, "Colonization Perspective," 58).
15. Shafir, *Half Century of Occupation*, 93–4.
16. On this subject, see David Nirenberg, *Anti-Judaism* (New York: W. W. Norton, 2013).

17. Neguib Azoury, *Le Reveil du Nation Arabe* (Paris: Librairie Plon, 1905), iii. See also Neville Mandel, *The Arabs and Zionism before World War I* (Berkeley: University of California Press, 1976), 50–52.
18. Benny Morris, *Righteous Victims* (New York: Vintage Books, 1999), 65, 66, 91, 94–95.
19. The question of how many of the Jews murdered in Hebron were non-Zionist is vexed and unsettled, as are many other questions about these murders. For a careful, thorough, and balanced study, see Hillel Cohen, *Year Zero of the Arab-Israeli Conflict: 1929* (Waltham, MA: Brandeis University Press, 2015), chapter 6. For the mufti's use of the *Protocols* to "prove" that the Jews had to be behind the Hebron riots, see Morris, *Righteous Victims*, 116.
20. Gilbert Achcar, *The Arabs and the Holocaust* (New York: Metropolitan Books, 2009), 131–34.
21. Morris, *Righteous Victims*, 100–101. See also Rashid Khalidi, *Palestinian Identity* (New York: Columbia University Press, 1997), 263n28.
22. Fawzi al-Qawuqji, quoted in Klaus-Michael Mallman and Martin Cuppers, *Nazi Palestine: The Plans for the Extermination of the Jews in Palestine*, trans. Krista Smith (New York: Enigma Books, 2010), 126–27. In light of this, Achcar's attempt to whitewash al-Qawuqji, suggesting that he was never "in the proper sense of the word, a partisan of Hitler's Germany" (Achcar, *The Arabs and the Holocaust*, 92), rings hollow.
23. Mallmann and Cuppers, *Nazi Palestine*, 211–2.
24. See Alex Yakobson and Amnon Rubinstein, *Israel and the Family of Nations*, trans. Ruth Morris and Ruchie Avital (London: Routledge, 2009), 49–53; and Benny Morris, *1948: A History of the First Arab-Israeli War* (New Haven: Yale University Press, 2008), 70–71. See also Norman Stillman, *The Jews of Arab Lands in Modern Times* (Philadelphia: Jewish Publication Society, 1991), 99–100, 142–46.
25. Rashid Khalidi, *The Iron Cage* (Boston: Beacon Press, 2006), 119.
26. See Hans Kohn, *Nationalism: Its Meaning and History* (Malabar, FL: Robert E. Krieger, 1982), 46–49; and Benedict Anderson, *Imagined Communities*, rev. ed. (London: Verso, 2006), 72–75.
27. Tessler, *History of the Israeli-Palestinian Conflict*, 441. Before the collapse of Faisal's rule in Syria, most Palestinians identified themselves simply with the wider Arab nationalist movement, aiming at a broad Arab state in Greater Syria that would include Palestine, rather than a separate Palestinian Arab state. The Nablus Youth Society, for instance, was established around the time of World War I in order "to protect the rights of the Arabs, to agitate for the good of the Arab people and for the good of Syria" (Mandel, *Arabs and Zionism*, 219).
28. Marxist Palestinians have also not always been anti-Zionist. When the State of Israel was founded, its Communist Party, comprising both Jews and Palestinians, initially supported it, considering Israel to represent a more advanced stage in the worldwide class struggle than Arab nationalism.
29. I use the word "nationalism" here for what some scholars call "ethnic nationalism" (or, sometimes, "ethnonationalism"), as opposed to "civic nationalism." Ethnic nationalists seek political representation for groups that are bound together by factors like shared language, religion, history, or kinship ties; civic nationalists hold that the citizens of a state do need to be bound together into an effective collective agent, but that a commitment to shared civic principles is sufficient to do that job. Ethnic nationalism is often associated with movements in Central and Eastern Europe; civic nationalism with the revolutions and political movements that built modern Britain and France. I believe that this distinction obscures more than it illuminates. "Civic nationalism" almost always has a strong ethnic component, even in Britain and France, and ethnic nationalism is the paradigm form of nationalism as a distinctive kind of politics (distinct *from* liberal and Marxist politics, especially). In the context of this essay, however, it doesn't matter if I am right to be skeptical of this distinction or not; to the extent that the distinction makes sense, both Zionism and Palestinian nationalism fall firmly on the ethnic side of it. My thanks to Omer Bartov for pressing me to clarify this point.
30. There is a vast literature on nationalism. For a variety of views on it, see Anderson, *Imagined Communities*; Walker Connor, *Ethnonationalism* (Princeton: Princeton University Press, 1994); Ernest Gellner, *Nations and Nationalism* (Oxford: Blackwell, 1983); Eric J. Hobsbawm, *Nations and Nationalism since 1780* (Cambridge: Cambridge University Press, 1990); Kohn, *Nationalism*; Elie Kedourie, *Nationalism* (London: Hutchinson, 1960); David Miller, *On Nationality* (Oxford: Oxford University Press, 1995); and Anthony D. Smith, *The Ethnic Origins of Nations* (Oxford: Blackwell, 1986).

31. For non-statist versions of Zionism before the 1940s, see Dmitry Shumsky, *Beyond the Nation-State: The Zionist Political Imagination from Pinsker to Ben Gurion* (New Haven: Yale University Press, 2018).
32. A nuanced account of this fraught subject can be found in Hobsbawm, *Nations and Nationalism*, 67–72.
33. It is sometimes said that the Jews cannot be a people because they are a religion and that the Arab nation is wholly distinct from Islam. Both of these claims are misleading, at best. In general, peoplehood is tied closely to religion. Greek and Russian peoplehood has been strongly tied to the Greek and Russian Orthodox Churches, marginalizing Jews, Muslims, and even non-Orthodox Christians; Polish, Croatian, Italian, and Irish peoplehood has been similarly bound up with Catholicism, despite the existence of Orthodox and Protestant minorities in these groups; Tibetan peoplehood is tied to Buddhism, despite the presence of Muslim and Bon minorities in its midst; and Iranian, Turkish, Malaysian, and Arab peoplehood has been identified with Islam by most Iranians, Turks, Malaysians, and Arabs, despite the non-Muslim minorities in these groups. It is only the ideology of secular nationalists that obscures these points.

    Zionists sometimes claim that the Jews have the unique distinction of being both a religion and a people, so the categories that apply to other peoples don't fit them. This too is misleading. Religion and culture may be more deeply interwoven for Jews than for most other peoples, but Jews are hardly unique in combining these two things. As we've just seen, other peoples are defined at least in significant part by a religion, and some groups (the Parsees, the Balinese, and aboriginal tribes in the Americas, Africa, and Australia) understand their collective identity in a way that intertwines religion and culture as fully as the Jews do.
34. See, for instance, Philip Carabott, "Aspects of the Hellenization of Greek Macedonia, ca. 1912–ca. 1959," *Kampos: Cambridge Papers in Modern Greek* 13 (2005): 21–61; and Karen Fleming, *Greece: A Jewish History* (Princeton: Princeton University Press, 2008), 54–66.
35. I am again grateful to Omer Bartov for pressing me to clarify this point.
36. "In order to believe that such a state would in fact be binational [let alone *non*-national], a number of wildly implausible assumptions need to be made: that the Arab-Palestinian people would agree over the long term that its state . . . would not have an Arab character and would not be regarded as part of the Arab world; that it would agree to be the only one among the Arab peoples whose state would not be officially Arab, would not be a member of the Arab League, and would not share, by declaration, the aspirations for Arab unity; and that the Palestinian people would agree to make this concession—a declared relinquishing of Palestine's 'Arabness,' something which no Arab nation has agreed to do in its own state for the sake of the non-Arab native minorities—for the sake of the Jews, widely considered 'foreign intruders' and 'colonialist invaders' in Palestine, whose very claim to constitute a nation is no more than 'Zionist propaganda'" (Yakobson and Rubinstein, *Israel and the Family of Nations*, 10).
37. For a constructive proposal along these lines, see the statement of principles of the Palestinian-Israeli group "A Land for All" (formerly called "Two States One Homeland"), https://www.alandforall.org/english/?d=ltr.

Select Bibliography

Khalidi, Mohammad Ali. "Formulating the Right of National Self-Determination." In *Philosophical Perspectives on the Israeli-Palestinian Conflict*. Edited by Tomis Kapitan. Armonk, NY: ME Sharpe, 1997.

Khalidi, Rashid. *Palestinian Identity*. New York: Columbia University Press, 1997.

Morris, Benny. *Righteous Victims*. New York: Vintage Books, 1999.

Muslih, Muhammad. *The Origins of Palestinian Nationalism*. New York: Columbia University Press, 1990.

Ram, Uri. "The Colonization Perspective in Israeli Sociology." In *The Israel/Palestine Question*. Edited by Ilan Pappé. London: Routledge, 1999.

Shafir, Gershon. *A Half Century of Occupation: Israel, Palestine, and the World's Most Intractable Conflict.* Oakland: University of California Press, 2017.

———. "Zionism and Colonialism: A Comparative Approach." In *The Israel-Palestine Question.* Edited by Ilan Pappé. London: Routledge, 1999.

Shumsky, Dmitry. *Beyond the Nation-State: The Zionist Political Imagination from Pinsker to Ben Gurion.* New Haven: Yale University Press, 2018.

Tessler, Mark. *A History of the Israeli-Palestinian Conflict.* 2nd ed. Bloomington: Indiana University Press, 2009.

Yakobson, Alex, and Amnon Rubinstein, *Israel and the Family of Nations.* Translated by Ruth Morris and Ruchie Avital. London: Routledge, 2009.

CHAPTER 14

THINKING ABOUT STATE DEMISE
THE CASE OF ISRAEL

IAN S. LUSTICK

Introduction

The spread of territorial state organizations across the planet was the single most transformative political phenomenon of modern times. But not all states prosper and grow. No state lasts forever. It is no surprise that states can disappear when conquered or that fragile states with insufficient governing capacities collapse.[1] But what of strong states that disappear without either being conquered or collapsing? How is it that capable states decline and even come to an end, often quite suddenly? The questions raised by the fates of powerful states, such as Yugoslavia, Czechoslovakia, the Soviet Union, Pahlavi Iran, Franco's Spain, Qaddafi's Libya, or apartheid South Africa, are crucial but rarely if ever addressed. This is an awkward lacuna in political science's engagement with its premier institution—a conceptual omission that makes it difficult to understand the case of Israel.

By most military, political, and administrative measures, Israel is a powerful state. Yet the citizens of no state on earth spend more of their political time discussing the possible or even likely disappearance of the state in which they live. Because powerful states do suddenly disappear and because so many Israelis believe it may happen to their state, the case of Israel raises questions about what the disappearance of a powerful state means and whether it is possible to gauge how likely or how imminent that outcome might be. In this chapter I use the wide-ranging debate in Israel over whether the state will survive to offer a theory of "state demise" based on understanding a "state" as a hegemonically institutionalized regime. I then use that theory to explain why the end of a seemingly robust and powerful state can be much closer and more possible than it may seem.

States as Projects

Max Weber's familiar definition refers to a state as "a human community that (successfully) claims the *monopoly of the legitimate physical force* within a given territory."[2] More useful for the problem posed here is another of his formulations. In *Economy and Society*, Weber described the state not as an apparatus of power per se, but as a set of stabilized expectations:

> A "state" ... ceases to exist in a sociologically relevant sense whenever there is no longer a probability that certain kinds of meaningfully oriented social action will take place. This probability may be very high or it may be negligibly low. But in any case it is only in the sense and degree in which it does exist that the corresponding social relationship exists. It is impossible to find any other clear meaning for the statement that, for instance, a given "state" exists or has ceased to exist.[3]

From this perspective, a state is a contingent institution that exists and reproduces itself, or not, as an array of stable intersubjective expectations.[4] This is the view of both Antonio Gramsci and Douglass C. North, who treat states as purposeful institutions seeking to enforce property rights. For Gramsci, this view leads naturally to a concept of the state as a kind of "project," a continuous effort to organize society that is always vulnerable to failure.[5] A state project is thus a political campaign to sustain a monopoly of authority over agreed upon populations for the purpose of defining and enforcing property rights—including law, taxation, and the coercive capacity to enforce them.

State projects begin as movements to serve the interests of ambitious elites. A successful state project establishes and consolidates a regime—a legal order combining judicial, legislative, administrative, and coercive institutions to standardize and regularize life within its territorial ambit. To the extent that populations subjected to the legal order experience and treat that regime as the permanent and unquestioned arena for pursuing political ambition, it can be said to enjoy hegemonic status, that is, its "stateness" is well-established.

If a state project manages to naturalize its regime into a hegemonic institutional order, its existence is shielded by embedded expectations of its permanence—a "regime" appears as a "state." If, however, that hegemony is subsequently lost, the project is exposed to questions about its viability, its serviceability for different groups, and its vulnerability to challenges. Accordingly, in line with Weber's conception that states are stabilized expectations about patterns of behavior, loss of hegemony should be considered movement toward, a form of, or a stage in state demise. The theory of state demise offered here predicts that political discourse focused on state survival would itself be a leading indicator of the vulnerability of the regime to drastic change and to further movement toward the demise of the state project.

To be clear, as long as the project's goals and norms are hegemonic, elites pursue their ambitions by treating those goals and norms as justificatory principles that themselves require no justification. Hence, if substantial political attention *is* explicitly directed to the defense of key elements of the regime, it is evident that some of the project's "stateness" has been stripped away. By putting question marks next to key features of the regime, this kind of discourse signals the potential for threats to be launched directly against the regime, unprotected by the walls of public presumption and routine surrounding a regime enjoying hegemonic status.

For well-established state projects, movement toward state demise entails loss of key elements of hegemonic status, but not necessarily—or perhaps even usually—the rapid disappearance of the state project as a regime. It follows from these considerations that evidence of state demise, or the potential for it, can be sought in the extent to which the regime is treated in dominant political discourses as problematically established. Moreover, when key elements of the state's political formula are treated as only contingently achieved, elites experience irresistible incentives to advance their particular agendas and interests by presenting themselves as saviors of the threatened state and defenders of its basic principles. A prominent discourse focused on state survival, or threats to it, thus not only signals the weakening of the institutional order, it also contributes to that weakening. Once some putatively hegemonic elements are treated as contingent, discursive dynamics can spread doubts about the integrity and future of the state project along any number of dimensions.

Assessing the stability of expectations of a regime's continuation means asking whether, how pervasively, and how explicitly elites contemplate the possibility of its disappearance. Assuming some significant measure of freedom to express oneself, the absence of such questions implies that the disappearance of the regime is effectively unimaginable. At the very least it means that ambitious elites present their views as if their audiences cannot imagine or do not concern themselves with that possibility. In other words, to the extent that a state manages to establish itself as hegemonic, its nature as a project—its fundamental artifactuality—is obscured by commonsensical apprehensions of its permanence, thereby protecting it from challenges associated with the vicissitudes of political life. On the other hand, just because a state achieves hegemony does not mean the project will forever enjoy that status. Even hegemonically established beliefs can be destabilized; there remains the crucial empirical question of what conditions make that destabilization possible or more likely.[6]

The Prominence and Pervasiveness of the State Survival Discourse in Israel

When Israelis talk politics, a great deal of what they talk about is whether their state will survive. Perhaps the most common political assertion in Israel follows this template: "If X occurs [or does not occur], the state will not survive." This is not a discursive tic. It prevails across the political spectrum and arises from a deep pool of worry. The Israeli writer David Grossman has argued that to advance toward peace, Israelis must first believe "that we, the Israelis, have a future. I am not speaking of a good future or a bad future at this point, but of the mere possibility of there being a future."[7] Michael Oren began his five-year stint as Israel's ambassador to the United States with a high-profile article describing the seven "existential threats" that Israel faced "on a daily basis."[8] An attempt to measure the prominence of existential fears in Israeli political discourse was offered by Uriel Abulof, who studied polling and articles in the Israeli press between 1994 and 2007 focused on "existential danger" or "existential threat." Abulof reported that "opinion polls consistently indicate that most Israelis believe that Israel's existence is acutely threatened." In the independent (liberal) Israeli newspaper *Haaretz*, Abulof found an average of approximately 150 articles per year that framed Israel as facing either "existential dangers" or "existential threats."[9]

Evidence from the internet suggests that discussions of Israeli state survival are substantially more prominent than with respect to any other country. On 21–22 June 2016, I used the Google search engine to collect data on the number of hits by country for the search "Will country_name survive?" The search was conducted for the twenty countries closest to Israel in population. While the median number of hits was only 4, the average was 417, indicating that a few very high scoring countries were featured in the data set alongside many countries with small or very small numbers of hits. Indeed, twelve of the twenty-one countries surveyed resulted in 0–4 hits. These included countries that relatively rarely attract the attention of English-language media or about whom questions involving "survival" refer not to the country per se, but to the prospects of the country's team in World Cup Football competition. The countries in this category, ordered by decreasing population, were the Czech Republic, Azerbaijan, United Arab Emirates, Tajikistan, Austria, Honduras, Papua New Guinea, Togo, Bulgaria, Laos, Paraguay, and Sierra Leone. Six of the 21 countries resulted in between 10 and 350 hits: Portugal, Belarus, Serbia, Switzerland, Hong Kong, and Libya. The remaining three countries reported numbers that were much higher. There were 1,520 hits for "Will Jordan survive?" and 1,970 hits for "Will Sweden survive?" But far exceeding these numbers was Israel, with 4,610 hits for "Will Israel survive?" As a check on these results, another search was conducted targeting countries immensely larger than Israel that also loom large in the global English-language media—China, India, France, Russia, and the United States. When the same search was conducted on these countries, the results were as follows: France 271; Russia 3,490; United States 2,830; India 1,070; and China 1,200. Perhaps unsurprisingly, of these countries, Russia registered the highest number of hits regarding the question of its survival, but even so, its 3,490 was still only three-quarters of (tiny) Israel's total of 4,610.

Inside Israel and within Israel-related communities of support, the discourse on state survival is pervasive. A sampling reveals how common is the trope, across virtually all areas of public debate, that Israel's existence hangs by delicate threads, the severing of any one of which could mean the end of the state. Not unusual is Abulof's observation that on one "uneventful day," *Haaretz*'s op-ed page

> featured three columnists describing what they consider the real existential threat: Yoel Marcus termed the bankruptcy of law enforcement in Israel an "existential danger from within"; David Landau depicted the Diaspora's silence in the face of radical right-wing activities as shirking historical Jewish responsibility for the "future of the country and its survival prospects," de facto accepting the imminent possibility of the destruction of the current Jewish commonwealth; Elia Leibovitch presented the immanent assaults on Israel's academic institutions as endangering the most vital foundation for our survival as a Jewish state in the Middle East.[10]

In 2010 Yossi Yonah, a leading Israeli intellectual and subsequently a member of Knesset, told the Zionist Congress meeting in Jerusalem that four imperatives would have to be met for the state to survive: embracing Israel's nature as a Middle Eastern country, determining its final boundaries, closing gaps between the rich and poor, and integrating Israeli Arab citizens.[11] The president of the Technion, Israel's premier center for science and technology, noted that students from Dubai and Croatia had outperformed Israelis in science. "Science education," he warned, had become "an existential issue for the State of Israel."[12] Daniel Doron, director of the Israel Center for Social and Economic Progress (ICSEP), identified the extent of "economic concentration" in Israel as "an existential threat."[13] A noted right-wing columnist told Prime Minister Benjamin Netanyahu that without permanent rule of the Jordan Valley, "Israel cannot survive."[14] Benny Morris, well-known revisionist historian turned nationalistic commentator, announced in 2011 that "a profound, internal, existential crisis" had arrived and asked whether the brain drain, unprecedented inequality, Islamization of Israeli Arabs, and trends toward illiberalism had already put an end to the State of Israel.[15]

Instead of seeking to accommodate international criticism of Israeli policies, many right-wing commentators and Jewish fundamentalists have warned that to survive, Israel should reject the liberal-dominated international order itself, abandon the ambition to be accepted as a "Western nation," and assert itself explicitly as an "ethnically Jewish state." The opposite is the case, responded two university professors. Instead it is precisely the Israeli Right's rejection of international law, enlightenment values, and liberal standards of legitimacy that "threaten to turn Israel into an anachronism."[16] While it is a commonplace of Israeli political and cultural speech that maintaining a fresh if painful memory of the Holocaust is crucial for Israel's survival, a nearly opposite argument is also made. As one leading Israeli scholar of the Holocaust put it, "I see no greater threat to the future of the State of Israel than the fact that the Holocaust has systematically and forcefully penetrated the consciousness of the Israeli public."[17]

Amid the continual cut-and-thrust of Israeli politics, it is common for warnings to be issued that one or another mundane problem will actually seal the country's doom if not handled properly. A 2011 *Haaretz* editorial protested the government's failure to enforce the law against illegal outposts in the West Bank. "The outposts must be removed immediately. Israel's future depends on it."[18] In 2012 Israelis were warned by a supporter of former IDF chief of staff and prime minister wannabe Shaul Mofaz that if the political center did not unify, it would be impossible "to save the project called Israel."[19] At the same time, one editorialist warned that the vigilante actions of the "Price Tag" group against Arabs in the West Bank "endanger the future and the security of the State of Israel. . . . One does not have to be an intelligence expert in order to assess that it is enough for only one lunatic to burn an entire forest."[20]

Palestinians are typically seen as posing threats to the state's survival along a variety of vectors. In 2012 the majority opinion in a Supreme Court case barring Palestinian women from joining their Israeli citizen spouses in Israel characterized the ruling as necessary for the survival of the state. "Human rights," read the opinion, "do not prescribe national suicide."[21] A much more comprehensive argument about the danger to Israel's survival is associated with Palestinians being given the "right of return" to their homes and lands. "Recognition of this right," even according to a dove such as the journalist Dani Rubinstein, "would mean the end of the Jewish identity of the State of Israel, and perhaps even the demise of state."[22]

When then foreign minister Tzipi Livni warned of the consequences for Israel of a European boycott in response to its settlement policies, Mark Langfan attacked what he characterized as her implicit support of the boycott as itself a threat to Israel's survival, insisting that "without all, I repeat ALL, the heroic Jewish settlers of Judea and Samaria, there will be no Negev, no Galilee. There will be no Israel, period."[23] In 2012 Israel's ambassador to the United Nations offered the judgment that Israel was at a "critical juncture" as a result of the Obama administration's retreat from the Middle East and that as a result "our very survival is once again at stake."[24] A staple of Israeli political discourse in the years prior to the Iran deal limiting that country's nuclear technology program was that the signing of such a deal "threatens the survival of the state of Israel."[25] Daniel Seaman, former head of the Israel Government Press Office, put the blame on Israeli government mistakes and the behavior of Israeli journalists, rather than on American foreign policy. "In light of the "ineptitude of the Israeli government," he told an interviewer, "that we survive here is the modern miracle."[26]

In his "Lamentation for the State of Israel," Ron Rosenbaum characterized Israel as a "one bomb state" in regard to the threat to its existence emanating from Teheran, but that was not, he wrote, the most important reason to think Israel's "days are numbered." Following a rash of "lone wolf" attacks in late 2015 on Israelis by young West Bank Palestinians wielding kitchen knives, he cited a poll according to which

80 percent of Israeli children had been "traumatized" by watching videos of these attacks, and that 64 percent of them "were afraid to leave their homes."[27] In 2015 the prominent Israeli journalist and author Ari Shavit added the difficulties faced by pro-Israel students in the United States to a long list of existential threats to the country. "Our fate," he concluded, "will not only be determined on the country's southern or northern borders, but on the quads of American campuses."[28]

Other Israelis portray conflicts among Jews and the fragility of the cultural ties binding them together as threatening the state's survival. The well-known journalist Aluf Benn blamed the accelerated growth of "tribes"—ultra-Orthodox Jews, religious Jews, and Arab Israelis—who neither shared in the core values of the country nor were capable of making the economic and military contributions required to sustain the state. He warned of "the question that should occupy every Israeli, certainly its political leadership . . . how a state divided into rival tribes, which suffers from underemployment and under-education, whose founding core is falling apart, persists."[29] A 2011 study by the University of Haifa concluded that "Israel is on its way to becoming a religious state—a reality that would pose a threat to its survival."[30] A former general, writing in October 2015 for a major right-wing think tank, warned against relinquishing rule over Arab neighborhoods in the greater Jerusalem area, maintaining that only by preserving intact the current expansive municipal boundaries of Jerusalem could Israel survive.[31]

In 2006 Israel's leading "futurologist" warned that even discussing the possibility of an end to Israel was itself a threat to its survival.[32] His concern was that public perseveration about state survival could act as a self-fulfilling prophecy. By encouraging timidity, loss of self-confidence, or emigration, it was liable to create dangers to the state's survival that otherwise would not exist. Indeed, by so regularly invoking the contingency of the state's survival, rival elites are incentivized to stress or even exaggerate the threats they see to survival and the urgency of the responses they favor to meet those threats. In this context, it is difficult for any ambitious politician to avoid invoking threats of state survival without ceding the field to their rivals ready and willing to embrace such rhetoric.

Just as striking as the pervasive invocation of threats to the country's survival is the absence of discussion of the chains of consequence upon which such claims rely. It seems that Israeli Jewish audiences are deemed to already understand what it would look like for Israel not to "survive" *and* prepared to treat any threat to Israel's survival as so automatically plausible that no justification is needed. This explains why Israeli discourse contains virtually no discussion of what is meant by "state survival," but begs the question of what Israeli Jews, who are ready to believe their state is at risk from so many directions, think the demise of the state would mean. By focusing on the three most regularly invoked types of threats, we will be in a better position to see what state survival and state disappearance mean in the Israeli context. These threats are Jewish demoralization, the future of the West Bank and Gaza Strip, and demography.

The Three Most Prominent Threats to Israeli State Survival
Jewish Demoralization

Warnings that the fate of the state hangs in the balance depending on the faith and dedication exhibited by Jews is the most common theme of right-wing, fundamentalist, or ultranationalist contributions to the "Will the state survive?" discourse. Such arguments hearken to Zionist slogans such as Herzl's "If you will it, it is no dream" or Ben-Gurion's dictum that what matters for the fate of the Zionist project is "not what gentiles think, but what Jews do." An influential example of this genre is Yoram Hazony's *The Jewish State: The Struggle for Israel's Soul*. When he published the book in 2000, Hazony—who previously worked as a ghost writer for Benjamin Netanyahu—was president of the Shalem Center, a Jerusalem think tank dedicated to promoting Jewish nationalism, territorial expansion, and Zionist renewal. Hazony's book condemned Israeli culture for becoming "a carnival of self-loathing." He blamed "cultural disintegration" on Israeli intellectuals who had betrayed Ben-Gurion's proud vision of a Jewish state by adopting liberal ontologies and Buberian attitudes. For Hazony, Israel's survival hinged on defeating these ideological traitors, restoring the nation's self-confidence, and rousing within it the dedication required to become an authentic *Jewish* state. "If we wish for the Jewish state to end otherwise than did the Soviet Union, then we must turn our attention back to the motivating idea that has grown faint and unintelligible."[33]

Eight years later, Daniel Gordis's 2009 book *Saving Israel* offered a more detailed version of the same argument. The state would not survive, he wrote, unless a deeper, stronger Jewish identity was forged among young Israelis.[34] He provided two apt epigrams for one chapter, entitled "The Withering of Zionist Passion." The first was Herzl's slogan, cited above, "If you will it, it is no dream." The second was a quote from the German-born and American-Israeli Nobel laureate in economic sciences Israel Aumann, well-known for his pronounced right-wing political views.

> The greatest [threat] of all does not come from Iran, nor from terrorist groups, nor from any external source. It comes from within us. . . . Without motivation, we will not endure. . . . What are we aspiring to here? Without [answers], we will not endure. . . . We are like a mountain-climber that gets caught in a snowstorm; the night falls, he is cold and tired, and he wants to sleep. [But] if he falls asleep he will freeze to death.[35]

In 2012 Danny Danon, a leading right-wing Israeli politician, published *Israel: The Will to Prevail*, promoting aggressive Israeli policies of unilateralism, maximalism, and annexation. According to him, the decisive element in Israel's ability to survive was the willpower and determination of the Jewish people. Emphasizing the crucial role of religious faith, Danon concluded his book with a declaration and a quotation from the Bible.

We have the will and with that we will prevail.

> The LORD will give strength unto His people;
> The LORD will bless his people with peace. —Psalms 29:11[36]

In 2010, Uri Elitzur, a veteran settler activist, former head of Prime Minister Netanyahu's office, and associate editor of the right-wing nationalist publication *Makor Rishon*, warned of the need to save Israel from the "disaster" of a Palestinian state by annexing the West Bank. This meant overcoming fears of increasing the Arab population of the country and the "panic" such fears trigger among Israeli Jews. Citing the biblical book of Numbers, Elitzur noted that conquest of the land required the Israelites to have faith in God and themselves despite the pessimism of spies charged to evaluate prospects of victory over the land's inhabitants. He called upon Jews to have that same kind of faith in large-scale immigration and in Israel's ability to pass laws maintaining its Jewish identity despite a larger Arab population.[37]

The Occupied Territories

Zionists have never agreed on the boundaries of the state they almost all sought to establish. Disputes over boundaries have been deep and even violent. So it is no surprise that after 1967 hawks and doves regularly warned that the survival of the state would be determined by the fate of the captured territories. Immediately after the Six Day War, some Israelis predicated that maintaining control over the West Bank and Gaza Strip would have catastrophic consequences for the state. A decade later this kind of rhetoric intensified in response to an aggressive program of Jewish settlement and de facto annexation decided upon by Prime Minister Menachem Begin and engineered by the minister in his cabinet in charge of settlement affairs, Ariel Sharon. Its purpose was to make it politically impossible for future governments to withdraw from the West Bank.[38] Since then, opponents of the steady incorporation of the West Bank into the polity and society of Israel have found themselves facing increasingly contradictory imperatives. On the one hand they have sought to convince Israelis to heed their warnings of imminent disaster if an end to the occupation is not achieved, while on the other assuring them that withdrawal from occupied territories is still possible, despite years and then decades of saying that it soon would not be.

In the early 1980s, Meron Benvenisti (a political geographer and former deputy mayor of Jerusalem) declared it was "five minutes to midnight," meaning that within three years there would be 100,000 Jewish settlers in the West Bank (excluding expanded East Jerusalem). This would constitute a "point of no return" beyond which the process of de facto annexation would be irreversible.[39] By 2018 nearly five times that number of Jews were living in Israeli settlements located in the West Bank—or more than 650,000, if those living in expanded East Jerusalem are included. Throughout the intervening three and a half decades, frantic warnings have continued of the threat posed by the settlement project to the survival of Israel, mainly by creating unbreakable bonds between the captured territories and the State of Israel in its 1949 boundaries. In his widely read 2013 book *My Promised Land*, Ari Shavit's treatment of the consequences of the occupation and the settlements that have made it so difficult to end was nearly hysterical. Shavit compared Israel's predicament to that of the Crusaders. "We live on a cliff facing east. . . . The howling winds of change . . . are turning into a hurricane that is sweeping the Middle East . . . the future of the fortress on the cliff is not clear." Israel, he wrote, is a project whose success means "walking a tightrope over the abyss," with the occupation a burden too heavy for the tightrope walker to bear without losing his balance. Unless it extricated itself from the West Bank, the country "will be politically and morally doomed."[40]

In the early 1990s, the Labor Party government of Prime Minister Yitzhak Rabin signaled its acceptance of the principle of the "two-state solution," a position that subsequently, officially at least, was adopted by Prime Minister Benjamin Netanyahu. With the emergence of the two-state solution as the operational meaning of "trading land for peace," warnings about Israel's demise have increasingly been framed around exhortations to realize that solution before its possibility vanishes. Perhaps the most succinct of these injunctions came from Prime Minister Ehud Olmert in 2008: "two states—or Israel's finished."[41]

Often these warnings focus on Israeli failures to pursue diplomatic options vigorously enough. In 2011, former Mossad head Meir Dagan urged the government to "adopt the Saudi Initiative [for negotiating a two-state solution] . . . not because [the Palestinians] are my top priority but because I am concerned about Israel's well-being and I want to do what I can to ensure Israel's existence."[42] Former prime minister Shimon Peres, while occupying the office of president, warned that the government's diplomatic foot-dragging meant that Israel was "about to crash into a wall. We're galloping at full speed toward a situation where Israel will cease to exist as a Jewish state."[43] For many others the government's lethargic diplomacy is but a reflection of a more profound pathology, namely, the domination of the Israeli polity by hard-right and fundamentalist religious elites.[44]

Early in 2013, former foreign minister Tzipi Livni warned that "Netanyahu is leading us toward the end of the Jewish state. . . . Israelis must choose between extremism and Zionism. Israel is in great danger and everyone must wake up now."[45] In December 2014, Livni was fired from the cabinet for denouncing the government as based on "extremism, provocativeness, and paranoia."[46] In 2015 a best-selling Hebrew novel depicted the rise to power of a messiah king, the complete annihilation or expulsion of Arabs from the entire country, the rebuilding of the Temple, suppression of all forms of Jewish dissent, and Israel's complete isolation from the non-Jewish world. The novel ends with a successful Arab invasion and the destruction of the state.[47] In 2016 Israel's oldest left-wing politician, journalist, and activist identified politically progressive Israelis who had emigrated as a crucial group whose return was necessary "to save the state from the hands of Netanyahu and his evil friends."[48]

Meanwhile, supporters of West Bank settlements insist that Israel's survival hinges on the presence of settlements and their expansion. From their point of view, only by keeping the entire West Bank can Israel be secure, and only by thoroughly settling it with Jews can it be permanently retained.[49] Aside from security considerations, they say abandonment of the "Jewish communities in Judea and Samaria" would fatally undermine the entire rationale for Zionism and the State of Israel.[50] The removal of seventy-five hundred settlers from Gaza enlivened right-wing concerns that the settlement project as a whole was threatened and with it the "dismantling of Israel."[51]

Demography

In Israel, *habe'ayah hademografit*—"the demographic argument"—is the claim that Israel's survival is threatened by a changing balance between Jews and Arabs (or non-Jews) living in the country. A fundamental tenet of classical Zionism was that in the new polity, Jews would be a majority of the population, not a minority as they were in every other country. No other single argument is as capable of producing as much moral panic from Israeli and Israel-supporting Diaspora Jews as the specter of Jews losing their majority. Israeli doves standardly characterize the demographic problem as a "time bomb."[52] Typical is the consternation expressed in 2013 by Daniel S. Abraham, a prominent (American Jewish) advocate for the two-state solution, for whom its absence means realization of a demographic nightmare and with it the end of the Jewish state.

> If Israel doesn't find a way to make an agreement now, the future is clear. The day will come when Palestinians so outnumber Jews that Israel will be forced to give them the vote. When the Israeli parliament has a majority of Palestinian delegates . . . the first bill to pass will be to change the country's name from Israel to Palestine . . . the second bill will enable the descendants of the original Palestinian refugees to move to Israel/Palestine. Israel as we know it will cease to exist.[53]

At the same time, many Israeli settlers and their supporters insist (against all evidence) that both official Palestinian and Israeli figures for the size of the Palestinian Arab population in the West Bank are wildly inflated. They fiercely condemn "leftist" hand-wringing about the supposed "demographic machete hanging over the neck of the Jewish state." While acknowledging Jewish demographic dominance is a matter of life or death for the state, they maintain that there are far fewer Palestinians in the country than is widely believed and that population growth rates favor Jews, not Arabs.[54]

In a 2014 analysis of the centrality of the demographic problem as an "existential threat" to Israel, Abulof showed that the Israeli obsession with the "demographic demon" had increased in recent decades, focusing with particular strength, not only on Arabs in the West Bank, but on Arab citizens of Israel. He noted that Israeli Jewish support for Sharon's disengagement from Gaza was based largely on the idea of ridding Israel of its 1.5 million Arabs, thereby "rescuing" the country from the demographic danger. "The securitization of demography [by which Abulof means treating it as a threat to the survival of Israeli state and society] motivated and legitimated the disengagement initiative, contributing significantly to its acceptance among the Jewish–Israeli public."[55] Abulof presented a content analysis of *Haaretz* newspaper articles over the twenty years from 1994 through 2013. It shows a close correlation over time between articles focused on existential threats in general and those stressing the demographic problem as a source of that threat. While the degree of anxiety retreated from a peak in 2005, just prior to the Gaza disengagement, it rose again in 2011 and 2012, even as other threats (specifically, perceived dangers associated with Iranian nuclear technology) took center stage. In the last year of the survey (2013) approximately 40 percent of all articles about threats to the state's survival were focused on demography.

The State of Israel as a Particular Regime

State demise includes the increased potential for the disappearance of a regime that has lost its hegemonic defenses. In Israel, that kind of threat is implicit in portrayals of the fate of the state as resting on the collective commitment of Jews and in apprehensions that demographic developments might make it impossible to preserve the privileged position of Jews without jettisoning the regime's liberal democratic features. In each of these domains, the actual referent for the end of the state is the end of a particular regime—a legal order whose particulars have taken on the very meaning of stateness for the overwhelming majority of Israeli Jews.

And what are those particulars? To what figure are Israelis gesturing when they warn of the end of the state? Analysis of the contexts within which forecasts of doom are made, and the exhortations typically associated with them, clearly indicates that what is meant is that the country will no longer be organized by a legal and political order qualified as representing the success of the Zionist project. In that circumstance, the regime known as "the Jewish state," with the particular meanings they attach to that phrase, will no longer exist.

Across a wide swath of political opinion there is agreement on the fundamental meaning of that regime: the legislative, executive, and judicial apparatuses of power, whether governed by black letter law or well-honored understandings, must reliably prioritize the interests and objectives of Jewish Israelis over extending civic protections and opportunities to all citizens, whether Jewish or not. Ruth Gavison is Israel's foremost legal theorist of statist Zionism (*mamlakhti'yut*). She uses the term "citizen" to designate all those within the ambit of the state who rightfully claim civic equality. According to Gavison, Israel has "an obligation . . . to treat them fairly and with respect." But she also insists that the key element making the state a fit vehicle for

Jewish self-determination is that it "offers special benefits to the people with whom the state is identified [and] at the same time . . . puts those citizens who are not members of the preferred national community at a disadvantage."[56] Passage by the Israeli parliament of Basic Law: Israel—the Nation State of the Jewish People in July 2018 is striking evidence that Gavison's depiction of the mission of the state as first to serve the interests of Jews and second to concern itself with needs of its citizens, which had been hegemonically understood as true and therefore not in need of legislation to make it so, no longer enjoys that status.

Thus Jewish privilege, fronted by an increasingly porous but still significant structure of liberal democracy, is the practical meaning of a regime often referred to as a "Jewish and democratic state."[57] Israelis, in other words, do not take the survival of their state for granted, but they do take for granted that the state whose survival they fret about is "Jewish and democratic" as I have characterized it.

State Demise in Israel: How Close to the Edge?

If what Jewish Israelis talk about when they talk about the end of their state is the end of a regime that obscures the privileged position it grants them, then exposure of that state-as-regime to real and pervasive questioning about its future signals that a process of demise is underway. This raises the question as to whether the process can be reversed and how close Israel may be to complete demise. Israeli political discourse contains three answers to this question. From one point of view, Israel has enough time to work in both political and cultural domains to secure its future. Such optimism is offered both by those who emphasize efforts to strengthen Jewish self-confidence and commitment and by those who stress the imperative for compromise with Arabs or with one another. For example, Israel's leading demographer, Sergio Dellapergola, frames the issue in terms of years or even decades. "Do current demographic trends," he asks, "in Israel and among Palestinians increase or decrease Israel's chances to be a Jewish and democratic state?"[58] Michael Oren answers this question by using Dellapergola's findings to describe how Israel, by losing its democratic character, would either cease to be Jewish or cease to be altogether. Arguing that the state "is predicated on a decisive and stable Jewish majority of at least 70 percent," Oren promotes the importance, and possibility, of extracting Israel from enough of the occupied territories to preserve it.[59]

The same time frame is used, with varying degrees of confidence, by most mainstream Israeli doves. They call for changes in Israeli diplomacy and settlement policy to preserve the two-state solution option as the only way to save the regime they experience as the State of Israel. Typical is a 2011 *Haaretz* editorial observing that "if Israel continues to prefer expanding the settlements to ensuring its status as a Jewish democratic state, we will lose the last Palestinian partner who could prevent its perpetuation as an isolated, condemned apartheid state."[60] Jeremy Ben-Ami, leader of

J Street, a dovish Israel lobbying organization, linked Israel's survival as a Jewish and democratic state to his movement's ability to achieve victory over the Israel lobby in the United States, so that American diplomacy could then effectively pursue a two-state solution. By focusing on the need to transform the context within which American presidents approach the Israeli-Palestinian conflict, Ben-Ami implies his belief that the question will remain open for multiple American election cycles.[61]

In other prominent formulations, the state, again indexed by a functioning "Jewish and democratic" regime, is not something that can survive for years or decades of consciousness raising, mobilization, political struggle, and diplomacy, but is in immediate peril, requiring emergency mobilization to save it. "The trend is clear," wrote Ari Shavit in 2013:

> Within a short time the number of settlers will increase dramatically, as will their ability to block any attempt to divide the land. If it continues this way, the Netanyahu-Lapid-Bennett government will put an end to the two-state solution, the Jewish democratic entity, and the Zionist dream ... it is a question of survival. Will Israel, at the last minute, stop flooding the occupied territories with settlers?[62]

Similarly, according to S. Daniel Abraham, "if Israel doesn't reach a two-state settlement with the Palestinians very soon, then one day—likely sooner rather than later—the Jewish state as we know it will cease to exist."[63] Despite the appearance of calm and prosperity, wrote Alon Ben-Meir, Israelis must "realize that the country is on a path of self-destruction. They must now rise and demand the restoration of Israel to the principles set by its founders: a free, democratic, and strong home for the Jews."[64]

For a third group, the state is either barely clinging to its existence or has already met its demise in the sense that the regime operating in the country is no longer Jewish and democratic. The challenge for this group is to fight against the currently established regime and eventually replace it with a re-institutionalized version of what has been reduced to only a dream. Markers of this perspective are invocations of the example of Weimar and use of terms such as "racist" and "fascist" to describe Israeli politics and society. As early as 1988, Yaacov Sharett, son of the former prime minister, warned of an imminent and catastrophic end to the Jewish democratic state. He advocated desperate measures such as "civil revolt" and underground resistance to save it and preparation for mass emigration in the likely event those efforts failed.[65] In 2012 Sami Michael, a prize-winning Israeli writer and president of the Association for Civil Rights in Israel, portrayed Israel as "the most racist state in the developed world" and provided evidence of the rise of "spiritual and cultural fascism." Israel was exposed, he said, to "severe existential dangers" as a result of the direction its leadership had taken, the extremism of the political forces dominating the country, and how intensely it was detested by the peoples of the Middle East. Too old to emigrate, Michael said he preferred "to remain a stranger in my own land."[66] During a 2014 Tel Aviv University symposium on a book about the effect of prolonged occupation in Israeli society, Ephraim Yuchtman-Yaar, head of the Tami Steinmetz Center for Peace Research, began his presentation by declaring "Fashism zeh kan!" (Fascism is here!).[67] Neither surprise nor shock was registered by the 150-person audience to this declaration.

In November 2011, a flood of proposed legislation targeting Arabs and Jewish dissenters was described by one prominent intellectual as dramatizing "the extent of fascism's domination of Israel."[68] According to Israel's leading scholar of fascism, Zeev Sternhell, the legislation was being advanced by members of the governing coalition whose worldview was fascistic. "Democracy," warned Sternhell, "can bring about its own demise, as we know from the history of the 20th century."[69] Noting the extent to which Israeli dissenters were invoking Weimar to describe what was happening in the country, one right-wing commentator agreed, identifying the threat that decadent cosmopolitanism posed to Germany in the interwar period as exactly the same as that posed to Israel by the population and culture of Tel Aviv.[70] Others argue that a Jewish and democratic Israel is no longer recoverable and that only enfranchising all Arabs under Israeli control, including West Bank Palestinians, has the potential to restore a democratic regime, by sacrificing its Jewishness.[71] Some hope for a military coup.[72]

Conclusion

In states, as Adam Smith famously observed about nations, "there is a great deal of ruin." Yet states do end. If, following Weber, the survival of a state is ultimately a function of the stability of human expectations about its existence, then the prominence and pervasiveness of questions about its survival themselves register its precariousness. By approaching all states as problematically institutionalized "projects," state demise can be considered a process of increasing precariousness. In this way, the theory of state demise offered here can explain how otherwise strong states, unprotected by hegemonic expectations of continued stability, can come to an end. In the specific case of Israel, it can also help explain the pervasiveness and intensity of questions about the Israeli state's survival—a peculiar pattern for such an ostensibly robust state.

This analysis can also help solve another puzzle. Israel was founded as a settler colonial state dedicated to the paramountcy of a particular ethno-national segment of the population, isolated in its region, and confronting a large aboriginal population. If one believes, as I do, that the two-state solution offered a historically unprecedented opportunity for Israel to avoid the fate of similarly situated and constituted states such as apartheid South Africa, Rhodesia, and French Algeria, then how is one to account for the astonishing fact that Israel did not pounce on opportunities to implement the two-state solution when it was available?

Part of the answer to this question is the weakness and increasing perforation of the hegemonic shield surrounding the Jewish-Zionist quasi-liberal regime. With the regime-as-state exposed directly to risks of its disappearance, Israeli elites were fundamentally unwilling to take the risk of regime breakdown that would be necessary to foster development of a viable Palestinian state in the West Bank and Gaza Strip. When France, under the Fifth Republic, faced the need to withdraw from Algeria, it did so as a political community that had weathered multiple regime changes in both the nineteenth and twentieth centuries. Spain, as a political community, survived both the end of its empire and a vicious civil war. In both France and Spain, regimes could fall but the state could re-emerge in the form of a successor regime because the political community, per se, was hegemonically established as natural and permanent. In Israel, however, since the regime defines the political community as Zionist, the state realized by that regime lacks the protection—the safety net—of a hegemonically established political community based on expectations more solidly anchored than beliefs about the integrity of the regime. Thus, when opportunities to consummate a deal with the Palestinians arose for Prime Ministers Yitzhak Rabin, Shimon Peres, Ehud Barak, and even Ehud Olmert, each chose to avoid fateful regime-threatening confrontations with opponents by shifting most of the political risks involved onto the Palestinians. In Israel, in other words, risking the regime not only means risking state demise, it means risking the end of the political community. Opportunities for a negotiated two-state solution no longer exist, but while they did, the relative shallowness of the institutionalization of the Israeli state made taking the risks necessary for securing its future too high to be run by any government that Israel was able to produce.

Ian S. Lustick is the Bess W. Heyman Professor of Political Science at the University of Pennsylvania. His research has focused on Jerusalem, Israeli-Palestinian politics, American foreign policy, historical institutionalism, computer modeling, and evolution. His most recent book is *Paradigm Lost: From Two-State Solution to One-State Reality* (2019).

Notes

1. On "state death," see Tanisha M. Fazal, *State Death: The Politics and Geography of Conquest, occupation, and Annexation* (Princeton: Princeton University Press, 2007). On state failure or collapse, see Daniel C. Esty, Jack Goldstone, Ted Robert Gurr, Barbara Harff, Pamela T. Surko, Alan N. Unger, and Robert Chen, "Failed States and International Security: Causes, Prospects, and Consequences," papers presented at the conference "Failed States," at Purdue University, West Lafayette, 1998; and by the same authors, "The State Failure Project: Early Warning Research for US Foreign Policy Planning," in *Preventive Measures: Building Risk Assessments and Crisis Early Warning Systems*, ed. John L. Davies and Ted Robert Gurr (Boulder, CO: Bowman and Littlefield, 1998), 27–38; Krista Hendry, "From Failed to Fragile: Renaming the Index," Fund for Peace, 24 June 2014, https://fundforpeace.org/2014/06/24/from-failed-to-fragile-renaming-the-index/.
2. Max Weber, "Politics as a Vocation," in *From Max Weber: Essays in Sociology*, trans. and ed. H. H. Gerth and C. Wright Mills (New York: Oxford University Press, 1958), 78. For a detailed discussion

of Weber's various formulations of this definition, see Ian S. Lustick, *Unsettled States, Disputed Lands: Britain and Ireland, France and Algeria, Israel and the West Bank/Gaza* (Ithaca: Cornell University Press, 1993), 3, 37, 457–458n, 468n.

3. Max Weber, *Economy and Society*, ed. Guenther Roth and Claus Wittich (Berkeley: University of California Press, 1978), vol. 1, https://archive.org/stream/MaxWeberEconomyAndSociety/MaxWeberEconomyAndSociety_djvu.txt.
4. Douglass C. North, *Structure and Change in Economic History* (New York: Norton, 1981), 17, 21.
5. On the party as "an embryonic State structure," see Antonio Gramsci, *Selections from the Prison Notebooks*, ed. Quintin Hoare and Geoffrey Nowell Smith (New York: International Publishers, 1971), 226, and also 194–95, 257–69.
6. Ian S. Lustick, "Thresholds of Opportunity and Barriers to Change in the Right-Sizing of States," in *Right-Sizing the State: The Politics of Moving Borders*, ed. Brendan O'Leary, Ian S. Lustick, and Thomas Callaghy (Oxford: Oxford University Press, 2001), 86–98.
7. David Grossman, "Contemplations on Peace," in *Writing in the Dark: Essays on Literature and Politics* (New York: Picador, 2008), 88.
8. Michael B. Oren, "Seven Existential Threats," *Commentary Magazine*, May 2009, https://www.commentarymagazine.com/articles/michael-oren-2/seven-existential-threats/. For similar treatments, see Jeffrey Goldberg, "Lesser Israel," *Foreign Affairs*, July/August 2013, 152–157; Benjamin Schwarz, "Will Israel Survive to 100?," *The Atlantic*, May 2005, https://www.theatlantic.com/magazine/archive/2005/05/will-israel-live-to-100/303896/; Victor Davis Hanson, "Can Israel Survive?," *National Review*, 29 January 2015, https://www.nationalreview.com/2011/09/can-israel-survive-victor-davis-hanson/; and Christopher Hitchens, "Can Israel Survive for Another 50 Years?," *Slate*, 12 May 2008, https://slate.com/news-and-politics/2008/05/can-israel-survive-for-another-60-years.html.
9. Uriel Abulof, "'Small Peoples': The Existential Uncertainty of Ethnonational Communities," *International Studies Quarterly* 53, no. 1 (March 2009): 227–48. See also Gil Troy, *Why I Am a Zionist: Israel, Jewish Identity, and the Challenges of Today* (Montreal: Bronfman Jewish Education Center, 2008), 139.
10. Abulof, "Small Peoples," 236.
11. Yossi Yonah, "The Return of Israel to the Middle East," *Tikkun*, July 2010.
12. Ori Kashti, "Technion Chief: Science Education in Israel on Brink of Collapse," *Haaretz*, 15 December 2010.
13. Ziv Heillman, "An Embarrassment of Riches?," *Jerusalem Report*, 11 April 2011.
14. Caroline B. Glick, "We Are Not for Sale," *Jerusalem Post*, 5 November 2010.
15. Benny Morris, "Is Israel Over?," *Newsweek*, 11 September 2011, http://www.newsweek.com/first-report-israel-over-67339.
16. Menachem Lorberbaum and Carlo Strenger, "Legitimacy without Ethnic Nationalism," *Haaretz*, 19 November 2010.
17. Yehuda Elkana, "The Need to Forget," *Haaretz*, 2 March 1988 (in Hebrew). See also Avraham Burg, *Victory Over Hitler* (Tel Aviv: Yedioth Ahronoth Books, 2007, in Hebrew); and Idith Zertal, *Israel's Holocaust and the Politics of Nationhood* (Cambridge: Cambridge University Press, 2005).
18. Editorial, *Haaretz*, 10 March 2011.
19. Leslie Susser, "The Rise and Fall of Kadima," *Jerusalem Report*, 27 August 2012.
20. Eshkol Nevo, "More Than Disgrace, 'Price-Tag' Violence Is Israeli Security Threat," *Yediot Acharonot*, 5 September 2012. See also Ben-Dror Yemini, "The Enemy Within: The Danger of Radicalism," Ynetnews, 26 December 2015, http://www.ynetnews.com/articles/0,7340,L-4744394,00.html.
21. *Jerusalem Post*, 30 January 2012.
22. Danny Rubinstein, "Bitter Anniversary," *Jerusalem Post*, 24 May 2010.
23. Mark Langfan, "A One-Way Ticket to the Zero-State Solution," Arutz Sheva, 22 January 2014, http://www.israelnationalnews.com/Article.aspx/14422#.UuEmEdlo7IV.
24. Danny Danon, *Israel: The Will to Prevail* (New York: Palgrave Macmillan, 2012), 2.
25. Toi Staff, "Netanyahu to Obama: Iran deal threatens Israel's survival," Times of Israel, 3 April 2015, http://www.timesofisrael.com/netanyahu-to-obama-iran-deal-threatens-israels-existence/. See also, for example, Mortimer Zuckerman, "Obama's Unforgivable Betrayal," *US News and World*

Report, 17 April 2015, http://www.usnews.com/opinion/articles/2015/04/17/obamas-iran-nuclear-deal-is-an-unforgivable-betrayal-of-israel.
26. Daniel Seaman, "Danny Seaman at Honest Reporting." Website no longer available.
27. Ron Rosenbaum, "Thinking the Unthinkable: A Lamentation for the State of Israel," *Tablet*, 15 December 2015, http://www.tabletmag.com/jewish-news-and-politics/195438/lamentation-for-israel. See also David Grossman, "The Desire to Be Gisella," in *Writing in the Dark*, 38.
28. Ari Shavit, "Israel Has Abandoned Young U.S. Jews in Fight Against BDS," *Haaretz*, 14 May 2015, http://www.haaretz.com/opinion/.premium-1.656352.
29. Aluf Benn, "Israel's Core Is Crumbling and It's More Important than Iran Deal," *Haaretz*, 17 September 2015.
30. Ben Hartman, "Israel Faces Threat of Becoming Religious State," *Jerusalem Post*, 3 April 2011.
31. Gershon Hacohen, "Is Jerusalem Divided?," Begin-Sadat Center for Strategic Studies Perspectives Paper no. 316, 25 October 2015, https://www.jstor.org/stable/resrep04426?seq=1#metadata_info_tab_contents.
32. Yehezkel Dror, "The Future of Israel between Thriving and Decline," Jewish People Policy Institute, May 2006, 5, http://jppi.org.il/uploads/The%20Future%20of%20Israel%20Between%20Thriving%20and%20Decline.pdf.
33. Yoram Hazony, *The Jewish State: The Struggle for Israel's Soul* (New York: Basic Books, 2000).
34. Daniel Gordis, *Saving Israel: How the Jewish People Can Win a War That May Never End* (Hoboken: Wiley, 2009), 204, and, for similar themes, 112, 124, 129, 186–92, 207, 210–13.
35. Gordis, *Saving Israel*, 112.
36. Danon, *Israel*, 188. See also Mitchell G. Bard, *Will Israel Survive?* (New York: Palgrave Macmillan, 2007), 235.
37. Uri Elitzur, "New Peace Initiative: Annex and Survive," *Makor Rishon*, 3 August 2011, http://www.israelnationalnews.com/News/News.aspx/142750. For particularly extravagant versions of this kind of argument, see Caroline Glick, "Post-Zionism Is So 1990s," *Jerusalem Post*, 17 April 2012; and Devin Sper, *The Future of Israel* (Scottsdale, AZ: SY Publishing, 2004).
38. For a detailed treatment of the debate over the "irreversibility" of de facto annexation, see Lustick, *Unsettled States, Disputed Lands*, 11–20.
39. "Summary of a Conversation with Meron Benvenisti," American Enterprise Institute, Washington, DC, 27 October 1982 (mimeo in author's files); Meron Benvenisti, "Israel's Deepening Wound," *New York Times*, 13 February 1983.
40. Ari Shavit, *My Promised Land: The Triumph and Tragedy of Israel* (New York: Spiegel & Grau, 2013), 394, 401. For other typical examples, see Avraham Burg, "The End of Zionism," *The Guardian*, 15 September 2003, https://www.theguardian.com/world/2003/sep/15/comment; Ephraim Sneh, "Bad Borders, Good Neighbors," *New York Times*, 11 July 2011.
41. Jerrold Kessel and Pierre Klochendler, "From 'Land for Peace' to 'Freedom for Self-Defense,'" *Jerusalem Report*, 7 January 2008. See also Dan Meridor, interviewed by Barak Ravid, "Deputy PM: Israel Must Cede Land to Remain Jewish and Democratic," *Haaretz*, 15 November 2010, http://www.haaretz.com/print-edition/features/deputy-pm-israel-must-cede-land-to-remain-jewish-and-democratic-1.324723.
42. Alon Ben-Meir, "Israel's National Security: Delegitimizing the Legitimate," 28 October 2013, http://www.alonben-meir.com/article/israels-national-security-delegitimizing-the-legitimate/.
43. Yossi Verter, "Peres Warns: Israel in Danger of Ceasing to Exist as Jewish State," *New York Times*, 28 June 2011, A5.
44. See, for example, Alon Ben-Meir, "Israelis Must Rise Up to Avert National Disaster," 10 January 2013, http://www.alonben-meir.com/article/israelis-must-rise-up-to-avert-national-disaster/?utm_source=Subscribers&utm_campaign=4e439c79c7-UA-5963141-2&utm_medium=email; and Carlo Strenger, "National-Religious Messianism Is Endangering Israel," *Haaretz*, 13 June 2012.
45. Dan Perry, "Analysis: Israel Left Wing Sees Jewish State's End," Associated Press, 11 January 2013.
46. Gil Stern, et al., "Livni: New Elections Are to Replace Extremist, Provocative, Paranoid Government," *Jerusalem Post*, 2 December 2014.

47. Yishai Sarid, *HaShlishi* [The third] (Tel-Aviv: Am Oved, 2015).
48. Uri Avnery, "To the Young Israelis of Berlin, Return to Israel," *Haaretz*, 29 July 2016.
49. Caroline B. Glick, *The Israeli Solution: A One-State Plan for Peace in the Middle East* (New York: Crown, 2014), 119.
50. Moshe Dann, "Settlements and the Future of Zionism," *Jerusalem Post*, 19 December 2013.
51. Ruth Matar, "Sharon Must Go," Arutz Sheva, 8 August 2004. See also Aaron Klein, *The Late Great State of Israel: How Enemies Within and Without Threaten the Jewish Nation's Survival* (Los Angeles: WND Books, 2009).
52. Ra'fat Aldajani and Drew Christiansen, "A Demographic Time Bomb in the Middle East," Berkeley Center for Religion, Peace & World Affairs, January 5, 2015, https://berkleycenter.georgetown.edu/essays/a-demographic-time-bomb-in-the-middle-east.
53. S. Daniel Abraham, "How Israel Will Be Destroyed without One Shot Being fired," *Haaretz*, 6 January 2013, http://www.haaretz.com/opinion/how-israel-will-be-destroyed-without-one-shot-being-fired.premium-1.492271.
54. See Yoram Ettinger, "The Myth of the Demographic Machete," *Makor Rishon*, 19 March 2007 (for an English translation [misdated], see http://maof.rjews.net/english/37-english/14785-the-myth-of-the-demographic-machete); Bennett Zimmerman, Roberta Seid, and Michael L. Wise, *The Million Person Gap: The Arab Population in the West Bank and Gaza* (Ramat Gan: Begin-Sadat Center for Strategic Studies, Bar-Ilan University, 2006). For the author's analysis of this fraudulent argument and its widespread acceptance, see Ian S. Lustick, "What Counts Is the Counting: Statistical Manipulation as a Solution to Israel's 'Demographic Problem,'" *Middle East Journal* 67, no. 2 (Spring 2013): 185–205.
55. Uriel Abulof, "Deep Securitization and Israel's 'Demographic Demon,'" *International Political Sociology* 8, no. 4 (December 2014): 408.
56. Ruth Gavison, "The Jews' Right to Statehood," *Azure* 15 (Summer 2003): 72, 74–75.
57. For a strained plea to avoid overly clear formulae as a way to disguise a state dominated by Jews and for Jews as a liberal democracy, see Aharon Barak, "Individual Freedom in a Jewish and Democratic State," *Haaretz*, 25 March 2018, https://www.haaretz.com/opinion/.premium-individual-freedom-in-a-jewish-and-democratic-state-1.5935245.
58. Sergio Dellapergola, "Israel's Existential predicament: Population, Territory, and Identity," *New York Times*, 28 June 2011.
59. Oren, "Seven Existential Threats."
60. Editorial, *Haaretz*, 25 January 2011.
61. Jeremy Ben-Ami, *A New Voice for Israel* (New York: St. Martin's Griffin, 2011), xii, 167, 178–79, 198–99.
62. Ari Shavit, "Israel's Spectacular Suicide," *Haaretz*, 13 June 2013.
63. Abraham, "How Israel Will Be Destroyed."
64. Alon Ben-Meir, "Israelis Must Rise Up To Avert National Disaster," 10 January 2013, http://www.alonben-meir.com/article/israelis-must-rise-up-to-avert-national-disaster/?utm_source=Subscribers&utm_campaign=4e439c79c7-UA-5963141-2&utm_medium=email.
65. Yaacov Sharett, *The State of Israel Is No More* (Tel-Aviv: Tesher, 1988, in Hebrew).
66. An English translation of this speech is available at Lisa Goldman, "Sami Michael: 'Israel—Most Racist State in the Industrialized World,'" +972 Magazine, 9 August 2012, http://972mag.com/author-sami-michael-israel-is-the-most-racist-state-in-the-industrialized-world/52602/.
67. Author notes, 27 February 2014.
68. Hanan Hever, "The Unmasked Law," *Haaretz*, 12 November 2010.
69. Eetta Prince-Gibson, "Legally Challenged," *Jerusalem Report*, 19 December 2011, 9. Sternhell has published several articles warning that Israel has become or was becoming a fascist state. See "The Birth of Fascism," *Haaretz*, 7 July 2016. See also Gideon Levy, "Stop Living in Denial, Israel Is an Evil State," *Haaretz*, 31 July 2016, https://www.haaretz.com/opinion/.premium-stop-living-in-denial-israel-is-an-evil-state-1.5418219.
70. Giulio Meotti, "The State of Tel Aviv—Israel's Weimar?," Arutz Sheva, 7 August 2012, http://www

.israelnationalnews.com/Articles/Article.aspx/12023. For an illustrative leftist evocation of Weimar, see Avraham Burg, *Victory over Hitler* (Tel Aviv: Yediot Aharonot Books, 2007, in Hebrew), 110.
71. Bradley Burston, "Fascism in Israel: It's Up to You," *Haaretz*, 22 December 2015, http://www.haaretz.com/opinion/.premium-1.693304; Bradley Burston, "One Thing Which Could Change Everything: Give the Palestinians the Vote," *Haaretz*, 12 April 2016, http://www.haaretz.com/opinion/.premium-1.714082; and Ian S. Lustick, *Paradigm Lost: From Two-State Solution to One-State Reality* (Philadelphia: University of Pennsylvania Press, 2019).
72. Ofra Rudner, "It's Better to Stick Your Head in the Sand," *Haaretz*, 21 July 2016 (in Hebrew), http://www.haaretz.co.il/opinions/.premium-1.3013147.

Select Bibliography

Abulof, Uriel. "Deep Securitization and Israel's 'Demographic Demon.'" *International Political Sociology* 8, no. 4 (December 2014): 408.
Burg, Avraham. *Victory Over Hitler*. Tel Aviv: Yediot Aharonot Books, 2007. In Hebrew.
Danon, Danny. *Israel: The Will to Prevail*. New York: Palgrave Macmillan, 2012.
Dellapergola, Sergio. "Israel's Existential Predicament: Population, Territory, and Identity." *New York Times*, 28 June 2011.
Gordis, Daniel. *Saving Israel: How the Jewish People Can Win a War That May Never End*. Hoboken: Wiley, 2009.
Lustick, Ian S. *Paradigm Lost: From Two-State Solution to One-State Reality*. Philadelphia: University of Pennsylvania Press, 2019.
———. "What Counts Is the Counting: Statistical Manipulation as a Solution to Israel's 'Demographic Problem.'" *Middle East Journal* 67, no. 2 (Spring 2013): 185–205.
Morris, Benny. "Is Israel Over?" *Newsweek*, 11 September 2011. http://www.newsweek.com/first-report-israel-over-67339.
Sarid, Yishai. *HaShlishi* [The third]. Tel Aviv: Am Oved, 2015.
Shavit, Ari. *My Promised Land: The Triumph and Tragedy of Israel*. New York: Spiegel & Grau, 2013.

CHAPTER 15

DECOLONIZING ISRAEL-PALESTINE
A DISCOURSE OR A POLITICAL PROGRAM?

ILAN PAPPÉ

Decolonization

Decolonization is associated, quite rightly, with a specific historical period, when the great empires collapsed and were dismantled. These were processes that allowed ethnic, cultural, and religious groups to demand nation-states in the name of self-determination. While in Europe this process referred to the creation of nation-states, in Africa and South America, in particular, it was described as the replacement of colonial rule with postcolonial movements of liberation.[1]

However, with the appearance of critical works on the postcolonial period, and with the realization that colonialization can take different forms long after empires collapse and physical occupation ends, quite a few scholars have come to appreciate that decolonization has not yet been completed.

Decolonization has thus become a popular and significant topic in academia, informing the production of knowledge and engaging with the colonialist and post-colonial periods (focusing on the European settler projects from the seventeenth century until the second half of the twentieth century). Decolonization has also re-emerged as a clear political program for social movements in places where the former empires are still controlling crucial aspects of life and remains a potent idea especially in settler colonial settings (this was and still is the discourse that accompanies the struggle of native peoples in Mexico, the First Nations in Canada, the Aboriginals in Australia, and the Native Americans).[2]

As an actual physical process on the ground, decolonization of settler colonial states has occurred recently in only two places: Algeria and South Africa. These two historical developments energized studies on decolonization and helped scholars to identify settler colonialism not just as a historical phenomenon but also as one that is still a relevant paradigm for analyzing many parts of the world today.

Recently, a number of scholars have framed the Zionist movement as a settler colonial movement and Israel as a settler state.[3] From this perspective, Israel as a settler colonial state—if this framing is accepted—is a project that could in theory still be decolonized. There is still a wide gap between this emerging and growing literature, which offers alternative visions for a decolonized future, and the hegemonic academic and public discourse on Israel and Palestine, which frames the conflict as one fought between two legitimate national movements or as an issue confined to the Israeli occupation of the West Bank and the Gaza Strip since 1967. Until now, therefore, mainstream academia, media, and the politicians involved in the so-called peace process regarded decolonization as a plan for the future rather than a possible scholarly framing of the conflict as a whole.

Indeed, until the 1980s, decolonization as a concept was absent from the academic discourse on Israel and Palestine; in that sense, the balance of power on the ground was also reflected in the production of knowledge about the region.[4] More recently, decolonization as a possible solution has entered the discourse about peace in Palestine, and the depiction of post-mandatory Palestine as a settler colonial reality has moved from the scholarly margins of academia into a more central place in knowledge production sites such as universities and research centers. As so often happens in the case of Palestine, ideological positions and scholarly stances have intermixed and fertilized each other.

The decolonization of scholarly knowledge about Palestine's history began in the late 1960s by way of interpreting the Palestinian struggle as anti-colonial and recently by analyzing Zionism and Israel as settler colonial phenomena. By now, numerous PhD students outside of Israel have employed the settler colonial paradigm to analyze the modern history of Israel and Palestine.[5] Many of these graduate students are also activists, and therefore their work engages with efforts to bring about decolonization as much as it does with analysis of the reality on the ground.

Political sociologists find it difficult to assess the influence and significance of young Palestinian or pro-Palestinian intellectuals within Palestinian society as a whole (needless to say they have no impact on Israeli Jewish society), but recent developments are noteworthy. What can tentatively be concluded so far is that even if this scholarly effort does not as yet impact national Palestinian politics and positions, it certainly has a potential to do so in the future.

There are two reasons for this prediction. The dialogue among Palestinian scholars and between them and interested scholars worldwide is much more feasible now in an age of accessible and ever-expanding cyberspace. Where once there were physical barriers that prevented such connections, now cyberspace allows Palestinians to spread and interact with new ideas and to strive to have wider influence than ever before. In a society that is very young (the Palestinian society between the Jordan River and the Mediterranean Sea and in the refugee camps), these ideas are spreading with extraordinary speed, making it difficult for us to fully assess their impact.[6]

The second possible trigger for such a development in the future is the resurfacing of the discourse of a one-state solution that—at least in part—perceives Zionism as a settler colonial movement, Israel as an apartheid settler state, and ergo decolonization as the precondition for peace and reconciliation. Cherine Hussein, in her excellent survey on the one-state conversation, insists that it is only a discourse and not a political movement on the ground (although her book does not cover the last five years).[7] In Gramscian terms, Hussein describes a counter-hegemonic discourse that follows the Fanonian trajectory on the way to liberation: decolonize the colonized mind before you can decolonize the colony.

It can thus be said that decolonization is a common term among activists and an appropriate academic one for describing the way forward toward peace in Israel and Palestine. But some questions are still hard to answer: What are the chances that such a discourse will inform the policies of future political elites and the powers that be? Does this discourse have a realistic chance of changing reality on the ground? Will this conflation of activism and scholarship be able to impact the Palestinian political discourse, given that all the official Palestinian representatives (Palestinian Knesset members, Palestinian Authority, the PLO, and Hamas) endorse the two-state solution? Moreover, "decolonization" as a proper term is also absent from the vocabulary employed by members of the international community working to find a solution to the Palestine issue. And there are only a handful of anti-Zionist activists in Israel who converse in this language.

However, there is a Palestinian consensus about the nature of the struggle even if the endgame—namely, whether it should be a struggle for a two-state or one-state solution—is under debate. The struggle, unlike the desired solution, is framed as a stubborn, at times bloody and violent journey that has become a way of life since the arrival of Zionism in Palestine. The interplay between the hope for any peace agreement and the intensity of the struggle (by whatever means) against Israel is an important factor that affects not only the reality on the ground but also the conversation over alternative solutions. The absence of such a hope has propelled this conversation forward and produced a new vocabulary. This vocabulary replaces the concept of peace with decolonization; the term "reconciliation" with "regime change"; "occupation" with "colonization"; and "the Nakba" with "ethnic cleansing"—among other entries.[8]

This new vocabulary is now employed extensively by young scholars writing on settler colonialism in Palestine, but not only by them. It is becoming an acceptable prism through which Palestinians and their supporters all over the world view the future. Recently, some of its entries, so to speak, have been inserted into the discourse employed by journalists, pundits, and politicians engaged with the question of Israel and Palestine. The spillover of this new vocabulary and the discourse of decolonization into more mainstream venues is caused by five discrete processes, as outlined below. Should these processes, which I outline here, continue and intensify, this new vocabulary will grow more acceptable and may even become predominant.

The first process is the incremental delegitimization of the current Palestinian representative bodies. While I was writing the final version of this chapter, new demonstrations occurred in Ramallah against the corruption of the Palestinian Authority (PA) and against Hamas in the Gaza Strip. Moreover, following a brief period of unity, when the Joint List of Arab parties ran for the 2015 Israeli elections, Palestinian politicians in Israel became once more embroiled in internal divisions and began losing their electorate's support; consequently, large numbers of especially young Palestinians boycotted the April 2019 elections. These were just a few instances of the crisis of confidence and representation in Palestinian politics, probably dating all the way back to the destruction of the PLO base in Lebanon in 1982. That traumatic event had disempowered the already fragmented Palestinian nation. Although the PLO survived until 1988 as the sole representative of the Palestinian people, the emergence of political Islamic groups and, even more so, the Oslo Accord eroded its legitimacy in many quarters of Palestinian society, wherever they were.

This void in Palestinian politics is ripe terrain for the growth of new ideas and for the evolution of a new discourse. In the case of Palestine, quite often, such a void is an opportunity for the revival of old ideas and their adaptation to present realities. And indeed, even among PA leaders and Palestinian politicians in Israel, more and more voices are now heard calling for a one-state solution.[9] In the case of official PA representatives, the one-state option is framed as a threat to the liberals in Israel and the West, in the sense that if the two-state solution fails, Israel would have to become a nondemocratic apartheid state encompassing the entire territory of historical (Mandatory) Palestine. For others, the one-state solution has remained the preferred model. In either case, if it unfolds as a reality, the new dictionary might become more relevant.

If indeed a consensus develops that the two-state solution is dead, then the very notion of decolonization will no longer seem so alien, even to the pragmatic politicians of the West and various Palestinian groups. This observation is further supported by a second recent development: the shift to the right in Israeli politics. This shift has been accompanied by intensive Judaization of the West Bank and by other discriminatory policies toward the Palestinian communities on both sides of the Green Line, creating a de facto one-state solution.

The legal and actual status of the Palestinians in Israel is still superior to those who live in the West Bank, and there are differences between the conditions of those living in areas A, B and C, respectively. Within a one-state solution envisaged by the right wing in Israel, the annexation of the West Bank, in particular area C (60 percent of the West Bank), will create a Greater Israel, with two small Bantustans (one consists of the remaining 40 percent of the West Bank and one in the Gaza Strip). The former, Israel of today and area C, would be governed by the same legal and constitutional system. The main challenge, against which the Zionist Left is warning, is the dramatic increase in the number of Palestinians, who would become Israeli citizens in such a case. This is why the new system, in order to maintain the Jewish nature of the state, would be equally discriminatory against Palestinians wherever they are in this new enlarged Israel so as to ensure that they have no impact on the state's identity, ideology, and strategy.

Political activism in Israel on the Palestine question has been focused, until now, on the question of whether to withdraw from the 1967 occupation. This dichotomy could change now as a result of the new focus on a one-state solution and generate a public debate on the nature of this future single state that at present is well on the way to becoming an apartheid state.

The third process is on the other side of the political divide in Israel, namely the disappearance of the Zionist Left (a process that already began twenty years ago).[10] Seen from within the paradigm of decolonization, and for that matter of settler colonialism, the Zionist Left is what Albert Memmi has called "the leftist colonizer." These are settlers who remain within the ideological framework of colonialism (or in this case, of settler colonialism) and, in the words of Memmi, either willingly or reluctantly are still "part of the oppressing group and will be forced to share its destiny." Accordingly, "even if he [the leftist colonialist] is in no way guilty as an individual . . . he shares a collective responsibility by the fact of membership in a national oppressor group."[11]

The "leftist colonizers"—namely, the liberal Zionists—are more susceptible to believing that international law does not challenge their ideology. More specifically, they believe that it does not challenge the privileges granted them by the settler colonial state and that an improved settler state could be created in conformity with international law, thereby leading to the necessary changes on the ground.

In the April 2019 elections the number of anti-Zionist members of Knesset was the same as those of the left Zionist parties (the Labor Party and Meretz), and in the September 2019 elections they had two members of Knesset more than the left Zionist parties. It seems that the Israeli electorate is not attracted to "leftist colonizers." This constituency had been most loyal to the two-state solution and to the basic principles informing the "peace process." Recognizing that there is very little Jewish electoral support for the two-state solution might open the way to a different framing at least among some left Zionist politicians, who might follow the path of Avraham Burg's journey from a two-state to a one-state solution. Avraham Burg is a veteran politician, the son of the famously almost eternal minister of the interior Yosef Burg, who also led the Religious National Party from the early days of statehood until the early 1980s. Avraham veered more to the left, joined the Labor Party, was elected speaker of the Knesset, and subsequently served as chairman of the Jewish Agency. In this century, after a short stint in the business world, he returned to politics, adopting a very critical view toward Zionism and supporting the one-state solution.[12]

The fourth process, which is also intertwined with the previous three, is the decline of the peace process, the Pax Americana, that had been attempted since 1967. The peace accord initially signed in 1993 was never pronounced officially dead, although it is very clear that in 2000 it petered out and disappeared. The final nail in the coffin was the election of President Donald Trump in 2016. His administration was eager to withdraw from any potential role in the peace process, on the one hand, and to endorse more openly, officially, and unconditionally Israel's unilateral actions on the ground, on the other. Trump's decision to recognize Israel's annexation of East Jerusalem and the Golan Heights further diminished any hope for a two-state solution as the American position (also included in his "deal of the century"—his proposal for peace). The Trump administration's stance undermined the role of international law as the legal infrastructure for any future solution. Without such an infrastructure, the two-state solution has nothing to offer to either side.

Finally, it is noteworthy that Palestinians are one of the youngest societies in the world. The United Nations Population Fund (UNFPA) already noted this fact in 2015 when it stated, "Palestine is facing a period of rapid population growth and a large youthful population with 69 percent below the age of 29."[13] This young generation's operating mode is different in many ways from that of its elders, as can be seen at various levels and through discrete actions and projects that so far have not been translated into a meaningful transformative movement, but may do so in the future.

One mode of action has been the "return march," known as the Great March, conducted along the border of the Gaza Strip, which began in March 2018. This was the initiative of a group of young Palestinians such as Ahmad Abu Arthima, who represents these new young Palestinian activists in the outside world.[14] Well-educated and highly committed, he and others have organized weekly demonstrations of thousands and at time tens of thousands of people along the Gaza border. The aim is twofold. The first is to attract world attention through courageous protest—resulting quite often in a high casualty count—against the long Israeli siege of the Gaza Strip. As a United Nations report has pointed out, this siege would render life in the Strip unsustainable by 2020.[15] Their second demand is to return to the villages and lands from which they had been expelled in 1948, located on the other side of the fence. From this perspective, the right of return is not an imaginary vision, especially not for refugees in the Gaza Strip, if a single democratic state were to be the solution. This is why the approximately 350,000 internal Palestinian refugees living in Israel today—namely, those who were expelled in 1948 from their villages and towns but remained within the Jewish state and their descendants, who are organized in an NGO called ADRID (Association for the Defence of the Rights of the Internally Displaced)—are supporting the one-state solution.[16] In other words, although the Palestinian refugee community, estimated at 5.5 million, is scattered all over the world, those in geographical proximity to Israel and dwelling in refugee camps deem such a scenario to be an endgame for their struggle.

Palestinians of a similar age, as well as a fair number of young progressive Israeli Jews, demonstrate quite regularly in solidarity with the demonstrators in Gaza. They are part of a larger conversation carried out by the younger generation of activists and scholars. They communicate easily and across borders and are networking among the various Palestinian communities around the globe. Their dialogues and communications, as I have tried to show in a recent article in the *South Atlantic Quarterly*, can be seen as a new stage in the Palestinian cultural resistance to Zionism.[17] They exchange projects of oral histories of the Nakba, as well as models of reconstructed villages destroyed in 1948 and of future villages to be built after the return of Palestinian refugees. Whereas the fragmentation of the previous generation was the product of hard borders, fences, and regional conflicts, this generation does not need, at this stage, to meet physically in order to form a joint agenda and vision.[18]

This discourse among digitally interconnected young Palestinians across the globe has not yet contributed to the emergence of an effective social movement. Efforts to do so have suffered from the lack of any significant institutional infrastructure, a deficiency that similarly undermined the more hopeful moments of the Arab Spring. This young generation is very skeptical about institutions, which have been deemed corrupt and ineffective. However, transformations of this magnitude will be impossible if the youth ignore existing institutions and do not build new ones.

In March 2018, I was part of the One Democratic State Campaign (ODSC), aimed at creating a joint space for the individuals and movements already acting on behalf of this idea. The wish in this program is to enhance a dialogue on the one-state solution and to locate the disagreements and the challenges ahead. It differs somewhat from similar attempts in the past, as it taps into a rich body of academic work that has been done on the topic in the last decade and thus focuses more clearly on translating what could rightly be described as a utopia into a more practical program through, for instance, social movement theories. (In this volume another attempt for a solution known as "two states, one homeland" is also discussed. The latter differs from the ODSC in that it frames the current reality as a struggle between legitimate national movements seeking an appropriate geopolitical arrangement. The ODSC frames the conflict as a struggle between a settler colonial movement and an indigenous population. Hence the ODSC is pursuing a way of decolonizing Palestine rather than another version of partition into two states, which is offered by this particular initiative.)

The One Democratic State Campaign[19]

The preamble of the ODSC plan, which I helped write, states the following:

> In recent years, the idea of a democratic state as the best political solution for Palestine has re-emerged and gained support in the public domain. It is not a new idea. The Palestinian liberation movement, before the Nakba of 1948 and after, had promoted this vision in the PLO's National Charter, abandoning it for the two-state solution only in 1988 (although

through the years there were indications that the PLO is willing both to give up the demand in the charter for all the Jews who came before 1948 to leave and that it is possible to establish a Palestinian state in the 1967 occupied territories as a first stage on the way to full liberation).[20] It was on this basis that, in September 1993, the Palestinians entered into the Oslo negotiations. The two-state solution was also endorsed by all the Palestinian parties represented in the Israeli Knesset. But on the ground Israel strengthened its colonial control, fragmenting the West Bank, East Jerusalem and Gaza into tiny, isolated and impoverished cantons, separated from one another by settlements, massive Israeli highways, hundreds of checkpoints, the apartheid Wall, military bases and fences. After a half-century of relentless "Judaization," the two-state solution must be pronounced dead, buried under the colonial enterprise on the territory that would have become the Palestinian state. In its place Israel has imposed a single regime of repression from the Mediterranean Sea and the Jordan River.

The main point in this opening paragraph is to accentuate the need for a Palestinian-led initiative that is based on the recognition of the Palestinian movement as a legitimate anti-colonial movement. In other words, this preamble uses the decolonization discourse explicitly.

The program appeared in Arabic, English, and Hebrew. It has sections that would be very difficult for an Israeli Jewish constituency to swallow, and some that Palestinians would find hard to accept. Thus, for instance, I realize how alien the following section in the program would sound to Israeli Jews:

> The only way forward to a genuine and viable political settlement is to dismantle the colonial apartheid regime that has been imposed over historic Palestine, replacing it with a new political system based on full civil equality, implementation of the Palestinian refugees' Right of Return and the building of a system that addresses the historic wrongs committed on the Palestinian people by the Zionist movement.

The main bone of contention here is indeed the promise to guarantee the right of return. However, this new approach is entirely based on transforming the hegemonic Zionist discourse and re-educating—as much as is possible—the privileged section of this unjust system by reframing past and present realities. Even in the case of South Africa, this kind of transformation was not a precondition to decolonization, but occurred on a significant scale only after decolonization came about. Yet it seems that in the South African case, and hopefully in the case of Israel, there was a need for only a small group to subscribe to the new framing that, in addition to other discrete processes, caused the transformation on the ground. Thus, in South Africa it was the decision of the United States to join the sanctions' regime after the Cold War ended that was a prime factor in bringing down the apartheid regime. The other two factors were the steadfastness of the jailed African National Congress (ANC) leaders and their liberation campaign. This campaign, at times quite violent, motivated a small number of whites to join the ANC. The multiethnic ANC convinced the more pragmatic members of the regime that the apartheid system had to be dismantled. Only subsequently did large sections of the white society acclimatize to the new reality in South Africa.

How to make the insistence on implementing the Palestinian right of return more palatable to Israeli Jews is one of the many projects that may benefit enormously from collaboration between scholars and activists. It is possible that a more detailed picture would soften resistance. In a recent book, Eitan Bronstein presents several surveys taken among the Jewish population inquiring about their positions on the right of return. It shows a clear increase in the consent among Jewish citizens in Israel to the right of return—around 30 percent of those sampled.[21] Salman Abu Sitta's work (see also his chapter in this volume), for its part, shows the possibilities of implementing the right of return without dislocating anyone in Israel.[22]

Palestinians will find it difficult to accept any section in the program that refers to the collective rights—and especially the national rights—of the Jews in a joint state:

> We, Palestinians and Israeli Jews alike, have therefore revived the one-state idea. Although possible different models range from bi-national to liberal, secular and democratic state, we are united in our commitment to the establishment of a single democratic state in all of historic [sic] Palestine.

Those involved in authoring the program hoped that the following way of articulating the national rights of the Jewish community in a one state, always a thorny issue in the eyes of many Palestinians, would help to allay Palestinian apprehensions:

> This Constitution will also protect collective rights and the freedom of association, whether national, ethnic, religious, class—or gender—based. Constitutional guarantees will ensure that all languages, arts and culture can flourish and develop freely. No group or collectivity will have any privileges, nor will any group, party or collectivity have the ability to leverage any control or domination over others. Parliament will not have the authority to enact any laws that discriminate against any community under the Constitution.

Thus, the collective national or ethnic identity of the original settler community can be maintained, but not on the basis of a privileged structure. This is closely connected to the question of future Jewish immigration, which is privileged and exclusive in the present regime of Israel. The program calls for a neutral policy of immigration, exempting the right of return. The program states that "normal procedures of obtaining citizenship will be extended to those willing to immigrate to the country." I suspect this balance between Jewish immigration and Palestinian return will undergo several rounds of revision if ever this program, or one similar to it, is seriously considered politically. Although it would be a huge challenge for Zionist Jews to give up the Law of Return and accept the right of return, it is very difficult to see how Palestinians would be willing to equate preferential immigration status to Jews around the world with the right of people who were expelled to return.

The future of such an initiative depends much on its ability to be sold as a practical, and not a utopian, political program. The translation of the program into a practical way forward can be done in the future by academics. There are today a large number of postgraduate programs focusing on Palestine, and quite a few of the doctoral dissertations produced there already cover the practical aspects of statehood. Some areas have not as yet been researched by scholars, such as the future constitution and the educational curricula of such a state. Other topics can be examined, such as the mechanisms of restitutive justice, the issue of compensation and return, and so forth.

Conclusion

In December 2018, the Israeli Knesset passed the Nationality Law, which recognizes only one nation within the undefined borders of the State of Israel. The law introduces two terms: one is the State of Israel (Medinat Israel), and the other is the Land of Israel (Eretz Israel). The latter refers to all the territory west of the River Jordan. The law declares that "the state regards the development of the Jewish Settlement [*Hityashvut*] a national value and would act toward expanding and consolidating it." Although it does not specify where these Jewish settlement projects would be expanded and consolidated, the law clearly implies that this would occur on the West Bank. Thus, in essence, the law is committed to expanding the "State of Israel" into "the Land of Israel."[23]

Both this law and Benjamin Netanyahu's commitment on the eve of the April 2019 elections to officially annex parts of the West Bank are indicators of the institutionalization of the one, nondemocratic state over the whole of historical Palestine. These developments continue what Oren Yiftachel recently termed "incremental apartheid." This is a valid analysis that describes the institutionalization of an apartheid state that can only be challenged through decolonization and not through partition (as the Bantustans—the South African autonomous kingdom established by the apartheid regime—did not serve as an alternative to apartheid South Africa).[24]

In the near future, the process of "incremental apartheid" will be accelerated by governmental legislation and policies on the ground, benefiting from ineffective global condemnation.

In the field of knowledge production, we will quite surely see the further application of the settler colonial paradigm to the Palestine case, along with more active, and younger, scholarship on Palestine taking the form of cultural resistance. Antonio Gramsci remarked once that cultural resistance is either the substitute for political action by the feeble or a grand rehearsal for political resistance.[25] Time will tell which of the two definitions is relevant to this case.

Finally, let me make two remarks about the future. First, it is noteworthy that decolonization cannot be a project of the colonizer, but that of the colonized. For decades, the so-called "peace process" was made up exclusively of Israeli initiatives. Decolonization is first and foremost a Palestinian initiative, which has not been attempted for a while. Secondly, decolonization can also be carried out from below. The hallmark of settler colonialism on the ground is segregation, whose antithesis is desegregation. This has recently happened on a small scale in towns that were built exclusively for Jews but are now binational, in joined schools operating despite a segregated educational system, and in joint workplaces and shopping malls. The imbalance of power is still evident in these locations, but it enhances a desegregated culture that can be transformed into a decolonized one in the future.

Professor Ilan Pappé was born in Haifa in 1954. He received his BA from the Hebrew University in Jerusalem (1979) and his DPhil from the University of Oxford (1984). Pappé taught at the University of Haifa in Israel until 2007. He is currently the director of the European Centre for Palestine Studies at the University of Exeter, UK. Pappé has written twenty books, among them *The Ethnic Cleansing of Palestine* (2007) and, most recently, *The Biggest Prison on Earth: A History of the Israeli Occupation* (2019).

Notes

1. On the emergence of nation-states after World War I, see Omer Bartov and Eric D. Weitz, eds., *Shatterzone of Empires: Coexistence and Violence in the German, Habsburg, Russian, and Ottoman Borderlands* (Bloomington: Indiana University Press, 2013).
2. On settler colonialism in Mexico see Rosaura Sánchez and Beatrice Pita, "Rethinking Settler Colonialism," *American Quarterly* 66, no. 4 (2014): 1039–55. On settler colonialism in Canada, see Adam J. Barker, "The Contemporary Reality of Canadian Imperialism: Settler Colonialism and the Hybrid Colonial State," *American Indian Quarterly* 33, no. 3 (2009): 325–35. There are a large number of publications on settler colonialism in Australia; I suggest consulting the Australian Historical Association website entry on the topic and the recommended literature there. As for settler colonialism in the United States, a basic and excellent book is Walter L. Hixon, *American Settler Colonialism: A History* (New York: Palgrave Macmillan, 2013).
3. Probably the best known among them is Lorenzo Veracini, *Israel and Settler Society* (London: Pluto Press, 2006).
4. On this pendulum, see Ilan Pappé, "Introduction: New Historiographical Orientation in the Research on the Palestine Question," in *The Israel/Palestine Question: A Reader*, ed. Ilan Pappé (London and New York: Routledge, 2007), 1–9.
5. Some of their works appear in the journal *Settler Colonial Studies*, in particular the issues (two of them so far) devoted to Palestine. See "Past Is Present: Settler Colonialism in Palestine," ed. Omar Jabary

Salamanca et al., *Settler Colonial Studies* 2, no. 1 (2012); and "Collaborative Struggle in Australia and Israel/Palestine," ed. Marcelo Svirsky, *Settler Colonial Studies* 4, no. 4 (2015). See also "Special Issue on Settler Colonialism in Palestine," ed. Francesco Amoruso et al., *Intervention*s: *International Journal of Post-Colonial Studies* 21, no. 4 (2019).

6. See the reference in note 11 for the demographics of young Palestinians.
7. Cherine Hussein, *The Re-emergence of the Single State Solution in Palestine/Israel* (London and New York: Routledge, 2015).
8. See discussion about this dictionary and further examples of possible entries in Noam Chomsky and Ilan Pappé, *On Palestine* (London: Penguin, 2015), 1–10.
9. See, for instance, David M. Halbfinger, "As a 2-State Solution Loses Steam, a 1-State Plan Gains Traction," *New York Times*, 5 January 2018, https://www.nytimes.com/2018/01/05/world/middleeast/israel-palestinians-state.html.
10. Ilan Pappé, "The Making and Unmaking of HADASH," in *Rebels against Zion: Studies on the Jewish Left*, ed. August Grabski (Warsaw: Jewish Historical Institute, 2011), 254–58.
11. Albert Memmi, *The Colonizer and the Colonized*, trans. Howard Greenfeld, 3rd ed. (London: Earthscan, 2003), 83.
12. Memmi, *The Colonizer and the Colonized*.
13. Youssef Courbag et al., *Palestine 2030—Demographic Change: Opportunities for Development* (UNFPA, December 2016), https://www.un.org/unispal/document/auto-insert-192874/.
14. See Oliver Holms and Hazem Balousha, "Time for Peaceful Resistance," *The Guardian*, 6 April 2018, https://www.theguardian.com/world/2018/apr/06/time-for-peaceful-resistance-says-gazas-new-movement.
15. World Food Program, "Gaza: A Livable Place?," https://www.wfp.org/countries/palestine; http://www.unic-eg.org/eng/?p=22516.
16. Nur Masalha, ed., *Catastrophe Remembered: Palestine, Israel and the Internal Refugees* (London: Zed Books, 2015).
17. Ilan Pappé, "Indigeneity as Cultural Resistance: Notes on the Palestinian Struggle within Twenty-First-Century Israel," *South Atlantic Quarterly* 117, no. 1 (2018): 157–17.
18. Pappé, "Indigeneity as Cultural Resistance."
19. See ODSC Facebook page, https://www.facebook.com/odsc.org/.
20. See ODSC Facebook page, https://www.facebook.com/odsc.org/.
21. Eitan Bronstein and Marza Bronsetin Eelenor, *Nakba in Hebrew* (Tel Aviv: Pardes, 2018, in Hebrew).
22. Salman Abu Sitta, "The Feasibility of the Right of Return" (ICJ and CIMEL paper, June 1997), https://prrn.mcgill.ca/research/papers/abusitta.htm.
23. See *The Book of Laws*, vol. 2743, 26 July 2018, Israeli Knesset, p. 898.
24. Oren Yiftachel, "The Dark Side of Modernism: Planning as Control of an Ethnic Minority," in *Postmodern Cities and Spaces*, ed. Sophie Watson and Katherine Gibson (Cambridge, MA: Blackwell, 1995): 216–34.
25. Antonio Gramsci, *Selections from the Prison Notebooks of Antonio Gramsci*, trans. Quintin Hoare and Geoffrey Nowell Smith (New York: International Publishers, 1971): 229–39.

Select Bibliography

Bartov, Omer, and Eric D. Weitz, eds. *Shatterzone of Empires: Coexistence and Violence in the German, Habsburg, Russian, and Ottoman Borderlands*. Bloomington: Indiana University Press, 2013.
Chomsky, Noam, and Ilan Pappé. *On Palestine*. London: Penguin, 2010.
Hixon, Walter L. *American Settler Colonialism*. New York: Palgrave Macmillan, 2013.
Hussein, Cherrine. *The Re-emergence of the Single State Solution in Palestine/Israel*. London and New York: Routledge, 2015.
Jabary Salamanca, Omar, et al. "Past Is Present: Settler Colonialism in Palestine." Special Issue, *Settler Colonial Studies* 2, no. 1 (2012).

Masalha, Nur, ed. *Catastrophe Remembered: Palestine, Israel and the Internal Refugees*. London: Zed Books, 2015.
Pappé, Ilan. "Indigeneity as Cultural Resistance: Notes on the Palestinian Struggle within Twenty-First-Century Israel." *South Atlantic Quarterly* 117, no. 1 (January 2018): 157–77.
"Settler Colonialism in Australia." Australian Historical Association. https://www.theaha.org.au/tag/settler-colonialism/.
Svirsky, Marcelo ed. "Collaborative Struggle in Australia and Israel/Palestine." Special issue, *Settler Colonial Studies* 4, no. 4 (2015).
Veracini, Lorenzo. *Israel and Settler Society*. London: Pluto 2006.

CHAPTER 16

What Would a Decolonized Archaeology of Israel-Palestine Look Like?

Raphael Greenberg

Introduction

While it is virtually a commonplace that the archaeology of Palestine, and later Israel, has been implicated in colonialist and nationalist enterprises, its ongoing importance in perceptions of the present and future of the region is often ignored; we are asked to forget the past and move on, in the spirit of the modernist and late capitalist project that foregrounds development (at the expense of preservation), mobility (at the expense of attachment to place), and commodified nostalgia (at the expense of history). In response to the caricature of archaeology that is often recruited in the service of national and religious agendas and to the neutered archaeology that is expected to provide fodder for the tourist market, a decolonized archaeology can offer a contemporary sense of continuity and a shared appreciation of the unique relationship between communities and their landscape in the deep history of Israel-Palestine. It recognizes that people—even in "modern" states—do not want to live in a sterile environment or to be deprived of the intimate relation between identity, place, and collective memory. This chapter will thus suggest accepting the distant and recent past as a player in the future accommodation between and shared existence of diverse communities, without giving it a bully pulpit.

Archaeology between East and West

Archaeology—or at least a significant part of the archaeological community—has been engaged in a decades-long struggle to escape its imperial and colonial past, a struggle that began with the recognition of its suppressed origins and continued with the establishment of explicitly postcolonial institutions (such as the World Archaeological Congress), legal instruments (such as the US Native American Graves Protection and Repatriation Act), and professional practices (such as collaborative community archaeological projects and exhibits).[1] The bulk of these efforts have, however, been conducted in the context of classic colonial encounters, where "pre-contact" and "contact" phases are clearly demarcated, and where Western epistemologies of modernity can be starkly contrasted with alternative indigenous (or Indigenous) values and modes of knowledge.[2] In pre-1948 Palestine and post-1948 Palestine-Israel (and, to some extent, Jordan), where colonialism itself has mutated from imperial-colonial to crypto-colonial and settler colonial projects, the locus and content of archaeological passions and their cultural-political connotations—and indeed, the very identity of the standard-bearers of archaeological activity—have also shifted.[3] Late nineteenth-century archaeological "pioneers" tasked themselves with the responsibility of bringing progress to the "immovable" East,[4] while retrieving the "birthright and sacred legacy" of European civilization.[5] The British Mandate promoted modern statehood by separating the present from the past through its bureaucratic definition and the "opening up" of Palestine to "scientific" excavation.[6] And the Zionist and, later, Israeli settlement project and state organs have alternated between seeing archaeology as an impediment to progress and development,[7] exploiting it as a magnet for tourists and as a prop for consumable images of antiquity,[8] promoting the scientific, secular values associated with Western archaeology,[9] and promoting archaeology as an instrument of the Jewish nation-state project.[10] Palestinian and Jordanian postcolonial institutions, for their part, have often adopted colonial legislation and value systems, attaching merit to archaeology either within a universalizing neoliberal economic discourse ("UNESCOization") or as part of an internal national narrative (however, see below on nongovernmental avenues of Palestinian heritage work).[11] Each of these uses of archaeology in Israel and Palestine finds its place in a different vein of colonial discourse (e.g., rescuing the remains of "great civilizations" from indigenes in imperial colonialism, serving as a locally sourced proxy for the construction of Western supremacy in crypto-colonialism, engaging in contract work for tourist development in economic colonialism, or excluding Palestinians from history in settler colonialism), allowing archaeologists to misrecognize their role in upholding the structural inequalities of the current local and global political and moral economy, while gleefully tarring their counterparts with accusations of bias and misplaced ideology.

In further contrast to Western and Southern Hemisphere colonialism, the concept of a "precontact" phase has very different implications in the Mediterranean/

West Asian theater, where east-west and north-south human interaction and movement are constant and normal, rather than remarkable, and where no pristine "European" versus "Indigenous" value systems can be posited. This is not to say that the modern Western effort to colonize the Levant (either directly or by proxy) did not employ or co-opt archaeology, but that archaeology does not necessarily reside entirely on one side of the divide, whether as a way of knowing the past or as a way of valuing its remains. On the contrary, numerous texts and oral traditions attest to long-standing—and indeed quite ancient—conceptions regarding the landscape as a palimpsest of past civilizations and of the existence of ancient peoples, migrations, and prior cultures. These include, for example, a strong interest evinced by Sumerian and later Mesopotamian kings in the continuity of temples built on the same spot since time immemorial or the Babylonian king Nabonidus's extraordinary interest in excavating buildings and inscriptions of earlier rulers.[12] Ibn Khaldun makes frequent reference to ancient structures and their possible function in his compendium of fourteenth-century historical knowledge the *Muqaddimah*, although his low opinion of "archaeologists" of his time reflects a fundamental intellectual distrust that was likely to have been widely shared in learned circles and may still resonate today:

> It should be known that many weak-minded persons in cities hope to discover property under the surface of the earth and to make some profit from it. They believe that all the property of the nations of the past was stored underground and sealed with magic talismans. . . . They approach well-to-do people with papers that have torn margins and contain either non-Arab writing or what they claim to be the translation of a document written by the owner of buried treasures, giving the clue to the hiding place. In this way, they try to get their sustenance by (persuading well-to-do people) to send them out to dig and hunt for treasure.[13]

In late Ottoman Palestine, official and local Arab interest in systematic archaeology was on the rise, reflected both in official policy and among the local intelligentsia.[14] But those engaged in its implementation, as noted by Dotan Halevy, were cognizant of the timeless cycle of ruination and rebuilding that permitted the redeployment of ancient materials in new structures. It was only under the British Mandate that bureaucratic separation of past from present—through the definition of "antiquities" as part of a broader program of social and ethnic compartmentalization—took on the clear outlines of colonial imposition, deeply embedded in the concept of modernity itself, and began to acquire the lineaments of "negative heritage" for Palestinians.[15] Archaeological "excavation houses" and archaeologists were targeted as early as the Palestinian uprising of 1936–39,[16] and archaeological finds are increasingly seen by Palestinians as weaponized relics.[17] Archaeology, as a methodical way of recovering (or recollecting) evidence of past lives and peoples, need not be viewed, therefore, as *inherently* antagonistic to non-Western or non-Zionist value systems in Palestine. But if it is to serve an emancipatory purpose, that is, liberating Israelis and

Palestinians from reductive religious and historical determinisms and demonstrating alternative perceptions of the past anchored in local tradition,[18] it must be itself freed from a good deal of its current ideological baggage. It is conceivable that where decolonization has been achieved, common ground can be found between currently antagonistic modern communities, based on non-colonial modes of defining the "common good" and of preserving, retrieving, interpreting, and presenting the material traces of the past. A decolonized archaeology can offer a true sense of continuity and a shared appreciation of the unique relationship between communities and their landscape in the deep history of Israel-Palestine. By accepting the need to protect the physical fabric of the past from complete annihilation by the destructive practices of the present, it recognizes that people do not want to live in a sterile environment or to be deprived of the intimate links between identity, place, and collective memory.

Dismantling Old Structures

Given the complex history of and the accretion of contradictory values by the archaeology practiced in Palestine (and later, in Israel and neighboring countries), the decolonization of archaeology cannot consist of the complete undoing or rejection of archaeological knowledge and institutional structures; such a reactionary response would most likely result in widespread destruction of cultural heritage.[19] Rather, decolonization should comprise a retooling of archaeology in a way that dismantles structural inequality, dispossession, and injustice and offers room for "alternatives to colonialist constructions of time, place and narrative."[20] Such a retooling has been initiated by Palestinian archaeologists and heritage professionals in nongovernmental institutions and organizations[21] but has not yet been taken up fully even by the Palestinian Authority,[22] let alone by Israeli or Western archaeologists working in the region. This may be explained only partly by the professed allegiances, national or cultural, of the individuals and institutions concerned; the nature of the overlapping colonialisms at work in the modern polities of Israel and Palestine conspires to disguise their hold on archaeological practice.

To decolonize archaeology in Israel-Palestine, archaeologists must recognize the ideological structures implicated in both overt (imperial or settler) and disguised (crypto-) colonial projects. These include not only the obvious discursive elements—such as the focus by most Israeli and Western archaeologists on periods and cultures viewed as "formative" for "Judeo-Christian civilization" or the characterization of cultures in terms of progressive technological or political evolution (placing Western modernity at the most evolved pole)—but the more insidious nondiscursive assumptions ingrained in archaeological practices and in the global hegemonic structures. The latter include the assumptions that archaeologists are uniquely privileged and legally empowered to interpret past places, that archaeological excavation is a value-neutral technical procedure, and that the more technologically advanced a procedure is, the more objective and value-free it must be, so that the best archaeology is that which is the most technologically endowed (thus ensuring a Western/global northern stranglehold on "acceptable" archaeological interpretation). Other unstated assumptions relate to the tacit acceptance of neoliberal economic policies that govern the funding of archaeological work, the inevitability of existing inequality, and the unquestioned merit of the global edifice of academic capital that invests leading anglophone universities, publications, and professors, as well as big labs, with ultimate authority and powers of arbitration, thus perpetuating the received wisdom on what is "worthwhile," "robust," and "serious," and ensuring the reproduction of the existing hegemony in local academic and institutional archaeology.

In terms of settler colonialism, where the incoming group envisions itself as ultimately replacing the pre-existing population, a decolonized archaeology would consciously move away from those aspects of archaeology and colonialism in Israel and Palestine that seek to minimize or erase the history of people and communities, that naturalize inequality and innate privilege, that value one history over another, and that promote injustice and exploitation. In terms of crypto-colonialism, where even indigenous actors are co-opted as defenders of Western values and interests, a decolonized archaeology must diminish its dependence on outside schemes of value. To this end, several structural changes in the discipline should be effected, wherever it is taught and practiced.

- Archaeology should encompass the entire range of past human existence. This implies not only the removal of the 1700 CE threshold imposed by the 1929 Mandatory Law of Antiquities and its Israeli (1978) and Jordanian (1988) successors, as already proposed by Palestinian heritage organizations, but the conceptual removal (at the source; i.e., in university curricula) of any temporal threshold for significant archaeological work. Archaeologists may define the archaeological as anything that has been buried[23] or, as I would suggest, anything that has been forgotten. Where bureaucratic definitions are required (as in the determination of sites, places, structures, or features to be protected from development), they can be linked to local institutional definitions of heritage and to accepted practices of public consultation.
- Archaeology must be decoupled from the historical, social-evolutionary, and clerical paradigms in which it was engendered in the nineteenth and twentieth centuries and emerge as an independent, critical discipline. This requires not only that academic training be clearly separated from biblical (Old Testament) and theological disciplines (as suggested long ago by "new" anthropologically oriented archaeologists of the 1970s and 1980s), but that seemingly neutral concepts such as "prehistoric," "Classical," or "Islamic" archaeology—all of which carry an enormous weight of colonial baggage—be abandoned. These divisions seem to be set in stone,[24] yet only by cutting loose from them and establishing new terms of reference will the necessary independence of the discipline

be accomplished. Critical historical surveys of the field should be a standard requirement, as should discussions of archaeological and scientific ethics and politics; ideologies must be made visible.
- Archaeologists must avoid the facile use of religio-ethnic categories for sites and finds. The atomization of society through its division into myriad identity groups was historically an effective political tool wielded by empires, not least in Palestine,[25] and currently tends to serve the ends of neoliberal economics and politics. In Israel, sites are consistently identified according to religious and ethnic categories (as if a site can "be" Jewish, Christian, Nabatean, or otherwise), and ancient finds are trotted out on appropriate dates or in appropriate settings to offer comfort and ontological security to the different identity groups (e.g., ancient Jewish coins on Independence Day; olive oil presses for Druze communities). A decolonized archaeology will not ignore cultural difference but will avoid reductionist identity branding.
- Archaeology must be grounded in negotiation with local communities and regulated (legally or professionally) in such a manner as to provide a buffer against interference by funding bodies or persons, whether they are evangelical institutions and individual donors who have historically maintained a strong presence in "Holy Land" archaeology, militant organizations (settlers, in the Israeli context) who have weaponized archaeology to serve nationalist ends, clerical institutions associated with the three major religions, or governmental institutions, local or national, bent on co-opting the past for political gain.
- A serious commitment must be made to escape the compartmentalization of archaeology as a middle-class diversion. This requires social (and, in Israel, ethnic) diversification in academic departments, including faculty and students, and a commitment to the politics of inclusion.

Redefining the Field

An archaeology of Israel and Palestine that has escaped the temporal and epistemic constraints of biblical and historical settings, distanced itself from exclusionary political and religious ideologies, recognized the complexities of identity, consistently engaged with local stakeholders, and diversified its community of practice will obviously be a discipline far removed from the one in which the present generation of archaeologists, myself included, have been trained and in which we participate. The following attempt to imagine the themes and practicalities of a decolonized archaeology is therefore offered only as an initial exploration, within the obvious limitations of my experience.

As a preliminary caveat I wish to suggest that even if we were to successfully weed out the manifold expressions of colonialism in archaeological practice—expressions that color almost every aspect of its activity—a disciplinary core would have to be maintained: a defensible and reproducible method of bringing traces of the past into the present and interpreting them. The disciplinary basis for a decolonized archaeology should probably be sought in the practices and performances that produce the "finds" and "contexts" that compose the "archaeological record": an assemblage of artifacts, texts, and images representing buried or forgotten things that have been reintroduced into the present and offer themselves to interpretation. These performative acts are governed by a set of largely arbitrary rules—such as those determining the layout of an excavation; the tools used for excavation and measurement; the conventions used to represent structures, deposits, and finds—and hence take on the character of empty signifiers. That is, the practices do not impose meaning by the mere fact of their existence. Rather, they are used by archaeologists to craft narratives in accordance with their broader aims.[26] The existence of such "pointless" practices (such as recovering, measuring, sorting, describing, identifying, dating, and presenting) permits them to be employed to various ends, including those that can be labeled decolonizing and emancipatory.

An example of the rededication of practice through a change in ideology might be the following: The imposition of a 1700 CE threshold for the scheduling of antiquities in Palestine, imposed by the Mandate authorities, relegated later remains—including virtually the entirety of Ottoman architecture and most elements in the traditional agricultural Palestinian village landscape—to the status of "modern ruins," effectively dematerializing premodern Palestinian history and removing it from the purview of archaeological research. It is, therefore, one of the most prominent symbols of colonial antiquities policy. If this arbitrary determinant were to be shifted—or even entirely removed—no change in archaeological technique, fieldwork methods, or training would be required. Likewise, postcolonial practices such as collaborative work in local communities or multivocality in presentation of archaeological sites can be seamlessly integrated with the existing rules of archaeological engagement. And while decisions on the constitution of heritage through selective remembrance and conservation are inherently cultural and political, a decolonized archaeology affords a starting point for the presentation of a past that does not naturalize conflict and subjugation.

In a decolonized archaeology of Israel and Palestine, disciplined fieldwork and the thrill of discovery—which lie at the heart of archaeological passion—will be placed in a new conceptual setting, offering new ways of viewing the land and its heritage that could be promoted as an antidote to the current, highly partisan modes of archaeological practice. In the context of our discussion, archaeology offers a way to distance ourselves from the familiar, immediately recognizable texts and visual symbols of ideology and conflict. An archaeology, even of contemporary material culture, reassembles the local through the lens of *habitus* and practice, investigates the mundane, and can supply surprising insights by recourse to "small things forgotten" while challenging automatic assumptions and ideologies associated with the more prominent monuments of the past. Instead of merely complementing extant historical scenarios, a decolonized archaeology can retell the history of the land and its people through a focus on "matters of concern." Below I offer a few potential fields of study that deal with such matters.

An Archaeology of Social Justice

"Conflict" has long been synonymous with "the Middle East" in popular and historical perceptions, and "conflict archaeology" has been a perennial favorite in regional conferences, attaining the standing of a subdiscipline in archaeology. There is, undoubtedly, no shortage of material manifestations of conflict to be studied in a decolonized archaeological setting, whether they be the physical traces of the Nakba or the material effects of ethnic discrimination within Israeli society. But conflict is never eternal, and although humans have an innate desire to live in peace and among friends and equals, we never hear of the archaeology of peace or an archaeology of social justice. Such archaeologies might draw on anthropological and archaeological studies of inequality, which have experienced a recent surge, along with archaeologies of cooperation and collective action,[27] and may provide an excellent platform for a sustained study of the long periods of relative peace and social solidarity in the deep history of Palestine-Israel. It would be especially instructive to identify such periods in the early history of sedentary societies, given that the process of Neolithization (the domestication of economic plants, livestock, and people) may be said to have originated along the Dead Sea rift valley and is often considered ground zero for sustained social inequality and conflict. The long local history of social critique, attested frequently in the foundational literature of the three monotheistic religions, was very likely a product of a local penchant for curtailing the power of elites—a penchant with broad and deep roots.

The effect of social leveling mechanisms can be observed in the archaeological record from the beginning of sedentary settlement, while in the Early and Middle Bronze Age they may be said to constitute a peculiar characteristic of south Levantine or Canaanite polities, clearly diverging from the neighboring regions of Syro-Mesopotamia and Egypt. In fact, during most periods of self-rule, the inhabitants of Canaan and the later Iron Age kingdoms seem to have deliberately played down hierarchical power and played up that of the collective of commoners. One of the most powerful innovations of Canaanite culture—alphabetic writing—was likely invented by migrant workers in the Egyptian turquoise mines in the Sinai Peninsula, and the subsequent history of alphabetic writing shows a preponderance of personal, rather than official, texts.[28] The rules of land tenure, which prevented individuals, families, or institutions from gaining control of excessively large estates and tethered labor, can be followed archaeologically from the earliest villages to the most recent ones, with their *musha'* (collective) strategies of common ownership and redistribution. Thus, regardless of common perception, direct evidence for warfare, despotism, and interpersonal violence can be quite rare during long stretches of antiquity, and a better understanding of the structures that permitted or promoted conflict resolution and social leveling and solidarity is long overdue.

Archaeology and the Agency of Landscape

Archaeologists, whether of periods as early as deep prehistory or as late as the contemporary past, often view the landscape as a resource for human subsistence and as a setting for the exercise of political and military power. There are, however, important alternative approaches that imbue landscape with agency.[29] Studies of the agency of landscape focus on the way it shapes human experience and memories. Often, landscapes or landmarks appear to have an identity, spirit, or even a will of their own, making them symmetrical actors with the people who move through them. Thus, landmarks and other features will be named; they will allow or prevent access; they will afford contact with the supernatural. Indeed, the land itself may judge, reward, or afflict those who tread on it.

While the agency of the "Promised" or "Holy" Land, reflected in myriad texts and traditions, requires no special pleading, its impact on the daily lives of people living in the land—rather than those imagining it, pining for it at a distance, or coming to it as pilgrims[30]—has attracted far less interest. Using the wealth of textual allusions as well as ethnographies describing the personification of natural features in Palestine,[31] archaeologists may compare contemporary or historically recorded human interaction with features in the natural world (e.g., alterations made in them, gifts offered to them, representations or replicas made of them) to archaeological evidence of possibly similar practices. Studies of this kind are relatively rare, perhaps because of modern scientific reticence regarding "irrational" behavior and a supposed absence of "hard evidence" that can be brought to the archaeological court of law. But they should be pursued as part of the decolonization project, which should turn its gaze from the history of outside engagement with the land to that of local communities.

Past Places of Memory

Sometimes termed "the past in the past," the study of past people's interpretation of the palimpsest of landmarks, ruins, and other traces of earlier existence is a corrective to our solipsistic tendency to view our own times and interests as novel, unique, or singular.[32] People of the ancient and recent past never really considered themselves as eternal or present from time immemorial. They were surrounded by a cultured landscape, that is, a land transformed by untold generations of human activity that left traces in the form of ruins, field fences and terraces, tombs and cemeteries, megaliths and standing stones, wells, dams, and irrigation channels, shrines and caves. These places were given names, attached to stories and to historical figures, mined for mementos, and generally used as resources. As one of the densest archaeological landscapes in the world, characterized by numerous mounded sites (tells) that, by definition, are palimpsests of human settlements, the interplay of place and memory within Palestine and Israel deserves close attention. Attending to "the past in the past" reminds archaeologists that they are merely the latest in a chain of scavengers, conjurers, and storytellers who extract value from the past and can relieve archaeology of some of the baggage with which it is often saddled.

Migration, Colonization and Identity: Being "In" and Becoming "Of"

Ever since groups of Homo Erectus first made their way up the Rift Valley, the Levant has been a target of colonizers and migrants. In recent years, the study of migrations, diasporas, internal and external boundaries, and cultural transmission and negotiation have proliferated, in line with almost universal anxieties about globalization and the permeability of borders.[33] The archaeology of migrations and border zones, whether prehistoric and surmised or historical and recorded in detail, often undermines popular notions of fixity, of boundedness, and of exclusion. "Obvious" physical boundaries (such as the Jordan River) are found to be ephemeral, "essential" ethnic differences (e.g., between "Egyptians" and "Semites") are found to be blurred, and "eternal" enmities (e.g., between medieval Franks and Muslims) are found to be subverted by the nature of everyday contact.

In the context of such studies, it would be particularly interesting to gain a perspective on the tipping point between being an expatriate or diasporic group *in* a "foreign" place and becoming *of* a place.[34] In a region that has never known fixed boundaries, nor a time during which people were not on the move, what *in the world* (i.e., not in the mind) makes someone "indigenous"? Continued study of these issues is clearly relevant to the essentialist reduction of ethnicities and naturalization of conflict that aim to keep history at a standstill in the "troubled Middle East," questioning the fixed nature of local identities.[35]

Each of the themes described above resonates with central concerns of the people living in Israel-Palestine, while challenging "common knowledge" by means of an independent research agenda. Without shying away from political relevancy, archaeologists can offer a fresh view of the past *from* the past—a view that can help redefine the meaning of locality and belonging in a postcolonial world. While not ensuring freedom from colonial structures embedded in the structure of the academic and scientific worlds, pursuing these themes can counter the evisceration of archaeology by the deterministic and mechanistic tendencies of "big data" and "big-science," establishing its relevancy as a human science.

Conclusion: Conditions for a Decolonized Archaeology

The challenge of decolonizing archaeology, decoupling it from its historical missions in the service of modernism, nationalism, Western appropriation of the Eastern "birthplace of civilization," and of course the central myths of the "Judeo-Christian" world is crucial to its ultimate survival as a viable avenue for shared understandings of the past in Israel-Palestine. It is the only way out of the zero-sum game of agonistic pasts, in which each side wills the other to disappear. The themes, suggested above, along which a decolonized discipline might coalesce are sufficiently broad, sufficiently cogent, and sufficiently attuned both to contemporary interest and to the archaeological potential of the land to provide a firm basis for the growth and continued relevance of the discipline. They do, however, require a radical transformation of academic practices, not only in Israel and the West, but in Palestine (and Jordan) as well, moving away from true and tried cultural-historical narratives (not to mention foundational myths) to a more independent—and exposed—position. Can such an archaeology be sufficiently viable and relevant to the people in Palestine-Israel to withstand the powerful combined forces of religious and nationalist fundamentalism (selective remembering) and unbridled growth and globalized "development" (intentional forgetting)? Is the approach to material heritage that fosters inclusion, rather than exclusion, a sustainable one? I see this as a central concern of the archaeological discipline, but one with implications for broader questions of heritage, memory, identity, and cultural survival. Although many archaeologists are extremely wary of being "political," it is a discussion that can no longer be postponed.

Barring a dramatic shift in global priorities and a reversal of the antidemocratic, authoritarian tide that has swept across the globe, decolonized archaeology will not become public policy in Israel or its neighboring states any time soon. It can only emerge from the bottom up, by personal example and through professional solidarity. This, I think, will eventually occur, because of the stark inequalities that are an inevitable corollary of the neoliberal/neocolonial project in academia—inequalities that will allow only a chosen few to flourish at the top while the rest languish in part-time or low-end employment—and because of the authoritarian turn in politics. It takes very little to prop up the caricature of archaeology that is often recruited in the service of national and religious agendas or the neutered archaeology that is expected to provide fodder for the tourist market. Authoritarian regimes have been historically supportive of deregulation and destructive development and suspicious of any form of intellectual curiosity and critical thinking.[36] To survive as a discipline and a profession, archaeologists will be forced to organize, to promote professional solidarity, and to broaden their public appeal. A decolonized archaeology can offer a contemporary sense of continuity and a shared appreciation of the unique relationship between communities and their landscape in the deep history of Israel-Palestine, securing both its own future and that of the heritage it aims to investigate.

Raphael Greenberg teaches archaeology at Tel Aviv University, focusing on the study of Bronze Age social formations, economies, and institutions and on the impact of archaeology in the present. He is cofounder of Emek Shaveh, a nonprofit that monitors the political role of archaeology in Jerusalem and beyond. His most recent book is *The Archaeology of the Bronze Age Levant* (Cambridge, 2000).

Notes

1. For archaeology's roots in nineteenth-century movements, see Bruce G. Trigger, "Alternative Archaeologies: Nationalist, Colonialist, Imperialist," *Man* 19, no. 3 (1984): 355–70; on the World Archaeological Congress, see Peter Ucko, *Academic Freedom and Apartheid: The Story of the World Archaeological Congress* (London: Duckworth, 1987); on legal instruments and professional practices, see, among others, Martin Nakata and Bruno David, "Archaeological Practice at the Cultural Interface," in *Handbook of Postcolonial Archaeology*, ed. Jane Lydon and Uzma Z. Rizvi (Walnut Creek, CA: Left Coast Press, 2010), 429–44; Sonya Atalay, *Community-Based Archaeology: Research with, by, and for Indigenous and Local Communities* (Berkeley: University of California Press, 2012); Gabriel Moshenska, ed., *Key Concepts in Public Archaeology* (London: UCL Press, 2017).
2. See Margaret M. Bruchac, Siobhan M. Hart, and H. Martin Wobst, eds., *Indigenous Archaeologies: A Reader on Decolonization* (Walnut Creek, CA: Lest Coast Press, 2010); Margaret M. Bruchac, "Decolonization in Archaeological Theory," in *Encyclopedia of Global Archaeology*, ed. Claire Smith (New York: Springer Reference, 2014), 2069–77.
3. Crypto-colonialism, as described by Michael Herzfeld, "The Absent Presence: Discourses of Crypto-colonialism," *South Atlantic Quarterly* 101, no. 4 (2002): 899–926, refers to the use of national projects as proxies for Western dominance, disguised as shared norms and interests; such nations are maintained by massive support from the West but remain a periphery in its eyes. Israel is also characterized as a settler colony with a stated or unstated agenda of displacing the previous Palestinian population and as a project of national self-determination; see Patrick Wolfe, *Settler Colonialism and the Transformation of Anthropology: The Politics and Poetics of an Ethnographic Event* (London: Casell, 1999); Lorenzo Veracini, *Israel and Settler Society* (London and Ann Arbor: Pluto Press, 2006); Lorenzo Veracini, "Introducing: Settler Colonial Studies," *Settler Colonial Studies* 1, no. 1 (2011): 1–12; Rachel Busbridge, "Israel-Palestine and the Settler Colonial 'Turn': From Interpretation to Decolonization," *Theory, Culture & Society* 35, no. 1 (2018): 91–115.
4. Philip J. Baldensperger, *The Immovable East: Studies of the People and Customs of Palestine*, ed. Frederic Lees (London: Sir I. Pitman & Sons, 1913).
5. James Henry Breasted, cited in *Pioneers to the Past: American Archaeologists in the Middle East, 1919–1920*, ed. Geoff Emberling (Chicago: Oriental Institute of the University of Chicago, 2010), 115.
6. Nadia Abu El-Haj, "Producing (Arti) Facts: Archaeology and Power During the British Mandate of Palestine," *Israel Studies* 7, no. 2 (2002): 33–61; Dotan Halevy, "Ottoman Ruins Captured: Antiquities, Preservation, and Waqf in Mandatory Palestine," *Journal of the Ottoman and Turkish Studies Association* 5, no. 1 (2018): 91–114; Raphael Greenberg, "150 Years of Archaeology and Controversy in Jerusalem," in *The Routledge Handbook on Jerusalem*, ed. Suleiman A. Mourad, Naomi Koltun-Fromm, and Bedross Der Matossian (New York and London: Taylor and Francis, 2018), 363–76.
7. Raz Kletter, *Just Past? The Making of Israeli Archaeology* (London: Equinox, 2006).
8. Uzi Baram "Appropriating the Past: Heritage, Tourism, and Archaeology in Israel," in *Selective Remembrances: Archaeology in the Construction, Commemoration, and Consecration of National Pasts*, ed. Philip L. Kohl, Mara Kozelsky, and Nachman Ben-Yehuda (Chicago: University of Chicago Press, 2007), 299–325.
9. Rachel S. Hallote and Alexander H. Joffe, "The Politics of Israeli Archaeology: Between "Nationalism" and "Science" in the Age of the Second Republic," *Israel Studies* 7, no. 3 (2003): 84–116.
10. Asher N. Silberman and David B. Small, *The Archaeology of Israel: Constructing the Past, Interpreting the Present* (London: Bloomsbury Publishing, 1997); Nadia Abu El-Haj, *Facts on the Ground: Archaeological Practice and Territorial Self-Fashioning in Israeli Society* (Chicago: University of Chicago Press,

2001); Maria Theresia Starzmann, "Occupying the Past: Colonial Rule and Archaeological Practice in Israel/Palestine," *Archaeologies* 9, no. 3 (2013): 546–71.
11. Elena Corbett, "Hashemite Antiquity and Modernity: Iconography in Neoliberal Jordan," *Studies in Ethnicity and Nationalism* 11, no. 2 (2011): 163–93; Elena Dodge Corbett, *Competitive Archaeology in Jordan: Narrating Identity from the Ottomans to the Hashemites* (Austin: University of Texas Press, 2014); Khaldun Bshara, "Heritage in Palestine: Colonial Legacy in Postcolonial Discourse," *Archaeologies* 9, no. 2 (2013): 295–319.
12. Pinhas Delougaz and Seton Lloyd, *Pre-Sargonid Temples in the Diyala Region* (Chicago: University of Chicago Press, 1942), 21; Harold D. Hill, Thorkild Jacobsen, and Pinhas Delougaz, *Old Babylonian Public Buildings in the Diyala Region: Excavations at Ishchali* (Chicago: Oriental Institute of the University of Chicago, 1990), 26–28, 61–64; Giulia Francesca Grassi, "Nabonidus, King of Babylon," *Middle East—Topics and Arguments* 3 (2014): 125–35.
13. Ibn Khaldun, *Muqaddimah* V, 4.
14. Halevy, "Ottoman Ruins"; Dotan Halevy, "Toward a Palestinian History of Ruins: Interwar Gaza," *Journal of Palestine Studies* 48, no. 1 (2018): 53–72; Khalil al-Sakakini, *Kazeh ani, rabotai: Mi-yomano shel Khalil al-Sakakini* [This is how I am, sir: Excerpts from the diary of Khalil al-Sakakini], trans. Gideon Shilo, 2nd ed. (Tel Aviv: Tzivonim, 2007, originally published in Arabic as *Katha ana, ya dunya*, ed. Hala al-Sakakini), 41; Salim Tamari, "Lepers, Lunatics and Saints: The Nativist Ethnography of Tawfiq Canaan and His Jerusalem Circle," *Mountain against the Sea: Essays on Palestinian Society and Culture* (Berkeley: University of California Press, 2009); Nadim Bawalsa, "Unpacking the Modern National Self: The Diary of Khalil al-Sakakini" (MA thesis, Georgetown University, 2010); Thomas M. Ricks, "Arab Jerusalem in the Age of Modernity and Empire: Oral Histories of a Palestinian City, Its Schools, and Childhood Days, 1907 to 1987," in *Reclaiming the Past for the Future: Oral History, Craft and Archaeology–Adel Yahya in Memoriam*, ed. Reinhard Bernbeck, Arwa Badran, and Susan Pollock (Berlin: Ex Oriente, 2018), 169–206.
15. The term "negative heritage" was coined by Lynn Meskell, "Negative Heritage and Past Mastering in Archaeology," *Anthropological Quarterly* 75, no. 3 (2002): 557–74, to indicate sites that carry negative connotations in the collective imaginary. See also Sandra A. Scham and Ann E. Killebrew, "Many More Rivers to Cross: Experiments in Shared Heritage," in Bernbeck, Badran, and Pollock, *Reclaiming the Past for the Future*, 95–108.
16. Tali Erickson-Gini and Ami Oach, "The Es Sbaita (Shivta) Visitors Book, 1934–1937: Negev Archaeology in British Mandate Palestine," *Michmanim* 28 (2019): 9*–22*.
17. Albert Glock, "Archaeology as Cultural Survival: The Future of the Palestinian Past," *Journal of Palestine Studies* 23, no. 3 (1994):70–84. See also "The Old City," survey results, *Emek Shaveh*, 21 September 2016, https://alt-arch.org/en/survery-shows-palestinian-residents-of-east-jerusalem-experience-the-archaeological-activities-as-a-tool-to-undermine-jerusalems-national-and-religious-identity/.
18. See, e.g., Walter Mignolo, "Epistemic Disobedience and the Decolonial Option: A Manifesto," *Transmodernity: Journal of Peripheral Cultural Production of the Luso-Hispanic World* 1, no. 2 (2011): 44–66.
19. Salah Hussein Al-Houdalieh, "Khirbet el-Lauz Revisited: Lessons from the Renewed Destruction of a Vulnerable Heritage Site," *Near Eastern Archaeology* 81, no. 4 (2018): 244–49.
20. Bruchac, "Decolonization."
21. E.g., Glock, "Cultural Survival"; Ghada Ziadeh-Seely "An Archaeology of Palestine: Mourning a Dream," in Kohl, Kozelsky, and Ben-Yehuda, *Selective Remembrances*, 326–45; Chiara de Cesari, "Heritage by NGOs in Palestine: Toward a Grassroots Politics of the Past?," in Bernbeck, Badran, and Pollock, *Reclaiming the Past for the Future*, 149–65; Nazmi Jubeh, "Cultural Heritage in Palestine: Challenges and Opportunities," in Bernbeck, Badran, and Pollock, *Reclaiming the Past for the Future*, 67–94.
22. Bshara, "Heritage in Palestine."
23. Assaf Nativ, "No Compensation Needed: On Archaeology and the Archaeological," *Journal of Archaeological Method and Theory* 24 (2017): 659–75.

24. They were, in fact, established by a committee convened in 1922, consisting of archaeological representatives of the victorious empires of World War I—Britain, France, and the United States: John Garstang et al., "A New Chronological Classification of Palestinian Archaeology," *Bulletin of the American Schools of Oriental Research* 7, no. 7 (1922): 9.
25. "The British strategy of distinguishing between the communities and organizing them according to religious-based lines signals, I argue, the end of the period in which fluid forms of identity were still possible." Abigail Jacobson, *From Empire to Empire: Jerusalem between Ottoman and British Rule* (Syracuse, NY: Syracuse University Press, 2011), 19.
26. Michal Shanks and Randall H. McGuire, "The Craft of Archaeology," *American Antiquity* 61, no. 1 (1996): 75–88.
27. E.g., David M. Carballo, ed., *Cooperation and Collective Action: Archaeological Perspectives* (Boulder: University Press of Colorado, 2013); David Wengrow and David Graeber, "Farewell to the 'Childhood of Man': Ritual, Seasonality, and the Origins of Inequality," *Journal of the Royal Anthropological Institute* 21, no. 3 (2015): 597–619; Charles Stanish, *The Evolution of Human Cooperation: Ritual and Social Complexity in Stateless Societies* (Cambridge and New York: Cambridge University Press, 2017).
28. Orly Goldwasser, "The Advantage of Cultural Periphery: The Invention of the Alphabet in Sinai (circa 1840 B.C.E)," in *Culture Contacts and the Making of Cultures: Papers in Homage to Itamar Even-Zohar*, ed. Rakefet Sela-Sheffy and Gideon Toury (Tel Aviv: Tel Aviv University, 2011), 251–316; Orly Goldwasser, "The Miners Who Invented the Alphabet—A Response to Christopher Rollston," *Journal of Ancient Egyptian Interconnections* 4, no. 3 (2012): 9–22.
29. Richard Muir, *Approaches to Landscape* (London: Macmillan, 1999); Bruno David and Julian Thomas, eds., *Handbook of Landscape Archaeology* (London and New York: Routledge, 2008).
30. For the physical and emotional impact of the land on those who visit it in a religiously receptive frame of mind, see, e.g., Hillary Kaell, *Walking Where Jesus Walked: American Christians and Holy Land Pilgrimage* (New York: New York University Press, 2014); or Beverly Butler, "The Efficacies of Heritage: Syndromes, Magics, and Possessional Acts," *Public Archaeology* 15, no. 2–3 (2016): 113–35.
31. Tawfiq Canaan, *Haunted Springs and Water-Demons in Palestine* (Jerusalem: Palestine Oriental Society, 1922); Tawfiq Canaan, *Mohammedan Saints and Sanctuaries in Palestine* (London: Luzac, 1927); Tamari, "Lepers, Lunatics and Saints."
32. Richard Bradley and Howard Williams, eds., "The Past in the Past: The Reuse of Ancient Monuments," Topical Issue, *World Archaeology* 30, no. 1 (1998); Gavin Lucas, *The Archaeology of Time* (London and New York: Routledge, 2005); Andrew Jones, *Memory and Material Culture* (Cambridge: Cambridge University Press, 2007); Raphael Greenberg, "The Afterlife of Tells," in *Proceedings of the 2nd International Congress on the Archaeology of the Ancient Near East, 22–26 May 2000, Copenhagen*, ed. Ingols Thuesen (Bologna: Department of History and Cultures, University of Bologna / Einebrauns, 2016), 337–43.
33. Stephen Greenblatt, *Cultural Mobility: A Manifesto* (Cambridge: Cambridge University Press, 2010); Peter van Dommelen, ed., "Mobility and Migration" (Topical issue), *World Archaeology* 46, no. 4 (2014).
34. Sarit Paz, "A Home Away from Home? The Settlement of Early Transcaucasian Migrants at Tel Bet Yerah," *Tel Aviv* 36, no. 2 (2009): 196–217.
35. Ali Qleibo, "Continuity and Discontinuity in Palestinian Cultural Expressions: Baal, El Khader and the Apotheosis of St. George," *Archaeologies* 9, no. 2 (2013): 344–55.
36. Michael L. Galaty and Charles Watkinson, *Archaeology under Dictatorship* (New York: Kluwer Academic/Plenum Publishers, 2004).

Select Bibliography

Abu el-Haj, Nadia. *Facts on the Ground: Archaeological Practice and Territorial Self-fashioning in Israeli Society*. Chicago: University of Chicago Press, 2001.

Atalay, Sonya. *Community-Based Archaeology: Research with, by, and for Indigenous and Local Communities.* Berkeley: University of California Press, 2012.

Bernbeck, Reinhard, Arwa Badran, and Susan Pollock, eds. *Reclaiming the Past for the Future: Oral History, Craft and Archaeology—Adel Yahya in Memoriam.* Berlin: Ex Oriente, 2018.

Bruchac, Margaret M., Siobhan M. Hart, and H. Martin Wobst, eds. *Indigenous Archaeologies: A Reader on Decolonization.* Walnut Creek, CA: Left Coast Press, 2010.

Corbett, Elena Dodge. *Competitive Archaeology in Jordan: Narrating Identity from the Ottomans to the Hashemites.* Austin: University of Texas Press, 2014.

Kohl, Philip L., Mara Kozelsky, and Nachman Ben-Yehuda, eds. *Selective Remembrances: Archaeology in the Construction, Commemoration, and Consecration of National Pasts.* Chicago: University of Chicago Press, 2008.

Lydon, Jane, and Uzma Z. Rizvi, eds. *Handbook of Postcolonial Archaeology.* Walnut Creek CA: Left Coast Press, 2010.

Silberman, Asher N., and David B. Small. *The Archaeology of Israel: Constructing the Past, Interpreting the Present.* Sheffield: Sheffield Academic Press, 1997.

Tamari, Salim. *Mountain against the Sea: Essays on Palestinian Society and Culture.* Berkeley: University of California Press, 2009.

Veracini, Lorenzo. *Israel and Settler Society.* London and Ann Arbor: Pluto Press, 2006.

Part V
Future Scenarios

CHAPTER 17

Reinstating Apartheid or Stating the Obvious?
1948 Palestinians and Israel's New Nation-State Law

Nida Shoughry

Introduction

In 2018 the Israeli Knesset approved a controversial law that was overwhelmingly criticized for constitutionally enshrining Jewish supremacy and reinstating Israel as the nation-state of the Jewish people. The new law, officially called Basic Law: Israel—The Nation State of the Jewish People, was met with strong opposition from 1948 Palestinians (Israeli Arabs), among others, and has been widely perceived as a turning point in the state's relationship with its Palestinian citizens. The law defines Israel as a Jewish state, promotes the creation of Jewish-only settlements, removes Arabic as an official language, and defines national self-determination as "the unique right of the Jewish people."[1]

This chapter will discuss the enactment of the Basic Law (hereinafter Nationality Law) as a grievance added to, and reviving, old 1948 Palestinian grievances and as contributing to political mobilization. It will provide an overview of the controversial clauses in the Nationality Law and will examine the response by 1948 Palestinian leadership, public, and civil society, noting the diversity of ideological positions concerning the relevance and value of political participation in Israeli elections. In order to better understand 1948 Palestinians' responses to the enactment of the law, a review of the complexities of 1948 Palestinian political history and reality will be included, together with an exploration of examples of past mobilization dynamics.

This chapter will employ social movement theory as a theoretical framework to understand the 1948 Palestinian reaction to the enactment of the Nationality Law, while taking into consideration past political mobilizations, as well as the mobilizing framing of 1948 Palestinian grievances, political opportunities, and resources. Mobilization has been defined as "the process of creating movement structures and preparing and carrying out protest actions which are visible movement 'products' addressed to actors and publics outside the movement."[2]

Social movements are among the main forms of group actions used by collectivities to express their grievances. And while grievances are among the alternative explanations given for the development of social movements, they are not sufficient on their own to mobilize people. The argument is that for mobilization to take place, it is not enough for people to feel aggrieved about some aspect of their lives; people also need to feel optimistic that acting collectively, they can redress the problem. Hence, without these two components, it is highly unlikely that people will mobilize even when afforded the opportunity to do so.[3]

In social movement theory, framing is considered a powerful leadership mechanism that displays how discourse can be used as a leadership resource. Framing is believed to help generate resonance and support for mobilization. Hence, the ability of a movement to transform the potential for mobilization into action depends on its success in framing certain issues in a way that resonates with likely participants. That is why 1948 Palestinian framing of political opportunities and resources, in addition to grievances, is crucial in accounting for any mobilization concerning electoral participation after the enactment of the Nationality Law.

Frame analysis is only one out of three social movement theory approaches. The other two, political-opportunities structure and resource mobilization, are useful to understand the nature of the 1948 Palestinians' political behavior and to explain its mobilization dynamics. Political-opportunities structure argues that the amount of resources available to a movement is not of primary importance in determining social movement mobilization; rather it is a question of what a movement can achieve with those resources given external conditions. In other words, without encouraging external conditions or a wider socioeconomic structure within which social movements operate, grievances will not necessarily lead to social movements.[4]

The resource mobilization approach focuses on the importance of structural factors and the rationality of participation in social movements.[5] According to this approach, the likelihood of effective collective action increases with the availability of diverse kinds of resources and the privileged access of social actors to them.[6] Hence, a change in access to resources, such as people, money, knowledge, frameworks, skills, and technical tools, which facilitates the processing and distribution of information in order to influence the public or, on the macro level, provides political opportunity, will enable people to mobilize.[7] Employing these three approaches provides a useful theoretical framework to understand the varied and sometimes conflicting responses of the 1948 Palestinians to their predicament.

1948 Palestinians

Commonly known as Israeli Arabs, 1948 Palestinians are those Palestinians and their descendants who remained on their land during and after the 1948 War that led to the establishment of Israel on two-thirds of historical Palestine, or what used to be British Mandate Palestine. At the conclusion of the war, those Palestinians found themselves within the borders of the new state and were given Israeli citizenship, either immediately or, in many cases, some decades later. The 1948 Palestinians account for 1.8 million people, over 20 percent of Israel's population.[8] Yet, despite holding Israeli citizenship, 1948 Palestinians have suffered and continue to suffer from racism, discrimination, and neglect. This ranges from public expressions of hatred toward them by Israeli officials to shortages or lack of services and funding, discriminatory laws, and even the targeting and killing of civilians.[9]

Concerning terminology, any reference to 1948 Palestinians tends to be contested and politicized, as reflected in the existence of over a dozen terms, including self-identifying labels used to refer to this minority. "Israeli Arabs," "Arabs in Israel," "the Arab sector," "the Arabs inside the Green Line," "the Arab citizens of Israel," "Israeli Palestinian-Arabs," and "1948 Arabs" are only a few of these terms. This confusion about identity, as expressed in the multiplicity of terms, is only one indication of the identity crisis of 1948 Palestinians.[10] This crisis began with the absurd reality created after the 1948 War, in which members of a non-Jewish Palestinian nation came under the rule of the Jewish Israeli state and were made into its citizens, and thereby into enemies of the remainder of their nation. The 1948 Palestinians were an integral part of the Arab and Palestinian nation. They shared the same history, language, heritage, culture, and reality until the establishment of Israel, at which point the 1948 Palestinians were cut off from the rest of their Palestinian and Arab nation.

Any attempt to understand the complex situation of the 1948 Palestinians' identity should take into account a number of factors. These Palestinians never endeavored to establish or to become part of the State of Israel. They did not immigrate to it, as minorities often do, but on the contrary, they were occupied by it. This occupation and incursion into Palestinian territories transformed 1948 Palestinians from a majority into a minority on their own lands and within the newly established political entity, Israel. Additionally, 1948 Palestinians have neither given up their sense of belonging to and affiliation with the Palestinian people and Arab nation, nor have they given up their rights and the right of the Palestinian refugees to their homeland. Most important, this problematic 1948 Palestinian identity goes to the heart of Israel's own self-definition as a "Jewish and democratic state" that is in constant conflict with its Palestinian and Arab neighbors. Hence, the enactment of the Nationality Law further contributes to this identity crisis.

Even prior to the enactment of this law, given the profoundly Jewish identity and Zionist character of the state, it was impossible for 1948 Palestinians to gain meaningful political power or social equality. Israel's definition as a Jewish homeland with a "right of return" for Diaspora Jews but no one else, its national symbols, such as a flag with a Star of David, portraits of Zionists leaders on its currency and stamps, and its national anthem proclaiming the "yearning" of Jews for Zion, all further excluded 1948 Palestinians and minimized their chances as non-Jews to ever be treated as equal and true citizens. The state of affairs of 1948 Palestinians is well described in the following quote:

> [1948 Palestinians] perceive a state that for the most part is unwilling either to respect their individual rights or to recognize their collective identity and seeks instead to limit their political weight and demographic presence. Increased tolerance within the Israeli polity for extremist rhetoric, combined with hostile legislation and participation in the government of parties openly advocating the transfer of Arab citizens beyond Israel's borders has further heightened tensions.[11]

The above quote explains in part why 1948 Palestinians are torn between their given Israeli identity and their "imagined" Palestinian one.[12] In addition, their willingness to come to terms with the existence of Israel is constantly being questioned, especially at times of conflict when their country (Israel) is at war with their people (Palestinians and Arabs).

The unfeasibility of becoming full citizens in a country that does not grant that right to a non-Jew has further pushed 1948 Palestinians to turn to their original Palestinian identity. However, that identity has become more imagined and less possible to retrieve. Together with their physical isolation from the Arab world and the complexity of their political situation, 1948 Palestinians were denounced by some Palestinians and Arabs as traitors for not resisting, for accepting Israeli citizenship, and for joining the Israeli political system and thereby legitimizing the Zionist cause. At times, 1948 Palestinians were also looked upon by their fellow Palestinians in the Occupied Territories with an envious eye for enjoying the benefits of holding an Israeli citizenship, which granted better living conditions and freedom of movement.

So, in addition to not being welcomed as full citizens by the Israeli state, 1948 Palestinians were growing further apart from their fellow Palestinians. Furthermore, despite voicing their solidarity with the Palestinian cause, 1948 Palestinians were mostly excluded from the Palestinian and Arab discourse, including the Israeli-Palestinian peace negotiation, and were treated with suspicion. Hence, the identity crisis of 1948 Palestinians further influenced and complicated their framing and perception of what political mobilization was possible and necessary.

To be sure, when speaking of an identity crisis, one cannot talk about a uniform identity for all 1948 Palestinians because of the richly diverse character of this minority. Like other national groups and societies, 1948 Palestinians are differentiated along regional, historical, socioeconomic, religious, and political lines. By religious affiliation, for example, the vast majority of 1948 Palestinians are Muslims, with a significant Christian minority, in addition to the Druze.

Furthermore, there are subgroups within that minority, such as the Bedouins or the Druze, that have a special status and relationship with the Israeli state. In Israel, the Druze are officially recognized as a separate ethno-religious minority, and their men are conscripted into the Israeli army.[13] Thus, apart from the identity confusion faced by all 1948 Palestinians, we need to take into account the existence of subgroups subjected to specific Israeli policies aimed at excluding them from the rest of the 1948 Palestinian minority.

While 1948 Palestinians account for over 20 percent of Israel's population, demographic studies predict that within a few years, 1948 Palestinians together with the Palestinians in the Occupied Territories will form the majority of Israel's population.[14] And while the birth rate of Palestinian citizens has dropped in recent years, this demographic fact continues to concern Israeli officials and politicians, who warn against the "Arab demographic threat."[15] They believe that the natural growth of the Palestinian population, both within and outside the borders of Israel, challenges the Israeli authorities' attempts to preserve the Jewish majority within Israel and threatens to change the Jewish nature of the state. Indeed, Knesset member (MK) Avi Dichter justified the Nationality Law by arguing that "enshrining this important bill into a law today [is intended] to prevent even the slightest thought, let alone attempt, to transform Israel to a country of all its citizens." Indeed, he asserted, the Nationality Law "is a response to Arabs—both Israeli citizens and those living in the West Bank—who believe that Israel would one day become a bi-national state of all its people."[16]

In addition, significant political events such as the mass protests of October 2000, which will be discussed later, or the unprecedented nomination of a 1948 Palestinian candidate for prime minister in the 1999 Israeli elections[17] have increased both the political awareness of 1948 Palestinians and the suspicion of the Israeli authorities and the general Jewish Israeli public toward this minority. These events also attracted the attention of the Arab and international community to this abandoned minority, suggesting that the long-neglected 1948 Palestinians can play a bigger role in Israeli and Middle East politics.

Historical Background

The many significant historical and political phases in the lives of 1948 Palestinians remain relevant to discussing any current or future political mobilization in the wake of the Nationality Law. These phases shaped the identity of 1948 Palestinians and defined their relationship with the State of Israel. As mentioned earlier, having been simply Palestinians until the 1948 War, the 1948 Palestinians became isolated from their fellow Palestinians as a result of the establishment of Israel. And unlike Palestinians in the West Bank or the Gaza Strip, 1948 Palestinians were given Israeli citizenship. Yet, until 1966, the 1948 Palestinians were placed under military rule and treated as enemies despite holding Israeli citizenship.

During those years and long after, the 1948 Palestinians were heavily discriminated against and were subjected to a wide range of both overt and covert policies that widened the gap between them and the Jewish citizens of Israel. Together with discrimination in providing municipal and state services, the 1948 Palestinians suffered from lower budgetary allocations and income and fell behind in education and health. Furthermore, the 1948 Palestinians continued to be targeted by the Israeli policy of land confiscation and were faced with restrictions on individual rights and opportunities. In addition, they could exercise their individual rights only as long as these rights did not conflict with the national goals or nature of the Jewish state.[18]

To be sure, 1948 Palestinians entered the Israeli political system right from the start, first through membership in different Zionist parties and the Israeli Communist Party, and later through their own parties. However, as citizens of a state that was essentially Jewish, 1948 Palestinians could not become an integral part of the state, since the relationship between the state and the individual was based on the common Jewish identity of both. In addition, the Israeli policy of land confiscation, which fiercely targeted 1948 Palestinians, did not make it possible for them to feel part of the state, and understandably, they could not relate to the Zionist mission of building a national home for the Jewish people on the land of Palestine.

Having been physically cut off from the rest of the Palestinians and Arabs and forced into a challenging political status, 1948 Palestinians could not retrieve their Palestinian Arab nationality even if had they wanted to. Moreover, their fellow Palestinians and the Arab nations appeared to have deserted them for good. As a result, 1948 Palestinian political identity and behavior came to be influenced mainly by autonomous factors dictated by the complicated reality they faced.

After twenty years of military rule that made 1948 Palestinians generally fearful of displaying any Palestinian national sentiment, the period between 1967 and the mid-1970s saw a reconciliation with their Palestinian identity. This increase in political consciousness, both generally and in the context of Palestinian nationalism, can be attributed, in part, to the 1967 War and the subsequent ease of contact with the Palestinians in the Occupied Territories. Moreover, the growing international recognition of the Palestine Liberation Organization (PLO) as the legitimate representative of the Palestinian people, together with the Israeli-Arab War of October 1973, contributed to the revival of Palestinian nationalism. Combined, all of these developments significantly increased the Palestinian component of the political identity of 1948 Palestinians.[19]

Indeed, a few years later, on 30 March 1976, which came to be known as Land Day, 1948 Palestinians used civil disobedience for the first time on a significant scale, to protest against the confiscation of their land for Jewish settlements in northern Israel. By the time this event ended, six 1948 Palestinians had been killed by Israeli forces. This was a pivotal moment in the history of 1948 Palestinian political mobilization and the first time in which their public organizations came into conflict with state authorities.

However, the years that followed witnessed a phase of Israelization for many 1948 Palestinians. The 1980s was a time when Israel was prospering economically, and 1948 Palestinians were offered some economic opportunities. However, these economic opportunities were given in return for political acquiescence and were not accompanied by integration into Israeli society. This ongoing marginalization of 1948 Palestinians became clearer during Yitzhak Rabin's government, in 1992–95, and during the peace talks in the mid-1990s. Its peak came after Rabin's assassination on 4 November 1995, which came in the wake of the Oslo II agreement,[20] for which Rabin was accused of giving away land while relying on the "illegitimate" votes of 1948 Palestinians. Rabin relied on the support of Palestinian Knesset members, thereby breaking a taboo that government decisions (certainly on this scale) must rely on a Jewish majority.[21]

The years that followed Rabin's assassination brought a great deal of despair to those who supported the peace process and the possibility of establishing a Palestinian state. At the same time, Israel was becoming more Jewish in its character, pushing 1948 Palestinians further away from any sense of belonging and from full citizenship.

Another key event in the history of 1948 Palestinians came in October 2000, in the wake of the second intifada, which marked the failure of the Oslo agreements. The mass protests of what became known as "Habbat October" (October Ignition) in Palestinian discourse, and the "October Events" in Israeli public discourse, refer to the Palestinian mobilization in Israel in response to the breakout of the Al-Aqsa intifada. On the first day of the general strike announced in solidarity with the Palestinians in the Occupied Territories, Israeli police and armed forces surrounded 1948 Palestinian towns and villages. Within a week, the violent reaction of the police in the Galilee left thirteen Palestinians dead and hundreds of civilian protesters injured by live ammunition, rubber-coated steel bullets, and tear gas.[22]

Many have identified the mass protests of Habbat October as a turning point for 1948 Palestinians, one that has had a major effect on their political mobilization.[23] They discovered that they would be dealt with by the Israeli security forces in the same brutal manner as the Palestinians in the Occupied Territories, despite being Israeli citizens.

Habbat October also affected the state's relationship with its Palestinian citizens. Following these events, Israel introduced new policies targeting 1948 Palestinians and created new laws to bolster the Jewish character of the state. Together with proposed bills that aimed to place severe restrictions on the citizenship rights of 1948 Palestinians, between October 2000 and July 2002 the Knesset enacted eight laws that discriminate against the Palestinian minority in various aspects. In addition, prosecutions of 1948 Palestinian Knesset members, the introduction of a new reunification law, the plans to transfer 1948 Palestinians or annex their towns to the Palestinian Authority,[24] and the warnings against the demographic growth of 1948 Palestinians were only some of the Israeli measures directed against 1948 Palestinians.[25]

From that point onward, the relationship between Israel and its 1948 Palestinian citizens has continued to deteriorate, especially with the subsequent radicalization of Israeli governments and politicians and the shift to the right, quite evident in the April 2019 Israeli legislative elections, which also witnessed the disqualification of 1948 Palestinian Knesset candidates.[26] It was also during that election campaign that Prime Minister Benjamin Netanyahu responded to comments supporting equality for 1948 Palestinian citizens of Israel by saying that "Israel was not a state of all its citizens" and that "according to the Basic Nationality Law we passed, Israel is the nation-state of the Jewish people—and only it." Netanyahu made similar comments at the opening of a cabinet meeting.[27] Furthermore, following the April 2019 elections, it was revealed that the Likud party had provided activists with hidden cameras "to monitor" 1948 Palestinian polling stations.[28]

In conclusion, any political mobilization of 1948 Palestinians, including future ones, is better understood by taking into account the complex political reality of this minority as explained throughout this chapter. On the one hand, 1948 Palestinians are "inferior" Arab and non-Jewish citizens in a Jewish and "democratic" country that is ostensibly in a state of war with its Arab neighbors. They are discriminated against and targeted by Israeli state policies and are often considered a fifth column and treated like state enemies. On the other hand, 1948 Palestinians are part of the Arab and Palestinian nation. While they sympathize with the Palestinian national struggle for independence, they realize they are abandoned by all outside players and must, therefore, conduct their own battle for survival against or within the State of Israel.

Furthermore, right from the start, 1948 Palestinians had to regulate their relationship with the Israeli state. Despite being placed under military rule, they were given the right to vote and thus, at least theoretically, could have a say in Israeli politics. Yet, the extent and nature of political participation in the Israeli Knesset continues to present 1948 Palestinians with major dilemmas. That is why it should come as no surprise that the enactment of the Nationality Law led to growing calls for boycott and to a low electoral turnout in April 2019 elections.

Political Mobilization

Analyzing the political mobilization of 1948 Palestinians in past decades helps clarify current and future mobilization following the enactment of the Nationality Law, especially because arguably their political reality retains similar characteristics as in the past. At first sight, it would appear that the 1948 Palestinians who found themselves defeated and deserted after the 1948 War were faced with the choice of either withdrawing into passive acquiescence, participating within the existing structures, or resorting to open resistance. However, none of these options were in fact fully available or affordable to 1948 Palestinians. Withdrawal meant giving up their national identity, rights, and existence as Palestinians in the State of Israel. Political participation and full integration were not possible in a country where granting civil rights is conditional upon being Jewish. Finally, open resistance was costly and required the presence of enabling political, social, and economic conditions and resources that were not available to a weak minority that barely survived a devastating war and mass expulsion.

Therefore, the 1948 Palestinian answer was to largely adopt survival mechanisms that could ensure them a reasonable level of personal safety and existence. While this might be directly understood as acquiescent behavior, the implementation of this survival mechanism was more complex—revealing forms of mundane resistance. The state of affairs of the 1948 Palestinians, especially under military rule, reflects a multifaceted reality with mixed behavior ranging from acquiescence, to participation, to resistance.

Even though at that stage the 1948 Palestinians did not seem to have the political opportunities or resources necessary to make open resistance feasible, and while they by and large acquiesced to Israeli sovereignty and put up with the discriminatory practices of military rule, there were still occasions on which the 1948 Palestinians resisted openly. Resistance under military rule and during the state of war and emergency declared in Israel was costly, especially in the early stages of the state's establishment. However, and against all odds, one can find spontaneous as well as planned instances of mobilization by 1948 Palestinians against state policies that targeted them, as part of their survival strategies. At the same time, we face a major challenge to define or characterize the behavior of the 1948 Palestinians, not least because this group cannot be referred to as a uniform entity with a united political stand or action. Rather, this is a politically and socially diverse minority with fluctuating responses and political behavior.

Understanding the 1948 Palestinian reaction to the enactment of the Nationality Law should take into consideration past political mobilizations of this population, hence the earlier preview of the complex historical background and political reality of 1948 Palestinians is vital. Using social movement theory as an analytical framework to study the mobilization of 1948 Palestinians has shown that the political mobilization of 1948 Palestinians over time has been influenced greatly by the mobilizing factors of grievances, political opportunities, resources, and their framing.[29] The core argument of these three approaches that the presence of grievances is not enough on its own to generate mobilization was found applicable when various case studies of 1948 Palestinian mobilization were examined. The theoretical argument that in order for people to mobilize they need to have the opportunity and resources to do so and need to frame their grievances and their predicament more broadly, in such a way that political mobilization becomes possible,[30] was also found valid.

As mentioned, social movements are carriers of grievances, which they can dramatize by engaging in various types of collective action and mobilization, as well as demanding that they be addressed.[31] While mobilization usually takes the form of demonstrations or public gatherings, it is not strictly confined to them. Examples from the history of 1948 Palestinians reveal a wider range of mobilization and various forms of civil disobedience, including engaging in awareness campaigns on the issue of land in the 1970s, the production of policy papers and documents such as *The Future Vision of the Palestinian Arabs in Israel*, issued in December 2006, or even the new trend of film production and rap music.[32]

In line with the core theoretical argument that the presence of grievances is not enough on its own to generate mobilization, one can find plenty of incidents in the history of 1948 Palestinians that generated or intensified grievances. However, the response to these grievances from 1948 Palestinians was a total acquiescence. This was, in part, because of fear of a hostile state response against those who challenge its policies or because of the perception of limited political opportunities and resources available to the 1948 Palestinians. Nonetheless, we can identify some cases, such as the Red Identification Document (ID) battle[33] and the al-Ard movement,[34] in which the 1948 Palestinians mobilized and resisted despite the many obstacles they confronted. These and other cases demonstrate that often enough, despite limited political opportunities and resources, the 1948 Palestinians took the risk and mobilized, notwithstanding the low chances of success and the costly price of challenging the state.

Social movement theory refers this kind of outcome (of taking action) to the positive framing or optimism of social movement participants that by acting collectively they can redress or at least more explicitly address the problem. This kind of positive framing, or cognitive liberation process, encourages social movement participants and helps them transcend the costly price of mobilization.[35] In addition, evidence from 1948 Palestinian case studies suggests that participants disregarded cost-benefit calculations in the heat of the events or as a result of a shock effect. This was true, for example, in incidents where 1948 Palestinians were met with unexpected state violence and participation was recorded despite circumstances with discouraging mobilization conditions.[36]

The analysis of the case studies of the 1976 Land Day and Habbat October makes it possible to identify some of the factors that contributed to the mobilization of 1948 Palestinians. Along with a strong grievance, these factors included, as social movement theory argues, the sum of political, social, and economic resources and opportunities, as well as positive framing. However, while the contributing mobilizing factors were similar in most incidents, the dynamics of mobilization varied. More interestingly, the analysis suggests that the mobilization dynamics of the 1948 Palestinians are better understood by taking into account the interplay between the various mobilizing components of grievances, political opportunities, resources, and their constantly changing framing. This dynamic contributes to changes in the cognitive liberation process[37] and in cost-benefit calculations, leading to changes in the nature and strategy of political mobilization.

The analysis also indicates two types of 1948 Palestinian mobilization, preplanned and spontaneous, with each type appearing to have its own mobilizing dynamics. The preplanned 1948 Palestinian mobilization is a more rational and better-calculated response, which self-consciously takes into account the political opportunities and resources available and works within their limits. Conversely, the spontaneous or the reactionary 1948 Palestinian mobilization usually includes impulsive reactions and takes place at either the beginning or the middle of a particular protest cycle. In contrast to preplanned mobilization, these impulsive reactions, seen during the violent clashes in both the 1976 Land Day and Habbat October, are less likely to take into account cost-benefit calculations, to undertake rational actions in accordance with the available political opportunities, or to efficiently use the sum of resources available for mobilization. Yet, in both case studies, even such spontaneous responses relied upon pre-existing networks, resources, and, up to a point, even perceptions of what was possible (e.g., unity across parties, areas).[38]

An analysis of the case studies of Habbat October and 1976 Land Day highlights the heat of the moment or the shock effect, which was found to have a temporary paralyzing effect on the cost-benefit calculations of social movement participation. In addition, it recognizes that the regional situation was an important factor in shaping the political opportunities of the movement, an aspect that the social movement theory has traditionally neglected. And, indeed, the political behavior of the 1948 Palestinians is highly context-specific.

In other words, it is dependent upon the circumstances of the case in question, and therefore triggers for past behavior are not always useful in predicting future behavior. As an example, while the presence of the security forces in Habbat October appears to have contributed to the escalation of events, it does not necessarily mean that their presence is likely to have the same effect in future contexts. Therefore, the ability of 1948 Palestinians to generate resonance and support for mobilization in response to the enactment of the Nationality Law is highly related to their ability to successfully frame issues in a way that resonates with likely participants, thus transforming the potential for mobilization in action.

The Nationality Law

The passage of the Nationality Law by the Israeli Knesset with a slim 62–55 majority and two abstentions[39] on 19 July 2018, as Israel's thirteenth Basic Law, gave it the status of a constitutional norm. In the absence of a constitution, Basic Laws serve as a guide for the legal system in Israel and can only be changed by a new or revised Basic Law, requiring a minimum of 61 votes out of the Knesset's 120 members.[40]

The Nationality Law was first proposed by Likud Knesset member Avi Dichter in 2001 and had been significantly revised since then because of the controversy it provoked. Apart from concerns over non-Jewish minority rights, criticism included the potential damaging impact this legislation could have on the democratic character and advancement of pluralism in Israel, its potential negative effect on the rights of Reform and Conservative Jews and the LGBTQ community, and even the possibility of undermining Israel-Diaspora relations.[41] Alongside the widespread condemnation, other responses from within Israel and abroad have been positive and supportive of affirming the Jewish character of the State of Israel.

As for 1948 Palestinians, the Nationality Law has raised significant concerns regarding their rights and status, their sense of belonging, and Jewish-Arab relations.[42] The law once again highlighted the argument that Israel's definition as a "Jewish and democratic state" failed to take into account the 1948 Palestinians' demand to live in Israel with full equal rights while maintaining their Palestinian national identity. Others compared Israel to apartheid South Africa, saying the legislation "codifies discrimination against Arabs."[43] For 1948 Palestinians, the Nationality Law deepened their sense of alienation and was widely perceived as an attempt to reinforce Jewish supremacy and reinstate the inferior status of 1948 Palestinians as second-class citizens.[44]

The clauses on language and Jewish settlements in Israel (not to be confused with illegal settlements in the occupied West Bank) are perhaps the most problematic elements in the Nationality Law as concerns their prospective ramifications for 1948 Palestinians. Despite its incomplete implementation, the status of the Arabic language as one of Israel's two official languages was perhaps the only collective right officially left to 1948 Palestinians. Therefore, declaring Hebrew to be the sole official language of the state and degrading the status of Arabic meant not only that the state no longer recognizes the language and culture of its 1948 Palestinian citizens, but that it also violates a commitment made upon Israel's establishment, thereby ultimately further degrading Israel's 1948 Palestinian citizens.

Furthermore, prioritizing Jewish settlement in Israel and viewing its development as a national value when there is a pressing housing crisis for 1948 Palestinian legitimizes the unequal allocation of resources and services and signals to 1948 Palestinians that they are indeed, at best, second-class citizens. This is especially true when bearing in mind that not a single new Arab community has been built for Arab citizens since the establishment of Israel in 1948, despite the massive population growth and a continuing Israeli policy of house demolitions in Arab villages and towns.[45]

During the debate against the Nationality Law, MK Ayman Odeh, chairman of the Joint List of Arab Palestinian parties, waved a black flag. "Just as [the 1956 massacre] in Kafr Qasim was a blatantly illegal order, with a black flag flying over it,[46] so is a black flag hoisted today over this evil law," Odeh said.[47] While receiving a round of applause from right-wing MKs, the approval of the Nationality Law caused outrage among 1948 Palestinian MKs, who "tore up copies of the bill and shouted their disgust, before some were thrown out of the chamber."[48]

Other members of the Join List expressed their anger and disapproval of the legislation. In a statement he released, MK Yousef Jabareen said, "The Nation-State Law is the last nail in the coffin of the so-called Israeli democracy which has been dying in recent years, suffering as it has from the chronic disease of racism, compounded by fascism and which has now been transform to Apartheid through the passage of this law."[49]

Social media was widely used by 1948 Palestinians as a protest tool, and numerous voices, including those of writers and activists, have publicly expressed "similar sentiments, with many also stating their steadfast pride in their identity and in the belief that there is a future for Jewish-Arab partnership."[50] Alongside such public statements, MK Zouheir Bahloul, a 1948 Palestinian and a member of the opposition Zionist Union party, resigned from the Knesset, having expressed his refusal to "sit on the fence" and give legitimacy to a "destructive, racist, extremist parliament." The High Follow-Up Committee for Arab Citizens of Israel turned to international advocacy, addressing the foreign policy chief of the European Union, the secretary-general of the United Nations António Guterres, and other international bodies, demanding their intervention against the legislation.[51]

Adalah, the Legal Center for Arab Minority Rights in Israel, submitted a petition to the Israeli Supreme Court to pronounce the law unconstitutional. The arguments put forward in the petition were that the Nationality Law supports and further strengthens the Jewish nature of the State of Israel, entrenches the Jewish identity of the state, and omits any reference to universal values, such as democracy, human dignity, freedom, justice, or equality, which are protected under the 1948 Declaration of the Establishment of the State of Israel or the Basic Laws of 1992.[52]

However, while modest protests took place in several 1948 Palestinian localities, including the city of Haifa, it took a while for a coordinated and unified response from the Arab leadership to be formulated, largely thanks to disagreement and a diversity of political views and ideologies in its ranks. Many people urged the Palestinian leadership in the Knesset to collectively resign in protest and to form a national 1948 Palestinian council. Others called for month-long boycott of the Knesset during its winter session, for holding a general conference of 1948 Palestinians, and for appealing to the UN and EU institutions to oppose the legislation.[53]

To the dismay of observers and the disappointment of the 1948 Palestinian public, despite recurrent and intensifying statements by key leadership members—such as Mohamed Barakeh, head of the High Follow-Up Committee for Arab Citizens of Israel, which warned of drastic protest measures—there was no strong response from the 1948 Palestinian political leadership beyond empty rhetoric. In fact, the first and forceful organized response came from the Druze community, who filed a petition to the High Court of Justice and quickly established a Special Forum Against the Nationality Law backed by Druze Israeli Defense Forces (IDF) reserve officers, which organized a major demonstration with over ninety thousand protestors in Rabin Square in Tel Aviv.[54]

The Druze, who serve in the IDF and mostly declare complete loyalty to the state, have therefore been even more deeply hurt by the Nationality Law than other Palestinians. The Druze were deeply offended because, as their leaders argued, they had spilled blood for Israel and had been proud of their sacrifice. Now, as they implied, they were treated "like Palestinians," namely, explicitly as second-class citizens.

The enactment of the Nationality Law, along with the failure of the Palestinian leadership to handle the crisis and respond with firm and forceful measures, followed by the disintegration of the Joint List of Arab Palestinian parties, have all contributed to an increasing number of voices demanding to boycott the April 2019 elections. The Joint List had been the first political alliance of 1948 Palestinian parties ever to come together. It was formed in the buildup to the 2015 elections and resulted in a turnout of 63.5 percent, the highest percentage of Palestinian voters recorded, of whom 82 percent voted for the Joint List, enabling it to win thirteen seats and thus to become the third-largest party in the twentieth Knesset. The breakup of the Joint List, which was blamed on narrow partisan interests, motivated 1948 Palestinian activists to launch online campaigns calling to punish Palestinian MKs by boycotting the elections.[55] The Joint List, activists said, had "failed to offer a united front with a clear agenda or strategy" even at times of great challenge such as the passage of the Nationality Law.[56]

Calls were also made to use this opportunity to rebel against traditional leadership and revisit electoral participation in the Israeli Knesset. By participating, 1948 Palestinians give legitimacy to the Israeli Knesset and its discriminatory nature and laws. Conversely, their parliamentary presence in the Knesset could be said to contribute to their recognition by the state and to the protection of some of their civil rights. While such protection of rights has proved to be of limited effectiveness, especially following the enactment of racist and discriminatory laws and in the wake of the Nationality Law itself, it is difficult to say whether the presence of Palestinian representatives in the Knesset has managed to block even more severe laws.

The elections of April 2019 witnessed a drastic 14 percent decrease in 1948 Palestinian participation, the lowest turnout since the first Knesset elections in 1949, in the immediate aftermath of the Nakba. A combination of disappointment and despair caused by disillusionment with Israeli politics, growing Israeli racism and the enactment of the Nationality Law, and the strained relations between the Palestinian parties have all contributed to the low turnout. This is a serious issue that should concern not only the 1948 Palestinian public and leadership, but also the larger Israeli society. The increase in grievances, together with the perception of limited political opportunities for activism and the expectation of unresponsiveness by the state to 1948 Palestinian demands, creates similar conditions to those that preceded, for instance, the Land Day events of 1976. The resort to what may appear on the face of it as acquiescent behavior of nonparticipation can also be seen as the development of a new, albeit low-key, 1948 Palestinian resistance movement.

Conclusion

The mobilization and dynamics explained in this chapter contribute to a better understanding of current and future 1948 Palestinian mobilization in response to grievances. While the enactment of the Nationality Law is widely perceived as a turning point in the state's relationship with its 1948 Palestinian citizens, the political situation in Israel at present continues to push 1948 Palestinians further away from the prospect of normalcy or full citizenship rights. There is a growing Jewish Israeli radicalization and shift toward the right, with the rise to power of radical right-wing leaders openly inciting against 1948 Palestinian population.

At the time of the writing of this chapter, the results of the September 2019 snap legislative elections are being released. While it is still early to reflect on the elections or their outcome, it is important to highlight the increase in 1948 Palestinian turnout, which resulted in reproducing the historic 2015 achievement of thirteen Knesset seats. The turnout remained unclear until just before Election Day, despite the reestablishment of the Joint List about two months earlier, the parties having understood the disastrous consequences of the split. The high turnout is being attributed in part to the highly racist Likud election propaganda against Arab voters.[57] The election results also challenge Israeli democracy with a pressing question of whether Israel is ready to have a 1948 Palestinian party, the third-largest party, in its government coalition.

The increasing political awareness of 1948 Palestinians, together with the continuation of Israeli discriminatory and racist practices against them, increases the chances of possible future confrontations. This is highly probable, considering the limited political opportunities and mobilization resources available to 1948 Palestinians and the high cost of mobilization against grievances, especially under a radical right-wing government, which is trying to make citizenship conditional on loyalty to and recognition of the Jewish character of the state. The coming period will likely present 1948 Palestinians with further challenges to be added to existing grievances, and the analysis given in this chapter will be useful in understanding or even foreseeing future 1948 Palestinian mobilization.

Nida Shoughry is a lecturer, researcher, and former journalist, with a PhD in politics and international relations from the University of Wales, Aberystwyth, UK, and a master's degree in journalism from Emerson College, Boston, USA. Shoughry has worked on several research projects in the fields of media and politics, focusing mainly on the Middle East, the Israeli-Palestinian conflict, and social movement theory. Shoughry is the author of *"Israeli-Arab" Political Mobilization: Between Acquiescence, Participation, and Resistance* (2012), and her work includes journalism articles, reports, and translations.

Notes

1. For the full text, see the Knesset website: https://main.knesset.gov.il/EN/activity/Documents/BasicLawsPDF/BasicLawNationState.pdf.
2. Dieter Rucht, "The Impact of National Contexts on Social Movement Structures: A Cross-Movement and Cross-National Comparison," in *Comparative Perspectives on Social Movements: Political Oppor-*

tunities, Mobilizing Structures, and Cultural Framings, ed. Doug McAdam, John D. McCarthy, and Mayer N. Zald (Cambridge: Cambridge University Press, 1996), 186.
3. Doug McAdam et al., eds., *Comparative Perspectives on Social Movements Opportunities, Mobilizing Structures, and Cultural Framings* (Cambridge: Cambridge University Press, 1996), 5.
4. For more, see Sidney Tarrow, *Power in Movement: Social Movements, Collective Action and Politics* (Cambridge: Cambridge University Press, 1994).
5. Bert Klandermans, "Mobilization and Participation: Social-Psychological Expansions of Resource Mobilization Theory," *American Sociological Review* 49, no. 5 (1984): 583–600.
6. Bob Edwards and John D. McCarthy, "Resources and Social Movement Mobilization," in *The Blackwell Companion to Social Movements*, ed. David A. Snow, Sarah A. Soule, and Hanspeter Kriesi (Hoboken: Blackwell, 2008), 116–52.
7. Rucht, "The Impact of National Contexts on Social Movement Structures," 186.
8. In 2016, Israel had 1.8 million Arab citizens, representing 21 percent of the country's total population. *Statistical Abstract of Israel*, Central Bureau of Statistics, 2016, table 2.1.
9. Key incidents include the killing of forty-eight Palestinians in 1956 in Kafr Qasim, the killing of six during the 1976 Land Day general strike against land confiscation, and the October 2000 killing of thirteen Palestinians. For more details, see *The Future Vision of the Palestinian Arabs in Israel* (Nazareth: National Committee for the Heads of the Arab Local Authorities in Israel, 2006), http://www.adalah.org/newsletter/eng/dec06/tasawor-mostaqbali.pdf; Hillel Cohen, *Good Arabs: The Israeli Security Services and the Israeli Arabs*, trans. Haim Watzman (Berkeley: University of California Press, 2010); Sabri Jiryis, *The Arabs in Israel*, trans. Inea Bushnaq (New York: Monthly Review Press, 1976); Katie Hesketh, *The Inequality Report: The Palestinian Arab Minority in Israel"* (Haifa: Adalah, the Legal Center for Arab Minority Rights in Israel, 2011), https://www.adalah.org/uploads/oldfiles/upfiles/2011/Adalah_The_Inequality_Report_March_2011.pdf.
10. For more on the identity crisis of 1948 Palestinians, see "Identity Crisis: Israel and Its Arab Citizens," International Crisis Group report, *Middle East & North Africa Report* 25, Amman/Brussels, 4 March 2004, https://www.crisisgroup.org/middle-east-north-africa/eastern-mediterranean/israelpalestine/identity-crisis-israel-and-its-arab-citizens.
11. "Identity Crisis: Israel and Its Arab Citizens."
12. The terms are borrowed from Benedict Anderson's concept of imagined community, which states that a nation is a community socially constructed or imagined by the people who perceive themselves as part of the same group. See Benedict Anderson, *Imagined Communities: Reflections on the Origin and Spread of Nationalism* (London and New York: Verso, 1991).
13. For more on the Druze in Israel and their special relationship with the state, see, Nabih Al-Qasim, *The Druze in Israel: The Historical and Current Dimension* (Haifa: Al-Wadi Press and Publishing House, 1995, in Arabic); Laila Parsons, *The Druze between Palestine and Israel, 1947–49* (New York: St. Martin's Press, 2000).
14. According to the Palestinian Bureau of Statistics, at the end of 2017 the Palestinians made up 49.9 percent of the population in historical Palestine. Also see Arnon Sofer, *Israel: Demography 2000–2020* (Haifa: University of Haifa, 2002, in Hebrew).
15. According to the Arab Association for Human Rights (HRA), a conference held on security issues in December 2003 and organized by the Institute of Policy and Strategy of the Interdisciplinary College in Herzliya proved that demographics have become a favorite topic among Israel's political elite. See HRA press release issued on 14 January 2004.
16. Charles Dunst, "Jewish? Democratic? Nation-State Law Raises Questions over Israel's Purpose," Times of Israel, 26 July 2018, https://www.timesofisrael.com/jewish-democratic-nation-state-law-raises-questions-over-israels-purpose/.
17. In 1999 Azmi Bishara was the first Arab citizen to run for prime minister election, but he dropped out of the race two days before election day in order to facilitate the election of Ehud Barak.
18. Amina Minns and Nadia Hijab, *Citizens Apart: A Portrait of the Palestinians in Israel* (London: I. B. Tauris, 1990); Yasir Zughaib, *1948 Palestinians: Identity, Reality, and Future* (Beirut: Baheth Centre for Research and Strategic Palestinian Studies, 2003, in Arabic); Ṣabri Jiryis, *Democratic Freedoms in*

Israel (Beirut: Institute for Palestine Studies, 1972); Nur Masalha, ed. and trans., *The Palestinians in Israel: Is Israel the State of All Its Citizens and "Absentees"?* (Nazareth: Galilee Center for Social Research, 1993).

19. Mark Tessler and Audra K. Grant, "Israel's Arab Citizens: The Continuing Struggle," *Annals of the American Academy of Political and Social Science* 555, no. 1 (1998): 97–113.
20. Also known as Taba agreement. The Israeli-Palestinian Interim Agreement on the West Bank and the Gaza Strip was signed 24 September 1995, in Taba, Egypt.
21. For more on the so-called illegitimacy of the Arab vote to determine the fate of the Jewish state, see Israel Shahak, "Questioning the Legitimacy of the Arab Vote in Israel as a Result of the Peace Process," *Middle East Policy* 2, no. 2 (1993): 61–73.
22. Marwan Dalal, *October 2000: Law and Politics before the Or Commission of Inquiry* (Haifa: Adalah, the Legal Center for Arab Minority Rights in Israel, July 2003), http://www.adalah.org/eng/features/commission/oct2000_eng.pdf.
23. See, for example, Nimer Sultany, *Citizens without Citizenship: Mada's First Annual Political Monitoring Report; Israel and The Palestinian Minority 2000–2002* (Haifa: Mada al-Carmel—The Arab Centre for Applied Research, 2003), 38–52; Laurence Louer, *To Be an Arab in Israel* (New York: Columbia University Press, 2007); Zughaib, *1948 Palestinians*; Marwan Dwairy, "October 2000: Defined Goals and New Mechanisms," Adalah's *Newsletter* 19 (October 2005); Raphael Israeli, *Arabs in Israel: Friends or Foes?*, trans. Joshua Schreier (Israel: ACPR Publishers, 2008); Dan Rabinowitz, Asad Ghanem, and Oren Yiftachel, eds., "After the Break: New Directions to the Government's Policy towards the Arabs in Israel: An Emergency Report by a Team of Inter-university Researchers, Presented to Israeli Prime Minister Mr. Ehud Barak" (Tel Aviv: unknown publisher, 2000, pamphlet in Hebrew).
24. In 2004, for example, the "Populated-Area Exchange Plan" was proposed by then Israeli foreign minister Avigdor Liberman to transfer the jurisdiction of towns in the "triangle" region southeast of Haifa to become part of a Palestinian state in any peace agreement in exchange for the illegal Jewish settlement blocs of the West Bank. In 2010 a similar plan was presented by Liberman in a speech before the UN General Assembly in New York.
25. Sultany, *Citizens without Citizenship*; Sultany, *The Palestinian Minority 2000–2002* (Haifa: Mada al-Carmel—The Arab Centre for Applied Social Research, 2003), 141–62.
26. Sawsan Zaher, "The Disqualification of Arab Knesset Candidates: A Critical Mass of Racism," *Adalah*, 8 April 2019, https://www.adalah.org/en/content/view/9723.
27. "Netanyahu Says Israel 'Not a State for All of Its Citizens,'" *Middle East Eye*, 10 March 2019, https://www.middleeasteye.net/news/netanyahu-says-israel-not-state-all-its-citizens.
28. "Israel Election 2019: Netanyahu's Party Places 1,200 Hidden Cameras in Arab Polling Sites," *Haaretz*, 9 April 2019, https://www.haaretz.com/israel-news/elections/likud-provides-activists-1-200-body-camera-to-monitor-arab-polling-sites-1.7105989. Also see "Adalah Calls for Criminal Probe into Likud's Planting of Hidden Cameras in Israeli Polling Stations," *Adalah*, 11 April 2019, https://www.adalah.org/en/content/view/9725.
29. See Nida Shoughry, *"Israeli-Arab" Political Mobilization: Between Acquiescence, Participation, and Resistance* (New York: Palgrave Macmillan, 2012).
30. Doug McAdam et al., "Introduction: Opportunities Mobilizing Structures and Framing Process—Toward a Synthetic, Comparative Perspective on Social Movements," and Doug McAdam, "Conceptual Origins, Current Problems, Future Direction," in Doug McAdam et al., *Comparative Perspectives on Social Movements*, 1–20, 23–40, respectively.
31. David A. Snow et al., "Introduction: Mapping the Terrain," in *The Blackwell Companion to Social Movements*, ed. David A. Snow et al. (Malden, MA: Blackwell, 2006), 3–16.
32. Shoughry, *"Israeli-Arab" Political Mobilization*, 26. Also see Joseph Massad, "Liberating Songs: Palestine Put to Music," *Journal of Palestine Studies* 32, no. 3 (2003): 21–38.
33. This refers to 1948 Palestinian attempts to resist Israeli plans to deport more 1948 Palestinians after the establishment of Israel by giving part of them temporary red ID cards that had to be renewed by the military governor, as opposed to permanent blue ID cards that granted their holder the right to reside in Israel.

34. The al-Ard movement is an all-Arab organization established in the aftermath of the violent clashes between 1948 Palestinians and Israeli security on May Day in 1958. The al-Ard was established to articulate the 1948 Palestinian grievances, especially those along national lines. The movement derived from the Arab Public Committee for the Protection of Detainees and Deportees, set up to protest the imprisonment of 1948 Palestinians following the 1958 May Day. For more, see Leena Dallasheh, "The Al-Ard Movement," in *The Palestinians in Israel: Readings in History, Politics and Society*, ed. Nadim N. Rouhana and Areej Sabbagh-Khoury, 2nd ed. (Haifa: Mada al-Carmel—Arab Center for Applied Social Research, 2011, e-book), https://www.mada-research.org/wp-content/uploads/2020/06/english.indd_.pdf.
35. Doug McAdam, *Political Process and the Development of Black Insurgency, 1930–1970*, 2nd ed. (Chicago: University of Chicago Press, 1999), 34.
36. Shoughry, *"Israeli-Arab" Political Mobilization*, 165–66.
37. It is a process that is comprised of feelings of injustice and efficacy. Cognitive liberation is usually attributed to cognitive processes between social actors and larger movements or activist organizations. For more, see Gregory C. Stanczak, *Engaged Spirituality: Social Change and American Religion* (New Brunswick, NJ: Rutgers University Press, 2006), 43.
38. Shoughry, *"Israeli-Arab" Political Mobilization*, 167.
39. MK Benny Begin, from the ruling Likud party, and MK Orly Levi-Abukasis (Independent).
40. For further information about the Nationality Law, see "Israel's Jewish Nation-State Law," *Adalah*, 20 December 2020, https://www.adalah.org/en/content/view/9569.
41. Jeremy Sharon and Gil Hofman, "Diaspora Clause in Nation-State Bill Called Patronizing," *Jerusalem Post*, 17 July 2018, https://www.jpost.com/Israel-News/Diaspora-clause-in-nation-state-bill-called-patronizing-562687.
42. See Yehuda Ben Meir, "The Nationality Law Is Redundant, but the Attacks by the Left Are Hysterical," *Haaretz*, 23 July 2018 (in Hebrew), https://www.haaretz.co.il/opinions/.premium-1.6295116.
43. Dunst, "Jewish? Democratic?"
44. As expressed by MK Ayman Odeh, the chair of the Joint List that represented the majority of 1948 Palestinians in the Knesset at the time. See "Jewish and Democratic," editorial, *Jerusalem Post*, 26 July 2018, https://www.jpost.com/Opinion/Jewish-and-democratic-563480.
45. For more, see "Demolition and Displacement reports of the Israeli Committee against House Demolitions ICAHD," numerous reports, most recent posted on 3 March 2021, https://icahd.org/?s=Demolition+and+Displacement+Report.
46. The Israeli Supreme Court debating Kafr Qasim defined unlawful orders as akin to having a black flag waving over them.
47. "'Black Flag' over Knesset as It Enacts Jewish Nation-State Law," Communist Party of Israel, 21 July 2018, http://maki.org.il/en/?p=15683.
48. "Israeli Arab MP Resigns over Controversial 'Nation State' Law," *BBC News*, 29 July 2018, https://www.bbc.com/news/world-middle-east-44995501.
49. "'Black Flag' over Knesset."
50. "Basic Law: Israel as the Nation-State of the Jewish People: Discourse and Implications for Arab Citizens of Israel," Inter-Agency Task Force on Israeli Arab Issues, 27 July 2018, https://www.iataskforce.org/sites/default/files/resource/resource-1624.pdf.
51. Itay Blumenthal, "Israeli Arabs Launch Struggle against Nationality Law," *Ynet News*, 8 July 2018, https://www.ynetnews.com/articles/0,7340,L-5324316,00.html.
52. See HCJ 5866/18: "High Follow-Up Committee for Arab Citizens of Israel et al. v. the Knesset," submitted on 7 August 2018. For further information about the law and the petition in English, see "Arab Leadership Takes Action Against Israel's New Jewish Nation-State Law," *Adalah*, 6 August 2018, https://www.adalah.org/en/content/view/9574.
53. Arik Bender and Yasir Okby, "Arab Politician Divided Over Protest against Nationality Law," *Maariv*, 30 July 2918, https://www.maariv.co.il/news/politics/Article-653680.
54. "Druze Leader: 'No One Can Teach Us What Sacrifice Is,'" *Ynet News*, 8 April 2018, https://www.ynetnews.com/articles/0,7340,L-5322434,00.html.

55. Joshua Mitnick, "How Israel Marginalizes Its Arab Citizen," *Foreign Policy*, 15 April 2019, https://foreignpolicy.com/2019/04/15/how-israel-marginalizes-its-arab-citizens/.
56. Abir Kopty, "The Collapse of the Joint List Is a Wake-up Call for Palestinian Politicians," *Middle East Eye*, 25 February 2019, https://www.middleeasteye.net/opinion/collapse-joint-list-wake-call-palestinian-politicians.
57. "Netanyahu's New Election Message: 'Arabs Want to Annihilate Us All,'" *Haaretz*, 11 September 2019, https://www.haaretz.com/israel-news/elections/.premium-netanyahu-s-new-election-message-arabs-want-to-annihilate-us-all-1.7832283.

Select Bibliography

Cohen, Hillel. *Good Arabs: The Israeli Security Agencies and the Israeli Arabs, 1948–1967*. Berkeley: University of California Press, 2011.

Dalal, Marwan. *October 2000: Law and Politics before the Or Commission*. Haifa: Adalah, the Legal Center for Arab Minority Rights in Israel, July 2003. http://www.adalah.org/eng/features/commission/oct2000_eng.pdf.

The Future Vision of the Palestinian Arabs in Israel. Nazareth: National Committee for the Heads of the Arab Local Authorities in Israel, 2006. http://www.adalah.org/newsletter/eng/dec06/tasawor-mostaqbali.pdf.

Ghanem, As'as. *The Palestinian-Arab Minority in Israel, 1948–2000: A Political Study*. Albany: State University of New York Press, 2001.

Jiryis, Ṣabri. *The Arabs in Israel*. New York: Monthly Review Press, 1976.

Lustick, Ian. *Arabs in the Jewish State: Israel's Control of a National Minority*. Austin: University of Texas Press, 1980.

McAdam, Doug, John D. McCarthy, and Mayer N. Zald, eds. *Comparative Perspectives on Social Movements: Political Opportunities, Mobilizing Structures, and Cultural Framings*. Cambridge: Cambridge University Press, 1996.

Pappé, Ilan. *The Forgotten Palestinians: A History of the Palestinians in Israel*. New Haven: Yale University Press, 2011.

Shoughry, Nida. *"Israeli-Arab" Political Mobilization: Between Acquiescence, Participation, and Resistance*. New York: Palgrave Macmillan, 2012.

Sultany, Nimer. *Citizens without Citizenship: Israel and the Palestinian Minority 2000–2002*. Haifa: Mada al-Carmel—The Arab Center for Applied Social Research, 2003.

CHAPTER 18

PALESTINIANS IN ISRAEL
THE UNDESIRABLE OTHERS

SAID ZEEDANI

Democratic and Jewish

As we all (should) know, the State of Israel is currently normatively defined as both a democratic state and a Jewish state.[1] It has been both a democratic and a Jewish state since its establishment in May 1948. It is a Jewish state in the sense that it is for Jews wherever they reside, whether inside Israel or in the Jewish Diaspora. The Jews inside Israel are "actual" citizens of the state, while the Jews outside Israel are "potential" citizens. The Law of Return (1950) and the associated Law of Citizenship (1952) are intended to easily bridge the gap between potentiality and actuality. Needless to say, the Law of Return is one of the defining features of the State of Israel. It applies only to Jews. According to this legal setup, any recognized Jew from anywhere can become an Israeli citizen simply by immigrating to Israel and signing certain documents. Israel is thus open to almost all Jews, but it is closed to almost all non-Jews.

Israel is also a Jewish state in the following additional respects: it is committed primarily to Jewish-Zionist aspirations, projects, and interests; it gives priority to Jews over non-Jews who are citizens of the same state; it excludes non-Jews from taking part in major decisions that affect the nature, borders, security, future, and order of priorities of the state; all state symbols, the official language, and national holidays are Jewish; and finally, it has official and semiofficial institutions (such as the Israel National Fund and the Jewish Agency) that provide services to and own property benefiting the Jews of Israel exclusively. It goes without saying that the Israeli state is for the Jews no matter how they conceive of their identity or orientation (whether religious or secular, Zionists or non-Zionists). The recent Basic Law: Israel—the Nation State of the Jewish People, passed by the Israeli Parliament (Knesset) in July 2018, legalizes, among other things, the supremacy of Jews over non-Jews who are citizens of the Israeli state.[2]

As a democracy, Israel is committed to treating all its citizens (Jews and non-Jews) equally, that is, with equal consideration and respect, as Ronald Dworkin puts it.[3]

But as a Jewish state in the senses mentioned above, it is also committed to something else. In the case of Israel, "Jewish and democratic" is, no doubt, an *oxymoron*. In other words, two sets of competing and often conflicting commitments flow directly from the normative definition of Israel as a Jewish and democratic state. The practices and policies of successive Israeli governments over the years reflect and manifest these competing and conflicting commitments. Given these competing and conflicting commitments, it is no accident that for over seventy years the Palestinian citizens, or *semi-citizens*, of Israel have been, and still are, victims of racial discrimination. They have been, and still are, condemned to the inferior status of second-class citizens. That is to say, they are more than permanent residents but less than equal citizens; more than tenants but less than the landlords. The basic democratic principle of single and uniform citizenship does not apply to Jews and non-Jews alike. This denial of equal membership in the political community is responsible for a host of abuses, which pervade all spheres of allocating and redistributing socially meaningful goods (security, wealth, office, opportunity, liberty, and political power). Furthermore, Palestinians in Israel are not supposed to overstep limits set for them by the Jewish majority, its political representatives and security agents. Palestinians in Israel are thus the "undesirable others," and as such they should know how to behave, or else!

Israel is a democratic state that neither claims nor even pretends to be neutral with respect to its citizens, not to speak of neutrality as far as the competing conceptions of the good are concerned. It is a democratic state that is dedicated to the Zionist idea and project (i.e., creating and sustaining a *Jewish* state in Palestine), an idea and a project whose realization has come at the expense (if not the ruin) of the Palestinians (Israeli Palestinians included). Pervasive discrimination against the Palestinians in Israel is the unavoidable by-product of this unholy marriage between Zionism and democracy in the State of Israel. From the perspective of the Palestinians in Israel (the victims of discrimination), Israel is more of an ethnic than a liberal democracy. The basic structures of the state as well as its practices and policies over the years have manifested this bias without ambiguity or equivocation. From the perspective of liberal theories of justice, these basic structures and state policies are inherently discriminatory and, hence, unjust.

Second-Class Citizens

Israeli Palestinians, or the Palestinians who are Israeli citizens, are those Palestinians who remained within the borders of Israel, and hence under Israeli sovereignty, following the tragic events of the Nakba (Catastrophe), or ethnic cleansing, of 1948. Their number was then about 160,000; their number now exceeds 1.5 million (about 18 percent of the total population of Israel, according to the most recent official statistics). More than half of them reside mainly in separate towns and villages in the Galilee (where they still constitute a numerical majority despite intensive efforts by successive Israeli governments since the 1950s to "redeem" the land and to "Judaize the Galilee"). Almost 30 percent of them reside in the coastal cities and in separate towns and villages in the Triangle district, not far from the city of Tel Aviv and its surrounding. And close to 17 percent of them (around a quarter of a million Bedouins) reside in separate towns and villages in the Negev desert in the south. More than a fifth of Israeli Palestinians are "internal refugees"—their villages were demolished in 1948–49 and their lands confiscated. Since then they have been labeled "present absentees," that is, internally displaced persons who have not yet been compensated for the loss of homes, property, and the related suffering.

In a broad sense, all Palestinians in Israel are "present absentees." Formally, they are equal citizens of the state; they carry its passports and exercise the right to vote and run for office. They pay taxes and are entitled to economic and social benefits. But due to pervasive discrimination, both legal and nonlegal, they have been economically and politically marginalized. Additionally, their feelings of discomfort and alienation are intensified whenever Israeli Jewish leaders (religious or secular right wingers) refer to them as a demographic or security threat and when they are threatened with transfer from their places of residence by ultra-nationalist Jews. With such a Jewish state they cannot and should not be expected to identify. The state simply does not inhabit their hearts. In a profound sense, they are aliens in their own homeland.

Two additional points should be kept in mind whenever we talk about the Palestinian citizens of Israel. First, they are an inseparable part of the Palestinian people. There should not be any doubt about the truth of this statement of fact. We should not forget for a moment that the Palestinian refugees are their relatives, fellow villagers, and fellow town dwellers. Secondly, they are an indigenous and distinct ethno-cultural minority in Israel. They are not intruders or infiltrators or immigrants or guest workers or aliens of any kind. Currently approximately 80 percent of Palestinian Israelis are Muslims; the rest splits almost equally between Christians and Druze. And they are all Arabs, regardless of their religious affiliation. Indeed, even the Jews of Palestine before the emergence of the Zionist movement were regarded as Arabs. And yet, instead of trying to come to terms with the far-reaching implications of these facts about the ethnicity of the population, the Israeli authorities have engaged consistently and tenaciously in a twofold denial: denial that the Palestinians in Israel are an inseparable part of the larger Palestinian people, a position maintained up to the late 1970s or early 1980s; and a denial that they constitute a distinct ethno-cultural minority and, as such, are entitled to collective rights. The Israeli governmental policies of control and containment, divide and rule, temptation and intimidation, carrots and bullets, and of treating Palestinians differentially as religious sects or confessions rather than as a distinct ethno-cultural minority are all part and parcel of this twofold denial. Whether and to what extent these policies have succeeded or failed is a worthy topic for a separate discussion.

In response to the above challenges, the struggle of Palestinians in Israel has been, and still is, for just peace and full equality: just peace between Jewish Israel and the

Palestinian people (themselves included), and full equality as citizens of the Israeli state. It is on the decades-long struggle for the twin ideas and values of a just peace and full equality that the following discussion will focus.

Full Equality

Full equality (as I conceive of it) entails at least three main commitments by Jewish Israel: first, commitment to a single and uniform concept of democratic citizenship, which in turn requires replacing the current ethno-cultural nationalism of Israel with citizenship nationalism;[4] second, commitment to end discriminatory distribution and redistribution of material and nonmaterial goods, or what Michael Walzer calls "socially meaningful goods";[5] and third, commitment to protect, promote, and sustain the distinct ethnic identity of the Palestinian minority. For these commitments to be adequately or satisfactorily met or honored, Israel should become a genuine liberal democracy, that is, a state of *all* its citizens, regardless of race or language, color or religion. But even if Israel becomes such a democracy, the predicament of the Palestinians in Israel would not necessarily evaporate. This is mainly because the danger of the tyranny of the numerical Jewish majority would still loom large. Hence, for the idea of full equality to be realized, the recent Nation-State Law, which legalizes the supremacy of Jews over the non-Jewish citizens of the state, should be abolished. In such a case, the reallocation of certain powers and resources within the state would be necessary, so as to facilitate some form of mutually agreed autonomy or internal self-government.

Consistent with the demands outlined above, the struggle of Palestinians in Israel for full equality has been proceeding, as it should in my opinion, on two parallel tracks: first, as an effort to gain more "integration" into Israeli society and the state, with the manifest emphasis on individual civil and political rights and entitlements; and second, as a demand for recognition by the state that Palestinians in Israel constitute a distinct ethno-cultural minority, with the resultant emphasis on group or collective rights. It is my belief that the two tracks of struggle complement each other. It is also my belief that group or collective rights should go beyond cultural rights so as to include or encompass, *inter alia*, collective property rights and rights to internal self-government.[6] Needless to say, this dual struggle poses enormous challenges to Jewish and democratic Israel.

But only the politically naïve and epistemologically blind would believe that full equality is realizable or attainable under the conditions of conflict between Jewish Israel and the Palestinians. To say the least, the absence of a just peace, like the overemphasis on the Jewish character of the state, is a major obstacle on the path to accomplishing full equality.

The Palestinians inside Israel constitute close to 15 percent of the Palestinian people as a whole. Almost two-thirds of the 1.2 million Palestinians were displaced in 1947–49. They became refugees in Gaza, in the West Bank, inside Israel (internally displaced), in the surrounding Arab countries, as well as in other parts of the globe. Some of them acquired the citizenship of their host countries (mainly Jordan and several non-Arab states), others remained stateless (e.g., in Lebanon, Syria, as well as in Gaza). The Israeli authorities demolished more than five hundred villages and almost completely emptied the major cities (e.g., Jaffa, Haifa, Acre, Ramla, Lod, Safed, Tiberias) of their original inhabitants. Many scores of documented massacres were committed by the Jewish militias in order to sow fear among the inhabitants and thereby expedite the process of expulsion and dispossession of the Palestinians. The massacre in Deir Yasin on 9 April 1948 was the best known, but not the gravest or the bloodiest of them. The Palestinian refugees left almost everything behind: homes, towns, villages, lands, relatives, cattle, orchards, and even crops and personal belongings. In a matter of months after the departure of the British in May 1948, the country changed owners and rulers. With this large-scale expulsion and robbery of private and public property (even the Islamic endowment was not spared), the major Zionist goal of creating a Jewish state in Palestine was realized. In this manner, Israel was created and the Jewish majority in the state was secured.

This Jewish majority has been maintained and consolidated by waves of Jewish immigrants. Needless to say, the suffering of the displaced and dispossessed Palestinians is simply inexpressible, and the magnitude of losses is simply indescribable. How can anyone harbor any doubt that the Jewish state was born in an unpardonable sin?[7] Additionally, Gaza and the West Bank, including East Jerusalem, have been under belligerent occupation since 1967. They are, of course, still under occupation, despite the illusions to the contrary created by the partial implementation of the 1993 Oslo Accords. As for the gross violations of human rights vis-à-vis the Palestinians in the Occupied Palestinian Territories (including the illegally annexed East or Arab Jerusalem) before, during, and after the Al-Aqsa intifada (2000–2004), suffice it to consult the abundant reports by human rights and humanitarian organizations, both local and international (including United Nations periodic reports).[8]

Born in sin or not, more than seventy years later, the Jewish state has emerged as a political, economic, technological, and of course, military regional superpower. It is also said to be a functioning democracy, at least as far as its Jewish citizens are concerned. And it has managed to attract and absorb several million Jews, who immigrated in waves to Israel from all corners of the world (about four hundred thousand of them are not yet recognized as Jews by the religious Orthodox establishment). From the perspective of its advocates and supporters, Zionism as realized by the Jewish State of Israel has proved to be a success story, a remarkable revolution. According to the Zionist ethos, the Jews returned to their homeland and exercised their historical right to it after almost two thousand years of exile, dispersion, and yearning. In it they can lead normal lives, defend themselves, revive and speak their own language, and be masters of their own destiny.

The problem, of course, is that the homeland they "returned to" is also, and to no lesser degree, the homeland of the Palestinian Arabs. The country they "returned to" was not, as they tended to imagine or think, without people, and the homes they either demolished or seized were not without owners and inhabitants. They were able to "redeem" the homeland only by committing barbarous acts of killing, destruction, mass expulsion, and dispossession. It is ironic that these barbarous acts reached their climax just a few months before the proclamation of the Universal Declaration of Human Rights by the UN General Assembly on 10 December 1948.

Two States, One Homeland

It is not my primary intention here to pass final or unqualified judgments on the justice or injustice of Zionism or more generally on the morality of the Jewish state.[9] It is, rather, to show that neither just peace nor full equality (for the Palestinians in Israel) is attainable as long as Israel is normatively defined as a Jewish state (i.e., as the nation-state of the Jews). Corollary to this, it is also my intention to show that the two-state solution, as envisioned by Israel and advocated by the US administration since President Clinton, is not the right path to genuine peace, full equality, and justice. It can be defended pragmatically as a practicable or plausible solution to the prolonged conflict. But its morality would remain fundamentally questionable. To put it bluntly, as long as Israel insists on being or remaining a Jewish state (in the senses mentioned above), there will be no just solution to the Palestinian question in all its aspects, and there will not be full equality for Palestinians who are also Israeli citizens.

Saying this does not mean or imply rejecting the two-state solution, however. What it means or implies is that even if the two-state solution is the only political game in town, it should be redesigned to address the main competing claims of the two parties to the conflict. Creating a Palestinian state alongside Israel even on the basis of the June 1967 borders, separated from Jewish Israel by a monstrous wall or repulsive fence or any other impenetrable physical barrier, will only perpetuate the separation of the Palestinians in Israel from the Palestinians in the new state, on the one hand, and will not provide for full equality within Jewish Israel, on the other. The short of the matter is: what is required is the kind of solution that is based, among other things, on democracy, equality of individual and collective rights, and respect for the attachment of both Israeli Jews and Palestinian Arabs (including the Palestinians in Israel) to their respective communities and to the country as a whole. Elsewhere I have argued that the "two states, one homeland" proposal is the one that satisfies the two main conditions of fairness and practicability.[10]

According to the two states, one homeland proposal:

- A democratic Palestinian state should be created along the 4 June 1967 borders.
- Israel should be recognized as a democratic and Jewish state, Jewish only in the sense that the majority of its actual citizens are Jews.

- Settlers who find themselves under Palestinian jurisdiction can become either equal Palestinian citizens or remain Israeli citizens with permanent resident status in Palestine (of course, without their current privileges).
- Palestinian refugees can freely return to the Palestinian state. Those who opt to return to Israel can become permanent residents of Israel, but citizens of Palestine.
- The two states should commit themselves to the values and practices of liberal democracy, as well as to the principle of nondiscrimination against ethnocultural minority groups.
- Separation between the two states is to be mainly political rather than geographic or demographic. Thus, the unity of the country can be preserved.
- The two states are fairly to share all the things that cannot or should not be divided. Above all, they are fairly to share the city of Jerusalem, which shall remain united and open to all.
- The attachments of both Palestinians and Israeli Jews to the whole country or to special places in it should be respected. The attachments of non-Palestinian Arabs, Muslims, and Christians, as well as of non-Israeli Jews, should also be respected.

The above revised or redesigned two-states proposal rests on two important distinctions: the first is between country (homeland) and state; the second is between citizenship and (permanent) residency. Accordingly, although I might end up as a citizen of either state, the whole country will be in some sense mine (as my attachment to it is being respected). In the other state, I can be a permanent resident enjoying equal civil rights. Thus, Israel can remain a Jewish and democratic state while Palestinians and Israeli Jews can still enjoy the whole country or homeland.[11]

Only in this kind of political setting or dispensation are Palestinians in Israel likely to enjoy to the full their equal democratic citizenship rights and hence to feel at home in their homeland. It has been argued that the one democratic state solution best accommodates the aspirations and rights of Israeli Jews and Palestinians (Palestinians in Israel included). But the main problem with such a solution is that it is being opposed and resisted by the overwhelming majority of Israeli Jews, who are still committed to one version or another of Zionism.

I am not one of those who believe that my country is my God or is God-given to me or to my people. And the God deserving of my worship is not the God of vengeance. But the fact remains that what I call "hard nationalism" (or religious fanaticism for that matter), whether Palestinian or Jewish Israeli, is the major obstacle to the kind of solution I am advocating. Hard nationalism and religious fanaticism breed and feed on resentment and violence and hence keep all of us away from the path of genuine reconciliation and mutual recognition and accommodation. But make no mistake about it, I am one of those who believe that discrimination, occupation, displacement, statelessness, and denial of other fundamental human rights are evils and therefore ought to be resisted. Yet if the long-term goal is coexistence in peace, equality, and respect for and tolerance of ethnic or cultural differences in one country or state, then violence or brute force is not the right means, nor is it the right way. Hard nationalism and religious fanaticism breed and feed on violence and erect psychological barriers and barriers of self-righteousness that stand in the way of the kind of accommodation I envision and advocate.

Summary Comments

Back to the predicament of the Palestinians who are also citizens of the Jewish state. They are being discriminated against for no other reason than for being Palestinian Arabs. But this discrimination is not a fact of nature, nor is it a fate that they should be urged to embrace or love. They have a moral right, some say they are even under a moral obligation, to resent and resist it. In this regard, I wish to make the following four summary comments:

First, two factors combine to frustrate the struggle of the Palestinians in Israel for full equality of rights (human rights and citizenship rights): the Jewish character of the State of Israel, on the one hand, and the prolonged conflict between Jewish Israel and the Palestinians, on the other. Each of these two factors is an insurmountable obstacle.

Second, in their struggle for full equality, and to their credit, Palestinians in Israel have on the whole not resorted to or practiced violence. They have not even practiced any serious acts of civil disobedience against unjust laws and immoral policies and practices. In this particular situation, and more generally in the struggle for equality of rights and entitlements within the one state, the resort to violence is most likely to defeat the purpose. If your goal is to replace ethno-cultural nationalism with citizenship nationalism, violence is not a defensible means of struggle. It can achieve only the opposite result. Violence can be justified, however, if the aim of the struggle is political and physical separation (given, of course, the moral and legal constraints on the use of force).

Third, the struggle of the Palestinians in Israel will not be crowned with success as long as the larger Palestinian Israeli conflict remains unresolved. Hence, their struggle for ending the larger conflict is inseparable from and intertwined with their struggle for full equality within the Israeli state. This does not entail, however, that the latter struggle is pointless unless the former succeeds. There are different degrees of success or failure in this regard. And degrees do matter.

Fourth, the struggle of the Palestinians in Israel for peace and equality should be guided, in my opinion, by a liberating and redeeming vision, one that addresses and accommodates the basic needs, vital interests, rights, and aspirations of the concerned parties (Israeli Jews included, of course). I am afraid that the two-state solution, as envisaged by the Zionist center-left parties in Israel, is not guided by such a liberating and redeeming vision. Only the one democratic state and the two states, one homeland proposals can be said to embody such a vision. The advantage of the latter vision is that it does not require the end of Zionism or, what amounts to the same thing, the end of the Jewish state.

A Personal Note

I wish to close this chapter with a personal note that has general moral and political implications. I am a Palestinian Arab who is also a citizen of the Jewish State of Israel. As an Israeli Palestinian citizen, I know from the inside how discrimination works and what it entails. My extended family on both my mother's and my father's sides lost two villages in 1948, and some of our relatives and fellow villagers have become refugees in Lebanon ever since. Their two villages in the Galilee, Damun and Birweh, were completely demolished in 1949, and the lands of their residents were expropriated. But I also I know from the inside the fears, concerns, and aspirations of Israeli Jews. For the past thirty-five years or so I have been living and working in the West Bank, occupied since 1967. And so, I have also been a witness to the atrocities of the occupation authorities.

As a human rights activist in 1990–92 (the first intifada) and 2000–2004 (the Al-Aqsa intifada), I was engaged in monitoring, documenting, and reporting on the violations of the human rights of the Palestinians in Gaza and the West Bank (including East Jerusalem) committed by the Israeli occupation authorities and the Jewish settlers. These human rights violations were identified and evaluated according to the applicable international standards and norms. Finally, I should add that I spent 1976–82 living and studying in the United States, the so-called land of freedom and opportunity. I have two daughters: the eldest lived, studied, and worked in France for eight years; the youngest has been living, working, and studying in the United States for the past fifteen years. I am personally a committed liberal democrat, animated by a strong sense of justice. And so, in a real sense, we are a cosmopolitan family.

Given all the above, what I am seeking is the kind of situation that would make me feel at home in my homeland as well as in the wider world. Feeling at home in the world requires commitments to and respect for universal ideals and universal, impersonal, or impartial moral values. In other words, it requires worship of the Right and the True and the Good, without xenophobia, racism, prejudice, or hatred of the ethnic or cultural other. It requires looking at different cultures as converging rather than clashing. It also requires commitment to genuine democracy and to what is truly universal in the human rights declarations and conventions. And so on. In my opinion, cultural particularity should not be accepted as a shield against universal values, ideas, and ideals. Feeling at home in the world requires, in other words, some degree of cosmopolitanism.[12]

It is ironic that in my personal case, as in the case of so many other Palestinians, feeling at home in the homeland proved to be no less difficult than feeling at home in the world. Feeling at home in the homeland requires, among other things, overcoming discrimination (the case of the Palestinians in Israel), ending the occupation of 1967, and addressing the problem of the Palestinian refugees since 1948 (inside as well as outside the country) in a fair and compassionate manner. For all of this to be realized, both Palestinian Arabs and Israeli Jews should find a way to live together in peace, justice, and equality of rights, in a country they should know how to share or to both divide and share. Physical separation by a repulsive wall or fence, ethnocultural nationalism, religious fanaticism, and the hatred, violence, and resentment they breed and nurture are inimical to this feeling of home in the homeland or, for that matter, to feeling at home in the wider world. For finally, it is the Nikhils (the seekers of harmony, rights, and freedom) rather than the Sandips (the demonic and tyrannical nationalists) of Rabindranath Tagore's *The Home and the World*, who should ultimately prevail, in Palestine, Israel, and elsewhere.[13]

Said Zeedani is an associate professor of philosophy at Al-Quds University. He obtained his PhD from the University of Wisconsin in Madison in 1982. He served as vice president for academic affairs at Al-Quds University in 2005–11 and as director general of the Independent Commission for Human Rights (ICHR) of Palestine in 2000–2004. He was also dean of arts at Birzeit University in 1995–98. Zeedani has edited five annual reports about the human rights situation in the Occupied Palestinian Territories, in addition to a book on the Oriental Jews in Israel (in Arabic). Additionally, he has coauthored a book titled *The Democratic Option* (in Arabic), along with numerous articles and book chapters about aesthetics, democracy, human rights, ethics and politics, and the Palestine-Israel conflict.

Notes

1. There are numerous books, articles, and conference proceedings about the Palestinians in Israel. For our purposes here I wish to recommend the following books by three Jewish writers: David Grossman, *Sleeping on a Wire: Conversations with Palestinians in Israel*, trans. Haim Watzman (New York: Straus and Giroux, 1993); Oren Yiftachel, *Ethnocracy: Land and Identity Politics in Israel/Palestine* (Philadelphia: University of Pennsylvania Press, 2006); Susan Nathan, *the Other Side of Israel: My Journey across the Jewish-Arab Divide* (London: HarperCollins, 2005). For official statistics about demographics and socioeconomic gaps between Palestinian Arabs and Israeli Jews in Israel, consult the periodic reports of Israel Central Bureau of Statistics. According to a twenty-seven-page report to the European Union, submitted by some consuls general of member states, 50 percent of the Palestinians in Israel live under the poverty line (as defined by the State of Israel), and they own less than 3 percent of the land. For a summary of the report, see the British newspaper *The Independent*, 27 December 2011.
2. The controversial basic law "Israel—the Nation State of the Jewish People" was passed by the Israeli Parliament (Knesset) on 19 July 2018. Article 1(c) of the law states: "The exercise of the right to

national self-determination in the State of Israel is unique to the Jewish People." And article 4 (b) of the law demotes the status of Arabic from its prior status as an official language to a language with a special status in the state.
3. Ronald Dworkin, "Liberalism," in *Public and Private Morality*, ed. Stuart Hampshire (Cambridge: Cambridge University Press, 1978), 113–43.
4. Shlomo Sand, *The Invention of the Jewish People*, trans. Yael Lotan (London and New York: Verso, 2009), chap. 5.
5. Michael Walzer, *Spheres of Justice: A Defense of Pluralism and Equality* (New York: Basic Books, 1983).
6. Will Kymlicka, *Liberalism, Community, and Culture* (Oxford: Clarendon Press, 1989).
7. Ilan Pappé, *The Ethnic Cleansing of Palestine* (Oxford: One World, 2006); Nur Masalha, *Expulsion of the Palestinians* (Washington, DC: Institute for Palestine Studies, 1992); Benny Morris, *The Birth of the Palestinian Refugee Problem* (Cambridge: Cambridge University Press, 1987); Adel Manna, *Nakba and Survival: The Story of the Palestinians Who Remained in Haifa and the Galilee 1948–1956* (Ramallah: Institute of Palestine Studies, 2016, in Arabic).
8. Jimmy Carter, *Palestine: Peace Not Apartheid* (New York: Simon and Schuster, 2006); Raja Shehadeh, *Palestinian Walks: Notes on a Vanishing Landscape* (London: Profile Books, 2007).
9. Chaim Gans, *A Just Zionism: On the Morality of the Jewish State* (Oxford: Oxford University Press, 2008).
10. The "two states, one homeland" initiative was launched in the summer of 2012 by a Jewish Israeli group led by Meron Rapaport and a Palestinian group led by Awni Almashni. The initiative was inspired by an article I published almost five years earlier. The impetus for the article and, later on, for the initiative is the perceived demise of the two-state solution, which served as the basis of the Oslo political process. See Said Zeedani, "Palestinians and Israeli Jews: Divide and Share the Land," *Israel-Palestine Journal* 14, no. 3 (2007): 104–9, https://pij.org/articles/1116/palestinians-and-israeli-jews-divide-and-share-the-land.
11. Said Zeedani, "A Non Modest Proposal for Resolving the Palestine-Israel Conflict: The Divide and Share Approach," in *Palestine Membership in the United Nations: Legal and Practical Implications*, ed. Mutaz Qafisheh (Newcastle-upon-Tyne: Cambridge Scholars, 2013), 434–39.
12. Kwame Anthony Appiah, *The Ethics of Identity* (Princeton: Princeton University Press, 2005), esp. chap. 6, "Rooted Cosmopolitanism," 213–72.
13. The Zionist Sandips (i.e., the fanatic religious/nationalist Jews) believe that Palestine was given by God to the Jews exclusively. It is fortunate that these Zionist Sandips do not yet command the allegiance of the majority of Jews in Israel.

Select Bibliography

Carter, Jimmy. *Palestine: Peace, Not Apartheid*. New York: Simon & Schuster, 2006.
Gans, Chaim. *A Just Zionism: On the Morality of the Jewish State*. Oxford: Oxford University Press, 2008.
Kymlicka, Will. *Liberalism, Community and Culture*. Oxford: Clarendon Press, 1989.
Manna, Adel. *Nakba and Survival: The Story of the Palestinians Who Remained in Haifa and the Galilee 1948–1956*. Ramallah: Institute for Palestine Studies, 2016, in Arabic.
Masalha, Nur. *The Expulsion of the Palestinians*. Washington, DC: Institute for Palestine Studies, 1992.
Nathan, Susan. *The Other Side of Israel: My Journey across the Jewish-Arab Divide*. London: HarperCollins, 2005.
Pappé, Ilan. *The Ethnic Cleansing of Palestine*. Oxford: One World, 2006.
Sand, Shlomo. *The Invention of the Jewish People*. Translated by Yael Lotam. London and New York: Verso, 2009.
Yiftachel, Oren. *Land and Identity Politics in Israel/Palestine*. Philadelphia: Pennsylvania University Press, 2006.

CHAPTER 19

THE DEMOGRAPHY OF RETURN

SALMAN ABU SITTA

Introduction

In the mid-twentieth century, Palestine witnessed a devastating event on a scale unseen in its four-thousand-year history.[1] The Nakba, or the Catastrophe, the forcible displacement of some 750,000–900,000 Palestinians[2] during so-called Arab-Israeli War of 1948, is one of the most comprehensive and longest-running campaigns of ethnic cleansing since the beginning of the twentieth century.[3] The Arab population that lived in 560 towns and villages was forcibly displaced in 1948–49; in areas that became the State of Israel, as many as three-quarters of all Palestinians were displaced.[4] In several districts incorporated into the newly created Israel, not a single Palestinian village remained intact by the time hostilities came to a close. Palestinian refugees and internally displaced persons (IDPs) from the first Arab-Israeli War were denied the right to return to their homes, lands, and properties by the State of Israel; by late 2014 they and their descendants numbered around 6.5 million.[5] Nearly seven decades after their initial displacement, a solution to their predicament has yet to be found.

The ethnic cleansing of Palestinians has its roots in the period before the 1948 War, when the Zionist movement first began to colonize Palestine with the aim of creating a Jewish state through immigration, acquisition of land, and settlement. At the beginning of the twentieth century, Jews composed a small percentage of the population and owned very little land in Palestine. The term "ethnic cleansing" is used here to describe the panoply of policies and practices, sometimes associated with the establishment of states, that aim to create an ethnically or religiously homogenous region through the forced displacement of a particular existing ethnic or religious group.[6] While there is no universally agreed nor codified definition, it is generally accepted that ethnic cleansing can occur on a mass scale through expulsion and forcible transfer propelled by terrorist acts,[7] as happened during the 1948 War, or it can take place gradually through a range of measures. This is how it began in Palestine in

 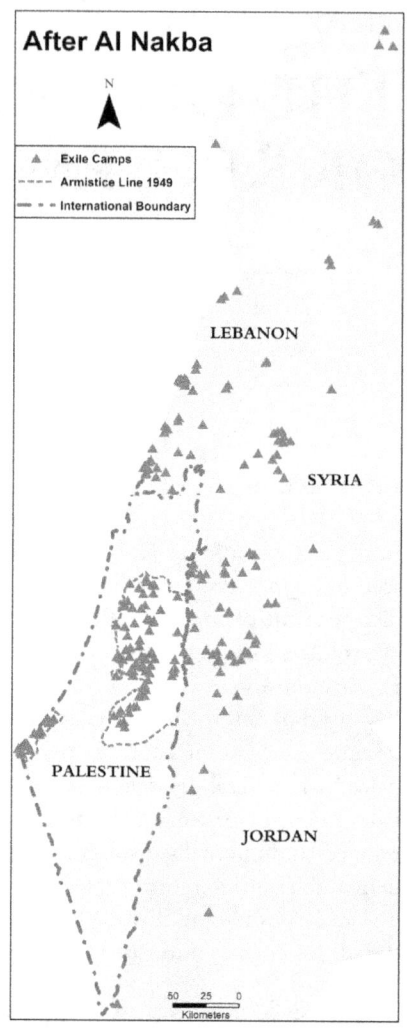

Map 19.1a. The Nakba. Over 500 Palestinian towns and villages were attacked and depopulated in 1948. Their population composes 85 percent of the inhabitants of the land in Palestine that became Israel. Source: Author compilation.

Map 19.1b. The refugee exile. The refugees sought safety in UN-run refugee camps in what is left of Palestine (the West Bank and Gaza Strip) and in neighboring Arab countries: Jordan, Lebanon, and Syria. They are still refugees there today. In 1967 Israel extended its occupation to the West Bank and Gaza Strip. Source: Author compilation.

the decades leading up to the first Arab-Israeli War. The war broke out following the United Nations General Assembly plan (Resolution 181, 29 November 1947), which recommended, against the wishes and rights of the majority of its population, partition of the country into two states. Among those displaced during the two and a half preceding decades of British Mandatory rule were Palestinians denationalized under the citizenship legislation drafted in consultation with Zionist leaders; Mutaz Qafisheh has described the denationalized as the "first Palestinian refugees."[8]

The two decades following the 1948 ethnic cleansing saw an ongoing expulsion and forcible transfer of Palestinians who remained within Israel.[9] During the 1967 Arab-Israeli War a second mass displacement of 350,000–400,000 Palestinians took place, of whom half were refugees from the previous war.[10] The ethnic cleansing of Palestine continued with Israel's occupation and colonization of the West Bank, including East Jerusalem and the Gaza Strip, which is now well into its fifth decade.[11] Israel's war on the Gaza Strip in 2014, the third in six years, displaced an estimated half-million Palestinians at its height and illustrates the ongoing war on Palestinians by one of the only surviving colonial projects in the world. Today an estimated two-thirds of all Palestinians are refugees or internally displaced persons; more than half of the displaced are living outside their historic homeland.[12]

Since its establishment during the 1948 Arab-Israeli War, the State of Israel has refused to allow displaced Palestinians, whether refugees or IDPs, to return to their homes, lands, and properties inside the Jewish state.[13] Initial arguments that return was impossible for economic, political, and security reasons were later supplemented by legal arguments drawn from developments in international law—in particular, the codification of return as a binding treaty obligation under international human rights law. While the prohibition of ethnic cleansing as a treaty rule does not exist, the illegality of ethnic cleansing stems from the fact that related policies and practices, including expulsion and forcible transfer, constitute serious violations of international law.[14] There is also a growing body of international and to a lesser extent national jurisprudence on the crime of forced displacement.[15] UN General Assembly Resolution 194, which calls upon the State of Israel to allow refugees wishing to do so to return to their homes at the earliest possible date, has been reaffirmed annually by a large majority of UN member states.

While the return of millions of displaced Palestinians to their homes, lands, and properties inside Israel and the additional territories occupied by it over the past fifty years is presented as raising a complex range of political, economic, and social challenges, the premise of this chapter is that there are no serious logistic reasons that should prevent their return. Indeed, this was the position taken by the United States, one of the main drafters of Resolution 194, during the 1948 War, notwithstanding the subsequent shift in American policy stemming from the evolving alliance with Israel.[16] Nor are there serious legal arguments that would prevent refugees from exercising their right to return to their homes, lands, and properties on either side of the 1949 armistice line "dividing" Palestine into what became the State of Israel in

1948 from the remaining territory Israel occupied in 1967. In addition to Resolution 194, along with a host of additional UN resolutions reaffirming the Right of Return for refugees and displaced persons, UN human rights treaty committees have consistently called upon Israel to revise or repeal legislation that currently prevents displaced Palestinians from returning to their places of origin.[17]

This chapter focuses on some of the practical aspects of voluntary repatriation, one of three durable solutions afforded to refugees and displaced persons, and the primary solution to forced displacement around the world. The study presented here is part of an ongoing comprehensive demographic, geographic, and legal research undertaken by the Palestine Land Society, established in 2000 with the aim of implementing the Right of Return.[18]

In planning for the eventual return of displaced Palestinians, three major elements should be examined: the people, the land, and legislation relevant to each. The latter two elements have been addressed sufficiently elsewhere (see table 19.1).[19] The following discussion, therefore, focuses on the population, which can be divided into three basic groups: non-refugee Palestinians, returning Palestinians (returnees), and the existing Jewish population in territories that compose the State of Israel. The discussion focuses, in particular, on refugees from the 1948 War who originate from areas inside Israel and compose the majority of the Palestinian refugee population. All figures used in this chapter are for the year 2008 unless otherwise stated.

Table 19.1. Elements of future Palestine.

The Element	The Components	Supporting Data
The land	Ownership and occupancy: well documented	The Ottoman Records. The British Mandate. The United Nations. Seized Israel records.
The people (2008)	Palestinians: 11 million natural inhabitants; Jews: 5.5 million	Palestinians: two-thirds refugees. Half under Israel rule on Palestine soil. Jews: immigrants/settlers. Now citizens. About 750,000 Israelis abroad. Excluding 300,000 foreign workers.
The law	Universal Declaration of Human Rights – 10 December 1948, international covenants against racism, apartheid, colonialism, war crimes and crimes against humanity, right of s elf-determination	UN Resolution 181 – 29 November 1947; UN Resolution 194 – UNCCP – 11 December 1948; Israel's Conditional Membership (Res. 273 III) – 11 May 1949. Subsequent UN and Security Council resolutions.

Source: Author.

Distribution of the Population

As of 2008, Palestine in its three main regions—Israel (Palestine 1948), West Bank, including East Jerusalem, and Gaza Strip—had a total population of about 10.5 million people. The number of Palestinians (4.7 million) and Jews (5.8 million) were roughly comparable.[20] The Jewish population cited above, however, was an overestimate, since it covered all those who were not Palestinians. This included an estimated 300,000 foreign workers, primarily from Thailand and Romania, and 1 million Russians, of whom about 40 percent were not certified as Jews by religious authorities. The actual parity between Palestinians and Jews, however, is not in itself important except for the fact that Israel's refusal to allow refugees to return stems from a desire to maintain a permanent Jewish majority. It should be recalled that while immigration contributed to a significant increase in the Jewish population in the decades leading up to the 1948 War, it was only through mass expulsion and the forced flight of Palestinians that the Zionist movement was able to achieve majority status. Important here are the privileges granted to Jews and the concomitant denial of many of the same rights to non-Jews, in particular to Palestinians.[21] This is evidenced most clearly in Israel's refusal to allow Palestinian refugees and IDPs to exercise their right to return to places of origin, whether inside Israel or within the territories it has occupied for over fifty years.

The impact of this discrimination becomes clearer when the above figure for the Palestinian population is broken down into refugees and non-refugees. Of the 4.7 million Palestinians who resided on either side of the 1949 armistice line "dividing" the State of Israel from the Palestinian territories that it occupied in 1967 as of 2008, about half (2.23 million) were refugees. The bulk of Palestinian refugees resided outside Palestine, primarily in a narrow ring along the borders of Palestine in three major host countries—Jordan, Lebanon, and Syria.

In total, the estimated Palestinian refugee population in 2008 was 6.77 million persons, the majority (4.67 million) of whom were registered to receive assistance from the UN Relief and Works Agency for Palestine Refugees (UNRWA), the agency set up in 1949 to provide emergency relief and longer-term development assistance until a solution to their situation could be found as set out in General Assembly Resolution 194. As of 2008, refugees, whether registered with UNRWA or not, made up two-thirds of the entire Palestinian people, one of several features of the Palestinian case that has made it different from refugee situations elsewhere since the beginning of the twentieth century.

Palestinians in Mandatory Palestine live either under Israeli rule or under Israeli military occupation.[22] Common to the Palestinians (whether displaced or not) on either side of the 1949 armistice line, as noted earlier, is the fundamental lack of equality in relation to Jews. Racism and apartheid dominate Israel's laws and practices.[23]

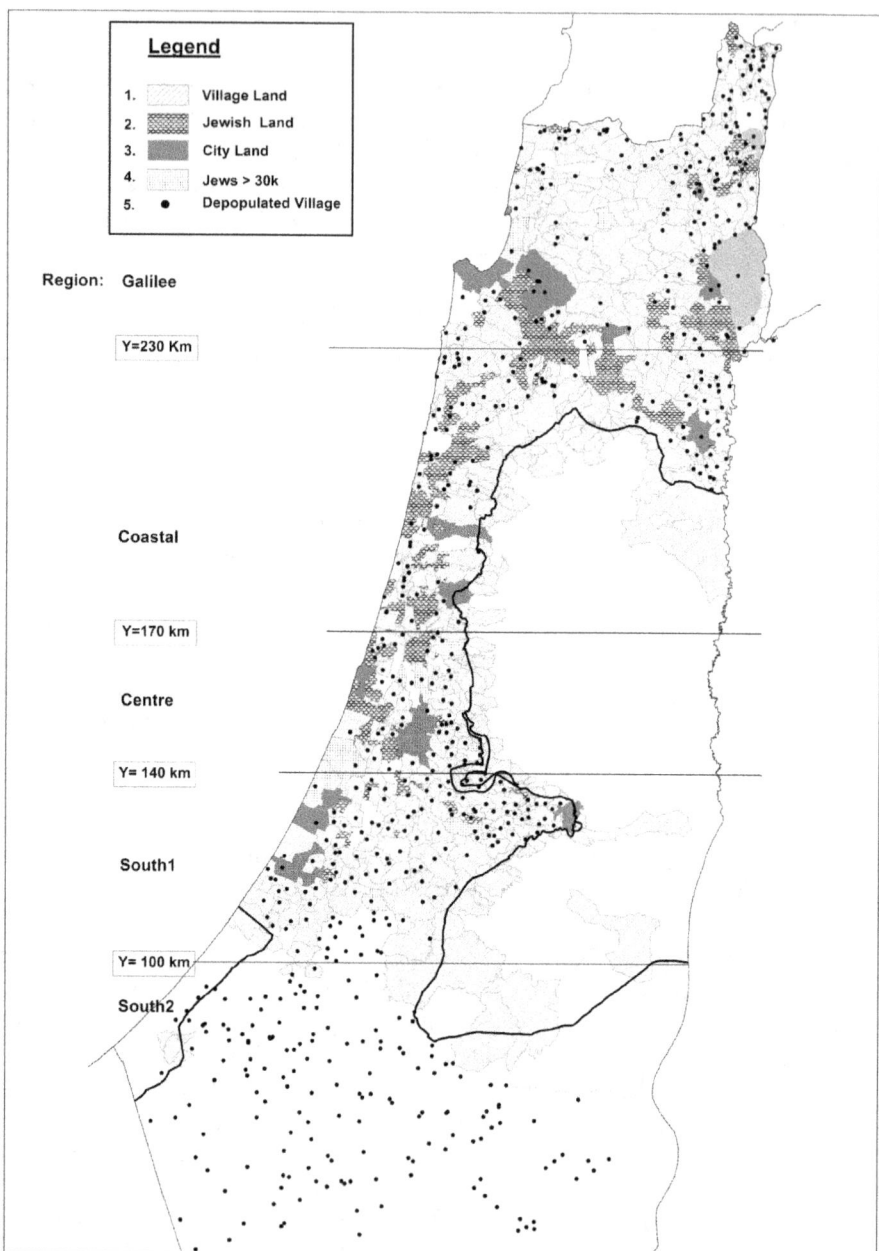

Map 19.2. Population distribution. The Palestinian population in village lands before 1948 is compared with the present Jewish settlers on each village land. The cities are identified. The village lands where Jews today are over thirty thousand are also identified. Source: Author compilation.

In order to examine the effect of return on the existing population, the present-day State of Israel can be divided, for the purposes of this study, into five geographical regions (see map 19.3): the Galilee in the north, the intermediate coastal region between the cities of Haifa and Jaffa, the central region (including the city of Tel Aviv) where most of the country's Jewish population resides, and two regions in the south—Gaza and Beersheba Mandate districts—which together compose the southern district.

In 2008 Jewish Israelis, with a total population of 5.8 million, resided in 924 localities within the 1949 armistice line, excluding West Bank settlements. The distribution of Jewish localities inside Israel is especially revealing. Of the total number of localities, only fourteen have a population of over 100,000, twelve have a population between 50,000 and 100,000, and twenty-nine localities between 20,000 and 50,000. In other words, 87 percent of Jewish Israelis reside in just fifty-five localities, or 5 percent of the total number of localities. These localities occupy fourteen hundred square kilometers, or 6 percent of Israel's total area. It is also interesting to observe that the area where the majority of Jewish Israelis currently live is almost the same area where they resided in Palestine during the British Mandate.

The remaining Jewish settlements inside Israel are comparatively small. As of 2008, for example, a total of 390,500 Jews, not including the small number located in the Beersheba district in the south of the country, resided in 638 kibbutzim and moshavim, at an average of 600 persons per locality. The average will be much smaller if we include the southern district of Beersheba. Set up to extend Jewish control across the country as part of the colonization process referred to earlier, Jewish settlements or colonies were also central to the policy and practice of "retroactive transfer," which aimed to prevent the return of Palestinian refugees to their homes, lands, and properties after the 1948 War.[24]

The Feasibility of Return

Despite the passage of time since the 1948 War, including the increase in the size of the Jewish population through immigration and natural growth, it is still possible for the majority of rural Palestinian refugees wishing to do so to return to their homes, lands, and properties without the displacement of most Jewish inhabitants of the country. In 246 Palestinian villages depopulated in 1948, for example, there are no Jews currently residing on village lands. The Jewish population in kibbutzim and moshavim located on the lands of another 272 depopulated Palestinian villages does not exceed 5,000, regardless of the number of such settlements on any one village land. These village lands are shown in map 19.3, shaded area 1. The figures exclude the Beersheba district, which is sparsely populated save for Beersheba city, now repopulated by Jews.

Land owned by Jews prior to the 1948 War is shown in map 19.2, shaded area 2, and is today fully populated. Cities, whether mixed (Palestinian and Jewish) or not, are shown in map 19.2, shaded area 3. Unlike depopulated Palestinian villages that were totally destroyed by Israel, the destruction of cities during the war was limited to old quarters, with the dual aim of facilitating Jewish settlement in newer quarters and concentrating Palestinians in a limited number of areas in order to contain the remaining non-Jewish population.[25] The 3,500-year-old archaeological artifacts and much of the old quarter of Tiberias, for example, were totally destroyed during and after the 1948 War. While the Jewish population of these mixed cities has expanded over time, many still retain a sizable number of Palestinians. There are, by way of contrast, few Palestinian villages that were depopulated during the 1948 War where the Jewish population today exceeds 30,000. These appear in map 19.2, shaded area 4, and are located adjacent to areas where Jews resided prior to the war.

The main Jewish population concentration remains in Tel Aviv metropolis, Haifa, and West Jerusalem.

As this brief overview illustrates, the voluntary return of the vast majority of Palestinian refugees could be carried out without the significant displacement of Jews from the lands of depopulated Palestinian villages.

In the Galilee in the north, the Little Triangle (an area some twenty kilometers south of Haifa annexed to Israel under the 1949 armistice agreement with Jordan), and Beersheba district in the south, there is already a sizable Palestinian population ready to welcome and help reintegrate their kith and kin.

Table 19.2. Land use in Israel.

Land Use	Km²	% of Total	Km²	% of Total	% Per group
	1994		2020		
Pop. centers	1,150	5%	1,800	8%	12%
Spaces in centers	640	3%	710	3%	
Military	5,860	27%	5,860	27%	88%
Open, protected	5,090	24%	5,090	24%	
Vacant	8,760	41%	8,040	37%	
Total	21,500	100%	21,500	100%	100%

Notes:
1. Total includes Golan (1.154 km²); net Israel area 20,346 km², as per source.
2. Population centers: includes built-up areas, roads, and railways within.
3. Spaces: includes army installations, bases, and factories.
4. Military: includes camps, training, maneuverings, and firing ranges.
5. Open protected areas: includes nature reserves, parks, panoramic scenes, forests, and woods.
6. Vacant: includes uninhabited areas, mining, quarries, roads, railways, and agriculture.
7. Cultivated area is 4,200 km² (1997) including irrigated land 2,000 km² (1979), reduced to 1,115 km² (2000).

Source: Adam Mazor, *Israel Plan 2020*, vol. 2 (Haifa: The Technion, 1997, in Hebrew), 188, table 12.1 (excerpts).

The vast tracts of sparsely populated areas in rural Israel have been known to planners in Israel for a long time. An expert study entitled *Israel 2020* conducted by 250 Israeli and international experts in 1994 already pointed out this little-known result (see table 19.2).

Thus, it becomes clear that the primary obstacle to the refugees' return to Israel, as noted earlier, is not the lack of living space inside Israel, but rather the system of racism and apartheid incorporated into Israel's laws.[26] With this obstacle removed, the return of refugees is readily possible. Granting equal rights to all persons is the fundamental requirement to ending the century-long conflict in Palestine.

Phases of Return

The Palestinian refugees with homes, properties, and lands inside Israel can usefully be divided into three groups. In the first group are the rural refugees, who compose by far the majority of Palestinians displaced in 1948 and represent the most pressing issue. In the second group are the refugees returning to areas where the majority of the Jewish population currently resides. In the third group are the refugees who originate from urban areas.

The third group originate from eighteen cities classified as follows: three coastal cities (Jaffa, Tel Aviv, Haifa), which were and are still mixed; two inland cities (Tiberias and Safed), which were mixed and are now wholly Jewish; three Palestinian cities (Acre, Lydda, Ramla), which were Palestinian and are now mixed; four Palestinian cities (Baysan, Beersheba, al-Majdal/Asqalan) along with the former village of Isdud, which were wholly Palestinian and are now Jewish populated; two Palestinian cities (Shafa Amr and Nazareth), which were and are still Palestinian; three Palestinian cities (Gaza, Tulkarem, Qalqilya), whose lands are located on the Israeli side of the 1949 armistice line, while urban areas remain Palestinian; and the western neighborhoods of Jerusalem, which were mixed and are now Jewish.

Let us now examine the major case, the return of the rural refugees (see table 19.3). The return of registered rural refugees can be further divided geographically into the following stages: the rural south in two phases, the rural Galilee in one phase, and central Palestine in one phase. During the ethnic cleansing of Palestinians in 1948, refugees escaped the ravages of war and massacres by seeking refuge in the nearest safe place. The Haganah, later the IDF, closed all exit routes except one left for escape. Refugees took the open route to safety. Most of the village population ended up in two regions, with lesser numbers in other areas. Therefore, the return of refugees from Gaza Strip camps, for example, must be accompanied by the return of their kith and kin from Jordan and the West Bank, and so on. For this study, refugee populations of less than two thousand per village were ignored. The number of localities (towns and villages) taken into account here were Gaza Strip (98), West Bank (80), Jordan (104), Syria (23), and Lebanon (49).

Table 19.3. Phases of return. The table shows the remaining refugees after the repatriation of each phase. It is clear that the repatriation of refugees in the Gaza Strip is the most dramatic.

Refugee Population in Thousands in 2008	West Bank	Gaza Strip	Lebanon	Syria	Jordan	Total
All registered refugees	754	1,060	417	457	1,931	4,619
Remaining after Gaza Strip repatriation	610	73	352	401	1,415	2,851
Remaining after Lebanon repatriation	551	72	58	208	1,245	2,134
Remaining after West Bank repatriation	153	60	54	188	686	1,141
Remaining after Jordan repatriation	94	40	52	169	175	530
Remaining after Syria repatriation	93	40	43	56	172	403
Total refugees repatriated >2000	661	1,020	374	401	1,759	4,215
Total repatriated and leftover	754	1,060	417	457	1,931	4,619

Note: Refugees in one region have relatives in other regions. For example, the majority of refugees from villages in the south found refuge in the Gaza Strip but many found refuge in the West Bank and Jordan. Source: Author compilation.

The Gaza Strip is one of the most densely populated areas of the world, with currently around two million residents. The situation of the refugees there, who reside in 1.3 percent of the area of Palestine, and compose 80 percent of the Gaza Strip's population, is in urgent need of resolution. These refugees were expelled from 247 villages in southern Palestine. Their situation has become even more dire since the imposition of an Israeli siege in 2007; the United Nations has warned that Gaza may be unlivable by 2020.[27] Further, they have been under constant Israeli land, air, and sea attacks, including three major Israeli assaults in the years 2008–21. Of all refugee cases, the return of Gaza refugees to their homes and lands in southern Palestine would be a major breakthrough in the one-hundred-year struggle for peace in the region.

Similarly, the return of rural refugees in Lebanon and Syria to their homes and lands in the Galilee could be effected without much population dislocation. Almost half of the present Galilee population is Palestinian.

The return of the refugees from the West Bank and Jordan to their homes in the central sector needs special consideration.

In summary, the voluntary return of rural refugees would make a significant contribution to resolving the Palestinian refugee situation and would have little impact in terms of secondary occupation on the present Jewish inhabitants of these areas. In this way, it is possible to arrange for the return of some three-quarters of all Palestinian refugees (including their descendants) from the 1948 War without any significant displacement of the existing Jewish population.[28]

As for the smaller number of Jews who reside on the lands of depopulated Palestinian villages, there are a range of possible solutions,[29] from leasing agricultural land from returnees who wish to repossess their lands to a shift in economic activity of kibbutzim and moshavim from agriculture to industry and tourism, which would require the use of smaller areas of land.

The Return to Heavily Populated Areas

By way of contrast, the return of refugees from depopulated villages in the central region of the country (between latitudes 170 and 230—see map) is less straightforward, for two major reasons. First, as mentioned earlier, there is a significant concentration of Jewish Israelis in the coastal region in the center of the country, which predates the 1948 War. Second, the refugees' return is further complicated by the presence of Jewish populations surrounding Palestinian villages. In this region of the country, voluntary return could nevertheless be accomplished in part through the creation of independent Jewish cantons, which maintain full administrative, social, and cultural autonomy.

The urban Jewish population in Israel can be grouped into three cantons: a central canton around the Tel Aviv metropolitan area, a northern canton around the city of Haifa, and a Jerusalem canton. The Jerusalem canton is beyond the scope of this chapter. The canton system, used successfully in Switzerland, will provide a solution for the Jewish desired independent mode of living and enable the Palestinian refugees to return to their homes and restore their property.

Cantons

The central canton (see map 19.3), which is exclusively Jewish, can be divided further into three sub-cantons, all of which are located on Jewish-owned land: the Tel Aviv canton, the Rishon LeZion canton, and the Herzliya canton. The division of the canton into sub-cantons, as evidenced on the map, is designed to facilitate movement between Palestinian villages located in the canton while maintaining lawful Jewish land ownership. To ensure physical continuity of the Jewish population between these three sub-cantons, some Palestinian bridging land may need to be added to these cantons.

In this especially crowded area, the lands of about two dozen depopulated villages (out of 560, or 4 percent) are over-built by post-1948 Israeli construction. In this region, the Jewish population exceeding thirty thousand on the lands of some Jaffa

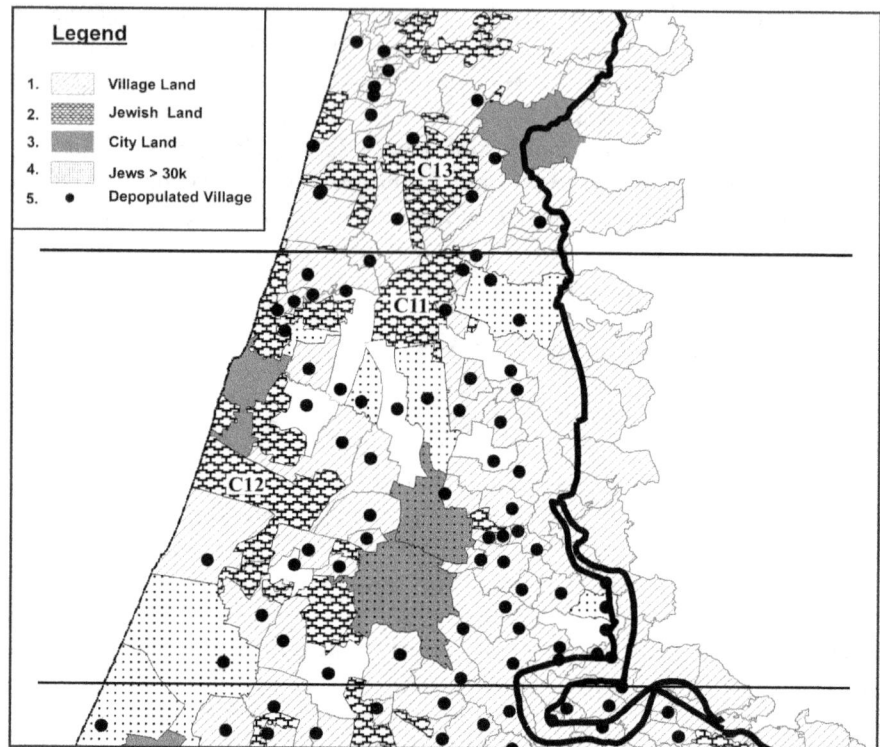

Map 19.3. Canton 1 Central. This canton shows the largest Jewish concentration mostly on Jewish purchased land during the Mandate. Continuity of Jewish areas is maintained. Source: Author.

villages is shown in map 19.3, shaded area no 4. This population could lease land from original owners wishing to repossess their lands while others may choose to relocate to one of the Jewish cantons. Relevant examples in such situations can be gleaned from the Bosnian repatriation scheme. According to UN plan, the ownership of the property remains vested in the original owner. The secondary occupant may lease, rent, or receive compensation for his costs from the first (legal) owner provided the secondary occupant has obtained this property "in good faith," in other words, it was not stolen, expropriated, or otherwise obtained against the consent of the original owner.[30]

The Haifa canton (see map 19.4) comprises the city of Haifa, its environs, and Jewish colonies or settlements located between Haifa and the city of Acre in the north. This canton is different from the Tel Aviv canton in that the eventual Palestinian population is comparable in size to the Jewish population. The return of refugees, however, is simpler because of the area's history of coexistence between Palestinians

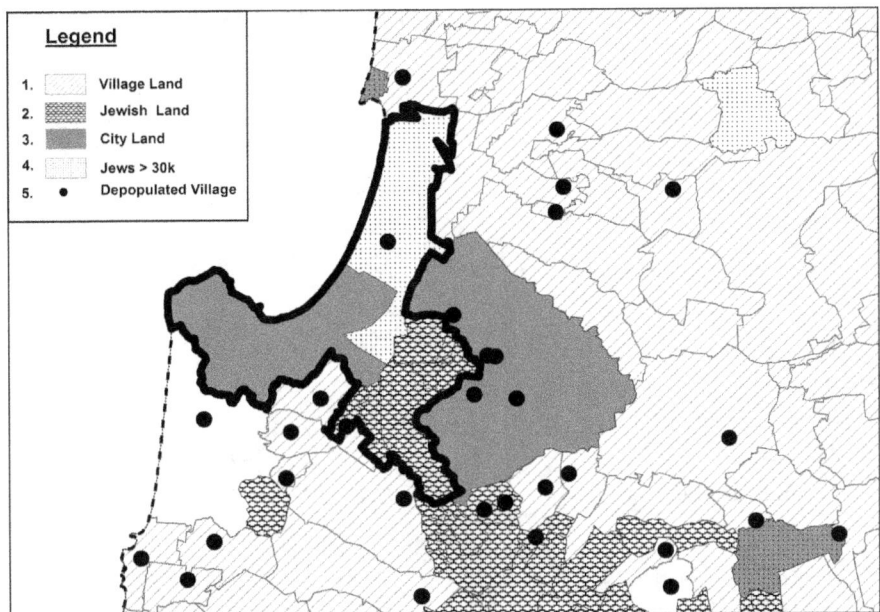

Map 19.4. Canton 2 Haifa. This canton in Haifa shows the second-largest Jewish concentration. It connects with Jewish settlements in the north and the east. Traditional coexistence with Palestinian quarters in Haifa and nearby villages is expected to remain. Source: Author.

and Jews and because the existing populations are not as interspersed as in the Tel Aviv canton. The Palestinian population of al-Tira, a village south of Haifa, which has been annexed to the city, could either choose to remain part of Haifa or may wish to become once again an independent municipality.

Rural Jewish Areas

The concentration of kibbutzim and moshavim in the coastal area and Galilee can be divided arbitrarily for the sake of discussion into five geographical blocks. The first block on the coastal plain (which has an area of 178 km^2) has a Jewish population of 372,253 and a small number of Palestinians (15,220). The Jewish population of the four remaining blocks is much smaller, with no Palestinians. In blocks two (119 km^2) and three (104 km^2) in upper and lower Marj Ibn Amer (Jezreel Valley) there are 51,671 and 50,475 Jewish inhabitants, respectively. Block four (123 km^2) has a Jewish population of 15,723, while block five (59 km^2) has a Jewish population of 6,757. The population and area of the abovementioned cantons and blocks are shown in table 19.4.

Table 19.4. Areas and population of cantons and blocks. Cantons are described above. Rural settlements blocks are small and spaced out. They can maintain local civil independence.

Canton/ Block	Area Km²	Jews, Thousands (2008)	All Palestinians, Thousands (2008)
Canton C1 Central	163	1,728	2
Canton C2 Haifa	131	476	602
Block 1	178	372	15
Block 2	119	51	—
Block 3	104	50	—
Block 4	123	16	—
Block 5	59	7	—
Total blocks	583	496	15
Total cantons and blocks	877	2,700	619
Other Jews		2,810	
of which:			
Living in Palestinian cities		1,312	
Living in Palestinian village lands—see breakdown		1,432	
Remaining Jews		66	
Jews in all Palestinians rural villages (no. 558)		1,432	
of which: only 32 villages lands have over 5,500 Jews		1,286	
Top 21 village lands with Jews over 20k (no. 21)		1,005	
Next 11 village lands with Jews from 5–20k (no. 11)		281	
Therefore 526 village lands have no or less than 5,500 Jews			

Source: Author compilation.

Problem Areas

It is of course naive to suggest that the return of Palestinian refugees to their homes, lands, and properties inside Israel some seven decades after their initial displacement could take place without so much as a hitch. While return is the preferred solution to forced displacement (and it is the refugees' constant demand), a detailed procedure is needed to achieve it, especially when large numbers of persons are involved. The ethno-national and settler colonial nature of the conflict in Palestine-Israel, characterized by an apartheid regime on both sides of the 1949 armistice line, further complicates solutions for Palestinian refugees and internally displaced persons. But a process of decolonization that would include constitutional guarantees for the fundamental principle of equality and prohibition of racial discrimination could nevertheless ensure that each group, however defined ethnically, religiously, or culturally, would be able to resume its life in an atmosphere of democracy and the rule of law. This would also entail other legal reforms that address both the political and economic consequences of colonialism, military occupation, and apartheid.[31] This is the reason for the establishment of Jewish urban cantons and Jewish rural blocks, which would enable municipal councils in these areas to apply their own religious or cultural preferences, such as worship, holidays, education, and the like. The same of course will be true for the Palestinian areas.

There remains the problem of Palestinian towns of origin in the south of the country—Isdud (Ashdod), al-Majdal (Asqalan), and Beersheba (Bir Es Saba')—which are inhabited today by Jewish Israelis. In Beersheba and Isdud there should be no problem, because the Jewish urban areas are removed from the original Palestinian areas. This is not the case in al-Majdal (Asqalan or Ashkelon). However, there is sufficient area for the refugees' return when al-Majdal is combined with the village of al-Joura in the south and further expanded toward the west and north in the direction of the Palestinian village of Hamama. Safed and Tiberias pre-1948 had a mixed population and should remain so. The Palestinian populations of Lydda, Ramla, and Beisan (Baysan) could return to rehabilitated old quarters, leaving the Jewish immigrants in the newer neighborhoods of these cities.

Reconstruction of Destroyed Villages and Repatriation

While over five hundred Palestinian villages depopulated during the 1948 War in Palestine-Israel have long been destroyed, their history has been preserved through a range of sources, including village books, oral history passed down through generations, UNRWA registration, British Mandatory Government of Palestine records, and aerial photographs of Palestine taken by the Royal Air Force during World War II.[32] These provide a rich source of information from which it is possible to begin planning for the return of refugees to their homes, properties, and lands inside Israel. Through existing records, it is possible to identify houses and possibly the owners of the houses by name and the location of the family in refugee camps and communities of exile in each of the major host countries. Refugees sought refuge mostly in one or two of the UNRWA's five areas of operation, namely, the West Bank, Gaza Strip, Jordan, Lebanon, and Syria. In many cases, refugees reside within sight of or at most a bus ride away from their villages of origin. It is thus possible to reconstruct Palestinian villages depopulated during the 1948 War, taking into account the growth of the refugee population and change of occupation over time.[33] Palestinians can rebuild their villages by their own labor and expertise. In recent years, Palestinian architects and engineers have begun to draw up plans for the reconstruction of refugee villages located inside Israel.[34] Palestinians also have many decades of experience building similar or much larger projects in the Arab Gulf. In fact, Palestinian builders are now an indispensable labor force in building Israel on both sides of the 1949 armistice line.[35]

It is worth noting, moreover, that the cost of reconstruction for about 1.5 million dwelling units is a small fraction of the aid to Israel provided by the United States and the European Union. Additionally, construction costs would be incurred only once, not annually as is the case of American foreign aid to Israel. It could be financed in part by Israel from the revenues collected by Israel from the refugees' property according to UN resolutions (e.g., General Assembly Resolution 72/83, 7 December 2017). The subject of compensation and reparations is beyond the scope of this chapter.

The UNRWA should also be able to employ its predominantly Palestinian staff to supervise the repatriation and rehabilitation of refugees to their homes, lands, and properties and provide reintegration assistance, which would be gradually transferred to relevant UN development agencies.[36] Although it is not the subject of this chapter, it is evident that the return of the refugees must be associated with the stringent application of many articles of international law and of similar precedents for postwar justice and restitution, such as compensation and reparation, recovery of lost income, war crimes trials, and measures to prevent the recurrence of such crimes, wherever such action is relevant.

The return of small numbers of displaced Palestinians—whether through family reunification or under the repatriation plan between Israel and Jordan mediated by the International Committee of the Red Cross after the 1967 War—provides an initial body of precedents and practices from which to draw lessons that could be applied to the return of refugees who have yet to find durable solutions to their situation.[37] The repatriation of millions of refugees after the end of the Cold War, during what former UN high commissioner for refugees Sadaka Ogato described as the Decade of Repatriation,[38] provides an equally rich source of comparative precedent and practice with lessons learned, which is also the focus of an emerging body of literature on the practical aspects of return in Palestine-Israel.[39] Special attention should be given to applicable lessons for repatriation drawn from protracted refugee situations, especially cases of ethno-national conflict, settler colonialism, military occupation, and apartheid.

Conclusion

This chapter began with the premise that there were no economic, political, or legal reasons for barring Palestinian refugees and internally displaced persons from returning en masse to their homes, lands, and properties inside the State of Israel. Noting that many of the policies and practices associated with ethnic cleansing, expulsion, and forcible transfer in particular constitute serious violations of international law, including war crimes and crimes against humanity, this chapter further emphasized the right of Palestinian refugees and displaced persons to return to their places of origin. It further noted that the primary barrier to their return is the State of Israel's lack of adherence to the fundamental principles of international law, including equality and the prohibition of racial discrimination. In March 2017 the UN Economic and Social Commission for Western Asia (ESCWA) issued a groundbreaking report, written by distinguished legal experts, on conditions in Israel and the Palestinian refugees in Palestine and in exile. The commission concluded that Israel was guilty of the crime of apartheid against Palestinians wherever they reside and called upon UN bodies, national governments, and civil society actors to examine measures that each should take in accordance with legal obligations under the Apartheid Convention to suppress and eliminate apartheid in Palestine-Israel.[40]

The fact that the ESCWA was forced to retract the report at the UN secretary-general's request, leading to the resignation of the commission's director, however, underscores the challenge ahead in attempts to bring about the decolonization of Palestine and the dismantling of the apartheid regime on both sides of the 1949 armistice line, which is a precondition to finding durable solutions for displaced Palestinians. The abolition of apartheid is nevertheless key to a peaceful future in Palestine/Israel. The region could be spared more wars and destruction; an end to apartheid would save the lives of thousands of Palestinians and hundreds of Israelis. Moreover, the billions of dollars currently being spent on arming and supporting one group against all tenets of international law should be diverted and used instead to bring peace and justice to the region. Once this has been accomplished, as the above discussion has illustrated, Palestinian refugees and internally displaced persons should be able to return to their homes, lands, and properties, with only a small number of problems arising in areas where existing Jewish settlements are located on the lands of refugee villages depopulated during the 1948 War.

Salman Abu Sitta is founder and president of Palestine Land Society, London (www.plands.org), which is dedicated to the documentation of Palestine's land and people. He has authored six books on Palestine, including the compendium *Atlas of Palestine 1917–1966* (English and Arabic editions) and the atlas *The Return Journey*, as well as over three hundred papers and articles on the Palestinian refugees, the Right of Return, the history of the Nakba, and human rights.

Notes

1. Nur Masalha, *Palestine: A Four Thousand Year History* (London: Zed, 2018).
2. UNCCP, *First Interim Report of the United Nations Conciliation Commission for Palestine* (United Nations, 1949); and Salman Abu Sitta, *Atlas of Palestine, 1917–1966* (London: Palestine Land and Society, 2010).
3. Comparisons are complicated by the absence of a universally recognized definition of ethnic cleansing. While there were larger cases of ethnic cleansing in the twentieth century, few if any have lasted as long as the situation in Palestine, which continues until the present day. See, e.g., the cases discussed in Michael Mann, *The Dark Side of Democracy: Explaining Ethnic Cleansing* (New York: Cambridge University Press, 2005).
4. Abu Sitta, *Atlas of Palestine*.
5. The estimate includes refugees registered with the UN Relief and Works Agency for Palestine Refugees (UNRWA), non-registered refugees, and internally displaced persons inside Israel. Nidal al-Azza and Amaya al-Orzza, eds., *Survey of Palestinian Refugees and Displaced Persons 2013–15* (Bethlehem: Badil Resource Center, 2015), https://www.badil.org/phocadownloadpap/badil-new/publications/survay/Survey2013–2015-en.pdf.
6. Robin Geiß, "Ethnic Cleansing," Max Planck Encyclopedia of Public International Law, 2012, https://opil.ouplaw.com/view/10.1093/law:epil/9780199231690/law-9780199231690-e789; Jennifer Preece Jackson, "Ethnic Cleansing as an Instrument of Nation-State Creation: Changing State Practice and Evolving Legal Norms," *Human Rights Quarterly* 20, no. 4 (1998): 817–42.
7. UN, *Progress Report of the United Nations Mediator on Palestine*, Submitted to the Secretary-General for Transmission to the Members of the United Nations (Paris: United Nations, 1948); and Geiß, "Ethnic Cleansing."
8. Mutaz Qafisheh, "An Ongoing Anomaly: Pre– and Post–Second World War Palestinian Refugees," *International Journal of Refugee Law* 27, no. 1 (2015): 60.
9. Benny Morris, *The Birth of the Palestinian Refugee Problem Revisited* (Cambridge: Cambridge University Press, 2004), 536.
10. UNSG, *Report of the Secretary General under General Assembly Resolution 2252 (EX-V) and Security Council Resolution 237 (1967)*, UN Doc. A/6797, 1967; and, George Kossaifi, *The Palestinian Refugees and the Right to Return* (Washington, DC: Center for Policy Analysis on Palestine, 1996), 6.
11. Kossaifi, *The Palestinian Refugees and the Right to Return*, 8; Jon Pedersen, Sara Randall, and Marwan Khawaja, eds., *Growing Fast: The Palestinian Population in the West Bank and Gaza Strip* (Oslo: Fafo, 2001).
12. Al-Azza and al-Orzza, *Survey of Palestinian Refugees and Displaced Persons 2013–15*, xiii.
13. Nur Masalha, *The Politics of Denial, Israel and the Palestinian Refugee Problem* (London: Pluto Press, 2003).
14. Geiß, "Ethnic Cleansing."
15. Federico Andreu-Guzman, "Criminal Justice and Forced Displacement: International and National Perspectives," in *Transitional Justice and Displacement*, ed. Roger Duthie (New York: Social Science Research Council, 2012), 233–78.
16. Donald Neff, *Fallen Pillars: US Policy towards Palestine and Israel Since 1945* (Washington, DC: Institute for Palestine Studies, 1995); and Irene Gendzier, *Dying to Forget: Oil, Power, Palestine & the Foundations of US Policy in the Middle East* (New York: Columbia University Press, 2015).
17. Terry M. Rempel, *Survey of Palestinian Refugees and Displaced Persons* (Bethlehem, 2002), https://www.academia.edu/40885701/Survey_of_Palestinian_Refugees_and_Internally_Displaced_Persons_2002; Office of the United Nations High Commissioner for Human Rights, Israel Homepage, https://www.ohchr.org/EN/Countries/MENARegion/Pages/ILIndex.aspx.
18. Palestine Land Society, http://www.plands.org/en/home.
19. Michel Fischbach, *Records of Dispossession: Palestinian Refugee Property and the Arab-Israeli Conflict* (New York: Columbia University Press, 2003); Sami Hadawi and Atif Kubursi, *Palestinian Rights and Losses in 1948: A Comprehensive Study* (London: Saqi Books, 1988); Thierry J. Senechal, *Valuation*

of Palestinian Refugee Losses: A Study Based on the National Wealth of Palestine in 1948, 18 June 2008, http://www.ajtransparency.com/files/2767.pdf; John Quigley, "Displaced Palestinians and a Right of Return," *Harvard International Law Journal* 39, no. 1 (1998): 171–230; Gail J. Boling, *The 1948 Palestinian Refugees and the Individual Right to Return*, 2nd ed. (Bethlehem: Badil, 2007), https://www.badil.org/phocadownloadpap/Badil_docs/publications/individualROR-en.pdf; Michael Lynk, "Compensation for Palestinian Refugees: An International Law Perspective," *Palestine Yearbook of International Law* 11 (2000–2001): 155–83; Paul Prettitore and Terry M. Rempel, "Restitution and Compensation for Palestinian Refugees and Displaced Persons: Principles, Practical Considerations, and Compliance," in *International Law and the Israeli-Palestinian Conflict*, ed. Susan Akram et al. (New York: Routledge, 2011), 69–112.

20. Abu Sitta, *Atlas of Palestine*.
21. Roselle Tekiner, "Race and the Issue of National Identity in Israel," *International Journal of Middle East Studies* 23, no. 1 (1998): 39–55; Don Handelman, "Contradictions between Citizenship and Nationality: Their Consequences for Ethnicity and Inequality in Israel," *International Journal of Politics, Culture and Society* 7, no. 3 (1994): 441–59; Virginia Tilley, ed., *Occupation, Colonialism, Apartheid? A Re-Assessment of Israel's Practices in the Occupied Palestinian Territories under International Law* (Cape Town: Human Sciences Research Council, 2009); Katie Hesketh, *The Inequality Report: The Palestinian Arab Minority in Israel* (Haifa: Adalah, 2011), https://www.adalah.org/uploads/oldfiles/upfiles/2011/Adalah_The_Inequality_Report_March_2011.pdf.
22. Yair Bäuml, "The Military Government," in *The Palestinians in Israel: Readings in History, Politics and Society*, ed. by Nadim Rouhana and Areej Sabbagh-Khoury (Haifa: Mada al-Carmel: Arab Center for Applied Social Research, 2011), 47–57, https://www.academia.edu/10514312/The_Palestinains_in_Israel_Readings_in_History_Politics_and_Society; Neve Gordon, *Israel's Occupation* (Berkeley: University of California Press, 2008).
23. Haidar Eid and Andy Clarno, *Rethinking Our Definition of Apartheid: Not Just a Political Regime* (Ramallah, 27 August 2017), https://al-shabaka.org/briefs/rethinking-definition-apartheid-not-just-political-regime/; Richard Falk and Virginia Tilley, *Israeli Practices towards the Palestinian People and the Question of Apartheid* (Beirut: United Nations, 2017), https://opensiuc.lib.siu.edu/cgi/viewcontent.cgi?article=1013&context=ps_pubs.
24. Morris, *The Birth of the Palestinian Refugee Problem Revisited*, 313.
25. Don Peretz, *Israel and the Palestine Arabs* (Washington, DC: Middle East Institute, 1958); Ian Lustick, *Arabs in the Jewish State: Israel's Control of a National Minority* (Austin: University of Texas Press, 1980); and Ahmad Sa'di, "Ominous Designs: Israel's Strategies and Tactics of Controlling the Palestinians during the First Two Decades," in *Surveillance and Control in Israel/Palestine*, ed. by Elia Zureik et al. (New York: Routledge, 2011), 83–98.
26. David Kretzmer, *The Legal Status of the Arabs in Israel* (Boulder: Westview Press, 1990); Adalah—The Legal Center for Arab Minority Rights in Israel, "The Discriminatory Laws Database," 25 September 2017, https://www.adalah.org/en/content/view/7771; Adalah's Position Paper, "Proposed Basic Law: Israel—The Nation State of the Jewish People," Haifa, 16 July 2018, https://www.adalah.org/uploads/uploads/Adalah%20Position%20Paper%20-%20Basic%20Law%20Jewish%20Nation%20State%20-%20ENGLISH%20-%2015072018%20-%20FINAL.pdf; CERD, "Concluding Observations of the Committee on the Elimination of Racial Discrimination," U.N. Doc. CERD/C/ISR/CO/14–16, 3 April 2012.
27. UNCT, *Gaza in 2020: A Livable Place?* (Jerusalem, August 2012), https://www.un.org/unispal/document/auto-insert-195081/#:~:text=To%20ensure%20that%20Gaza%20in,the%20face%20of%20all%20difficulties.
28. A comprehensive overview of refugee returns in the twentieth century can be found in Katy Long, *The Point of No Return: Refugees, Rights and Repatriation* (Oxford: Oxford University Press, 2013). For repatriation statistics, see UNHCR, Population Statistics, https://www.unhcr.org/refugee-statistics/.
29. Eitan Bronstein, "The Nakba—Something That Did Not Occur (Although It Had to Occur)," in *Rights in Principle, Rights in Practice: Revisiting the Role of International Law in Crafting Durable Solu-*

tions for Palestinian Refugees and Displaced Persons, ed. by Terry M. Rempel (Bethlehem, 2009), 315–26, http://www.badil.org/phocadownloadpap/Badil_docs/publications/ex-forum-layout-final-S.pdf.
30. Michael Kagan, "Restitution as a Remedy for Refugee Property Claims in the Israeli-Palestinian Conflict," *Florida Journal of International Law* 19, no. 2 (2007): 422–89; Scott Leckie, ed., *Returning Home: Housing and Property Restitution for Refugees and Displaced Persons* (Ardsley, NY: Transnational, 2003).
31. Eid and Clarno, *Rethinking Our Definition of Apartheid*; Falk and Tilley, *Israeli Practices towards the Palestinian People*; Adalah, "Proposed Basic Law."
32. Rochelle Davis, *Palestinian Village Histories: Geographies of the Displaced* (Stanford: Stanford University Press, 2011); Abu Sitta, *The Atlas of Palestine*.
33. Salman Abu Sitta, "Future Scenarios in Israel-Palestine," https://vimeo.com/267407386/4a9d6adfbe.
34. Examples of projects can be found at Palestine Land Society, http://www.plands.org/en/home.
35. Andrew Ross, *Stone Men: The Palestinians Who Built Israel* (London: Verso, 2019).
36. Terry M. Rempel, *The UN Relief and Works Agency for Palestine Refugees and Durable Solutions for Palestinian Refugees* (Bethlehem: Badil, July 2000), http://www.badil.org/phocadownloadpap/Badil_docs/bulletins-and-briefs/Brief-No.6.pdf; Salman Abu Sitta, *The End of the Palestinian-Israeli Conflict: From Refugees to Citizens at Home* (London: Institute for Palestine Studies, 2001); Lex Takkenberg, "The Search for Durable Solutions for Palestinian Refugees: A Role for UNRWA?," in *Israel and the Palestinian Refugees*, ed. Eyal Benvenisti et al. (Berlin: Springer, 2007), 373–86; Michael Dumper, *The Future for Palestinian Refugees: Toward Equity and Peace* (London: Routledge, 2006).
37. Peretz, *Israel and the Palestine Arabs*; Avi Raz, *The Bride and the Dowry: Israel, Jordan and the Palestinians in the Aftermath of the June 1967 War* (New Haven: Yale University Press, 2012); Ron Wilkinson, "Rafah Canada Camp Relocation," Back to Basics 19 (2003), https://www.badil.org/en/publication/periodicals/al-majdal/item/811-don't-confuse-relocation-with-return-18-years-to-move-two-kilometers.html.
38. Statement by Mrs. Sadako Ogata, United Nations High Commissioner for Refugees, at the International Management Symposium, St. Gallen, Switzerland, 25 May 1992, https://www.unhcr.org/admin/hcspeeches/3ae68faec/statement-mrs-sadako-ogata-united-nations-high-commissioner-refugees-international.html. The 1990s saw both large-scale returns and new refugee situations arising in large part from genocide, the dissolution of states, and related ethno-national conflict.
39. Michael Kagan, "The (Relative) Decline of Palestinian Exceptionalism and Its Consequences for Refugee Studies in the Middle East," *Journal of Refugee Studies* 22, no. 4 (2009): 417–38; BADIL-Zochrot, "Thinking Practically about Return," *al-Majdal* 49 (2012): 39–55.
40. Falk and Tilley, *Israeli Practices towards the Palestinian People*.

Select Bibliography

Al-Azza, Nidal, ed. *Survey of Palestinian Refugees and Displaced Persons 2013–15*. Bethlehem: BADIL Resource Center for Palestinian Residency and Refugee Rights, 2015.

Boling, Gail. *The 1948 Palestinian Refugees and the Individual Right to Return*. Bethlehem: BADIL Resource Center for Palestinian Residency & Refugee Rights, 2001.

Falk, Richard, and Virginia Tilley. "Israeli Practices towards the Palestinian People and the Question of Apartheid." *Palestine and the Israeli Occupation*, no. 1. Beirut: UN Economic and Social Commission for Western Asia, 2017.

Fischbach, Michael. *Records of Dispossession: Palestinian Refugee Property and the Arab-Israeli Conflict*. New York: Columbia University Press, 2003.

Hadawi, Sami and Atif Kubursi. *Palestinian Rights and Losses in 1948: A Comprehensive Study*. London: Saqi Books, 1988.

Mallison, Thomas W., and Sally V. Mallison. *An International Law Analysis of the Major United Nations Resolutions Concerning the Question of Palestine*. New York: Division for Palestinian Rights, 1979.

Masalha, Nur. *The Politics of Denial: Israel and the Palestinian Refugee Problem.* London: Pluto Press, 2003.
Prettitore, Paul, and Terry M. Rempel. "Restitution and Compensation for Palestinian Refugees and Displaced Persons: Principles, Practical Considerations, and Compliance." In *International Law and the Israeli-Palestinian Conflict*, edited by Susan Akram et al., 69–112. London: Routledge, 2011.
Quigley, John. "Displaced Palestinians and a Right of Return." *Harvard International Law Journal* 39, no. 1 (1998): 171–230.
Tilley, Virginia, ed. *Occupation, Colonialism, Apartheid? A Re-Assessment of Israel's Practices in the Occupied Palestinian Territories under International Law.* Cape Town: Human Sciences Research Council, 2009.

CHAPTER 20

WHEN UTOPIA BECOMES TOPIA
MAPPING THE FUTURE IN ISRAEL-PALESTINE

DEBBY FARBER AND UMAR AL-GHUBARI

Introduction

It appears that nothing arouses the resistance of the Jewish Israeli public more than the right of return of Palestinian refugees and internally displaced persons to their homeland. For Jewish Israelis, this is the greatest taboo: the very thought of its possible realization appears to be a senseless utopia or worse—a monstrous dystopia, a colossal collapse of the normative order. The opposition of the Jewish public in Israel to Palestinian return is so total, so widespread, that it seems impossible to think of it as a concrete political plan. It is therefore defined by Adi Ophir as *utopia*, given that this precondition for realizing the Palestinian demands for justice appears to be unrealizable. We do not know what return would look like nor what factors could set such a process in motion; the thought of return seems like a leap of faith into a future that is completely detached from the present. It is the total otherness of this imaginative place that transforms return into utopia.[1]

In Greek, *utopia* means "no-place," or a place that does not exist. In popular discourse, labeling political action as utopian frames it as abstract, unattainable, or inconceivable, thereby denying utopia its transformative civic political potential.[2] Against this commonly held view, Martin Buber reminds us in his seminal *Paths in Utopia*[3] that we must always think in terms of the *topia*, which is "the place." We must bring what is seen as no-place together with the place and endeavor to think how "the line of separation, which should be stretched and re-stretched toward the proper fulfillment from time to time, is the conscience that [should] guide us."[4]

In that vein, this chapter discusses questions related to that inability to think, to imagine, and to visualize the return: Why is the return experienced as a dystopia by the majority of the Jewish public in Israel? How can we constitute an alternative discourse that does not reject the potentialities of return? Is it possible to produce a place out of a no-place, and if so, how? These questions will be examined through the ongoing work of Zochrot (זוכרות), an NGO engaged in promoting the Israeli public's recognition of and accountability for the injustices of the Nakba (النكبة) and the realization of the right of return of the Palestinian refugees. We will focus on how Zochrot identifies and studies the current space, while revealing and creating new spaces and innovative paths for future implementation that challenge the conception of return as utopia. As we will show, the radical shift of Zochrot's discourse and practice away from the utopian or abstract nature of the commonplace discourse on return—that which constructs it as delusional—toward the topian dimension, as a force that constitutes feasible action, enables us to imagine, see, and think return in concrete terms.

We begin with the history of Zochrot, starting with its emphasis on producing a counter-hegemonic knowledge about the Nakba and its historical and spatial ramifications in the present. This is followed by an examination of the change in Zochrot's emphasis from raising awareness about the silenced and denied memories of the past to a new emphasis on practical thinking about a future that includes return. We conclude with an analysis of the various creative strategies employed by Zochrot over the years, allowing us to suggest a new path to generate decolonization processes in both the present and future.

Revisiting the Ghost of the Nakba

Before establishing Zochrot in 2002, its Jewish Israeli founders had been involved for many years in organizing and facilitating dialogue and awareness-raising workshops on the Israeli-Palestinian conflict, as well as in extensive political activism.

Something in these workshops, however, was dissatisfying, if not frustrating. The dialogue did not address the main in-depth issues and historical junctures that shape the power relations between Palestinians and Israelis. The discussions revolved automatically and quite naturally around the occupation of the West Bank and the Gaza Strip in 1967 as the single prism through which we could examine the conflict. The participants made great efforts to come up with a peaceful solution based on Israeli withdrawal from the Occupied Palestinian Territories. It was as if they were all trapped in a narrow concept of the conflict, as conventionally presented in the official political discourse in the region. In other words, these encounters adhered to long-standing and rigid discursive boundaries. Consciously or not, the students were ensnared in the illusion of symmetry between two enemies—shedding each other's blood on the same piece of land, as if they were almost equally responsible for both the problem and its solution.

In other words, these discussions failed to address the conflict's constitutive disaster,[5] namely, the Nakba that began in 1948 and has still not ended today; they consequently also failed to acknowledge the wrongs and atrocities perpetrated by Israel and the Zionist movement in the pre-statehood period on the Palestinian people. There were thus no in-depth discussions over the Nakba and its multiple ramifications, including the ethnic cleansing of the Palestinians, the denial of return, the destruction of hundreds of Palestinian towns and villages whose inhabitants had been expelled or forced to abandon, and the Judaization of space and privileging of Jews over Palestinians.

The evasion of these challenges inspired the idea of establishing Zochrot. Zochrot's name means "remember" in the feminine plural form, alluding to its obligation to promote alternative forms of remembering, forms that enable the expression of other memories often kept silent. The NGO's aim was defined as raising the awareness of Jewish Israeli society about the Nakba; this is the first and only Israeli organization that has undertaken this political educational mission. The point of departure of Zochrot's founders was that as long as Israelis did not acknowledge their responsibility for the Nakba and recognize the right of return as its redress, there would be no real chance for just peace.

Zochrot's first steps, literally, in learning and teaching other Jewish Israelis about the Nakba, were made in tours to the remains of Palestinian localities within the sovereign territory of the State of Israel. During the Nakba, and mainly in 1948, Jewish militias and armed forces took over 78 percent of the territory previously under the control of the British Mandate of Palestine and proceeded to expel more than 750,000 Palestinians from their homes in some six hundred cities, towns, and villages.[6] Many of those homes were destroyed during and after their residents were driven out, while others were settled by Jewish immigrants. Some were destroyed later, once they were no longer useful to Israel. With rare exceptions, by now all Palestinian villages and neighborhoods throughout the country have been completely demolished, leaving only scattered remains that can easily be ignored by Jewish Israelis. Over some of those ruins, Jewish settlements were built. In the large cities, some of the neighborhoods were destroyed in order to make room for new Israeli construction, while others were preserved, but without their original owners.[7]

Only about 150,000 Palestinians remained in what became the State of Israel and were made into its nominal citizens, through no choice of their own. About a quarter of them were internally displaced persons whose new forced Jewish citizenship did not help them return to their home villages.[8] As for the Palestinian refugees, they currently represent the largest long-lasting refugee population in the world, numbering some 5.4 million people registered by the UNRWA and an estimated 7.5 million if all unregistered refugees are also included.[9] Many still live in refugee camps in the Middle East, including in the territories occupied by Israel in 1967, experiencing exclusion, precarious living conditions, and extensive poverty.[10] Many of the refugees, particularly in Lebanon and Syria, were uprooted in devastating wars when their neighborhoods were engulfed by violent fighting. Second, third, and even fourth generations of stateless Palestinian refugees have come to bear the same fate of displacement and dispossession.[11]

Thus, for the Palestinians, the Nakba is not a singular historical event that occurred in the past; rather, while it began in 1948, it is still happening today. As Ahmad Sa'di and Lila Abu-Lughod remind us, the Nakba is a process that has taken various shapes and involved different practices over the years but continues to occur in the present.[12]

The average Jewish Israeli will not learn or hear about the catastrophic impact of the Zionist colonization of the land on its Palestinian inhabitants. Since 1948, the education system, public discourse, and mainstream Israeli media have gone to great lengths to banish the existence of Palestinians in the country and, above all, the expulsion of the bulk of the Palestinian population from the territory that became the Jewish state from the minds and consciences of Jewish Israeli citizens. A wide range of state apparatuses are actively engaged in the systematic denial of the Nakba, while simultaneously disavowing any Israeli responsibility for its perpetration.

Zochrot's tours, then, seek to deconstruct the mechanisms of denial and suppression and to expose the history shaped by the Zionist takeover of the land. Even though local observers rarely notice it, the Nakba can in fact be traced in the present Israeli space through the remains of Palestinian villages and towns that have become part of the landscape, albeit without any official reference to or public interest in them. Many Jewish Israelis encounter remains of Palestinian houses throughout the country, sometimes even near their own homes. Often, they do not ask any questions, and if they do, they receive no answers.

The tour then enables some fifty participants, mostly Israelis, to have physical contact with the remains of the emptied site, to learn its history, and to hear the testimonies of Palestinians refugees uprooted from that village or town. This experience makes it impossible to evade the basic facts: the site had been populated for centuries; the community that lived there was forced out; when the inhabitants tried to return, they were prevented from doing so by the Israeli state, which demolished their houses, appropriated their lands and belongings, and let Jewish citizens reap the benefits. Mediated to Jewish Israelis, these facts must form part of their coming to terms with the past and the process of confronting their own denials and obfuscations, a necessary precondition for dismantling fear and political paralysis.

One of the most powerful moments of the tour occurs when the refugees post a sign with the original name of their village or town, long erased from Israeli road signs and maps and on the brink of total oblivion. The sign with the name is complemented by others posted during the tour, indicating the locations of former buildings such as the school, the cemetery, the mosque, or the church. Together, these visible markers of the Palestinian past represent an act of resistance to the current colonial situation and convey a message of civic refusal to come to terms with the destruction of Palestinian identity. The silent presence of those signs on the ground is disturbing to most Jewish Israelis, and they are quickly uprooted following the conclusion of the tour. Nevertheless, the encounter with the sign, symbolizing the Nakba, cannot be easily erased from consciousness. It undermines the normative order and challenges what Jewish Israelis take for granted.

It should be noted that in the past, colonial powers commonly used touring as a way to discover supposedly new sites in occupied lands, map them, learn about them, and "improve" them. Conversely, Zochrot uses the tours as an act of decolonization. It employs the same colonial practice to expose what was hidden and erased by the colonial act.

The erasure of Arabic names from Israeli maps, combined with their obliteration from space and mind, has served the Zionist movement's goals of Judaization and Hebraization, creating an Israeli nomenclature almost completely free of Arabs and Arabic after centuries of Arabic cultural and linguistic domination. With time, the names of Palestinian cities and villages disappeared from Israeli linguistic usage. New names appeared to replace them, some borrowed from the Bible, others from modern Zionist sources, which were themselves often based on translations or transliterations of Arabic names.[13]

In order to raise awareness of this linguistic erasure, Zochrot has once again adapted a colonial mapping tool as a means of decolonization, by publishing the first Nakba map in Hebrew. This counter-map includes the names of over six hundred Palestinian villages and cities destroyed in the Nakba. The map with the Arabic names was superimposed on the country's current map, which includes present-day Jewish Israeli and Palestinian communities. The map invites Israelis to see space differently, since the illusion of a "neat" Jewish Israeli space is disrupted by a map that reflects the painful and quite intentionally suppressed truth. The map has been printed in thousands of copies, distributed widely in Zochrot's tours and events, and uploaded to Zochrot's website.[14]

Additionally, Zochrot launched a smartphone application called iNakba, in Arabic, Hebrew, and English. The application includes all the information from Zochrot's website about the destroyed Palestinian localities.[15] It uses GPS to direct users to the sites of erased Palestinian localities; indeed, it is the only navigation app in the world that can take its users to sites that no longer exist. It is an uncanny experience to hear the app announcing that you have arrived at your destination, which is usually invisible, and to observe the presence of an absence. The app also enables users to send updates from the site and to upload photos, transforming them from passive observers into active participants in documenting the ongoing Nakba.

Zochrot thus allows thousands of users to confront the wreckage of what was Palestinian life, view space with critical eyes, and see what lies underneath. This activity runs counter to the goal of the Israeli regime, which has created a space designed to mold an Israeli consciousness blind to Palestinian existence. In its unique way, Zochrot manages to challenge this practice.

Unlike the map and the app, in its education activities Zochrot targets a specific population within the wider Israeli public: students and teachers. The Israeli education system completely ignores the Nakba. If mentioned at all, the Palestinian people is usually referred to negatively, as the initiator of irrational violence against Jews, as having rejected the 1947 UN Partition Plan, and as being opposed to peace. Given the lack of any serious discussion of the Palestinian people, its identity, history, and culture, there is also no mention of its loss.

Since Zochrot is not allowed into classrooms to meet with teachers and students, it has organized alternative symposiums and workshops for educators outside the schools. Teachers have been invited to discussions on the Nakba, its absence from textbooks, and the educational implications of this lacuna. One of the most important products of Zochrot's education project is the kit "How Do We Say Nakba in Hebrew?" The result of research work by the study group participants themselves, the kit includes thirteen learning units that refer to various aspects of the Nakba. Intended for teachers in Jewish high schools, the kit covers the historical events of the twentieth century in Israel-Palestine—before, during, and after the establishment of the State of Israel.[16]

How Do You Say *'Awda* in Hebrew?

Over the years, the Zochrot kit and other educational materials about the Nakba have met with frequent protests by teachers, parents, and students, and even by government ministers—attesting once again to the great Israeli fear of the Nakba's memory. As Ophir reminds us, however, that same fear conceals the even more primal dread of return, since acknowledgment of the catastrophe contains an acknowledgment of the Palestinian refugees' moral right to return and to be compensated for their loss.[17] The Nakba and return can therefore not be uncoupled.

Recognizing the right of return, or *'Awda* (العودة), has always been central to Zochrot's ideology and activism. A just, equitable, and democratic space for Palestinians and Jews cannot exist without recognition of the right of the refugees and their descendants to return to their homeland and places of origin as part of the country's decolonization. The right of return is anchored in international law, the 1948 Universal Declaration of Human Rights, UN Resolution 194 adopted in the immediate aftermath of the 1948 War, and the 1949 Geneva Convention. In Israel, from 1948 to this day, the right of return has been rejected entirely by the hegemonic discourse in Israel. The return has become the greatest source of fear for Jews in Israel, a constant cause of anxiety. For them, it is an existential threat, implying the apocalyptic destruction of the Zionist state as they know it.[18]

As the fear of Palestinians was never consistent with the asymmetrical present-day power relations, a persistent public education campaign evolved over the years to constitute the Palestinian as a murderous and inhuman demon, who would take advantage of the first opportunity to annihilate Jews. Israel's racist and paternalist propaganda managed to construe the country's Jews as cultured Europeans, and the Palestinians as potential terrorists. This propaganda was used, in turn, to justify any violent act by the Zionists and Israel, including the ongoing dispossession of Palestinians, and all the more so to prevent their return.[19]

For the Palestinians, the right of return is pivotal to the struggle for freedom; it defines their national identity and cannot be transferred or diluted. In every formal or public institution or assembly, in every discussion or negotiation, they are adamant in refusing to settle for anything less. For the Palestinians, this right is carved in stone, and no person can deny it, not even a Palestinian leader. It is both a collective and an individual right. For more than seventy years of refugeehood, the Palestinians have cultivated respect and awe for return, to the point of even sanctifying it; they keep sustaining the dream of *'Awda*—the return to the lost paradise. It often feels as though this dream is far from realization, if at all possible. Burdened by weakness and despair and the urgent present struggle for basic necessities, it appears that the Palestinians are simply waiting for a miracle—for there is no actual struggle for implementing the return, nor any action plan.

The discussion of return is usually conducted, if at all, among small organizations or in informal meetings between Israelis and Palestinians and remains stuck in the gap between the Jewish fear and the Palestinian dream. Thus, in most cases, this has been a sterile, theoretical conversation causing both sides to become entrenched in their positions and emotions. In response to this conundrum, Zochrot has been forced to answer complex and challenging questions raised by many Jewish Israelis wishing to know, for example, what the country would look like, on the ground, after the return, and what it would mean for the Jews who live here. Moreover, what needs will have to be met for the refugees in order to be reabsorbed? How would major social institutions be reorganized to prepare for return?

In order to respond to these questions, Zochrot has undertaken an innovative tactic: actual planning for return, and the imagining of its spatial consequences. This approach seeks to decenter the rights-based approach to return, shifting discussion from legal and political principles to concrete practices.

Together with Palestinian organizations, mainly with the Badil Resource Center for Palestinian Refugees in Bethlehem, Zochrot has initiated a process of joint learning about the practical meanings of return. Lessons of return and processes of restitution for displaced people around the world have helped tremendously in the planning of potential visions for a sustainable return.

In working to dismantle the maze of Jewish Israeli anxiety and to enable rational deliberation over the creation of an equitable civic space, Zochrot aims to challenge the binarism of eternal occupier or victim. Thinking about return in practical terms also helps the Palestinians ground their lofty dream of return, convert the abstract and passive concept into active initiatives, think rationally about planning the post-return space, and engage in political steps to promote it.

Gradually, the practicalities of return have begun to permeate all of Zochrot's activities, thereby leading to a focus on shaping the desirable future rather than settling for recognition of painful memories of the past. Destroyed Palestinian sites came to be seen not only as symbolic memorials of the Nakba, but also as sites of potential return. The landscape was imagined as a space for return in what could be called an exercise of guided imagery designed to promote political change and justice. This served as a new approach to address the space in the present. Thus, Zochrot's tour has become a kind of symbolic return, involving dynamics from the imagined future, as exemplified in the use of both the Arabic and Hebrew languages during the tour and the encounter with the Palestinians participating in the tour.

As Norma Musih argues, thanks to the tour's multilayered temporality, the participants are able "to experience a different kind of togetherness," since the tour "offers a glimpse into a potential moment of return, which means not only the redress of a historical wrong but the creation of a new relationship."[20] This new relationship also makes it possible to undo the current colonial relations between Israelis and Palestinians, not only through the act of recognizing Palestinian memory, but also by way of reversing the colonial relationship, whereby Jewish Israelis become guests and the refugees act as their hosts.

Zochrot has also mobilized its partners to promote actual return. Following a decade of study and activities, significant progress has been made in scrutinizing the practicalities of return and in formulating possible visions for sharing the land in the future. Groups of Israelis and Palestinians have created visionary documents and planning proposals for specific locations following academic seminars held in Israel-Palestine or abroad. These include the Cape Town Document, written following a tour in South Africa, which outlines potentials paths and phases to imagine and envision a post-Zionist Palestine, drawing on the experiences of the return process of displaced South Africans in Cape Town.[21] Similarly, the Yaffa Documents, written by an Israeli-Palestinian group, outlined a plan for a return to Yaffa (Jaffa) and considered the political, sociocultural, and other implications of this plan for the city.[22] Finally, a number of Palestinian and Israeli authors have written short stories about the imagined future collected in the Arabic-Hebrew book *'Awda: Imagined Testimonies from Potential Futures*.[23]

Mapping the Future

To anchor the imagined return in reality, the destroyed village of Miska in central Israel was selected for replanning. In 2010 a group of internally displaced Palestinians from the village, currently residing in the town of Tira, a ten-minute drive from Miska, met with a group of Jewish Israelis, some of whom were also living in the area, and set about designing what the rebuilt village would look like. This "counter-mapping" workshop was moderated by Einat Manoff, a scholar specializing in alternative planning, including for marginalized populations. The product was rudimentary, yet revolutionary. For the first time, refugees and settlers thought about a future life as it could or should be lived in a rebuilt Palestinian village and about relations with neighbors, both Jews and Palestinians.[24]

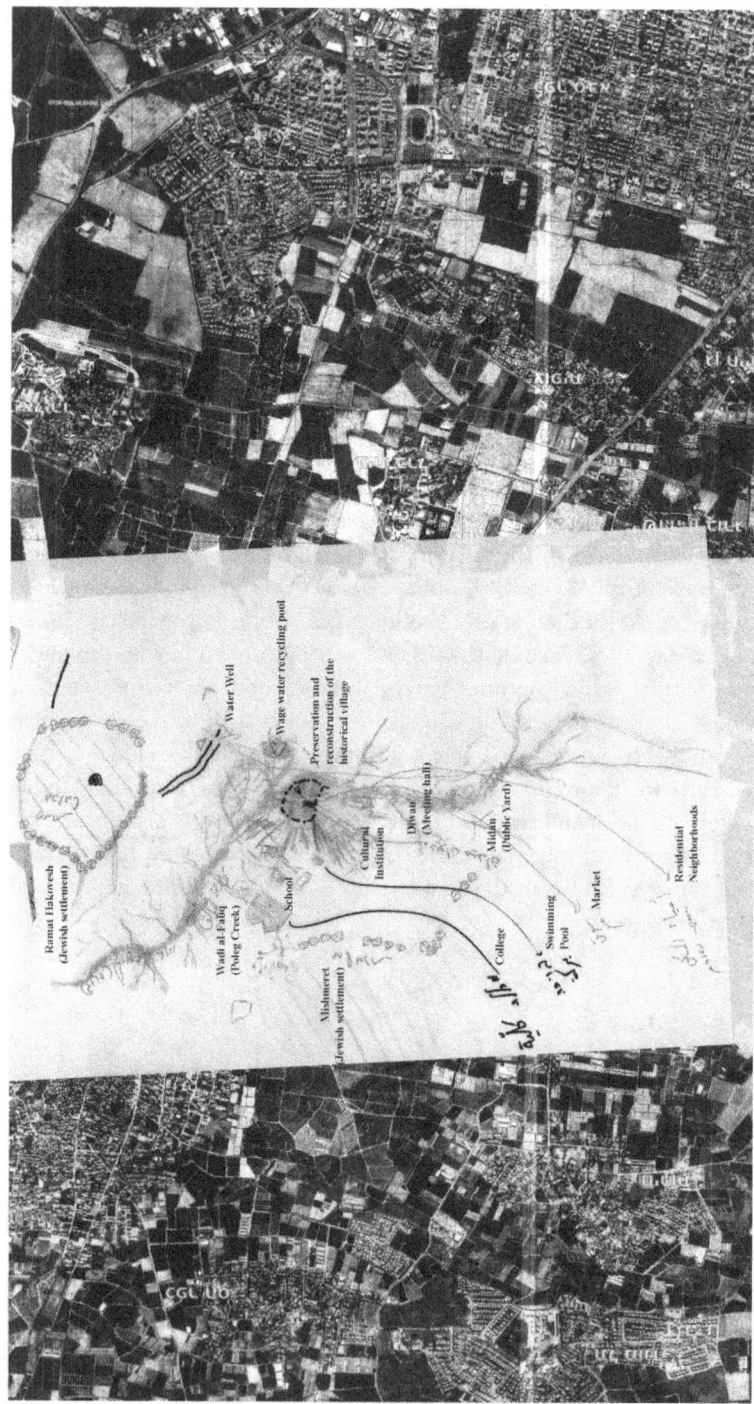

Map 20.1. The Miska return map: superimposition of historical aerial photo with a contemporary bilingual mental map created by the counter-mapping workshop members, including the names of the current Jewish settlements. Source: Zochrot. Published with permission.

A group of Palestinian youths from Nazareth, whose families had been uprooted from the nearby village of Ma'lul, also participated in a workshop organized by Zochrot for planning the return to their destroyed village. It was almost inconceivable that for seventy years, living only three miles away from their village, they had never thought or imbibed ideas from their parents about an actual return. The experience of discussing return in pragmatic terms was fascinating and challenging for them. As in other cases of planning the return, certain concrete issues came up that had never occurred to them before. For example, how would all the uprooted be housed in the village, considering that they had multiplied tenfold since the Nakba? The necessities of life had also changed entirely over the past seventy years. Would there be enough land for all? Which institutes should be built? What about workplaces? How could the returnees be prepared for their new life, mentally and socially? Should the vernacular nature of the old village architecture be reserved in the new imagined village to be built?

In 2012 the Association for the Defense of the Rights of the Internally Displaced, the Baladna Arab Youth Association, and the Arab Association for Human Rights—all Palestinian NGOs active within the sovereign State of Israel—joined Zochrot in a trailblazing project for planning return to destroyed Palestinian localities. The project participants were young, internally displaced Palestinians of the third and fourth Nakba generation, who planned return to their own communities and addressed the questions arising from the process of planning their future villages. The project was named *Udna* (عدنا), meaning "We Have Returned." Every class took upon itself the planning of several locations. Plans for twenty villages have already been drawn, proposing various paths of future return to the sites of dispossession through films, three-dimensional models, and exhibitions.

The return models were translated into Hebrew and presented to Israeli audiences for feedback. Some of the proposals were even covered by the Israeli mainstream media as an unprecedented step, whereby displaced Palestinians took responsibility for their future, publicly announced their desire to return to their villages, and actively planned their future shape. Such acts are directly opposed to the current political trends in Israel that push further and further away any likelihood of opening this issue for negotiations.[25]

Two of the models created in 2013 by project groups, for the destroyed villages of al-Lajun and Mi'ar, are discussed below as test cases for Zochrot's vision of actual return becoming a tool for radical sociohistorical change. The village of al-Lajun is located some ten miles west of Jenin, on the key juncture connecting northern and central Israel. Its strategic location contributed to its development before the Nakba. Al-Lajun had a clinic serving other villages in the area, well-developed agriculture, two mosques, schools, a thriving market, and a bus station. It was also one of the largest villages in Palestine—comprising nineteen thousand acres—and home to 1,280 people. Following its occupation in late May 1948, the Israeli army destroyed the village and expelled its population to nearby Umm al-Fahm. Apart from the mosque, a cemetery, and a few houses in the center of the village, there are no visible remains. The ruins are built over by Kibbutz Megiddo, founded in 1949.[26]

Supervised by the architect Shadi Habib-Allah, thirteen of the third generation of internally displaced Al-Lajunites currently living in Umm al-Fahm created an architectural model of the future village (see figure 8.10). They also produced a film called *In Our Hands*, which provides a three-dimensional simulation of the model, depicting life in the village after the return. This model was based on preparatory work that included historical research, interviews with first-generation displaced persons, historians, town planners, and lawyers, and tours to the village. This preparatory work allowed the participants to reconstruct the architecture of the past in order to plan the architecture of the future, considering the socioeconomic and cultural changes experienced by the community, which is currently estimated at sixteen thousand people.

The group chose to rebuild the village center on the basis of traditional pre-Nakba architectural forms as remembered by the refugees and reconstructed from the ruins. The idea was to preserve the village's human and historical heritage by retaining al-Lajun's typical building techniques. In doing so, the young planners sought to prevent any emotional trauma resulting from a gap between the returnees' memories of the village and a reconstructed modern space and to soften the shock involved in the return to the village after so many years in exile.

At the core of the architectural concept is the *hosh*, or inner courtyard, which traditionally formed the central part of the Palestinian house (or of several dwellings), the family's (or community's) shared space and meeting place.[27] The *hosh*, a kind of symbolic *lieu de mémoire* (site of memory), as defined by geographer Haim Yacobi following Pierre Nora,[28] will serve as a community square with an open-air amphitheater for cultural activities and a lowered stage for meetings and performances.

It is the group's hope that the new industrial zone will become a center for industrial and agricultural development, providing employment and academic opportunities, and shared with the nearby Kibbutz Megiddo and other Jewish settlements in the area, thereby becoming a binational space and a model of decolonization and shared living on equal terms.

Against the common myth in Israeli society claiming that return is impractical since the country is completely settled by Jews, this model demonstrates that the return of al-Lajun's refugees does not involve uprooting the Jews of Kibbutz Megiddo, but rather construction on uninhabited agricultural areas. In this sense, the model aims to challenge the demon of return that haunts Israeli Jews, showing us how by turning to the past, recognizing the right of return, and planning its practicalities, we can imagine al-Lajun as an equitable space for all of its inhabitants, Jews and Palestinians alike.

As defined by Albert Smith, the architectural model has been used throughout history as an effective tool for imagining the future built environment.[29] According to Smith, the model enables the viewer to visualize, measure, examine, and make the invisible visible. As also suggested by Yael Padan, architectural models are part of the cultural effort of fashioning a collective identity, providing the infrastructure for building and legitimizing a desirable national vision by embodying and simulating collective issues such as identity, nationality and history through the material model often presented in public venues.[30]

Al-Lajun's 3D model is based on the familiar methodology of the present-day architectural model. It offers a combination of concrete properties: the concept of a specific place and the use of geography and topography to connect the model to a mapping format; the concept of time, related to the choice of representing future prospects; and educational aspects related to selecting and presenting the objects included in the model. Unlike conventional public architectural models, however, it undermines the teleology of the national narrative presented through the traditional model as authentic and as a representation of "reality," by constructing a topian counter-model that enables us to imagine the invisible as visible—not in the past or present, but in the future. Al-Lajun's model is topian in that, unlike utopian architectural models,[31] it re-concretizes the political and civic potential that can be elicited from the utopia, namely, it reaches out from the no-place to the place.

The second model plans the return to the village Mi'ar, situated on a rocky hill some eleven miles east of Acre, with a land area of twenty-seven hundred acres. Occupied on 15–18 July 1948, its 900 inhabitants were expelled.[32] As early as mid-1949, they tried to return, reoccupy their undestroyed houses, and rebuild the rest, but the army forced them out and blew up the houses, putting an end to any further attempts to return.[33] Today, the Mi'ar refugees are estimated at 8,600–10,000 people, including about 1,400 in Lebanon, Syria, and Jordan, as well as internally displaced persons living in Haifa, Nazareth, and various nearby villages nearby in the Galilee—many of whom frequently visit the village site.[34] Three Israeli villages were built on the village lands: Segev (in 1953; today, Atzmon-Segev), Ya'ad (in 1975), and Manof (in 1980). The village ruins include stone walls and graveyards. The JNF (Jewish National Fund) planted trees on the village lands, which are currently used by travelers and vacationers.[35]

In 2013 a group of third-generation internally displaced youths, who were then living in the nearby Arab town of Kabul, began planning the return to Mi'ar and produced a short film summarizing their work process. The film includes historical photos of the village prior to the Nakba, testimonies of first- and second-generation refugees about life in pre-1948 Mi'ar, and interviews with the participants describing their own personal experiences with the project, particularly a renewed sense of belonging to and ownership of the village. Between interviews, animated visuals reconstruct the village's main buildings: the mosque, the school, sitting areas, and houses, in a contemporary style and with optimistic colors symbolizing change and hope. As in the case of al-Lajun, Mi'ar's lands are mostly uninhabited, and the film shows the viewers how, out of the ruins, the village can be built anew.

The film presents two ways of realizing the return. The first is Ahmad Shehade's (b. 1933) symbolic return visit.[36] Similar to many other internal refugees, Shehade lives near his village of origin, allowing him to visit its ruins frequently and to keep its memory alive. In a moving interview with him, he says that he keeps returning to the village to remember. The film documents his modest pilgrimage ceremony: Walking by the ruins, he tells the third generation about the life that is no longer, mentally charts the village map (where the mosque and cemetery used to be, etc.), and lingers between the remains of houses, terraces, cactus fences, and trees for several hours. Shehade's return to his village evokes a different perception of time, allowing the Palestinian past to be contained within the present, and thus enabling a return to a lost time and space.[37]

The second, topian type of return, designed and imagined by the members of the third-generation youth, transcends the past-present framework of Shehade's pilgrim-

Figure 20.1. The Mi'ar Mosque—before (above) and after the village's mosque had been reconstructed digitally (below). Source: Zochrot and Baladna. Published with permission.

age by manipulating time, locating the return in the present as well as extending it into the future. In this return, the buildings come to life in each of the destroyed village's historical sites, allowing us momentarily to suspend our perceptions of destruction and absence and to imagine the re-creation of a Palestinian space. In the film, the youths travel among the ruins with Shehade, imagining how the village could have looked had it not been destroyed and how it would look in the future.

From the monochromatic village ruins, the film's animation rebuilds houses. From the site of rubble and thorns where the mosque had once stood, the different landscape emerges, filled with vegetation and imaginary stairs leading future visitors to the mosque, which is designed in a traditional style with stone cladding. In a desolate grove planted on the ruins of the school, a new and modern school appears. The residential homes, meeting areas, and children's playgrounds similarly rise to fill the vacuum. The group's leader Shadi Akri describes how for the group members, the model does not express a dream or longing for the lost paradise, but rather represents a realistic vision: "The young people of Mi'ar have the abilities and qualities to rebuild Mi'ar. If anyone thinks this is an imaginary scenario, I'll tell them they're wrong."[38]

Conclusion

The two village return plans, cited here as paradigmatic examples of return models produced within the framework of the Udna project, are based on a heterotopic conception of space: they embody a double place, simultaneously containing what is and what was and, on top of that, adding what is to be in the future.[39] According to Michel Foucault, heterotopia is a place both detached from normal space and challenging its actual existence: a space that is at the same time material and mythical, physical, and imagined.[40] On the one hand, it connects to the real space surrounding it; on the other, it overturns its properties and subverts both its topography and its symbolic or linguistic codes. The models of return to the villages of al-Lajun and Mi'ar are therefore multi-spatial but also multi-temporal, since as heterotopias they operate in a manner that is detached from and transcends our traditional perception of time.[41] The models create a combination of concrete reality and imagination that enables a new temporal consciousness; they cross the boundaries of Zionist historical time, which dispossessed the Palestinians and denied them their space and time; and they venture into a temporal horizon that offers empowerment and liberation from the dependence on the hegemonic time frame.[42] Thus, the models define the place of return in a way that merges pre-1948 Palestinian time, its memories, and the life that used to be with the life that can be.

Planning the practicalities of return is thus a practice of resistance against the present reality. It produces specific topian sites that contain a rich life, thereby challenging Jewish fears by showing that return does not require a new injustice or further atrocities.[43]

Since its inception, Zochrot's work on the practicalities of return has facilitated an unprecedented experience in the discourse of "return" for Palestinians and certainly for Israelis. Suddenly, "return" acquires a twist, a different approach. It can be touched and felt. It seems real. Many of the participants in the processes described above have found the project of planning the return to be one of the most optimistic of their lives. This is a surprising description, given earlier images of Jewish fears or Palestinian dreams.[44]

Einat Manoff suggests that the inability to imagine return is related to the lack of what geographer David Harvey calls "geographical imagination"—the inability to think or imagine the future physical space configuration that will take place should return materialize.[45] Given the ability to think and imagine the shared decolonial space, however, it would be possible to see, for example, where the refugees would return to, where they would live and next to whom, and what potential possibilities and opportunities this return would offer to the whole country and the region's inhabitants. Zochrot's proposition thus lays the groundwork for planning different future spaces. It holds the transformative potential to redesign not only the way we see the present space, but to actively imagine new possibilities of shared life.

By opening cracks in the Zionist discourse in Israel, Zochrot seeks to open a way to future radical political change. This change will not take place without transforming worldviews, exposing the truth, disseminating knowledge about the past, and proposing a better alternative for the present. But it is important to note here that while raising awareness about the Nakba in Hebrew can challenge its denial, the problem still remains of dismantling the regime of justifying past atrocities. Moreover, even acknowledging the Nakba will not necessarily lead to active acceptance of responsibility. Thus, although knowledge and acknowledgment are necessary, they remain insufficient preconditions for decolonization. A radical transformation in conscience, so we believe, can only come about through understanding the fundamental inseparability between responsibility and return. At this point, just as we have striven to introduce the Nakba into an Israeli discourse that denied it, we are now active in promoting the 'Awda.

Debby Farber is the former curator of the gallery of the NGO Zochrot. Between 2012 and 2014, she served as the Civil Transitional Justice Program director at Zochrot, where she established the first unofficial Truth Commission in Israel for the events of 1948 in the Negev/Naqab. Debby is a PhD candidate in the Politics and Government Department at Ben-Gurion University in the Negev and recently completed a visiting fellowship at the Leibniz Institut für Jüdische Geschichte und Kultur—Simon Dubnow, Leipzig.

Umar al-Ghubari is the director of the Space for Return program of the NGO Zochrot. He is a professional group facilitator, a political educator, a "Nakba tours" guide, and a lecturer on Palestinian-Israeli history. Prior to joining Zochrot in 2006, he was the coordinator of the political youth workshops for Palestinian and Israeli students at the School for Peace at Neve Shalom–Wa'hat al-Salaam. Umar received his BA in Arabic literature and general studies with focus on Middle Eastern history and education at the Hebrew University of Jerusalem and trained as a group facilitator at Neve Shalom–Wa'hat al-Salaam. He was born in Mushierfeh, a Palestinian village inside the State of Israel, and currently resides with his family in Wahat al-Salam–Neve Shalom village.

Notes

1. Adi Ophir, "Return as Utopia," *Sedek* 4 (2009): 97–103 (in Hebrew).
2. Ernst Bloch, *The Spirit of Utopia*, trans. Anthony A. Nassar (Stanford: Stanford University Press, 2000); Karl Mannheim, *Ideology and Utopia*, trans. Louis Wirth and Edward Shils (London: Routledge & Kegan Paul, 1976); Tali Hatuka, "Against the Silencing of Utopian Discourse," *Blok* 3, "Y-Topia" (2006): 6–12 (in Hebrew).
3. Martin Buber, *Paths in Utopia* (Tel Aviv: Am Oved, 1983, in Hebrew), 196.
4. Buber, *Paths in Utopia*, 196.
5. The term "constitutive violence" was coined by Ariella Azoulay in her book *Constitutive Violence 1947–1950: Genealogy of a Regime and "a Catastrophe from Their Point of View"* (Tel Aviv: Resling, 2008, in Hebrew).
6. Baruch Kimmerling, "Al-Nakba," *Theory and Criticism: Year Zero: 50 to 48*, no. 12–13 (1999): 33–37 (in Hebrew).
7. Walid, Khalidi, *All That Remains: The Palestinian Villages Occupied and Depopulated by Israel in 1948* (Washington, DC: Institute for Palestine Studies, 1992); Benny Morris, *The Birth of the Palestinian Refugee Problem, 1947–1949* (Cambridge: Cambridge University Press, 1987); Ilan Pappé, *The Ethnic Cleansing of Palestine* (Oxford: Oneworld, 2007).
8. Pappé, *The Ethnic Cleansing of Palestine*.
9. Badil, *Survey of Palestinian Refugees and Internally Displaced Persons*, vol. 8, *2013–2015*, Bethlehem, 2016, https://www.badil.org/phocadownloadpap/badil-new/publications/survay/Survey2013-2015-en.pdf.
10. Ilana Feldman, "Reaction, Experimentation, and Refusal: Palestinian Refugees Confront the Future," *History and Anthropology* 27, no. 4 (2016): 411–29.
11. "Syria Crisis," UNRWA.org, 25 September 2019; "Protection Brief Palestine Refugees Living in Lebanon," UNRWA.org, 25 September 2019.
12. Ahmad H. Sa'di and Lila Abu-Lughod, eds., *Nakba: Palestine, 1948, and the Claims of Memory* (New York: Columbia University Press, 2007).
13. Meron Benvenisti, "The Hebrew Map," in *Sacred Landscape: The Buried History of the Holy Land since 1948*, trans. Maxine Kaufman-Lacusta (Berkeley: California University Press, 2000), 11–54; Umar Al-Ghubari, "God Willing, Al-Quds Is Erased from Space and Mind," *HaOkets*, 20 November 2015 (in Hebrew), English translation: https://dikflantz.wordpress.com/2015/11/22/umar-al-ghubari-with-the-help-of-hashem-theyre-erasing-alquds-from-the-land-and-the-mind/; Noga Kadman, *Erased from Space and Consciousness: Israel and the Depopulated Palestinian Villages of 1948*, trans. Didi Rieder (Bloomington and Indianapolis: Indiana University Press, 2015).
14. For the map in Zochrot's website, see https://zochrot.org/en/article/54772.
15. For the iNakba app in Zochrot's website, see https://www.zochrot.org/en/keyword/45323.
16. See the kit in Zochrot's website, https://www.zochrot.org/en/educationUnit/all.
17. Ophir, "Return as Utopia," 97.
18. Ophir, "Return as Utopia," 97.

19. For an excellent analysis of root causes of the Israeli's regime of fear, see, for example, Talal Asad, *On Suicide Bombing* (New York: Columbia University Press, 2007), 1–76; and Nadera Shalhoub-Kevorkian, "Palestinians, Education, and the Israeli 'Industry of Fear,'" in *World Yearbook of Education 2010: Education and the Arab "World"; Political Projects, Struggles, and Geometries of Power*, ed. Andre Elias Mazawi and Ronald G. Sultana (New York and London: Rotledge, 2010), 335–49.
20. Norma Musih, "To Look at the Landscape, to See a Place and to Call It by Its Name: About the Tours of Zochrot NGO," in *Names of Places and Spatial Identity in Israel-Palestine*, ed. Amer Dahamshe and Yossi Schwartz (Tel Aviv: Resling, 2018, in Hebrew), 190.
21. The Cape Town document can be viewed here: https://zochrot.org/uploads/uploads/1e00cb835033f77873fe93c7ab1ae4fc.pdf.
22. The Jaffa Documents can be viewed here: https://zochrot.org/en/article/54827.
23. For the book page in Zochrot's website, see https://zochrot.org/en/sedek/56235.
24. To read more about the project, see https://zochrot.org/uploads/uploads/fc0d7cbe64a2d95b697bd2c811d8e3fc.pdf.
25. It is important to note here that Zochrot is well aware of the limitations of its mandate regarding the return as it promotes its objectives in working with its target audience, the Jewish public in Israel. For Zochrot, work on return is limited to raising suggestions and developing ideas, learning, and encouraging discussions about it. We have no intention of appropriating solutions for return. It is up to the refugees and internally displaced to decide in this matter. Therefore, Zochrot's learning processes have been conducted from the beginning jointly with Palestinian partners.
26. Eitan Bronstein, ed., *Remembering Al-Lajun* (Tel Aviv: Zochrot, 2004, in Hebrew), https://zochrot.org/uploads/uploads/250d6a7aa544b96121bd2321769f90d8.pdf; Khalidi, *All That Remains*.
27. Ron Fuchs, "The Palestinian Arab House and the Islamic 'Primitive Hut,'" *Muqarnas* 15, no. 1 (1998): 157–77.
28. Pierre Nora, "Between Memory and History: Les Lieux de Mémoire," trans. Marc Roudebush, *Representations* 26 (1989): 7–25.
29. Albert C. Smith, *Architectural Model as Machine: A New View of Models from Antiquity to the Present Day* (Boston: Elsevier, 2004).
30. Yael Padan, *Modelscapes of Nationalism: Collective Memories and Future Visions* (Amsterdam: Amsterdam University Press, 2017), 18.
31. Francois Choay, *The Rule and the Model: On the Theory of Architecture and Urbanism* (Cambridge, MA: MIT Press, 1997).
32. Khalidi, *All That Remains*.
33. Tovi Fenster, "One Place, Different Memories: The Case of Ya'ad-Mi'ar," in *Memory, Forgetting, and the Construction of Space*, ed. Tovi Fenster and Haim Yacobi (Jerusalem and Tel Aviv: Van Leer Institute and Hakibbutz Hameuhad, 2011, in Hebrew), 210–31.
34. Fenster, "One Place, Different Memories."
35. Umar Al-Ghubari, *Remembering Mi'ar* (Tel Aviv, 2013, in Hebrew), English translation: https://www.zochrot.org/en/activity/52179; Khalidi, *All That Remains*.
36. Efrat Ben-Ze'ev, "The Politics of Taste and Smell: Palestinian Rituals of Return to the Destroyed Villages," *Alpayim: Journal for Contemporary Thought and Literature* 25 (2003): 73–88 (in Hebrew).
37. Ben-Ze'ev, "The Politics of Taste and Smell."
38. The quote was taken from the interview with Akri in the film in Zochrot's website: https://zochrot.org/en/video/56334.
39. Ophir, "Return as Utopia."
40. Michel Foucault, "Of Other Spaces," trans. Jay Miskowiec, *Diacritics* 16, no. 1 (1986): 22–26.
41. Yehouda Shenhav, "The Chronotope of Refugee Return," *Sedek* 6 (2011): 2–11 (in Hebrew), English translation: https://zochrot.org/uploads/uploads/3d2f0b63fc330f0bb1004e2b5fa73440.pdf.
42. Amal Jamal, "The Struggle for Time and the Power of Temporariness: Jews and Palestinians in the Labyrinth of History," in *Men in the Sun*, ed. Tal Ben Zvi and Hana Farah-Kufur Birim (Herzliya: Herzliya Museum for Contemporary Art, 2009, in Hebrew), 44–54, http://www.men-in-the-sun.com/HE/amal-jamal-part-1, http://www.men-in-the-sun.com/HE/amal-jamal-part-2.

43. Nevertheless, it's important to note here that the Jews will obviously have to part with some of their privileges, acquired by violence against the Palestinians, so that the country's space can be reallocated in a way enabling the return.
44. In the last ten years, we can notice similar innovative research dealing with practical return, i.e., the architecture student competition for the deconstruction of destroyed Palestinian villages organized by the Palestine Land Society in the UK (http://www.plands.org/en/competition), the work of Badil on community empowerment workshops (http://www.badil.org/en/campaigning-networking/campaigning/community-empowerment.html), and the work of DAAR—Decolonizing Architecture Art Residency based in Beit Sahour, Palestine (http://www.decolonizing.ps/site/site3-returns/).
45. David Harvey, "The Sociological and Geographical Imagination," *International Journal of Politics, Culture and Society* 18, no. 3 (2005): 211–55; Einat Manoff, "Counter-Mapping Return," *Sedek* 6 (2011): 1–10 (in Hebrew), English translation: https://zochrot.org/uploads/uploads/fc0d7cbe64a2d95b697bd2c811d8e3fc.pdf.

Select Bibliography

Badil. *Survey of Palestinian Refugees and Internally Displaced Persons*, vol. 8, *2013–2015*. Bethlehem, 2016.
Buber, Martin. *Paths in Utopia*. Tel Aviv: Am Oved, 1983 (in Hebrew).
Harvey, David. "The Sociological and Geographical Imagination." *International Journal of Politics, Culture and Society* 18, no. 3 (2005): 211–55.
Hatuka, Tali. "Against the Silencing of Utopian Discourse." *Block* 3 (2006): 7–12 (in Hebrew).
Feldman, Ilana. "Reaction, Experimentation, and Refusal: Palestinian Refugees Confront the Future." *History and Anthropology* 27, no. 4 (2016): 411–29.
Khalidi, Walid. *All That Remains: The Palestinian Villages Occupied and Depopulated by Israel in 1948*. Washington: Institute for Palestine Studies, 1992.
Manoff, Einat. "Counter-Mapping Return." *Sedek* 6 (2011): 1–10 (in Hebrew).
Morris, Benny. *The Birth of the Palestinian Refugee Problem, 1947–1949*. Cambridge: Cambridge University Press, 1987.
Ophir, Adi. "Return as Utopia." *Sedek* 4 (2009): 97–103 (in Hebrew).
Pappé, Ilan. *The Ethnic Cleansing of Palestine*. Oxford: Oneworld, 2007.

Afterword
Between Talbiyeh and Me

Alon Confino

Introduction

When evenings came, my mother used to cook dinner for us. Although she grew up in a kibbutz and the dinner menu in our home was quite basic, with a lot of schnitzel and mashed potatoes, she was of Italian origins and loved Mediterranean spices. We lived on the fourth floor, and she used to send me downstairs to the backyard to fetch some rosemary, which grew wild around our house and in the Talbiyeh neighborhood in Jerusalem. I can still smell today the scent of this rosemary, my personal madeleine.

I grew up in Talbiyeh in the 1960s and 1970s.[1] It was an elegant, homey neighborhood inhabited by university professors, liberal professionals, and government officials. My childhood was a good one. There were many children around, and many of us went to the same school, which was down the hill toward the neighborhood of Katamon. There an open lot served us as a soccer field, with two big stones designating the goalposts. We used to play until the ball became indistinct in the falling evening and would then climb the hill back home exhausted. It was safe, and as children we enjoyed a freedom that is unimaginable today. My parents knew many people in the neighborhood. Some were connected to my mother's growing up in Palestine in the 1930s and 1940s and her activity in the 1948 War, such as the poet Haim Gouri; others were from my father's social and professional circle as a professor at the Hebrew University. Our house was at the square that was and still is the heart of Talbiyeh. Interspersed among the houses there were wide fields we used as our playground. They were inhabited by all sorts of interesting animals and carpets of crocuses, scarlet anemones, pink cyclamen, and squills. Behind our house there was a huge field where I used to wander and daydream. It was slowly built on: the Van Leer Jerusalem Institute and the Israel Academy of Sciences and Humanities were erected there in the early 1960s, followed by the Jerusalem Theater and Israel's President's House in 1971. A stone's throw away was the YMCA, opposite the King David Hotel, with its swimming pool and the adjacent soccer pitch. Down the hill in the direction of the Old City, I used to frequent the Khan Theater, opposite the old railway station.

As a child, I knew that Arabs had once lived in Talbiyeh. We called the Palestinians in those days "Arabs." It was a vague, undefined knowledge—the word "knowledge" itself seems too cerebral—that did not trigger awareness, acknowledgment, or curiosity. It was simply there, like a natural fact, the information that Arabs were once here and since 1948 were not here anymore. Still, the Arab character of the neighborhood was all around us and in a sense part of us. In line with the massive project to Hebraize the names of sites in the new Israel and erase the Palestinian past, in 1958 Talbiyeh was named Komemiyut (independence in Hebrew), Katamon became Gonen (to defend), and the square where I lived was named Orde Wingate Square, commemorating the colonialist, pro-Zionist British officer who trained Yishuv military forces in the late 1930s against the Palestinians and for a while lived a few houses away from the square.[2] But no one ever called these sites by their Hebrew names, and this is true also today. The square has always been called Salameh Square, and it was said that Salameh was a builder who owned many houses in the area. His house at the square was unmistakable, a majestic three-story building that later served as the Belgium consulate. For us, it seemed like a palace, its fence flushed with jasmines that smelled divine. This house had secrets. We used to stick out our necks and stand on our tiptoes to peek into the yard (see figure 21.1). Down the hill there was another splendid villa that I passed by every day on my way to school; I often stopped and admired its grand staircase and yard.

We could all identify the "Arab houses," as we called them, in the neighborhood; they were considered elegant compared to the new buildings constructed after 1948.

Figure 21.1. Salameh Square and the majestic villa of Constantin Salameh, which has been the Belgium consulate since 1948. Photo: Alon Confino.

They were expensive. There were tales about how, after the war, some Jews acquired an Arab house for free. References to the Arab past of these houses were always imprecise, brief, brushing the topic aside, or just declaring that their owners had "left." The Arab past was there and not-there; hinted at and denied. On one level, it did not disturb me; on another, I sensed here a topic veiled by adult avoidance. Children feel it when adults avoid a topic. But these feelings were buried under what appeared to be a state of nature: The Arabs were here once, and they left. They lost the war that we miraculously and justly won. What else was there to say?

There was another Arab house that became a reference point for me. It was on the way from Salameh Square to the Rehavia neighborhood, where I had friends and later attended high school. This house was on Balfour Street near the Terra Sancta Catholic monastery compound and opposite the building that in those years housed Israel's foreign minister Abba Eban and has served as the Israeli prime minister's residence since 1974. What drew my attention was the gate announcing "Villa Salameh" in art deco letters (see figure 21.2). Every time I passed by this house, I looked at its gate. I did not know why, but there was something personable about it, a name and a family who owned and lived in the house. It would be imprecise to describe the Arab past of the neighborhood as repressed; after all, the Jews knew exactly what they had done to the Palestinians. The Arab past was present, but it lacked an awareness that brings accountability. I was reminded of this mental state of affairs when I recently read in Deborah Levy's stirring memoir *The Cost of Living* "that the things we don't want to know are the things that are known to us anyway, but we do not wish to look at them too closely. Freud described this wish to unknow what we know as motivated forgetting."[3]

Figure 21.2. The gate of Villa Salameh. Photo: Alon Confino.

The years passed. As I write this chapter, I am cognizant of the massive incongruence between the story I had believed in during my childhood about Talbiyeh, and by extension Palestine and Israel, and the way things actually happened. In the search for truthful accounts of the past, the historian is, at one and the same time, an insider and an outsider. Historians can never reach a cultural Archimedean point from which they can interpret the world from the "outside." They are always "inside" culture; they are products of the intellectual tradition and historical mentality of their societies, while attempting at the same time to explain and criticize them. And yet, the historian's vocation is to represent the past accurately. The truth of this story is never stable, for it is socially and culturally constructed, and it can never tell the whole truth about the past. But the foundation of all serious historical work is the intent for truth and fairness in the representation of the past.

In what follows I would like, first, to draw out some of the main themes that emerge from this stimulating volume; then, building on it while changing the register, I shall link my childhood biography to my work as a historian of the period by choosing elements that were missing from my childhood story of Talbiyeh, Palestine, and Israel and that are decisive for telling a story based on truth and fairness in the representation of the past.

The Volume

Israel-Palestine: Lands and Peoples puts into sharp focus an interpretative approach that is becoming central in mainstream historiography of Palestine and Israel, though it is still an exception in Zionist historiography: that the rivalry between Jews and Palestinians since 1882, when the first Zionists immigrated to Palestine, is not simply a symmetrical story between two national movements that resided in a given land, but is, rather, an asymmetrical story of the conflict between those who lived in Palestine and those who had recently arrived. Indeed, the very word "conflict" may be a misnomer, because it implies a symmetry that in reality did not exist. The Arabs in Ottoman Palestine had no national conflict with the Jews who lived in their midst; the national conflict was brought by the Zionists who came from Europe. This story does not deny the *reasons* for which Jews fleeing antisemitism and discrimination in Europe immigrated to Palestine; but at the same time it emphasizes the *consequences* of this act for Palestinians over the last hundred years. On one level, this is not a new assertion. It has long been part of literature and history writing by different scholars and laypersons. It has certainly been part of Palestinian culture, and this is the reason I refer above to "mainstream historiography," as distinct from what has always been part of Palestinian telling about the past. But there is a difference between a general, and often vague, knowledge and transforming this knowledge into one of the theoretical, methodological, and interpretive organizing principles for how we tell the history of Palestine and Israel.

Let me illustrate this claim by discussing briefly how one particular distinguished body of work within the historiography of Zionism, written by excellent historians and writers with an explicit Zionist perspective, has approached the history of Palestinian nationhood and of the Nakba. Anita Shapira has been perhaps the doyen of the historiography of Zionism in the last forty years, producing admirable books endowed with superb scholarship and a flair for storytelling. But they tell a one-sided story where Zionists, who have faces, characters, and full- fledged history, progress inexorably toward their just vision of a Jewish state, only to be obstructed by Palestinians, whose faces and characters are blurred and whose history exists only as a function of Zionism. It is not only that Palestinians are marginal to this history, but that something is missing in the motivations and practices of Zionists and in the larger context of the Zionist project that gave it meaning. An essence of the Zionist project—a denial of indigenous national rights—is either ignored or seen as natural and transparent to the story and the analysis. The aim of the Palestinian national movement for independence in its homeland is viewed as a thorn in the legitimate national aim of the Zionists, not as equally if not indeed more legitimate, since the Arabs were the indigenous people of the land when the Zionists arrived. This historiography has often uncritically reproduced the terminology that the Zionists themselves employed in order to understand their history, including such demeaning references used over the decades to the Palestinian struggle for nationhood as "Arab terror" and to Palestinian fighters as "gangs."[4]

One important case in this trend is the uncritical adoption by historians of the Zionist term "the Arab question" (or "the Arab problem"). Shapira writes in her book *Land and Power* of the Zionists' debates about the 1942 Biltmore Plan that finally reached "the painful topic, which is the Arab question."[5] This is stated without critical examination. What was the meaning and what were the consequences of the recently arrived European settlers' sentiment that the existence of the majority of the population was a painful problem? By coming to Palestine, even as refugees, did the Jews not create a Jewish problem for the Palestinian inhabitants? What is the relationship between the Jewish problem in Europe and the Arab problem created by the Jews in Palestine? Similar to the term "the Jewish problem," coined by non-Jews in Europe, one key meaning of the term "the Arab problem" was not so much that it called forth various proposals to solve the problem, but the construction of an ethnic or religious group as a problem to begin with. First you create the group as a historical problem, then you rack your brain to find ways to solve it. One difference between "the Jewish problem" and "the Arab problem" was that in Europe it was the majority who constructed a minority as a problem, while in Palestine it was the minority who constructed the majority as a problem.[6]

In her studies, Shapira represents a whole body of work that, in the main, writes about the Jews in Palestine and Israel since the onset of Zionism as an island unto itself. These studies focus on the historical reasons for Zionism and on Jewish victimhood, yet the consequences of the Zionist movement for the Palestinians' way of life and national aspiration do not become an inherent part of the story. Shapira's books are learned when it comes to describing the Jewish side; they are silent about the Palestinian side. This is not the kind of complex historical writing historians have come to expect when they explore topics that call for commingling and reciprocal relations, as well as for an evaluation of the ethical consequences of a given history. I can think of the recent historiographies of the relations of metropole and colonies, of whites and Blacks in the American South, or of the recent book by Omer Bartov on Buczacz that integrates Jews, Poles, Ukrainians, Germans, and Russians and that by Hillel Cohen on 1929 that integrates Jews and Arabs.[7] The result is a history that makes the sound of one hand clapping.

About the Nakba, Shapira is apologetic, minimizing Jewish responsibility for it. She views it as the fault of the Palestinians, who are seen as responsible for the 1948 War by rejecting the United Nations Partition Resolution in 1947, and whose society and governance collapsed, leading to mass flight. This interpretation, which is in decline among mainstream scholars of the war, views the Yishuv in 1948 as an observer in the story of a Palestinian exodus with which it had very little to do.[8] Others have described the Nakba in great detail. We can think of Benny Morris, who has contributed to our knowledge of the Jewish role in the Nakba more than any other historian in the last generation, and of the journalist Ari Shavit, with the evocative chapter "Lydda, 1948" in his book *My Promised Land*. They are both straightforwardly honest about the Jewish expulsion of the Palestinians. They admit the crimes. But they justify the expulsion as necessary, as a just alternative to Jewish existence after centuries of antisemitism and the Holocaust. They accept expulsion as a solution, and so, on a profound level, they own no moral responsibility for the destruction of Palestinian way of life in Palestine. Shapira, Morris, and Shavit, while telling different stories, share a storytelling that shirks responsibility. The honest reporting by Morris and Shavit, which is certainly better in terms of historical accuracy and willingness to confront the Nakba than Shapira's obfuscation, avoids a commitment to assume responsibility and hence, in the end, amounts to self-exoneration. They justify the war crimes and thus write about the Nakba in order to remove it from Israeli consciousness. This has methodological and interpretative consequences with respect to the questions we ask and the answers we seek, for example, about the motivations of the wrongdoers and the cultural diffusion of an expulsion mentality before 1948.[9]

There are different ways of producing—in historiographical, interpretative terms—the sound of both hands clapping, and this volume shows us some of them. Here lies its contribution. I would like to point out some of the main points that emerge from the volume and that enrich the overall story of Palestine and Israel. Perhaps the first impression that emerges from reading the chapters from first to last is the relentless Zionist encroachment on Palestinian rights and the unshakable principle of separation that has characterized the Zionist project from its inception. Embedded in this principle of separation was, implicitly or explicitly, consciously or unconsciously, a denial of the right of Palestinians, as the majority and indigenous inhabitants, to decide their future and the future of their land. While this notion has changing historical twists and turns, as every historical notion over a period of time, it appears as a continuous streak right from the beginning of the book and the beginning of Zionism, when Hannan Hever cites Ze'ev Dubnow, one of the Bilu (a First Aliyah settler group), who wrote on 1 January 1882 that "our ultimate goal is to conquer the *Land of Israel* and restore the political independence stolen from the Jews two thousand years ago." Variations of this disregard of the Palestinians, this book shows, have continued until the present.

A second theme that runs through the volume concerns who is allowed to tell the story, and how. The Zionists saw it as self-evident that they have the right to make a claim not only to the land but also to telling the story of the land through collective memory and national narrative. Original chapters in the volume illuminate this telling in such fields as architecture, geography, civic rituals, and education. Remembering and forgetting were complementary in this Zionist tale, not contradictory, as reflected in the erasure of Palestinian voices and pasts. These stories appear in unexpected places, as shown in the history of the urban planning of Netanya told by Noah Hysler Rubin. She writes that "the planning history of the cities of Palestine, whether old or new, is a partial history. It provides no account of alternative geographies, alternative people, or alternative visions; not only descriptive and monolithic, it is bluntly committed to the classical Zionist narrative."

A third important theme in the book is the link between settler colonialism, indigenous studies, and Zionism. I shall return to this topic later in the chapter. What I'd like to stress here are two points. First, the book presents diverse views of settler colonialism, one critical (Fleischacker) and several who find the notion illuminating on various grounds (Hysler Rubin; Pappé; Cohen and Gordon). This is now part of the conversation on Palestine and Israel, much as the Nakba is hovering over many if not indeed all of the chapters. Things have changed. In 1978 the young historian Rashid Khalidi wrote a foreword to Nafez Nazzal's book, *The Palestinian Exodus from Galilee*, based on oral history conducted in Lebanon and Syria, describing the "*colonial settler* nature of Zionism."[10] Then it was a voice in the dark; today settler colonialism—however one wants to apply it, interpret it, or argue with it—is one element in providing the sound of clapping. But second, and as important, is the undeniable sense that emerges from these chapters that over the decades the settlers have become native themselves and that when one thinks of possible solutions, as the final essays attempt to do, this fact has to be taken into consideration.

The value of this book is that it heightens our awareness of the sounds of the past that make the historical picture richer and more complete. However just the Zionist quest for rights and justice, for a political life free of antisemitic persecutions in the Land of Israel, might have been and was, this quest meant an antidemocratic imposition and later a denial of the national rights of the Palestinians, the majority of the population. The grand, overarching story of Palestine and Israel's modern history is the commingled creation and destruction embedded in it: the Zionists' creation of a homeland rested on the destruction of Palestinian society; building a state with a robust Jewish majority produced ethnic cleansing. Finding a home and losing a home were not contradictory, but complementary. It is the merit of this book to remind us of this predicament in a series of excellent chapters.

Talbiyeh

I might as well continue by telling the history of Talbiyeh I was not told during my childhood. Talbiyeh was one of several elite neighborhoods in West Jerusalem—together with Katamon, Baq'a, the Greek Colony, the German Colony, and Namamra—that housed upper-middle-class Palestinian professionals. Scholars have meticulously and gracefully reconstructed Palestinian life in these neighborhoods, not least by relying on memoirs written by its inhabitants.[11] My description below is tremendously indebted to these studies. Developed during the years of the British Mandate, these districts were mostly inhabited by Christian Arabs, Greeks, and Armenians. At the end of 1947 the number of inhabitants in these Arab southern neighborhoods reached 22,000, of whom 9,000 were Muslims, 13,000 Christians, and 550 Jews. The residents belonged to an emerging bourgeois elite, carrier of a Palestinian indigenous modernity commingling modern with local, traditional ways of life, new habits with old values, Palestinian nationhood with Arab pride. This was a self-conscious elite, proud of its refined cultural tastes, Palestinian yet cosmopolitan visions, and professional accomplishments. It saw itself as the elite of a future, post-colonial, post-Mandatory political structure in Palestine, whatever its shape might be. The future belonged to it.

The neighborhoods combined elegance and a sense of social cohesion. Hala Sakakini, daughter of Khalil Sakakini, a Jerusalemite educator, intellectual, and public figure, recalled that these Arab quarters "formed a garden city, as they consisted mainly of villas surrounded by gardens. All houses, almost without exception, were built of stone . . . every house had individuality; somehow it was marked by the personality of its owner." Residents were mindful of the appearance of the interior and exterior of the houses and of its courtyard. A stone fence surrounded the house, and an iron gate let to the courtyard and into a staircase leading to the main door. The gate and main door were often adorned, representing the personality of the owner, as in the case of one gate whose bars were in the shape of musical notes.[12]

Streets had no names and houses no numbers; they were known by their owners' family name. Mail was delivered to Villa Salameh, Sakakini house, and the like. Hala writes that "people living in the same quarter were like one large family. Everyone knew everyone else." This was a common sentiment.[13] Even if there is an element of nostalgic idealization in these descriptions, this was also true. The Palestinian families in the neighborhoods were, among others, merchants, lawyers, businessmen, educators, physicians, contractors, bankers, and officials in the Mandate administration. Many of the families were connected by commercial, political, and social ties. Close to the Sakakinis lived the Karmi and the Toubbeh families. The three families were acquaintances. Hasan Karmi was an official in the Mandatory education department, while Issa Mikhail Toubbeh, of especially elevated social standing, was the mukhtar of the Eastern Orthodox Christian Arab community in Jerusalem. Khalil was a frequent visitor at the Toubbeh home, and he and Issa used to puff their narghiles and exchange views on current affairs.[14]

There was more than a grain of truth in the description of the neighborhoods as a garden city. They were integrated with nature and with the Arab villages surrounding Jerusalem. The neighborhoods were modestly inhabited, leaving in between wide fields and rolling hills. They were flushed with plants, flowers, and fruit trees. The Karmi family garden, recalled Ghada, the youngest daughter, had five apricot trees, an almond, a plum, and a pear tree, and one lemon tree just under her parents' bedroom window.[15] This was not exceptional. Pomegranates, apple, and olive trees were common, as well as pines, pepper, and cypress trees. The area was known for its pink scented roses. The Baq'a area was known as Wadi al Ward, or Rose Valley, and some of the blossoms were harvested to prepare rose water for local churches. After the first rain, fields between the houses and the surrounding countryside filled with flowers among the rocks—crocuses, scarlet anemones, and pink cyclamen. As all over Palestine in those days, there was active wildlife, with rabbits, owls, sparrows, gazelles, and also hyenas appearing from time to time.[16] John Melkon Rose, who lived in Baq'a and wrote a moving memoir, recalled that the nights were silent and dark, and the crisp Jerusalem air echoed with the incantatory sounds of Palestine: the bark of a fox, hooting of an owl, howling of a jackal.[17]

Education was highly important as a marker of status and a path to success. Sakakini's son Sari spent six years in the United States, completing a master's degree at the University of Michigan. His daughters Dumia and Hala received private English lesson from Clarissa Graves, sister of the author Robert Graves, and learned to play the piano with a German teacher in Baq'a. Children went to the best private schools, where they studied in several languages—German, English, or French, depending on the denomination of the school—apart from speaking Arabic and other languages, such as Greek or Armenian, at home. In their opening horizons, stress on education and languages, this elite conformed to and shaped the cosmopolitan character of Jerusalem during the Mandate, whose residents were Jews, Arabs, Muslims, Christians, Greeks, Armenians, and British.

This Palestinian elite combined Arab mores and modern habits. Ghada Karmi described her mother as a middle-class woman "keen on the latest fashions coming from Europe, as portrayed in Egyptian films," be they hairstyles, dresses, and silk stockings. With the Arab and the new European Jewish bourgeoisie, provincial Jerusalem began having an interesting social life. There was the Zion Cinema, which was Jewish owned, and then the Rex Cinema opened, which was Arab owned and replaced the Jewish cinemas for Arab audience. There were new cafes in the 1930s, the best of them newly opened by Jews. They brought a Viennese atmosphere, like in the movies, and delicious chocolate cakes and apple strudel. Cinema Edison was a famous entertainment venue, which also hosted the concerts of the Palestine Philharmonic Orchestra.[18]

Life was lived, with its share of conflicts. Living in these neighborhoods may have been like living in one large family, but then family is the quintessential space for tensions. The new ways of life brought cultural tensions that split society, and families debated how to be modern while keeping Arab tradition. Furthermore, the West Jerusalem Christian elite lived within a Muslim society. Most of the Christians were Arab, but that was not the case for Armenians and Greeks. In Jerusalem and the rest of Palestine there was silent discrimination of Christians by Muslims. Muslim society in Jerusalem was stiflingly conservative. Palestinian political power in the city and the country overall was in the hands of Muslim families, particularly the grand Jerusalemite Husayni, Nashashibi, Alami, and Khalidi families, among others. If the social, economic, and educational position of the Christian elite was undeniably the backbone of Palestinian indigenous modernity, its access to political power was nonetheless circumscribed. There were gender tensions between a nascent middle-class Arab women's movement and conservative values. There were tensions between Palestinian nationhood and Arab nationalism, between Palestinian aspirations for self-determination and the opposing interests of neighboring Arab states, particularly Transjordan. And there were political tensions, of course, between Jews and Arabs. Life was lived.

New patterns of consumption were emerging. American consumer goods began arriving from overseas; some people owned cars, and Heinz ketchup and Kellogg's cornflakes became markers of bourgeois consumption. Sari introduced to the Sakakini family an unexpected and amazing American food: the lemon pie! Dumia and Hala loved it. An important space of social, athletic, and intellectual activity was the YMCA, opened in 1933 opposite the King David Hotel. Hala and Dumia played tennis and joined the gym and swimming classes. Ghada Karmi was also a regular. The YMCA had an auditorium for concerts and lectures, a library, and a cafeteria. It was a space of interaction and entertainment, and as Ghada writes, "not the least of its attractions was that it provided a venue for young men and women to meet."[19]

Leisure and family traveling in and around Jerusalem, Palestine, and the Levant was a feature of this social class. One of the favorite trips of the Sakakinis was to Ein Karem, where Khalil and his wife Sultana used to stroll together when he courted her. Often the Sakakinis stopped by to see family friend Shukri Deeb, who had an estate a mile or two from Ein Karem along the main road, situated in a large area on a mountainside, from which there was a splendid view. It was common for families to travel within Palestine to visit relatives. Well-to-do families loved going to Jaffa, to picnic on the beach and swim in the sea. And beyond Palestine, popular destinations were Beirut and Cairo.[20] Sakakini loved traveling. "We visited Nazareth, Tiberias, Safed. . . . Everywhere we saw sunrise, prosperity, blossoming, as if nature went out of its way to welcome us," he wrote in a letter to Sari on December 1935 about a trip he and Sultana took to the Galilee, confiding his sensual love for his homeland. "I shall only write you that the whole of Palestine, with its mountains and valleys and plains, is a slice of paradise."[21]

The elite represented broader trends in Palestinian society and much of the Levant. It was a mobile society and region. Wadi Said was born in Jerusalem and married a Palestinian from Nazareth. Later in life he moved to a house in Talbiyeh, halfway between Salameh Square and Villa Salameh, with a wide marble staircase and a nice garden. Some members of his extended family lived nearby in the neighborhood, and the children used to play with their cousins. His daughter, Jean, recalled the neighborhood and Jerusalem as an intimate space, endowed with a succession of scents, jasmine and orange blossom, squeezed lemon, cinnamon sticks in syrup, and the bay leaf and olive oil smells of the Nablus soap they used to wash with. Jean's brother recalled that "we knew everyone else" in the area. At some point Wadi moved his successful stationery business to Cairo, and the family followed. It was Jean's brother, Edward, who later coined the term "Orientalism" and became a key Palestinian scholar and voice.[22]

My neighborhood started to come to life. The majestic villa on Salameh Square was constructed by the businessman and builder Constantin Salameh. It was the most splendid and grand building in the neighborhood, perhaps in all of Palestinian West Jerusalem, combining oriental, neoclassicist, and art deco motifs. Downhill from Salameh Square, the splendid villa I saw every day on the way to school was built by the businessman Hanna Ibrahim Bisharat in 1926. Although a Christian, Bisharat named his new home Villa Harun al-Rashid, celebrating the eighth-century Muslim caliph famous for his knowledge and wisdom, who established the House of Wisdom library in Baghdad. The gate adorned with "Villa Salameh" was built for Hana Salameh, the commercial agent of General Motors in Palestine and Jordan.[23]

The 1948 War arrived. When the United Nations passed the resolution to partition Palestine on 29 November 1947, the joy of the Yishuv knew no bounds. For the Palestinians, their homeland, political future, and way of life were now in danger. Sami Hadawi sat that evening in his new home in Katamon, a few houses away from Sakakini. He was born in Jerusalem in 1904 to a Christian family and during the Mandatory period worked for the British administration. Upon hearing of the UN resolution, Hadawi struggled "to recover from the news." He got up and tightly closed the shutters of his home.[24]

The Sakakinis left Katamon in late April 1948, when the full force of the war reached the neighborhood. By that time, most of the Palestinian inhabitants of West Jerusalem had left, fearing for their lives, to stay with family and friends in East Jerusalem, Beit Jala, or elsewhere in the Levant. They locked the door behind them, leaving their household intact, since they expected to return soon. Already in February 1948, after a Haganah soldier patrolling the neighborhood was wounded in an exchange of fire, Jews expelled Arab inhabitants of Talbiyeh. "The Arabs of Talbiyeh are leaving following the demand of the Haganah," wrote *Davar* (the newspaper of

Mapai, the main political party in the Yishuv) on 12 February 1948. "A Haganah car [with a loudspeaker] drove through the Talbiyeh neighborhood yesterday afternoon and called the Arabs to evacuate the neighborhood. Many Arabs left."[25] When the Jews conquered the Palestinian neighborhoods in April, a massive outbreak of plunder ensued. These two moments, of expulsion and plunder, articulated the gist of the Jewish demographic war. The meaning of spoliation of Palestinian property cannot be reduced to acquiring material possession. It reflected a popular outpouring to remove Palestinians that required no official order, clearly signaling that they were not coming back. Moshe Salomon was a company commander in the forces that occupied Katamon. On 28 April 1948 he wrote in his diary:

> Katamon was occupied during the previous week. . . . As a rich neighborhood, [it] provided opportunities for looting, and everybody, army privates and commanders, were swept away by this temptation. . . . The guys broke into the houses and lunged at the radios, elegant household items, and the like. It is difficult to describe what wealth there was in these houses. A craving for property engulfed everybody. . . . This ravenous hunger seized me too, and I could hardly control myself. In this area there is no limit to what one is able to do. . . . The craving for hoarding almost drove me crazy.[26]

New Jewish residents entered the houses in the Palestinian neighborhoods shortly thereafter, some arriving as destitute refugees from the Old City's Jewish Quarter, even as the violently interrupted lives of Palestinian families were still suspended in the rooms.

The 1948 War

In May 1973, when I was in eighth grade, my school commemorated Israel's twenty-fifth anniversary with a competition on the 1948 War of Independence. I prepared by reading three booklets about the war distributed free by the main daily in Israel at the time, *Ma'ariv*. I knew every operation and campaign of the war. It was a war of the few against the many, good against bad, innocence against evil. The uprooting of the Palestinians was not part of the story. I won first prize. There was a short circuit between my knowledge of the War of Independence and the Arab houses that stood silently in the neighborhood as I passed by them every day.

Part of what I learned and identified with was important and historically accurate: the Jewish anxiety during the Arab siege on the city—with the loss of thirty-five Haganah fighters on their way to assist Gush Etzion settlements south of Jerusalem, the Hadassah medical convoy massacre in April 1948 (of its connection to the massacre of Deir Yassin, which happened a few days earlier, I did not know from my teachers and books), the fall of Gush Etzion—this anxiety of Jewish Jerusalemites about their personal and national future was real. But there was also a short circuit between my knowledge of the war—knowledge that included more Jewish collective memory of the war than history of it—and a more sophisticated picture of the 1948 War. Scholars agree now that the Yishuv enjoyed social, economic, and military organization far superior to what Palestinian society could master. The Jewish military forces were larger and better organized, enjoying central command and control, than the fighting units of the Palestinians, who did not have an army to speak of, and the armies of the Arab states.[27]

But the short circuit was more profound. The two years between 1947 and 1949 are justifiably described as revolutionary by way of creating victors and victims. In 1882 the Palestinian Arabs made up about 97 percent of the population, while the Jews composed 3 percent; by 1918 the Arabs made up 92 percent and the Jews 8 percent. Even after the massive Jewish immigration of the 1930s, following Hitler's rise to power, at the end of the decade Arabs made up two-thirds of the population and Jews one-third; this was the population also in 1947.[28] But now a massive demographic change was to follow. In early 1949, only 160,000 Palestinians remained within the borders of the new state of Israel out of the 860,000 who had lived there before the war. Conversely, between 1948 and 1951, as many as 750,000 new Jewish immigrants arrived in the state, Holocaust survivors and Jews from the Arab Middle East and North Africa, who found in Israel a home, a homeland, and a haven from persecution.[29] During the same period, some 700,000 Palestinians were expelled or coerced to leave during the war, and their return home was denied.

The new state of Israel moved quickly to establish an institutional basis, a flourishing Hebrew culture, and a functioning democracy for Jews only. The Arab minority was under military rule until 1966, and structural discrimination has continued since. To the Jews this seemed like a national redemption, particularly after Auschwitz, as if the days of the Messiah had arrived. They also set out to erase the traces of Palestinian civilization in the land. Hundreds of Arab villages were destroyed. A special committee was set up in 1949 to give Hebrew names to all human and natural sites. Arab names were erased and replaced with Hebrew names, some bearing biblical and historical links, others simply invented. As Meron Benvenisti has observed, within a decade or so, this resulted in "erasing an entire universe" of Palestinian life, society, and culture that went back hundreds of years. The creation of a Jewish state and the destruction of Palestinian society were complementary.[30]

For the Palestinians, toponymy and violent reality coalesced. The name "Palestine" was erased from the map, the land divided now between Israel, Jordan, and Egypt. Palestinian civilization, with its cities, villages, culture, and social life, was torn asunder. We don't have an exact number of the uprooted Palestinians, but there is a general agreement among scholars on approximate figures. Some 90,000 Palestinians were uprooted from their homes to Lebanon, and 60,000 to Syria; some 200,000 were uprooted to the area of Mandatory Palestine ruled by Egypt after 1949, and 350,000 to the area of Mandatory Palestine ruled by Jordan or to Jordan beyond the river.³¹ They lost their entire property—lands, houses, goods, and bank accounts—all looted or expropriated by Israel.

Palestinian society, with its family, cultural, and commercial relations, its exchange of ideas and geographical mobility within and beyond Palestine into the larger Arab Middle East—all this was cut off. Take the city of Gaza, for example. On the eve of the 1948 War, it had 40,000 inhabitants. The town was linked to the markets of Bir Saba'a (today Beersheba) and Jerusalem, while inhabitants owned land in the adjacent areas toward Majdal (today Ashkelon) and the Naqab (Negev). All this changed in 1948: Gazans lost their lands that remained in Israel; the city and its inhabitants lost the geographical hinterland of Palestine and the direct land access to Palestinians now living in Israel and Jordan; and the expulsion of Palestinians during the war increased dramatically the population of the city and its environs with refugees from Jaffa and south Palestine. The city's population doubled to 80,000 souls. In the area that became the Gaza Strip, before the war there were some 70,000 inhabitants; immediately after the war the number grew to 270,000 people. Even an area flush with prosperity and resources would have found itself in dire situation. Most of the people living there were now poor, propertyless refugees. The Gaza Strip itself was an outcome of the war; it had no social, cultural, or economic logic: what was once a regional city connected to Palestine, the Middle East, and the eastern Mediterranean became a tiny strip encircled by Israel, Egypt, and the sea that made up 1 percent of Mandatory Palestine yet comprised 18 percent of its total population and 27 percent of its Palestinian inhabitants.³²

The war transformed Jerusalem from a cosmopolitan city under British control to a divided city along ethnic lines: Jewish Jerusalem in the west, the capital of Israel; and Arab Jerusalem in the east, under Jordanian rule.

As a result of 1948, the fate of national self-determination of Jews and Palestinians could not have been more different. Jews, some of them only recently arrived, enjoyed an independent state, with few Arabs. Palestinians who had lived in Palestine for ages lost not only home and homeland, but also faced a broken society, with no independent state to pick up the pieces. The expulsion of the Palestinians belonged within a larger history of ethnic cleansing in the modern world, particularly in the 1940s. But whereas the ethnic German expellees from Eastern Europe after 1945 and those of India and Pakistan in 1947 found a home in states that absorbed them, this was not the case in Palestine. In spite of the Partition Resolution, a Palestinian state was not established. The Palestinian expellees thus neither were allowed to return to their erstwhile homes nor did they have a Palestinian state to move to at the end of the crisis that caused their refugeehood, a state that would have seen the expellees as part of its national community and would have cared for them on multiple levels.

The Palestinians who remained in Israel lived under military rule from November 1948. They received ID cards from the state that had occupied them and expelled their relatives. Overnight they became people who needed to justify their existence and ask for favors in their own homeland. They were allowed to move only with a permit from the military administration. Hanna Abu-Hanna was born in 1928 in the village of al-Rina in the Galilee. "I obtain a permit to visit Nazareth" after its occupation in June 1948, he wrote. "At the crossroads . . . soldiers check the permits. The situation is humiliating." Anxiety about making ends meet and identity concerns coalesced when the military administration made a proposal that was halfway between ironic evil and insensitivity. "The military governor of Nazareth suggests that workers be sent to gather corn from the Saffurieh plain, olives from Lydda, Ramleh, Hittin and others. A few months ago, these crops were eagerly awaited by their owners. They planted them, our people who were made refugees. Shall workers from Nazareth and the district go to pick the crops of others in return for a daily wage to satisfy their hunger?" Abu-Hanna was a teacher. The school year 1948–49 was about to begin: "A peculiar feeling: You stand in front of the students you taught two months ago. The world has changed, but they haven't. Have you changed yourself?"[33]

Settlers, Natives, and Settlers Who Feel Native

When I was young, any comment that questioned the immaculate Zionist narrative was dismissed as antisemitic, and the person was dubbed as someone who loves Arabs. The use of the notion of antisemitism was quite broad. When the Israeli national soccer team lost (and it happened quite often), the saying went that the referee was antisemitic, and if he came from a country in Europe that sent Jews to their death in the Holocaust, then this was given as a proof for his prejudices. Referees from the Netherlands and Denmark were spared this judgment. I cannot recall now how serious we were in this utterance; I think it was uttered with an ironic smile. After all, we loved and played soccer and could judge for ourselves the level of the Israeli national team—it was not Italy or Brazil. But the saying had cultural significance in itself, showing the explanatory power of the victimhood of antisemitism, even if used with a sense of irony.

The years passed. Antisemitism still exists and is still used and misused as an explanation. But nothing perhaps represents the intricacy of Palestine and Israel better than the inseparability of antisemitism and settler colonialism. This pairing may seem incongruous, even outrageous, given the sharply diverging opinions about Zionism and settler colonialism.[34] And yet, antisemitism and settler colonialism belong together, as each describes a different facet of Zionism: antisemitism describes the reasons for the immigration of Zionists to Palestine and their justified claim for an independent polity, while settler colonialism describes its results.[35] Oren Yiftachel has coined the useful term "colonization of refugees."[36] Raef Zreik gives meaning to this duality in poetic words:

> Zionism is a settler-colonial project, but not only that. It combines the image of the refugee with the image of the soldier, the powerless with the powerful, the victim with the victimizer, the colonizer with the colonized,

a settler project and a national project at the same time. The Europeans see the back of the Jewish refugee fleeing for his life. The Palestinian sees the face of the settler colonialist taking over his land.[37]

Scholarship on the Zionist project as settler colonialism has grown tremendously in the last generation. It has contributed to our understanding of Zionist settlement, expansion, and political practice, while eliciting heated, even polarizing debates. Settler colonialism cannot explain everything about Zionism for the simple reason that an idea that explains everything ends up by explaining nothing, because it is deterministic and views history as moving inexorably toward a defined and unchangeable aim. But the notion of settler colonialism does point out important characteristics of the Jewish national movement, without which Zionism turns into a tautological, apologetic Jewish story. I cannot possibly do justice here to the field, its contribution, and its critics; but I do wish to briefly describe some main insights from this body of work that help us understand why my childhood view of Zionism was so ingenuous as to be historically inadequate.

The initial intent of Zionists to build a Jewish polity in the Land of Israel emerged from persecutions in Europe and was not, strictly speaking, determined by colonialist perceptions of Palestine's population. There was an ideological element of homecoming in Zionism based on the historical link between Jews and the land. Zionism was a case of a Diaspora national liberation movement that sought a land outside of Europe, but not a case of citizens who took control over an overseas land belonging to their empire. They came not as conquerors but as members of a persecuted minority. Zionism was an idea about nationhood and not an imperialist project.

But from the moment Zionists stepped on Palestine's shores, they became settlers whose project, fundamentally—with the good and bad intentions, the contingencies and unpredictability of history, the plans to live with and without the Arabs—denied Palestinians their full political independence in their homeland. Zionism fits quite comfortably within a definition of settler colonialism articulated by Caroline Elkins and Susan Pedersen:

> Settlers sought to construct communities bounded by ties of ethnicity and faith in what they persistently defined as virgin or empty land. Indeed, insofar as there was a logic to their approach to the indigenous populations, it was a logic of elimination and not exploitation: they wished less to govern indigenous peoples or to enlist them in their economic ventures than to seize their land and push them beyond an ever-expanding frontier of settlement.[38]

Two issues are fundamental to settler colonialism: the emotional struggle over the land, and the structural inequality set up by settlers between them and the native population. Ultimately, they wish not to integrate with the natives but to replace them and take over their land.[39] Zionism fit and still fits this historical portrait.

Zionists described their project in terms of settler colonialism, even if unintentionally. They saw the land as a virgin, uncultivated territory that had lain dormant for hundreds of years waiting for them as pioneers to redeem it. In their minds the land was empty, not in the sense that Zionists thought no one lived in Palestine, but in the sense that they thought its inhabitants were not at the same civilizational level and therefore deserved fewer national and political rights, if any.[40] They defined their identity as hermetically excluding the native on an ethnic, religious, and historical basis. They made the principle of political inequality between them and the natives into a tenet of their project, be it in the Balfour Declaration and the Mandate Treaty, which recognized Jews but not the natives as having national political rights, or in their opposition to the principle of democracy whereby the majority of the inhabitants of the land would decide its future. They made the issue of purchasing land ("redeeming" it in Zionist parlance) central. They did not want to exploit the natives economically, advancing the notion of Hebrew labor, but wished to acquire their land. "Judaizing the land" was a term from the lexicon of settler colonialists whose aim was to be rid of the natives in order to make space for themselves. Zionists were everyday settler colonialists, consciously or not, down to their most basic actions in Palestine.

I use the term "settler colonialism" without thrill or accusation. Several modern societies originated from settler colonialism, such as Canada, Australia, and the United States. Their current legitimacy is not questioned, but coming to terms with the past is required. No argument offends Israelis more than the idea that Zionism is, among others, a settler colonialism. They resent it in the most emotional way. One can see why, but this claim has more than a trace of historical truth and hence demands coming to terms with: Zionists arrived from Europe to an inhabited land not to integrate within the social and political framework of the local population, but to replace this framework and the population with a political community of their own. Zionists did not see their project as settler colonialism, and subjective experience is important to understand history, because their original intent to flee persecution had no connection to colonialism, and because colonialism itself stood in contradiction to their experience as a persecuted minority. They did not see themselves at all as immigrants but as *olim* (those who ascend) who "returned" to their homeland after a historical hiatus, though somewhat long, of two thousand years. The Zionist term *aliyah* (ascent) to the Land of Israel derived from the ancient Jewish notion of *aliyah la-regel*, namely, the ascent to Jerusalem during the three Jewish pilgrimage festivals. Thus a link was made between old Jewish and new Zionist practices. Every national story is made of facts and fables. One reason for the tremendous power of national stories is what they choose not to tell. The Zionist story chose to ignore the fact that the land did not really wait two thousand years empty and barren for East European Zionists to arrive. To the son of the land Sakakini, his Palestine was a paradise. The story Zionists told themselves did not change the fact that they came to an inhabited land to build a political community without asking permission of the locals.

There was another reason why mainstream Zionists did not view themselves as settler colonialists: it undermined the image dear to Zionists of the absolute morality embedded in their project. The Zionist idea of returning to the ancestral land emanated from Jewish culture, but it also served to obfuscate the moral problem inherent in the project: the land was not empty, the native population did not want the newcomers, and most Zionists, somehow, overall, would have preferred to find the land empty. They behaved like all people by building their identity as a commingling of challenges and contradictions; they knew and refused to know, they saw the Arabs and disregarded them, they devised plans to live with them and ignored their wishes, culture, and language. They lived for the moment, knowing full well that there were Arabs in the land, and at the same time they also dreamt of a *Jewish* state. Zionists saw their project as "cultivating the wasteland"; it represented perhaps that which they would have liked to see, a fantasy, a dream, of the Land of Israel as a blank slate.

The Zionist story thus becomes much more interesting and human, if not always humane, from the simplistic story I had believed in my youth, because it included unexpected twists and turns, lofty intentions and destructive consequences, and the lies and embellishments we all tell ourselves to give meaning to our lives. Zionism as a migrating national movement changed its character as it traveled in space from Europe to Palestine. Its adherents journeyed from Eastern Europe with Jewish national liberation ideas in mind. Landing in Palestine, they found themselves denying the national liberation of Palestinians. Its justified causes were different from its destructive results. Its essence comprised these two elements and should not be reduced to only one of them. Once Israelis put aside a sense of insult, once they free themselves of the need to feel always right and to divide the world into Jews as victims and Palestinians as perpetrators, then this way of thinking makes Israelis more—not less—connected to the land, because it allows understanding my history not as an island unto itself in the Land of Israel, as a Zionist-centric history, as a Jew in Talbiyeh as a neighborhood without a past, but as part of the history of the entire land and within the history of the Palestinians its inhabitants.

Conclusion: Telling the Story of Palestine and Israel

I still go back to Talbiyeh to visit my aging mother, who lives in the same house (figures 21.3 and 21.4). My childhood story of Talbiyeh, in which the Palestinians simply left and the Jews had nothing to do with it, turned out to be a fable of national memory. The word "Nakba," unknown in those days, is a household term today, and whether one acknowledges it or denies it, talking about it calls it into being. The Nakba was an ethnic cleansing undertaking, historically belonging within the context of the borderlands of the Austro-Hungarian, German, Russian, and Ottoman Empires, a geographical area of multiethnic coexistence that turned in the first half

Figure 21.3. Salameh Square in the 1940s. The two-story house on the left was known as the Montserrat monastery, housing from 1930 to 1941 a Spanish Catholic institute devoted to translating the Bible into Catalan. The grand Salameh villa is off the photo to the right of the house at the center. Photo: Hannah and Efraim Degani.

Figure 21.4. The house where I grew up on 4 Marcus Street just off Salameh Square, previously the Montserrat house. In the 1950s two nondescript floors were added to the beautiful building, and my parents moved to the fourth floor in the early 1960s. Photo: Ofra Confino.

of the twentieth century into a locus of ethnic cleansing and genocide in state-authorized suppression of ethno-religious difference.[41]

Even when Israeli Jews open themselves to a truthful historical account of 1948 and the modern history of Palestine and Israel, it takes time and an emotional journey to account for the past. I can think of myself. Some ten years ago I wrote an essay on the expulsion of the inhabitants of Tantura in 1948. I observed that I prefer to use the term "forced migration" over "ethnic cleansing," on grounds of method and of opening up a conversation rather than shutting it down, because the term "ethnic cleansing" is often associated in public and scholarly discourse with creating a tribunal atmosphere that causes an immediate scandal and reflexive denials.[42] This was correct on some level, but it also reflected, I now understand, my own process of coming to terms with the past. Today, I would use the term "ethnic cleansing," for two reasons. First, from the standpoint of evidence and of comparative history, the burden of proof is now on scholars who argue that the Nakba was *not* an ethnic cleansing. And second, I use this term, too, without thrill, but rather with a sense that coming to terms with the past is an ethical obligation. I have been a scholar of modern mass violence and the Holocaust for some time and have thus shared with my colleagues the professional and ethical concern of bringing the voice of the victims into the mainstream of historical writing on these events. There is an ethical duty to put front and center the victims of the 1948 War, the Palestinian civilian population, and to demand justice for it (whatever this may be in terms of historical acknowledgment, financial compensation, and politics).[43]

It took me some years to realize that my childhood in Talbiyeh was based on the ruins of the Sakakinis and their peers. The Khan Theater in Jerusalem was once the summerhouse—located outside of the city walls—of the family of Sultana Abdo, Khalil's wife. It was known before 1948 as Haririyyeh, "the silk factory," recalling the shop that had occupied the space in the past.[44] The estate of Shukri Deeb, whom the Sakakinis used to visit on the way to Ein Karem, is today Mount Herzl. The gate adorned with "Villa Salameh" is only some thirty meters away from the entrance to the residence of Israel's prime minister. But in another sense the distance is immeasurable. It represents the rejection by Israeli Jews of the fundamental interdependence in 1948, namely, that Israel's independence was made possible by the Nakba, and their unwillingness to come to terms with this national history of violence in 1948 and in the present occupation. On the other hand, the gate is there, a reminder for Jews that one can open it and enter.

The history that created the current situation in Palestine and Israel cannot tolerate utopian or perfect solutions. An adequate solution must take into consideration two facts. First, the Palestinians deserve full national rights in their homeland and an end to their dispossession, occupation, and existence as a people without rights; the Nakba should be acknowledged by Israel, and proper compensation offered. Second, the Jews have created in Palestine and then Israel in the last one hundred years a distinct national culture and society; the settlers have become natives, and they, too, deserve full national rights in their homeland. A political configuration that has any hope of success should include these two elements. Any solution that desires to be just and humane, whatever its political arrangement, ought to confer full political, national, civil, and human rights to all the inhabitants of the land between the river and the sea. Of course, there is the possibility of inhumane solutions: continuation of Israeli occupation in the West Bank and Gaza, deepening of the apartheid regime, perhaps Israel's annexation of the West Bank or part of it, or ethnic cleansing of Palestinians under specific historical circumstances.

Today, as I write these final sentences in 2020, it is difficult if not outright impossible to be optimistic about any humane solution to the conflict. The massive disparity of power between the two sides is detrimental to a negotiated settlement. The Jewish ethno-nationalists' future scenarios seem more realistic. The 1948 War ended, with its winners and losers. But, in a sense, it is still going on today, every day. And then again, I recall the wonder of history: Who ever imagined a year before 9 November 1989 that the Berlin Wall would fall, unleashing the end of dictatorships? Who could imagine in the 1980s the end of apartheid in South Africa? Could I have imagined in my childhood the evolution of my own Talbiyeh story? We don't know what tomorrow may bring. Hope remains, even if constrained, as long as we keep the human capacity to see the world through the eyes of others, to tell the story of Palestine and Israel, because telling a story, be it as a writer or a historian, enables us to look outward and provides a way of seeing the world, of being in it, of offering the possibility of freeing our imagination. Maybe. I'd like to believe in these words. No one knows what tomorrow may bring. I am waiting, then, for the unpredictable, for history to pleasantly surprise me. And why not? I am entitled, perhaps, for a new daydream.

Acknowledgments

I am grateful to Omer Bartov, Amos Goldberg, and Ofra Confino for their illuminating comments on earlier drafts of this paper and for sharing with me their insights in conversations. Yochi Fischer was important to sharpening some key ideas in the final stages of this text.

Alon Confino is the Pen Tishkach Chair of Holocaust Studies and professor of history and Jewish studies at the University of Massachusetts at Amherst. He has written extensively on modern German history, nationhood, memory, and Palestine and Israel. His most recent book is *A World without Jews: The Nazi Imagination from Persecution to Genocide* (Yale University Press, 2014), for which he received a Guggenheim Fellowship. He is now at work on a book on 1948 in Palestine, crafting a narrative that captures the experience of Palestinians, Jews, and the British based on letters, diaries, and oral history, while placing 1948 within the global perspective of decolonization, ethnic cleansing, and partitions.

Notes

1. The title of this chapter is inspired by Ta-Nehisi Coates, *Between the World and Me* (New York: One World, 2015).
2. I am grateful to Shira Wilkof for sharing with me her work on the topic.
3. Deborah Levy, *The Cost of Living: A Working Autobiography* (New York: Bloomsbury, 2018), 77.
4. These terms are common in the description of the Palestinian Revolt in 1936–39 and of the 1948 War. Anita Shapira, *Land and Power: The Zionist Resort to Force, 1881–1948* (New York: Oxford University Press, 1992), 230–33, 250. The description of Palestinian nationhood as terror has remained to the present.

AFTERWORD | 423

5. This is the wording in the original Hebrew edition of the book, where the word "painful" has clear meaning of a disturbing and unwelcomed problem. The English translation reads differently—the deliberations "ultimately arrived at the issue of the Arab question"—which replaced the emotions embedded in "painful" with neutral language. Shapira, *The Sword and the Dove: Zionism and Power, 1881–1948* (Tel Aviv: Am Oved, 1992, in Hebrew), 382; and Shapira, *Land and Power*, 281.

6. On the relationship between the Jewish and Arab questions, see Bashir Bashir and Leila Farsakh, eds., *The Arab and Jewish Questions: Geographies of Engagement in Palestine and Beyond* (New York: Columbia University Press, 2020). On how Europeans in the nineteenth century and later formed social and political issues as problems to be solved, see Holly Case, *The Age of Questions* (Princeton: Princeton University Press, 2018).

7. Omer Bartov, *Anatomy of a Genocide: The Life and Death of a Town Called Buczacz* (New York: Simon and Schuster, 2018); Hillel Cohen, *1929: Year Zero of the Arab-Israeli Conflict* (Waltham, MA: Brandeis University Press, 2015).

8. See, for example, Anita Shapira, *Israel: A History* (Waltham, MA: Brandeis University Press, 2012), 158, 162, 168, 174–75.

9. Benny Morris, *The Birth of the Palestinian Refugee Problem Revisited* (Cambridge: Cambridge University Press, 2004); Ari Shavit, *My Promised Land: The Triumph and Tragedy of Israel* (New York: Spiegel & Grau, 2013). On Shavit's book, see Ian Lustick, "Making Sense of the Nakba: Ari Shavit, Baruch Marzel, and Zionist Claim to Territory, *Journal of Palestine Studies* 44, no. 2 (2015): 7–27. For a thoughtful discussion of the Nakba and Jewish historical responsibility, see Hannan Hever, "The Crisis of Responsibility in S. Yizhar's *The Prisoner*," and "Expulsion Never Solves Anything: On S. Yizhar's *Khirbet Khizeh*," in *Hebrew Literature and the 1948 War: Essays on Philology and Responsibility* (Leiden: Brill, 2019), 78–104, 105–21.

10. Nafez Nazzal, *The Palestinian Exodus from Galilee* (Beirut: Institute for Palestine Studies, 1978), ix (italics in the original).

11. Lena Jayyusi, "Introduction: Arab Jerusalem and Colonial Transformation," in *Jerusalem Interrupted: Modernity and Colonial Transformation, 1917-Present*, ed. Lena Jayyusi, (Northampton, MA: Olive Branch Press, 2015), xiii–xviii; Rochelle Davis, "The Growth of the Western Communities, 1917–1948," in *Jerusalem 1948: The Arab Neighbourhoods and Their Fate in the War*, ed. Salim Tamari (Jerusalem: Institute of Jerusalem Studies, 1999), 32–73; Itamar Radai, "The Rise and Fall of the Palestinian-Arab Middle Class under the British Mandate, 1920–39," *Journal of Contemporary History* 51, no. 3 (2016): 487–506. Dorit Naaman headed a fantastic digital project, *Jerusalem, We Are Here*, re-creating pre-1948 Katamon, which included maps, videos, biographical information of the families and their houses, and "Katamon Tours" of the neighborhood: https://info.jerusalemwearehere.com/.

12. Hala Sakakini, *Jerusalem and I: A Personal Record* (Amman: Economic Press,1990), 105. On life in the neighborhood, see also Jacob Nammar, *Born in Jerusalem, Born Palestinian: A Memoir* (Northampton, MA: Olive Branch Press, 2012), 1–44. On the history and architecture of the neighborhood, see the excellent studies by David Kroyanker: *Jerusalem Neighborhoods: Talbiyeh, Katamon and the Greek Colony* (Jerusalem: Keter, 2002, in Hebrew), 22–24, 180, 239, 272; *Jerusalem Architecture* (New York: Vendome Press and St. Martin's Press, 1994); and *Jerusalem: The German Colony and Emek Rephaim Street* (Jerusalem: Keter, 2008, in Hebrew).

13. Sakakini, *Jerusalem and I*, 104. For a similar sentiment, see the recollections of John Melkon Rose, who grew up in Baq'a to a British father and an Armenian mother: *Armenians of Jerusalem: Memories of Life in Palestine* (London: Radcliffe Press, 1993), 94–96. See in general, Rochelle Davis, "Growing up Palestinian in Jerusalem before 1948: Childhood Memories of Communal Life, Education, and Political Awareness," in Jayyusi, *Jerusalem Interrupted*, 187–210.

14. Jamil Toubbeh, *Day of the Long Night: A Palestinian Refugee Remembers the Nakba* (Jefferson, NC: McFarland, 1998), 18–20, 67–68. On Issa and Maria Balsam Toubbeh, see the recollections of their grandson, Michel Moushabeck, in Naaman, *Jeruslaem, We Are Here* https://jerusalemwearehere.com/#/mapping/way-163932762. See also Ghada Karmi, *In Search of Fatima: A Palestinian Story* (London: Verso, 2004), 28.

15. Karmi, *In Search of Fatima*, 26.
16. Tahir al-Nammari, "The Namamreh Neighborhood in Baq'a," in Tamari, *Jerusalem 1948*, 279; Rose, *Armenians of Jerusalem*, 93, 108
17. Rose, *Armenians of Jerusalem*, 103–4, 110.
18. Karmi, *In Search of Fatima*, 22, 36–37.
19. Karmi, *In Search of Fatima*, 37.
20. Sakakini, *Jerusalem and I*, 92–93.
21. Khalil al-Sakakini, *Kadha Ana Ya Dunia* (Such am I, oh world: The diaries of Khalil al-Sakakini), ed. Hala Sakakini (Jerusalem: Commercial Press, 1954), 278, entry for 26 December 1935.
22. Jean Said Makdisi wrote a memoir centered on three generations of women in the family—her grandmother, mother, and herself: *Teta, Mother and Me: An Arab Woman's Memoir* (London: Saqi, 2005), 19, 31. Edward Said wrote a memoir several years earlier: *Out of Place: A Memoir* (New York: Knopf, 1999), 21.
23. Kroyanker, *Jerusalem Neighborhoods*, 24, 43–46, 119–20, 156–57; George Bisharat, "Talbiyeh Days: At Villa Harun al-Rashid," *Jerusalem Quarterly* 30 (2007): 88–98; David Kroyanker, *The Terra Santa Compound, Jerusalem. Biography of a Place—Profile of a Period, 1926–1999* (Jerusalem: Hebrew University in Jerusalem, 1999, in Hebrew).
24. Larry Collins and Dominique Lapierre, *O Jerusalem!* (New York: Simon and Schuster, 1972), 41.
25. *Davar*, 12 February 1948.
26. "Moshe Salomon: From the Diary of a Company Commander in the War of Independence," ed. Mordechai Bar-On, in *Alei Zayit ve-Herev*, vol. 6, *Jews and Arabs in a Protracted Struggle*, ed. Assnat Shiran (Tel Aviv: Defense Ministry, 2006, in Hebrew), 78. Kroyanker, the architecture historian of Jerusalem, who was born in the city in 1939, later recalled similar plunder. Kroyanker, *Jerusalem Neighborhoods*, 12.
27. An excellent starting point on this topic is Mordechai Bar-On, "Balance of Power in Combat Situation and Myth: 'David against Goliath' in the War of Independence," *Israel* 20 (2012): 107–52 (in Hebrew).
28. Justin McCarthy, *The Population of Palestine: Population History and Statistics of the Late Ottoman Period and the Mandate* (New York: Columbia University Press, 1990), 37.
29. Israel Central Bureau of Statistics, Statistical Abstract of Israel, 2017, no. 68: 2.2., http://www.cbs.gov.il/reader/shnaton/templ_shnaton.html?num_tab=st02_02&CYear=2017.
30. Meron Benvenisti, *Sacred Landscape: The Buried History of the Holy Land since 1948* (Berkeley: University of California Press, 2000), 39. And see Nur Masalha, *The Palestine Nakba: Decolonizing History, Narrating the Subaltern, Reclaiming Memory* (London: Zed Books, 2012), 88–119.
31. I am grateful to Fatina Abreek-Zubiedat and to Benny Morris for sharing information with me. See also Charles Smith, *Palestine and the Arab-Israeli Conflict*, 2nd ed. (New York: St. Martin's Press, 1992), 146.
32. Fatina Abreek-Zubiedat, "Architecture of Negotiations: Gaza and Yamit Cities as a Case Study for the Israeli Construction beyond the Green Line, 1967–1982" (PhD diss., The Technion—Israel Institute of Technology, 2018), 71.
33. Hanna Abu Hanna, "From a Diary of Fateful Years," *Palestine-Israel Journal* 5, no. 2 (1998), online, no page numbers, entries after 16 July 1948: http://www.pij.org/details.php?id=221.
34. The literature is huge by now. A good start are the three special issues devoted to Palestine and Israel in the journal *Settler Colonial Studies* 2, no. 1 (2012); 4, no. 4 (2015); 21, no. 4 (2019). For differing views, see Derek Penslar, "What If a Christian State Had Been Established in Modern Palestine," in *What Ifs of Jewish History: From Abraham to Zionism*, ed. Gavriel Rosenfeld (Cambridge: Cambridge University Press, 2016), 142–64; Arnon Golan, "European Imperialism and the Development of Modern Palestine: Was Zionism a Form of Colonialism?," *Space and Polity* 5, no. 2 (2001): 127–43.
35. I have been influenced by the work of Baruch Kimmerling, *Zionism and Territory: The Socio-Territorial Dimensions of Zionist Politics* (Berkeley: University of California Press, 1983), 28 in this instance.
36. Oren Yiftachel, "Between One and Two," in *Israel and Palestine: Alternative Perspectives on Statehood*, ed. John Ehrenberg and Yoav Peled (Latham, MD: Rowan & Littlefield, 2016), 317–47.

37. Raef Zreik, "When Does a Settler Become a Native? (With Apologies to Mamdani)," *Constellations* 23, no. 3 (2016): 358–59.
38. Caroline Elkins and Susan Pedersen, "Introduction: Settler Colonialism: A Concept and Its Uses," in *Settler Colonialism in the Twentieth Century: Projects, Practices, Legacies*, ed. Caroline Elkins and Susan Pedersen (New York: Routledge, 2005), 2.
39. The seminal article is Patrick Wolfe, "Settler Colonialism and the Elimination of the Native," *Journal of Genocide Research* 8, no. 4 (December 2006): 387–409.
40. Beshara Doumani, "Rediscovering Ottoman Palestine: Writing Palestinians into History," *Journal of Palestine Studies* 21, no. 2 (Winter 1992): 8.
41. See Mark Levene, "Harbingers of Jewish and Palestinian Disasters: European Nation-State Building and Its Toxic Legacies, 1912–1948," in *The Holocaust and the Nakba: A New Grammar of Trauma and History*, ed. Bashir Bashir and Amos Goldberg (New York: Columbia University Press, 2018), 45–65; Omer Bartov and Eric D. Weitz, eds., *Shatterzone of Empires: Coexistence and Violence in the German, Habsburg, Russian, and Ottoman Borderlands* (Bloomington: Indiana University Press, 2013)
42. Alon Confino, "Miracles and Snow in Palestine and Israel: Tantura, A History of 1948," *Israel Studies* 17, no. 2 (Summer 2012): 39–40. See also Alon Confino, "The Warm Sand of the Coast of Tantura: History and Memory in Israel after 1948," *History and Memory* 27, no. 1 (Spring/Summer 2015): 43–82.
43. See Alon Confino, "When Genia and Henryk Kowalski Challenged History, Jaffa 1949: Between the Holocaust and the Nakba," in Bashir and Goldberg, *The Holocaust and the Nakba*, 135–53.
44. Salim Tamari, "Sultana and Khalil: The Origins of Romantic Love in Palestine," in *Mountain Against the Sea: Essays on Palestinian Society and Culture* (Berkeley: University of California Press, 2009), 117.

Select Bibliography

Benvenisti, Meron. *Sacred Landscape: The Buried History of the Holy Land since 1948*. Berkeley: University of California Press, 2000.

Confino, Alon. "Remembering Talbiyah: On Edward Said's *Out of Place*." *Israel Studies* 5, no. 2 (Fall 2000): 182–98.

Hever, Hannan. *Hebrew Literature and the 1948 War: Essays on Philology and Responsibility*. Leiden: Brill, 2019.

Jayyusi, Lena, ed. *Jerusalem Interrupted: Modernity and Colonial Transformation, 1917–Present*. Northampton, MA: Olive Branch Press, 2015.

Naaman, Dorit. *Jerusalem, We Are Here*. 2018. https://info.jerusalemwearehere.com/.

Radai, Itamar. "The Rise and Fall of the Palestinian-Arab Middle Class under the British Mandate, 1920–39." *Journal of Contemporary History* 51, no. 3 (2016): 487–506.

Ram, Uri. "Ways of Forgetting: Israel and the Obliterated Memory of the Palestinian Nakba." *Journal of Historical Sociology* 22, no. 3 (2009): 376–95.

Shafir, Gershon. *A Half Century of Occupation: Israel, Palestine, and the World's Most Intractable Conflict*. Berkeley: University of California Press, 2017.

———. *Land, Labor and the Origins of the Israeli-Palestinian Conflict, 1882–1914*. Updated edition. Berkeley: University of California Press, 1996.

Tamari, Salim, ed. *Jerusalem 1948: The Arab Neighbourhoods and their Fate in the War*. Jerusalem: Institute of Jerusalem Studies, 1999.

Zreik, Raef. "When Does a Settler Become a Native? (With Apologies to Mamdani)." *Constellations* 23, no. 3 (2016): 358–59.

Index

Abdelqader, Senan, 176, 177
Abdo, Sultana, 411, 421
Abdul Hamid (Sultan), 106
Aboriginals, Australian, 141
Abraham (biblical figure), 34, 200–202, 206
Abraham, Daniel S., 292, 295
Abraham of Kalisk, R., 28, 30, 31
absentee property, land and, 120, 126, 158
Absentee Property Law (1950), 158
Abu Assad, Hany, 67
Abu-Hanna, Hanna, 416
Abulafia, R. Abraham, 26
Abulof, Uriel, 285–86, 292, 293
Abu-Lughod, Lila, 387
Aburabia, Safa, 2
Abu-Saad, Ismael, 243
Abu Sitta, Salman, 310
Achcar, Gilbert, 271, 279n22
Adenauer, Konrad, 53, 55
African National Congress (ANC), 310
Afula Illit, 163, 164
agrarian festivals, 224
The Agricultural Colonization of the Zionist Organization in Palestine (Ruppin), 266
Ahad Ha'am, 36, 267
Akri, Shadi, 397
Alatout, Samer, 116n32
Algeria, 14, 87, 267, 268, 269, 296, 302
allegory, symbol and, 26–27
Allenby, Edmund, 101
All That Remains (Khalidi, W.), 142
Almashni, Awni, 362n10
American Jewish Committee (AJC), 44
American Palestine Exploration Society (APES), 101
Amoco, 115n15

Anatolian Railway Company, 106
ANC (African National Congress), 310
Anderson, Benedict, 30, 348n12
Anglo-Persian Oil Company (APOC), 105, 115nn14–15
annexation, populations and, 124–25
antisemitism, 44–46, 264, 269–72, 416–17
anti-Zionism, as antisemitism, 269–72
apartheid, Israel and, 16, 367
  historical background, 337–40
  incremental, 14, 311
  Nationality Law and, 343–47
  1948 Palestinians and, 335–37
  political mobilization, 340–43
  reinstating, 333–34, 346–47
Arab Christians, 119, 122, 409
Arabic, 187–92
Arab Revolt (1936–1939), 107, 110, 112
Arabs, 48, 270, 335, 342, 403, 414
  attitudes toward Arabic and, 187–92
  Christians, 122, 409
  Hasidism and, 30, 32
  population, 363
  violence and, 24
Arab schools
  first period (1950s–1970s), 244–46
  history curriculum comparison, 243–54
  percentage of all history hours in, 246
  percentage of required history units for, 247
  second period (1970s–1990s), 246–48
  stated objectives of history teaching in, 245
  stated objectives of teaching of history in, 249
  third period (late 1990s), 248–54
  wording of new history curriculum for, 252

INDEX | 427

Arab village, in Israel-Palestine, 157, 176, 177
  apartment for Kafr Oasim, 169
  Ashkelon urban scheme, 161
  Be'er Sheva map, 160
  building in Gilo neighborhood, 171
  housing for younger generation in castle, 173
  housing project in Afula Illit, 164
  Khirbet Yama, 170
  al-Lajun return project, 175
  in 1950s as unique planning problem, 158–62
  in 1960s with vernacular "but not quite," 162–70
  in 1970s with architecture as exhibition, 170–74
  private home in Beit Safafa, 176
  public housing in Fureidis, 168
  Ramla urban scheme, 162
  Terrace Houses project, 163, 164
  Umm al-Fahm, 167
Aragon, Louis, 47
Aran, Gideon, 30
archaeology. *See also* Israel-Palestine, decolonized archaeology of
  agency of landscape and, 323
  between East and West, 316–18
  of social justice, 322–23
  structural changes, 319–20
Architecture without Architects exhibit, MoMA, 162–63
al-Ard movement, 342, 350n34
Arendt, Hannah, 46
Arieli, Zvi, 216
Asad, Talal, 68, 69
Ashkelon urban scheme, 161
Ashkenazim, 28, 29, 30–31
el-Assad, Hafez, 271
Association for the Defence of the Rights of the Internally Displaced (ADRID), 307
Attlee, Clement, 47
aura of sanctity, Zionist ceremonies with, 11, 223
auto-emancipation, 32–33, 36, 38
Auto-Emancipation (Pinsker), 32, 38
'Awda (right of return), 336. *See also* return

for Palestinians, 287, 307, 309–11, 366, 384, 385, 386, 389–91
  recognition of, 394, 398
Azoury, Neguib, 270

Ba'al Shem Tov. *See* ben Eliezer, Israel
Baghdad Concession (1899), 106
Baghdad-Haifa Railway, 108, 111
Bahloul, Zouheir, 345
Balfour Declaration, 23, 121, 202, 418
Balibar, Ettiene, 72, 73
Barak, Ehud, 297, 348n17
Barakeh, Mohamed, 345
Bar-Gal, Yoram, 199
Barnai, Ya'acov, 31
Barr, James, 101
Bar-Tal, Daniel, 243
Bartal, Israel, 25
Barth, Karl, 50
Bartov, Omer, 407
Bashir, Bashir, 62, 72–73
Basic Law, 294, 333, 343, 345, 352, 361n2
Bechtel, corporation, 108, 117n48
Beckman, Binyamin, 144, 146–47
Bedouins, 54, 103, 123–24, 129–31, 337
Be'er Sheva, 159, 160
Begin, Menachem, 290
Behar, Nissim, 186, 187, 189, 191
Beit Safafa, 176, 177
Beldjoudi v. France, 87
Ben-Ami, Jeremy, 294–95
Ben-Ami, Oved, 137, 142, 144
Ben-Avi, Itamar, 144
ben Eliezer, Israel (Ba'al Shem Tov, the Besht), 23, 25, 28, 30–31
Ben-Gurion, David, 114, 289
Benjamin, Walter, 27
Ben-Meir, Alon, 295
Benn, Aluf, 288
Benvenisti, Meron, 290, 414
ben Yehuda, Eliezer, 186
Ben-Yishai, Ron, 70, 71
ben Ze'ev, Yisrael, 195n30
Berdichevsky, Michah Joseph, 31, 35–36
Bereaved Family Circle, 68
Berlin-Baghdad Express, 106, 107
the Besht. *See* ben Eliezer, Israel

Between the World and Me (Coates), 422n1
the Bible, 140, 145, 200–201, 290
　Leviticus, 25, 29, 33, 35
Bidermanas, Izraels "Izis," 51–52
Biltmore Plan (1942), 406
Bilu immigrants, 36–37, 408
biocriminal, 131
biospatial politics, Israel, 118–19, 132–33
　with colonial leviathan recoiling, 129–31
　racial-spatial logic and, 120–24
　territorial expansion, 124–28
Bisharat, Hanna Ibrahim, 412
Bitosh Comforti, 166, 168
Blueprint Negev, 131
Blum, Léon, 47
Bnei Binyamin (The Sons of Benjamin), 142, 147
Bonaparte, Napoleon, 24, 143
borderless map, 205, 216
Bostoni, R., 166, 167
Bowman, Humphrey, 191
BP, 103, 105, 115n15
Braier, Michal, 125
Brawer, Abraham, 199, 203, 206, 211, 219n37
Brit Shalom, 39
Bronstein, Eitan, 310
Brown University, 1, 2
Buber, Martin, 31, 39, 289, 384
Buddhists, 122, 265, 280n33
Burg, Avraham, 306

Cadman, John, 108
Camus, Albert, 48, 49
cantons, return, 373–75
Carbon Democracy (Mitchell), 104, 107, 110
Cartier-Bresson, Henri, 50
Central Bureau of Statistics (CBS), 121–22, 124, 130, 132, 361n1
Chatterjee, Partha, 31–32
Chayut, Noam, 70
chemical weapons, 116n31
children, 70–71, 193n4, 193n10, 210, 219n35, 288
Christian Mission School, 188

Christians, 205, 318, 336, 411
　Arab, 122, 409
　tourists in Palestine, 24
Churchill, Winston, 46, 107–8
circumcisions, 31
climate change, oil and, 106
Clinton, Bill, 357
coal miners' strike, Great Britain, 107
Coates, Ta-Nehisi, 422n1
cognitive liberation, 342, 350n37
Cohen, Albert, 44
Cohen, Hillel, 407
Coletti, Duilio, 48
colonialism. *See also* decolonization; settler colonialism
　crypto-colonialism, 316, 319, 326n3
　international law and, 82
Colonial Settler Studies (journal), 140–41
colonization, 12–15, 140, 266, 324
Combatants for Peace, 68
Come to Netanya, 143–44
Commission of Inquiry (2010), 92
community, non-national, 30–31
Compagnie Française de Pétroles (CFP, Total), 103, 105, 115n14
Comparing the Incomparable (Detienne), 72
comparison in extremis, 63, 67–71
concentration camps, 43, 48, 50, 58, 59, 76n50
conflict, reconciliation and, 1–3
　education and ideology, 9–12
　future scenarios, 15–18
　nationalism, settler colonialism and decolonization, 12–15
　with space redrawn, 7–9, 401n43
　trauma and displacement, 4–7
conflict resolution, nonviolent, 68
constructivist approach, 218n15
The Cost of Living (Levy, D.), 404
Crampton, Jeremy, 199
Croce, Benedetto, 44
Crossman, Richard, 49
crypto-colonialism, 316, 319, 326n3

Dagan, Meir, 291
Dahiya Doctrine, 63
Dahl, Roald, 110, 116n30

Dajani, Aref Pasha, 270
Danon, Danny, 289–90
Davar (newspaper), 412–13
David (King), 29, 203
Dayan, Moshe, 112, 125
Daybreak for a Nation (Van de Poll), 50–51
decolonization, 12–15. *See also* Israel-Palestine, decolonization of; Israel-Palestine, decolonized archaeology of
De Gaulle, Charles, 44–45
Deir Yasin massacre (April 1948), 356, 413
Dellapergola, Sergio, 294
De Meyer, J., 87
demography, Israel and state demise, 13, 292–93
demolitions, 126, 130, 344
demonstrations, against Hamas, 305
demoralization, 13, 288, 289–90
Denmark, 87, 416
depopulation, 49, 125, 154, 364, 369–70, 373, 377
Derrida, Jacques, 63
detention centers, at US-Mexico border, 59
Detienne, Marcel, 72
Deutsche Bank, 105, 106, 107, 112, 113
Ein Deutscher sieht Israel (*A German sees Israel*) (Lüth), 54
Deutsche Welle, 68
Dichter, Avi, 337, 343
Dinur, Ben Zion, 29, 41n18
displacement, trauma and, 4–7
Doisneau, Robert, 50
Doron, Daniel, 286
Drexler, Yehuda, 163, 164, 165
Dreyfus Affair, 45
Druze, 122, 166, 246, 336–37, 345
Dubnow, Simon, 29, 36
Dubnow, Ze'ev, 36–37, 408
Dushkin, Alexander, 190–91
Dworkin, Ronald, 352–53

The Earth Cries Out (*Il grido della terra*) (film), 48
Eban, Abba, 404
Economic and Social Commission for Western Asia, UN (ESCWA), 379
economy, 90–93, 111–13, 379

Economy and Society (Weber), 283
ecstasy, 26
education, 193n4, 410. *See also* Arab schools; Hebrew education, modern; Jewish schools; schoolbook maps, Israeli
  ideology and, 9–12
  Jewish, 184–85
  system in Israel, 241–42
Egypt, 127, 271, 322
Eichmann, Adolf, 233, 271
Elboim-Dror, Rachel, 193n4
elite
  IDF, 113
  Palestinian, 188, 409–13
  political, 348n15
  professional, 169
Elitzur, Uri, 290
Elkins, Caroline, 417
empathic unsettlement, 72–73
Engels, Friedrich, 267
Enlightenment, 33–34, 38, 184, 185, 273
Entre Nous (Levinas), 72
Epstein, Yitzhak, 186, 194n16
equality, 31, 71, 72, 73, 355–57, 359, 371
equivalence, 71, 72, 73
erasure, Holocaust guilt and, 53–55
Eshkol, Levi, 118
Esprit (newspaper), 48
ethnic cleansing, 38, 304, 363, 380n3, 420–21. *See also* the Nakba
Ethnocracy (Yiftachel), 361n1
European Convention on Human Rights and Fundamental Freedoms (ECHR), 85
European Court of Human Rights (ECtHR), 85–87, 89
Even-Chen, Aharon, 144, 147
Even-Zohar, Basmat, 193n4
Even-Zohar, Itamar, 222
exclusiveness, Hebrew revived with pedagogy versus, 192–93
Exodus 1947 saga, 47
Exodus Border, Tribes' Estates and, 205–16
expulsion, prohibition of mass, 84
extermination camps, concentration and, 43
ExxonMobil, 103

Fauda (television show), 157
Feige, Michael, 199
Feisal ibn Hussein (King of Iraq), 108
Felski, Rita, 63
fertility rates, 129
Fieldhouse, D. K., 265
Filastin (newspaper), 270
Firer, Ruth, 203, 210, 217
First Aliyah, 223–25
Firsting and Lasting (O'Brien), 141
First Zionist Congress (1897), 36
Folman, Ari, 6, 69, 70, 71
foreign aid, to Israel, 17, 378
The Forgotten Palestinians (Pappé), 135n21
Foucault, Michel, 131
France, 44–45, 47, 49, 87, 104, 105
Frenkel, Walter, 144, 147
Freud, Sigmund, 404
Friedman, Susan Stanford, 63
"From Gaza to Warsaw" (Rothberg), 73n3
Frumkin, Arieh Leib, 37
Fureidis, 166, 168
The Future Vision of the Palestinian Arabs in Israel, 342

Galilee, Judaization of, 135n21, 163, 275
Gamerman, Giora, 167, 170
Gassmann, Vittorio, 45
Gavison, Ruth, 293–94
Gaza, 58–59, 64, 65, 73n3, 134n6, 372, 415
Geertz, Clifford, 221
Geneva Convention of 1949, Fourth (GCIV), 80–81, 82, 83, 389
geographical imagination, 398
Georges-Picot, Francois, 102
Germany, 43–44, 45, 105, 106–7, 115n17
Gershon of Kuty, R. Abraham, 25, 30–31
ghost railway, oil and, 108–11
Gilbert, Mads, 64, 65, 68
Gilo neighborhood, building in, 171
Girard, René, 24, 33
Glubb, John Bagot "Glubb Pasha," 110, 112
God, 50, 202, 206
  the Bible and, 145
  revenge and, 33, 34, 35, 37

Godwin, Mike, 73n2
Goethe, symbol and, 26
Golan Heights, land seizures in, 135n28
Goldberg, Amos, 62, 72–73
Gollwitzer, Helmut, 50
Gonen, Amiram, 139
Gordis, Daniel, 289
Gouri, Haim, 402
Gramsci, Antonio, 283, 312
Graves, Clarissa, 410
Graves, Robert, 410
Grazowski, Yehuda, 217n1
Great Britain, 107, 113, 139
  oil and, 103, 104, 105, 108, 112
  Zionist civic rituals and mandate of, 225–29
Greece, 274, 280n33
Green Line, 118, 125–27, 132, 276, 305, 335
Grossman, David, 68, 285, 361n1
guilt
  erasure and Holocaust, 53–55
  of perpetrator, 69, 70
Gulbenkian, Calouste, 115n14
Gurevitch, Zali, 30

Haaretz (newspaper), 285, 286, 287, 293, 294
Habbat October (October Ignition), 339, 342, 343
Habib-Allah, Shadi, 175, 394
Hadawi, Sami, 412
Hague Regulations (1907), 80, 81, 82
Haifa, 72, 108, 116n46, 375
Haifa-Tripoli-Kirkuk pipelines map, 109
hakham ha-kahal (wise man of the community), 28
Halevy, Dotan, 188, 195n17, 317
Halpern, Israel, 25
halutzim (pioneers), 36–37, 49, 222, 418
Hamas, 59, 65, 68, 305
  charter of, 74n20, 270
  Israel compared to, 63–64, 69, 75n24
Hamdan, Saleh, 142
Hannibal Protocol, 63
Harlan, Veit, 54
Harley, John Brian, 199

Harvey, David, 398
"Ha-shavui" ("The Prisoner") (Yizhar), 66
Hasidic-Haredi (ultra-Orthodox), 37, 128–29, 187, 194n16, 288
Hasidic Jews. *See* Palestine, Nakba and Hasidic immigration to
Hasidism, 23, 26–27, 28, 29–30
  nonviolence and, 24, 34, 37, 38
  Zionism and, 4, 25, 32–33
Hassan, Sharaf, 254
hate speech, criminalization of in France, 45
Hazan, Yaakov, 195n17
Hazony, Yoram, 289
Hebraization, 183, 388
Hebrew education, modern, 183. *See also* Jewish schools
  attitudes toward Arabs and Arabic, 187–92
  exclusiveness versus pedagogy for reviving, 192–93
  "How Do We Say Nakba in Hebrew?," 389
  Palestine and revival of Jewish and, 184–85
  with pedagogy or segregation, 185–87
Hebrew in Hebrew (*Ivrit be-Ivrit*), 185–87, 190, 191
Hebron riots, 270–71, 279n19
Herder, Johann Gottlieb von, 272
Hershman, Salo, 171–74
Hever, Hannan, 66, 408
High Court of Justice, 92, 345
Hijaz Railway, 107, 110–11
Hirsch, Marianne, 72, 73
Hitler, Adolf, 43, 44, 52, 267, 271
Holliday, Clifford, 142, 148–49
Holocaust, 5, 6, 43, 47, 61
  guilt and erasure, 53–55
  memory, 58–59, 60
  with pro-Jewish empathy, 46
Holocaust comparisons
  competitive forms, 59–60, 61
  with difference recognized, 71–73
  Israel-Palestine discourse and, 58–73
  in media, 58–60, 65–66, 68
  mirror and no, 63–67

moral equivalence and, 58–60
  Nakba and, 4, 60–63, 70, 74n14
  reciprocity and recognition, 67–71
The Holocaust and the Nakba (Bashir and Goldberg), 61, 62, 72–73
homeland
  exile in, 25
  two states, one, 16, 357–60, 362n10
homes, right to noninterference in, 86–87
The Home and the World (Tagore), 361
Hotam, Yotam, 35
Hourani, Rida Blaik, 242
housing, 166
  projects in Afula Illit, 163, 164
  for younger generation in castle, 173
"Housing for the Arab and Druze Sector" (Ministry of Housing), 166
Hovevei Zion (Lovers of Zion) movement, 32, 37
humanist photography, 50
L'Humanité (newspaper), 47
human rights, 357, 389. *See also* international human rights, West Bank Israeli settlers and
Human Rights Committee (HRC), 85–87
"Human Values in Urban Architecture" (Karmi, R.), 172
Hussein, Cherine, 304
Hussein, Saddam, 116n31, 265, 274
al-Husseini, Hajj Amin, 112, 270–71
hydraulic fracturing, oil and, 116n29
Hyman, Benjamin, 142, 148, 149
Hysler Rubin, Noah, 408

Ibn Khaldun, 317
ID cards, 349n33, 415
Idel, Moshe, 26, 27
identity
  cards, 349n33, 415
  migration, colonization and, 324
  nationality and, 121–22
  settlers with, 268
ideology, education and, 9–12
IDF. *See* Israel Defense Forces
immigrants
  Bilu, 36–37, 408
  Hasidic, 28–29

immigration. *See* Palestine, Nakba and Hasidic immigration to
iNakba app, 388
incremental apartheid, 14, 311
independence, Zionist civic rituals with Israeli, 225–29
indigenous people, 141, 144–46, 317
injustice, redress for historical, 89–90
In Our Hands (film), 394
Intended Border, 200, 203–4
Interim Agreement (1995), 89
International Covenant on Civil and Political Rights (ICCPR), 84–86
international human rights, West Bank Israeli settlers and, 78–79
  economy and property restoration, 90–93
  grounds for limitations on, 88
  historical injustice redress and, 89–90
  law and repatriation obstacles, 83–87
  law and settlements project, 80–83
  necessity and proportionality, 88, 90–93
  public order and national security, 88–89
international law
  colonialism and, 82
  legal regulation of repatriation of settlers, 82–83
  settlements project and, 80–83
  in West Bank, 80–81
Iraq, 104, 110, 115n7, 116n31
Iraq Petroleum Company (IPC), 102–5, 108, 111–12, 115n15, 117n48
Isaac, R. Levi, 29–30
Israel. *See also* apartheid, Israel and; Arab village, in Israel-Palestine; biospatial politics, Israel; Palestinians, in Israel; planning history, Israel; schoolbook maps, Israeli
  Arabs in, 335
  with Bedouin fields plowed, 130
  borders of state of, 212–16
  contemporary map of state of, 215
  foreign aid to, 17, 378
  The Future Vision of the Palestinian Arabs in Israel, 342
  Hamas compared to, 63–64, 69, 75n24

  Jewish schools and educational system in, 241–42
  Joshua with conquest map of, 209
  Kingdom of Israel in Solomon era map, 203, 204
  land use in, 370
  military doctrines of, 63
  occupation with Auschwitz spirit, 58
  oil and, 110
  Palestine and, 419–22
  Palestinian population in, 335
  Peace with, 54
  symbol for State of, 237n24
  urban studies, 140–41
  Zionist civic rituals with independence of, 225–29
Israël (Bidermanas), 51
Israel (Danon), 289
Israel, R., 28
Israel, state demise, 282, 297
  demography, 13, 292–93
  how close to, 294–96
  Jewish demoralization, 13, 289–90
  occupied territories, 13, 290–92
  as projects, 283–84
  as regime, 293–94
  survival discourse and, 284–88
Israel 2020 study, 371
Israel Defense Forces (IDF), 38, 113, 167, 230, 235, 287
  concentration camps and, 58, 76n50
  Druze and, 345
  role of, 114, 371
  war crimes by, 75n24
Israel-Gaza war (2008–2009), 58
Israel-Hamas war (2008 and 2014), 59, 74n20
Israeli Jews, 50–52. *See also* international human rights, West Bank Israeli settlers and
Israeli origin, 121–22
Israeli Supreme Court, 81, 96n55, 122, 287, 345, 350n46
Israel My Homeland (Shifman), 202
Israel-Palestine, decolonization of, 312
  as discourse or political program, 302–8
  ODSC plan, 308–11

Israel-Palestine, decolonized archaeology of, 315
  agency of landscape, 323
  being in and becoming of, 324
  conditions for, 324–25
  between East and West, 316–18
  with field redefined, 320–24
  memory and, 323–24
  with old structures dismantled, 318–20
  social justice, 322–23
Israel-Palestine, future of, 384, 398
  'Awda and, 389–91
  ghost of Nakba, 385–89
  mapping, 391–97
  Mi'ar Mosque, 396
  Miska return map, 392
Israel-Palestine conflict, 263–64, 277
  anti-Zionism as antisemitism, 269–72
  nationalism clash with, 272–76
  settler colonial paradigm, 265–69
Israel-Palestine discourse, Holocaust comparisons and, 58–73
"Israel-Palestine: Lands and Peoples" (research project), 1
Italy, 45, 49
Ivrit be-Ivrit (Hebrew in Hebrew), 185–87, 190, 191

Jabareen, Yousef, 344
Jabotinsky, Ze'ev, 267
Jasin v. Denmark, 87
Jaspers, Karl, 46
Jerusalem, We Are Here (digital project), 423n11
Jerusalem Times (newspaper), 271
Jewish calendar, 224, 226, 230, 232, 234, 236n11
Jewish education, 184–85
Jewish National Fund, 111, 130
Jewish question, 32, 34–36, 37, 43
Jewish schools, 255–56
  educational system in Israel, 241–42
  first period (1950s–1970s), 244–46
  history curriculum, 242–43
  history curriculum comparison, 243–54
  percentage of all history hours in, 246
  percentage of required history units for, 247
  second period (1970s–1990s), 246–48
  stated objectives of history teaching in, 245
  stated objectives of teaching of history in, 249
  theoretical framework, 239–41
  third period (late 1990s), 248–54
  wording of new history curriculum for, 252
The Jewish State (Hazony), 289
Jews, 30–31, 44, 45, 60, 64, 122, 336
  Israeli, 50–52
  Mizrahi, 120, 121–22, 128
  nationalist, 36–39, 354
  "Nazism" of, 63, 65, 70
Jordan, 104, 110, 116n29, 126, 414
Jordan River, 14, 101, 103, 110, 211, 309
Joshua (biblical figure), 208–10, 219n29
Judaization, 126, 305, 309, 386, 388
  of Galilee, 135n21, 163, 275
  of land, 118–20, 131–32
Jud Süß (film), 54
Jumblatt, Kamal, 271
June 1967 War. *See* Six Day War

Kafr Qasim, 167, 169, 344, 348n9, 350n46
Kahn, Dorothy, 144, 145, 146
Kalvarisky, Haim Margaliot, 186, 187, 190–91
Kanafani, Ghassan, 72
Karmi, Ghada, 410, 411
Karmi, Hasan, 410
Karmi, Ram, 172
Katamon, 402, 403, 409, 412, 413, 423n11
Katznelson, Berl, 227, 228, 231–32
Kedar, Alexander, 121
Kedar, Mordechai, 75n23
Keller, Haim, 190
Kessel, Joseph, 49
Kesselman, Moshe, 142
Al-Khaledi, Ottman Effendi, 187–88
Khalef, Amin, 188, 195n17
Khalidi, Rashid, 272, 408
Khalidi, Walid, 142–43

Khirbet Khizeh (Yizhar), 6, 66
Khirbet Yama village, 167, 170
Khmelnytsky Uprising (1648), 28
Khoury, Elias, 61, 74n14
Kielce pogrom (July 1946), 43
Kimenich, Otto, 53
Kimmerling, Baruch, 268
King-Crane Commission, 270
Kingdom of Israel in Solomon era map, 203, 204
Kirkuk-Banias pipeline, 117n48
Kisch, Frederick, 191
Kitchener, Herbert, 102
Kizel, Arie, 243
Klein, Menachem, 185, 187
Korenfeld, Zvi, 144, 149
Krieger, John, 199

labor unions, 111–12
LaCapra, Dominick, 69, 72–73
al-Lajun return project, 175
land, 141, 224, 291, 366, 370, 401n44.
    See also Netanya
  absentee property and, 120, 126, 158
  acquisition and indigenous dispossession, 144–46
  Judaization of, 118–20, 131–32
  rural Jewish areas, 375–76
  seizures, 120–21, 125, 126, 130, 135n28, 415
  territorial expansion, 124–28
"Land, Identity, and History" (Aburabia), 2
Land and Power (Shapira), 406
Landau, David, 286
Land Day (1976), 338, 342, 343, 346, 348n9
landscape, archaeology and agency of, 323
The Land and Its Regions (Brawer), 211
Langfan, Mark, 287
language. *See also* Hebrew education, modern
  children and, 193n10
  segregation and, 187–92
Lawrence, T. E., 102, 116n41
Lawrence of Arabia (film), 107
Lazare, Bernard, 45–46
Lebanon, 104, 110, 371

Le Corbusier, 47–48
legal regulation, repatriation of settlers and, 82–83
Leibovitch, Elia, 286
Lenin, Vladimir, 273
"Let Us Make an End to Falsities" (Buber), 39
leviathan, recoiling of colonial, 129–31
Levinas, Emmanuel, 72
Leviticus, 25, 29, 33, 35
Levy, Deborah, 404
LGBTQ community, 343
Libération (newspaper), 47
Liberman, Avigdor, 349n24
"Living with Political Depression in Tel Aviv Is Harder Than Dying in Gaza" (Shatz), 65
Livni, Tzipi, 287, 291
Locke, John, 146
Lockman, Zachary, 112, 116n41
London Review of Books, 65
Lovers of Zion (Hovevei Zion) movement, 32, 37
Lufenfeld, Moshe, 167, 170
Luria, Yosef, 191
Lüth, Erich, 54, 55

Maas, Herman, 55
Maggid of Mezherich, 28
Malraux, André, 43, 51–52, 53
Manoff, Einat, 391, 398
Marchandeau Law, France, 44–45
Marcus, Yoel, 286
Maritain, Jacques, 46
Marker, Chris, 50
marketing
  for Netanya, 137
  scarcity and oil, 111–13
Marx, Karl, 267
Massignon, Louis, 53
Maté, Gabor, 64, 65, 68
Matisse, Henri, 47
Mauriac, François, 51
Mazor, Lea, 208
McMeekin, Sean, 106
media
  Arabs depicted in, 48

INDEX | 435

Holocaust comparisons in, 58–60,
  65–66, 68
Jews portrayed in, 45
Meir, Golda, 118
Memmi, Albert, 306
memory
  Holocaust, 58–59, 60
  motivated forgetting, 404
  Multidirectional Memory, 72, 73n3
  past places of, 323–24
  rituals of, 226
Mendel of Przemyślany, R. Menahem, 28
Mendel of Vitebsk, R. Menahem, 28, 29, 31
Mexico, detention centers at US border, 59
Mi'ar refugees, 395
Michael, Sami, 295
Middle East. *See* oil, Middle Eastern
  sovereignty and
migration, colonization, identity and, 324
militarization, of oil, 103, 104, 110
military doctrines, of Israel, 63
Miska return map, 392
Mitchell, Timothy, 104, 107, 110
Mizrahi Jews, 120, 121–22, 128
Mofaz, Shaul, 287
Monmonier, Mark, 208
Morag, Raya, 69, 70
Morris, Benny, 286, 407
motivated forgetting, 404
Muhanna, Elias, 101
multiculturalism, 255–56
Multidirectional Memory (Rothberg), 72,
  73n3
Muntez, Ali, 114
Muqaddimah, 317
Musih, Norma, 391
Muslim Brotherhood, 271, 274
Mussolini, Benito, 48
My Holocaust Thief (Chayut), 70
My Promised Land (Shavit, A.), 291, 407

Naaman, Dorit, 423n11
Nabonidus (King of Babylon), 317
Nahman of Braslav, R., 26
the Nakba, 4, 6, 12, 15, 17–18, 24,
  33–34, 38, 39–40, 50, 52–55, 60,
  61n14, 62, 66, 70, 72, 142, 158,
  175–76, 304, 308, 322, 346, 353,
  364, 385–90, 393–95, 398, 406–8,
  413–16, 419, 421. *See also* Palestine,
  Nakba and Hasidic immigration to;
  philosemitism, Nakba in 1950s and
  Western European
depopulation, 364
Holocaust and comparisons to, 4, 60–63,
  70, 74n14
The Holocaust and the Nakba, 61, 62,
  72–73
"How Do We Say Nakba in Hebrew?,"
  389
IDF with ethnic cleansing in, 38
iNakba app, 388
with 1948 Palestinians and apartheid,
  335–37
revisiting ghost of, 385–89
violent role of, 24, 33
narcissism, 65, 66, 73
Nathan, Susan, 361n1
nationalism, 12–15, 27, 202, 217n3,
  272–76, 279n29
nationalist Jews, 36–39, 354
nationality, 27, 121–22
Nationality Law, 132, 311, 343–47
national projects, 31–32
national security, public order and, 88–89
Native Americans, 141
Nazareth, Terrace Houses project in, 163,
  164
Nazis, 43–44, 46, 48–49, 61, 64
"Nazism," of Jews, 63, 65, 70
Nazzal, Nafez, 408
Near East Development Corporation
  (NEDC), 105, 115n14
the Negev (al-Naqab), 129–31
Netanya
  celebration photos, 152
  Come to Netanya, 143–44
  land acquisition as indigenous
    dispossession, 144–46
  marketing for, 137
  as modern resort, 146–48
  as Palestinian-Israeli planning history
    case study, 142–51
  plan, 150

story of, 138
urban planning and, 148–51
Netanyahu, Benjamin, 286, 290, 291, 295, 311, 340
Netherlands, 44, 45, 49, 416
neutrality, Jewish question and, 43
New York Review of Books, 59
New York Times (newspaper), 68
+972 Magazine, 65
1948 Palestinians
apartheid and, 335–37
Nationality Law and, 344–47
1948 War. *See* the Nakba
non-Arab Christians, 122
nonviolence, 24, 34, 37, 38, 67, 68. *See also* violence
Nora, Pierre, 394
Nordau, Max, 267
North, Douglass C., 283
La Nuit (*Night*) (Wiesel), 51

Obama, Barack, 287
O'Brien, Jean, 141, 144, 146, 148
Ocasio-Cortez, Alexandria, 59
Occupied Palestinian Territories (OPT), 6–8, 13
occupied territories, Israel, state demise and, 13, 290–92. *See also* West Bank
October Ignition (Habbat October), 339, 342, 343
Odeh, Ayman, 344, 350n44
ODSC (One Democratic State Campaign) plan, 308–11
Ogato, Sadaka, 378
oil, Middle Eastern sovereignty and, 116n29, 116n46
with concessions made, 104–5
end of line and, 113–14
ghost railway and, 108–11
Haifa-Tripoli-Kirkuk pipelines map, 109
IPC, 102–5, 108, 111, 115n15, 117n48
marketing scarcity and, 111–13
militarization of, 103, 104, 110
pipelines in sand, 101–2
subjects of, 103–4
with trains and conveying power, 105–8
Olmert, Ehud, 291, 297

One Democratic State Campaign (ODSC) plan, 308–11
On Suicide Bombing (Asad), 68
Ophir, Adi, 384
Oren, Michael, 285, 294
Orientalism (Said, E.), 53
The Origins of Totalitarianism (Arendt), 46
Ornan, Uzi, 195n30, 196n44
Orwell, George, 44
Oslo Accords, 127–28, 305, 356, 362n10
Oslo II agreements, 339
The Other Side of Israel (Nathan), 361n1
Ottoman Empire, 28, 101, 104–7, 274
Our Homeland (Brawer), 211
Oz, Amos, 65, 66, 68

Pabst, Georg, 45
Pada, Yael, 394–95
Palestine, 101, 139, 266, 305, 335, 342. *See also* Arab village, in Israel-Palestine; Holocaust comparisons; Israel-Palestine, decolonization of; Israel-Palestine, decolonized archaeology of; Israel-Palestine, future of; Israel-Palestine conflict
children in Warsaw Ghetto and, 70–71
elements of future, 366
Hasidism in, 4, 23–24
Holocaust and, 61
Israel and, 419–22
oil and, 104, 110
OPT, 6–8, 13
urban studies, 140–41
Zionists in, 23–24
Palestine, Nakba and Hasidic immigration to, 24, 40
auto-emancipation, 32–33
exile in homeland, 25
immigrants, 28–29
with Jewish question imported, 34–36
nationalist Jews, 36–39
national project, 31–32
non-national community, 30–31
revenge, 33–34
spiritual connection, 4, 23, 29–30
symbol and allegory, 26–27
turning point, 28

INDEX | 437

Palestine Exploration Fund (PEF), 101, 115n1
Palestine Land Society, 366, 401n44
Palestine Liberation Organization (PLO), 250, 304, 305, 309, 338
Palestine Review, 144
Palestinian Authority (PA), 127, 250, 304–5, 318, 339
Palestinian Revolt (1936–1939), 107, 110, 112–13, 144, 146, 422n4
Palestinians, 6, 19n4, 135n21, 414
  elite, 188, 409–13
  population, 121, 353, 355, 409
  rape of women, 64, 75n23
  right of return for, 287, 307, 309–11, 366, 384, 385, 386, 389–91
Palestinians, in Israel
  democratic and Jewish, 352–53
  full equality, 355–57
  personal note, 360–61
  as second-class citizens, 353–55
  summary comments, 359–60
  two states, one homeland, 357–60
The Palestinian Exodus from Galilee (Nazzal), 408
Pappé, Ilan, 135n21, 140
Paradise Now (film), 67, 68
Paris Peace Conference (1919), 270
Parkes, James, 54
Partition Plan, UN, 33, 39, 113, 123, 133, 271, 388, 407
Pasolini, Pier Paulo, 50
Patriarchs' Border, 200, 201–2
Pax Americana, 306–7
Peace with Israel, 54
pedagogy. *See also* Hebrew education, modern
  exclusiveness versus reviving Hebrew with, 192–93
  with ideology and education, 9–12
  Ivrit be-Ivrit as tool of segregation or, 185–87
Pedersen, Susan, 278n7, 417
Peel Commission, 113, 116n40, 133
Peled, Mati, 246
Peres, Shimon, 291, 297
Peres, Yeshayahu, 187

Perez, Rafi, 254
Le Péril juif universel (Azoury), 270
perpetrator trauma, 69
"Philosemite" (van Messel), 45
philosemitism, Nakba in 1950s and Western European, 43
  from antisemitism to anti-antisemitism, 44–46
  erasure and Holocaust guilt, 53–55
  Israeli Jew portrayals, 50–52
  philo-Zionism from, 46–50
philo-Zionism, 46–50
Pines, Yechiel Michal, 195n30
Pinsker, Leo, 32–34, 38
pioneers (*halutzim*), 36–37, 49, 222, 418
pipeline, oil, 108–11
place, rituals of, 226
planning history, Israel, 137–38, 152–53
  comparative discourse, 141–42
  Netanya as case study for Palestinian and, 142–51
  new paradigm, 139–42
police violence, 339
politics, elite in, 348n15
Le Populaire (Blum), 47
Porter, Libby, 140–41, 146, 148
Preminger, Otto, 48
Prewitt, Kenneth, 121–22
primordialist approach, 218n15
Prince Hassan air base, 116n31
"The Prisoner" ("Ha-shavui") (Yizhar), 66
Promise Border, 200, 202–3, 205–6, 208, 216
Promised Land map
  Borderless and Tribes' Estates Border, 205
  Intended Border, 203–4
  in Israeli schoolbooks, 200–205
  Kingdom of Israel in Solomon era, 203, 204
  narrative aspects of, 201–4
  Patriarchs' Border, 201–2
  Promise Border, 202–3, 215
  theology, history, nation, 205
Protocols of the Elders of Zion, 63, 74n20, 270, 271

Der Prozess (The Trial, film) (Pabst), 45
public order, national security and, 88–89

Qafisheh, Mutaz, 365
al-Qawuqji, Fawzi, 271, 279n22

Raban, Zvi, 144
Rabin, Yitzhak, 235, 291, 297, 339
race, space and, 118, 119
racial-spatial logic, 120–24
racism, apartheid and, 367
Radhakrishnan, R., 68, 71
railways, 106–11, 115n17
Ramla urban scheme, 162
Rapaport, Meron, 362n10
rape, of Palestinian women, 64, 75n23
Rashi, 35
Razi, Tami, 140
Raz-Krakotzkin, Amnon, 202–3
redemption
  Hasidism and, 25, 29
  symbols and, 27
Réflexions sur la question juive (Sartre), 45
Remembrance Day for Fallen Soldier of the IDF, 230
reparations, for Jewish survivors, 44
repatriation
  international human rights law and obstacles to, 83–87
  reconstruction of destroyed villages and, 377–78
  of settlers and international law with legal regulation, 82–83
residential segregation, 121, 132
Resnik, Julia, 243
return, 363–65, 379
  cantons, 373–75
  distribution of population, 367–69
  feasibility of, 369–71
  to heavily populated areas, 373
  al-Lajun return project, 175
  law of, 311, 352
  mapping future of Israel-Palestine and, 389–91
  Miska return map, 392
  phases of, 371–73
  problem areas, 376–77
  reconstruction of destroyed villages and repatriation, 377–78
  right of, 287, 307, 309–11, 336, 366, 384–86, 389–91, 394, 398
  rural Jewish areas, 375–76
"Returning to Haifa" (Kanafani), 72
Le Réveil de la Nation Arabe (Azoury), 270
revenge
  cyclical narrative of, 34–35
  God and, 33, 34, 35, 37
  Zionism and, 33–34
right of return. *See 'Awda*
rights. *See also* international human rights, West Bank Israeli settlers and
  ADRID, 307
  ICCPR, 84–86
  of individuals and attachment to country, 84–86
  with mass expulsion prohibited, 84
  to noninterference in homes, 86–87
  with repatriation of settlers, 84–87
  against torture or degrading treatment, 87
Rinot, Moshe, 195n29
rituals, Zionist, 226. *See also* Zionist civic rituals, nation-building and
Rivlin, Joseph Joel, 37
Robbins, Bruce, 68, 69
Robinson, William, 58
Rodinson, Maxime, 265
Rohingya Muslims, 133, 265
Roman Catholic Church, 49
Romania, 367
Rose, John Melkon, 410
Rosenbaum, Ron, 287
Rothberg, Michael, 58–59, 71, 72, 73, 73n3
Rothschild (Baron), 278n13
Rousset, David, 48
Royal-Dutch Shell, 105, 116n29
Rubinstein, Amnon, 280n36
Rubinstein, Dani, 287
Ruppin, Arthur, 266, 278n6

Sabbagh-Khoury, Areej, 2
Sabbateanism, 28
sabra, 210, 219n35
Sa'di, Ahmad, 387

INDEX | 439

Said, Edward, 53, 61, 157
Said, Wadi, 412
al-Said, Nuri, 117n48
Said Makdisi, Jean, 412, 424n22
Sakakini, Dumia, 410, 411
Sakakini, Hala, 409, 410
Sakakini, Khalil, 409, 411–12
Sakakini, Sari, 410, 411–12
Salameh Square, 403, 404, 412, 420
Salomon, Moshe, 413
Salomon, Yoel Moshe, 37, 195n30
Samuel, Herbert, 271
Sandercock, Leonie, 139
Saramago, José, 58, 76n50
Sartre, Jean-Paul, 45, 46, 50
Saul (biblical character), 29
Saving Israel (Gordis), 289
Schmitt, Carl, 37
Scholem, Gershom, 26, 27, 29, 39
schoolbook maps, Israeli (1903–1967), 198–99
    Exodus Border and Tribes' Estates Border, 205–16
    Promised Land map, 200–205
Schori-Rubin, Tzipora, 193n4
Seaman, Daniel, 287
Sea of Galilee, 103
second-class citizens, 345, 353–55
security. *See* national security
Segev, Tom, 69
segregation
    Ivrit be-Ivrit as tool of pedagogy or, 185–87
    language and, 187–92
Separation Wall, 67
Sephardim, 28, 29, 30–31
Sergeants affair (August 1947), 44
settlements project, international law and, 80–83
settler colonialism, 148, 319, 418
    decolonization, nationalism and, 12–15
    in Israel/Palestine urban studies, 140–41
    paradigm, 265–69
settlers
    with identity, 268
    international law with legal regulation of repatriation of, 82–83
    natives and, 416–19

Shafir, Gershon, 140, 265–66, 267–68, 278n13, 278n14
Shapira, Anita, 228, 406–7
Sharett, Yaacov, 295
Sharon, Arieh, 158–59
Sharon, Ariel, 290, 293
Sharon Plan (1951), 158–59
Shatz, Adam, 65, 66, 68, 69
Shavit, Ari, 65, 288, 291, 295, 407
Shavit, Yaakov, 193n4
Shehade, Ahmad, 395–97
sheikh of the Jews (*sheikh al-yahud*), 28
Shell, company, 103, 105, 115n14
Shemesh, Hana, 242
Shenhavi, Mordechai, 195n17
Shifman, David, 202, 216
Shimshoni, D., 167, 169
Shohat, Ella, 122, 134n14
Sitton, Shoshanna, 193n4
Six Day (June) War (1967), 118, 119, 124, 174, 198, 231, 233, 290
Sleeping on a Wire (Grossman), 361n1
Slivenko v. Latvia, 89
Smith, Adam, 263, 296
Smith, Albert, 394
social justice, archaeology of, 322–23
Solomon era map, Kingdom of Israel in, 203, 204
The Sons of Benjamin (Bnei Binyamin), 142, 147
South Atlantic Quarterly, 308
sovereignty. *See* oil, Middle Eastern sovereignty and
space
    Judaization of, 386
    Oslo Accords and division of, 127–28
    race and, 118, 119
    redrawing, 7–9, 401n43
    residential segregation of, 121, 132
spatial imagination, 9, 10, 198–200, 208, 211
Spender, Stephen, 50
spiritual connection, Hasidism and, 4, 23, 29–30
spiritual consanguinity, 46
Spivak, Gayatri Chakravorty, 63, 65, 67, 70, 71

Standard Oil, 105
Stav, Shira, 61, 70
Stern, Frank, 55
Sternhell, Zeev, 296, 300n69
subhuman (Untermenschen), 64
suicide bombings, 67, 68, 70, 287
survival discourse, 284–88
Sykes, Mark, 102
Sykes-Picot Agreement, 102, 105
symbol
    allegory and, 26–27
    with nationality and salvation, 27
    of State of Israel, 237n24
Syria, 104, 108, 110, 271, 371

Tagore, Rabindranath, 361
"Taking Possession of Village Lands and Expulsion of the Land Tenants" (Sabbagh-Khoury), 2
Talbiyeh, 402–3, 405, 409–13, 419
Tamari, Salim, 115n1
Témoignage Chrétien (newspaper), 53
Terrace Houses project, 163–65
time, rituals of, 226
Toronto Star (newspaper), 64
torture, rights against, 87
Total (Compagnie Française de Pétroles, CFP), 103, 105, 115n14
Toubbeh, Issa Mikhail, 410
towns, Bedouin villages and, 129
Toynbee, Arnold, 53
trains, oil and, 106–11, 115n17
Transjordan, 111, 112
translatability, Derrida and, 63
trauma, 4–7, 69, 70, 288
Treaty of Guarantee (1960), 97n67
The Trial (*Der Prozess*) (Pabst), 45
Tribes' Estates Border
    borderless map and, 205
    Exodus and, 205–16
    as historical, 206–8
    to Israeli State border, 212–16
    Joshua's conquests as historical maps, 208–10
    map, 207, 213, 216
    territorial aspects, 210–12

Trump, Donald, 133, 307
tunnels, Hamas, 64, 68
Turkey, 97n67, 105, 111
two states, one homeland plan, 16, 357–60, 362n10
tzabar (prickly pear), 219n35

ultra-Orthodox (Hasidic-Haredi), 37, 128–29, 187, 194n16, 288
Umm al-Fahm, 166, 167, 393–94
United Nations (UN), 47
    Economic and Social Commission for Western Asia, 379
    Holocaust and, 5
    Partition Plan, 33, 39, 113, 123, 133, 271, 388, 407
    Peel Commission map and, 113
    Relief and Works Agency for Palestine Refugees, 367, 377, 380n5
    right of return an, 366, 389
    Universal Declaration of Human Rights, 357, 389
United Nations Population Fund (UNFPA), 307
United Nations Relief and Works Agency for Palestine Refugees (UNRWA), 367, 377, 380n5
United States (US), 59, 105
United States Holocaust Memorial Museum (USHMM), 59
Universal Declaration of Human Rights, UN, 357, 389
L'univers concentrationaire (Rousset), 48
Unlearning the Colonial Cultures of Planning (Porter), 141
Untermenschen (subhumans), 64
urban planning, Netanya and, 148–51
urban studies, Israel/Palestine, 140–41
Uris, Leon, 48
utopia, connotations, 384. *See also* Israel-Palestine, future of

Van de Poll, Willem, 50–51
van Messel, Saul, 45
Ventura, Avraham, 163, 164, 165
Vercors, 47

village, with Bedouin towns and, 129. *See also* Arab village, in Israel-Palestine
Villa Salameh, 403, 404, 409, 412, 421
violence
  antisemitism and, 44
  Arabs and, 24
  comparison in extremis and, 63, 67–71
  equality and, 359
  military doctrines with, 63
  the Nakba and, 24, 33
  nationalism and, 275
  nonviolence and, 24, 34, 37, 38, 67, 68
  police, 339
  rape, 64, 75n23
  sovereignty, 37
  suicide bombings, 67, 68, 70, 287
  torture, 87
  Zionism and, 4, 24, 34–35, 37–38

Wahabi Akhwan, 103
Waltz with Bashir (film), 6, 69–70, 73
Walzer, Michael, 355
war crimes, 17, 75n24, 80, 378–79, 407
War of Independence (1948 War), 158, 208, 210n35, 230, 232–33, 252–53, 335, 337, 340, 363, 365–67, 369–70, 373, 377, 379, 389, 402, 406n4, 407, 412–16, 421–22
Warsaw Ghetto, 58–59, 64, 65, 70–71
Watson Institute for International and Public Affairs, Brown University, 1
Watzman, Haim, 361n1
Weber, Max, 283, 296
Weizman, Chaim, 267
West Bank. *See also* international human rights, West Bank Israeli settlers and
  international law in, 80–81
  Judaization of, 126, 305
  Palestinian population in, 6, 19n4
  population, 126, 127–28
  territorial expansion and, 124–28
West Germany, 49
White Paper (1938), 116n40
Wiesel, Elie, 51
Wilkomitz, Simhah, 189
women, rape of Palestinian, 64, 75n23

Wood, Denis, 199
World Cup Football, 285
World War I, 108, 112, 186–87, 189, 196nn39–40, 223–26, 328n24
World War II, 43, 50, 83, 271, 377

Ya'ar, Ora, 163, 164, 165
Ya'ar, Ya'acov, 163, 164, 165
Yacobi, Haim, 394
Yaffa Documents, 391
Yakobson, Alex, 280n36
Yehoshua, A. B., 65
Yellin, David, 187, 189, 194n5, 194n13, 195n29
Yemen, 271
Yiftachel, Oren, 121, 140–41, 311, 361n1, 416
Yishuv period, 218n5
Yizhar, S., 6, 66
Yonah, Yossi, 286
Yuchtman-Yaar, Ephraim, 296

Zaslavsky, David, 159
Zelkin, Mordechai, 194n16
Zevi, Sabbatai, 28
Zionism
  antisemitism and, 264, 416–17
  anti-Zionism as antisemitism, 269–72
  ceremonies with aura of sanctity, 11, 223
  with *Exodus 1947* saga, 47
  Hasidism and, 4, 25, 32–33
  nationalist Jews and, 36–39
  philosemitism to philo-, 46–50
  Protocols of the Elders of Zion, 63, 74n20, 270, 271
  revenge and, 33–34
  rituals, 226
  settler colonial paradigm and, 265–69
  transformation of, 5
  violence and, 4, 24, 34–35, 37–38
Zionist civic rituals, nation-building and, 221–22, 235
  from British mandate to Israeli independence, 225–29
  from First Aliyah to end of World War I, 223–25

from foundation of state to early twenty-first century, 229–34
Zionist Organization, 142, 191, 196n44, 211, 225

Zionists, 23–24, 280n33
Zochrot, 18, 175, 385–86, 388–93, 398, 400n25
Zreik, Raef, 416–17

www.ingramcontent.com/pod-product-compliance
Lightning Source LLC
Chambersburg PA
CBHW071328080526
44587CB00017B/2772